COUNS   & HIGHER EDUC

DAVENPORT

COUNSELLING

The BAC *Counselling* Reader

EDITED BY
Stephen Palmer, Sheila Dainow *and* Pat Milner

British Association for Counselling

SAGE Publications
London • Thousand Oaks • New Delhi

SAGE Publications Ltd
6 Bonhill Street
London EC2A 4PU

SAGE Publications Inc
2455 Teller Road
Thousand Oaks, California 91320

SAGE Publications India Pvt Ltd
32, M-Block Market
Greater Kailash – I
New Delhi 110 048

British Library Cataloguing in Publication data

A catalogue record for this book is available from the British Library.

ISBN 0 8039 7476 0
ISBN 0 8039 7477 9 (pbk)

Library of Congress catalog record available

Typeset by Mayhew Typesetting, Rhayader, Powys.
Printed in Great Britain by The Cromwell Press Ltd, Broughton Gifford, Melksham, Wiltshire.

Contents

v

Contents

Part Two **Counselling Contexts and Practice**

Part Three **Counselling Issues**

Contents

Contents

Foreword

The title 'British Association for Counselling' is often misrepresented in articles or minutes of other organizations as the 'British Association of Counselling'. The error suggests a more partisan, trade union focus than is the case. The Association is necessarily concerned with ethics and standards of training and practice but the *for* of the title points to a larger concern with the field of counselling as a whole and its well-being in the same way that the individual counsellor has the well-being of his or her clients at heart. This excellent collection of readings from the Association's journal *Counselling* makes the same point through their breadth, diversity of stance and the authors' evident willingness to enter into debate.

The vitality of the field depends on the contribution of its counsellor members and friends – and critics – in the related and over-lapping fields of psychotherapy and psychology whose writings here set out the leading questions of the day. Articles on competing and seemingly competing theoretical models of practice, the special requirements of particular client group and setting, accreditation, supervision, research and the future of counselling and the Association jostle for the reader's attention. Mostly they seek to make a point and, hence, point up their ancestry. They are written with vitality because the author wanted to either address an issue or enter into issue with another's view. The reader can do the same, electively using the discussion points that end each chapter.

Counselling is a human activity which attests to the willingness of one person to help another in his or her psychological journey through life. The counsellor brings to this work varying degrees of training and practical experience but, always, a professional attitude and the insights of his or her own experience of living. In the *Reader*, counsellors explore and debate issues of central concern. For the reader, this is an opportunity to enjoy and from which to learn.

Mark Aveline
President
British Association for Counselling

For Maggie, Kate and Tom.

Stephen Palmer

To the clients, students, colleagues, supervisors and counsellors with whom I have worked over the years and from whom I have learned and am still learning. Specifically, my thanks as always go to Cyl in appreciation for constant unconditional positive regard and the ever-pouring teapot.

Sheila Dainow

For my great-niece and nephews in order of appearance:
Joanna, Russell, David and Jacques.
With love from Pat.

Pat Milner

Introduction

The current internationally recognized name of the British Association for Counselling is built on a foundation of many years of voluntary work in many areas. People have attended meetings, worked to evolve structures, processes, codes of ethics and given freely and loyally of their time in other ways because they believe that counselling is an important activity which is worthy of their support. Some people contributed to the growth of BAC by writing for its journal, which has played a major part in enhancing the wider recognition of the association.

The *BAC Counselling Reader* reflects some of the best work of its time published in *Counselling, Journal of the British Association for Counselling*, over the past fifteen years. In addition, the choice of articles gives a historical perspective of the development of counselling in Britain.

The Reader has been compiled and edited by Sheila Dainow, Pat Milner and Stephen Palmer, all of whom have been editors of *Counselling* during the time of its recent rapid growth in size and stature, which has seen it become an internationally recognized counselling publication. Stephen Palmer suggested that fifteen years of *Counselling* was worth celebrating and so the idea of a book based on key articles from the journal was conceived.

This is a book aimed at students of counselling, experienced counsellors and trainers of counsellors who will find amongst the wide range of stimulating topics covered a springboard for discussion, debate and reflection. Authors were invited to bring their pieces up to date and each chapter includes four suggested discussion issues to help initiate further deliberation. Trainers and lecturers may also find suitable essay subjects in some of the discussion issues.

There are four main sections in the book: Counselling Approaches, Counselling Contexts and Practice, Counselling Issues, and Counselling and Research. The final part, The Last Word, contains a description of the development of BAC itself, and looks to the future of counselling in Britain. Journal articles have stemmed from the interests of journal authors and they have not necessarily presented a comprehensive view of the counselling field. Consequently a small number of chapters were specially commissioned, to represent certain key topics and developments which had not been adequately covered in the journal.

There are 78 chapters in total, providing a representative selection which should offer some reading of interest to both trainees and experienced counsellors alike, whilst also celebrating fifteen years of *Counselling*.

Acknowledgement

The editors would like to acknowledge the British Association for Counselling's consultant, Douglas Hooper, who helped them with this project.

1

Person-Centred and Psychodynamic Counselling: a Dialogue

John McLeod and Sue Wheeler

The person-centred approach to counselling has evolved from the work of Carl Rogers and his colleagues (Rogers, 1961), and represents a humanistic orientation to counselling and psychotherapy. Psychodynamic counselling originates in psychoanalysis and the work of Sigmund Freud, but has also been significantly influenced by the ideas of writers such as Klein, Winnicott, Bowlby and Erikson. Person-centred and psychodynamic counselling are two of the most widely used therapeutic orientations currently used in Britain. Moreover, the majority of counsellors who employ one of these approaches are informed about, and aware of, the other approach. There are also some counsellors who attempt to integrate these perspectives, or to combine techniques from them in an eclectic manner. However, despite the close relationship between the approaches in everyday practice, there has been little debate in recent years over the issues involved in bringing together what can be seen as two very contrasting styles of counselling.

In this chapter we seek to explore the similarities and differences between person-centred and psychodynamic counselling. One of us (Sue Wheeler) is a psychodynamic counsellor and trainer, whose initial training was with Ellen Noonan at London University. The other (John McLeod) is a person-centred counsellor and trainer who received his training through the Person-Centred Therapy (PCT) Institute. We have engaged in a dialogue, trying to be clear about what are the distinctive core assumptions and methods associated with our approach, but at the same time being open to the large areas of overlap and agreement that exist. Most of the time this process was fun, but sometimes it was painful. It can be difficult to accept that someone you respect does not necessarily understand what you are saying or share your experience or beliefs. Nevertheless, we both felt that we learned a lot from engaging in this kind of dialogue, and hope that it will continue, not only between the two of us but involving the wider counselling community.

The main features of the person-centred approach

Person-centred counselling has been an important part of the humanistic movement in psychology. In the 1950s, humanistic psychologists such as Maslow, Buhler, Jourard and Bugental argued that it was essential for psychology to begin to take more account of dimensions of human experience such as fulfilment,

This chapter was first published in *Counselling, Journal of the British Association for Counselling*, vol. 6, no. 4, pp. 283–7 (1995).

creativity and choice. One of the leading members of this movement, Carl Rogers, was the key figure in the development of what was originally known as the 'client-centred' approach to counselling and psychotherapy. As this approach came to be applied in group and organizational settings as well as with individual clients, it became more accurate to refer to it as a *person*-centred approach. Rogers and his colleagues were among the first to engage in systematic research into the process and outcomes of counselling and psychotherapy, and person-centred theory is supported by a substantial amount of research evidence.

At its heart, person-centred counselling is a way of using the relationship between client and counsellor to facilitate the development of the client. If the counsellor is able to offer the client a relationship characterized by the 'core conditions' of empathy, acceptance and congruence, and if the client is able to perceive and appreciate these qualities, then the client will feel safe enough to begin to disclose aspects of self that are painful, shameful and hidden. Within thi. therapeutic relationship, the fact that the counsellor is able to accept these previously disowned parts of the self helps the client to be able to accept them too. An important goal of person-centred counselling is, therefore, that of promoting greater self-acceptance in the client. This process can also be understood as involving a shift in the *locus of evaluation* used by the client. At the beginning of counselling, clients can often be caught up in making judgements and decisions based on the standards, values and wants of other people. For example, clients may often talk about how they 'should' do something. As the person becomes more willing to accept their own feelings and needs, they can make decisions based on a sound sense of their own values as well as being more able to respond to others in a genuinely caring way.

In person-centred counselling, the counsellor approaches the client with an attitude of deep *respect*. This respect includes an acceptance of whatever it is the client chooses to talk about. As a counselling perspective that has been strongly influenced by existential philosophy, the person-centred approach employs a *phenomenological* approach toward understanding and knowing. In phenomenology, the knower arrives at deeper understandings by 'bracketing-off' his or her assumptions, in order to explore, in so far as it is possible, the totality of meanings associated with a particular experience or situation. As a result, the person-centred approach is theoretically lean. What matters to the person-centred counsellor is the theory or model of the world held by the client.

Person-centred counselling is also a *process*-orientated approach. Central to the approach is the belief that people are always engaged in a search to fulfil themselves, to actualize, to become. There is, therefore, no final result, solution, answer or insight that can be achieved. Person-centred counsellors are very cautious about any attempts to diagnose or categorize clients, because such labels are static and deny the growth or movement in a person's life, and because, most of the time, such categories are derived from the frame of reference, world-view or purposes of the counsellor rather than those of the client.

The concept of *experiencing* is another core idea in person-centred counselling. The work of Gendlin (1984) has been instrumental in enabling person-centred practitioners to make sense of the ways that cognitions, ideas and symbols interact with bodily or organismic feelings to constitute the raw experience of life, and to appreciate the importance in this on-going experiencing of what he calls the 'edge of awareness', the client's openness to new possibilities for life.

Historically, person-centred counselling has not placed great emphasis on technique. Rather, the person and presence of the counsellor, and his or her capacity to engage with the world of the client, are paramount. An ability to apply techniques and interventions in the absence of a genuine relationship with the client would be seen as misguided and unhelpful from a person-centred stance. Person-centred and experiential counsellors are more likely to describe their work in terms of the types of process that occur (see, for example, Greenberg et al., 1993) or the quality of the relationship (see Mearns and Thorne, 1988), rather than in terms of technical operations.

This brief summary can only convey some of the main ideas of person-centred counselling. Readers seeking a fuller account are advised to consult Rogers (1951, 1961), Mearns and Thorne (1988), McLeod (1993) and Mearns (1994).

The main features of the psychodynamic approach

Psychodynamic counselling has its origins in psychoanalytic theory, from which it has drawn the basic assumptions about human growth and development. The *dynamic* part of the word psychodynamics refers to the regulation of the psyche, in which defensive manoeuvres take place to regulate or control impulses or anxiety that is generated from within the self or in response to external stimuli. It also describes the relationship between counsellor and client, which provides an arena for a fluid interchange of thoughts, feelings and projections. The counsellor–client relationship also invites the development of transference, in which the counsellor is experienced by the client in a way that resembles their relationship with significant others in their past or present.

Psychodynamic counsellors use psychoanalytic theories to inform their work and to make a formulation of client difficulties. The continuing debate about the differences between counselling and psychotherapy is particularly relevant in the arena of psychoanalytically based therapies. Psychodynamic counsellors generally use some techniques derived from psychoanalytic practice and some aspects of the stance of the psychoanalyst but are unlikely to engage in intensive psychotherapy with the objective of psychic restructuring, and will focus on specific issues or life events that the clients have sought counselling to resolve.

The psychodynamic counsellor is interested not only in the presenting problem that the client brings but also his/her life history. The relationship with the client is central to the work, first and foremost in establishing a therapeutic alliance, the real relationship between two (or more) people which fosters respect, trust, common purpose and commitment. The task of the counsellor is to facilitate the client's insight and understanding through linking past and present, interpreting some of the client's communication as metaphor and interpreting transference in terms of past and present relationships. The counsellor reveals as little as possible about him- or herself to the client so that there can be as much clarity as possible about the nature of the transference. Time boundaries are kept strictly to preserve the sanctity of the therapeutic hour (or fifty minutes) and to highlight unconscious communication that regularly occurs at the beginning or end of sessions and before or after breaks.

Psychodynamic counselling is informed by a wealth of literature, both from its roots in psychoanalysis (see, for example, the complete works of Freud, 1976) and in more recent texts that put these theories into a counselling context (Brown and Pedder, 1989; Jacobs, 1985, 1988; Malan, 1979; McLeod, 1993; Noonan, 1983).

Similarities between the approaches

These summary descriptions of the main features of psychodynamic and person-centred counselling map out significant areas of similarity as well as pointing up some quite clear contrasts between the two approaches. From the point of view of the authors of this chapter, the main ways in which the two approaches converge are:

1   They are exploratory, and take as their goal the aim of helping the person to develop understanding and find/clarify meaning. These approaches are clearly different from behavioural perspectives on counselling, and from family systems models, which have the objective of achieving change without necessarily producing insight and awareness.
2   Both person-centred and psychodynamic counselling operate primarily through dialogue and conversation.
3   Both emphasize the importance of the counsellor–client relationship as a vehicle for promoting learning and understanding (although the nature of the recommended therapeutic relationship is different in each). The notion of the *therapeutic alliance* can be applied equally well to both approaches.
4   Person-centred and psychodynamic counsellors work with the person-in-relationship (rather than with the system or merely with individual behaviour). There is an interest in the relational world in which the client operates.
5   There is a requirement that the counsellor will have undertaken a significant amount of work on self, usually through personal therapy.
6   Both are broad-based approaches, that have tended to incorporate practitioners with different shades of opinion under the same banner.

The key concepts in this list of similarities are *therapeutic alliance/relationship*, *exploratory* and *conversational*. The existence of these shared core ideas suggests that person-centred and psychodynamic can be located in the same general 'space' within the spectrum of therapy as a whole.

The main differences between the approaches

Having discussed the similarities between the models we turn to the differences, which are considerable. Table 1.1 briefly lists some of the differences, which cover

Table 1.1 *Differences between person-centred and psychodynamic counselling*

Person-centred	Psychodynamic
Conscious processes	Unconscious processes
Dream work not emphasized	Use of dreams
Therapist congruence (may include self-disclosure)	Therapist opaque stance no self-disclosure
Shows warmth	Professional distance
Focus on experiencing feelings	Focus on the underlying anxiety
Expression of feelings	Understanding feelings
Focus on past, present or future	Linking past and present
Sees people as fundamentally good	Sees people as destabilized by bad/hostile/self-destructive instincts
Allows client to make their own interpretations	Makes interpretations for client
Allows client to determine what they talk about: the client is right	May see reluctance to engage with a topic as resistance
Accepts the client where they are	Looks for what is hidden
Does not make an initial assessment: mutual negotiation	Assessment an essential part of the work
The past sometimes irrelevant	History-taking essential
Some flexibility with time boundaries	Time boundaries fixed
Theory genderless	Theory gender-orientated
Adaptable to cultural diversity	Less flexible to cultural diversity
Promotes personal growth	Promotes self-understanding
Limited theoretical literature	Vast theoretical literature

important areas such as model of personality, therapeutic aims, aspects of theory, general applicability and technique, and underlying 'image of the person'.

While person-centred theory takes as one of its basic tenets the notion of the human potential for self-actualization, psychoanalytic theory proposes that human beings have an instinct towards life, love and procreation as well as an instinct towards self-destruction or the destruction of others. Whereas person-centred theory sees self-actualization and individual fulfilment as blocked by lack of self-awareness and unexpressed emotions, psychodynamic theory explains that instincts are curbed by defence mechanisms that are both functional and dysfunctional. In the latter model one of the objectives of counselling is to challenge dysfunctional defences, while preserving those that are necessary for survival, while the former model has the objective of enabling clients to express their full range of feelings in order to experience themselves more fully, become more self-accepting and hence able to use more of their own untapped resources.

Psychoanalytic theory takes no account of cultural difference but postulates that the psychological development of men and women is different. Boy children develop their sexual identity during the phase of resolution of the Oedipus complex, during which they increase their identification with father, while girls identify closely with their mothers from an early age and do not have to relinquish that identification. The theory is often criticized for being phallocentric, having been formulated by members of an oppressive male elite. Person-centred theory does not account for gender differences in the same way or attract the same types of criticism. It also lends itself more readily to the acceptance of cultural differences with more flexibility to modify technique for a non-white middle-class population.

While psychodynamic counsellors would embrace some aspects of the core conditions of empathy, positive regard and congruence, there are differences in both language and usage of the notion of congruence. Some aspects of congruence are described by the psychodynamic term countertransference, meaning the feeling response from the counsellor to the client or to material presented by the client. A person-centred counsellor might choose to share their response to the client in a direct and immediate way (congruence) whereas a psychodynamic counsellor would examine their emotional or physical response (counter-transference) to the client carefully in order to make sense of it, which may or may not lead to an interpretation. A psychodynamic counsellor would be unlikely to answer any client's personal questions about them without thinking about the meaning of the question with the client, which can be contrasted with the person-centred recommendation for openness on the part of the counsellor. Moreover, while a person-centred counsellor is urged to display warmth and acceptance, the psychodynamic practitioner would be encouraged to maintain a professional distance or opaqueness that reveals little about themselves. Such a stance facilitates the recognition and subsequent interpretation of the transference relationship. Lastly, a major difference between the two models is in the use of assessment and history-taking as an essential aspect of the counselling work. Person-centred counselling advocates exploratory work and mutual decision-making at a first meeting to determine the viability of a counselling relationship. Psychodynamic counselling requires an assessment session to be conducted by the counsellor based on a detailed personal history of the client, which leads to a formulation of client difficulties to be held in mind, although sometimes modified, throughout the counselling if they decide to take the client on.

It is perhaps not surprising that such a long list of differences can be constructed. Whereas the similarities we identified could be viewed as comprising some very broad-based shared general principles, at the level of practical application many more contrasts in style and technique are visible. These contrasts can be understood as arising from two fundamental differences: *level of theoretical elaboration* and *attitude towards authority*. Psychodynamic counselling can draw upon a detailed and elaborate theoretical structure, whereas person-centred counselling is committed to a more phenomenological, theory-free approach. Psychodynamic counselling intentionally re-creates the authority relationship that existed between parent and child, while person-centred counselling strives to create a relationship of equality and mutuality.

Psychodynamic counselling from the point of view of a person-centred counsellor

One of my (J.McL.) main reservations about the psychodynamic approach is the sense that the therapist is the expert who knows where the client's story will lead. My impression is that psychodynamic therapists use their theory and assessment skills to build up a model of the client's pathology, and then induce the client to share this interpretation (I realize that this is an exaggeration). A dramatic example of this would be the two generations of psychoanalysts who did not accept their patients' accounts of having been sexually abused. As a person-centred counsellor, I always want to be following the client, half a step behind him/her, rather than knowing the 'answer' to the puzzle. Another big criticism is of psychodynamic therapists who refuse to be known, for example on principle not answering questions. I think this is humiliating for clients. These two criticisms are, I believe, connected to the fact that psychodynamic work is still based in a model of therapist–patient relationship borrowed from medicine. A third criticism is that I do not believe that an understanding of current psychological and emotional difficulties is *necessarily* facilitated by exploring childhood memories and fantasies. Undoubtedly this is *sometimes* helpful but there are many occasions when it is quite irrelevant. For me, many of the differences between psycho-dynamic and person-centred counsellors are a matter of the style with which a therapist sets about doing 'exploratory' or 'meaning-making' therapy. However, these two factors of the *power relationship* and the *assumption of a childhood origin for problems* are very fundamental, and are indicative of contrasting and non-compatible images of the person and philosophical/epistemological positions.

I would say that I have learned a lot from psychodynamic therapists, trainers and writers. Psychodynamic theory is powerful, intellectually satisfying and, for me, a valuable source of starting points for making sense of myself and my clients. The concepts of psychodynamic theory have often helped me to get a 'handle' on what is going on in therapy. For example, the work of feminist psychodynamic therapists has enabled me to begin to understand the importance of gender. Concepts such as parallel process and projective identification open up new ways of 'seeing' relationships. In writing this I realize something that had not been clear to me before. I use psychodynamic concepts in thinking about therapy, but in my way of being with clients I draw on a humanistic tradition of which person-centred counselling is one element.

I feel driven to add that I also have many criticisms of the person-centred approach, so my critique of the psychodynamic approach is definitely not coming from a stance that the person-centred school has all the answers.

Person-centred counselling from the point of view of a psychodynamic counsellor

For me (S.W.) the person-centred counselling model is an excellent foundation for counselling training and a good starting point for learning to see the world from another person's perspective. The theory challenges counsellors to recognize and tolerate individual differences and to truly hear and participate in communication from their clients. Contrary to the assertion that the person-centred approach places little emphasis on technique, it is my experience that the model lends itself to being reduced to a series of skills including listening, reflection, immediacy and the communication of empathy, that can be taught by trainers who have mastered little more than the basics themselves. A little skill goes a long way, or can be quite harmful depending on the circumstances and I fear that many so-called person-centred counsellors have never fully embraced the full depth of theory and skill involved in competent and effective use of the model, nor embraced the full complexity of human problems they seek to treat.

While I have no doubt that a sophisticated or expert person-centred practitioner can offer the highest standard of counselling, I fear that the terms congruence, genuineness and immediacy can be unhelpfully misinterpreted. Immediately responding to a client with self-disclosure, or offering inappropriate spontaneous feedback, can be unhelpful if not harmful. Similarly while I can see that being warm and accepting will be both comforting and encouraging to some clients, it may lead to a false expectation of friendship or worse by some or deter others from exposing the parts of themselves that are less than warm and friendly, sometimes envious, murderous or distraught. As a psychodynamic counsellor my aim is to help the client to internalize a carer who can help them make sense of their thoughts and feelings both inside and outside of the counselling room in order to deal with them in an appropriate and adult way.

A serious reservation that I have about person-centred counselling is the belief in humankind being inherently good. In my experience, Freud's (1915) concepts of Eros and Thanatos, the life and death instincts, and Klein's (1946) defence mechanism of splitting into good and bad, love and hate, are fundamental to all relationships, including the counselling relationship. Particularly when working with women, giving permission and legitimacy to talking about thoughts and feelings such as envy, murderous rage, bitterness and hatred can often be the most energizing and productive aspects of the work. Such feelings are often deeply repressed, disguised by politeness and servitude, producing depression and guilt, and it is only through repeated reference to these less acceptable aspects of the self that they can be acknowledged and integrated. I can think of many clients who would have avoided looking at their aggressive feelings for ever had the words and concepts not been introduced by the counsellor.

My other major criticism of person-centred counselling is the lack of theory of human growth and development to underpin the practice, and the subsequent disregard for assessment. Not everyone can engage in a therapeutic relationship or indeed a relationship of any kind and it can be very difficult for a person-centred counsellor to choose not to take someone on for counselling when they have entered into a mutual selection process contract with a potential client. I suspect that this sometimes leads to clients being taken on against the better judgement of the counsellor because it was difficult to turn them away. There is little written about assessment or quasi-assessment from a person-centred perspective which is a deficit. Acceptance and non-labelling of people is a laudable ideal but one which may prevent some people from receiving the treatment they need, wasting both time and money.

Having said all this, person-centred counselling has a lot to offer the counselling world. It is a perfect model for working with some client difficulties such as bereavement and is admirable in its anti-intellectual, non-racist, heterosexualist or sexist standpoint. The core conditions provide a solid underpinning for the therapeutic alliance and are crucial to the early stages of a therapeutic relationship. I would like to see more written about the person-centred approach, so that the theory can be expanded to ensure that potential counsellors can be well equipped to cope with the full range of clients they are likely to encounter.

Conclusions

Some writers have attempted the difficult task (Wheeler 1993) of integrating psychodynamic and person-centred theories. Kahn (1985), for example, has discussed the similarities between Rogers and Kohut. Some of the issues related to integration are discussed in Norcross and Goldfried (1992) and McLeod (1993). The task of integrating theories and approaches in counselling is complex, and we would wish to be tentative in any recommendations or conclusions that we might make. Nevertheless, what emerged for us quite powerfully from this exercise was a strong sense that person-centred and psychodynamic counsellors have a lot to offer each other. Psychodynamic theory can potentially fill in some of the gaps in the person-centred approach, and vice versa. The key idea here is that practitioners in one approach can usefully be *informed* by knowledge of the other approach. However, when the differences between the approaches are examined there are significant areas of contradiction and incompatibility. On questions such as congruence vs. countertransference, empathy vs. interpretation, being a companion on a journey as against being Sherlock Holmes on a case it seemed essential to us that counsellors must make a clear and definite decision about which side of the line they stand. Attempting to straddle both theories, adopting both positions at the same time, risks confusing the client and diluting your skills. So it may be that in the end the integration of person-centred and psychodynamic approaches to counselling will take place at a personal level, as individual counsellors trained within one or the other of these approaches find fresh insights and ideas from the other. It may never be possible to achieve coherent integration, to create the new 'grand theory', but let the dialogue creatively continue!

References

Brown, D. and Pedder, J. (1989) *Introduction to Psychotherapy. An Outline of Psychodynamic Principles and Practice*. London: Tavistock/Routledge.

Freud, S. (1915) *Instincts and their Vicissitudes*, in S. Freud (1976), *The Pelican Freud Library*. Harmondsworth: Penguin.

Freud, S. (1976) *The Pelican Freud Library*. Harmondsworth: Pelican. (Texts reprinted unabridged from the Standard Edition of the Complete Works of Sigmund Freud, 24 volumes, Hogarth Press, 1953–74.

Gendlin, E.T. (1984) 'The client's client: the edge of awareness', in R.F. Levant and J.M. Shlien (eds), *Client-Centered Therapy and the Person-Centered Approach: New Directions in Theory, Research and Practice*. New York: Praeger.

Greenberg, L., Rice, L. and Elliott, R. (1993) *Facilitating Emotional Change: the Moment-by-Moment Process*. New York: Guilford.

Jacobs, M. (1985) *The Presenting Past*. London: Harper and Row.

Jacobs, M. (1988) *Psychodynamic Counselling in Action*. London: Sage.

Kahn, E. (1985) 'Heinz Kohut and Carl Rogers – a timely comparison', *American Psychologist*, 40: 893–904.

Klein, M. (1946) 'Some notes on defence mechanisms', in J. Mitchell (ed.) (1986), *The Selected Melanie Klein*. Harmondsworth: Penguin.

Malan, D.H. (1979) *Individual Psychotherapy and the Science of Psychodynamics*. Oxford: Butterworth-Heinemann.

McLeod, J. (1993) *An Introduction to Counselling*. Buckingham: Open University Press.

Mearns, D. (1994) *Developing Person-Centred Counselling*. London: Sage.

Mearns, D. and Thorne, B. (1988) *Person-Centred Counselling in Action*. London: Sage.

Noonan, E. (1983) *Counselling Young People*. London: Methuen.

Norcross, J. and Goldfried, M. (eds) (1992) *Handbook of Psychotherapy Integration*. New York: Basic Books.

Rogers, C.R. (1951) *Client-Centered Therapy*. Boston: Houghton Mifflin.

Rogers, C.R. (1961) *On Becoming a Person*. Boston: Houghton Mifflin.

Wheeler, S. (1993) 'Reservations about eclectic and integrative approaches to counselling', in W. Dryden (ed.), *Questions and Answers on Counselling in Action*. London: Sage.

Discussion issues

1 What are the main similarities and differences between the person-centred approach and psychodynamic counselling?

2 What is a 'process-orientated approach'?

3 Why is the psychodynamic counsellor interested in the client's life history?

4 Can therapies ever be coherently integrated?

2

Person-Centred and Systemic Models

Martin Payne

'John, with his hands over his eyes, lapsed into silence. I asked him what he was thinking, and he replied that he was worried about what I would think of him for crying. I said, "If you are crying on the inside and not on the outside at the same time, you will drown your strength."'

'We believe that "therapy" is inadequate to describe the work discussed here. The . . . dictionary describes therapy as the "treatment of disease, disorder, defect etc., as by some remedial or curative process." In our work we do not construct problems in terms of disease and do not imagine that we do anything that relates to a "cure".'

The therapeutic process . . . 'necessitates the active involvement of persons in the reorganization of their experience'.

These quotations are not from a person-centred therapist but from Michael White, a family and marital therapist at the Dulwich Centre in Adelaide, South Australia (White, 1986; White and Epston, 1989), whose work is becoming increasingly influential internationally (cf. S. Gilligan and R. Price, 1993). Systemic concepts rooted in the writings of Gregory Bateson underlie the approach (White, 1986, 1989), for example in its insistence on the importance of political, relational and social contexts in influencing people's perceptions of their situations, but White's practice incorporates original emphases and departures. As a person-centred counsellor I find White's ideas invigorating, exciting, and convincing, with enough common ground between Carl Rogers and White to make their integration enriching to my work – at a time when there is some movement in family therapy to recognize the relevance of concepts more usually associated with the person-centred tradition (Ceccin, 1985; Boscolo, 1989; Hoffman 1990; Wilkinson, 1992; O'Hanlon, 1993) and some person-centred therapists are looking at systemic perspectives in working with couples (e.g. Warner, 1989).

Externalizing the problem

On first reading White I recognized that his key concept of *Externalization of the Problem* matched my own experience in a personal crisis some years ago, when I had found hope and strength by instinctively personifying my depressive

---

This chapter was first published as 'Down-under innovation: a bridge between person-centred and systemic models', in *Counselling, Journal of the British Association for Counselling*, vol. 4, no. 2, pp. 117–19 (1993).

symptoms as 'The Enemy' something apart from my 'True Self' which could be fought.

Michael White's therapeutic approach is described by Karl Tomm as 'simple in the sense that what is basically entailed is a linguistic separation of the distinction of the problem from the personal identity of the patient (*sic*). This intervention opens "conceptual space" for patients (*sic*) to take more effective initiatives to escape the influence of the problem in their lives. What is complicated and difficult is the delicate means by which it can be achieved' (Tomm, 1989).

'The externalizing of the problem and the re-authoring of lives and relationships' (1989) is perhaps White's most accessible and complete summary of his approach and its theoretical base. It is not a universal method and there are many circumstances where White modifies it or uses a different approach; but he has found it particularly effective in helping couples, families and individuals where despair and defeat have become predominant, often with one family member identified as 'having' a problem 'incorporated in' them.

Examples in the paper include a soiling child, a child who has sleep problems, and young people previously diagnosed as 'schizophrenic'. A consistent therapeutic framework underpins a variety of creative responses geared to the needs, circumstances and characteristics of the persons (White does not use the term 'client') and the description of method which follows is a simplified, generalized outline.

The 'Problem Saturated Account'

White first invites persons to describe their problems in detail. Often these accounts convey a sense of being overwhelmed by and at the mercy of events. White encourages the account to include the problem's effects on all who encounter it, and extends it by questioning – using linguistic forms which begin to refer to the problem as a factor external to the individual, couple or family. An example is his reference to an encopretic child's family's problem as 'Sneaky Poo' (a characteristically humane and humorous touch). White's question 'encourages persons to map the influence of the problem in their lives and relationships . . . to identify the problem's sphere of influence, and this can include in the behavioural, emotional, physical, interactional and attitudinal domains . . . rather than restrict the investigation of the effects of the problem to the relationship between the problem and the person ascribed the problem, these questions identify the effect of the problem across various interfaces; between the problem and various persons, and between the problem and various relationships' (White, 1989).

White's term for this first description by persons of the problem and its effects on their lives is the 'Problem Saturated Account'. In his articles he gives least space to this initial process and yet clearly it is seen as crucial – a point confirmed by John Burnham (Burnham, 1991). For a person-centred therapist this would be when Rogerian Core Conditions were established, accompanying the client's experiencing the relief of sharing pent-up distress. In White's own stated terms, it is the first of two complementary descriptions to be drawn from the persons, which together will comprise 'Double Description' (Bateson's term, related to the impossibility of any one viewpoint adequately describing any reality (Bateson, 1979).

White contends that persons' views of their relationship with a problem are limited by mental set – 'dependent upon how it fits with the network of pre-suppositions' (White, 1986). Persons presenting problem-dominated situations tend to see only the influence of the problem, not their actual and potential resistances to and victories over it. The Problem Saturated Account is one, but only one, possible description. White does not deny or invalidate that experience; unlike with a cognitive behavioural approach, he does *not* wish to represent to the persons that they are 'thinking wrongly'. Through the therapist's firstly exter-nalizing the problem then questioning, a second, different description of the same events is encouraged (*not* imposed by the therapist) where the painful experiences begin gradually to be seen in a contrasting, more hopeful perspective as persons start to recognize that they have unknowingly been resisting the problem's attempts to dominate their lives.

A second account – drawing forth awareness of strengths

As in person-centred therapy, White's assumption is that persons are capable of working out their own solutions once they have gained a recognition of their own potential to do so; that no matter how defeated persons appear to be, they are in fact always fighting back, are to an extent succeeding, and have potential for further success. The aim of White's approach is to help persons recognize, call on and trust these strengths in their movement towards what White calls 'personal agency'. He uses Erving Goffman's term 'Unique Outcomes' (Goffman, 1961/1987, p. 119) for persons' previously unrecognized, successful resistances to their problems, and he calls the process of encouraging Double Description 'Relative Influence Questioning' (White, 1988, 1989). The questions are designed to 'assist in engaging persons in . . . ascription of new meaning . . . involve them in . . . the re-authoring of their lives and relationships' (White and Epston, 1990). Some examples (White, 1988):

> 'Can you recall an occasion when you could have given in to the problem and didn't?'
> 'What do you think Fred could have noticed about how your relationship coped on this occasion that could have been surprising to him?'
> 'What difference does knowing this about yourself make to how you feel about yourself?'
>
> (To encopretic children, White, 1984) – 'Are you more the boss over the Sneaky Poo or is it more the boss over you?'
>
> 'When do you think you will deal the Sneaky Poo a decisive blow?'

The groundwork for Relative Influence Questioning is the problem's having already been characterized, implicitly, as external to the person, a deviation from their norm (what a Rogerian therapist would call the True Self). White firmly stresses that behaviour which directly damages others, such as sexual abuse or violence, should never be externalized: 'When these problems are identified, the therapist would be more inclined to encourage the externalizing of the attitudes and beliefs that appear to compel the violence, and those strategies that maintain persons in their subjugation; for example the enforcement of secrecy and isolation' (White, 1989).

The effort to define the problem in a way that is acceptable to the persons concerned is in itself therapeutic: 'At times when families or couples present for therapy . . . externalizing can establish a mutually acceptable definition of the problem, and this facilitates conditions under which persons can work effectively together in their efforts to resolve their problems' (White, 1989). (He also claims that defining and externalizing the problem can counteract past stereotyping, e.g. with psychiatric 'labels'). White quotes a family where parents identified their adolescent son's 'irresponsibility' as the problem. The young man saw the problem as his parents' 'nagging' and 'hassling'. After talking about their feelings concerning what might happen if things did not change, all expressed considerable anxiety; this was the problem then agreed as at the centre of their difficulties, and the sessions became cooperative and productive (White, 1989).

Discoveries made through Relative Influence Questioning may produce still further re-definitions of the problem to be externalized, 'particularly . . . when persons have been undergoing some struggle to identify terms of description that adequately identify their experience of the problem' (White, 1989).

Persons become aware of their choices

White's next step is to point out that the persons face the choice of cooperating with the problem or challenging it; he calls this 'Raising the Dilemma' (White, 1986). If persons decide that they do not wish to confront the problem or are not yet ready for the stresses this may produce, then other possibilities are discussed – such as a pause in therapy, a longer time scale, a referral or abandoning therapy altogether. If they do choose to attempt to challenge the problem (and most do) then this is in itself a Unique Outcome and therapy proceeds with what Tomm calls 'the careful use of language in a therapeutic conversation (through which) the patient's (*sic*) healing initiatives are mobilized' (Tomm, 1989).

White congratulates the persons on their courageous choice but warns that there will be a real struggle, with 'hangovers' – times when the problem will fight back by achieving partial or temporary successes. He encourages and assists the persons to explore what these discoveries of unrecognized strengths might mean 'for them in the present and the future and in so doing to 'revise their relationship with the problems' (White, 1989) as they 're-write' a 'new life story' including past, present and potential successes in defeating the problem's demands. Sometimes this is all that is needed – 'I have consistently found that relative influence questioning, of itself, precipitates significant changes that are empowering to family members' (White, 1988). This process – encouraging persons to 're-story' their perceived life history to include previously forgotten or ignored resourcefulness and capacities, with the aim of encouraging a wider, more realistic and hopeful self-view as a springboard to solving their problems, is central to White's approach. It is one of several aspects differentiating it from Steve de Shazer's superficially similar but more functional 'Solution Focused' therapy (White and de Shazer, 1993).

The 're-writing their story' and 'performing new meanings around Unique Outcomes' (White, 1989) emerge from the persons and are not imposed by the therapist. It 'is not suitably described as "pointing out positives". In response to the invitation to attend to unique outcomes, family members entertain new descriptions of themselves, others, and their relationships. In this process, the therapist is not required to convince anyone of anything' (White, 1988).

White's accounts of his sessions make inspiriting reading. They convey a sense of warmth, creative joy and even fun, reinforcing his claim that his approach 'frees persons to take a lighter, more effective and less stressed approach to "deadly serious" problems' (White, 1989). White describes helping a child to defeat night fears by externalizing them as Monsters, and externalizing the mother's nervous attempts to deal with the boy's fears as 'cooperating with the fears' by taking away his personal agency in fighting. Among other battle plans the boy is encouraged to draw pictures of his monsters, lock the pictures in a box and put it in the garden at night because the 'Third Law of Monsters' states that monsters are 'fearsome with night practice and more funny with day practice', and finally he takes part in a ceremonial award of a Diploma in Fear Busting (White, 1985, pp. 31–3).

Rogers and White

Person-centred therapists may be feeling uneasy. Is it not fundamental to Rogers that the opposite of externalization must happen – indeed, that therapy enables clients to cease to externalize their problems and fully to accept them as aspects of themselves? Rogers writes that in early stages of therapy 'Problems are perceived as external to the self' and that through therapy this is changed for the better; 'there are no longer "problems", external or internal. The client is living, subjectively, a phase of his problem. It is not an object' (Rogers, 1961).

These are complementary positions. White, through externalization of persons' problems, helps them to separate from their limited-vision-based perceptions – aspects of the self that are out of key with what he calls 'lived experience' (White, 1989). He does *not* suggest externalization of *responsibility* for actions and attitudes (see the quotation above concerning sexual abuse and violence) and indeed claims that 'as these practices assist persons to become aware of and to describe their relationship with the problem, they enable persons to assume a responsibility for the problem that they could not do beforehand' (White, 1989). Rogers' reference is to a defensive avoidance of responsibility. Rogerian therapy, by its very concern to establish acceptance of clients (as distinguished from their actions) as an essential condition for therapy, *itself* encourages externalization of and relinquishment of those aspects of the Self which are damagingly derived from the internalization of others' values and perceptions (Rogers, 1951).

A short paper cannot do justice to White's approach (I omit details of his rigorously argued debt to Bateson and Foucault and his recent development with David Epston of using letters to persons as part of therapy (White and Epston, 1990)).

Rogers and White come from different traditions and certainly differ in many significant ways. My aim here has been to stress their common ground, which includes a significant range of positive, humanly optimistic perspectives including the belief that clients always have a potential for self-derived growth and change; a rejection of 'unconscious' explanations and processes as unknowable and of limited usefulness; respect for rather than denial of client perceptions; a belief that the therapist should follow the client; a belief that the central aim is to promote empowerment of the client; and the concept of clients' potential for reorganization of 'interiorized' experience as a route to overcoming longstanding problems.

I cannot resist ending with quotations from Rogers and White which show a similarly engaging, self-deprecating humour.

(a) Rogers (at a public demonstration of person-centred therapy):

> *Client*: [*dubiously*] So even though I'm getting older, I can still be a naughty little girl?
> *Rogers*: Well, I don't know . . . I'm only eighty, but I can still be a naughty little boy.
> [*Much laughter and applause.*] (Rogers, 1990)

(b) White (extract and footnote from an article on 'vicious and virtuous cycles' in relationship patterns):

> When events are considered within the context of mutually causative deviation-amplification feedback-processes, they can be understood as the 'virtually inevitable' outcome of vicious or virtuous cycles.*
>
> * This classification depends entirely upon the consequences. I recently had a fall which resulted in hospitalization and surgery. I was riding downhill on a child's cycle at a birthday party for one of my daughter's friends . . . the inevitable happened. I still don't know how it all started but this accident can be classified as the consequence of a vicious (child's) cycle. (White, 1984, p. 154)

References

Bateson, G. (1979) *Mind and Nature: a Necessary Unity*. New York: E.P. Dutton. (Quoted in Keeney, B.P. (1983) *Aesthetics of Change*. New York: Guilford Press. p. 27).

Boscolo, L. in Cornwell, M. (1989) 'Falling in love with ideas – an interview with Luigi Boscolo', *Australia and New Zealand Journal of Family Therapy*, 10(2): 97–103.

Burnham, J. (1991) 17th April: Kensington Consultation Centre workshop on the White/Epston Model at Little Plumstead Hospital, Norwich.

Ceccin, G. (1985) in D. Campbell and R. Draper (eds), *Application of Systemic Family Therapy: the Milan Approach*. London/New York: Grune and Stratton. p. 26.

Goffman, E. (1961/1987) *Asylums*. London: Penguin.

Hoffman, L. in Carr, D. (1990), 'Developments in systemic approaches', Cardiff AFT Conference report, *Context*, 61(2): 4.

O'Hanlon, W.H. (1993) 'Possibility theory', in S. Gilligan and R. Price (eds), *Therapeutic Conversations*. New York/London: W.W. Norton. pp. 6, 7, 14.

Rogers, C.R. (1951) *Client Centred Therapy*. London: Constable.

Rogers, C.R. (1961) *Becoming a Person*. London: Constable.

Rogers, C. (1990) *The Carl Rogers Reader* (eds H. Kirschenbaum and V. Land Henderson). London: Constable.

Rogers, C.R. et al. (1990) *Dialogues* (eds H. Kirschenbaum and V. Land Henderson). London: Constable.

Tomm, K. (1989) 'Externalizing the problem and internalizing personal agency', *Journal of Strategic and Systemic Therapies* (Halifax, Canada).

Warner, M.S. (1989) 'Empathy and structure in the family system', *Person Centred Review*, no. 4, 324–43.

*White, M. (1984) 'Pseudo-encopresis: from avalanche to victory, from vicious to virtuous cycles', *Family Systems Medicine (Australia)*, 2(2).

*White, M. (1985) 'Fear busting and monster taming: an approach to the fears of young children', *Dulwich Centre Review*.

White, M. (1986) 'Negative explanation, restraint and double description', in *Selected Papers*. Adelaide: Dulwich Centre Publications. pp. 85–99.

*White, M. (1988) *The Process of Questioning: a Therapy of Literary Merit?* Adelaide: Dulwich Centre.

*White, M. (1989) 'The externalising of the problem and the re-authoring of lives and relationships', *Newsletter* (Dulwich Centre, Adelaide), Summer.

White, M. and Epston, D. (1989) *Literate Means to Therapeutic Ends*. Adelaide: Dulwich Centre. Reissued 1990 as *Narrative Means to Therapeutic Ends*. New York: W.W. Norton.

White, M. and de Shazer, S. (1993) in S. Gilligan and R. Price (eds), *Therapeutic Conversations*. New York/London: W.W. Norton.

Wilkinson, M. (1992) 'How do we understand empathy systemically?', *Journal of Family Therapy*, 14(2): 193–205.

*Also reprinted in White, M. (1989) *Selected Papers*. Adelaide: Dulwich Centre. Available in UK from Kensington Consultation Centre, Publications Dept. 2 Wyvil Court, Trenchard Street, London SW8 2TG or from Brief Therapy Press, 4d Shirland Mews, London W9 3DY.

Discussion issues

1   Michael White claims that his approach 'frees persons to take a lighter, more effective, and less stressed approach to "deadly serious" problems'. What might be (a) the disadvantages and (b) the advantages of sometimes lightening the atmosphere in therapeutic sessions about serious issues?

2   Michael White's accounts of his work reveal that persons he helps seldom need to attend more than a few, often widely spaced sessions for significant and lasting changes to occur in their abilities to cope with and/or overcome their problems. What might this suggest about the assumptions underlying some other counselling models which assume the need for many sessions, at regular weekly intervals?

3   What (a) advantages and (b) disadvantages might result for clients in a therapist's using *either* of these approaches:
    (a) taking a very long time, perhaps over many sessions, to listen to and mutually clarify the client's problem?

continued

(b) moving as swiftly as possible, perhaps in the first session, to drawing out the client's past and present successes with aspects of the problem?

4 Rogers died before Michael White's approach started to become widely known. He was always open to new ideas that might enrich his own work. From your reading of Rogers, what do *you* think his opinion might have been of White's approach?

3

Systems Theory

David Bott

This chapter is concerned with understanding the relationship between psychological and systemic thinking in an integrated model of counselling.

In the practice of counselling we can only decide to do one thing rather than another by reference to explanations about what people are like and how they can be helped. This is a question of epistemology, or 'rules one used in making sense of the world and making sense of others' (Bateson, 1971). As Bateson (1977) argues: 'All descriptions are based on theories of how to make descriptions. You cannot claim to have no epistemology, to claim so is to have nothing but a bad epistemology' (p. 147).

There is a range of theories and models which inform counselling, notably: humanistic psychology, psychodynamic theory and learning theory. Recently systems theory has come to assume increasing importance. Systemic thinking with its emphasis on relationship and circular causality represents a revolutionary epistemological shift. In locating difficulties in the context of a set of relationships as opposed to the psychology of an individual it is much more than the application of a new set of therapeutic practices (Auerswald, 1986). Where, in the practice of counselling, it is possible to assimilate and integrate what are often competing and conflicting explanations (Egan, 1986), systems theory is problematic. Practitioners who have been used to focusing on the individual are challenged by systemic thinking and sometimes offended by systemic methods. This does not mean that it can be ignored. Systems theory has been central to the development of family and couple therapy (Hoffman, 1981) and outcome studies suggest very favourable results in relation to a wide range of problems and populations (Gurman et al., 1986). Significantly, systemic approaches may provide a framework for developing interventions in work with clients from different cultures (Bott and Hodes, 1989).

Epistemological considerations are of no interest to those practitioners who make sense of their work by reference to a discrete theory or school. Even so, it follows that they are still adherents of an implicit epistemology. They will look for increased understanding and effectiveness by further study of their existing set of explanations to the exclusion of others. An alternative view is that, in setting out to explain similar and related phenomena, each approach has the possibility of enriching understanding of the others. Saying this is not to advocate crude eclecticism but a disciplined study of theory both in relation to other theories and in historical and social context.

This chapter was first published as 'Epistemology: the place of systems theory in an integrated model of counselling', in *Counselling, Journal of the British Association for Counselling*, vol. 1, no. 1, pp. 23–5 (1990).

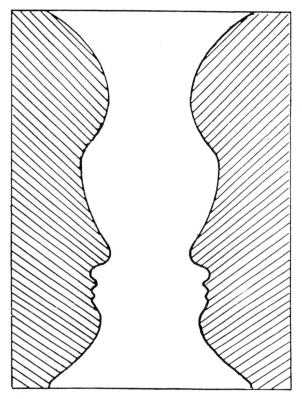

Figure 3.1

The problem remains of how to reconcile what appear at first sight to be very different epistemological frameworks. One option is to go for the discrete theory stance and view the approaches as mutually exclusive. Here, practitioners have to decide whether to be psychological or systemic counsellors or therapists. The disadvantage is that each camp is deprived of the insights and understanding available to the other. Experience suggests that they are often also rendered incapable of talking to each other at all without coming close to blows. A second possibility is to see each approach as complementary to the other merely filling in what the other leaves out. In ignoring fundamental epistemological differences between systemic and psychological thinking, this invites the charge of mindless eclecticism. The attempt to see an individual and a system at the same time tends to confuse rather than illuminate. A third alternative is to establish systems theory as metatheoretical to individual psychology. The latter is subordinated and incorporated into the former (Rocco Cottone, 1988). This is theoretically tidy and logical but risks losing the individual in the system.

The view taken here is that these are false alternatives and each might be the case depending upon where the perceiver is standing, what they are looking at and when they are looking. Here the classic Gestalt experiment can be used (Figure 3.1). It is only possible to see figure at the expense of ground and in that sense they are mutually exclusive. Equally both are needed in order to see either. Above all, it is the relationship between the two that gives them meaning.

An example: epistemology and student counselling

To illustrate this, take the case of a student coming to a college counselling service (Bott, 1988) presenting with concerns about isolation and suicidal thoughts. The way in which the counsellor makes sense of the difficulties and decides to work with them is a question of epistemology.

The counsellor taking a humanistic view will assume that the difficulties are associated with a damaging self-concept (Rogers, 1974). Adopting Rogers' necessary and sufficient conditions the student may be facilitated in the expression of an authentic self and the emotions associated with this. From a psychodynamic perspective, the problem may be understood in terms of difficulties in completing the developmental tasks of separation and individuation exacerbated by the 'environmental separation experience' (Masterson, 1971) of coming away to study. Here the counsellor will work with the client in uncovering and illuminating the past and a transference relationship will provide the central vehicle for change. A behavioural approach (Krumboltz and Thorenson, 1976) will frame the problem in terms of skill deficits. Social skills may be developed with the support of a behavioural programme.

There are fundamental differences between each of these approaches in terms of philosophy and theory. In practice, however, counsellors have found it helpful to integrate supportive/expressive, transferential and behavioural principles (Egan, 1986). This is possible because, while they differ in their descriptions of what people are like, they share a common perspective in locating difficulties within the individual and helping is seen in terms of working with mental processes with a view to self-actualization, resolving intrapsychic conflicts or increasing skills and abilities.

Systems epistemology, with its focus upon context and pattern, does not lend itself readily to integration. Here the figure of the individual's mind becomes ground as perception shifts looking for the meaning of a symptom in a complex set of relationships. This follows from a radically different conception of the nature of mind. Bateson (1971) rejects linear cause and effect epistemology on the grounds that thinking cannot be located in the mind of an individual. The brain inside a person is part of larger systems residing in balance with the environment. What thinks is the total circuit. Counselling, then, focuses upon patterns of transactions over time rather than individual experience. Difficulties or symptoms are viewed as communications within circular causal loops (Hoffman, 1981). The counsellor looks for the function or meaning of a symptom within a relationship system (Keeney, 1979). In practice this usually means seeing a family together, having the members communicate with each other and identifying patterns from which structure can be inferred and family themes and transgenerational issues identified. This shift in perspective is put succinctly by Haley (1980): 'the problem is a malfunctioning deviant organisation: that organisation requires peculiar communicative behaviour and therefore peculiar thought processes' (p. 29).

Systemically, the student's difficulties are placed in a set of relationships over time. As a system the function of the family is to: 'produce and train new sets of humans to be independent, form new families and repeat the process' (Hoffman, 1981, p. 160).

It follows that family life is by its nature problematic in that there is an inherent tension in the need to provide stability while accommodating development. This is worked through in a series of discontinuous rearrangements of relationships interspersed with periods of comparative calm. The developmental phase when young people are leaving home presents a multiple challenge to the existing arrangement of relationships in a family (Carter and McGoldrick, 1989). At the same time the grandparent generation may be facing failing health, increasing dependency and death. The middle parenting generation, while carrying increasing responsibilities for their parents, are faced with having to work out a new relationship as a couple. There are particular difficulties for the young person who has carried family responsibility for diverting conflict (Minuchin et al., 1978). From this perspective the distressed or acting out student can be understood as providing a solution to a family crisis where the developmental pressure for change has not been met by appropriate and sufficient transformation of the family system or its structure (Bott, 1988).

Systemic intervention will be aimed at helping the young person separate and become independent in a way that is constructive for all family members. This may take the form of family meetings or of helping the individual change the part they play in the family process.

Psychological and systemic epistemologies

In making sense of difficulties the counsellor is left with the dilemma of whether to focus on the psychology of an individual, a system of relationships, or to attempt some synthesis of both. One option is to see psychological and systemic thinking as mutually exclusive. Haley (1987) takes this view from a systemic position. He argues that attempts at rapprochement are founded upon a misunderstanding of what systemic thinking is about in that: 'When you focus on an individual I don't think you can see simultaneously what is happening to the system . . . to bring them together and say that they are all true is just to confuse the issue' (p. 39).

Others, notably British family therapists who have come to systemic thinking from work in individual and group analysis, see the possibility of integration (Dare, 1981; Skynner, 1986). Drawing on object relations theory, they take the view that the internalized experiences within the family of origin are not only crucial to the formation of the adult personality but help create the systemic structure of the individual's new family. Dare suggests that: 'each member of a person's family is recorded within his memory and the patterns of interaction between himself and the persons of the family of origin are repeated as potential for interactions when he is making a family' (p. 284).

One view is that psychological and systemic approaches are incompatible, the other is that they are complementary. What is the case is that, in making sense of difficulties, they are concerned with intervention at different levels of abstraction. To quote Dare: 'The family therapist intervenes on those external processes that are beginning to be internalised ... psychoanalytic psychotherapy is directed to the point where the internal world is being externalised' (p. 288).

To do the former requires a perspective that gives primacy to the realm of relationship. The latter demands that attention be given to individual meaning and identity. Apart from this each needs different skills. In individual counselling the relationship with the counsellor is the vehicle for change as the client works through internal processes. The systemic therapist is concerned with the external world and affiliates in order to actively manoeuvre for changes in relationships. Clearly when past distortions are worked through and resolved current relationships change. Equally, realignments of relationships impinge on an individual's internal world.

Frameworks for Practice

Recent additions to the counselling and therapy literature are beginning to address the practical implications of combining individual and family approaches while recognizing the epistemological distinction between psychological and systemic thinking. Jenkins and Asen (1992) propose a systemic framework for working with individuals where the work focuses upon the social context of the client rather than transference or internal feeling states. In a similar way, the author (Bott, 1994) has outlined a model for working contextually with individuals which emphasizes the value of particular systemic approaches at different stages of the therapeutic process.

Another response, also proposed by the author (Bott, 1992), has been to suggest an integration of psychological and systemic approaches where the focus moves over time from individual characteristics to context and relationships. Empathic understanding and the examination of the counselling relationship, which are a feature of the earlier stages of intervention, also model the means by which the client can approach actual family members with a view to changing unproductive patterns.

Conclusion

At the level of theory there are two broad sets of explanations about how to relieve distress exhibited by an individual. Each is directed towards different phenomena – the structure of individuals and that of relationships. In the author's experience much energy can be expended on establishing which is right and which is wrong with individual and family counsellors dividing up into different and often hostile camps. At the same time crude atheoretical eclecticism only serves to confuse. Haley is right when he argues that the individual and the system cannot be seen simultaneously. However integration is possible by moving from figure to ground, making ground figure, and moving back again. It follows that different theoretical perspectives, while requiring different thinking, do not necessarily need different counsellors. A practitioner can make sense of things in terms of sequences, processes and structure – the externals of family life. The same practitioner may focus instead on the internalized family in the form of the self-concept of humanistic counselling, developmental failure in psycho-analytic thinking or faulty learning. Where they will run into trouble is in attempting to do both at the same time. Systemic epistemology does have a place in an integrated model of counselling but to argue this is not to suggest that integration is a simple process of addition.

References

Auerswald, E. (1986) In C. Fishman and B. Rusman (eds), *Evolving Models of Family Change*. New York: Guilford Press.

Bateson, G. (1971) 'A systems approach', *International Journal of Psychiatry*, 9: 242–4.

Bateson, G. (1977) '"The thing of it is"', in M. Katz, W. Marsh and G. Thompson (eds), *Explorations of Planetary Culture at Lindisfarne Conferences: Earth's Answer*. New York: Harper and Row, pp. 142–5.

Bott, D. (1988) 'The relevance of systemic thinking to student counselling', *Counselling Psychology Quarterly*, 1(4): 367–75.

Bott, D. (1992) '"Can I help you help me to change?" Systemic intervention in an integrated model of counselling', *Counselling, Journal of the British Association for Counselling*, 3(1): 31–3.

Bott, D. (1994) 'A family systems framework for intervention with individuals', *Counselling Psychology Quarterly*, 7(2): 105–15.

Bott, D. and Hodes, M. (1989) 'Structural therapy for a West African family', *Journal of Family Therapy*, 11: 169–79.

Carter, E. and McGoldrick, M. (1989) *The Changing Family Life Cycle*. New York: Alleyn and Bacon.

Dare, C. (1981) 'Psychoanalysis and family therapy', in S. Waldrond Skinner (ed.), *Developments in Family Therapy*. London: Routledge and Kegan Paul.

Egan, G. (1986) *The Skilled Helper*, 3rd edn. Pacific Grove, CA: Brooks Cole.

Gurman, A., Kniskern, D. and Pinsof, W. (1986) Research on the process and outcome of marital and family therapy. In S. Garfield and A. Bergin (eds), *Handbook of Psychotherapy and Behavior Change*, 3rd edn. New York: Wiley.

Haley, J. (1980) *Leaving Home*. New York: McGraw Hill.

Haley, J. (1987) 'The disappearance of the individual', *Networker*, March–April.

Hoffman, L. (1981) *Foundations of Family Therapy*. New York: Basic Books.

Jenkins, H. and Asen, K. (1992) 'Family therapy without the family: a framework for systemic practice, *Journal of Family Therapy*, 14: 1–14.

Keeney, B. (1979) 'Ecosystemic epistemology: an alternative paradigm for diagnosis', *Family Process*, 18(2).

Krumboltz, J. and Thorenson, C. (1976) *Counselling Methods*. New York: Rinehart and Winston.

Masterson, J. (1971) *The Diagnosis and Treatment of the Borderline Adolescent*. New York: Wiley Interscience.

Minuchin, S., Rosman, B. and Baker, L. (1978) *Psychosomatic Families: Anorexia Nervosa in Context*. Cambridge, MA: Harvard University Press.

Rocco Cottone, R. (1988) 'Epistemological and ontological issues in counselling', *Counselling Psychology*, 1(4): 357–66.

Rogers, C. (1974) *On Becoming a Person*. New York: Houghton and Mifflin.

Skynner, A.C.R. (1986) 'What is effective in group psychotherapy', *Group Analysis*, 19: 5–24.

Discussion issues

1 How does the understanding of epistemology help you in your work as a counsellor?
2 'Epistemological considerations are of no interest to those practitioners who make sense of their work by reference to a discrete theory or school.' Discuss.
3 Provide examples of the practical application of epistemological ideas.
4 In what way are psychological and systemic approaches complementary?

4

An Existential Framework

Emmy van Deurzen-Smith

People who turn to a counsellor or a psychotherapist often hope to find someone who can do more than just listen or understand. It is rarely sufficient for them to find someone who is an accomplished technician, capable of working with them on their personal problems in an insightful and efficient manner. It is not enough for them to be prompted, coaxed, challenged and supported. Deep down, all along they know that it is something else that they hanker after. It is not the embracing warmth and love of a mother, it is not even the comradeship and loyalty of a friend. Neither is it the admonishments and good advice of a father figure. What they really crave is the wisdom of someone capable of putting their present worries and doubts into some perspective. What they long for is the voice of experience reminding them of the possibility of consulting their own conscience and making sense of their life in terms of its ultimate significance. In brief what people are often looking for is the answer to the question: what is the meaning of my life?

All too often counselling and therapy detract from this fundamental question rather than encouraging the client's quest for an answer. If the therapist emphasizes the client's pathology which has so far stood in the way of a satisfactory way of life, the client may sink into a morass of morose self-doubt and negativity. If the therapist emphasizes the client's potential and need for growth a simplistic and unrealistic self-congratulatory spurt of energy may ensue which often fails when new troubles appear at the horizon. It is therefore important for any form of therapy and counselling to insert itself within a wider framework which can provide the background investigation of fundamental issues. The existential approach provides just such a framework.

An existential approach consists of a philosophical investigation of life. The focus is on the problems inherent in being in the world, not primarily on those of personal pathology or achievement. Clients are encouraged to explore their most intimately held opinions and values in order to discover for themselves what it is that really matters to them when it comes down to it. The most basic question here can be formulated as: what is worth living for? It can also be expressed as: what would it be worth dying for?

In a more moderate and modest form the objective is to find those values, rules and insights that one would be able to live by and commit oneself to. And of

This chapter was first published as 'The need for an existential framework for psychotherapy and counselling', in *Counselling, Journal of the British Association for Counselling*, no. 62, pp. 6–8 (1987); and the detailed case study was first published in 'Existential Therapy', in W. Dryden (ed.), *Individual Therapy in Britain* (London: Harper and Row, 1984), pp. 172–7.

course in the first instance such an enquiry starts from the consideration of those rules, values, and assumptions that one is in fact already living by, be it without express knowledge of them and their impact on one's life.

There are a number of therapeutic approaches that take such considerations into account. Worth mentioning are Daseins-analysis and existential analysis, which are both existentially oriented forms of psychoanalysis (May 1958; Boss, 1963, 1975). On the humanistic scene there are many approaches that have been inspired by existential philosophy and that have integrated some of its ideas. Gestalt therapy is by far the most clear representative of these, although its technique is anything but existential. Person-centred counselling also has a similar base, but it stops short of in-depth investigation. In the cognitive mode rational emotive behaviour therapy and personal construct therapy both come close to existential exploration, but their ultimate concern is very different from that of finding meaning. In many ways it is Frankl's logotherapy that represents the existential stream most effectively, in spite of his insistence on paradoxical interventions and in spite of his heavily pastoral interpretations. (Frankl 1946, 1967). R.D. Laing is an important representative of the existential approach in the UK (Laing, 1960, 1961).

Of course there are a number of American authors who have provided inspiration for those wishing to work from an existential perspective. Rollo May's writings in particular have done much to stimulate thinking along these lines (see May, 1958, 1969, 1983).

Yalom was one of the first to define a structure of existential investigation (Yalom, 1980). This is rather new because the existential approach has always maintained a very low profile on technique as it sets out to fight against technology and the alienation that it can produce.

The outline of an existential framework for counselling and therapy must necessarily remain sparse and basic (see van Deurzen-Smith, 1988). It should be an essential map of human living, rather than a detailed description of how to tackle specific personal issues. In the last analysis such a framework would provide the outline for the art of living, rather than for the art of psychotherapy and counselling. It should be a guide for those who want to examine their life in an exhaustive manner without being held back by any particular religious, social and psychological dogma.

Existential philosophers talk about the basic concerns that human beings sooner or later are confronted with. These include death, isolation, loneliness, fate, time, illness and absurdity. They may be dealt with by people's obsession with them or by their active attempt to overcome them through exclusive focus on their opposite, life, communion, love, responsibility, eternity, health and meaning.

The existential view is that it matters enormously to reflect on such issues and on one's ways of dealing with them. As an intrinsically philosophical approach existential therapy and counselling does not pretend to cure or change the person, but simply to assist in coming to terms with life and living. It often seems that once this is possible personal problems and strivings become more easy to tackle as they are now seen against the background of a vast and far more significant purpose which becomes a guiding light.

This was precisely the case with Marie-Louise, who came to counselling to get a better grasp of her own values and in order to glean a sense of direction and meaning in life.

Case example

Marie-Louise was a 24-year-old Frenchwoman, who presented herself in the first interview as a small, but sturdy, colourfully dressed and generously made-up young lady. She worked in England as an au pair and had done so for the last nine months. She left France because she did not know how to solve some of the situations she was involved in. She had broken off a three-year relationship with her boyfriend because he wanted her to marry him and move with him to another town where he had just been promoted. She felt this was a trap and that she would be unable to maintain her independence if she went along with him; independence was one of the main concepts that Marie-Louise's choices were based on. Of her three sisters (all older than she) two were married and installed in 'bourgeois' family life. Marie-Louise had obvious contempt for this.

The third sister had an alternative life-style but was unable to manage her life satisfactorily. The parents were divorced after many years of fighting. Marie-Louise's picture of marriage was that of a battlefield where no one can win. Her picture of her own and her sister's alternative life-styles was that of a romantic voyage into nowhere.

Marie-Louise fled to England to escape from the impossible choice between marrying her boyfriend and becoming like the two elder sisters and her mother, or opting for a bohemian life-style and ending up like her other sister. She was working for an upper-middle-class family in Richmond and spent all her time off with a group of free-floating people of her own age, around Hammersmith.

The problem she experienced was that of not knowing what to do with her life; every possible option seemed to carry potential destruction. Once, she thought she could solve things by starting a new life in England; now she had realized everything was still the same, or worse. The French ex-fiancé had taken up a relationship with another woman. In the gang she hung out with in England, there was a total denial of the value of a personal relationship. While she was pregnant a few months ago, the other women in the group supported her in obtaining an abortion while using the occasion to cut her off from her privileged relationship with one of the men in the group. They called her 'Marylou' and did not seem interested in hearing about her past life in France. She was able to talk quite freely about her French life with Mildred, her employer, but she sensed Mildred's pressure on her to conform and settle down into a 'mature marriage'. At this point in time there was no one she trusted implicitly: everyone seemed out to make her give up something, and nobody really knew her. This theme recurred many times throughout the weekly therapy sessions that took place over a four-month period. Her trust in me was based chiefly on the fact that I at least admitted what I wanted from her: a fee for the session and a commitment to working towards total frankness. What I offered in return seemed most attractive to her: a joint building up of an understanding of her experience in all its many facets and complexity; permission for her to explore the completeness of self that had been lost between her fear of being reduced to a conventional, 'maturely' marrying, dependent Marie-Louise and a fear of being doomed to become Marylou, an outlaw and desperately lonely.

In the second session, Marie-Louise talked about a letter she had received from François, her ex-fiancé. He tried to make her feel jealous and offered her marriage again, more on his terms than ever. To Marylou it seemed like a last chance to become 'mature' and 'dependent': if she refused this time to go straight, she would have to be an outcast ever after – that is how she viewed the dilemma. Most of the session was spent on exploring the definitions and fantasies that constituted the dilemma in her mind. What did it mean to be married? What did it mean to be an outcast? What was her own world like inside, beyond those definitions of a way of life? What essential qualities of life could not be found in either of those accounts of reality?

Slowly, Marie-Louise started to talk about what life 'should be like' or 'could be like' instead of focusing on the two thus far impossible realities she had envisaged. It transpired that what mattered most was to find a life where she could be with people who could listen to her and talk about those things that mattered such as independence *and* romantic love, instead of one *or* the other. We talked about her image of independence and dependence. She discovered that what she really valued was autonomy, i.e. the ability to be a person in her own right, strong enough to remain true to herself while relating deeply to others.

Her Hammersmith group was of course, in favour of 'independence', but this implied that love could not exist: to maintain independence one must reject commitment to anything or anybody. That is not what Marie-Louise wanted although it had often seemed the only way out of smothering relationships. She was starting to disidentify with the ideas of Marylou. She was starting to identify her own personally meaningful ideas and aspirations. She was afraid it would not be realistic to live according to her own ideas, following her own conscience rather than the norm of some existing group in society; she did not think anyone would understand or agree. She wondered where I would want to push her: would I stand by her side when she made her real self known, or would I come down in judgement, in favour of independence or dependence?

The next session she challenged me. She broke down in despair and cried for nearly half an hour uninterruptedly. There was no direct cause other than her expectation of me letting her down and trying to perk her up in spite of herself. She feared I might propose a solution, announcing my bias by choosing the 'right life-style' for her. It was only because I did not do this and instead related to her isolation and despair, to her fear, by letting her know that I respected it and would allow it, it is only because I showed her this respect, first by saying these things and then by letting her cry her own sorrow through, that she started to feel some confidence – not only in my understanding of her reality but chiefly and for the first time in her own right to be just exactly the way she was.

The next session was different. Marie-Louise did not wear make-up. 'It only messes up when I cry anyways,' She wanted to sort out her part in the relationship with François. She had still not replied to the letter he sent her two weeks ago; she was still overflowing with resentment for his treatment of her, his expectations of her fitting in with his life. I reminded her several times of the importance of examining her active part in the relationship rather than focusing on her feelings about what he did to her. She discovered that by doing this she could not only get insight into her own character and actions, but also build up a stronger image of herself as an active human being who does not exclusively respond, react and feel but also creates, initiates and acts.

This new way of viewing her relationship inspired her to write a letter to François the following week. She was pleased with herself for having formulated for the first time what she wanted out of a relationship. She considered the relationship ended because she now knew what she did want to experience with a man.

During those weeks the sessions focused on her slowly building self-esteem. My interventions were all geared to help us explore her inner frame of reference. The Catholic values were much more intrinsically present than she ever wanted to acknowledge herself. She was only able to acknowledge her own rights once she had been able to acknowledge her own 'guilt' in terms of the Catholic Church. Sleeping around and having an abortion were not things that she could easily forgive herself for; in order to live that life of 'freedom' she had had to disown her conscience; she had had to live in 'bad faith', with the created image of the independent Marylou. She lost her substance in the process. Gradually, she was now rebuilding her own sense of substance and identity. Some time during these two months she received a letter from Bernadette, her actress sister, who informed here of the attempted suicide of one of their mutual friends. Marie-Louise understood that act as the only possible way out of the emptiness that follows the flight away from one's own inner reality. She was determined not to flee any more. She had several open disagreements with both her friends in Hammersmith and Mildred, her employer. She concluded that she could not any longer 'play the part' in either case. She decided towards the middle of the third month in therapy that the time had come for her to explore a more creative future; and she planned a trip to France to investigate training courses in social work. Her idea was to find a place in the world where she would be able finally to be herself and help other people to do so too.

She had now been in England for exactly a year and thought herself ready to go back to face her sisters, her parents, even François if she happened to meet him. She was determined to stick to the values she had discovered as her own. To be autonomous rather than dependent or independent was the most crucial decision in terms of her relationship to her family. She feared, however, that no one would understand her new self, although she found that Mildred had been more respectful of her since she applied for the social work courses.

We had already arranged for the last review session before her trip to France when she phoned me in a panic one day. François had arrived in England without giving her any notice. He had come to see her in order to persuade her to come back and marry him. He affirmed that he would respect her new sense of self, but he did not want to listen to her plans for study. Marie-Louise feared that her new autonomy would melt in front of this proposal, which for the first time included her as a person important enough to make a trip to England and abandon his current girlfriend for. She was sure it would not last if she gave in now, but she was also sure, suddenly, that she loved him and wanted him to love her. She decided to tell François all of that and then go off on the trip as planned, alone. The review session was spent considering her growing sense of direction in the midst of all the distractions and disappointments that she feared she would meet on her way. We discussed the middle way between turning her back on people or situations because they had not allowed her sense of self and merging into other people's opinions or ways of life for the sake of it, giving up inner reality. Marie-Louise decided that her commitment to a course of study was of essential importance to her because she needed time to establish her new reality more concretely and substantially. She still feared it would mean a choice away from the relationship with François. She struggled with doubts, anxiety and guilt about walking out on François a second time, albeit this time for positive reasons.

When she came back to England a few weeks later, it was only to fetch her luggage and say her goodbyes to Richmond, Mildred, Hammersmith and me. We had two sessions during this time. Marie-Louise looked very different from the way she did four months before. She had found her own image somewhere between the classic woman and the renegade. She had obtained a place on the desired course, but was already disappointed with the curriculum. We examined her expectations and her attitudes towards the course. At the end, she seemed clear enough about what it was she wanted from the course without having to expect it to provide her with the ultimate answer.

A letter, fifteen months later, indicated that Marie-Louise had had all the disappointments she expected. Her views on social work were certainly less idealistic than at the outset. She had, however, continued with her course of study and was finding satisfaction in her own ability to do so. She was seeing François at weekends and holidays, and there was a possibility of his obtaining a post near Marie-Louise's college. She said that she would feel ready to live with him and commit herself to him if he were prepared to make his commitment clear by that move towards her. She sounded confident.

It would have been easy to pin her down on a number of personal problems in the therapy and ignore her desire to find her own way in disentangling these eventually. It would have been interesting to let her play with her own desires and resentments, helping her to express these in ever fuller ways. But in the event it was only a kind of new courage that Marie-Louise wanted to find for herself so that she could take care of the rest herself. What she wanted more than anything else was to be able to get a clear idea of what she would be able to make of her life, a sense of how and what she had been neglecting or forgetting. Then she was able to look at her emotional life in a fresh way, which allowed her to emerge from it rather than go under again and again. Of course she needed to disentangle herself from the emotional weeds that were impeding her swimming out of the trouble that she was in. Of course she had to relearn how to proceed and swim.

But in the end all that mattered was for her to have gained some understanding of the shores that would be within her reach. It was only when she gained the will to swim again, because there was a direction worth swimming into, that she found the motivation to do whatever else would be necessary to succeed.

References

Boss, M. (1963) *Psychoanalysis and Daseins-analysis*. New York: Basic Books.
Boss, M. (1975) *Existential Foundations of Medicine and Psychology*. New York: Jason Aronson.
van Deurzen-Smith, E. (1984) 'Existential psychotherapy', in W. Dryden (ed.), *Individual Therapy in Britain*. London: Harper and Row.
van Deurzen-Smith, E. (1988) *Existential Counselling in Practice*. London: Sage.
Frankl, V.E. (1946/1964) *Man's Search for Meaning*. London: Hodder and Stoughton.
Frankl, V.E. (1967) *Psychotherapy and Existentialism*. Harmondsworth: Penguin.
Laing, R.D. (1960) *The Divided Self*. Harmondsworth: Penguin.
Laing, R.D. (1961) *Self and Others*. Harmondsworth: Penguin.
May, R., et al. (1958) *Existence*. New York: Basic Books.
May, R. (1969) *Love and Will*. New York: Norton.
May, R. (1983) *The Discovery of Being*. New York: Norton.
Yalom, I. (1980) *Existential Psychotherapy*, New York: Basic Books.

Discussion issues

1 Do you agree that what most people are looking for is the answer to the question, 'What is the meaning of life?'
2 How are the ultimate concerns of rational emotive behaviour therapy and personal construct psychology different from those of the existential approach?
3 What did you learn from the case study?
4 How does your philosophy of life inform your counselling?

5

Personal Construct Counselling

Fay Fransella and Helen Jones

The background

Like so many attempts to come to an understanding of the complexities of human existence, George Kelly's theory has its roots in the counselling setting. In the early 1930s, Kelly had the role of student counsellor placed upon his reluctant shoulders. Reluctant because his whole training had been in science; first as a physicist and mathematician, and then as a physiological psychologist. An assuredly unlikely candidate for the job of helping university students with their problems in the famous 'dust-bowl' of the central United States at the height of the economic depression. But counsellor indeed he became.

Faced with the very real problems students were experiencing, Kelly found his training in psychology useless; it gave him no guidance on how to understand these students let alone help them with their problems. He turned to Freud and found that some students were indeed helped by 'Freudian' interpretations. But his scientific training led him to question whether or not it was these particular Freudian-based interpretations that were of help or whether *any* interpretation would do. He found that any interpretation was helpful *providing* it was directly relevant to the student's problem and offered that student an alternative way of looking at his or her problem, at him- or herself and at life in general.

From these early encounters the *psychology of personal constructs* (1955/1991), the philosophy of *constructive alternativism* and the model of the *person-as-scientist* were born.

The psychology

Kelly presented his theory in the unpalatable form of a fundamental postulate and the eleven corollaries which elaborate it. Every word of the postulate and corollaries is defined, making it the most explicit and elaborated theory in modern psychology.

It is first and foremost a theory about the total person. We are not divided up into motives, emotions, thoughts, perceptions and behaviours. We are complete, unified individuals. In order to understand ourselves and our clients we must discover and pin-point the interpretations we or others place on events in the world which lead us to experience things in the ways that we do. The

This chapter was first published in *Counselling, Journal of the British Association for Counselling*, vol. 6, no. 4, pp. 299–301 (1995).

interpretations (or constructions) we place on events are our construings of those events. These are by no means always consciously and neatly tied up with verbal labels. For instance, we may construe a person or happening with constructs which served us better as children.

Construing is not simply a verbal activity. It is any way in which we 'discriminate' between events, people or objects in our world. For instance, the young child soon sees some similarities between events which involve the same face; these, in turn, are associated with warmth, comfort and a full stomach. The child responds to its construing of these events which it has 'seen' repeating themselves. There are no verbal labels here. Consider the child who comes to construe 'mother' as unpleasant because of the emotions and feelings evoked. In that case the person might experience problems in adult life when making relationships with women. If that were how the counsellor formulated the problem, it might be useful to help the client attach some words to the feelings about 'mothers' in general and this mother in particular and so be better able to work out whether it is reasonable to let 'mothers' influence adult life in such a deleterious way.

The process of reconstruction is under way. This is the aim of all personal construct counselling. The person with a psychological problem is seen as being 'stuck'. Their present construing of life and the world around them are found to be inadequate in some way and they cannot continue developing. And since Kelly sees us each as a form of motion, being psychologically stuck and not able to deal with the ever-shifting course of events is an undesirable state to be in. An example of being 'stuck' is given in the case study at the end of this chapter.

The philosophy of constructive alternativism

Kelly's psychology is a hopeful psychology. We need not be stuck for long. The underlying philosophical statement is that there are always alternative ways of construing any event; 'no one needs to paint himself into a corner; no one needs be completely hemmed in by circumstances; no one needs be the victim of his biography'. This philosophical statement relates to the basic assumption of his theory that *all our present interpretations of the universe are subject to revision or replacement*. For Kelly there is indeed a reality 'out there', but no one person has direct access to it. All we can do is look at our world through our system of personal constructs which enables us to place interpretations upon events and thereby predict outcomes. Thus, we may make ourselves a victim of our biography if we construe it that way.

The model of the person-as-scientist

Since no one has direct access to the truth, personal construct psychology has no dogma. Kelly uses the 'as if' approach. He suggests we might usefully look at all of us 'as if' we were scientists and see whether this gives us any different insights into human beings and leads us to ask different questions about our complexities.

Basically, scientists aim to predict events in the natural world and we, as part of that natural world, may be seen as doing the same. The better able we are to predict events, the more control we have over those events. Scientists have theories and derive hypotheses from those theories. So do we. Scientists conduct experiments to test these hypotheses. So do we. Scientists look to see whether the hypotheses turn out to be right or wrong. So do we.

Our current system of constructs is the equivalent of a system of theories about the world which we have developed over the years. When we construe someone as 'kind' we thereby predict certain types of behaviour from that person. We test out this prediction by behaving in a certain way and look to see whether or not the person responds in a 'kindly' way or not. If the person does, we have been validated; if they spit in our eye, we have been invalidated.

The most unusual aspect of this model is that *our behaviour becomes an experiment*. Instead of trying to understand someone by interpreting their behaviour from our own standpoint, it can be quite illuminating to ask 'what experiment is this person conducting which leads them to behave in this way?' 'What ways of construing is this person testing out?' Not only can useful insights into another's world be gained by such questioning, but it puts into practice an essential aspect of personal construct psychology; that the only way to understand another is to, as far as is humanly possible, get inside that other's shoes and look at the world through that other's eyes.

Personal construct counselling

For Kelly 'counselling is a situation in which one person helps another achieve a psychological reconstruction of life'. Thus, the aim of counselling is to open up the personal world of experience in which the person feels 'stuck' so that they may find alternative ways of coping with the world of events which confronts them. This is by no means always easy, as we are all too well aware. But the personal construct counsellor's starting point is the present personally construed world of the client.

Kelly says his first principle is 'if you do not know what is wrong with someone, ask him (*sic*), he may tell you'. He created the self-characterization sketch to ask that question. By credulous listening we gain our first insight into how our client may construe his or her world. The counsellor will, at the outset, explain to the client something of the nature of the relationship. This is of two people jointly tackling a problem, with the client having to struggle with gaining some understanding of how their present construing is resulting in something not being how they wish it to be. Emphasis is placed on the client and not the counsellor having the answers; it is the client's and not the counsellor's personal construing which is causing the problem. Kelly puts the situation thus:

> The client needs to assume that something can be created that is not already known or is not already there – the fortunate client has a partner, the counsellor – he (*sic*) does not know the answer either, they face the problem together. They formulate hypotheses jointly and upon each other . . . take stock of outcomes and common hunches. Neither is

the boss – the counselling room is a protected laboratory where hypotheses can be formulated, test-tube sized experiments performed, field trials planned and outcomes evaluated . . . the interview is an experiment in behaviour. (Kelly, 1969, p. 229)

With its focus on the person as an ever-moving entity, as a self-creator and thus a potential re-creator, and as the possessor of the final answer to the problem, personal construct counselling has either very few or else an infinite array of 'tools' depending on which way you look at it.

Apart from the *self-characterization*, he designed the *repertory grid*. Kelly saw the grid as enabling the client as well as the counsellor to get a deeper understanding of the client's construing of themselves and their problem. In some grids the client rates, say, their mother on a set of constructs elicited from the client which have been formed into scales. Does the client see their mother as *selfish* or its opposite *unselfish*, as *caring* or *uncaring, independent* or *dependent*. The client will also rate other people in the same way. Such grids yield figures that can be statistically analysed. But grids need not be used in this way. The case study given later uses a 'resistance-to-change' grid because that seemed the most useful type of grid with this particular client. Grids come in many shapes and sizes. For some worked examples of grids and the self-characterization the reader is referred to the book *Personal Construct Counselling in Action* (Fransella and Dalton, 1990).

The personal construct counsellor also makes great use of role play. This is ideally suited for the testing out of new behavioural experiments. The counsellor is not limited to these methods. If it seems that the client cannot move psychologically because she construes events in such a 'tight' manner that there is no room for manoeuvre, then some 'loosening' techniques such as guided fantasy, relaxation or free association may be beneficial. The techniques employed are determined by the needs of a particular client at a particular time. This does not mean that there is no cohesion in what takes place. For the counsellor has the very elaborate and explicit theory guiding her. But within that firm constraint, client and counsellor are free to be inventive together, each seeking to solve the one problem and so help the client 'get on the move again' and take charge of the business of living. The following account of work with a client shows some of these points in action.

Personal construct counselling in practice: being stuck – working with a doctor facing career change

Background

Most doctors make their career choices at the age of seventeen or eighteen when they apply to Medical School. And, at least until recently, they have anticipated a thirty-year tenure when they eventually become Consultants, or GPs.

In the current climate of change in the NHS doctors' futures are no longer quite so certain and far more doctors now seek help with their career development. A personal construct approach can be a powerful way of helping.

Felix

Felix is a Consultant Radiologist. As his name suggests, he looked the happiest of men. His appearance belied the truth – which was that he was a very unhappy man, locked, as he perceived himself to be, in a career as a Consultant Radiologist chosen because he had taken the advice of his teachers and colleagues instead of following his own real interests.

Initially he described himself as 'bad at making decisions – I can never make up my mind what I really want . . . all I know is that I'm doing the wrong thing'.

It is hard for Medical Consultants to change direction once a specialty has been chosen. Doctors who change their minds after many years of training are often regarded as failures. They are seen as not being up to the strain; not clear about their purpose as Medical Consultants. Their identities are called into question.

Character sketch

One of George Kelly's approaches to discovering what people are about was to invite them to write a character sketch. 'I should like you to write a character sketch of Felix, just as if he were a character in a play. Write it as it might be written by a friend who knew him very *intimately* and very *sympathetically*, perhaps better than anyone ever really could know him. For example start out by saying, "Felix is . . . ."' (Kelly, 1991, p. 242)

Felix's sketch began, 'Seeing myself as others might is very difficult for me . . . however here goes. He is a cheerful looking person, perhaps giving the impression of being a bit intense but hiding the fact that he is interested in many things besides work . . . .' He ended by saying, 'when committed to something, he will give it full attention . . . unfortunately he has no sense of direction or enthusiasm or organization . . .'. Both the beginning and the end of a character sketch are of interest to the counsellor.

The early statements for Felix were exactly right. He did look cheerful and was polite and friendly and charming. This was a clear statement about his public image. He physically disguised, almost perfectly, the sad state of affairs indicated in his last sentence.

We talked about the difficulty of maintaining his public image as a Consultant when the uncertainty tormenting him had to be kept secret. He was in enough pain to agree almost immediately to doing something which might help him to understand why he was so unhappy.

Resistance to Change Grid

A Resistance to Change Grid seemed appropriate. Felix chose the names of about thirty significant characters in his life, past, present and some future like 'my ideal self'. These were used, in threes, to establish the similarities and differences between them (a procedure known as 'eliciting personal constructs'). The personal constructs revealed were then 'laddered'. ('Laddering' is a technique which enables the client to identify the underlying values, or core constructs, which underpin his or her approach to life.) Both 'laddering' and the 'Resistance to Change Grid' were developed by D.N. Hinkle (1965).

Several sessions were taken on these procedures as Felix found the discoveries he was making to be fascinating.

When he had chosen eight particularly important 'core constructs' (those without which he could not imagine living) and indicated which pole of the construct he preferred to describe him, the grid was begun. In this grid each bi-polar personal construct is compared with every other one. Fransella's modification (1972) of Hinkle's question was used:

'If, tomorrow morning, you were to wake up and find that you could choose to keep only one of these two preferred positions (in capital letters) and therefore had to accept one of the non preferred options which would it be?'

Felix's example was:

pleasing myself vs PLEASING OTHERS
MAKING A DIFFERENCE vs having a secure life

Felix chose without hesitation to keep MAKING A DIFFERENCE and to put up with 'pleasing myself'.

Results

For a person describing his main problem as 'indecisiveness' this should have been a very difficult thing to do. However, for Felix, there was no difficulty in making choices at this very deep level. It quickly became apparent that he was suffering because he was making choices to please other people and had been doing so for years. For Felix the really important choice was that the work he did should be capable of changing the human condition for the better. Radiology, for him, did not achieve this aim. Radiology reflected 'reality and improved diagnosis' but did nothing tangible to change the patient's condition.

For Felix this discovery was amazing. He began to recall episodes in his life where he had not been stuck; where his life felt full of purpose and meaning. All these occasions had been when he was being intellectually stretched and in a mode of discovery. For a while it seemed that laboratory work was the answer, but this did not, for him, have that human quality which is implicit in direct contact with patients. It became obvious that a field of work where new discoveries are constantly being made and patients are helped directly would be the right choice for Felix. Oncology came to mind.

Felix lost his view of himself as lacking decisiveness. Despite opposition and difficulties about retraining, he decided what he must do.

It would be simplistic to say that doing a Resistance to Change Grid changed Felix for ever more. However it was a powerful technique for him. The main advantage, as he saw it, was that he participated in every stage of the counselling process. He chose the elements; he discriminated between them; he identified the values which underpinned the personal constructs which emerged; and he made the difficult choices when comparing each core construct with another. He did not have to wait for his grid to be 'analysed' – it was self-evident.

References

Fransella, F. (1972) *Personal Change and Reconstruction*. London: Academic Press.

Fransella, F. and Dalton, P. (1990) *Personal Construct Counselling in Action*. London: Sage.

Hinkle, D.N. (1965) 'The Change of Personal Constructs from the Viewpoint of a Theory of Implications', Unpublished PhD thesis, Ohio State University.

Jones, H. (graphics by D. Jancowicz) (1995) 'Cookery Corner: Recipe 4: Resistance to Change Grid', *European Personal Construct Association NEWSLETTER*, April.

Kelly, G.A. (1955/1991) *The Psychology of Personal Constructs*, vols 1 and 2. London: Routledge.

Kelly, G.A. (1969) 'Personal construct theory and the psychotherapeutic interview', in B. Maher (ed.), *Clinical Psychology and Personality: Selected Papers of George Kelly*. New York: Wiley.

Discussion issues

1 How is personal construct psychology a theory about the total person?
2 In what ways is personal construct psychology similar and dissimilar to person-centred counselling?
3 Would you use a Repertory Grid in a counselling session? Discuss.
4 The authors state that 'Kelly's psychology is a hopeful psychology'. Discuss.

6

The Lifeskills Helping Model

Richard Nelson-Jones

This chapter describes significant changes between my revised five-stage model of the helping process, DASIE (Nelson-Jones, 1993a, 1993b), and its predecessor, DOSIE (Nelson-Jones, 1987, 1988). In addition, I outline and describe the revised helping model.

Some changes between the models

Following are some differences between my revised and former helping process models.

Towards an altering problematic skills emphasis

A useful distinction exists between managing problems and altering the underlying problematic skills that sustain problems. To date helping process models have emphasized managing problems rather than altering problematic skills. DOSIE was presented as 'a five-stage model for problem management counselling and helping' (Nelson-Jones, 1987, p. 2). Egan describes his model as a 'three-stage problem-management model of helping . . .' (Egan, 1990, p. v). The model's three stages – identifying and clarifying problem situations and unused opportunities; developing a preferred scenario; and formulating strategies and plans – clearly indicate its problem management focus. Carkhuff's helping model also emphasizes managing problems (Carkhuff, 1987). His model's four stages are: attending – facilitating the helpee; responding – facilitating exploring; personalizing – facilitating understanding; and initiating – facilitating acting.

Problem management helping models are useful since clients frequently require help to manage immediate problems. However, the big drawback of such models is that they inadequately address *the repetition phenomenon*, the repetitive nature of many clients' problems. Consequently, helping models only assisting clients to manage problems are open to the charge of band-aiding. Clients' self-defeating behaviours may repeat themselves both vertically into the future and horizontally across a range of current situations. An example of vertical repetition is that of people who keep losing jobs because of poor relating to employers' skills. An example of horizontal repetition is that of people shy in home, work and recreation situations. Such clients require assistance in developing skills and not just in

This chapter was first published as 'Hello DASIE! Introducing the lifeskills helping model', in *Counselling, Journal of the British Association for Counselling*, vol. 5, no. 2, pp. 109–12 (1994)

managing a specific current problem. Often in reality, practical considerations, such as client wishes and helper caseload, limit how much time and effort they expend addressing underlying skills weaknesses.

Skills language and lifeskills helping theory

The new helping model uses lifeskills language and is based on lifeskills helping theory. Skills may be defined in three main ways: as an area of expertise, as a level of expertise and as a process. Virtually any skill may be viewed as a lifeskill, for instance getting dressed. However, lifeskills helping (LSH) in particular focuses on skills with a large psychological or 'mind' component in them, for instance managing anger. Lifeskills are viewed as sequences of choices in specific psychological skills areas. Within each lifeskills area, people can make effective choices, or possess skills strengths, or ineffective choices, or possess skills deficits, or a mixture of both. Put simply, the criterion for skills strengths or deficits is whether they help or hinder people to assume personal responsibility for their happiness and fulfilment. The object of lifeskills helping is to assist clients, in one or more lifeskills areas, to shift the balance between strengths and deficits more in the direction of strengths. Clients need to develop self-helping skills not just for now but for after the helping process.

Lifeskills helping distinguishes between helpers and clients' inner game or how they think and their outer game of how they act. Thinking skills comprise such areas as: owning responsibility for choosing, coping self-talk, possessing realistic personal rules, perceiving accurately, attributing cause accurately, predicting realistically, setting realistic goals and making rational decisions (Beck, 1976, 1988; Ellis, 1980, 1989; Nelson-Jones, 1989). Action skills tend to vary according to skills areas: for instance studying for examinations or self-disclosing when taking someone out for the first time. Nevertheless, it can help to think of action skills in terms of four main ways of sending messages: verbal messages, or words; voice messages, such as volume, speech rate and emphasis; body messages, such as gaze and facial expressions; and action messages, or how people act when not in direct contact with another, for instance sending flowers (Nelson-Jones, 1990). Feelings represent people's basic animal nature. As such, feelings cannot accurately be viewed as skills. However thinking skills and action skills are feelings-related skills when used to enhance either experiencing feelings, expressing feelings or managing negative feelings.

Skills language means consistently using the concept of skills to analyse and describe both helper and client behaviours. Skills language is central to lifeskills helping theory and practice. Lifeskills helping has a psychological education theoretical framework that has been stated elsewhere in terms of four main categories: assumptions, acquiring lifeskills, maintaining lifeskills, and change and self-development (Nelson-Jones, 1991, 1993a). The framework attempts to integrate concepts from the existential, humanistic, cognitive and behavioural theoretical positions. Space limitations preclude further discussion of the lifeskills framework other than to say that skills language has been used to ensure consistency between its model of the person and its model of practice. Furthermore, within lifeskills helping's model of practice, skills language provides coherence between individual helping, group helping and self-helping.

People-centredness and consolidating lifeskills

The revised lifeskills helping model attends more than its predecessor to what clients take away from and retain after helping. It is a people-centred approach that empowers clients to be their own best helpers. Though necessary, it is insufficient for most clients to feel understood during helping (Rogers, 1957, 1975). In addition clients require assistance to develop specific self-helping skills for afterwards. Consequently, the language of helping must lend itself to client self-instruction.

In any helping contact, there are present at least four possible languages: namely, helper and client inner and outer speech (Nelson-Jones, 1986). People-centred helpers use language not just to communicate to clients, but to develop clients' inner speech so that they can understand their problems and instruct themselves through sequences of choices to prevent and manage them when on their own. Contrast this emphasis with person-centred therapy. Person-centred helpers operate out of a theoretical framework, for instance terms like self-actualizing and conditions of worth, that is rarely, if ever, explicitly communicated to clients (Rogers, 1959; Raskin and Rogers, 1989). To a certain extent person-centred helpers talk one language to themselves and another to clients. At no stage do they directly try to influence client's inner speech so that they are better able to retain gains post-helping.

Helpers as psychological educators

Through somewhat implicit in the earlier model, in the revised model helpers are explicitly psychological educators. Within the context of supportive helping relationships, they use training skills to assist clients not only to manage problems, but also, where possible, to develop longer-term self-helping skills. Just as helpers are educators, clients are learners. Table 6.1 depicts modes of psychological education and modes of learning in both individual and group lifeskills helping (Nelson-Jones, 1991).

The revised model stresses supportive helping relationships. Supportive helping relationships fall into two broad, overlapping categories: (1) facilitating clients to disclose, explore and experience themselves and (2) supporting assessment and training. Helpers need flexibly to offer both kinds of support. Facilitative support builds rapport and allows clients to feel prized as unique persons. It is the gentle, sensitive companionship described by Rogers as an empathic way of being (Rogers, 1975). If disciplined about respecting clients' best interests, helpers can show their tender hearts. Furthermore, helpers who understand clients and clients who feel understood are each better prepared for the training part of helping. When introducing and using training interventions, supportive helping relationships assist clients to work through fears about learning and change. Furthermore supportive relationships provide a secure base for clients to try out new skills inside and outside helping.

Table 6.1 *Modes of psychological education or training and of learning*

Psychological education or training mode	Learning mode
Facilitate	Learning from self-exploring and from experiencing self more fully
Assess	Learning from self-monitoring and self-assessment
Tell	Learning from hearing
Show	Learning from observing
Do	Learning from coached rehearsals and homework assignments
Consolidate	Learning from developing self-helping skills in all the above modes

Helpers as psychological educators require good skills at delivering interventions. It is insufficient to know *what* interventions to offer without being skilled at *how* to offer them. A whiteboard is an essential training tool. Helpers work much of the time with the three modes of 'tell', 'show' and 'do'. 'Tell' entails giving clients clear instructions about how to implement targeted skills. 'Show' means demonstrating the skills. 'Do' means arranging for clients to perform structured activities and homework tasks. From their initial contacts with clients, helpers assist them to consolidate and retain trained skills as self-helping skills.

The DASIE Helping Model

DASIE is a systematic five-stage model for helping clients both to manage problems and also to alter problematic lifeskills. The model provides a framework or set of guidelines for helper choices. The use of the acronym is deliberate to assist beginning helping trainees, anxious about working with clients, to remember the five stages. DASIE's five stages are:

D **Develop** the relationship, identify and clarify problems
A **Assess** problem(s) and redefine in skills terms
S **State** working goals and plan interventions
I **Intervene** to develop self-helping skills
E **End** and consolidate self-helping skills

The labels of the five stages of the model bear a surface similarity to DOSIE, its predecessor. However, when helpers work within the new model, they are likely to find it very different. Now I briefly describe each of DASIE's stages rather than keep making comparisons between the two models.

Stage 1 Develop the relationship, identify and clarify problems

Stage 1 may either be completed sometime in the initial interview or take longer. Its two goals are to initiate a supportive helping relationship with clients and to work with them to identify, break down and clarify their problems. During stage 1, helpers use basic counselling skills such as reflective responding, summarizing and understanding the cultural and other contexts of clients' problems. However, helpers do not always stay within clients' frames of reference. Rather they use questions and probes, interspersed with reflective responses, to help clients identify their real agendas and break them down into their component parts. For instance, a client may use a work relationship difficulty as a 'calling card' to discuss a more important loneliness problem. Together, helper and client break down loneliness into its component problem areas: boredom at work, little social life, poor relationships with family of origin, shortage of money, being overweight and so on. They are now in a position to start developing hypotheses about how the client's thinking and action skills deficits contribute to sustaining each problem area.

Skills language can be introduced during initial session structuring. One possibility is to start the session with an open-ended question encouraging clients to tell their stories. After they respond, the following statement might structure the remainder of the session.

> You've given me some idea of why you've come. I work within the lifeskills framework. Together I'd like us to explore your problem(s) further so that we can identify which skills you may need to cope better. Once we agree on which skills might help you, then we can look at ways to develop them. Does this way of proceeding sound all right?

Stage 2 Assess problem(s) and redefine in skills terms

It is in stage 2 of the model, that the lifeskills emphasis becomes more pronounced. Stage 2 may be completed in the initial session, but also reverted to in subsequent sessions for either the same or for different problems. In stage 2, helpers use focused questioning to look for 'handles' on how to work for change. While the major focus is on pin-pointing skills deficits, attention is also paid to identifying skills strengths and resources.

Stage 2 ends with redefinitions of one or more problems in skills terms. Redefinitions of problems in skills terms are essentially hypotheses, based on careful assessment of available information, about clients' thinking and action skills deficits. Redefining problems in skills terms can be difficult. Mistakes in redefinition not only lead to wasted time and effort, but may contribute to clients being even less able to manage problems.

Clear and simple skills redefinitions are essential. Often it helps to write redefinitions on whiteboards. Visual communication makes it easier for clients to participate in the process and, if necessary, suggest alterations. Helpers may use a simple T diagram to present thinking and action skills deficits that sustain each problem. Figure 6.1 illustrates in the T format the hypothesized thinking and action skills deficits of Susan, a recently promoted office manager in a teaching hospital department, with difficulty supervising the secretaries. Susan demonstrated similar thinking skills deficits across a range of other situations: collecting maintenance payments from her ex-spouse, negotiating where to live with her present partner, and conducting an important negotiation over her realistic difficulties in honouring a previous business contract.

Susan's problem: Difficulty supervising secretaries

Thinking skills deficits	Action skills deficits
Unrealistic personal rules about approval and being the perfect office manager Anxiety engendering self-talk Misperceiving – insufficiently acknowledging own strengths and support from medical staff	Not giving instructions assertively Poor getting support skills

Figure 6.1 *Simple T diagram for presenting redefinitions of problems in skills terms*

Stage 3   State working goals and plan interventions

Stage 3 consists of two phases: stating goals and planning interventions. Goals can be stated at different levels of specificity. First, there are overall goals. For example, Susan may have an overall goal of managing secretaries better not only now, but in future. However, overall goals refer more to ends than to means. Second, goals may be stated in terms of the broad skills required for attaining overall goals. This is the level of specificity required in stage 3. Working goals are the flip-side of redefinitions – positive statements of skills strengths to replace existing skills deficits. For example, Susan's thinking skills goals are: to develop realistic personal rules about approval and her own performance standards; to use coping self-talk; and to perceive accurately her strengths and the degree of support she has from other staff. Susan's action skills goals are to give instructions assertively and to develop good getting support skills. Third, goals can be stated still more specifically. For instance, in subsequent sessions, getting support skills may be broken down into various 'how to' sub-goals.

Statements of working goals provide bridges to choosing interventions. Interventions are intentional behaviours, either on the part of helpers or clients, designed to attain working goals. Plans are statements of how to combine and sequence interventions. Where time is very limited, helpers and clients may develop plans to manage immediate problems. Given more time, helpers and clients may develop plans to alter problematic skills. Here they have a choice between: structured plans, predetermined step-by-step packages of interventions: open plans, using material clients bring to helping sessions as the basis for training interventions: or partially structured plans, setting aside some sessions for predetermined structured work and leaving others open.

Stage 4   Intervene to develop self-helping skills

Stage 4 focuses on delivering specific thinking and action skills interventions. Within the context of supportive relationships, helpers aim for educational efficiency. The importance of helpers possessing good training skills has been stressed. Thinking skills interventions tend to entail three steps: increasing awareness of targeted thinking skills deficits; challenging faulty thinking; and training in effective thinking. Action skills interventions include assisting clients to develop: self-monitoring skills, time-tabling skills, generating and evaluating alternative actions and action skills, and using self-reward skills. Role-play rehearsals inside helping, and conducting experiments in which clients try out behaviour changes outside helping, are additional action skills interventions (Nelson-Jones, 1993a, 1993b). Frequently work done in one problem area has great relevance for other problem areas, especially when focusing on thinking skills.

Stage 5   End and consolidate self-helping skills

Helpers can stress the finite nature of helping and consequently the need for clients to develop self-helping skills. Consolidating learned skills as self-helping skills takes place at the end of and between each session. Homework assignments are negotiated so that between-sessions time is used productively. In addition clients listen to cassette recordings of their last sessions before coming to the next ones. Listening to session cassettes can assist both self-exploring and also learning specific points about targeted skills. Transfer and maintenance of skills is encouraged throughout the helping model by developing clients' self-assessment and self-instructional skills.

Most often either helpers or clients bring up the topic of ending before the final session. This allows both parties to work through various task and relationship agendas attached to ending. As part of this process, helpers and clients can consider when to end, whether to meet less frequently, schedule one or more booster sessions, or arrange follow-up phone calls. As part of the ending stage, helpers work with clients to identify potential difficulties and stresses that may lead to lapses and relapses. Coping strategies to manage such contingencies are identified and rehearsed. Also helpers may assist clients to identify people who will support them in maintaining skills. Helpers may also provide information about further skills-building opportunities.

Concluding comment

DASIE is a helping model of central tendency. Helpers need to use it flexibly and not allow it to become a straitjacket. The lifeskills helping model requires helpers to possess a wide range of skills and interventions. When first using the model, beginning helpers are likely to be like centipedes learning to walk – they find it difficult to coordinate the parts. Even experienced helpers will discover that proficiency in using the lifeskills helping model is a lifetime challenge.

References

Beck, A.T. (1976) *Cognitive Therapy and the Emotional Disorders.* New York: New American Library.

Beck, A.T. (1988) *Love is Never Enough: How Couples Can Overcome Misunderstandings, Resolve Conflicts, and Solve Relationships Problems Through Cognitive Therapy.* New York: Harper and Row.

Carkhuff, R.R. (1987) *The Art of Helping*, 6th edn. Amherst, MA: Human Resource Development Press.

Egan, G. (1990) *The Skilled Helper: a Systematic Approach to Effective Helping*, 4th edn. Pacific Grove, CA: Brooks Cole.

Ellis, A. (1980) 'Overview of the clinical theory of rational-emotive therapy', in R. Grieger and J. Boyd (eds), *Rational-emotive Therapy: a Skills Based Approach.* New York: Van Nostrand Reinhold. pp. 1–31.

Ellis, A. (1989) 'Rational-emotive therapy', in R.J. Corsini and D. Wedding (eds), *Current Psychotherapies*, 4th edn. Itasca, IL: Peacock. pp. 197–238.

Nelson-Jones, R. (1986) 'Toward a people-centred language for counselling psychology', *The Australian Counselling Psychologist*, 2: 18–23.

Nelson-Jones, R. (1987) 'DOSIE: a five-stage model for problem management counselling and helping', *Counselling*, 61: 2–10.

Nelson-Jones, R. (1988) *Practical Counselling and Helping Skills: Helping Client to Help Themselves*, 2nd edn. London: Cassell.

Nelson-Jones, R. (1989) *Effective Thinking Skills: Preventing and Managing Personal Problems.* London: Cassell.

Nelson-Jones, R. (1990) *Human Relationship Skills*, 2nd edn. London: Cassell.

Nelson-Jones, R. (1991) *Lifeskills: a Handbook.* London: Cassell.

Nelson-Jones, R. (1993a) *Practical Counselling and Helping Skills: How to Use the Lifeskills Helping Model*, 3rd edn. London: Cassell.

Nelson-Jones, R. (1993b) *Training Manual for Counselling and Helping Skills.* London: Cassell.

Raskin, N.J. and Rogers, C.R. (1989) 'Person-centered therapy', in R.J. Corsini and D. Wedding (eds), *Current Psychotherapies*, 4th edn. Itasca, IL: Peacock. pp. 155–94.

Rogers, C.R. (1957) 'The necessary and sufficient conditions of therapeutic personality change', *Journal of Consulting Psychology*, 21: 95–103.

Rogers, C.R. (1959) 'A theory of therapy, personality and interpersonal relationships as developed in the client-centered framework', in S. Koch (ed.), *Psychology: a Study of Science*, Study 1, vol. 3. New York: McGraw-Hill. pp. 184–256.

Rogers, C.R. (1975) 'Empathic: an unappreciated way of being', *The Counselling Psychologist*, 5(2): 2–10.

Discussion issues

1　What is the difference between a model and an approach?
2　What are the limitations of a problem-management approach?
3　What are skills and skills deficits?
4　How would you introduce the DASIE model to your clients?

7

Reality Therapy

Robert Wubbolding

Reality therapy is a practical, directive, yet empathic method for counsellors to use with virtually any client. It began in a mental hospital and a correctional institution in Los Angeles, California. William Glasser, MD, the founder of reality therapy, was trained in the traditional psychodynamic, insight-centred theories which aimed at helping clients get in touch with their early childhood and work through their transference. The problem he faced was that even though these processes achieved their goals there was often little change in the client's behaviour.

Rather, he found that by holding people responsible for their behaviour instead of accepting the fact that they were condemned to remain sick, they were able to make dramatic changes (Glasser, 1965). The ideas were then used in schools where they were applied to large groups (Glasser, 1968). Since then, the system has been refined and applied to nearly every other kind of counselling setting; private practice, addictions centres, probation and parole, group homes and others.

Also it has been applied to many psychological issues. Wubbolding (1979) and Edelwich (1980) discussed how to use it with burn-out. Special tools for the use of reality therapy as a self-help method have also been formulated (Good, 1987; Wubbolding, 1990a). Because the ideas are applicable to any human interaction, special applications have been developed for coaching and managing employees (Wubbolding, 1990b). Most recently Brickell (1992) has applied the WDEP system (described in this chapter) throughout the United Kingdom to the issue of stress.

Theory

The theory underlying the practice of reality therapy has not been extensively discussed in the psychological or counselling texts. Nevertheless, there is a tradition of control theory or control system theory. Powers (1973) stated that the human brain generates behaviour not because of external stimuli received from the environment nor because of past unresolved conflicts. Rather human motivation for behaviour is current. Thus reality therapy is radically different from both behaviourism and psychodynamic theory.

Glasser (1985) has expanded control theory by incorporating the human need system as the source of behaviour and has further adapted it to counselling, educational practice, and human relationships (Glasser, 1990, 1993, 1995).

Like many current theories, reality therapy contends that human beings are responsible for their behaviour. It differs from such theories as rational emotive

---

This chapter was first published as 'Reality therapy: what is it?', in *Counselling, Journal of the British Association for Counselling*, vol. 5, no. 2, pp. 117–19 (1994).

behavioural therapy by emphasizing the central importance of human needs as sources of motivation, and it rejects the detailed labelling of human interactions of transactional analysis. On the other hand it is existential in that it sees human choice as a major factor of the human condition, yet it adds a precise delivery system which is lacking in existentialism. Brief therapy seems to incorporate some components of reality therapy; defining wants, describing actions, and making plans, but the self-evaluation of the client, the heart of reality therapy is seen by reality therapists as a major contribution to the work of effective counselling.

More specifically, the fundamentals as they relate to counselling practice, are summarized into five principles (Wubbolding, 1988).

1 Human beings are motivated to fulfil needs and wants. Human needs are common to all people. Wants are unique to each individual.
2 The difference (frustration) between what human beings want and what they perceive they are getting from their environment produces specific behaviours.
3 Human behaviour – composed of doing, thinking, feeling and physiological behaviours – is purposeful; that is, it is designed to close the gap between what the person wants and what the person perceives he or she is getting.
4 Doing, thinking and feeling are inseparable aspects of behaviour and are *generated from within* and not from external stimuli. Thus most of them are choices.
5 Human beings see the world through perceptual levels. There are two general levels of perception: low and high. The low level of perception implies knowledge of events or situations. A high level of perception gives values to those events or situations.

In summary, the source of all behaviour is seen to be in the 'here and now'. Whatever human beings do, think and feel has a purpose – to fulfil current wants and needs. And so control theory differs from other explanations of human behaviour that stress the influence of past, unconscious conflicts, or external stimuli.

The delivery system of reality therapy is divided into two major strategies: establishing an environment conducive to change and intervening by means of the WDEP system (Wubbolding, 1991).

Establishing the environment

The counsellor using reality therapy establishes an atmosphere similar to that which is recommended in other counselling theories. Clients must feel safe to discuss their inner worlds – thoughts, feelings and actions – without fear of criticism or blame. Counsellors attempt to communicate that they will be active, will ask questions and will cling relentlessly to the belief that the client can improve. Practitioners of reality therapy assume that the client can make better choices *now*. Therefore they actively intervene using the skills described below to help the client make even a microscopic change in behavioural direction. Specific skills for establishing the therapeutic environment are more fully explained elsewhere (Wubbolding, 1988, 1992).

Intervening with the WDEP system

The counsellor uses a structured but not rigid series of procedures for helping clients take more effective control of their lives. Each of the letters of the system represents a cluster of ideas. It must be emphasized that they comprise a system and thus are not steps to be used simplistically one after the other. On the contrary, whatever is useful at a given moment with a client is taken from the system and applied.

W Explore the client's **wants** and perceptions. Helping clients define what they want is a powerful tool. The mere clarification and articulation of a want is a major step toward achieving it. Emerson once remarked that we would do well to be cautious about what we want, for in all likelihood we will get it. Clients are asked most especially to determine how hard they want to work and what they will settle for in the event they cannot have everything they desire. A student, for example, might say, 'I want my parents off my back. I want to be left completely alone'. A counsellor using the WDEP system would ask, 'What are you willing to settle for?', 'What is your second want?', 'What are you willing to give up to get what you want?'

Similarly, part of the W is to explore the client's perceptions, especially their perceived locus of control. The principles of control theory state that the control is always inside the person. But many people do not agree. They see themselves as victims of society, controlled by the external world or imprisoned by their own past history. Consider the following statements and where the speaker perceives his/her control to lie:

'My teacher is a pain in the neck.'
'This weather gets me down.'
'The traffic *causes* me aggravation.'
'A fit of depression came over me.'
'I had an anxiety attack.'
'My parents are to blame for the way I am.'
'My job causes me stress.'

A counsellor using reality therapy gradually, gently and empathically leads the person to see that help is available, change is possible, a better life can be lived. And part of this process involves the client's change of viewpoint from seeing control and fulfilment of wants and needs as 'out there' to inside.

D Explore **doing**; actions, thinking and feelings. A skilled counsellor using reality therapy helps clients explore how they feel and what they think. But the emphasis in the dialogue is on action. The client describes exactly how he or she is living. Sometimes this is in general terms. But ideally the person describes 'exactly what happened'. This description can resemble a segment of a video tape. Such a description does not represent the events of a typical day. The description is specific, unique and precise. The counsellor helps the client in this disclosure so that it is generally quite a painless process. The reason for emphasizing the action component of total behaviour is that the client has the most control over this element. Negative feelings are changed by action. So the major part of the counselling time is spent on what is most easily controllable, i.e., the action component.

E Help clients self-**evaluate**. The heart of reality therapy or the WDEP system is the self-evaluation of the client. Therefore, the counsellor asks for specific judgements such as:

'Is what you're doing helping or hurting you?'
'Is what you're doing getting you what you want?'
'Is what you're doing to your best advantage?'
'Are your actions helping your family?'
'What impact does your behaviour have on your work, etc?'
'Is your overall life direction the way you want to go?'
'Is what you want realistic?'

These and literally hundreds of other forms of self-evaluation constitute the cornerstone of the practice of reality therapy. We change our behaviour only when we believe it is not taking us in the desired direction. So too, with the human behavioural 'car'. We will change our direction when we reach a judgement about the effectiveness of our choices.

Thus the counsellor using D and E holds a mirror before the client and says, 'describe what you're doing and is what you're doing working for you to your fullest advantage?'

P Help clients make action **plans**. The process of counselling using the WDEP system culminates in 'SAMIC' planning. The plan should be simple, attainable, measurable, immediate and controlled by the planner. Though not every client can make plans and not every session requires a plan, still it is best if the client leaves the counselling appointment with a sense of direction. The plan should not be overly complicated. A realistically attainable plan which is to be put into action as soon as possible is desirable. Finally it should not be an 'if' plan – one that is dependent on the actions of someone else. 'I'll study tonight if my friend does not phone me' is not a good plan. A more effective plan is, 'I will study tonight from 19.30 to 20.00 at my desk with the television turned off. I'll ask my mother to tell any callers to ring me later.'

This type of planning is more likely to succeed because it has the characteristics of an effective plan.

Elements of change

When William Glasser (1965) first used reality therapy in a mental hospital and a correctional programme in the 1960s, he achieved amazing results. Patients left the hospital and did not need to return. Residents of the girls' correctional school went on to live productive lives. Since then, reality therapy, or as it is often described, the WDEP system, has been widely used and practised in many countries. The question is 'What makes it work?' This author believes there are several elements that help to explain its effectiveness:

1 Emphasis on relationship and environment. In reality therapy there is heavy emphasis on the relationship between counsellor and client. In fact, with the appropriate use of the WDEP system, the relationship is deepened. In some forms of counselling, clients are rarely asked what they want. It could be argued that they even more rarely are asked to evaluate their behaviour. And so, a professional person who believes that clients' wants and judgements are important can enhance the counselling relationship by discussing them and by avoiding arguments and disputations.

2 Emphasis on action. The significance given to action rather than mere talk helps clients take control and move their lives in a different direction, yet the practitioner of reality therapy believes that feelings are important. They are like the lights on the dashboard of an automobile and thus are the indicators of a healthy or unhealthy motor or behavioural system. But when the emotions are discussed in reality therapy they are not ventilated endlessly. Temporary relief serves only a limited purpose. Thus discussions of feelings are linked with actions. The reason for this linkage is that a person can control actions more easily and more directly than feelings. Secondly, negative emotions are not the source of human problems. They are the symptoms and are generated when there exists a deeper problem: unmet wants and unfilled needs.

3 Total system. The suggestions for establishing an atmosphere (Wubbolding, 1992) are not elaborated on in this brief article, but are comprehensive and can be applied to any kind of client. So too, the WDEP system allows for application to virtually every type of client. Furthermore, the system is an open system not a narrow doctrinaire approach to clients. In fact, the reader is encouraged to incorporate techniques from other theories into this system. Our goal in counselling is to help our clients, not to maintain a cleansed theory.

4 Metacommunication. Under the deceptively simple methodology is a bedrock of messages that are provided in the skilful use of reality therapy. The clients come to believe they are in charge of their lives, that there is hope, that they are not prisoners of their past, that they can feel better, that it is more helpful to make plans than to blame others for their problems, and that they are motivated by internal sources 'here and now'.

Such messages are far beyond the simple questioning that is on the surface of the WDEP system. These profound messages and lessons are implied and though the system is direct and straightforward, very often the most helpful messages are the result of the effective use of the WDEP system.

Research

Reality therapy has been used in a variety of settings with efficacious results. Glasser (1965) first utilized the basic principles in the Veteran Administration

Neuropsychiatric Hospital in Los Angeles with paranoid and schizophrenic patients. The average stay in the hospital was fifteen years. After two years of a reality therapy programme, 100 of the 210 persons were well enough to be released.

Other studies indicate enhanced self-esteem and a lessening of court referrals (Shea, 1973), improvement in classroom behaviour (Hart-Hesler et al., 1989) and fewer behaviours requiring disciplinary action (Poppen et al., 1976). Yarish (1985) found significant differences in clients' perceived locus of control after being counselled with reality therapy. Other studies showed that reality therapy had a positive impact on institutionalized adolescents (German, 1975), and negatively addicted inmates (Chance, 1990; Honeyman, 1990).

In summary, reality therapy formulated in the WDEP system is a practical method based on control theory, a solid theory of brain functioning. Its applications range from clients who need minimal help with developmental tasks to the severely disturbed. Included in the delivery system is emphasis on the client's own self-evaluation of the attainability of their wants and their specific choices.

References

Brickell, J. (1992) 'The reality of stress and pressure', *Counselling News*, 7: 18–19.

Chance, E. (1990) 'Lifeline: a drug/alcohol treatment programme for negatively addicted inmates', *Journal of Reality Therapy*, 9: 33–8.

Edelwich, J. (1980) *Burn-out*. New York: Human Sciences Press.

German, M. (1975) 'The effects of group reality therapy on institutionalized adolescents and group leaders', *Dissertation Abstracts International*, 36: 1916.

Glasser, W. (1965) *Reality Therapy*. New York: Harper Collins.

Glasser, W. (1968) *Schools Without Failure*. New York: Harper Collins.

Glasser, W. (1985) *Control Therapy*, New York: Harper Collins.

Glasser, W. (1990) *The Quality School*. New York: Harper Collins.

Glasser, W. (1993) *Quality School Teacher*. New York: Harper Collins.

Glasser, W. (1995) *Staying Together*. New York: Harper Collins.

Good, P. (1987) *In Pursuit of Happiness*. Chapel Hill: New View.

Hart-Hesler, S., Heuchert, C. and Whittier, K. (1989) 'The effects of teaching reality therapy techniques to elementary students to help change behaviors', *Journal of Reality Therapy*, 8: 13–18.

Honeyman, A. (1990) 'Perceptual changes in addicts as a consequence of reality therapy based on group treatment', *Journal of Reality Therapy*, 9: 53–9.

Poppen, W., Thompson, C., Cates, J. and Gang, M. (1976) 'Classroom discipline problems and reality therapy: research support', *Elementary School Guidance & Counselling*, 11: 131–7.

Powers, E. (1973) *Behavior: The Control of Perception*. New York: Aldine Press.

Shea, G. (1973) 'The effects of reality therapy oriented group counselling with delinquent, behavior disordered students', *Dissertation Abstracts International*, 34: 4889–5000.

Wubbolding, R. (1979) 'Reality therapy as an antidote to burn-out', *American Mental Health Counsellors Association Journal*, 1(1): 39–43.

Wubbolding, R. (1988) *Using Reality Therapy*. New York: Harper Collins.

Wubbolding, R. (1990a) *A Set of Directions for Putting (and Keeping) Yourself Together*. Cincinnati: Real World.

Wubbolding, R. (1990b) *Managing People: What to Say When What You Say Doesn't Work*. Cincinnati: Real World.

Wubbolding, R. (1991) *Understanding Reality Therapy*. New York: Harper Collins.
Wubbolding, R. (1992) *Cycle of Counselling*, 6th rev. Cincinnati: Center for Reality Therapy.
Yarish, P. (1985) 'Reality therapy and locus of control of juvenile offenders, *Journal of Reality Therapy*, 6: 3–10.

Discussion issues

1 How does reality therapy differ from the psychoanalytic, person-centred and rational emotive behaviour approaches?
2 Describe why reality therapy is called a system based on human motivation as originating internally rather than from an external stimulus.
3 Why are the client's self-evaluations the centrepiece in the WDEP system?
4 What points would you emphasize if you were to teach this system to a client? To a colleague?

8
Using Neuro-Linguistic Programming
Alex Hossack and Karen Standidge

Introduction to NLP

We exist in that world that everyone is a part of. However, each individual has their own unique way of interpreting the information in the world around them. Neuro-linguistic programming (NLP) aims to access the structure of the individual's subjective experience, to appreciate the unique 'mental map of the world' which is constructed via sensory impression. The practitioner aims to assess the individual's sensory mode by which information is primarily selected, processed and subjectively interpreted. Thus, any dysfunctional distortions or limitations in the processing of the information can be reconstructed or reorganized to provide a more beneficial outcome. NLP theorists propose that problems arise not from a lack of any personal resource but from an inability to access existing internal resources.

The following chapter explains some of the basic principles of NLP. It provides an example of how it can be utilized creatively to provide a resource to attenuate pervading states of anxiety.

Stress management techniques

Stressors are an intrinsic part of everyday life and, depending on the degree of stress, they can be productive by motivation, or destructive when accumulative. When the individual's coping resources are insufficient to reduce or stabilize the effect of the accumulating stressors there are two immediate choices: we can stay and deal with it, or remove ourselves from the aversive situation (flight or fight response). The members of this stress management group were resident in a maximum security hospital and therefore environmental constraints rarely afforded the freedom to retreat. Consequently the aim of this programme was to assist in developing a means of dealing with overwhelming feelings of anxiety.

Traditional relaxation techniques of somatic tension and release (Jacobsen, 1938) have been utilized with mildly anxious individuals for many years. However this technique can often be inefficient with particular anxiety patients as focusing on muscular activity may paradoxically accentuate tension.

This chapter was first published as 'Using NLP to enhance the effectiveness of guided imagery in a stress management and relaxation programme', in *Counselling, Journal of the British Association for Counselling*, vol. 2, no. 2, pp. 53–6 (1991).

Guided imagery (GI) is a method of inducing relaxation which may succeed by diverting or re-focusing attention without focusing on the physical aspects of anxiety. May and Johnson (1973) conclude that mental imagery permits the client to enter more fully into the therapeutic experience and that, creating automatic, affective responses within the patient, mental pictures prove equally as effective as the real situation. It is this functional equivalence between real and imagined stimuli that is the crucial aspect of imagery's power to mediate therapeutic change. Imagery not only permits the creation of experience but facilitates the storage and recall of significant events (Singer, 1979). Guided imagery has been used success-fully in a variety of clinical settings: to reduce the effects of anxiety, to reduce the side effects of chemotherapy (Lyles et al., 1982), to strengthen patient ego and facilitate grief reduction (Melges and Demaso, 1980). Simonton et al. (1983) found guided imagery effective in programmes designed to reduce the effects of anxiety in the terminally ill. Pelletier (1979) reports success using imagery as a metaphoric analogy to strengthen patient ego and to create future fantasies which are used to establish goals and study patient psychodynamics.

When employed successfully GI may succeed by disassociating the person from their present (external or internal) anxiety-provoking experience by focusing on a novel mental image. If the image is of sufficient intensity the individual's per-ceptual position is diverted from an external stimulus to an internal stimulus. By re-focusing to 'appropriate' internal stimuli the individual's range of attention is attenuated and the potential for effecting a reduction in physiological and psychological arousal increased. Traditionally guided imagery requires the presen-tation of a highly visual scene of sufficient intensity to permit a re-focusing of attention. However, individuals differ in their ability to form visual images. Kosslyn et al. (1984) suggest that visual imagery involves a fixed number of processing subsystems and that individual differences in generating visual imagery may be due to the efficacy of neural pathways within these systems. An alternative explanation can be accommodated within a neuro-linguistic programming (NLP) framework (Bandler and Grinder, 1976, 1979; Dilts, 1983). NLP theorists propose that individuals take in information about the environment and themselves through five sensory modalities and of the five there are three major systems, visual (V), auditory (A) and kinaesthetic (K). Further, normal cerebral organization processes visual information, using imagery, auditory information, using sounds and kinaesthetic information, using feelings and bodily sensations (Thomason et al., 1980). Of the three major systems there will be one preferred representational system (PRS) by which information is processed. Consequently different modalities will have different methods of absorbing and mapping out information. According to the model proposed by Bandler and Grinder, there are two ways of assessing the PRS:

1   through eye movements which indicate the sensory modality in use (Figure 8.1).

To establish PRS through eye scanning patterns the individual is presented with a series of questions that require an affirmative response, e.g. 'Can you imagine

Top left
Visual constructed

Top right
Visual remembered

Horizontal
Auditory constructed

Horizontal
Auditory remembered

Bottom left
Kinaesthetic

Bottom right
Auditory digital

Figure 8.1   *Assessment of PRS through eye scanning patterns (after Bandler and Grinder, 1979)*

yourself with green hair?'. NLP theorists suggest that if information is being processed visually then an external assessment can be made through the eye scanning patterns. The question above may produce an upward left eye movement (Visual construct, Figure 8.1). Untrained observers may have problems with subjects who appear to dissent from the model (Krugman et al., 1985; Thomason et al., 1980). If we use the above example and the individual is not primarily visual but kinaesthetic, they may initially access a kinaesthetic experience feeling what it is like to have green hair before generating a visual image. The resulting eye movement may be bottom left to access a feeling, then an upward left eye movement to construct, or right to remember a visual image. Evaluation studies to assess the validity of eye movement patterns have reported mixed results. Buckner et al. (1987) support the proposition that specific eye movements exist, but suggest trained observers are needed for reliable assessment. Dilts (1983) found a high correlation between visual and auditory processing and eye scanning patterns. Dorn (1983) concluded eye scanning patterns did not indicate sensory experience but suggests that research has been unable to develop a method sensitive enough to assess PRS preference. Thomason et al. (1980) did not support eye movement as a means of assessing PRS.

2   The second means of assessing the primary representational system is made linguistically through a predominance of sensory-based predicates.

The predominant use of perceptual predicates such as, 'I SEE what you mean' or 'It's CLEAR to me now' would advise the therapist of visual processing, or using words like 'TONE/VOLUME/SOUND', auditory processing. Alternatively 'it FEELS right to me' or 'it's a HEAVY day' etc. indicates a kinaesthetic PRS. It can be beneficial to identify PRS and utilize this information in a counselling situation.

Paxton (1981) found counsellors who frequently use empathy predicate responding more positively influenced the client's perception of the relationship than counsellors who infrequently matched – confirmed by Falzett (1981). Yapko (1981) found sensory predicate matching in a relaxation programme using hypnotic induction facilitated relaxation. Owens (1977) found agreement between perceptual predicates and eye movement, but not with subjects' verbal report of the experience.

Linguistic assessment can be obtained through everyday conversation or by presenting an imaginary scenario incorporating all sensory modalities, for example:

> 'Imagine walking through a forest on a WARM sunny day, NOTICE the SOUNDS of the birds and FEELING of the breeze as it RUSTLES through the tress, SEE CLEARLY the COLOUR of the leaves.'

The individual can be asked to express their interpretation of the imagery. The description can help identify modality preference.

Limited modality functioning – sensory deprivation?

If an individual is found to have a limited sensory awareness, i.e. communicating from one sensory modality, then it is possible that they acknowledge and respond to a given situation from one level of communication. They may acknowledge and respond to what is visually apparent, but not to what they feel or hear. It follows that such individuals are virtually suffering from a form of sensory deprivation.

Counter-conditioning effects of imagery

The present study aimed to utilize the therapeutic physiological and psychological effects of relaxation as a resource to counteract the negative physiological and psychological effects of anxiety and stress. If we have maximum sensory experience, a relaxing imaginary scenario becomes overwhelming because it is seen, heard and felt. Thus by adding other dimensions of experience to guided imagery (or indeed communication generally) the individual is supplied with a counter-conditioning resource. When the resource is utilized it can effectively depolarize the overwhelming feeling of anxiety reducing physiological and emotional arousal (Figure 8.2). Hossack and Standidge (1993) successfully used visual and kinaesthetic recall of positive life events to attenuate moderate depression, anxiety and agoraphobia in an individual hospitalized for clinical depression.

The need for immediate access to a relaxed state

For this method to be of practical consideration it must be applicable to situations of impending danger, e.g. when there is a feeling of losing control or an impending panic attack. Therefore a minimum temporal contiguity must exist between the acknowledgement of anxiety and the ability to experience the physiological and emotional calm associated with appropriate imagery.

Tatchell (1987) suggests an affirmation technique as an experiential anchor to trigger into the effects of a relaxing imaginary scenario. Based on the learning

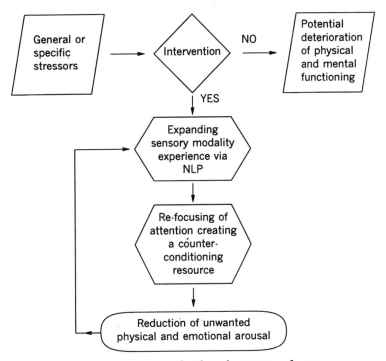

Figure 8.2 *Improving stress management by the enhancement of sensory experience*

theory principle of paired association a word is elicited which summarizes an imaginary or real scenario with calming associations. This is the 'affirmation' word which conjures up visual, auditory and kinaesthetic experience, at the same time this is paired with a finger-and-thumb tension and release action. The practised effect produces an immediate association between imagery and behaviour (finger and thumb action) which becomes the trigger to re-focus attention. The method is as follows:

> 'Press together very slightly your thumb and finger of both hands while taking a deep breath. Hold that breath for the mental count of four. On exhalation relax your fingers and mentally repeat your affirmation word.'

Thus the individual is supplied with a trigger which enables the affirmation experience and the potential for shifting the individual's perceptual position from an external to an internal stimuli is increased.

Development of the Relaxation Group Programme

The group consisted of six females resident in a maximum security hospital. All patients were in their twenties, chosen because they experienced anxiety, problems

RESULTS

SUBJECT	PRE	POST
1	V–K	V–K–A
2	V	V–K
3	A	A–K–V
4	K	K–V–A
5	K	K–V
6	V	V–A–K

Figure 8.3 *Sensory modality experience of guided imagery – pre- and post-intervention results*

with impulse control or insomnia. One patient suffered from visual hallucinations and one patient suffered from auditory hallucinations. Group sessions were of a three-hour duration, twice a week for four weeks.

A major component of the stress management programme initially utilized traditional guided imagery which emphasized the visual aspects of a scenario. The scene varied on each presentation. However, the individual's 'affirmation situation' was used to anchor a place of safety, thus providing a place of emotional security from which to explore further imaginary scenarios.

It became apparent during the early sessions that most of the group were experiencing difficulties in forming visual images. It was also apparent that they were unable to spontaneously generate abstract thought, often a requirement of guided imagery. A concrete presentation such as 'imagine a box covered in green velvet cloth' was easier to generate than 'make a note of the box contents'.

NLP theorists propose that some individuals have limited sensory modality processing. If we consider this in relation to members of the group and hypothesize that if individuals were functioning in one modality and having little or no access to others, that there would only be an acknowledgement of and response to the environment from one sensory experience. For example, there may be an acknowledgement of what they see and not primarily what they hear or feel. As a result the individual is unable to obtain maximum sensory experience from imagination or *in vivo*, and the potential of guided imagery as a diversionary tactic may be limited.

The next stage was to assess group members regarding their PRS. Using NLP assessment criteria and patient report of sensory experience results revealed that all but one group member functioned in a single modality (Figure 8.3).

Development of Secondary Modalities

Involvement in guided imagery produces a temporary dissociated state of consciousness (Hilgard, 1970). This study attempted to utilize full sensory experiences of imagery to evoke a dissociated state of consciousness.

To overcome the restrictions of functioning in one modality NLP originators Bandler and Grinder (1979) suggest 'overlapping' modality exercises. This method initially utilizes the primary processing modality. Secondary systems are gradually introduced with the expectation of making available to the individual what virtually amounts to 'novel' sensory experiences. If the 'quality' of imagery is improved then the possibility of increased sensory involvement in the image may activate the re-focusing of attention. An appropriate relaxing image has the potential for reducing anxiety. Overlapping exercises consisted of most of the course content and became the cornerstone for expanding sensory experience. An example of such exercises is given below:

1   V to K – Imagine a frog, LOOK closely at its COLOUR, OBSERVE its eyes, feet. Experience how it FEELS against your skin.
2   A to V – Remember the SOUND of a dog BARKING, NOTICE how its mouth LOOKS, OBSERVE the teeth.
3   K to V – FEEL the SENSATION of RELAXING in a WARM soapy bath. WATCH the bubbles as they burst.
4   K to V – Take the FEELING of having your hand in a jar of WET maggots. Turn that into a PICTURE of having your hand in a jar of £1.00 coins.

Assessment of Overlapping Exercises

An assessment of twenty hours of overlapping exercises such as those above revealed that patients were *all* functioning in at least one more modality than they were at the beginning of the programme. Post group assessment was taken by patient self-report of their sensory experience of imagery and facilitator observation of behaviour during the guided imagery presentation (Figure 8.3). Four members of the group were experiencing imagery in three sensory modalities. Group members verified the affirmation technique as an expedient method of accessing a relaxing scenario, effecting a reduction in arousal.

Summary

Research by Barr-Taylor et al. (1977), Bali (1979) and Zurawski et al. (1987), concluded that relaxation as a form of stress management can be more effective than (a) non-directive therapy alone; (b) elaborate physiological measurement; (c) skin conductive biofeedback exercises; (d) placebo-based exercises. The effectiveness of visualization, systematic desensitization and rational emotive behaviour therapy as methods of anxiety reduction were compared by Ayres and Hopf (1987). They discovered that visualization was as effective as the other two methods and that it is an easier and more convenient method to perform without utilizing excessive resources.

Research into NLP theory has been made from the late seventies to the present day with varying conclusions. An extensive review of the experimental evidence has been made by Heap (1988), much of this concerning assessment of PRS through eye scanning patterns and predicate choice. He concludes that there is a lack of empirical evidence to sustain many NLP claims and suggests trained practitioner investigation is necessary before NLP can be presented with conviction.

This study has focused on single modality functioning which has been largely ignored in previous literature where the focus of modality preference has typically been on choice of profession and activities (Heap, 1988). It is suggested that single modality functioning is a form of sensory deprivation and that it is possible to develop impoverished secondary modalities the benefits of which are suggested below:

1 Creating a greater sensory awareness has the potential for maximizing the use of guided imagery in a relaxation programme by adding another dimension of experience previously unavailable or greatly impoverished. If that experience is intense then guided imagery may succeed as a diversionary tactic by attenuating the individual's range of attention and re-focusing their perceptual position from an external stimulus to an internal stimulus.
2 Acknowledging and experiencing other elements of communication may be fundamental in the development of an empathic response. Lipton et al. (1987) suggest that impaired social perspectives may go far in contributing to the aetiology of offending behaviour.

The following anecdote is given to illustrate point (2).

A female member of the group, June, reported feeling quite distressed when a male member of her ward habitually stood behind her while she was in conversation. The male patient was socially unskilled but enjoyed 'being on the fringe'. June had been assessed as kinaesthetic, and we therefore deduced she may be disregarding other aspects of communication. As the course progressed the use of her secondary modalities increased and she gradually became aware of other aspects of his communication. She was able to acknowledge his quiet timid voice, his poor eye contact and the fact he was much smaller than June. This appeared to alter her perception of the situation which she now perceived as non-threatening, attenuating her feelings of anxiety.

3 In counselling or psychotherapeutic situations it can assist the facilitator in accessing the client's internal frame of reference.
4 Some studies have shown that the acknowledging and using of empathy predicate responding can build rapport between counsellor and client (Paxton, 1981; Yapko, 1981), the counsellor perceived as having greater empathy and understanding compared to control groups.
5 Imagery has no side-effects unlike pharmacological intervention and encourages the individual to take personal responsibility for problems.
6 Guided imagery can often be light relief compared to other forms of intervention with the added potential for increasing involvement in the sessions.

This stress management group was never intended to be an empirical study. However, the assessments made at different stages of the programme produced results which seemed to concur with the NLP propositions of preferred modality information processing and the development of secondary modalities to a level of functionality.

The two patients who experienced visual and auditory hallucinations were found to function in a visual and auditory mode respectively. Post course assessment discovered that both patients now functioned to some degree in the three primary modalities and the hallucinations had ceased. A three-month follow-up assessment revealed that the hallucinations had not returned.

The results of the present study may be viewed as a preliminary investigation into the effects of 'overlapping' modalities. To determine if overlapping exercises were solely responsible for increased modality functioning it would be necessary to utilize a control group as a standard of comparison to determine if the treatment condition, i.e. overlapping exercises, was responsible for the effect of additional modality functioning. Further studies will use a control group experiencing identical imagery instructions without overlapping exercises to elicit whether a statistical difference exists between the groups.

It is possible that the observed single modality functioning pre-training was an artefact due to restrictive effects of anxiety as proposed by Loomis and Cohen (1984). They maintain that an anxious individual focuses on one modality only. The individuals in this study may have demonstrated additional modality functioning post test merely as a result of anxiety reduction.

NLP propositions have been extensively studied with varying conclusions. Many of the studies have fundamental errors in presentation. Krugman et al. (1985) failed to substantiate NLP claims. However, in this study no PRS was identified prior to the presentation and all subjects were given instructions to access a visual modality in a relaxation programme. Individuals with a preferential kinaesthetic or auditory processing system would therefore have been disadvantaged.

Studies have focused on eye movement patterns to determine PRS. Thomason et al. (1980) did not support the eye movement hypothesis. In this study individual reactions were monitored to sensory/modality specific questions. However an individual who primarily processes information kinaesthetically is presented with a visual question, their first mode of accessing or relating to the information may be to access a feeling or tactile sensation from which they generate a visual image. The resulting eye movement would be bottom left to top right or left (Figure 8.1). Thomason et al.'s study does not account for the variation in response and therefore the NLP model is likely to be assessed as erroneous. However, not all studies have glaring experimental errors such as these.

In conclusion, the authors concur with the opinions of Heap (1988), Dilts (1983) and Buckner et al. (1987) proposing that trained observers are needed to produce more empirical research evidence to validate or refute NLP claims. Many studies misunderstand the model they are studying or use naive presenters and so apparent deviant responses from the model are classed as erroneous.

References

Ayres, J. and Hopf, T.S. (1987) 'Visualization, systematic desensitization and rational emotive therapy: a comparative evaluation', *Communication-Education*, 36(3): 326–40.
Bali, L.R. (1979) 'Long-term effects of relaxation on blood pressure and anxiety levels in essential hypertensive males', *Psychosomatic Medicine*, 41.

Bandler, R. and Grinder, J. (1976) *Transformations*. London: Real Press.

Bandler, R. and Grinder, J. (1979) *Frogs into Princes*. London: Real Press.

Barr-Taylor, C., Farquar, J.W., Nelson, E. and Agras, S. (1977) 'Relaxation therapy and high blood pressure', *Archives of General Psychiatry*, 34: 339–42.

Buckner, M., Meara, N.M., Reese, E.J. and Reese, M. (1987) 'Eye movement as an indicator of sensory components in thought', *Journal of Counselling Psychology*, 34(3): 283–7.

Dilts, R. (1983) *Roots of NLP*. Cupertino, CA: Meta.

Dorn, F.J. (1983) 'Assessing Primary Representational Systems (PRS) preference for Neurolinguistic Programming (NLP) using three methods', *Counselor Education and Supervision*, 23(2): 149–59.

Falzett, W. (1981) 'Matched versus unmatched primary representational systems and their relationship to perceived trustworthiness in a counselling analogue', *Journal of Counselling Psychology*, 28: 305–8.

Heap, M. (1988) 'Neurolinguistic programming – an interim verdict hypnosis', in *Current Clinical Experimental and Forensic Practices*. London: Croom Helm.

Hilgard, J.R. (1970) *Personality and Hypnosis: a Study of Imaginative Involvement*. Chicago: University of Chicago Press.

Hossack, A. and Standidge, K. (1993) 'Using an imaginary scrapbook for neurolinguistic programming in the aftermath of a clinical depression', *The Gerontologist*, 33(2): 265–8.

Jacobsen, E. (1938) *Progressive Relaxation*. Chicago: University of Chicago Press.

Kosslyn, S.M., Brunn, J., Cave, K.R. and Wallch, R.W. (1984) 'Individual differences in mental imagery ability: a computational analysis'. Special Issue: Visual Cognition. *Cognition*, 18(1–3): 195–243.

Krugman, M., Kirsch, I., Wickless, C., Milling, L., Golicz, H. and Toth, A. (1985) 'Neurolinguistic programming treatment for anxiety: myth or magic?', *Journal of Consulting and Clinical Psychology*, 53(4): 526–30.

Lipton, D.N., McDonel, E.C. and McFall, R.M. (1987) 'Hetero social perception in rapists', *Journal of Consulting and Clinical Psychology*, 55: 17–21.

Loomis, M.E. and Cohen, M.Z. (1984) 'The test of relationship between stress and primary representational systems', *Transactional Analysis Journal*, 14(1): 80–2.

Lyles, J.N., Burlish, T.G., Krozely, M.G. and Oldham, R.K. (1982) 'Efficacy of relaxation training and guided imagery in reducing the aversiveness of cancer chemotherapy', *Journal of Consulting and Clinical Psychology*, 50(4): 509–24.

May, J.R. and Johnson, H.J. (1973) 'Physiological activity to internally elicited arousal and inhibitory thoughts', *Journal of Abnormal Psychology*, 82: 239–45.

Melges, F.T. and Demaso, D.R. (1980) 'Grief resolution therapy: reliving, revising and revisiting', *American Journal of Psychotherapy*, 34(1): 51–61.

Owens, L.F. (1977) 'An investigation of eye movements and representational systems'. Unpublished doctoral dissertation, Ball State University.

Paxton, L.K. (1981) 'Representational systems and client perceptions of the counselling relationship', *DAI*, 41, 4,3888A.

Pelletier, A.M. (1979) 'Three uses of guided imagery', *American Journal of Psychotherapy*, 22(1): 32–6.

Simonton, O.C, Mathews-Simonton, S. and Creigton, J.L. (1983) *Getting Well Again*. New York: Bantam.

Singer, J.L. (1979) 'Imagery and affect in psychotherapy', in A.A. Sheikh and J.H. Shaffer (eds), *The Potential of Fantasy and Imagination*. New York: Brandon House.

Tatchell, P. (1987) *AIDS: A Guide to Survival*. London: GMP Publishing. ch. 3.

Thomason, T.C., Arbuckle, A. and Cady, D. (1980) 'Test of the eye movement hypothesis of neurolinguistic programming', *Perceptual and Motor Skills*, 51(1): 230.

Yapko, M.D. (1981) 'The effects of matching primary representational systems predicates on hypnotic relaxation', *American Journal of Clinical Hypnosis*, 23(3): 169–75.

Zurawski, R.M., Smith, T.W. and Houston, B.K. (1987) 'Stress management for essential hypertension: comparison with a minimally effective treatment, predictor and response to treatment, and effects on reactivity', *Journal of Psychosomatic Research*, 31: 453–62.

Discussion issues

1 What criteria would you use to assess how vivid the quality of your client's mental images are?
2 How can you assess which modality your client primarily uses to represent their internal experience?
3 Under what conditions do you find it easier to create guided imagery experience yourself?
4 How can you help expand your client's imagery experience when they are functioning in one modality?

9

The Insights of Alfred Adler

James Hemming

In this chapter I have put forward the case that during this century, in the fields of psychotherapy and counselling, no one has been more generally influential than Alfred Adler; yet, at the same time, no one has been less fairly acknowledged. The anomaly arises because, as Dr Joel Kovel pointed out in *A Complete Guide to Therapy* (1978), the school of psychologists described as Neo-Freudian – Karen Horney, Erich Fromm, Harry Sullivan et al. – were not Freudian at all. Actually they moved, not in a Freudian, but in an Adlerian direction, that is towards seeing the individual as a unique person, struggling towards fulfilment within a formative social milieu.

Other schools of thought – Rogerian, transactional analysis, construct theory, attribution theory and others – have also used, or been consistent with, Adlerian insights. Jungian approaches – which have been gaining ground recently – make their own specific contribution but are in accord with Adler in describing the individual as engaged upon the attainment of an actualized and integrated self, which, as a condition for this fulfilment, will need to be 'in unconditional, binding, and indissoluble community' with the world – a very Adlerian viewpoint. Jung was also at one with Adler in pointing out that people are liable to trade a false front with the world – the persona.

The time is ripe, then, to reconsider Adler's particular contribution to the understanding of our human situation.

The psychodynamics of personal growth

All psychologies have a central theme which aims to show how the individual moves towards maturity. Freud maintained that all personal development was to be accounted for by the individual's need to express his/her instinctive sexual impulses over and against the suppressive demands of society. Hence arose repressions, the Oedipus complex, and the rest. These theories have become less and less satisfactory as time passed. But all psychologies agree that the way the child experiences the early years of life is of profound significance to ultimate development. If repressed infantile sexuality and its consequences is not the dynamic, what is?

Adler – and those who think like him – start with the here-and-now situation of the infant as his/her self-awareness emerges. At a very early age, ideas about

This chapter was first published in *Counselling, Journal of the British Association for Counselling*, vol. 2, no. 2, pp. 50–2 (1991).

oneself, and oneself in relation to life and others, sink unquestioned into the depths of the unconscious. This has to be so because, without such social imprinting, society would have to start again with each generation of children; there would be no enduring pattern to cultures.

One inescapable idea for the infant is that he/she is small and weak among giants upon whom he/she totally depends. Even before the child acquires speech, the language of the environment offers a powerful message to the human beginner: 'You have a long way to go to catch up.' Thus, it comes about that all children are imprinted with a sense of personal inadequacy. The healthy, encouraged child responds to this challenge by plunging enthusiastically into the exploration of the world around him/her. This is revealed by, among other things, the infant's unconscious dedication to the tasks of learning to stand, walk and speak. A sense of 'being behind' must give a huge impetus to striving.

This urgency to be, and to become, is of profound evolutionary significance. We humans are an evolving species. Each one of us is born with a unique endowment of potentialities seeking to find the means to expression and growth within the surrounding environment. Consequently, every infant is motivated by two major drives: the drives to overcome initial inferiority and the urge to find expression within the environment for his/her own inherited potentialities. This linked unconscious determination to overcome initial incapacity, and to find ways of interacting formatively with the world, is nothing less than the raw energy for the psychosocial evolution of humankind.

This dynamism can have positive or negative consequences. If the child is loved, respected, encouraged and brought into things at an early stage as an involved participant, he/she will boldly seek to make a mark by his/her achievements and relationships. There will be set-backs of course, but a child in good heart will 'baffled, get up and begin again'. Every day will bring opportunities for exploration, growth, fulfilment and enhanced self-respect. He/she learns, by positive encounters with those around, that other people are to be trusted and that personal success is best to be gained by working with others, not against them; by coming out, as Adler used to say, 'on the useful side of life'.

If, instead, a child is deprived of affection and respect, is criticized and rejected, denied the encouragement which is an essential nutrient for all human beings, and is taught by the way he/she is treated to resent and fear other people, the message that will reach the child is 'You are no good as you are. You must be different.' Thus is implanted a conviction of inferiority. This leads to difficulties because these beginners acquire a false evaluation of themselves and society.

The child's inevitable response to an overwhelming feeling of inferiority is to retreat into subterfuge, fantasy, frightened shyness, habitual showing off, excessive revolt, or some other tactic to make good the gap in self-esteem. In this way a false strategy for dealing with life – compensatory subterfuge in place of courageous encounter – may be built in at an unconscious level, and obstruct creative relationships with the world.

The issue is whether, during the ups and downs of growing up, the individual has gained the confidence, courage and trust in self and others, to carve out a path of personal fulfilment and achievement or whether instead, he/she is caught up in the pressing need to prove his/her worth by any self-centred means that are available. Furthermore, the discouraged personality is liable to take on, as his/her unconscious goal of striving, not just to be equal to others but to become superior to them. Alternatively, an individual who has been too much put down by experience may go into retreat from the challenges of life, depending on fantasy for a sense of significance.

Difficult beginnings

Inferiority feelings are not only the result of inadequate parenting; conditions right outside parental control may be the cause. Adler called one of these 'organ inferiority' – the misfortune of being born, or developing, physical attributes that put the individual at a disadvantage *vis-à-vis* others. Feeling that he, or she, is excessively short or fat, or has weak eyesight, faulty hearing, ugly teeth or some other imperfection may be interpreted by the child as profound inadequacy. From this largely unconscious self-assessment will arise an urge to compensate for the inadequacy.

Position in the family can also influence the concept of self-worth. Every oldest child commonly experiences early adulation followed by the need to adjust to the sometimes rather sudden intrusion of a rival. Youngest children, for their part, may feel rather overwhelmed by the distance ahead that their siblings have already attained. A clumsy boy in the middle of two athletic brothers may well feel a sense of grudge at his situation. In one such case – a 'slow' child between two 'bright' ones – the disadvantaged girl started to steal in spite of dedicated efforts on the part of parents to help her feel good about herself.

The influence of organ inferiority and family situation may go either way. When the child is loved and encouraged, a personal disadvantage may lead to super-human effort to make up for it. An often quoted case is that of Demosthenes who overcame a stutter to become the greatest orator of his times. Beethoven had a hearing defect. A more modest modern example: the youngest of four boys in a robust athletic family, and the shortest of them all, turned himself into a sensitive, friendly young charmer whom everybody adored. The generation of a positive style of life comes down to keeping courage intact and being sustained by caring, cooperative relationships with others. But *not*, Adler emphasized, on actual pampering by overconcerned parents and others. The spoilt child is put right out of step with life by being given a false impression of his/her central importance.

The evidence for enduring inferiority feelings

Some writers, who have given Adler only cursory attention, have accused him of over-emphasizing the significance of inferiority feelings – and the resulting yearning for superiority – in personal and social life. However, the general evidence strongly supports Adler. We all hate being put down in any way. Gaffes of long ago return to haunt us when something reminds us of them. People show themselves to be eager for status symbols that give them the edge over others. Lies have been told, men slain in duels, even wars started, in order to save face. All the horrors of revenge are engendered by a perceived insult. A young hoodlum who knifed another boy in a cinema was asked by the magistrate why he had done it. His reply was: 'Because he give me a look.' It is now recognized that, throughout history, strategies for domination, including the domination of women, have been manifest world-wide. Some early potentates even demanded that they should be treated as gods – as did Alexander the Great. Despots – from the Roman Emperor Tiberius to more recent dictators – have frequently employed secret police whose task was to 'disappear' anyone voicing criticism. How are we to account for all this tetchy nervousness about losing face except in terms of the fear of being seen to be inferior, and the neurotic compensation for it evidenced by extreme claims to superiority?

Social interest

What keeps the energies of the human psyche on a creative track? Adler's answer was what he called 'Social Interest' – concerned involvement in the well-being of others. Alder believed that social involvement is man's natural mode of being but that early acute discouragement and sense of rejection can drive the individual towards an egocentric, self-seeking lifestyle which impairs the capacity for personal and social relationships. Through social interest the urge 'to arrive' is rescued from neurotic forms and the impotence of despair.

Our lives, Adler suggested, are characterized by certain inescapable tasks, notably those of work (creative contribution), friendship and love. How we respond to these challenges manifests the dynamics of our lifestyle. The proper framework for fulfilment through these – and other – commitments to life is cooperation. A distorted lifestyle will approach these tasks, not as the framework for working with others, but as opportunities for personal advantage at the expense of others.

Immorality, to Adler, was limitation, a failure to see ourselves in the context of others. The brute is erroneously seeking to establish his superiority at any cost; the liar has been trained by unfortunate circumstances and relationships not to trust the truth; the sexual pervert is withdrawing from the full challenge of a passionate relationship; cheats have failed to grasp that getting ahead at the expense of others cannot lead to anything but parasitical isolation.

On crime – very much in the news at present – Adler can speak for himself:

> We find the same kind of failure exhibited in criminals as in problem children, neurotics, psychotics, suicides, drunkards and sexual perverts. They all fail in their approach to the problems of life; and, in one very definite and noticeable point, they fail in the same way. Every one of them fails in social interest. They are not concerned with their fellow beings. Even here, however, we cannot distinguish them as if they were in contradiction to other people. No one can be held up as an example of perfect cooperation or perfect

social feeling; and the failures of criminals are only a more acute degree of common failures.

It should be noted that, for Adler, crime was essentially an act against a fellow being, as distinct from a justified revolt against autocracy.

Adlerian counselling

People come for therapy or counselling when they feel that life has lost its meaning or that the future for them seems blocked. Either way a lot of stress is involved. It is usually stress that tips the situation over from the ordinary unavoidable difficulties of living into the need for additional insight, support and help. We should note that the objective of counselling is guidance and encouragement, not identifying what has happened with some 'guilty' person. Off-loading the blame can be a temptation and a distraction from the main aim: facing the task of dealing with personal problems. Counsellors search into background and causes to increase understanding, keeping alert for ideas, attitudes and feelings that indicate sources of vulnerability in the style of life.

So here is the person in need. What should we ask about him or her? How do you see yourself and your situation? How do you come to be where you are? Where would you like to be? What is the way forward? What is getting in the way? What is your pattern of relationship with family and friends? And so forth. This is essentially a here-and-now approach to a human situation. But, at the same time, it has to be an exploration of the past because present behaviour emerges from past experience, and what is significant in the present may go right back to infancy, when the roots of a fulfilling, or destructive, style of life are laid down.

So the counsellor has to keep the past and the present constantly in mind together, and to share both with the person in difficulties. Talking it through, with the counsellor or in a group, can itself be a healing process. Mutual acceptance, respect and appreciation are vital elements in the healing exchange. 'Me doctor; you patient' has no place in Adlerian therapy but knee-to-knee collaboration, an exchange of common humanity.

Pertinent, considerate questioning can lead to a gradual unravelling of people's experiences, difficulties, attitudes and aspirations. Adler believed that clues to attitudes can come from early memories and dreams. Dreams of flying are sometimes described as sexual in origin; they are more likely to indicate ambition, according to the Adlerian viewpoint.

A driving, successful man, who ran into problems of readjustment when kept at home for an extended period by a bout of illness, described an early memory of being pushed along in a sort of go-cart by one of his older sisters while another older sister walked ahead. His mother, leaning out of an upstairs window, was telling his sisters to take him to the recreation ground at the end of the road. Early resentment at being at the mercy of women may have accounted, in part, for his ceaselessly striving personality, and for his initial sense of irritation and lostness at being confined to his home. With a little help, he saw the relevance of this early memory to his present condition and set about learning to relax without feelings of anxiety, and to value women as partners instead of fearing them.

Adlerian therapy is not about doing things *to* people but about exploring a situation together. The curative power is in the shared understanding and shared humanity. Many years ago, in *The Origins of Love and Hate* (1945), Dr Ian Suttie came to the conclusion that it was not the content of theory but the context of caring and insightful reciprocity – or, simply, love – that generated the healing power of counselling. How else can we account for the fact, Suttie asked, that counsellors/therapists of all persuasions achieve some success. The healing, Suttie held, derives not from theory but from personalities in relationship. This does not, however, alter the fact that practitioners need a framework of ideas within which to operate, and training opportunities to develop their powers. Adlerian psychology seeks to provide both framework and training in a comprehensible and readily available form.

The democratic era

Adler's teachings have something further to offer to our times. Hopefully we are living through the last era of despotism and moving towards the establishment of genuine, participant democracies. This could be the world growing up to the realization that the future of the planet lies with shared responsibility and cooperation for the general good, not with people and nations seeking to outsmart one another. Half a century ago, Adler saw the need for such changes. In his last book, *Social Interest: A Challenge to Mankind* (1938), he wrote:

> A careful consideration of individual and collective existence, past and present, shows us the struggle of mankind for a stronger social feeling. One can scarcely fail to see that humanity is conscious of this problem and is impressed by it. Our present-day burdens are the result of the lack of a thorough social education. It is the pent-up social feeling in us that urges us to reach a higher stage and to rid ourselves of the errors that mark our public life and our own personality . . . . The justified expectation persists that in a far-off age, if mankind is given enough time, the power of social feeling will triumph over all that opposes it.

We can recognize in that the worldwide struggles we are living through today. Global survival and personal mental health are aspects of one another. Adlerian insights are an important link between them.

References

Adler, Alfred (1952) *What Life Should Mean to You*. London: Allen and Unwin. p. 197.
Adler, Alfred (1938) *Social Interest: A Challenge to Mankind*. London: Faber & Faber. p. 285.
Jacobi, J. (1942) *The Psychology of C.J. Jung*. London: Kegan Paul. p. 120.
Kovel, J. (1978) *A Complete Guide to Therapy*. Harmondsworth: Pelican. p. 123.
Suttie, I. (1945) *The Origins of Love and Hate*. London: Kegan Paul. Ch. 12.

James Hemming

Note

New translations of two of Adler's books – *What Life Could Mean to You* and *Understanding Human Nature* – have recently been published by Oneworld, Oxford.

Discussion issues

1 What contributions has Adler to make in the field of counselling?
2 How are all small children imprinted with a sense of personal inadequacy?
3 Is personal inadequacy and a sense of inferiority the same?
4 How does the Adlerian approach link self-development and social awareness?

10

Cognitive Therapy and Counselling

Stephen Palmer and Kasia Szymanska

This chapter will cover the development of cognitive therapy and counselling from a historical perspective, describing the main principles of cognitive counselling and the therapeutic rationale. Key psychotherapeutic techniques and methods used in cognitive counselling will be included and case study, Emma, is used to illustrate different aspects of the cognitive counselling approach.

Development of cognitive therapy and counselling

Cognitive therapy and counselling was derived from a number of different roots: the phenomenological perspective, structural theory, behavioural and cognitive psychology. The phenomenological approach had its origins in the Stoic school of philosophy, in particular, the work of the philosopher Epictetus in the first century AD, who suggested that people 'are not disturbed by things but by the view they take of them'. Later, philosophers such as Kant emphasized the concepts of the self and the personal world. The work of Watson (see Watson and Rayner, 1920), the 'father' of the behavioural approach, and Pavlov was influential in the first half of the century. Later post-Freudian analysts such as Adler (1936) re-emphasized the importance of the personal world of the individual as an important factor in the determination of behaviour. In the 1950s, Kelly (1955), dissatisfied with the application of the behavioural paradigm, was one of the important writers who paved the way for the development of cognitive therapy. Subsequently, in the 1960s and the 1970s, the work of Ellis (1962), the founder of rational emotive behaviour therapy, Meichenbaum's (1977) cognitive behaviour modification and Beck's (1976) cognitive therapy drew further attention to the importance of cognitive processes. In Britain cognitive therapy and counselling is growing in recognition and is currently used in a variety of settings including the NHS and private practice. Cognitive forms of counselling have also been adapted for use in industrial settings for group stress management or 'managing pressure' workshops (see Palmer and Dryden, 1995). A recent survey (BAC, 1993) of the British Association for Counselling's members indicated that 19% of them adhered to a cognitive or cognitive-behavioural model.

This chapter was first published as 'An introduction to cognitive therapy and counselling' in *Counselling, Journal of the British Association for Counselling*, vol. 6, no. 4, pp. 302–6 (1995).

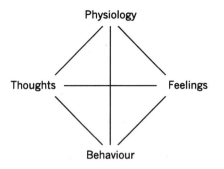

Figure 10.1 *The relationship between the modalities*

Therapeutic rationale

In this section we will consider the cognitive model of psychopathology. This will include the relevance of automatic thoughts, cognitive distortions and underlying schemata in general emotional disturbance, in particular, anxiety and depressive states.

Automatic thoughts

In their simplest form, the cognitive, cognitive-behavioural, and rational emotive behavioural models of counselling suggest that an individual's emotional response to a negative situation is largely determined by her/his views about the specific situation. These views may be in the form of negative-biased thoughts, basic attitudes and underlying assumptions. Of special interest are automatic thoughts which are a type of cognition consisting of private thoughts or internal dialogue that can occur spontaneously. If the thoughts are negative they tend to heighten anxious or dysphoric moods. This may also have an effect on the individual's behaviour and physiological response to a given situation, e.g. avoiding a stress scenario and an increase in heart rate. As clients often have difficulty recognizing automatic thoughts, cognitive counsellors may need to help them to identify and record this type of cognition (see Appendix 1).

A practical and clear model which serves to illustrate the interrelated effects of physiology, feelings, behaviour and thoughts is highlighted in Figure 10.1. This diagram can be used to help clients understand the interrelationship between these four modalities. To illustrate the contributory factor of automatic thoughts to emotional disturbance, a further analysis of a specific anxiety-provoking situation can be undertaken, as in Table 10.1.

Whilst in the example in Table 10.1 the activating event is an incident, it can also be a thought, a daydream, a bodily sensation or an image. The automatic thoughts may consist of inaccurate inferences or interpretations about the activating event which may be unrealistic and therefore exacerbate the emotional, behavioural and physiological responses. In this example Emma misinterpreted her

Table 10.1 *Analysis of a specific anxiety-provoking situation*

A	**Activating event**:	Emma is stuck in a lift for one hour by herself
B	**Beliefs about event**	
	Automatic thoughts:	The air could run out
		I may be stuck in here for ages
		I can't stand this situation
		I'm having a heart attack
		Somebody must help me
C	**Emotional consequence**:	High anxiety
	Behavioural response:	Cries
		Keeps on pressing lift buttons and shouting for help
	Physiological response:	Rapid heartbeat, sweating, hyperventilation

physiological reaction of anxiety for a heart attack. This greatly exacerbated her anxiety. Not surprisingly, her future behavioural response was the avoidance of lifts.

Cognitive distortions

A number of cognitive information processing errors have also been found to contribute to emotional disturbance. These are commonly known as cognitive distortions. The key errors are (adapted from Beck et al., 1979): overgeneralization; labelling (self or others); emotional reasoning, all-or-nothing thinking; fortune telling; mind reading; catastrophic thinking; selective abstraction; personalization and blaming; disqualifying the positive; arbitrary inference; musts and shoulds; magnification and minimization. Selective abstraction is when a person perceives a situation on the basis of a detail taken out of context, ignoring other information. This tends to be associated with depression. Arbitrary inference occurs when a person reaches a conclusion about an event with insufficient evidence. This tends to be associated with anxiety (see Blackburn and Eunson, 1988).

Schemata

Schemata are unspoken rules of life or basic underlying beliefs usually learnt from an individual's early development which help to make sense of the world and other people. They may summarize a number of similar experiences into a set template and, once activated, the schemata tend to act as fast-acting filters and aid interpretation of many future external (and sometimes internal) events. Essentially, schemata shape incoming information in order to confirm preconceived ideas. A specific schema is activated when an event occurs that relates to the rule or theme. For example, in Table 10.1 Emma's schema turned out to be 'I am vulnerable when I am alone'. The underlying schemata effect or 'powerdrive' the automatic thoughts, cognitive distortions and subsequent behaviours a person has or does in stress scenarios. In the previous example, if Emma did not have this underlying schema it is likely that being stuck in a lift for an hour would have triggered moderate concern instead of high levels of anxiety. There are five main classes of schemata: cognitive (abstraction, recall and evaluation); control (self-monitoring and directing actions); affective (feelings); instrumental (action-orientated); motivational (desires and wishes) (see Nelson-Jones, 1995).

Typical schemata for depressed clients include:

Everybody must love me
I must always perform well
If others don't like me it means that I'm no good

Typical schemata for anxious clients include:

If I lose control I will go crazy or die
The world is a dangerous and overwhelming place
If others look at me they will be critical

Main principles and characteristics of cognitive therapy

Cognitive counselling is normally short-term, structured, and a problem-orientated form of psychotherapy or counselling which gives clients a clear rationale for their emotional disturbance, worrying thoughts and maladaptive behaviour. In cognitive counselling the counsellor assists clients to become aware of the automatic thoughts, cognitive distortions and underlying schemata and helps them to modify the stress-inducing beliefs by using both cognitive and behavioural strategies.

Without disregarding childhood experiences, cognitive counsellors work in the 'here and now', focusing on current difficulties and implementation of strategies. Once mastered by the client, these strategies can be used to deal with future negative events, without further professional assistance. In other words, the client becomes his or her own therapist. Some of the main characteristics of cognitive counselling are detailed below.

Main characteristics

1 Cognitive counsellors adopt a collaborative and psychoeducational approach to therapy (see 'Collaborative empiricism' in Beck et al., 1979).
2 Therapy is goal-orientated. The counsellor and client mutually agree on goals based on their shared understanding of the client's problems.
3 Sessions, which usually last an hour, are structured with an emphasis on negotiating and setting an agenda for each session.
4 Homework assignments are considered of great value. The client is asked to collect data such as automatic thoughts, check the validity of hypotheses, and put into practice cognitive and behavioural strategies and skills. Also homework assignments can include bibliotherapy, i.e. reading self-help books and literature.

Table 10.2 *Session structure in cognitive counselling*

1	Review client's current state
2	Negotiate an agenda for the session
3	Review homework assignments carried out since last session
4	Work on specific session targets previously agreed when negotiating the session agenda, e.g. define problem, identify negative beliefs, modify beliefs
5	Negotiate homework assignments that relate to the session's targets. Check what may prevent the client from undertaking the agreed assignment and then attempt to overcome these obstacles
6	Obtain session feedback from client, e.g. how is the client feeling; did the client become upset about anything the counsellor said or did; check that everything in the session was understood; reschedule any important issue raised for the next session

5   In contrast to many other approaches in cognitive therapy, the counsellor adopts an active and directive role. This may involve didactic teaching sequences and socratic questioning.

6   Therapy is time-limited and the client is seen once or twice a week, for a total of twelve to twenty-two sessions over three to four months. However, therapy may last longer with clients suffering from severe difficulties such as personality disorders (see Beck et al., 1990).

Session structure

The structure of counselling sessions is similar to that of behaviour therapy and is summarized in Table 10.2.

Case formulation

Cognitive counselling is not a haphazard application of cognitive and behavioural techniques to help the client overcome difficulties. It is underpinned by a formulation of the client's problems which helps to guide the counselling programme (see Persons, 1989). Usually by the end of the first or second counselling session the counsellor has obtained sufficient data to make a tentative case formulation. At this stage the key issues that should be considered are:

1   The main problem.
2   The problem list.
3   The hypothesized underlying psychological mechanism.

The counsellor needs to examine the main problem(s) and the problem list which the client wants to overcome or manage. Then information about the origins of the main problem, the maintaining mechanisms, automatic thoughts and 'possible' underlying schemata are considered. In Emma's case, one of her maintaining mechanisms was that she stopped using lifts which reinforced her problem even though she worked in an office serviced by lifts. The hypothesized underlying schema which exacerbated her problem was 'I am vulnerable when I'm alone'.

Three more important issues are then considered:

4 The counselling programme.
5 Possible obstacles to counselling.
6 How to overcome possible obstacles.

In Emma's case, the provisional counselling programme was going to focus on behavioural exposure to using lifts again, reality-testing of her automatic thoughts and cognitive distortions, use of the 'downward arrow' technique (*see later*) to bring to her awareness the main schema, and then to seek evidence for and against the schema by socratic questioning and behavioural assignments. Because of her statement in session one, 'I really can't stand the awful feelings when I have a panic attack', the counsellor believed that the physiological effects of anxiety triggered by behavioural exposure to using lifts again would be a large obstacle to her counselling programme. To overcome this potential problem, Emma would probably need to be taught a relaxation technique. It would also be important to demonstrate that she really did suffer from a panic attack and not a heart attack when she was stuck in the lift.

The case formulation is updated as more information is obtained and if new difficulties are encountered.

Techniques and strategies

There are two main types of techniques used in cognitive therapy: behavioural and cognitive. (Imaginal techniques are considered as cognitive.) This next section covers a number of the commonly used interventions. They are applied in concert with the case formulation and *not* at random.

Behavioural strategies

Behavioural strategies and techniques have a variety of purposes. For example, initially depressed clients may be encouraged to undertake small assignments that previously gave them pleasure or simply just to counter withdrawal. Behavioural techniques are also used for reality-testing the client's dysfunctional thoughts. Relaxation techniques are often used to reduce the physiological aspects of anxiety.

Graded exposure

This technique focuses on helping clients to face their anxieties or phobia's step by step, starting with the least anxiety-provoking step first, either during the session using imagery or *in vivo*. For example, Emma was first encouraged in the counselling session to imagine using a lift again before undertaking a behavioural assignment of entering a lift with a trusted friend.

Monitoring activities

This involves asking clients to complete a form detailing their activities throughout the day. Each activity is rated on a scale of 1–10 for Mastery (M) and Pleasure (P) (see Blackburn and Davidson, 1990). This can give depressed clients an insight into which specific activities improve their mood.

Scheduling activities

To increase the client's activities the counsellor and client schedule a number of activities into the day. This technique and monitoring activities both are particularly successful with clients who are depressed, with low motivation levels, poor control and lack confidence in their own abilities.

Behavioural experiments

These are used to reality-test unhelpful automatic thoughts, cognitive distortions and underlying schemata. For example, Emma had a panic attack during the counselling session when she was describing her experience in the lift. When she said 'I can't stand these awful feelings of a panic attack', the counsellor encouraged her to 'stand them a bit longer' by asking her not to use the relaxation technique immediately.

Relaxation techniques

These techniques are used to reduce the negative physiological aspects of anxiety. They may work by acting as a cognitive distraction (see Palmer and Dryden, 1995).

Cognitive techniques

Cognitive techniques and strategies are used to help elicit, identify, examine, reality test and modify automatic thoughts, attitudes and schemata. Cognitive techniques also involve providing a rationale for the therapeutic approach and why techniques are being used. This section will cover a limited number of techniques but sufficient to highlight the approach. Further reading is recommended for those interested in having a greater insight into the wide variety of cognitive techniques and strategies, e.g. Beck, 1976; Blackburn and Davidson, 1990; Hawton et al., 1989; McMullin, 1986; Palmer and Dryden, 1995; Trower et al., 1988.

Questioning

Through the use of direct questioning counsellors help clients to examine their unhelpful beliefs. Awareness-raising questions include: 'What is going through your mind at this very moment?' Socratic questions focusing on reality testing, correcting automatic thoughts and modifying schemata include the following logical, empirical and pragmatic components (Palmer and Dryden, 1995):

Logical: How does it logically follow . . .?
Empirical: Where is the evidence for . . .?
Pragmatic: Where is holding on to the belief going to get you . . .?

Other typical questions include (adapted from Fennell, 1989, and from Palmer and Dryden, 1995):

'Are you disqualifying the positive?'

'Are you expecting yourself to be perfect?'

'Are you thinking in all-or-nothing terms?'

'Are you jumping to conclusions?'

'Are you magnifying the importance of this event?'

'Are you fretting about how things should be, instead of accepting and dealing with them as they are?'

'What else could explain her/his behaviour?'

'Could this be an example of you mind-reading?'

'Are you making a thinking error (i.e. cognitive distortion)?'

Cost–benefit analysis

The counsellor and the client focus on looking at the advantages and disadvantages of a particular belief (see Burns, 1990). These can be noted down on a whiteboard or flip chart paper. For example, this technique is usually very helpful for clients with rigid perfectionist beliefs who become anxious about undertaking some activity and, paradoxically, perform less well than they demand. Often in these cases the behavioural component of anxiety is procrastination and displacement behaviour, e.g. not preparing for the task and cleaning the car instead.

Double standard method

Clients often censure their own thoughts or behaviour more strongly than they would do those of others. The aim of this technique is to ask them how they would treat others in the same situation and why are they more harsh on themselves.

Alternative perspectives

The client is asked to look at the situation from a different perspective, e.g. how their closest friend would view it. Usually the friend's perspective is more realistic.

Re-attribution

Clients are encouraged to look at their problems objectively and to think about what other factors may have contributed to their problems instead of totally blaming themselves for them.

Testing out the validity of their beliefs

Having modified their unhelpful belief with a more realistic one, clients are encouraged to test their thoughts in the form of behavioural experiments.

Automatic thought form (see Appendix 1)

This form can be introduced in the counselling session to help the client see how their thoughts influence their emotions. Having written down the stress-inducing situation in the first column, the client is asked to list the automatic thought(s) in the second column, and emotion(s) in the third column. After examining the automatic thoughts, a more helpful alternative response is written in the fourth column. The new effective outcome is noted in the last column. There are a number of different versions of this automatic thought form which instruct the client to rate, using 0–100 scales, their belief in the automatic thoughts and the new rational response, and also rate the intensity of their emotion before and after the exercise (e.g. see Blackburn and Davidson, 1990).

Downward arrow technique

This important technique is used to access the client's underlying schemata. The counsellor usually starts with an expressed automatic thought and each thought is assumed to be true from the client's point of view. A dialogue with a female client went as follows:

> *Client*: My partner must ask me to marry him. It will be dreadful if he doesn't.
> *Counsellor*: Let's suppose he doesn't want to marry you. What would be so upsetting about that?
> *Client*: It means that he doesn't love me or care for me enough.
> *Counsellor*: And if that was the case, what does that mean to you?
> *Client*: That I'm unlovable.
> *Counsellor*: Does this indicate that unless somebody is prepared to marry you, you believe that '**I am unlovable**'. (*suggested schema*)

When the counsellor suggests the possible underlying schema, the client may correct or modify it.

Present and future developments in cognitive approaches to counselling

At present, cognitive counselling is used with individuals, couples and groups. It has been used with clients with specific problems such as substance abuse, personality disorders, hypertension, eating disorders, sexual dysfunction, chronic fatigue, phobias, obsessional disorders, somatic problems, post-traumatic stress disorder (PTSD) and schizophrenia (see Beck et al., 1990, 1993; Hawton et al., 1989; Scott and Stradling, 1992; Wright et al., 1993). Future developments are likely to focus on additional research and evaluation of the current applications to specific disorders and particular client groups. This may well include more in-depth studies with client groups that are generally difficult to help such as those suffering from personality disorders or PTSD clients with concurrent depression.

Three factors may influence the potential increase in the use of cognitive, cognitive-behavioural and multimodal-based approaches to counselling over the next decade:

1 Increased public awareness of the effectiveness of cognitive counselling for specific problems such as anxiety, phobias and obsessive-compulsive disorders. This has been reiterated many times in the media through magazines, on radio and television programmes. There has also been an increase in self-help books looking at cognitive-behavioural and rational emotive behavioural (REB) approaches to dealing with anxiety and depression.

2 The demand for research-based cost-effective counselling in medical and work settings has increased. Cognitive and cognitive-behavioural approaches are well

researched, and are easily applied to brief counselling settings. In addition, counsellor competencies are readily assessed and monitored (see Cognitive Therapy Scale in Blackburn and Davidson, 1990).

3 Qualified counsellors and psychotherapists offering cognitive counselling and psychotherapy are now on national registers, e.g. United Kingdom Council for Psychotherapy has a cognitive section, and the Association for Rational Emotive Behaviour Therapists has an REB therapy register. In addition, training programmes are becoming more easily available for counsellors interested in qualifying as cognitive counsellors and therapists.

In conclusion, we predict a steady increase in the use of cognitive approaches to counselling in Britain over the coming years as it becomes more easily available, and the desire for brief and effective counselling continues to grow, fuelled by both the service providers and, more importantly, the consumer.

Appendix 1 Example of an automatic thought form

SITUATION/ PROBLEM	AUTOMATIC THOUGHTS	EMOTIONAL RESPONSE	RATIONAL RESPONSE	NEW APPROACH TO PROBLEM
If I get stuck in a lift at work again:	It would be awful I couldn't stand it Nobody will help me	High anxiety	Last time it did happen, it was bad but not really awful Even though it felt bad, I'm living proof that I can stand it It's **very** unlikely that I won't be rescued. It took an hour last time but that was probably exceptional. In fact, it's very unlikely that the lift will break down again with me in it!	I'm going to have another go at using the lift at work. If it does break down again, which is unlikely, I'm going to press the alarm, use the relaxation exercise and remember my rational response. This should help me to stay reasonably calm.

References

Adler, A. (1936) 'The neurotic's picture of the world', *International Journal of Individual Psychology*, 2: 3–10.
BAC (British Association for Counselling) (1993) Membership Survey. Mountain & Associates, Marketing Services Ltd, Keele.

Beck, A.T. (1976) *Cognitive Therapy and the Emotional Disorders*. New York: International Universities Press.

Beck, A.T., Freeman, A. and Associates (1990) *Cognitive Therapy of Personality Disorders*. New York: Guilford Press.

Beck, A.T., Rush, A.J., Shaw, B.F. and Emery, B. (1979) *Cognitive Therapy of Depression*. New York: Guilford Press.

Beck, A.T., Wright, F.D., Newman, C.F. and Liese, B.S. (1993) *Cognitive Therapy of Substance Abuse*. New York: Guilford Press.

Blackburn, I.V. and Davidson, K.M. (1990) *Cognitive Therapy for Depression and Anxiety*. Oxford: Blackwell Scientific Publications.

Blackburn, I.V. and Eunson, K.M. (1988) 'A content analysis of thoughts and emotions elicited from depressed patients during cognitive therapy', *British Journal of Medical Psychology*, 62: 23–33.

Burns, D.D. (1990) *The Feeling Good Handbook*. New York: Plume.

Ellis, A. (1962) *Reason and Emotion in Psychotherapy*. New York: Lyle Stuart.

Ellis, A. (1977) 'The basic clinical theory of rational-emotive therapy', in A. Ellis and R. Greiger (eds), *Handbook of Rational-Emotive Therapy*. New York: Springer.

Fennel, M.J.V. (1989) 'Depression', in K. Hawton, P. Salkovskis, J. Kirk and D. Clark (eds), *Cognitive Behaviour Therapy for Psychiatric Problems: a Practical Guide*. Oxford: Oxford University Press.

Hawton, K., Salkovskis, P.M., Kirk, J. and Clarke, D.M. (eds) (1989) *Cognitive Behaviour Therapy for Psychiatric Problems: a Practical Guide*. Oxford: Oxford University Press.

Kelly, G. (1955) *The Psychology of Personal Constructs*, vols 1 and 2. New York: Norton.

McMullin, R.E. (1986) *Handbook of Cognitive Therapy Techniques*. New York: Norton.

Meichenbaum, D. (1977) *Cognitive Behaviour Modification: an Integrative Approach*. New York: Plenum Press.

Nelson-Jones, R. (1995) *The Theory and Practice of Counselling*. London: Cassell.

Palmer, S. and Dryden, W. (1995) *Counselling for Stress Problems*. London: Sage.

Persons, J.B. (1989) *Cognitive Therapy in Practice*. New York: Norton.

Scott, M.J. and Stradling, S.G. (1992) *Counselling for Post-Traumatic Stress Disorder*. London: Sage.

Trower, T., Casey, A. and Dryden, W. (1988) *Cognitive-Behavioural Counselling in Action*. London: Sage.

Watson, J.B. and Rayner, R. (1920) 'Conditioned emotional reactions', *Journal of Experimental Psychology*, 3: 1–4.

Wright, J.H., Thase, M.E., Beck, A.T. and Ludgate, J.W. (1993) *Cognitive Therapy with Inpatients: Developing a Cognitive Milieu*. New York: Guilford Press.

Discussion issues

1 Why is case formulation important?

2 Compare and contrast personal construct counselling with cognitive therapy and counselling.

3 What are schemata and how do they affect an individual's personality and behaviour?

4 What are the purposes of using cognitive and behavioural techniques in cognitive therapy and counselling?

11

Multimodal Assessment and Therapy

Stephen Palmer

Why multimodal therapy?

Karasu (1986) estimated that there were at least 400 'schools' of psychotherapy. London (1964, p. 33) noted that 'however interesting, plausible and appealing a theory may be, it is techniques, not theories, that are actually used on people. Study of the effects of psychotherapy, therefore, is always the study of the effectiveness of techniques.'

If each 'school' of psychotherapy has its own basic techniques and, assuming Karasu and London are correct, a therapist adhering to eclectism could use literally hundreds of different techniques. However, the number is reduced if the different approaches use similar techniques.

A problem may occur when choosing what techniques to use for a specific problem. Palmer and Dryden (1991, p. 1) stated, with reference to stress management training, and psychotherapy, 'from the array of techniques that can be taught within a psychoeducational framework, it is possible that the trainer/therapist may not choose or suggest the most appropriate techniques that would be in the client's best interest'. Lazarus (1989a, p. 249) suggests that 'unsystematic eclecticism is practised by therapists who require neither a coherent rationale nor empirical validation for the methods they employ'.

This is in contrast to systematic prescriptive (technical) eclectics who 'do not simply choose "whatever feels right." They case their endeavours on data from the threefold impact of patient qualities, clinical skills and specific techniques', p. 249.

Norcross and Grencavage (1990, p. 10) believe, 'the common thread is that technical eclecticism is relatively atheoretical, pragmatic, and empirical'. The technical eclectic does not necessarily apply the meta-belief systems of the different 'schools' of psychotherapy.

During the 1960s and 1970s, Lazarus gradually developed multimodal therapy which advocates technical eclecticism. One of the most useful aspects of multimodal therapy in its application to stress management, counselling and psychotherapy by 'its comprehensive, yet straightforward assessment procedures, which aid a trainer/therapist to develop and negotiate with a client an individual programme' (Palmer and Dryden, 1991, p. 3). The fundamental premise is that 'clients are usually troubled by a multitude of specific problems that should be dealt with by a similar multitude of specific treatments ... the multimodal approach stresses that all

This chapter was first published as 'Multimodal assessment and therapy: a systematic, technically eclectic approach to counselling, psychotherapy and stress management', in *Counselling, Journal of the British Association for Counselling*, vol. 3, no. 4, pp. 220–4 (1992).

therapy needs to be tailored to the individual requirements of each person and situation' (Lazarus, 1981, cover). The therapy is flexible enough to be tailored to fit the individual needs of the client, rather than the client needing to fit the therapy or its belief system. Interestingly Maslow's comment, 'if you only have a hammer you treat everything like a nail' is probably nearer the truth than can be imagined. Norcross and Grencavage (1990, p. 21) believe that the 'history of psychotherapy has repeatedly confirmed this observation'. The practise of multimodal therapy should overcome this problem. Although Beitman (1990, p. 65) criticized multi-modal therapy he believed that 'counsellors must build flexibility into their approaches to their clients. This flexibility may be imagined as the counsellor's moulding around the other, a fitting with the client rather than forcing the patient into the therapist's own theoretical bed'. Lazarus (1989a, p. 248) believes that many therapists 'overlooked the false conclusions of meta-analysis and contend that all treatment outcomes are similar'. He alleges that 'to ignore technique specificity is a serious breach of professional responsibility as specificity is a serious breach of professional responsibility as specific treatments can be recommended for specific problems', p. 248. Examples of technique specificity would be response prevention for obsessive–compulsive disorders (see Grayson et al., 1985) and exposure for phobics (Marks, 1987).

Multimodal therapy (Lazarus, 1981) goes further than just an application of a collection of techniques. It 'operates within a consistent theoretical base, and endeavors to pinpoint various processes and principles' (Lazarus, 1989a, p. 252). The multimodal framework is underpinned by general systems theory, social learning theory, group and communication theory (Lazarus, 1987).

This chapter illustrates the comprehensive assessment and treatment procedures of multimodal therapy applied to counselling, psychotherapy and stress management.

Rationale and method

Lazarus believes that the entire range of personality can be covered within seven specific modalities (Lazarus, 1991, 1989b). This helps the therapist achieve a (w)holistic understanding of an individual. The seven modalities are:

Behaviour
Affect
Sensation
Imagery
Cognition
Interpersonal
Drugs/Biology

This blueprint is known by the acronym BASIC I.D. and is used for the assessment of clients.

The initial interview is used to derive thirteen determinations (Palmer and Dryden, 1995, p. 19).

1 Are there signs of 'psychosis'?
2 Are there signs of organicity, organic pathology or any disturbed motor activity?
3 Is there evidence of depression, or suicidal or homicidal tendencies?
4 What are the persisting complaints and their main precipitating events?
5 What appear to be some important antecedent factors?
6 Who or what seems to be maintaining the client's overt and covert problems?
7 What does the client wish to derive from counselling, therapy or training?
8 Are there clear indications or contraindications for the adoption of a particular therapeutic style?
9 Are there any indications as to whether it would be in the client's best interests to be seen individually, as part of a dyad, triad, family unit and/or in a group?
10 Can a mutually satisfying relationship ensue, or should the client be referred elsewhere?
11 Has the client previous experience of counselling, therapy or relevant training. If yes, what was the outcome?
12 Why is the client seeking therapy at this time and why not last week, last month or last year?
13 What are some of the client's positive attributes and strengths?

To investigate the modalities and problem identifications in further depth, at the end of the initial interview the client is asked to complete a fifteen-page Multimodal Life History Inventory (MLHI, see Lazarus and Lazarus, 1991) at home. In addition, the MLHI looks at the client's expectations of therapy, including what personal qualities they think the ideal therapist should possess. This enables the therapist to match, if necessary, their approach to the expectations of the client, e.g. being directive as opposed to being non-directive. Others may want a 'tough, no-nonsense' approach and would find a 'warm, gentle' approach not helpful which could lead to a client dropping out in the early stages of therapy. One client expected the ideal therapist to possess 'objectivity, experience, extensive knowledge and honesty'. This client also thought that therapy was about 'helping me to overcome my problems and feel happier'.

Information obtained from the initial interview and the MLHI helps the therapist to produce a comprehensive Modality Profile. An example is see in Table 11.1. This consists of a modality analysis of identified problems.

Many adults are capable of writing up their own Modality Profile if they are given an instruction sheet explaining each modality of the BASIC I.D. The modality profile is the link between assessment and therapy. Each specific problem may need a specific treatment intervention. The problem checklists serve as 'working hypotheses' which may be modified or revised as additional factors come to light (Lazarus, 1987). The Modality Profile can be completed with the specific treatment strategies noted down (see Table 11.2).

A Structural Profile is drawn (Figure 11.1) to elicit more clinical information. This is obtained by asking the client to rate subjectively, on a score of 1–7, how they perceive themselves in relation to the different modalities. This is now usually derived from a part of the MLHI. However, typical questions asked are:

Table 11.1 *Modality Profile (or BASIC I.D. chart)*

Behaviour	Avoidance of social events
	Avoidance of public transport
	Sleep disturbances
Affect	Anger and irritability
	Anxiety attacks
	Guilt
Sensation	Tension
Imagery	Images of physical abuse
	Frequent nightmares
Cognition	Must perform well
	Life should not be unfair
	Self-downing statements
	Low frustration statements like 'I can't stand It'
Interpersonal	Passive/Aggressive in relationships
	Few close friends of long standing
Drugs/Biology	Smokes 10 cigarettes daily
	Lack of exercise
	Aspirin for headaches
	Unhealthy diet

B How much of 'doer' are you?
A How emotional are you?
S How 'tuned in' are you to your bodily sensations?
I Do you have a vivid imagination?
C How much of a 'thinker' are you?
I How much of a 'social being' are you?
D Are you health conscious?

It can be seen from Figure 11.1 that this client would probably respond well to behavioural tasks/assignments and cognitive restructuring. The Structural Profile is altered as new information is obtained. It is useful to ask the client in what way they would like to change their profile. The desired Structural Profile can be drawn (Figure 11.2). It can be seen that this client wanted to improve her Drugs/Biology modality as she felt this would help her overall physical and mental health.

In marital or couples therapy, profiles are compared and discussed.

One of the roles of the therapist is to use their experience and knowledge to indicate what particular intervention/techniques may be helpful in tackling a specific problem. In the Behaviour Modality in Table 11.2 a number of possible techniques are listed which may help in dealing with sleep disturbance. The client can choose which particular intervention they may wish to use. If a client has a strong belief that self-hypnosis would be beneficial then this may be indicated. Meeting client expectancies seems to lead to more positive outcomes (Lazarus, 1973a).

Table 11.2 *Modality Profile (or BASIC I.D. chart)*

Behaviour	Avoidance of social events	Exposure programme and cognitive restructuring
	Avoidance of public transport	Exposure programme
	Sleep disturbance	Self-hypnosis tape or Benson relaxation response
Affect	Anger and irritability	Anger management/calming self-statements
	Anxiety attacks	Breathing exercises
	Guilt	Dispute irrational beliefs
Sensation	Tension	Biofeedback/relaxation training (or self-massage)
Imagery	Images of physical abuse	Imaginal exposure
	Recurring nightmares	Mastery imagery intervention
Cognition	Must perform well Life should not be unfair Self-damning statements Low frustration statements e.g. 'I can't stand it'	Cognitive re-structuring and disputing irrational beliefs
Interpersonal	Passive/Aggressive in relationships	Assertion training
	Few close friends of long standing	Friendship training
Drugs/Biology	Smokes 10 cigarettes daily	Behavioural stop smoking programme self-hypnosis
	Lack of exercise	Fitness programme
	Aspirin for headaches	Relaxation training
	Unhealthy diet	Nutrition programme

It may be that the multimodal therapist is not sufficiently experienced to teach, for example, self-hypnosis or biofeedback. Therefore the client would require a referral to another therapist who was trained in these techniques. However, the client would still stay with the primary therapist to work on the other modalities if necessary.

Individual sessions become task-orientated as the specific problems across the client's BASIC I.D. are covered. The client may decide which particular specific problem they would like to resolve first. However, a glance across the Modality Profile may indicate that one specific technique could be a useful intervention for problems in different modalities. In Table 11.2 it can be seen that relaxation training may be very appropriate as it appears to be the preferred intervention across three modalities.

The aim is not necessarily to eradicate all of the problems on the modality profile. Large unattainable treatment goals are a hindrance and are to be avoided.

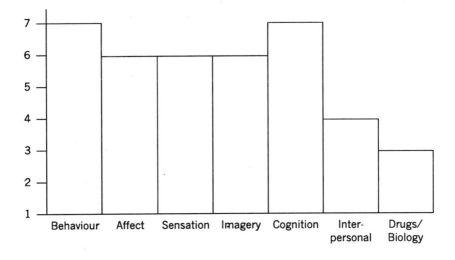

Figure 11.1   *A Structural Profile*

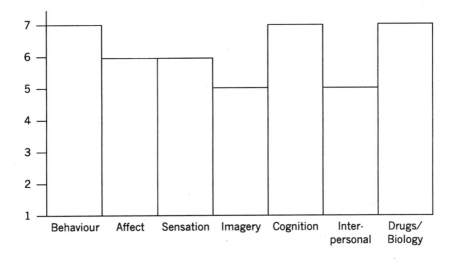

Figure 11.2   *Desired Structural Profile*

Termination of therapy usually occurs when clients have dealt with the major problems on their modality profile or feel that they can cope with the remaining problems. Some clients do not respond well to a multimodal intervention. Although a BASIC I.D. assessment can still be undertaken, a unimodal or bi-modal approach is applied.

Firing order   Modality

1	Sensation	–	Rapid heartbeat
↓	↓		↓
2	Cognition	–	'I'm going to have a panic attack'
			'It will be awful'
↓	↓		↓
3	Imagery	–	Image of collapsing in public with a crowd of people
			looking at him
↓	↓		↓
4	Behaviour	–	Escape from the situation

Figure 11.3   *Modality 'firing order' sequence*

Second-order BASIC I.D.

A second-order BASIC I.D. assessment is undertaken when the most obvious techniques have not helped resolve a problem. The second-order assessment concentrates in more detail on the specific problem, as opposed to the initial assessment which looks more at the overview. For example, an individual who tried, without success, relaxation training to cope with anxiety attacks when speaking publicly may reveal on a close investigation that the cognition *'I must perform well'* increased the problem. Cognitive restructuring and the disputing of the irrational belief would then be preferred intervention.

Tracking

It is often useful to look at the 'firing order' of the different modalities. A 'late' modality intervention may be unsuccessful. For example, an individual first recognized a bodily sensation of a rapid heart beat, then had the cognitions *'I'm going to have a panic attack. It will be awful'*. Then he had an image of collapsing in public with a crowd of people looking at him. This would happen within seconds and then he would react behaviourally by escaping from the situation, e.g. getting out of a lift. This was a S-C-I-B sequence (see Figure 11.3). If it happened again he was instructed to use momentary relaxation and simultaneously say subvocally *'it's only my heart beat getting faster. It feels bad, but it's not awful. It's not the end of the world. I can stand it'*. If he still had an image of himself collapsing then he would replace this with a pleasant relaxing image. He was instructed not to leave the situation as this would not help him overcome the problem. The 'firing order' of the modalities is matched with a sequence of specific modality interventions. A different 'firing order' would need a different order of interventions. This may explain why relaxation techniques only work with some individuals who suffer from panic attacks. The other modalities need to be considered.

Bridging

Often a client has a preferred modality which they may use to communicate with the therapist, e.g. talking about the sensation or images they may experience. Bridging is a procedure whereby the therapist may initially 'key into' the client's preferred modality before exploring a modality that the client may avoid, e.g. affect/emotions (Lazarus, 1987). This is undertaken if the avoided modality may be clinically useful to examine.

Techniques

Many techniques are used in multimodal therapy. Table 11.3 (Palmer and Dryden, 1991, 1995; adapted Lazarus, 1981) consists of those most frequently used.

If applying a multimodal approach to stress management training other techniques such as stress mapping (Palmer 1990), time management, stability zones and rituals (Palmer 1989), can be included (Table 11.4). A multimodal therapist would need a working knowledge of the different techniques. However, if less experienced in some areas, then a referral to another therapist or specialist may be required. Therefore a theoretical knowledge of the techniques available would be essential to make a 'judicious' referral when necessary. The Drugs/Biology modality may require training in exercise, nutrition and other health-related matters. Referral to medically trained practitioners is sometimes necessary. Multimodal therapists require good basic counselling skills in addition to their general working knowledge of techniques.

Additional applications

Multimodal therapy and counselling has been applied to a range of clients in different settings which include helping alcohol abuse (Lazarus, 1965); schizophrenia (Lazarus, 1973b); career education (Gerler, 1977); children (Keat, 1979) and marital/partner therapy (Lazarus, 1981). The author has also found the assessment procedure useful with clients diagnosed as suffering from post-traumatic stress disorder or athletes with performance anxiety. Multimodal group work is also undertaken. It is usually goal-orientated, task-orientated and time-limited. Group members would formulate their own individual modality and structural profiles with help from the facilitator. In addition, the author has applied a multimodal approach to stress management training in industry. In a one-day workshop the ABCDE paradigm of Ellis can be taught; problems and symptoms then discussed; a structural profile produced for each delegate and then techniques and interventions covering the entire BASIC I.D. explored.

Table 11.3 *Frequently used techniques*

Behaviour

Behaviour rehearsal	Empty chair
Exposure programme	Fixed role therapy
Modelling	Psychodrama
Reinforcement programmes	Response prevention/cost
Self-monitoring and recording	Stimulus control
Shame attacking	Risk-taking exercises
Paradoxical intention	

Affect

Anger expression	Anxiety management	Feeling identification

Sensation

Biofeedback	Threshold training
Hypnosis	Meditation
Relaxation training	Sensate Focus Training

Imagery

	Anti-future shock imagery
Associated imagery	Aversive imagery
Coping imagery	Positive imagery
Implosion and imaginal exposure	Time projection imagery
	Rational-emotive imagery

Cognition

	Self-acceptance training
Thought stopping	Challenging faulty inferences
Bibliotherapy	Disputing irrational beliefs
Cognitive rehearsal	Problem solving
Positive self-statements	Correcting misconceptions
Focusing	Problem-solving training
	Rational proselytizing

Interpersonal

Assertion training	Communication training
Contracting	Friendship/intimacy training
Graded sexual approaches	Paradoxical intentions
Fixed role therapy	Social skills training
Role play	

Drugs/Biology

Lifestyle changes, e.g. exercise, food, etc.	Alcohol reduction programme
Referral to physicians or other specialists	Weight reduction programme

Conclusions

This chapter was intended to be a brief overview of multimodal therapy and counselling. It did not include multimodal techniques such as 'deserted island' or delve with any depth into bridging, second-order BASIC I.D.s or the different techniques suggested in Table 11.3. Similar to other broad-based eclectic psycho-therapeutic approaches, multimodal therapy is multidimensional, multifactorial

Table 11.4 *Stress management training*

Lifestyle, i.e. diet, exercise, smoking, weight, alcohol/drugs
Relaxation techniques
Coping techniques
Problem-solving techniques
Life and time management
Communication skills training
Assertion training
Role play
Awareness of healthy stress (eustress) and unhealthy stress (distress) or pressure versus stress
Recognition of stress in self and others
Psychological, physiological, and behavioural aspects of stress
Occupational, organizational, family and social issues
Changing maladaptive cognitions and behaviour including Type A
Constructive self-talk
Rational-emotive therapy, ABCDE paradigm
Stability zones and rituals
Stress mapping
Emotional outlets
Formulation of a personal action plan

Adapted from Palmer, 1991

and multifaceted. The main difference is that in its assessment procedures specific attention is given to the entire seven modalities of the BASIC I.D. and nothing is left to chance or 'to the individual clinician's perspicacity' (Lazarus, 1988). The chapter is best concluded with a remark made by Lazarus (1989a),

> I have tried to provide a systematic, comprehensive psychotherapeutic structure that pragmatically contrives techniques, strategies and modalities, and addresses specific assessment and treatment operations. I have called this approach 'multimodal therapy' and offer it as a heuristic for diagnosing and treating discrete and interactive problems within and among each vector of 'personality'. (p. 255)

References

Bandura, A. (1986) *Social Foundations of Thoughts and Action: a Social Cognitive Theory.* Englewood Cliffs, NJ: Prentice-Hall.

Beitman, B.D. (1990) 'Why I am an integrationist (not an eclectic)', in W. Dryden, and J.C. Norcross (eds), *Eclecticism and Integration in Counselling and Psychotherapy.* Loughton: Gale Centre Publications.

Dryden, W. and Gordon, J. (1990) *What is Rational-Emotive Therapy?* Loughton: Gale Centre Publications.

Gerler, E.R. (1977) 'The "BASIC ID" in career education', *The Vocational Guidance Quarterly*, 25: 238–44.

Grayson, J.B., Foa, E.B. and Steketee, G. (1985) 'Obsessive-compulsive disorder', in M. Hersen and A.S. Bellack (eds), *Handbook of Clinical Behavior Therapy with Adults.* New York: Plenum Press.

Karasu, T.B. (1986) 'The specificity versus nonspecificity dilemma: toward identifying therapeutic change agents', *American Journal of Psychiatry*, 143: 687–95.

Keat, D.B. (1979) *Multimodal Behavior Therapy with Children*. New York: Pergamon Press.

Lazarus, A.A. (1965) 'Towards an understanding and effective treatment of alcoholism', *South African Medical Journal*, 39: 736–41.

Lazarus, A.A. (1973a) '"Hypnosis" as a facilitator in behavior therapy', *International Journal of Clinical and Experimental Hypnosis*, 21: 25–31.

Lazarus, A.A. (1973b) 'Multimodal behavior therapy: treating the BASIC I.D.', *Journal of Nervous and Mental Disease*, 156: 404–11.

Lazarus, A.A. (1981) *The Practice of Multimodal Therapy*. New York: McGraw-Hill.

Lazarus, A.A. (1987) 'The multimodal approach with adult outpatients', in N.S. Jacobson (ed.), *Psychotherapists in Clinical Practice*. New York: Guilford Press.

Lazarus, A.A. (1988) 'A multimodal perspective on problem of sexual desire', in S.R. Leiblum and R.C. Rosen (eds), *Sexual Desire Problems*. New York: Guilford Press.

Lazarus, A.A. (1989a) 'Why I am an eclectic (not an integrationist)', *British Journal of Guidance and Counselling*, 17: 248–58.

Lazarus, A.A. (1989b) *The Practice of Multimodal Therapy*. Baltimore, MD: Johns Hopkins University Press.

Lazarus, A.A. and Lazarus, C.N. (1991) *Multimodal Life History Inventory*. Champaign: Research Press.

London, P. (1964) *The Modes and Morals of Psychotherapy*. New York: Holt, Rinehart and Winston.

Marks, I. (1987) *Fears, Phobias and Rituals*. Oxford: Oxford University Press.

Norcross, J.C. and Grencavage, L.M. (1990) 'Eclecticism and integration in counselling and psychotherapy: major themes and obstacles', in W. Dryden and J.C. Norcross (eds), *Eclecticism and Integration in Counselling and Psychotherapy*. Loughton: Gale Centre Publications.

Palmer, S. (1989) 'The use of stability zones and rituals/routines to reduce or prevent stress', *Stress News*, 1(3): 3–5.

Palmer, S. (1990) 'Stress mapping: a visual technique to aid counselling or training', *Employee Counselling Today*, 2(2): 9–12.

Palmer, S. (1991) 'Behaviour therapy and its application to stress management', *Health and Hygiene*, 12: 29–34.

Palmer, S. and Dryden, W. (1991) 'A multimodal approach to stress management', *Stress News*, 3(1): 2–10.

Palmer, S. and Dryden, W. (1995) *Counselling for Stress Problems*. London: Sage.

Discussion issues

1 Can the entire range of personality be conveniently represented by the seven modalities of the BASIC I.D.? Discuss.

2 What is a Modality Profile? How is it used by the counsellor and the client?

3 In what ways does multimodal therapy differ from other forms of eclectic counselling?

4 What is meant by the term 'tracking'?

12

Rational Emotive Behaviour Therapy

Jack Gordon and Windy Dryden

Theories about the intrinsic nature of the person are at least as old as psychology itself. Freud viewed the person as determined by his or her past history while proponents of classical behaviourism saw the person as a product of environmental conditioning. Although poles apart in their theoretical modes of treatment of human emotional disturbance, both the orthodox psychoanalytic and classical behaviourist psychologies were pessimistic concerning the person's ability to freely choose and control his or her own emotional fate. Yet, just as the earlier models of human mental functioning studied in academic psychology have given way in recent years to the concept of an information-processing system implemented through a rich variety of complex cognitive structures assumed to exist in the human brain, so too have the traditional psychotherapies seen the emergence of new cognitive-behavioural theories of personality which emphasize the primacy of cognition. Cognitive therapies largely deal with beliefs, attitudes and values rather than focus on stimuli and responses. For that reason the cognitive therapies are in the vanguard of those methods that can be effectively employed to psychotherapeutically further man's humanization (Beck, 1970; Ellis, 1962, 1970, 1971, 1985a, 1987, 1988, 1990a, 1991a, 1994; Kelly, 1955). Prominent among the cognitive therapies is rational-emotive therapy, a theory of personality and a method of psychotherapy developed by Albert Ellis, a clinical psychologist, in the 1950s. The subsequent change of name from rational-emotive therapy to rational emotive behaviour therapy was made to emphasize the fact that REBT has always been cognitive, emotive and behavioural, especially cognitive-behavioural (Ellis, 1995). The name, rational emotive behaviour therapy, shows what the therapy really is.

The philosophic origins of rational emotive behaviour therapy (REBT) go back to the Stoic philosophers, particularly Epictetus and Marcus Aurelius, who publicized Stoic philosophy in his famous *Meditations*. The essence of REBT is captured in that famous saying attributed to Epictetus, who in the first century AD wrote in *The Enchiridion*: 'Men are disturbed not by things, but by the view which they take of them.' Other major philosophic ideas that have influenced the development of REBT can be traced to Kant, Spinoza and to philosophers of science such as Popper (1959, 1963), Reichenbach (1953), and Russell (1965). Ellis was also influenced by the work of the general semanticists (e.g. Korzybski, 1933) who showed that our emotional processes are strongly influenced by the way we

This chapter was first published as 'Rational emotive therapy; values and goals', in *Counselling, Journal of the British Association for Counselling*, no. 61, pp. 12–18 (1987) and no. 62, pp. 18–26 (1987).

think and the type of language we employ. The two main points of REBT philosophy may be summarized thus: human emotions are basically ideogenic in their origin; and that to control or change even one's most intense feelings, one had better mainly change one's ideas. In his earlier work Freud noted that 'a great number of hysterical phenomena, probably more than we suspect today, are ideogenic' (Freud and Breuer, 1957). It seems that Freud never followed through this insight and in his subsequent writings implied that emotions exist in their own right, quite divorced from thinking.

There have been many important precursors of the rational emotive approach to psychotherapy. Perhaps the most influential was Alfred Adler who wrote: 'The individual . . . does not relate himself to the outside world in a predetermined manner, as is often assumed. He relates himself always according to his own interpretation of himself and of his present problem . . . It is his attitude toward life which determined his relationship to the outside world' (Adler, 1958). The REBT theory of personality disagrees with the orthodox behaviourist position that the stimulus (S) causes the response (R). Instead, REBT theory holds that the organism (O) intervenes between (S) and (R), and that human responses are strongly influenced by the reactions of the organism to all the various stimuli. Adler (1958) aptly noted:

> No experience is a cause of success or failure. We do not suffer from the shock of our experiences – the so-called *trauma* – but we make out of them just what suits our purposes. We are *self-determined* by the meaning we give to our experiences; and there is probably something of a mistake always involved when we take particular experiences as the basis of our future life. Meanings are not determined by situations, but we determine ourselves by the meanings we give to situations. (p. 14)

Since Adler, and during the early 1950s when Ellis was first formulating the basic ideas of REBT, a number of well-known workers in the cognitive psychology field began independently to arrive at some theories and methodologies which significantly overlap with the methods subsequently outlined by Ellis (1962). Notable among these investigators were Eric Berne (1964), George Kelly (1955) and Joseph Wolpe (1958).

With the philosophic background to REBT as a stepping stone let us now consider the core values and goals of REBT.

Values in REBT

There is probably no such thing as a value-free system of psychotherapy; even if there were it is highly doubtful that it would be of much benefit to anyone. Just as each one of us posits some values by which we choose to live our lives so too does the practising psychotherapist choose certain goals and values when treating the individual who comes seeking help with some emotional problem. It is also probable that the goals and values of the particular therapeutic system adopted by the therapist are consonant with the therapist's own personal value system. If they were not, it is unlikely that the therapist would feel comfortable in the client–therapist relationship nor effectively help the client to get better.

REBT starts frankly with a *human* value system. That is to say, it espouses a scientific form of humanistic psychology which studies the whole individual for the purpose of helping him or her live a happier, more self-actualizing and more creative existence. Ellis (1973) characterizes this approach to humanistic psychology as scientific in the following:

> One of the advantages – and ironies – of adding ethical humanism to psychological humanism is that the latter becomes truly scientific. For when Abraham Maslow (1962) originated the so-called 'third force' in psychology and added humanism to behaviourism and psychoanalysis, he had no intention of becoming unscientific. But many of his followers have rushed pell-mell into astrology, magic, ESP, fortune-telling and all kinds of nonscientific and anti-scientific realms in their frantic need to 'push back the boundaries of the human mind', and, in the process, they have practically thrown 'humanistic psychology' back into the dark ages and have dogmatically espoused all kinds of unverified and unverifiable claptrap.
>
> Ethical humanism, however, goes hand in hand with the scientific method. For its fundamental postulate is that, until someone proves otherwise, there is nothing beyond human existence; and that for a human being to substantiate, or scientifically validate, any hypothesis, this hypothesis must be backed by some form of data which are, in some final analysis, observable and reproducible. Any hypothesis which cannot be backed by evidence which ordinary humans can observe and replicate is deemed to be a theological, supernatural, or magical hypothesis, and is not considered in the field of general or psychological science. (Ellis, 1973, p. 2)

Given this definition, humanistic psychology, according to Ellis (1973) becomes a study which:

> completely accepts people with their human limitations; it particularly focuses upon and employs their experiences and their values; it emphasizes their ability to create and direct their own destinies; and it views them as holistic, goal-directed individuals who are important in their own right, just because they are alive and who (together with their fellow humans) have the right to continue to exist and to enjoy and fulfil themselves. This concept of humanistic psychology, which includes both an ethical and a scientific orientation, has been espoused, at least implicitly and often explicitly, by many leading psychological theorists and practitioners . . . . (p. 3)

The emergence of humanistic psychotherapy in the 1960s and subsequent decades was accompanied by an emphasis, on the part of many of its leading exponents, on experiential, non-verbal and physical approaches to personality change. In part, this may have been a reaction to the increasingly technologized society in which we are now living, and in part to the seemingly mechanistic procedures employed by the practitioners of classic behaviourism or the too intellectualized approaches of traditional Freudian analysts. These humanistic approaches may well have yielded some benefit to those who felt oppressed and alienated by what they perceived as a dehumanized society and thus contributed to the actualizing of human potential through such means as encounter groups and other 'consciousness-raising' groups (Burton, 1969).

While Ellis recognizes the importance of these encounter-orientated therapies, he nevertheless does not lose sight of what is perhaps our most human trait; our ability to think and especially our ability to think about our thinking – probably, in Ellis's view, our most unique and most human quality. It is this capacity for high-level thinking possessed by the human animal that confers upon the person a potential for development and personality enrichment unavailable to other species of the animal kingdom. REBT sees humans as remarkably complex, thinking-feeling-behaving organisms. Our cognitive abilities – alas, often under-used or even neglected – represent our most important weapon in combating and over-coming our strong individual and societal tendencies to 'dehumanize' ourselves. But these cognitive abilities cannot in practice be separated from the emotions nor can these be separated from action and behaviour. While REBT may focus upon the thinking component at any given moment, it does not neglect the importance of feeling and behaviour. It is, indeed, the potent interlinking of all three modalities that makes the human personality what it is in the first place, and that can bring about personality change in the second place. In REBT humans tend to perceive, think, emote and behave simultaneously (Ellis, 1978). According to Ellis (1978):

> They therefore, at one and the same time, are cognitive, conative and motoric. They rarely act without also cognizing, since their present sensations or actions are appre-hended in a network of prior experiences, memories and conclusions. They seldom emote without thinking, since their feelings include, and are usually triggered by, an appraisal of a given situation and its importance. They rarely act without perceiving, thinking and emoting, since these processes provide them with reasons for acting. Just as their normal behaviour is a function of their perceiving, thinking, emoting and acting, so, too, is their disturbed behaviour. To understand self-defeating conduct, therefore, it is advisable to understand how people perceive, think, emote and act. (pp. 185–6)

In REBT the therapist looks for clients' philosophies and tries to show how these philosophies may be the root cause of many of the problems currently besetting them. More specifically, clients are taught during the course of therapy how to distinguish the rational or reality-based components from the irrational or fantasy-based components present in their philosophy or way of dealing with life, and how their irrational illogical views create and sustain their dysfunctional emotions and patterns of behaviour. Once this understanding is achieved the therapist's goal is to show clients how to uproot their negative self-defeating views, and attitudes and replace them with saner reality-orientated ideas. In many respects, rational emotive behaviour psychology overlaps with George Kelly's psychology of 'personal constructs' (Diamond, 1984/85); for REBT not only tends to teach clients rational or appropriate behaviours but also teaches them how to dispute irrational ideas and inappropriate behaviours and to internalize rules of logic and scientific method. It agrees with Karl Popper that hypotheses are provisional, that they should preferably be checked and re-checked against hard, factual evidence and never be taken to be final or unchangeable representations of reality. We may hold that some things may be probably, or partly, true, but never completely or certainly true. In REBT, therefore, there are no absolutes.

The goals of REBT

The goals of REBT can be stated quite simply: REBT aims to help humans to achieve their basic goals or values. As Morris and Kanitz (1975, p. xiii) put it,

REBT is a method of solving emotional problems and its basic goals are, especially, to help individuals:

1 To survive, exist and remain alive.
2 To be relatively happy.
3 To live successfully within a social group.
4 To experience a meaningful relationship with one or more selected individuals.
5 To work productively and creatively at some kind of remunerative activity.

All of these goals postulate certain values. Some of them are probably biologically based. For example, if we did not have the values of surviving and being happy, etc., we would probably die. None of us *have* to have these values, of course. You might choose to live as a hermit or as a member of say, a hippy-style commune in the desert. You could even choose not to go on living or to survive miserably by wearing a hair shirt all your life in the hope of attaining eternal bliss in some hereafter. In rational-emotive theory, therefore, 'rational' has no absolute meaning; 'Rationality means that after I start with certain values, goals and purposes, I try to efficiently (rationally) achieve them. It's just a technique. It doesn't exist in itself' (Morris and Kanitz, 1975, p. 41). In other words, given that humans are social animals with the power to choose to live happily rather than miserably, to prefer pleasure to pain, and to strive through some long-range, goal-directed activity for the achievement of an important ambition or to maximize their capacity for the enjoyment of life, *rational* in REBT theory means 'that which helps people to achieve their basic goals and purposes, whereas *irrational* means that which prevents them from achieving these goals and purposes' (Dryden, 1984, p. 238). Thus, in sum, in REBT, we do not use rationality in any absolute sense, but see it as relative in nature.

As a corollary to that, it is important to note that REBT takes a definite stand on the question of morality. The first principle of morality is Shakespeare's dictum: To thine own self be true. This principle is closely followed by the second principle of morality: Do not commit any deed that needlessly or deliberately harms others. Ellis (1964) sees morality as having meaning only in social context. Thus:

> Morality has to do with principles of right social conduct and not with personal like or dislike. We normally should treat other people properly, or at least refrain from needlessly harming them, whether we personally like them or not. And we should do so, primarily, because *we* want to be, in our turn, treated properly by others; *we* want to help create, by our right conduct, the kind of world that is safe and beneficial for *us* to live in; and *we* want to avoid reprisals, in case we do treat others badly. In the final analysis, then, morality is based, when it is sensible, on the golden rule: we try to do unto others as we would like them to do unto us. Consequently, far from being self-sacrificing, morality is based on highly rational, self-interested motives. (p. 1)

Ellis (1964) is emphatic that 'happiness' is meaningful only when it is associated with the individual.

> To be real, human happiness must include the well-being of a maximum number of *individual men and women*, rather than the 'happiness' of some abstract community, state, government, nation, fatherland, county, city, race, creed, or religion. However honored

their history or sacred their background, institutions and ideologies should be designed to serve mankind. As soon as they are maintained for their own mystical sakes, or for that of some ruling clique, they become perversions, the foci of inevitable dangers. (p. 2)

REBT, however, does not espouse a 'Let's live today for tomorrow we die', philosophy. Virtually all of us are hedonistic in the sense of having a strong biological tendency to stay alive and to achieve a reasonable degree of happiness during our earthly span of existence. We seek to avoid needless pain and to achieve freedom from chronic pain through the use of drugs and medications. However hedonism is a choice, not an absolute necessity. We could deliberately choose to be fairly unhappy or in pain throughout our lives on the supposition that we will later achieve happiness in heaven. Most people, it seems, try to achieve happiness in this life although *not* all succeed. If some people consciously choose to go for immediate and easy gratifications, 'Life is short, who knows how long I'll be here!' and if these people fully accept the consequences of that decision – for example, the fact that they may get lung cancer or other related disabilities because of the endless cigarettes they keep smoking today – that is their perogative, and their behaviour is not necessarily irrational. If, however, these people choose immediate gratification over future happiness and then demand that they have the latter as well as the former and bitterly complain when things do not turn out that way, that is not rational behaviour since they are not accepting the logical consequences of their choices. On the other hand, if you decide to focus on long-range hedonism and say to yourself something like – 'I may live for 75 years or so and since I want to be happy during most of my life and not just at the moment I had better discipline myself somewhat and put off many immediate gratifications in favour of future gains and try to ration my happiness over most of my earthly existence,' your behaviour is rational. It is rational because you accept reality and because you are prepared to follow the self-disciplined kind of existence that will probably accord you the goal you seek. But equally, if you choose long-range happiness, but then stubbornly refuse to follow the path of self-discipline you are being self-contradictory and hence irrational.

REBT, therefore, makes growth and happiness – achieved through action, work and self-discipline – the relevant core of a person's intrapersonal and interpersonal life. While REBT helps people maximize their self-actualizing tendencies by encouraging them to assume responsibility for their own lives, to become vitally absorbed in some creative pursuit or goal and to become sensibly self-interested and self-directing, REBT also puts emphasis on social interest. Social interest is usually rational because most people choose to live and enjoy themselves in a social group; and if people do not act morally, have some consideration for the rights and legitimate aspirations of others in the group and abet social survival, it is unlikely they will create the kind of world in which they themselves can live comfortably and happily.

While REBT deals primarily with disturbed human evaluations, emotions and behaviours and is highly rational and scientific, it uses rationality and science in the service of humans in an attempt to enable them to live and be happy. It hypothesizes that nothing superhuman probably exists and that devout belief in superhuman agencies tends to foster dependency and increase emotional disturbance. It assumes that no humans, whatever their antisocial or obnoxious behaviour, are damnable or superhuman. It particularly emphasizes the importance of will and choice in human affairs, even although it accepts the likelihood that some human behaviour is partially determined by biological, social and other forces.

Rational emotive behaviour therapy is deeply philosophic and re-educative. Whenever possible, it strives for the more elegant kind of personality-restructuring solutions rather than with the less elegant types of symptom-removal solutions to human problems. It is thus psychoeducational as well as therapeutic and it is now being applied to a large number of fields of human endeavour.

To appreciate how the ideals and goals of REBT are realized in practice it is necessary to understand the basic clinical theory of REBT.

Basic clinical theory and practice

The ABC of REBT

We will now present REBT's famous theory in its simplest form, although it should be noted that Ellis (1995, 1991b) has proposed an expanded version of his theory.

Unlike some systems of counselling and psychotherapy REBT does not start with the assumption that humans *get* conditioned by external circumstances such as early learning experiences. While these external conditions may carry important consequences for everything people do, and may well influence their development, humans still have strong innate or biological tendencies to think, feel and behave in certain ways. It would appear that the human animal functions are a product of both innate and acquired tendencies. Thus we can largely, but not exclusively, control our own destinies, particularly our emotional destinies. We do so by our evaluations, by the way that we feel about and interpret, or choose to look at, the events that occur in our lives and by the actions that we choose to take in response to our evaluations of these occurrences. We shall put this in REBT's ABC framework with an illustrative example as follows.

Suppose you have a good job which you definitely like and wish to hold on to but you get fired. We call this point A: A stands for an Activating Experience or Activating Event, something that occurs. At point C, you react to the happening at point A: C stands for your emotional and/or behavioural Consequence. Let us assume that at point C you feel quite depressed about your job loss and tend to stay at home most of the time moping about and thus avoid going out to look for another equivalent job. You observe that the emotional and behavioural Consequence (C) follows immediately and directly after the occurrence of the Activating Experience (A) and you (and others who know you) assume that A *causes* C. You say to yourself something like: 'I lost this good job and *that* has depressed me and made it difficult for me to get my heart high enough to go out and look for another job.'

REBT maintains that this conclusion is a non-sequitur, for C did not *automatically* follow A. Instead, the consequence (C) followed your Beliefs about A. What beliefs? Actually, you have two sets of beliefs or evaluations at B. One is a rational set of beliefs which we shall denote 'rB', and can be expressed thus: 'I liked the job I had and because it meant a lot to me to keep the job, I consider its loss unfortunate and disadvantageous. I wish I hadn't lost the job.' This evaluation is rational because you can produce evidence for it being true. You could point to the loss of income, for example, to the loss of a possible promotion had you stayed in the job, and so on. Thus if you *merely* desired to retain the job and told yourself: 'I definitely would have liked to keep that job, but I didn't. Tough! I find that pretty unfortunate, but hardly the end of the world', you would then tend to feel disappointed, sorry and regretful at C, after you experienced your job loss at A.

However, you actually felt *depressed* at the loss of your job. In REBT we would contend that in addition to your set of rational beliefs, (rB), you were also holding and maintaining a second set of irrational beliefs or evaluations which we shall denote (iB). These irrational beliefs (iBs) might be expressed this: 'I desperately *need* this job. I can hardly exist without it and I find it absolutely awful to lose it! I *must* have it!' If you hold these beliefs you will then experience something like despair, depression and complete inadequacy at point C. You will feel quite unable to go out and look for another job, and you will probably spend a lot of time in bed or sitting around instead of forcing yourself out to try for other jobs. A comparison of your (iBs) with your (rBs) will pinpoint the basic difference. Your rational beliefs can be empirically validated. You can *prove* that material disadvantages will follow from losing a good job. Since you cannot be expected to jump with joy at the fact or prospect of losing income for a time, you naturally will feel sad and disappointed about what has happened to you. And that is quite appropriate and functional in the circumstances. However, when you go beyond this rational philosophy and escalate into it the illegitimate conclusions that 'I'll never find a good job again! Life seems too hard to bear!', you are making illogical conclusions from limited data. For if you go after a new job and keep getting rejected by potential employers, your data from the job-hunting experience merely inform you that you cannot *quickly* find a suitable position and that you will probably get many more rejections before you do find one. You will therefore justifiably conclude that your life will continue to have difficulties and your frustrations will continue. But if you conclude that you will *never* get a reasonable job again you are over-generalizing from the available data. Your conclusions go beyond and distort reality and make things worse than you actually find them. If you challenge these anti-empirical conclusions by asking yourself: 'What evidence exists that I'll *never* find a job again? What makes my life *too* hard to bear?' you will tend to interrupt and negate them.

Not all irrational beliefs merely consist of unrealistic or unempirical statements. According to Ellis (1977):

> For the most part, however, you tend, as a human, to make anti-empirical overgeneralizations because you have a hidden *must*urbatory' agenda in your thinking. You sensibly want or desire to find a good job quickly, and you foolishly demand: 'I therefore

must immediately get what I desire'. And, again, you sanely prefer a rather easy and enjoyable life and you insanely command that you *have* to get it right now, immediately, pronto! With such desires *and* demands, you will find it almost impossible *not* to make anti-empirical conclusions about the world. For if you *must* get a good job *right* now, *this minute*, you will naturally conclude, when you do not immediately get it: 'I'll never find a good job again. Life seems too hard to bear!' If you rigorously stayed with the rational Belief (rB): 'I'd prefer to get a good job quickly, but if I don't, I don't', you would then tend to conclude: 'Well, I haven't found a good job yet; but if I keep trying, I'll most probably find one in the not too distant future.'

Almost always, therefore, irrational beliefs (iBs) do not merely stem from your human tendency to see the world somewhat distortedly and to make anti-empirical statements about what has happened and what probably will happen to you, but from your demanding, commanding statements about what *should* and *must* happen so that you can *absolutely* and *necessarily* get what you desire. If you really stayed with desires and preferences, and virtually never escalated them into needs and necessities, you would relatively rarely make anti-empirical statements to yourself and others. But just as soon as you make your desires into dire needs, such unrealistic statements almost inevitably follow – and follow, frequently, in great numbers! (p. 9)

If you follow the REBT approach, then when you feel anxious, depressed, self-downing, guilty, hostile, or otherwise emotionally upset, you can assume on theoretical grounds that you are strongly telling yourself some kind of absolute *should* or *must*. Look for those absolutes or magical demands! Ask yourself: 'What *should*, or what *must* do I keep telling myself to *create* my disturbance?' 'Do I have them in my social life? My sex life? My school life? My career? Where?' Quite quickly you will start to find them once you get adept at looking for your demands.

Does all emotional disturbance stem, then, from our demandingness? Not quite. Ellis (1977) maintains that:

various kinds of disturbance, such as dyslexia, mental retardation, hypoglycemic irritability, and neurological deficiencies that have physical, toxic or other causes do seem to exist. So let us not over-categorize and insist that *all* behavioural disorders exclusively consist of demandingness et al. They most probably don't. But the vast majority of what we normally call emotional problems probably do. Look even a little closely at behaviour that we tend to call 'neurotic', or 'disordered' and probably 90% or more of it involves a person's absolutistically demanding something, awfulizing about not getting what he or she demands, whining persistently about not getting it, and/or stupidly concluding that he or she, or someone else, is despicable for acting in a particular way. Certainly we can, if we look hard enough, find other forms of 'emotional disturbance'. But not very often! (p. 11)

Having detected and discriminated the (iBs) from the (rBs) the next step in REBT is point D. D stands for Disputing. By means of what is virtually a Socratic-type dialogue, clients in REBT are encouraged to question and find evidence for the irrational ideas which generate and sustain their emotional upsettedness and dysfunctional behaviour. Provided individuals persistently and vigorously dispute the unrealistic notions that they hold and replace them with saner empirically validatable propositions, after a period of time the previously held irrational ideas will loosen their hold and strike the individuals as having much less credence than hitherto. The end result of REBT consists of clients acquiring a new philosophy which enables them to think about themselves, others, and the world in a more sensible way in future. In the job loss which we used as an example above, when you acquire this new Effect, which we call E, you not only acquire a new cognitive Effect (cE), or new philosophy, but most importantly, you will, if you truly believe in it and follow what you believe, acquire a new emotive Effect (eE) and behavioural Effect (bE) as well. Thus, you will no longer feel depressed (though still sorry) about losing your job, you will feel unanxious (though still concerned) and, instead of avoiding looking for a new job, you will tend to actively and assertively look for the kind of employment you would feel happy about.

While Disputing is the main method in the therapeutic armamentarium of REBT, it is by no means the only one as will be shown later in this chapter. A number of other techniques are employed, such as rational-emotive imagery, shame-attacking exercises, and therapists showing the client unconditional acceptance. REBT also places much emphasis on a large variety of behavioural homework assignments (particularly action-orientated, *in vivo* desensitizing exercises). Ellis (1977) explains:

> For its theory, while stressing the cognitive components in human disturbance and personality change, also states that people *strongly, forcefully*, and *dramatically* hold on to their ideas and behaviours and that to make real and lasting changes, they had better therefore strongly, forcefully and emotively work at modifying their dysfunctional conduct. . . . RET theory and practice forcefully says, therefore, that only by doing your A-B-C's and your D-E's many many times and only by doing them in an emotive and action-oriented framework, will you likely undo your irrational Beliefs and keep them permanently undone. In fact, rational-emotive therapy postulates that your tendency to think irrationally, emote inappropriately and act dysfunctionally has a strong biological as well as a significant learned element to it: it therefore seems highly unlikely that you will ever behave as a completely rational un-self-defeating creature. However, if you learn your A-B-C's of RET really well and back them up with vigorous and persistent emotive and behavioural action, you can go surprisingly far in this lovely direction! (pp. 31–2).

REBT in action

The following case will demonstrate the rational-emotive approach in action. As is usual in REBT, the therapist uses the A-B-C model to structure the presenting problem. When the client indicates to the therapist that he or she truly understands and accepts the genesis of the disturbed feelings, the therapist proceeds to show the client how to dispute his or her irrational ideas at point D; and by persistently and vigorously challenging them, to wind up with new Emotional Effects (E) or rational philosophies. Ellis (1985c) presents the following transcript as a typical example of an REBT session with a female having difficulties in encountering suitable partners of the opposite sex:

> Cognitively, an RET practitioner will have the following kind of dialogue with a female client who wishes to meet men she might relate to emotionally but who rarely does very much to initiate or facilitate encounters.

T: When you see what you consider to be an attractive and personable man at a dance, a party or other social situation and you want to talk to him but run away from doing so, what do you tell yourself to make yourself retreat?

C: I tell myself that he's not for me – that he already has a woman, or something like that.

T: Well, that's a rationalization. You're giving yourself an excuse, which seems to be plausible (but really isn't), so that you don't have to talk to him. But what's your reasons behind your rationalization? What are you really telling yourself that makes you afraid to talk to him?

C: I don't know.

T: Yes, you do! 'If I go over and talk to him . . .?' What?

C: 'He may not like me. He may reject me.'

T: Right! That's what you're saying to yourself. 'And if he doesn't like me, if he rejects me . . .?' What?

C: 'I'll never get anyone I want. No good man will want me.'

T: Yes, that's what you're saying to yourself. But that's an antiempirical or unrealistic statement that follows from some absolutistic philosophy – from some should or must. What do you think that absolutistic philosophy is?

C: 'I must not ever get rejected by a man I really want. I should win them all. Otherwise, I'm unlovable and will never get one.'

T: Right. Now let's go over that set of irrational beliefs. At A, Activating Event, you encounter a man you really would like to talk to, probably date, and maybe eventually to mate with. At B, your irrational set of Beliefs, you tell yourself that you must not get rejected by him or any other decent man; that you should win every man who is good for you. Then, at C, emotional and behavioural Consequence, you feel anxious and you withdraw and refuse to talk to this man.

C: Yes, that's the way it always seems to go.

T: That's the way you make it go. But let's get you to make it go otherwise: help you approach many or most men you find desirable.

C: How?

T: First, by going on to D – Disputing. Let's you and I now do some active disputing. First of all, Why must you get all the desirable males you meet? Where is it written that you should not get rejected by them?

C: Uh–. Because it's so uncomfortable not to get what I want.

T: So it's uncomfortable! Why must you be comfortable?

C: Because I want to be.

T: Why must you get what you want?

C: Uh–. I guess I don't have to.

T: 'But I really should!'

C: (*laughs*): Yes, I guess I feel I really should.

T: And where will that should and must get you?

C: Anxious – and withdrawing.

T: Exactly! But you'd better go over that – better show yourself, very carefully and in detail, that as long as you insist that you must do well and get what you want, you'll almost inevitably be anxious and withdrawing.

C: Mmm.

T: Yes – Mmm! Suppose you don't get this attractive man, you really try and you still don't get him. How would you feel about that?

C: Awful!

T: Why would it be awful to get rejected?

C: Because I wouldn't like it.

T: That's why it would be bad. Uncomfortable. A pain in the ass. But why would that badness be awful?

C: Well, I guess it really wouldn't be.

T: Why wouldn't it be?

C: Well, uh, because it would only really be inconvenient. And there are other men available.

T: Right. And if it were awful, it would be totally bad or inconvenient – or 101% bad. And it hardly is that! No matter how inconvenient it is, you can probably always live and be happy – and then look for something less inconvenient.

C: Yes, I suppose so.

T: You'd better say that more enthusiastically!

C: Yes, I guess I could be happy without this one man. But suppose I never got a good lover or husband. Could I then be happy?

T: Why not? You wouldn't be as happy as if you did get one. But you could certainly be happy in some way, couldn't you?

C: Oh, yes. I see what you mean. Even if I never succeeded in love I could still be happy in other ways, with other things.

T: Damned right!

In this manner, the therapist keeps cognitively, philosophically, showing the client that she can risk rejection, and that if she does not, she is likely to be much less happy than if she does. The RET practitioner takes her absolutistic views and her unrealistic derivatives of them, rips them up, and shows her how to dispute them herself. She learns to use the scientific method to keep proving to herself that (1) she does not have to find love; (2) it is hardly horrible if she doesn't find it; (3) she can stand males rejecting her; (4) her worth as a human does not decrease when she gets rejected; (5) men who treat her badly in encountering situations are behaving inconsiderately but are not total bastards; and (6) it would be nice if conditions made it easy and enjoyable for her to meet a good many men until she finally found a suitable love partner, but the world is hardly a terrible place if things are difficult and if she has to keep striving to get what she wants.

RET uses, with clients like this one, some of its other common cognitive techniques, such as: (1) She is shown how to make a list of all the advantages of taking risks and getting, probably, many rejections while doing so, and all the disadvantages of 'comfortably' refusing to take such risks and waiting like a sitting duck for personable men to come to her. (2) She is given information on where are some of the best places to go to meet men and what methods of approach she can use to encounter them. (3) She is taught techniques of cognitive distraction, such as Jacobsen's (1942) relaxation techniques, when she makes herself quite anxious in an encountering situation. (4) She is shown how to imagine herself encountering men and talking to them in a sustained manner. (5) She is given bibliotherapy materials to read on RET and encountering, such as *The Intelligent Woman's Guide to Dating and Mating* (Ellis, 1979) and *First Person Singular* (Johnson, 1977).

Emotively, RET again uses its common techniques with clients who are having trouble encountering others and finding love partners, such as: (1) Forceful self-statements: helping clients to say to themselves, very forcefully, statements such as: 'It's hard to encounter new potential partners; but it's much harder if I don't!' 'If I fail in my encountering methods, too damned bad! It's better to have tried and lost than never to have encountered at all!' (2) Rational-emotive imagery: showing clients how to imagine themselves failing miserably at encountering others and only feeling sorry, regretful, frustrated and annoyed, and not depressed or self-downing. (3) Role playing: giving clients practice through role playing, in meeting partners they consider suitable, and showing them how they make themselves anxious, and need not do so, when they do encountering. (4) Shame-attacking exercises: inducing clients deliberately to do something they consider foolish or shameful in their encountering procedures: such as wearing outlandish clothing or deliberately saying the wrong thing; and showing them how to feel unashamed and self-accepting when they do so.

RET uses a number of behavioural methods in helping clients overcome their fear of encountering possible love partners: (1) *In vivo* desensitization: helping them to take homework assignments of actually encountering potential partners at least several times a week, until they become desensitized to rejection. (2) Implosive assignments: inducing clients to encounter potential partners many times in a row, say, twenty times a day, until they soon see that there is no 'danger' in doing so. (3) Reinforcement: showing clients how to reinforce themselves every time they carry out one of their encountering homework assignments. (4) Penalization: showing clients how to penalize themselves every time they refuse to carry out an encountering homework assignment. (5) Skill training: giving clients skill training (or sending them to someone who gives it) that will help them encounter others – for example, assertion training, communication training, and sex training. (pp. 40–4)

Although all the major psychotherapies employ a variety of cognitive, emotive and desensitizing techniques, including a few of those mentioned above, not all of them are equally effective in terms of therapeutic time and effort. In REBT we strive for long-lasting changes to clients' cognitions and behaviours. We believe that highly cognitive, active-directive, homework-assigning and discipline-orientated therapies such as REBT undoubtedly is, are likely to be more effective, and in fewer sessions, than therapies which employ less cognitive, less directive, less self-disciplining methodologies. The whole object of using role-playing, desensitizing, humour and all those other techniques mentioned above is to enable the client to achieve a deep-seated cognitive change. In REBT we are not really interested in mere symptom removal except when it seems that this is the only kind of change likely to be accomplished. REBT is designed to induce people to examine the philosophies they live by, and to change some of their most basic values – especially those values that help to keep them prone to emotional disturbance. REBT holds that virtually all serious emotional disturbances spring from magical thinking that cannot be empirically validated (Ellis, 1978). When the irrational Beliefs underlying such thinking are empirically checked and logically assailed, they tend to evaporate. Once people acknowledge that it is their own tendency to think crookedly that creates their emotional malfunctioning and that it is their own continuous self-indoctrinations and habituated behaviours that maintain this magical thinking, and that only *hard work and continual practice* will correct these irrational beliefs – only then are they likely to undo their self-defeating tendencies and begin to live more enjoyably.

Summary

Rational emotional behaviour therapy (REBT) is a comprehensive system of personality change. It employs a wide variety of cognitive, emotive, and behaviour therapy methods which are based on a clear cut theory of emotional health and disturbance. The main hypotheses of REBT are related to child-rearing, education – *particularly* education – social and political affairs, and for the extension of people's intellectual and emotional horizons. REBT fosters the use of reason, science and technology in the interests of man and woman with a view to abetting their unique potential for growth. As Ellis (1978) puts it:

> RET . . . is thus realistic and practical, as well as idealistic and future oriented. It helps individuals more fully to actualize, experience, and enjoy the here and now, but it also

espouses long-range hedonism, which includes planning for their own (and others') future. It is what its name implies: rational *and* emotive, realistic *and* visionary empirical *and* humanistic. As, in all their complexity, are humans. (p. 226)

References

Adler, A. (1958) *Social Interest: a Challenge to Mankind*. New York: Capricorn Books.

Beck, A.T. (1970) 'Cognitive therapy: nature and relation to behavior therapy', *Behavior Therapy*, 1: 1984–200.

Berne, E. (1964) *Games People Play*. New York: Grove Press.

Burton, A. (ed.) (1969) *Encounter*. San Francisco, CA: Jossey-Bass.

Diamond, A.T.P. (1984/5) 'Tinker, tailor, . . . scientist, psychologist, student, inquirer: an introduction to personal construct theory', *The New Psychologist*, May: 45–51.

Dryden, W. (1984) 'Rational-emotive therapy', in W. Dryden (ed.), *Individual Therapy in Britain*. London: Harper and Row.

Dryden, W. and DiGiuseppe, R. (1990) *A Primer on Rational-Emotive Therapy*. Champaign, IL: Research Press.

Dryden, W. and Gordon, J. (1991) *Think Your Way to Happiness*. London: Sheldon Press.

Ellis, A. (1962) *Reason and Emotion in Psychotherapy*. New York: Lyle Stuart (rev. edn, New York: Carol Publishing, 1994).

Ellis, A. (1964) *The Essence of Sexual Morality*. New York: Institute for Rational-Emotive Therapy.

Ellis, A. (1970) 'Rational-emotive therapy', in L. Hersher (ed.) *Four Psychotherapies*. New York: Appleton-Century-Crofts.

Ellis, A. (1971) 'Psychotherapy and the value of a human being', in J.W. Davis (ed.), *Value and Valuation: Essays in Honor of Robert S. Hartman*. Knoxville: University of Kentucky Press.

Ellis, A. (1973) *Humanistic Psychotherapy: the Rational-Emotive Approach*. New York: Julian Press.

Ellis, A. (1977) 'The basic clinical theory of rational-emotive therapy', in A. Ellis and R. Grieger (eds), *Handbook of Rational-Emotive Therapy*. New York: Springer.

Ellis, A. (1978) 'Rational-emotive therapy', in R.J. Corsini (ed.), *Current Psychotherapies*, 2nd edn. Itasco, IL: Peacock. pp. 158–229.

Ellis, A. (1979) *The Intelligent Woman's Guide to Dating and Mating*. Secaucus, NJ: Lyle Stuart.

Ellis, A. (1985a) 'Intellectual fascism', *Journal of Rational-Emotive Therapy*, 3(1): 3–12.

Ellis, A. (1985b) 'Expanding the ABCs in rational-emotive therapy', in M.J. Mahoney and A.J. Freeman (eds), *Cognition and Psychotherapy*. New York: Plenum.

Ellis, A. (1985c) 'Love and its problems', in A. Ellis and M.E. Bernard (eds), *Clinical Applications of Rational-Emotive Therapy*. New York: Plenum.

Ellis, A. (Speaker) (1987) 'The enemies of humanism – what makes them tick?', Cassette recording, no. 108. New York and Alexandria, VA: Audio Transcripts.

Ellis, A. (1988) *How to Stubbornly Refuse to Make Yourself Miserable about Anything – Yes, Anything!* Secaucus, NJ: Lyle Stuart.

Ellis, A. (1990a) 'Is rational-emotive therapy (RET) "rationalist" or "constructivist"?', in A. Ellis and W. Dryden (eds), *The Essential Albert Ellis*. New York: Springer. pp. 114–41.

Ellis, A. (1990b) 'A rational-emotive approach to peace'. Paper delivered at the 98th annual convention of the American Psychological Association, Boston.

Ellis, A. (1991a) 'Achieving self-actualization', in A. Jones and R. Crandall (eds), *Handbook of Self-actualization*. Corte Madera, CA: Select Press.

Ellis, A. (1991b) 'The revised ABCs of rational-emotive therapy', in J. Zeig (ed.), *Evolution of Psychotherapy* 11. New York: Brunner/Mazel. (Expanded version in *Journal of Rational-Emotive and Cognitive-Behavior Therapy*, 1991, 9(3): 139–72.

Ellis, A. (1991c) 'Using RET effectively: reflections and interview', in M.E. Bernard (ed.), *Using Rational-Emotive Therapy Effectively*. New York: Plenum. pp. 1–33.

Ellis, A. (1994) 'Secular humanism and rational-emotive therapy', in F. Wertz (ed.), *The Humanistic Movement: Recovering the Person in Psychology*. Lake Worth, FL: Gardner Press. pp. 233–42.

Ellis, A. (1995) 'Fundamentals of rational emotive behavior therapy for the 1990s', in W. Dryden (ed.), *Rational Emotive Behaviour Therapy: A Reader*. London: Sage.

Freud, S. and Breuer, J. (1957) *Studies in Hysteria*. New York: Basic Books.

Jacobsen, E. (1942) *You Must Relax*. New York: McGraw-Hill.

Johnson, S.M. (1977) *First Person Singular*. New York: New American Library.

Kelly, G. (1955) *The Psychology of Personal Constructs*. New York: Norton.

Korzybski, A. (1933) *Science and Sanity*. San Francisco: International Society of General Semantics.

Maslow, A.H. (1962) *Toward a Psychology of Being*. Princeton, NJ: Van Nostrand.

Morris, K.T. and Kanitz, H.M. (1975) *Rational-Emotive Therapy*. Boston: Houghton Mifflin.

Popper, K.R. (1959) *The Logic of Scientific Discovery*. London: Hutchinson (rev. 3rd edn, 1972).

Popper, K.R. (1963) *Conjectures and Refutations: the Growth of Scientific Knowledge*. London: Routledge & Kegan Paul (rev. 4th edn, 1972).

Reichenbach, H. (1953) *The Rise of Scientific Philosophy*. Berkeley, CA: University of California Press.

Russell, B. (1965) *The Basic Writings of Bertrand Russell*. New York: Simon & Schuster.

Wolpe, J. (1958) *Psychotherapy by Reciprocal Inhibition*. Stanford, CA: Stanford University Press.

Discussion issues

1 What are the two key philosophic insights of REBT?

2 In what way are cognition, emotion and behaviour related? In the ABC model of emotional disturbance, what do the letters ABC denote?

3 Given the values and goals of REBT, what criteria would you use to distinguish rational from irrational thinking and behaviour?

4 REBT frankly upholds a hedonistic value system. Does this imply that REBT espouses a 'Live for today for tomorrow we die' philosophy? Discuss.

13

In the Counsellor's Chair

Stephen Palmer interviews Dr Albert Ellis

Your first degree was a Bachelor of Business Administration. This seems an odd start to your well-known career in counselling and psychotherapy. What later encouraged you to undertake training in your current sphere of work?

I took the degree to become a writer and not to depend on my writing income, because I knew that good writing doesn't necessarily sell, so I was going to be an accountant to support my writing and retire at 30 with a million dollars. Unfortunately while I was at commercial high school the 1929 depression occurred and it didn't look like I'd make the million dollars, so I took the Business Administration degree anyway and wrote and wrote and wrote but none of my writing sold at the time. After I graduated from college with a BBA degree I kept taking odd jobs and was in business with my brother for a while in order to support the writing, because I was mainly interested in being an author. My novels and plays didn't sell, so then I decided to write non-fiction. Up to the age of 28 I wrote about 20 complete manuscripts of plays, poems, novels and non-fiction books, and then decided that the non-fiction that might sell would be on sex, love and marriage. So I started writing on that subject and wrote a book called *The Case for Sexual Liberty*, which was not published until a good many years later. Knowing that I was writing in this area, people came to me with their sex, love and marriage problems. I found to my surprise that I was able to give them very good answers and help them, although they were just friends of mine and not regular clients. I saw that counselling was enjoyable and that I might make it my profession; and in 1942, eight years after I graduated from college, I went to Columbia University and started taking my degree in Clinical Psychology. I didn't officially do counselling, but I started an institute, the LAMP (Love & Marriage Problems Institute) and I did unofficial counselling. In 1942 when I was 28 years of age I started in Columbia University in the Clinical Psychology Department after having unofficially done a great deal of counselling with my friends, relatives, and other people.

In the 50s you became a leading sexologist and then later were investigated by the FBI into the views you held. Why do you think you were heavily criticized for your beliefs?

My sex beliefs or my general beliefs?

Probably both!

This chapter was first published in *Counselling, Journal of the British Association for Counselling*, vol. 4, no. 3, pp. 171–4 (1993).

Well, my sex beliefs – at the time I started writing on sex – my articles were first published in the late 1940s – they were very liberal and my first book *The Folklore of Sex* was published in 1951, followed by *The American Sexual Tragedy* in 1954. They became very popular in paperback form, they didn't sell very well in hardback. But in paperback form I soon became known as a leading sexologist. Many psychologists resented that, because they were not very liberal sexually, and my first books were popular. Psychologists in the United States have often looked down on popular writers. Because I was a popular writer and because I was very liberal in my sex view, I was criticized severely. I was also a supporter of Kinsey and his liberal sex views, and many people objected to that. Then, when I started REBT in 1955, most psychologists, including Rogerians and Gestalt therapists, were very opposed to my views. I think I can safely say that almost everybody was against me for my psychotherapy views as well as my sex views.

Dryden has described you as the 'father of rational-emotive therapy and the grandfather of cognitive-behavioural therapy'. Can you explain some of the history behind your contribution in the development of these two therapies?

I was first a sex, love and marriage therapist and all the well-known people in the field, like Iwan Bloch, August Forel and Havelock Ellis were active-directive. They were physicians and would ask their patients about their sex, love and marriage problems and tell them what to do to solve them. I followed them and found that in a few sessions of active sex or marital therapy I could help people overcome many of their difficulties. Then I foolishly thought that psychoanalysis was deeper and more intensive than 'superficial' therapy. So I got analysed and did control work with a psychiatrist, a training analyst of the Karen Horney Institute. He analysed me and then volunteered to do supervision work, which he wasn't supposed to do according to his Institute. But he supervised me for a couple of years in psychoanalysis and I became an analyst. I had already been somewhat analytically inclined. I was not Freudian, because I thought that Freud made huge mistakes about sex, especially his idea that general neurosis stemmed from Oedipal problems. But I followed psychoanalytic principles even when I was a sex therapist. I was an unorthodox analyst, like Karen Horney, Erich Fromm and Harry Stack Sullivan, then I saw that almost all psychoanalysis was foolish and ineffectual. As I often say, I have a gene for efficiency whereas poor Sigmund Freud had a gene for inefficiency, as most analysts do! So in 1953 I actually gave up doing psychoanalysis and called myself a psychotherapist instead. I went back to philosophy, which has been my hobby since the age of 16. I adapted the views of Epictetus, Marcus Aurelius, and the early Asian philosophers, Confucius, Lao-Tse, and Buddha. They all said pretty much the same thing – that we largely upset ourselves rather than get upset by environmental influences. I welded this phenomenological view with behaviour therapy, which I had often used on myself at the age of 19. I was then phobic about public speaking. I always avoided it and was panicked about it. I read the experiment of John B. Watson, who took a long table, put a little child at one end and a feared animal at the other end and gradually moved the animal closer and closer to the child. After about 20 minutes or so the child got over his fear and was petting the animal. So I thought I'd try that on myself while using the idea that philosophers had also said: that if you do what you're afraid of doing, you finally get over your fear. So I made myself speak and speak in public and got over my phobia completely in about 10 tries.

I began to enjoy speaking and, as I say now, you can't keep me away from the goddamn public speaking platform! Then I asked myself, 'What's even more important than public speaking?' My answer was 'Sex', because I was quite terrified about picking up women and being rejected by them. At the Bronx Botanical Gardens I flirted with them and some of them were very interested, but I never dared talk to them. So I gave myself a famous homework assignment, which I later incorporated into REBT. I made myself, no matter how uncomfortable I was, go to the Gardens every day in the month of June, when I was 19 and off from college for the summer. My assignment was to sit on the same bench with any woman who was seated and to give myself no more than one minute – yes, one minute – to talk to her. I found 130 women sitting alone and immediately sat next to all of them and, following my stiff assignment, started to talk to every single one of them within one minute – thus breaking my lifetime habit of phobically avoiding such approaches. Was I successful? Definitely not! Out of the 100 women to whom I talked, I only made one date – and she didn't show up! But I saw cognitively, which I prepared myself for in advance, that nothing terrible happened. I had pleasant conversations – and did much better with the second hundred!

When I started in 1952 to give up psychoanalysis, I worked in developing REBT for the next two years and made it the pioneering cognitive-behavioural therapy. I began to practice REBT in January 1955. At that time there was a little behaviour therapy, following John B. Watson and B.F. Skinner, but very little. Joseph Wolpe and Hans Eysenck were little known. The only outstanding cognitive therapist was Alfred Adler, who was unpopular in the United States and today is still not popular. So I started RET which was called rational therapy, then rational-emotive therapy, and recently I have changed its name again to Rational Emotive Behaviour Therapy (REBT). About ten years later Aaron Beck got started, followed by William Glasser, Donald Meichenbaum, and other cognitive-behaviourists. They all clearly followed most REBT theories and practices. Some of them gave credit and some of them didn't. The only leading therapist who at first acknowledged the virtues of REBT was Rudolph Dreikurs in Chicago. When he heard about REBT he wrote me and we corresponded. When I read Aaron Beck's first papers on cognitive therapy in 1963 and I wrote to him, we corresponded and he invited me to the University of Pennsylvania to speak to their Psychiatry Department in 1967. Most of what is called cognitive-behaviour therapy directly stems from REBT. So I think that I am rightly called the father of rational emotive behaviour therapy and the grandfather of cognitive-behavioural therapy.

We often read about successes of therapy. In your experience can you comment on the successes and failures in REBT?

All psychotherapy, including REBT, which I hope is the most efficient of a bad lot, has many failures because one of the *main* aspects of the human condition is both to construct change and to resist it. When you see something that's wrong in your life, you try to change it or your reactions to it. Even animals, if they come up against some problems, try to rectify it. You wouldn't survive without being able to be somewhat flexible and to try to change.

But the human condition is also to not change. We have considerable evidence that humans resist change. People continually say they'll exercise and they say they'll quit smoking. Often, of course, they don't. Humans normally are con- structivists – who contradictorily resort to self-actualization and to self-defeat. So in REBT, I think if people would really do what we show them how to do to help themselves, if they consistently and forcefully follow more effective ways of getting what they want and avoiding what they abhor, most of them would considerably improve. But they don't. They have Low Frustration Tolerance or Short Range Hedonism and they resist improving. They try healthy dieting, non-smoking, and other 'rational' behaviours – and then, often, they fall back. Just as they do with good health plans, they use REBT for a while, find it fairly effective – and then start to use it sloppily, or hardly at all. Even most of the people who do change with REBT and feel much better about it, quit early after relatively few sessions, and don't persist at it and push through to what I call the elegant solution, in the course of which they not only make themselves less disturbed but also significantly less disturbable.

So that's too bad and I would prefer it otherwise, but I have to face the fact that people who use REBT by no means use it the way I would like to see them use it: persistently, consistently, strongly, and thoroughly – some only use its cognitive methods, and avoid using its emotive behavioural aspects. They refuse to do what I did when I was 19, when I gave myself the brilliant homework assignment of trying to pick up a hundred women within one month. Because I was determined to make myself uncomfortable until I became comfortable and then enjoying. Most humans won't do that. They will make themselves a little uncomfortable but not too much or very quickly. Thus, only if they're in serious trouble will they diet, exercise or take needed medication. Even then, for example, most diabetics are overweight and most people with this condition fail to eat and exercise well. Most of them! Similarly, most people in therapy, including in REBT, do relatively little of the work and practice that they'd better do to improve. Therefore they either improve mildly or moderately, or sometimes not at all. Though clients desire to change, they often insist on changing easily, slowly, and minimally. Why? For many reasons, including abysmal Low Frustration Tolerance!

In Britain, REBT has been relatively slow to take off. Have you any explanation for this?

I'm not sure why that is. My impression is that a great deal of cognitive-behaviour therapy is done in England, even more than psychoanalysis and person-centred therapy is used. But it's often called behaviour therapy. England has always been rather solid, as far as I can tell, on behaviour therapy and its behaviour therapists do considerable REBT but they still just call it behaviour therapy. Another reason is that Melanie Klein came along and the English therapists still haven't seen how nutty her ideas are. She rightly saw that people mainly upset themselves about their interpersonal relations – which she and her followers rather foolishly call object relations. Object relations psychology is better than the Freudians in some respects because Freud stupidly said that you get disturbed mainly because of your Oedipal complex. Well, I've practically never found any evidence for that! Neurotics rarely are hung up about wanting, consciously or unconsciously, to go to bed with their mothers. So Melanie Klein rightly said that what's wrong with people is that they don't function well in human relationships. In the States, we had Harry Stack Sullivan, who called it interpersonal relations which is a better term than object relations.

Anyway, Kleinians think that you get to have a personality disorder because your mother looks at you cross-eyed at the age of six months. We have new studies in the United States that show that children remember practically nothing until they're three or four because they don't have language and to have a good memory of what's happening you need language. So Melanie Klein was right and wrong, and so are most of the other object relations analysts, who write brilliant garbage – which is particularly highly thought of in England. In my view, most psychoanalysts are allergic to scientific thinking and the object relations people are hardly an exception in this respect.

On many counselling courses in Britain, the students still watch the rather dated 'Gloria' film. If you could re-shoot it now, how would your interventions differ do you think?

Well, I have several times. The American Counselling Association did three films with me back in 1973. Two were with adult women and one was with a child. The trouble with the Gloria film was that it was my first film and I tried to get too much in too quickly and persuade Gloria what to do about looking for a man. It had, as I recall, practically none of the emotive and just a bit of behavioural aspects of REBT and included mostly cognitive restructuring. She went along with what we did and she wrote me favourably about the film. She kept in contact with Carl Rogers and also with me. She said my session with her was very helpful and it helped her get married.

In the Gloria film we were all supposed to talk about the same problem. We didn't! At the end of my segment there's a section with Everett Shostrom interviewing Gloria. He encouraged her to say in the interview that all of us, including Fritz Perls, were helpful. But I saw her come out of the Perls session really upset because Fritz screwed up, as he often did, and was negative and hostile to her. Robert Dolliver interviewed her in 1980 and she said she hated Fritz. He got the truth out of her, and confirmed what she told me right after her session with Fritz. I found her crying and depressed because of his 'cruelty to me'.

So if I were to do the Gloria film over, I would not try to get so much into it in only 20 minutes. I would cut down on the cognitive side and show the emotive and the behavioural side of REBT. That was the worst session of recorded psychotherapy I ever had and it's quite different from my later sessions.

In your opinion, what were the disadvantages of Rogers' approach with Gloria?

Oddly enough, I was a little surprised myself that Gloria said to Rogers that he was just like a father to her. That wasn't his goal, he wasn't trying to be fatherly, he was trying to give unconditional acceptance. Apparently, she took him as a nice person who gave her conditional rather than unconditional acceptance and encouraged her to like herself because he seemed to like her in a fatherly manner. I saw Carl Rogers demonstrate several times. He got nowhere in any of the demonstrations that I personally witnessed. The clients had nice conversations with him, like Gloria had, but they only ended up by feeling, but not getting, better. He didn't antagonize anybody and he was diametrically opposed to Fritz, I guess that's why people were so horrified with Fritz compared to Rogers. So Carl's clients liked him and liked their sessions, but they, like Gloria, seemed to change very little.

Some approaches to counselling concentrate on abreaction and catharsis. Clients sometimes say they feel better after this experience and that the expression of anger is a great release. What are your views on approaches that use these techniques?

Well, I said many years ago and I still largely say that every once in a while they work because a person has unexpressed anger and now at least is expressing it and feels good about expressing it. Also when people feel angry and don't express it they hate themselves for being weak and wimpish. So once you encourage them to express it they no longer hate themselves. What's more, therapists obviously often reinforce catharsis, saying 'Oh that's right, do it, do it, do it! That's great!' So consequently clients express their feelings and think that because the therapist has told them that they're really going to get rid of their anger they will actually do so.

We have about 400 experiments that show that when you express your anger by, say, pounding a pillow, and you 'let it all out', you actually become more angry. Why? Because when you're pounding a pillow, what are you telling yourself? 'That lousy S.O.B. shouldn't be the way he is!' So you *increase* your rage. Temporarily you get exhausted and you feel good, because you congratulate yourself for 'strongly' letting it all out. But there's no evidence that you permanently rid yourself of your anger.

I often tell the story of what happened in one of my groups. I had a woman in the group and she asked if I would see a friend of hers, another woman, because her friend was in a Gestalt therapy group and the leader was encouraging the members to show their feelings and if they were angry, to tell people off. 'Yeah, let it all out!' What happened was that this woman came to group one day and they were going through the same thing. She was a small woman, about 5' 2, and there was this big guy about 6' 2, a foot taller than her. He said to her, 'You know I really hate you, I don't like you at all. You're no goddamn good!' He slapped her in the face and he took her new cashmere sweater and he ripped it down right off her, leaving her naked to the waist. He slapped her again, and she was stunned. But everybody started cheering him. 'You're really letting out your feelings!

You're really right in touch with things! You are right on the ball there!' She was really stunned.

She had a raincoat, so she put that on and went home and said she'd never go back to that group again. But then she thought about it and told herself 'Maybe they didn't really mean it. I can try the group at least once more to see if they really do.' She went back the next week and was shocked to see them cheering this guy again. 'Look what you did. Boy, isn't that great! You came out with your real feelings!' So she wouldn't go near them, she wouldn't go near *any* therapy again. That's the trouble with a lot of these methods. They turn people off and they won't go for any therapy after that. Her woman friend told her about my group and convinced her that we don't allow anything like that. If anyone gets physical, we stop them right away. If they yell and they scream, then we say, 'What are you telling yourself to make yourself enraged?' They can still do that and that's OK. But not physical violence! She came to my group and she was in it about six months, became significantly improved, but never forgot her gruesome Gestalt group experience (see Chapter 14).

Then I had one other client, a male about 18 with behaviour problems. He was a bright boy, but avoided studying at school. He was a member of a Gestalt therapy group and saw me for individual therapy, which was an unusual combination of therapy. After a few weeks of REBT he said, 'You know it's very odd but every time I go to the Gestalt therapy group I get more and more angry and every time I see you I get less and less angry.'

So I say that anything will work at times with some people. You never know, because clients are different. But by and large, the clinical data and the experimental data tend to show that when you vent your feelings you often feel better immediately. But not always, because sometimes you then get guilty. 'Oh, shit! I told that person off, I hit him. That makes me a rotten individual!' In REBT we show enraged people that others may indeed be acting badly but they, the angry individuals, are still making themselves enraged and are defining others as total worms because they sometimes act wormily. Abreaction and catharsis of course sometimes work. But watch their dangers!

In your opinion in 25 years from now what approaches to counselling will be in the decline and which will be in the ascendant?

I'm really not sure, because if humans were sane and sensible then there's no question in my mind that some forms of cognitive-behavioural therapy and REBT would be employed by practically all therapists. In the United States today, incidentally, the distinct majority – about 70% – of therapists often use cognitive-behavioural methods. They sometimes call themselves analysts, Gestalt therapists, or by other names. But most of them are sneaking in cognitive-behavioural methods because they find that they work. So I predict that therapy will tend to become more eclectic, more integrative, more cognitive-behavioural. But on the other hand people are so crazy and therapists are so devout that psychoanalysis may take another hundred years to die out, and recently in the United States it's been revived by object relations analysts. Very few therapists do classic Freudian analysis any more and the object relations analysts often include inter-personal relationship and other cognitive-behavioural methods. Therapists are often anti-scientifically hung up on highly ineffectual procedures. So I would hope that most kinds of intensive psychoanalysis would die out, but I'm not sure it will. It may take several more centuries before it is finally buried!

You've written many articles and books. Which one piece of work would you like to be remembered for as your contribution to the field of counselling and psycho-therapy?

That's a little difficult because my writings overlap. What I hope I will be remembered for is my pioneering work, *Reason and Emotion in Psychotherapy*, especially in the revised edition, which I'm now working on and will probably finish by the end of the year. If I revise it the way I intend to, I'll change it around somewhat and make important additions. But some of my other books, such as the ones I did with Windy Dryden, seem worth remembering. Also, some of my books that I've done for the public, such as *A New Guide to Rational Living* and *When AA doesn't work for you: Rational Steps to Quitting Alcohol*.

You are now nearly 80 years old. Assuming you're not on tour, can you describe your average working week when you're back in the USA?

My average working week is as follows: Let's take the days I'm in New York, which is most days, because I go out of town maybe one day a week on the whole. Sometimes I go on longer trips like this one to England or the one to Australia. In March I went on a week's tour of Seattle, Portland, San Francisco, Los Angeles and San Diego, five days in a row. Most of the time, however, I'm at the Institute in New York three or four days a week, sometimes five or six.

My regular schedule is to start at 9 o'clock and talk with our administrator for a while about all kinds of logistic arrangements and administrative issues. Then at 9.30 I begin clients, usually my individual clients, until 1.30. I mostly hold half-hour sessions and I don't have breaks in between. At 1.30 to 2.00 I eat and sometimes have other things to do, such as interviewing candidates for our fellowship programmes.

Then from 2.00 till 5.00 I have a series of individual sessions again and 5.00 to 5.30 I eat. Being diabetic, I also eat regular sandwiches while I am seeing some of my clients. At 5.30 I come back and work sometimes uninterruptedly until 11 at night, mostly with individual clients. But on Monday, Tuesday and Wednesday evenings I have five different groups for an hour and a half. On Friday night 8.30 to 10.00 I have my famous Friday Night Workshop, where I interview people in public.

On Saturday I work from 9.30 in the morning until 8.30 in the evening with clients, with two half-hour breaks for hot meals. On Saturday night I'm working on books, writing and all kinds of things. On Sunday, if I'm in New York, I'm at the Institute, where I also live. I work on research, writing letters, special meetings and workshops, and various other things.

So much of the time I'm working. When I'm out of town I frequently leave the night before, like I'll leave on Sunday night for some town like Detroit, Cleveland, New Orleans, and get there late at night. Then I give a workshop the next day, from about 9.00 till 4.30, and then I take a plane back to New York. Sometimes I have to stay over because there's no bloody plane so I go back the next morning.

That's my normal kind of working schedule. I also do a lot of work writing and reading on planes, trains, etc. I get a great deal of my writing done these days by writing it down in speedwriting, a form of shorthand, which I give to our people to put on a word processor for me to edit . . . So that's the sort of thing I normally do.

How many clients do you see, approximately, in a week?

Well, I have half-hour sessions and some full hour. The vast majority are half-hour, so in a week if I'm mainly in New York, I generally see about seventy individual clients and five therapy groups, each of which has ten members. So I usually see 120 or so clients in a week.

If you could take one book to Arnold Lazarus' deserted island, which one would it be?

I wouldn't take one of my own books because I know the contents, so I wouldn't want to read one of those! I might take it to re-write, to change it, add to it and presumably improve it. The one book I might take certainly *wouldn't* be the Bible! It might well be the Encyclopaedia Britannica, that has 20 volumes. It's very hard to pick just one book, but I might choose the collected writings of Bertrand Russell, one of my favourite authors. But just one book would become very boring!

Is there anything else you would like to add?

I can't think of anything at the moment. You covered the field very nicely!

Dr Albert Ellis, thank you for sitting in the counsellor's chair.

Discussion issue

1 What was Ellis' contribution in the development of rational-emotive therapy and cognitive-behavioural therapy?
2 Ellis is well known for his critical views about different forms of therapy. Discuss.
3 Ellis usually sees about seventy individual clients in a week and also runs five therapy groups. Discuss.
4 What are Ellis' views about failures in counselling? In what way do they differ from your views?

14

Modern Gestalt

Jennifer Mackewn

Gestalt has often been misrepresented or trivialized, as I think it was in Stephen Palmer's *In the Counsellor's Chair* interview with Albert Ellis (see Chapter 13). This chapter sets out to provide a counter-balance to Ellis' views. It distinguishes 'Perls-ism' from Gestalt, describes the modern Gestalt approach to counselling, considers some of the misunderstandings associated with Gestalt and explores possible reasons for those misunderstandings, as well as giving practical guidance about how to find a professionally reputable Gestalt counsellor or training course.

Gestalt is an integrative, ethical and exceptionally versatile approach to counselling/psychotherapy, which can be adapted to most people in many settings. It has, for example, been successfully used with depressed and alcoholic clients (Carlock et al., in Nevis, 1992). It has been modified for psychiatric settings (Harris in Nevis, 1992), GP surgeries and for people who have eating disorders (Merian, 1993). Gestalt has enabled people to solve problems, to regain a sense of authorship of their life and a delight in their being. It has led many to psychological health or spiritual search.

Gestalt counselling and therapy began in the early 1940s as an exciting and innovative development of and reaction to psychoanalysis. Since then it has evolved and matured and it recently celebrated 50 years of theoretical and practical development. Gestalt counselling/therapy was founded by Fritz Perls (originally trained as a Freudian psychoanalyst), Laura Perls (a Gestalt psychologist, influenced by Buber's existential philosophy) and Paul Goodman (social philosopher and creative writer). Perls, Hefferline and Goodman collaborated in 1951 to write the first full theoretical and practical exposition of the Gestalt approach to therapy. As illustrated in Figure 14.1, Gestalt counselling/therapy draws from and integrates a diverse range of sources.

Distinguishing 'Perls-ism' from Gestalt

In the 1960s two distinct branches of Gestalt therapy and counselling grew out of this integrative and dynamic beginning. One of these branches was led by Fritz Perls at the Esalen Institute in California (one of the first and most influential centres for growth and humanistic counselling). Here Perls gave up doing long-term psychotherapy in favour of large demonstration workshops, in which he would invite participants to come up to a 'hot seat' and work with him for a while.

This chapter was first published as 'Modern Gestalt – an integrative and ethical approach to counselling and psychotherapy', in *Counselling, Journal of the British Association for Counselling*, vol. 5, no. 2, pp. 105–8 (1994).

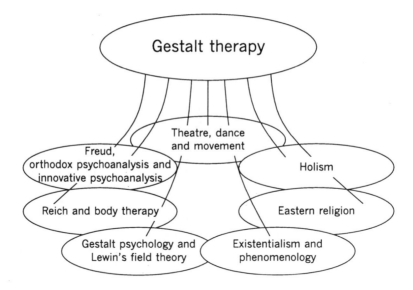

Figure 14.1 *The sources of early Gestalt therapy*

This later work of Fritz Perls was much publicized so that many people believe that Perls' demonstration work is synonymous with Gestalt. It is not. It is only one style of practising and demonstrating the Gestalt approach; and indeed even Perls differentiated his demonstration work from psychotherapy. Towards the end of his life, Perls realized how his theatrical style of demonstrating had contributed towards a trivialization of Gestalt and spoke out against over-simplifications of the approach.

The style of Perls' Esalen workshops has been called 'Perls-ism' or 'Perlsian Gestalt' to distinguish it from the Gestalt approach proper, which is now described.

A second branch of Gestalt counselling and therapy was practised and taught by the other founders and early contributors to Gestalt therapy such as Laura Perls (1991), Isadore Fromm, Jim Simkin (1974), Erving and Miriam Polster (1974), Joseph Zinker (1978), Elaine Kepner (1980). This approach also drew from the rich diversity of sources illustrated in Figure 14.1 and unlike Perls, these other practitioners of Gestalt were not tempted to reduce the rich complexity of the synthesis.

Modern Gestalt counselling

Modern Gestalt counselling/psychotherapy combines both the freshly creative qualities associated with the best of Perls' work with careful holistic investigation of both process and content in a dialogic approach to the therapeutic relationship. In encompasses a broad and integrative theoretical base and infinite possible variations of practical style. It is based in field theory and emphasizes the exploration of all aspects of the individual and his/her lifespace, as well as the immediacy of the moment.

Aims and philosophy

The aim of Gestalt counselling is to heighten the clients' perception of their current functioning in relation to their environment, including aspects of their present ways of being which may be out of their awareness. This increase in practical awareness helps people realize the ways in which they contribute to their own life circumstances. They may thus recognize options and develop more creative ways of relating to other individuals or events.

Essential to the Gestalt view of the self is the observation that people define, develop and learn about their ever-changing selves in relationship to others; so the shifting relationship co-created between client and therapist is both an important way in which clients can share different aspects of themselves and can develop or change themselves.

Another key premise of Gestalt counselling/therapy is that the power to heal lies not in the therapist or even in the client alone but in what happens between them, the contact between one person and another in an 'I–You' relationship. The person-to-person relationship is now widely recognized as a principle component of healing across the field of counselling and psychotherapy but was a startling innovation when Perls first suggested shifting some of the emphasis from transference to contact around 1940.

Methods of Gestalt counselling

Dialogic relationship

The Gestalt counsellor therefore grounds the work in a dialogic relationship, that is counsellor and client meet as two equal human beings, each with different skills and expertise. Together they explore and study the client's process of being and relating, of moving towards and separating in rhythmic alternation. Counsellors make themselves available for 'I–You' contact with the client by practising inclusion and presence. This means that counsellors honour and enter the clients' subjective world, accepting and confirming them as they currently are. At the same time counsellors are trained to stay in touch with themselves sufficiently to know and judiciously show themselves, rather than act 'as if' they were something else. Gestalt counsellors are committed to non-exploitation, so they try to meet the other in full humanity rather than treating clients as cases to be analysed or cured, which can be subtly objectifying.

Holistic and cooperative enquiry

The meaning that individuals give to their perception of the world is unique. The Gestalt counsellor therefore profoundly recognizes the impossibility of knowing another person's truth and avoids interpreting clients' behaviour, trying instead to help clients uncover their own unique sense of meaning through cooperative enquiry, description and exploration. In practice this means that the counsellor sets aside previous assumptions and focuses on the immediate experience of both client and counsellor, while adopting a genuinely investigative stance. The Gestalt approach is holistic – the counsellor does not rely on verbal exchange alone but encourages clients to notice and describe their bodily, emotional and spiritual reality as well; so that insights or awarenesses gained are not merely cognitive but based in the *experience* of the whole person.

Practical methods for exploring the past

Such fine attention to present process does not however mean that the Gestalt counsellor ignores the client's past. There is a common misapprehension that Gestalt therapists only deal with present phenomena. This is not true. By closely following the client and counsellor's co-created experience, 'unfinished business' from the past often arises spontaneously. One of the strengths of the Gestalt model of counselling is that it offers creative ways to bring those past situations alive in the present, to explore them actively and to find emotional resolution for them.

Creative and experimental approaches

Gestalt counselling is experimental from moment to moment, in the sense that neither counsellor nor client is controlling or able to predict the unfolding process of the session. A further strength of the Gestalt model is that the counsellor is trained to design experiments, in which the client tries out new behaviours and *sees what happens*. Gestalt experiments may include creative elements, such as silence, fantasy, visualization, exaggeration, role-playing, movement, drawing, dance, voice and language changes.

I stress that such experiments are not suggested *in order to* change the clients' behaviour but so as to investigate their functioning and increase their awareness of aspects of themselves or their surroundings that they may have pushed out of awareness. The challenge for the counsellor is to co-design experiments which are real enough to provoke the clients' unaware feelings and yet 'safe' enough for them to be willing to try.

The best modern Gestalt counsellors and therapists never work with experiments in isolation but always in the context of the dialogic relationship. Hopefully clients have a fresh experience of relationship in which they can risk trying new relational options. They may then assimilate this experience and experiment with those new options outside the counselling session.

Growing body of theory and research

Increasingly the practice of Gestalt counselling is supported by a growing body of high-quality theory and research (Lieberman et al., 1973; Greenberg and Clarke,

1986; L.S. Greenberg, 1979; Nevis, 1992; Wheeler, 1991; Yontef, 1980, 1988, 1992; Erving Polster, 1987; Miriam Polster, 1993; Parlett, 1993). Gestalt theorists have also continued to assimilate knowledge from other therapeutic approaches in response to the changing circumstances of the world and to the needs of those who seek counselling:

> We have always been an integrating framework. That's one of the things I love about Gestalt . . . We don't have to recreate the wheel. We take what we need from the total field . . . we emphasize the importance of people knowing what they need and finding sources to meet the need. (Yontef, 1988, p. 6)

For example, Gestalt writers have integrated contributions from self psychology and objects relations to enhance their theories of the self (Tobin, 1982; E. Greenberg, 1989); deepened their understanding of transferential processes (Mackewn, 1991; Robine, 1988) and judiciously assimilated psychiatric diagnostic skills in order to improve the efficacy of their approach (Delisle, 1993). In the 1960s one of Fritz Perls' favourite slogans was 'lose your mind and come to your senses'. This and other similar simplifications have become the yardstick by which Gestalt is too often judged, leaving many people unaware of the considerable contributions that Gestalt has made to the theory of counselling and psychotherapy. Some of the early Gestalt concepts and practices have been unconsciously assimilated into the mainstream of psychodynamic psychotherapy or been reinvented during the past two decades when psychoanalysis has found new life, particularly through the developments of object relations and self psychology. For example Fritz and Laura Perls popularized the synthesis of body and psychotherapies in the 1950s. Such ideas were rejected by psychoanalysis at the time but have since been re-evaluated and re-integrated into psychoanalytic theory (Bohart and Todd, 1988). For a wider discussion of the influence of early Gestalt on the whole field of counselling and psychotherapy, see *Fritz Perls* (Clarkson and Mackewn, 1993), Chapter 5.

Answering some criticisms of Gestalt

A number of specific criticisms of the Gestalt approach to counselling include Masson's (1989) accusations that Fritz Perls behaved unethically; that Gestalt consists of doing 'two-chair' work; Ellis' (Palmer and Ellis, 1993) implication that Gestalt over-emphasizes cathartic release and his allegation that a client was destructively confronted by a fellow participant in a Gestalt group. Here I will briefly explain how some of these allegations are largely based on misunderstanding, while referring the interested reader to (Clarkson and Mackewn, 1993), where these and related issues are discussed in more depth.

1   *Criticism regarding unethical behaviour.* Clarkson and Mackewn (1993) have fully acknowledged that although Perls was in some ways a therapeutic genius, he was capable of highly irresponsible behaviour. Modern Gestalt therapists adhere to ethical guidelines which preclude exploitative or sexual contact between client and therapist. They are held accountable for transgressions of

this limit, *in exactly the same way* as psychotherapists of other orientations, or members of other professions (see below). Perls' unethical behaviour would certainly not be tolerated by the Gestalt communities of the 1990s and it was abhorred by many Gestalt therapists at the time. Without in any way trying to justify Perls' behaviour, he was certainly not alone amongst psychotherapists, psychoanalysts or other professionals in transgressing ethical boundaries (Rutter, 1990).

2   *Misunderstanding about 'two-chair' work.* The single biggest misconception of Gestalt is that it means doing 'two-chair' work, holding conversations between different aspects of the self or becoming parts of the dream. Fritz Perls' demonstration work in the 1960s contributed to this misconception for he did often suggest that the client hold a dialogue between two parts of the self. These 'conversations' were taped/filmed and widely circulated. Modern Gestalt counsellors, on the other hand rarely repeat stale techniques. They are trained to co-create with the client unique experimental situations, to explore each fresh dilemma or situation as it arises. Many Gestalt counsellors/therapists would be barely affected if every supposedly 'Gestalt technique' (including 'two-chair' work) were never used again.

3   *Misunderstandings about catharsis.* An almost equally clichéd misrepresentation of Gestalt (which Ellis unfortunately reiterated) is that it consists of pounding pillows and raging. Some of Fritz Perls' demonstration sessions appeared to be aimed at dramatic catharsis. However, most Gestalt counsellors have a complex understanding of feelings and a through training in assessment skills and appropriate interventions depending on the individual client and circum-stances. They fully realize for example that anger may mask other emotions such as grief or loss. In each case they are likely to carefully consider whether expression, containment or exploration of feelings is most needed and help clients fine-tune expressive behaviour to their unique needs and character structure. So while some expression of anger or grief may be invaluable to one client, it might be counter-productive for another.

One considerable advantage that Gestalt counsellors have is their training in a *whole range* of creative means of communication. For instance Gestalt counsellors may suggest a client silently visualize or draw a feeling. They may help a client to transform a feeling, give it a voice or express itself as a metaphor. The means of containment and expression are finely calibrated.

4   *Misunderstanding concerning the confrontation of clients.* Ellis does not give details regarding the alleged incident of destructive confrontation, which makes it hard to consider the validity or relevance of the anecdote to modern Gestalt. It is possible that such an event took place but does that justify Ellis in 'often telling [a] story', which perpetuates a distorted picture of modern Gestalt? Present-day Gestalt counsellors establish a fundamental agreement that group participants may experiment with different behaviours, as long as they do no harm to self and others or to the property and environment. A crucial question here of course is what constitutes harm? Again some distinction is needed between 'Perls-ism' and Gestalt. The situation is complex. Fritz Perls' style of demonstration *could be* extremely confrontative and some clients felt

humiliated and shamed by him, while others emphasized how attentive, tender, playful and supportive he could also be. Recently Gestalt theories (Wheeler, 1991; Yontef, 1992) have explored the phenomenon of shame in some depth and explained the delicacy with which Gestalt (and other) counsellors must work if they are to ensure that they do not humiliate or re-traumatize clients. Gestalt counsellors/therapists who attend to their own professional development have integrated these contributions and work with appropriate care and respect.

High standards of training and assessment

In the 1960s almost anyone could start working as a psychotherapist. Many participants in Perls' workshops either copied Perls' more crude, repetitive or confrontative work or did what Perls *appeared* to do without Perls' thorough clinical background and without understanding Gestalt theory. I hope that I have illustrated that fully trained modern Gestalt counsellors are unlikely to perpetuate the behaviours described by Masson and Ellis. If they do so (and of course there is always a possibility of unprofessional practice in Gestalt counselling as in any other profession) then they are nowadays accountable for their behaviour through an ethical code and a complaints and grievance procedure.

Along with other counselling and therapeutic orientations, modern Gestalt has developed standards for ethical practice and sound training of its practitioners. For example several Gestalt Training Institutes are members of BAC and of the UK Council of Psychotherapy (UKCP) and have established minimum requirements for entry into Gestalt Psychotherapy Training and a core curriculum for trainee Gestalt psychotherapists. They have designed stringent criteria for assessment of their candidates, including independent moderators and examiners from other orientations. Their graduates may apply for accreditation with BAC and/or registration with UKCP.

A number of BAC Accredited Counsellors have done extensive training in Gestalt. Recently specific Training Courses in Gestalt Counselling have been initiated.

Ethical standards and accountability

UKCP Registered Psychotherapists and BAC Accredited Counsellors must adhere to the Code of Ethics and Guide Lines for Practice of their respective professional body. The Codes of Ethics of these professional bodies are available upon request; and any qualified Gestalt counsellor/psychotherapist should be able to show prospective clients the Code of Ethics by which they practise. Both BAC and UKCP have a Complaints and Grievances Procedure; so qualified Gestalt counsellors/psychotherapists are fully accountable for the standards of their work.

Clients who believe that a psychotherapist/counsellor of any orientation has behaved unprofessionally (as for example in the way described by Albert Ellis) may complain, either verbally or in writing, to the counsellor/psychotherapist concerned. If clients are not satisfied, they may complain to the professional body with which the counsellor/psychotherapist is registered/accredited.

Advice about Gestalt counselling or training

Prospective clients seeking a Gestalt (or any other type of) counsellor/psycho-therapist should ask about the qualifications of the counsellor they are considering consulting, specifically enquiring whether the counsellor is accredited with BAC or registered with UKCP; belongs to a professional body and works to a Code of Ethics. If counsellors fulfil these criteria, they are professionally accountable for the quality of their work. Prospective clients may also be wise to explore the style, values and type of training of the Gestalt practitioner (in terms of some of the issues raised in this article, for instance).

People seeking training in Gestalt counselling/psychotherapy need to enquire about the credentials of the trainers offering the training course and the possibilities for successful graduates of the course becoming registered with the UKCP or accredited with the BAC. They may approach the UKCP for information about training in their area and look in professional journals such as *Counselling* or the *British Gestalt Journal* for details of courses. A full training in Gestalt counselling is likely to take two to three years and a full training in Gestalt psychotherapy is likely to take between four and six years. Many training centres also offer shorter training courses, which could complement other person-centred or integrative counselling courses.

Conclusion

The whole that is Gestalt counselling is greater than and different from the sum of its parts. It is perhaps a controversial approach just because it *is* an effective instrument for change, which works creatively and enjoyably with whole people-in-their-environment and questions the status quo and the habitual both at an individual and communal level. Gestalt therefore requires respect, discipline, great skills, years of training and real responsibility from the counsellors/psychotherapists who practise it.

References

Bohart, A. and Todd, J. (1988) *Foundation of Clinical and Counselling Psychology*. New York: Harper Collins.

Clarkson, P. and Mackewn, J. (1993) *Fritz Perls*. London: Sage.

Delisle, G. (1993) *Personality Disorders: a Gestalt Perspective*. Highland, NY: Gestalt Journal Publications.

Greenberg, E. (1989) 'Healing the borderline', *Gestalt Journal*, 12(2): 11–55.

Greenberg, L.S. (1979) 'Resolving splits: the two-chair technique', *Psychotherapy: Theory, Research and Practice*, 16: 310–18.

Greenberg, L.S. and Clarke, K.M. (1986) 'Differential effects of the Gestalt two-chair intervention and problem solving in resolving decisional conflict', *Journal of Counselling Psychology*, 33(1): 11–15.

Kepner, E. (1980) 'Gestalt group process', in B. Federand and R. Ronall (eds), *Beyond the Hot Seat*. New York: Brunner/Mazel. pp. 5–24.

Lieberman, M.A., Yalom, I.D. and Miles, M.B. (1973) *Encounter Groups: First Facts*. New York: Basic Books.

Mackewn, J. (1991) 'Transference and countertransference: a Gestalt perspective', Unpublished paper.

Masson, J. (1989) *Against Therapy*. London: Collins.

Merian, S. (1993) 'The use of Gestalt psychotherapy with clients suffering from bulimia', *British Gestalt Journal*, 2(2): 125–31.

Nevis, E. (1992) *Gestalt Therapy: Perspectives and Applications*. New York: Gardner Press.

Parlett, M. (1993) 'Towards a more Lewinian Gestalt therapy', *British Gestalt Journal*, 2(2): 115–21.

Palmer, S. and Ellis, A. (1993) 'In the counsellor's chair', *Counselling, Journal of the British Association for Counselling*, 4(3): 171–4.

Perls, F.S., Hefferline, R.F. and Goodman, P. (1973) *Gestalt Therapy: Excitement and Growth in the Human Personality*. London: Penguin Books. (Originally published in New York by Julian Press, 1951).

Perls, L. (1991) *Living at the Boundary*. Highland, NY: Gestalt Journal Publications.

Polster, E. and Polster, M. (1974) *Gestalt Therapy Integrated: Contours of Theory and Practice*. New York: Vintage Books.

Polster, E. (1987) *Every Person's Life is Worth a Novel*. New York: W.W. Norton.

Polster, M. (1993) *Eve's Daughter: The Forbidden Heroism of Women*. San Francisco, CA: Jossey-Bass Publishers.

Robine, J.-M. (1988) *La Question du transfert en Gestalt-therapie*. Private publication.

Rutter, P. (1990) *Sex in the Forbidden Zone: When Men in Power – Therapists, Doctors, Clergy, Teachers and Others – Betray Women's Trust*. London: Unwin (first published 1989).

Simkin, J. (1974) *Gestalt Therapy Mini-Lectures*. Millbrae, CA: Celestial Arts.

Tobin, S.A. (1982) 'Self disorders, Gestalt therapy and self psychology', *Gestalt Journal*, 5(2): 3–44.

Wheeler, G. (1991) *Gestalt Reconsidered: A New Approach to Contact and Resistance*. New York: Gardner Press.

Yontef, G.M. (1980) 'Gestalt therapy: a dialogic method', Unpublished manuscript.

Yontef, G.M. (1988) 'Assimilating diagnostic and psychoanalytic perspectives into Gestalt therapy', *Gestalt Journal*, 11(1): 5–32.

Yontef, G.M. (1992) *Awareness, Process and Dialogue: Essays on Gestalt Therapy*. Highland, NY: Gestalt Journal Publications.

Zinker, J. (1978) *Creative Process in Gestalt Therapy*. New York: Vintage Books (first published 1977).

Discussion issues

1 In what ways can 'Perls-ism' be distinguished from Gestalt?

2 How did Ellis (see Chapter 13) possibly misrepresent modern Gestalt?

3 How can the client be safeguarded from unprofessional practice?

4 Why is Gestalt often considered a 'controversial approach'?

15

Uncovering a TA Script with Pictures

Sheila Dainow

The idea that people's adult life patterns are influenced by childhood experience is central to many psychological approaches. Transactional analysis (TA) offers the idea that each person writes the script of his or her own life story. The process begins at birth when each of us, faced with the questions 'Who am I?', 'Where am I?' and 'Who are all these others?', searches for our own answers. With these answers we lay down our own specific script for our life. Eric Berne, the originator of transactional analysis, asserted that our script takes the form of a drama with a clear-cut beginning, middle and end.

As infants, not only were we physically vulnerable but we found ourselves in a world peopled by giants whose language we did not understand. Even before we had words, each of us had to interpret other people's messages so that we could begin making sense of the world. If a mother holds her baby closely and warmly the baby is likely to get the message, 'I'm wanted and loved'; if she is nervous and tense, the baby might decide, 'There's something wrong here, I'm not wanted; I don't feel safe'. It is important to remember that these early decisions are made on the basis of the baby's perception of what is going on. This may be very different from what is actually intended; a mother's tenseness may stem from her love and anxiety that she will do the wrong thing. However, the baby only experiences the physical manifestation of her anxiety and makes general deductions.

In *Principles of Group Treatment* (1966), Eric Berne described a life script as 'an unconscious life plan' and in *What Do You Say After You Say Hello?* (Berne, 1972) he added 'a life plan made in childhood, reinforced by the parents, justified by subsequent events and culminating in a chosen alternative'. There are, of course, other theories of cognitive and emotional development. Jean Piaget (1954) for instance believed that all children pass through development stages, each one of which grows out of the one which preceded it. From the sensory-motor period when the child learns to integrate its various sense impressions into percepts, to the preoperational stage when the child learns to speak and deal with the world in symbolic terms; then the child moves into the stage of concrete operation, learning to differentiate itself from the outside world and finally gains the ability to think in purely abstract terms. Sigmund Freud (1927) theorized that, at birth, our thoughts lie in the unconscious realms of the mind and are aimed at satisfying our biological needs. He, too, described developmental stages through which he believed personality evolved. He suggested that ego develops as the infant interacts with its environment. The life script theory of TA suggests an understanding of how the child negotiates its way through the developmental processes.

This chapter was first published in *Counselling, Journal of the British Association for Counselling*, vol. 6, no. 4, pp. 291–3 (1995).

Although there is no way of being certain about what is actually going on in the infant's mind, most theorists describe a process in which the child tries to make sense of the world it is experiencing. TA practitioners work on the basis of Berne's idea of the script as a 'life plan *made* in childhood' implying that the child *decides* upon the life plan. It is not solely determined by influence from the parents or the environment. This means that even when children are brought up in the same family they may decide upon very different life scripts. Berne gives the example of two children being told by a parent 'You'll end up in a mental hospital'. One becomes a psychiatrist and the other a patient!

Although the life script we write so early is highly influential, it remains largely outside our awareness. Perhaps the nearest we come to recalling our earliest years are flashes of memory, fantasies and dreams.

Script work is a central aspect of therapy

For many clients, the task of uncovering original script messages is a central aspect of their therapy. The TA approach places a high priority upon understanding the process whereby we make early decisions which continue to influence our thinking, feeling and behaviour.

There are many ways of helping clients to engage in working on their script. Making cartoons is one very creative and effective way in to an event which became part of someone's script. Liesl Silverstone (1993), person-centred art therapist, observes that psychotherapy attaches great importance to the spoken word and suggests that other modes of expression need to be found. The now-famous research, often referred to as the 'split-brain' studies led by Roger W. Sperry (1973) mainly at the California Institute of Technology, established that the right and left hemispheres of the brain carry different functions. The mode of the left brain is thinking, analytic, judgemental, verbal; the right brain non-verbal, spatial, spontaneous, intuitive, creative, non-judgemental. In *Drawing on the Right Side of the Brain*, Betty Edwards (1979) describes how 'Inside each of our skulls, therefore, we have a double brain with two ways of knowing.'

Recognizing early script decisions often means connecting with and expressing repressed material. Some of this material may raise painful or confusing feelings; some may be difficult to put into words; some may be only barely understood. Introducing imaging allows the client to draw upon the right-brain mode of functioning. This is a very useful approach, for instance, with clients who find it hard to express their feelings in words – or for those who use words as a defence, covering their inner selves. It is invaluable for working with people for whom English is not their mother-tongue. The power and meaning of the image can shine through the tangle of grammar.

Clients usually approach therapy with great seriousness. They prepare for a solemn session in which I will ask them many deep questions and they will search diligently for the right answers. Their expectation is that after a great deal of hard and painful work they will discover their script from which will emerge the secrets which have been hidden from them all these years. Cure will then be a short step away. I take great pains to point out that this 'magic' is not likely to come about and that 'cure' (whatever that means) will be the result of our collaboration in the work that is necessary. Although clients usually nod knowingly and accept that this is reasonable, I am sure that for many there is still the hope that 'magic' will happen.

Many clients, knowing that my approach is based on years of TA training have already read *What Do You Say After You Say Hello?* (Berne, 1972). They are prepared for having to answer the 220 items on Berne's Script Check List. Although that list remains a wonderful guide for opening up important areas of script, it is also possible, by using other methods, to get to important script decisions in enjoyable and creative ways.

Cartoon of a memory

One such method which I have used many times is based on encouraging people to make a cartoon of a memory. At a relevant point in the client's work I ask him or her to take a large sheet of paper and sketch out, using simple matchstick figures (to overcome anxieties about 'not being able to draw'), a significant childhood scene in which he or she was involved.

Then I ask the client to give the cartoon a title and we begin talking about the picture. I ask him or her to describe what is going on and the story begins to emerge. I draw speech balloons coming out of the characters' mouths and encourage the client to write in the remembered or imaged dialogue. I cue the client to keep the language as near to child speech as possible. This is an important part of the process for it is the child perception which we are aiming to understand.

I will ask the client *how* the characters speak to uncover clues about his or her perception of the emotions involved (for example, 'sarcastically', 'sadly', 'sneakily' or 'like he was bored', 'as if she didn't care'). This also gets written into the balloons.

It may be that people who are important to the story – a parent or someone else of consequence – are not actually present at this particular event. In that case, I will ask what they might be saying about what was going on if they knew about it. These figures and their balloons are put in the picture.

I encourage the client to recount the story in the present tense so that a feeling of immediacy is developed. The work can become a fascinating, imaginative and often profound exploration for the client and myself. This approach is very rewarding when done in a group, so that group members can also experience the unfolding of the work.

The sketch, which may be very crude, becomes a realistic, often moving story as elements of the script emerge almost without effort. It becomes possible to see how Games, Rackets, Decisions, Permissions and Injunctions and other elements in the script developed.

I might ask questions like, 'So what did the little girl decide?' or 'What could the little boy have done differently?' My intention is to help the client recognize the choices which may be available now that he or she is a grown-up. I take care to point our that as a child, the client was making decisions in difficult circumstances. Since those decisions were effective in that they helped the client to survive, the child is to be congratulated rather than criticized. As an adult, the client can make a new decision, based on information and resources which were not available at the time.

The technique at work

1   The hospital visit

Jenny is a middle-aged woman who is having difficulty reconciling a 'happy' marriage which has lasted 16 years and produced three children with her attraction to another man working in the same office as herself. She doesn't want to leave her husband, whom she says 'would feel hurt and probably fall apart', neither does she want to relinquish her lover, who is pressing her to leave her husband.

Through previous work Jenny has identified the TA game of 'Harried' as one which she plays a great deal. Her job, which carries a great deal of responsibility, keeps her very busy. She feels anxious and guilty because she believes she does not spend enough time with the children or her husband. She is placatory almost to the point of ingratiation and sees herself as having a dilemma which she cannot resolve.

In answer to a question about the difficulties she has in confronting the men in her life, she recalls the anxiety she used to feel when she was about seven and visiting her brother in hospital after he had been badly hurt in a road accident.

I suggested to Jenny that she draw the scene and then we filled in the balloons. In Figure 15.1 the nurse is bringing Jenny's brother, his leg in plaster, to see her mother and herself in the hospital day room. Her father refused to visit the hospital, being too upset to do so. Her younger sister was still a baby and considered too young to go along. Mother makes Jenny into 'someone special' by taking her. She believes she has to stand by her mother and try to ensure that she does not have to suffer more than is absolutely necessary.

The only spoken dialogue in Figure 15.1 is the mother's 'How is he?' to the nurse and the nurse's response, 'He's doing fine'. All the rest of the dialogue is fantasized by Jenny. Her grandma, who loved her deeply, is the only one whom she felt ever gave her permission to be herself.

As we discuss the picture, we write down the messages that come up for Jenny and which still influence her life. The decisions which have become part of her script are:

Women are saintly
Men need to be looked after
I'm sad (If I'd been good enough Dad would have come)
I'm angry (If Dad really loved me he would have come)

Figure 15.1 *The hospital visit*

I want to leave but I've got to look after Mum
I mustn't show that I need anything
I've got to make life meaningful for everybody
I have to earn the right to live
I'm to blame
I mustn't criticize anyone

Need to rethink early beliefs

TA sees personal change in terms of a decisional model, and a premise of all TA therapy is that these early decisions can be changed (Stewart and Joines, 1987). The process whereby the client comes to understand the original structuring of the script is seen as an important element in therapy. It provides the client with a framework for thinking in a new way. If Jenny is to change her situation she is going to have to rethink her early beliefs that women are saintly and men need to be looked after; she also needs to reconsider her belief that she is responsible for how people behave and that she should not show her own needs. She needs to take stock of how her life consists of meeting other people's needs. I suggest that maybe her 'busyness' helps to keep her anger and sadness at bay so that her belief that men won't like her unless she does her best to prove herself loveable is never challenged.

We contract to continue to work on how Jenny can give up her script feelings of guilt, anxiety and fear so that she can clearly understand her autonomous (rather than script) needs and seek to meet them in more satisfying ways.

Figure 15.2 *The family picnic*

2 The family picnic

John is due to retire from his job as a production manager. He is not looking forward to the prospect and has been feeling depressed and miserable. His relationship with his wife is deteriorating; he feels she doesn't understand how fearful he is of the future. Whenever friends who are still working say how much they envy him the freedom that retirement will bring, he says he 'doesn't know how to respond'. He sees the future not as freedom but more like a prison sentence.

We were talking about the importance of his working life, when I suggested we might check up on how his script might be making it difficult for him to move happily into this phase of life. I asked him whether any childhood memory came to mind, and he described a family picnic when he was about seven years old.

In the cartoon (Figure 15.2) John is trailing behind the others – mother, father and older brother and sister. Everyone has been given something to carry – he has the rug which he keeps tripping over. In his memory the hill they are climbing is very steep. His father is saying, 'Come on, John, we can't start till we have the rug'; mother says nothing but looks cross. The rest of the dialogue is John's fantasy of what they were thinking.

In our discussion of the cartoon, John talked about the messages which he identified:

> Life is hard.
> I've got to keep going till you get to the top.
> Everyone is relying on me.
> I'm sad and angry (No one is going to help me).
> I don't like being left behind.
> I can't rest.
> They won't love me if I don't make it.

Open-ended script unhelpful for future

This memory led John to explore how his script has supported him in his work. Through hard work he has 'reached the top' in his career. As a manager, he was responsible for the care of the production workers, enjoying and feeling fulfilled by that role. However, as retirement looms, this script is unhelpful to say the least. He laughed as he said, 'You know, retirement makes me feel as if I'm over the hill!'

Among the main script themes identified by Eric Berne (1972) is the 'open-ended' script. This is the script which seems to have a particular cut-off point, leaving the person with no direction. It's like reading a book and discovering that the last chapter is missing. It could apply to a parent when the youngest child leaves home or a sports player when they are no longer physically able to continue. It applies to John, who has no script for free time.

Our contract is for John to complete his script, so that he can enjoy the next phase of his life. He will have the chance to re-decide how he can live; re-assess his belief that he is only loveable if he is working hard; reconsider his attitude towards time unstructured by authority. He will have the chance to get up the hill and down the other side, moving on through his journey.

References

Berne, E. (1966) *Principles of Group Treatment*. New York: Oxford University Press.
Berne, E. (1972) *What Do You Say After You Say Hello*? New York: Grove Press, 1972; London: Corgi, 1975.
Edwards, Betty (1979) *Drawing on the Right Side of the Brain*. London: Souvenir Press.
Freud, Sigmund, (1927) *The Ego and the Id*. London: Hogarth Press.
Piaget, Jean (1954) *Construction of Reality in the Child*. New York: Humanities.
Silverstone, Liesl (1993) *Art Therapy – the Person-Centred Way*. Autonomy Books.
Sperry, R.W. (1973) 'Lateral specialization of cerebral function in the surgically separated hemispheres', in F.J. McGuigan and R.A. Schoonover (eds) *The Psychophysiology of Thinking*. New York: Academic Press.
Stewart, I. and Joines, V. (1987) *TA Today*. Nottingham: Lifespace Publishing.

Discussion issues

1 Is there a place for using images in other therapeutic approaches?
2 How far do you think that early script messages could be eradicated or changed?
3 How would you approach the next session with each of the 'clients' described in the article?
4 What drawbacks do you see in working in this way?

16

Art Therapy the Person-Centred Way

Liesl Silverstone

What is person-centred art therapy? It is the bringing together of two strands, neither of which is as yet in the mainstream of our cultural thinking and practice. Each has vast potential for health and growth, and its combination is of even greater effectiveness and has particular scope in the realm of counselling.

First, the person-centred approach based on the belief that the person knows best, is responsible, and can reach her or his own potential in a climate of empathy, acceptance and congruence. Intellectually it is easy to embrace the model as it makes abundant sense on many levels – therapeutic, social, political. Yet we grow up in a climate where the very opposite model is the norm. In every system – family, school, work, health, religion, politics, even therapy – there are those professing to know best, to judge, criticize, advise others. In order to avoid rejection, we collude with this system, giving up our power, denying aspects of ourselves (Alice Miller's (1987) 'poisonous pedagogy') and because we know of no other, we perpetuate the model. Much personal work is needed to uproot the authoritarian model, to become available to the person-centred way.

I am committed to the person-centred way and have experienced its benefit for myself. In offering it as a counsellor and as a trainer, I know that personal development can occur in a climate of acceptance, empathy and genuineness. When an individual is regarded as trustworthy, he or she can move towards a more autonomous way of being. It is a therapeutic model with a vast amount of recorded evidence as to its effectiveness. So why weave in the other strand: art?

Through research conducted mainly at the California Institute of Technology by Roger Sperry (1973), the separate functions of the two hemispheres of the brain were revealed, showing that each hemisphere perceives reality in its own way. The mode of the left brain is thinking, analytic, judgemental, verbal; the right brain non-verbal, spatial, spontaneous, intuitive, creative, non-judgemental. Sperry says: '*Modern society discriminates against the right hemisphere.*' In education, science and the workplace, academic knowing rather than intuitive knowing is favoured as a selection criterion, a value-judgement.

In therapy – a microcosm of society – it can happen that by 'talking about' the client can stay in her/his left side of the brain and not connect with repressed material on the right side of the brain, the very material needed for integration.

By introducing imaging made visible in art form and working with it in a person-centred mode, that integration can occur. The person-centred mode, so

This chapter was first published as 'Person-centred art therapy' in *Person Centred Practice*, vol. 2, no. 1, Summer (1994), and later published in a modified form as 'Art therapy the person-centred way: its relevance in counselling', in *Counselling, Journal of the British Association for Counselling*, vol. 5, no. 4, pp. 291–3 (1994).

akin to the creative mode, both being non-judgemental, accepting and existential, makes for a natural, harmonious partnership. Images contain messages from the subconscious – perhaps hopes or fears – needing to be known. When thoughts are pushed aside, spontaneous images can emerge; symbolic aspects of the self, in need of recognition.

Integration of person-centredness and imaging

There are four stages in this integration:

1 *Imaging* – allowing images to present themselves to the inner eye. To aid the shift from the thinking to the creative mode, a theme or a guided fantasy can be a helpful vehicle. Whilst imaging, we aim to push aside censoring, thinking. To illustrate a *thought*, you are unlikely to learn anything new. Allow the image to float up. Trust it. Let it come.

2 *Making the image visible in art form* – Simply the process of externalizing the image, illustrating some event or feeling, can in itself be healing. The picture releases, expresses and contains within a manageable boundary hitherto repressed material.

   Alice Miller (1987) writes: 'The spontaneous images I began to do helped me not only to discover my personal story but also to free myself from the intellectual constraints and concepts of my upbringing and my professional training.'

3 *Trying to elicit the meaning of the image with a person-centred facilitator* – The image is a projection of the self, made visible. Thus, when incorporated into the counselling dialogue, the meaning of the symbolic aspect can emerge and contribute significantly to the therapeutic process. As with words, the person-centred counsellor respects the ability of the client to know for her/himself. As with words, the counsellor's task is to hold up the mirror – in this case to a picture – to allow the client to see – or not to see. If counsellors stick their own reflection into the mirror, by identifying or interpreting, they get in the way of the client's reflection, and of the ability to see that reflection for him/herself. The danger of identifying is even greater when working with images, because of their powerful emotive impact, and awareness is needed by a facilitator to push one's own reactions aside.

   If counsellors are able to immerse themselves in the fairy-tale language of symbols the client may be enabled to give them voice. In a guided fantasy a client could choose what she wants in a magic gift shop; she needs to relinquish something for it.

   'So you want to take away this mirror. It's dusty and you'll wipe it clean. In order to have the mirror, you'll leave behind this good little girl with an expressionless face.' A graphic description of what the client needs to do in order to move on. As the image came to her, as she made it visible in art form, she had no idea of its meaning. Only when her person-centred counsellor reflected the symbolic story to her, did she bring the unaware knowing to awareness. The very purpose of person-centred art therapy.

Violette Oaklander (1978) says: 'I believe there is no way you can make a mistake if you have goodwill and refrain from interpretation and judgement. Most of us have the goodwill, few of us refrain from judgements, or even notice that we are interpreting.'

4 *Working on the emerging issue in counselling* – The image can release its gift quickly. That is not the end of the story. The gift, brought to awareness, may need to be worked on in counselling. This may take rather longer. A client says: 'I *saw a strong serene tiger. What I drew is a fluffy cuddly pussycat.*' She cries. She cries that she keeps her tiger hidden, and shows only her pussycat. Now she needs to explore ways of making her tiger visible.

Aspects of working therapeutically with art

The counsellor needs to develop a shift of focus to incorporate three new aspects in working therapeutically with art.

1 The mirror is held up not only to words but to the picture.
   The counsellor reflects position and size:
   – 'You put yourself on the edge of the picture.'
   – 'What about the size of this shape?'
   That which is missing can be significant:
   – 'I notice there are no hands.'
   – 'You have left this part blank.'
   Wider reflections can be fruitful:
   – 'You drew mother in red paint, yourself in grey chalk.'
   – 'Last week you used small paper, today a large sheet.'
   Size, colour, material used may be reflected:
   – 'This is the only bit you did in red.'
   – 'You used black chalk for the whole picture.'
   The counsellor may reflect the whole process of image-making, not just the end product:
   – 'You took a piece of paper and folded it in half.'
   – 'You began with this shape, ended with this mark.'

2 The picture is an extension of the self made visible in symbolic form. Therefore the facilitator needs to help the client towards recognition of such projected material by making 'bridges' from the picture to the client.
   – 'This stag is in Scotland.'
      'Does that ring bells for you – the stag in Scotland?'
      'My grandfather was Scottish. I come from South
      Africa. I need to know I have roots here too.'
   – 'I need to define the shape of this cat.'
      'Can you associate with that? Defining the shape of the cat?'
      'Oh yes, I need to define *my* shape. ME!'

3 In face-to-face counselling not everything the client brings needs to be reflected. When talking about an image, the client becomes less self-conscious, the words more spontaneous, uncensored, of potential significance. These the client needs to hear: 'I couldn't bear to draw the image, it disturbed me so much, these three black roses.' These spontaneous words lead to denied feelings about the three children who have left home, the client's changing role as mother. Working with images, the words themselves being unpremeditated take on a right-side of the brain quality, more spontaneous than words carefully edited.

Working with art is in itself a creative spontaneous process, as the counsellor moves from words to image, to body language, to wider reflections, wherever the focus of the moment, both counsellor and client proceeding on to a journey into the unknown.

The scope of counselling and art

Counselling with the therapeutic use of art is most scopeful. Imaging can be suggested 'on the hoof' during a session to explore a feeling, a situation, an emotive word further. A client talked about a friend who had promised to ring her the previous night, and did not do so. She felt disappointed, abandoned. I suggested she close her eyes and let an image come to do with 'abandoned'. She drew a baby in a cot, crying; a wall, and a woman the other side of the wall, turned away. She spoke of herself, the baby, and the mother who never came when she wanted her. She was amazed. A memory from pre-verbal times, and her work in earlier therapy to do with issues of inclusion/exclusion had not brought up this crucial memory.

Imaging can be very effective in groups. To offer a group picture to a family will reveal the group dynamic more accurately than lengthy discussion. Who keeps apart, who is busy everywhere, who dominates, who splits the family, all made visible on the shared picture. It is difficult to deny, conceal, avoid, with the image before you. Much progress can be made based on such symbolic evidence.

That which is missing can be the needed trigger. A child is referred whose mother had committed suicide six months ago. The girl is ever cheerful. I suggest she draws her house. 'This is my bedroom. This, my brother's. Here, my dad and his girlfriend are watching TV. The front door. The bathroom.' I say: 'There's no kitchen.' 'That's where mum was talking to me' – and the floodgates open.

Art therapy has relevance in couples work. A couple come to look at their relationship. During the first session they draw a 'conversation' on paper; one makes marks on one side of the paper, the partner on the other. There is a space in between. The two sets of marks in their separate territories, never touching. This is an exact illustration of their relating, our contact made visible. During the last session the picture was more balanced, the two colours intertwining, together, separate, both.

143

Images and potential

Person-centred art therapy is most effective in counsellor training. A woman in counsellor role, receives feedback repeatedly that she reflects in a vague way, leaving out the pertinent material. Later the woman talks about her image of 'mother': 'Here a warm glow in the middle. I had difficulty sticking it down. Here I am on the edge, flitting around in my head. I need to pinpoint a tunnel to the central point.'

As she talks about the picture, she says about mother: 'She couldn't express what she felt. I longed for her to be honest with me.' A link between her early experience around not sharing the personal, and, many years later, her own inability to focus on such material as a counsellor. The image helped her to make this valuable connection.

Images help us away from cerebral, verbal judgemental processes, and into the here-and-now world of imagination, intuition, inspiration. The paradox applies that by thinking less it is possible to know more. By making visible our images we can tap into material from the subconscious denied to the forefront of our awareness and gain valuable insights leading to growth and self-awareness. We need to engage both the thinking and intuitive mode of knowing to become integrated.

Some schools of thought believe in interpreting images, telling the client the meaning of the image. To work with an image in a person-centred way enables the client to discover the message of the image for her/himself, thus gaining self-awareness as well as moving towards a more autonomous way of being. We are born creative, even though our culture may not value creativity. With art we can rediscover our creative force, move towards our potential.

Maslow (1977) says: 'Creating tends to be the act of the whole person. He is then most unified, most integrated. In moments of here and now we don't reject or disapprove, we become more accepting. Spontaneity allows the honest expression of our whole uniqueness.'

Conclusion

It is my hope that the counselling world will come to acknowledge ever more the need to incorporate the non-verbal as well as the verbal, the intuitive as well as the intellectual, the symbolic as well as the spoken wisdom in the counselling process as an invaluable means towards wholeness and growth.

I believe that this recognition needs to be reflected in our literature, in supervision, in accreditation, in counselling training and practice – in all areas of counselling, right-side of the brain knowing incorporated in that which we do.

I am thinking of the 'hundredth monkey syndrome': on an island in the Galápagos one monkey discovered how to open a certain plant to reach the food within. Another monkey found out how to do this, then another, and another. When the hundredth monkey knew how to open the plant, all the monkeys on neighbouring islands also knew.

Perhaps, as more and more people discover for themselves the power and potential of person-centred art therapy, the time is approaching when, à la hundredth monkey, an energy of knowing will be released, and spread, and be acknowledged.

The person-centred approach, at first developed in counselling, was then seen as relevant in a far wider range of settings: education, management, family, religion, industry, politics. Perhaps similarly the person-centred approach linked to the creative modes has relevance in a wider field. Integrating both the verbal and non-verbal way of knowing could bring about the capacity to function more fully to persons, wherever they may be.

What an exciting notion! Imagine!

References

Buber, M. (1970) *I and Thou*. Edinburgh: T. and T. Clark.
Maslow, A. (1977) *Therapy and the Arts*. Edinburgh/New York: Harper.
Miller, A. (1987) *The Drama of Being a Child*. London: Virago.
Oaklander, V. (1978) *Windows on our Children*. Moab, Utah: The Real People Press.
Sperry, R. (1973) 'Lateral specialization of cerebral function in the surgically separated hemispheres', in F.J. McGuigan and R.A. Schoonover (eds), *The Psychophysiology of Thinking*. New York: Academic Press.

Discussion issues

1 What is the relevance of art therapy in counselling?
2 How can person-centred art therapy be used in counsellor training?
3 Can you think of times when it would have been useful to have used art therapy in your counselling?
4 How does the person-centred approach to art therapy differ from traditional art therapy?

17

Photographic Images

Merav DeVere

The photo-language technique (PLT) uses photographic images portraying a wide variety of existing everyday social situations. Clients are presented with photographs and are requested to respond and relate to the familiar social images. The subjective interpretation of these images is subsequently used to address attitudes and emotions.

PLT was first introduced by the French psychoanalyst Alaine Baptiste, who presented workshops all over the world, in several of which I participated. He saw the main objective of the technique as encouraging discussion in groups.

A group of us have since developed the technique adapting it for use in multi-ethnic Britain in one-to-one counselling and groupwork, under the name Photo Language Workshop (PLW).

PLT aims to raise awareness of the subjective nature of a person's interpretation of reality. The technique can be administered in several forms:

- Clients are requested to choose pictures which they like/dislike, or pictures disclosing certain features of themselves. They may choose in this case to use the photos as a tool to help them disclose difficult or unpleasant features or experiences. In groups this can help participants to get to know each other better.
- Clients may be asked to choose pictures that surprise them or confirm their ideas. This can be a useful way to tackle stereotypes, images and fixed ideas that clients might hold.
- Clients may be asked to make up a story around a picture. The story can subsequently be self-analysed by the client with the counsellor's help if necessary.

The article suggests some guidelines for the analysis of stories and photo-interpretation. In particular it examines how projection, stereotyping and life experiences feature in one's story and/or interpretation. The article also illustrates how the technique can be used for both diagnosis and treatment.

The photo-language concept and application

PLT uses pictures as the communication medium. Much has been said about the special characteristics of pictures as a means of communication; 'a picture is worth a thousand words' is only one way of conveying the compactness and complexity

This chapter was first published as 'Photographic images as a diagnostic and therapeutic tool', in *Counselling, Journal of the British Association for Counselling*, vol. 5, no. 2, pp. 113–16 (1994).

contained in pictures. Pictures make their entire linguistic composition instantaneously available, which depending on the eyes of the beholder can be prone to various personal interpretation. PLT attempts to make use of both the compact complexity contained in pictorial images as well as the subjective aspects which underlie the personal interpretation of such pictorial images (DeVere and Rhonne, 1990).

Projection

PLT's prime concern is to help clients to gain insight into their present perceptions, and to emphasize the different accents people put on their 'here and now' interpretations based on features and events from their lives. Thus, clients may choose to use the pictures to describe their feelings towards their counsellor or people within their group. The picture of a child sitting on a chair, laughing or shouting, in the market (Figure 17.1 – *picture 21*) was described by a client as a girl who had lost her mother. Analysing her story the client claimed that she projected on to the child in the picture her own feelings 'here and now' of being lost and lacking control in her counselling sessions.

This example can illustrate the falseness of the rigid diagnostic–therapeutic dichotomy and supports the view that diagnosis is treatment (Brody and Waters, 1980). The diagnostic process in this case, the story analysis, functions as a type of treatment. The client diagnosed her problem as having no control, and started addressing and examining her relationships with her counsellor.

The use of pictorial (as well as verbal) language can be described as entailing three interpretational levels, starting with the formal level, through the social norm level, to the personal level. The first is based on the premiss that all communicating parties agree to share the formal meaning and interpretation attributed to the rules and components of that language. Without such a premiss, a language is nonsensical (Lindsay and Norman, 1977). In terms of the projective aspects of PLT, this level is concerned with the concrete and factual features in the picture, the realistic experience. The second level of interpretation is less formal and includes features which are not factually evident in the picture, but which are read into and attributed to the picture by the client's projection of acquired social norms, stereotypes, cultural myths, etc. The third level of interpretation and the one in which the widest deviation exists is the personal level. At this level of interpretation clients tend to draw on 'inner' experiences and fantasies as well as on the emotional aspects of personal relationships they have experienced.

Beyond and on top of the obvious variations on all levels of interpretation, Wyatt suggests that sometimes omission and distortion of prominent features in the picture take place (Wyatt, 1947). These are usually no accident and well worth addressing and are illustrated by the following examples of distorted interpretations given by different sex offenders on different occasions:

- Two young women chatting in a cafe (Figure 17.2 – *picture 24*) were described by a sex offender as looking at him and saying 'Hey, good looking!'

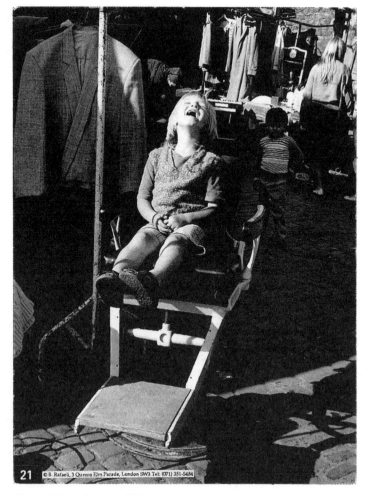

Figure 17.1 *(picture 21)*

- A young girl feeding pigeons in Trafalgar Square (Figure 17.3 – *picture 64*) was seen by another sex offender as stretching her arm out, inviting him.

Both examples give an insight into the distorted vision sex offenders can have of themselves and the world around them, which in turn supply them with the justification for attacking and offending.

Although distortion is evident in these interpretations, they are also an expression of the ideology of sexism which structures masculinity and femininity so that women are regarded as being responsible for and therefore appropriate targets for male aggression. Moreover, women (and girls) are commonly objectified in imagery in many respects. They are used as enticements for the sale of products in advertisements in which they are usually either sexy or servicing or

Figure 17.2   *(picture 24)*

both (Jukes, 1990). It is not surprising then that any images of girls and women as innocent as they may be can be distorted in the manner described above.

Latest thinking in counselling programmes dealing with violent or abusive men, promote a highly confrontational and challenging approach. The denial of responsibility through excuses and justification is a major issue for any anti-violence or anti-abuse programme, including sexual offence. Once the offender has begun to take responsibility for the nature of his actions and is struggling to renounce his abusiveness, time for exploration of his own pain can be granted. To do this before genuine work has been done on his nastiness results in phony self-pitying remorse and sentimentality (Jukes, 1990).

This area of work is another example of diagnosis and treatment being insepar-able. The distorted interpretations given to the photographic images by the

Figure 17.3   *(picture 64)*

offenders are diagnostic in the sense that they provide insight into the private world and perceptions of these offenders. At the same time they supply an opportunity to confront and challenge these perceptions immediately and with concrete 'evidence'. This challenge can take place in one-to-one sessions, where the client is pushed to make firm distinctions between hypotheses, feelings, fantasies and hard facts. It can also take place in group sessions, where group members do the challenging and confronting. Although most offenders are unable to detect their own distorted perceptions, they can effectively detect and challenge those of other offenders.

Stereotyping

When children of nine to ten years in different parts of England were given a free choice to fantasize on where they would like to go, Europe, America and the White Commonwealth were overwhelmingly preferred. When invited to write about somewhere they did not want to get landed in by mistake, they produced a narrow range of stereotypes, descriptions of jungles, 'primitive' natives brandishing spears, and dirty, thin people, Africans, Indians, and even Brazilian Indians were jumbled up in one confused notion of primitive, poor, uncivilized people (Worrall, 1980).

Images, both pictorial and verbal, are among the most powerful influences on our perception of the world and thus, are potentially a major source of stereotypes. Stereotypical images have a powerful role to play in perpetuating and sustaining racist, sexist, homophobic and any other dominant ideology. This power is illustrated in recent findings from a primary school in Birmingham, where a visual literacy project was conducted with eight- to nine-year-olds. A session looking at magazines and newspapers produced the following observations of how black people were represented: murderers; rapists; 'Standing outside shops when the shops have been burnt out'; sports stars; pop stars (Chawdry, 1989).

Sex-role stereotyping assigns domestic service and attendance upon infants to the female, the rest of human achievement, interest and ambition to the male (Millett, 1971).

Photographs can be a powerful resource for raising awareness about visual bias. Through responding to photographs one can identify and challenge stereotypes; recognize one's way of responding to an image, the personal feelings and attitudes it evokes, and identify issues which arise from these images. PLT uses various sets of photographic images portraying people of different ages and races individually or in groups, each having a distinct facial expression. Some also portray landscapes. The photos mostly portray existing, everyday, commonplace social situations; situations in which anyone could easily feature and which we come across quite often. Attributing stereotypical motives to these 'innocent' photos, and then realizing that no evidence or facts in the picture can actually support those attributions, can be an eye-opener. Consider this example.

- When asked to choose three pictures that he likes and three that he dislikes, a probation officer chose black people as all his dislikes. Explaining his choices he described the black men he chose as being drug dealers, or aggressive men, trying to steal his girlfriend.

Moreover, photographs of groups of young black men (Figure 17.4 – *picture 2*) regularly produce stories with violence or drugs or both in them.

The above incidents were elicited from people working in the social welfare sector and it is disconcerting that they have such negative and stereotypical perceptions of black people. It is likely that this perception influences the way they perceive black clients, which in turn perpetuates their clients' mistrust in them, and might further increase their resentment towards their clients. This negative image is hardly surprising, however, considering the almost exclusively negative images of black people in the media, where they are portrayed either as violent cunning criminals, or as sexually and physically fit bodies. These negative images might provide justification for racism. Hospital studies and much anecdotal evidence suggest that in mental institutions, black patients, especially Afro-Caribbean ones, are perceived as being violent and are therefore prescribed stronger medication, for longer periods of time, than white patients are. There are also reported incidents of the physical and mental abuse, motivated by racism, of black patients in mental hospitals by hospital staff and by fellow patients (Capstick, 1990).

Similarly, the extent of sex-role stereotyping within traditional psychiatric practice has been extensively discussed in feminist critiques of the mental health system (Penfold and Walker, 1984).

Figure 17.4 *(picture 2)*

Raising the awareness of workers in the social welfare and mental health sectors to the resentment they might be feeling towards some of their clients is of paramount importance and should be an ongoing component of their training, counselling and supervision. Doing that through photographic images may prove powerful, effective and less threatening, even though other methods and techniques could and should also be employed.

Experiences

There is no clear-cut distinction between projection, stereotyping and experiences. It is particularly difficult to distinguish between experiences and stereotyping, since human experience is so versatile and therefore can supply 'evidence' to any

Figure 17.5   *(picture 31)*

stereotype. In some of the examples given some clients pointed to their work experiences as the main source for the existence of drugs, violence and other criminal elements in their stories. Moreover, the assumption that the term 'experience' contains within it any human emotion, thought, attitude, etc. makes its definition particularly subjective. The following example demonstrates one subjective interpretation of a story in which projection, stereotyping and experiences all play a significant role.

The picture consists of two children, the older one holding a plastic bag and the younger one standing barefoot and smiling (Figure 17.5 – *picture 31*). The story behind it, told by a woman counsellor, suggests that the children are brother and sister. The sister, Lucy, is the older one. They were sent by Mum to buy food and when they returned home, Mum looked at the boy's bare feet and started telling

Lucy off. 'What happened? Where did you lose his shoes?' Lucy tried to tell Mum that her brother took his shoes off and then started running away from her. She ran after him and forgot the shoes. The boy said to his sister 'It is not true. You always blame me.' He ran to his mum who cuddled him and sent Lucy off to look for the shoes. Most of the feelings attributed to Lucy in the story were seen by the client as projection of how she felt as an older sister and how she still feels sometimes, needing to be loved; feeling victimized; angry with and hurt by mother's refusal to believe her, favouring her brother and burdening her with adult's responsibilities; anger with brother for being a boy, boys getting a better deal than girls; low self-worth; not feeling confident in herself; feeling guilty.

This client identified experiences in her story. She was an older sister who was expected to take too much responsibility, to take care of her brother and always behave herself.

She identified stereotyping in her assumption that it was a working-class family, based on the children's appearance. She then attributed stereotypical working-class characteristics to it, such as working-class women tend to shout and working-class families oppress the females. The mother in her domestic role was also identified as a stereotype.

The above example is another illustration of the point made earlier that diagnosis and treatment overlap, showing that the client's awareness is an important component of her treatment.

Summary

One of the apparent strengths of PLT lies in the social dimension of the photographs. The captured images and situations were deliberately selected to convey low-key situations. The low-key nature of the pictured situations is inducive to the elicitation of on-going perceptions, emotions, etc.

In terms of clients'/participants' feedback and evaluation, these were generally of a positive nature. The task seems to be interesting and often entertaining to the client. People enjoy the multi-layered experience, the sophistication and complexity of issues emerging from any of the pictures, which tend to divert the client's attention away from him/herself and thus reduce embarrassment and defensiveness. The self-analysis which follows makes the process even less threatening. It should be noted, however, that this point can be in certain circumstances a limitation, because the client might be 'soft' on him/herself and deny any unpleasant interpretations. Being challenged by either a group or a counsellor, is crucial in such cases.

On the conceptual level the technique allows for the exploration of stereotypes and perceptions, and for the examination of their effect on social positions and behavioural codes. On the affective level it provides the space for clients to examine their emotions. Moreover, the subjective interpretation of the photographs captures individual's feelings 'here and now', encouraging him or her to introspect, examine and reflect upon these feelings in relation to their background at home, at work and in society at large.

Appendix: Summary of keypoints for photo interpretation

(Can be distributed for self-analysis of participants' stories)

1 Projection

    (a) Identify the heroes in your story.

    (b) Make a list of your hero's motives, needs, feelings, etc. as they appear in the story.

    (c) Check for projection: do some of the feelings, needs, etc. that you have attributed to the hero, describe your own? Which are they? Does it represent your feelings, motives in general or is some of it unique to the way you feel here and now, within the group?

    (d) Identify the outcome of your story. Do you think it has a happy or unhappy ending? Does the hero in your story make things happen or do things happen to her/him? Can you identify projection here?

2 Stereotyping

In order to understand your own prejudice, while analysing your photo interpretation you can try to make distinctions between facts and opinion and explore how a blurring of these distinctions can be used to distort the underlying facts:

    (a) Distinguish between hypothesis and facts.

    (b) Distinguish between feelings and facts.

    (c) Look at the idea of evidence.

    (d) Question your assumptions/stereotypes.

3 Experiences

Look carefully at your story and identify all features in it which might be emanating from your everyday reality and experiences. These can include your job experiences, your family and social life or even a book or a film you have recently read/seen which made an impression on you.

References

Brody, H. and Waters, D. (1980) 'Diagnosis is treatment', *Journal of Family Practice*, 10(3): 445–9.

Capstick, L. (1990) 'Black and ethnic communities and mental health', in *MIND Information Sheet*, June.

Chawdry, T. (1989) 'Framing the subject', in *Whose Image?* Birmingham: Building Sights. pp. 9–12.

DeVere, M. and Rhonne, O. (1990) 'The use of photographs as a projective and facilitative technique in groups', in *Groupwork*, 4(2).

Jukes, A.E. (1990) 'Working with men who are violent to women', *Counselling*, 1(4): 124–6.

Lindsay, P.H. and Norman, D.A. (1977) *Human information processing*. Orlando, FL: Academic Press.

Millett, K. (1971) *Sexual Politics*. London: Virago Press.

Penfold, P. and Walker, G. (1984) *Women and the Psychiatric Paradox*. Milton Keynes: Open University Press.

Wyatt, F. (1947) 'The scoring and analysis of the thematic apperception test', *Journal of Psychology*, 24: 319–30.

Worrall, M. (1980) 'New era', in *Whose Image?* Birmingham: Building Sights (1989).

Discussion issues

1 What are the advantages and disadvantages of using photographic images as a diagnostic and therapeutic tool?
2 In what other ways could photographic images be used in therapy?
3 What might be the benefits of using the client's photographs in therapy?
4 Could the use of photographs be integrated into your own therapeutic approach?

18

The Counsel in Drama and the Drama in Counsel

Sue Emmy Jennings

Dramatherapy, or in the USA drama therapy, is a form of direct work with children and adults through the medium of theatre art. By theatre art I mean the entire range of methods and structures that belong to what we conventionally call 'drama and theatre'. Thus dramatherapy is not just a collection of techniques such as role play, but a theory and method together with an underlying philosophy that may be applied in a wide variety of client settings as well as being incorporated within other frames of reference.

I first became involved in this area whilst at drama school thirty-five years ago, when the superintendent of a local psychiatric hospital suggested that I took on the job of a nursing auxiliary, in order to be able to do some drama work on the wards. He did not reckon with the demands of the Sister, who insisted that all my other work must be completed first! This included helping with the electro-convulsive therapy, which was then administered without an anaesthetic, and the usual bedpan and urine-sample routine. However, it proved an important marker for me in the direction in which I was later to specialize. My professional career in the theatre as actress and dancer continued for some years until I raised a family and then moved forward into artistic and therapeutic work once again.

I am often asked at what point I realized that drama could be therapeutic, but there was no sudden dawning of light, or a particular dream or guru that pointed me on the right path. The more I studied theatre, the more it became obvious that it already existed as a healing form, and had been so for many thousands of years. The more I studied anthropology, the more it became clear that curative rituals are a healing form of drama and theatre. The more I studied myself, the more it became apparent at a personal level, that theatre art had proved very therapeutic. All this was happening in the 1960s when so many other new ideas were coming to the forefront in the 'growth movement', Laing and his innovatory beliefs, new thinking in education and medicine, especially in psychiatry.

Since then most of my life has involved working with theatre art in one way or another, but especially as therapy. This life journey has taken me to the Malaysian rain-forest to do fieldwork with a tribe who had very elaborate dramatic rituals, both for prevention and cure, to Australia and New Zealand, to the USA and Israel, as well as much of Europe, where people show interest and enthusiasm to develop the practice of dramatherapy.

My current work is at the School of Oriental and African Studies (University of

This chapter was first published in *Counselling, Journal of the British Association for Counselling,* vol. 4, no. 3, pp. 182–5 (1993).

London) where I teach dramatherapy to medical anthropologists, and as director of training programmes for fertility counsellors (London Hospital Medical College and City University). My work in the professional theatre and television constantly informs my clinical work and teaching, and indeed the other way round too!

Dramatherapy

What then actually *is* dramatherapy? It is the application of theatre art with individuals or groups of people who are seeking personal growth or change in their current lives. Such people may be populations in hospitals, prisons, day-centres, special units of various kinds, as well as those being helped in private practice. Dramatherapy works through movement, voice, theatre games, improvisation, role and mask play, script and chorus. Whereas psychodrama usually uses the immediacy of an individual's personal 'life script', dramatherapy assists people to connect their life script with 'Life Scripts', the bigger drama or story within which we all can find our own story. Thus dramatherapy emphasizes the importance of the dramatic metaphor as well as ritual and symbol.

Some popular misconceptions

It is important here to clarify certain assumptions that are often taken for granted about dramatherapy and indeed about theatre itself.

Drama is 'only' acting: the issue here is the pejorative association with the emphasis on 'only' as if it is unimportant. What is crucial *is* that it is only acting, otherwise we would be very confused. The dramatic imagination necessary in this acting process means that we can hypothesize about how life might be in the future and whether or not our perception of it can change from that of the past.

Drama is life: drama is *about* life but that is not the same as saying that drama *is* life. What is important is that drama and theatre enable us to establish a distance from everyday life so that we can see it in new and unexpected ways. For most of our lives, we are too close to events to be able to take them in all at once.

Dramatherapy encourages fantasy: and the sub-text of this statement is that fantasy is dangerous! Dramatherapy establishes 'dramatic reality' as being a separate space from 'everyday reality'. The space of dramatic reality allows for imagery, metaphor, risk-taking and experiment. It is within this space that we can challenge and be challenged in new and creative ways. Fantasy occurs in all our realities and should not be confused with the developed use of our imagination.

Dramatherapy is role play: indeed, role play, one of the methods that dramatherapists may use in their practice, is also used by other professions – family therapists, psychologists and counsellors themselves. However, we must remember that 'role' derives from the roll or 'role' of paper on which an actor's script would be written. The tendency now is to use the term role when a focused piece of work is being enacted such as 'this is my role when I am at work' (as contrasted with my role at home); increasingly I use the word 'character' in dramatherapy to encompass the fulsome person in the scene. Thus characters in a play or scene, and indeed all of us, have many roles.

Dramatherapy with people experiencing infertility problems

In the Rowan Clinic at the London Hospital, I notice that the one word my clients see before any other is *Fertility* (or infertility), therefore handouts with a heading *Counselling* or *Support group* or *Stress management* are quite simply not seen. They have no immediate connection with the suffering of the drama of people's lives. In fact it is a useful exercise to ask clients what they would want written on posters, handouts and so on.

The counselling space itself can be compared with a private theatre space, where the drama of the life of the client will unfold. It is a special place set apart with a different set of rules and roles and clients need to know the conventions of this space and also its limitations. What does your handbill say about this space? How reassuring can you be in order for people to come in the first place, but also to know that you are offering something different from tea and sympathy? What words, for example, make us stop and read something?

In my preparation before seeing a client(s), I often use the analogy of 'programme notes'. What do I need to know before the drama starts to unfold to guide me on the way. Usually an entire case history is too much, and quite literally takes on the work of the historian, whereas a client is coming in the present and very much the 'living present'. When we see a play it is 'in the now', even if it involves themes of antiquity. We need to remember when we have been to the theatre to see a new play, the minimum information that we needed to start with, and similarly, when we go to an old play, what sort of information prompted us to see this old story in a new way?

As the counselling work develops, it is possible to make even more use of the theatre metaphor and the following sorts of questions or statements have proved helpful in the recent past:

- What is the title of this play?
- Who is the author of this play or scene?
- Who is the star or chief actor?
- It seems that someone is not allowed onstage.
- Who (or what) is waiting in the wings?
- I'm not sure which scene we are in.
- Authors can write new endings.
- Is the scenario always the same?
- Who is wearing a mask here?
- It sounds as if the play is unfinished.
- How many characters are important in this drama?
- I sense there are some silent characters too.

That the metaphor of the theatre can be helpful to a counsellor is illustrated by two examples from my clinical work, both involving clients' needs to mourn the child they never had.

Example 1

Mrs Jones has been attending several clinics for her infertility problem and each time she is told by a gynaecologist that she has no chance of conceiving, she insists that her GP refers her for another opinion. After several such attempts, she is referred to me for fertility counselling and I see this piece of work falling into the category of 'bereavement counselling' when people have the chance to come to terms with the loss of their fertility and to the fact that they have no children.

(I was inspired to develop this aspect of my work after fieldwork with the Temiar tribe of the Malaysian tropical rain-forest. Here in their naming system all parents are referred to by their children as 'parents of a boy' or 'parents of a girl'. Included in the naming system are 'parents' called 'parents of no children', 'parents of dead child' and also 'parents of many still-born births'.)

Mrs Jones arrived very angry and tearful at being 'stopped' by all the doctors from being able to undertake treatment and saying that they kept 'blocking' what she wanted to do (an irony since her fallopian tubes were completely blocked with adhesions). I asked her if she had expressed her anger and she said that she would not dare because that could mean that treatment is withheld.

> *S.J.*: So in this script you are being a 'good girl' in order to get what you want.
> *Mrs J.*: (*tears increase*) It's the only way I know – to keep quiet and not say what you feel and then you get what you want and you don't get punished.

(Note the enormous sub-text emerging here.)

> *S.J.*: So the role of the good girl is the one you have always played and it feels like a punishment that you still have not got a baby.

(Flooding tears, during which time I acknowledge that her feelings are very legitimate and are the tears of grieving the baby she is unable to have.)

> *Mrs J.*: I'm mourning the child I will never have – I know so well what sort of child it will be – but it won't happen.

Even the brief intervention concerning her 'fixed role' of the good girl, enabled her to move on and begin the legitimate grieving for the loss of her fertility and her 'dream baby'. Now was not the time to work further with the fixed role, but she elected to come for further work after she had courageously worked through three grieving sessions.

Example 2

Mrs Smith saw me for counselling before having three attempts at treatment none of which allowed her to take home a baby. She arrives to see me again depressed and angry, but very silent and sits there, holding in her feelings.

I use the analogy of theatre immediately and remark that she has seen the inside of an operating theatre many times in her treatment, and each time the play has ended in tragedy for her.

> Mrs S.: (*as if she had already been speaking*) and I am really scared. I feel so violent, I could kill someone.
> S.J.: But maybe it feels as if someone has already been killed in your tragedy . . .
> Mrs S.: Of course . . . oh my god . . . the babies . . . (*very heavy tears as she moves into a grieving process*)

These examples show how the analogy of the theatre assists the counselling process for client and counsellor.

Counselling for dramatherapists

Most dramatherapists during their training undergo personal counselling for their own support and development, in addition to the two-year requirement to participate in a closed dramatherapy group. The counselling is not only for an individual to examine their own personal lives but also for them to understand the counselling process itself. The counselling process enables the dramatherapist to develop their reflective capacities and to understand the importance of the 'stillness within the action'. Probably from counselling more than from other areas, they have also been able to come to grips with management of time. And here I am not referring to just the timing of a session in itself, but the time decisions involved in short-, medium- and long-term interventions. Counsellors have experience in all those modes and are able to 'role-model' what can be achieved even in a single session.

Dramatherapy for counsellors

Increasingly in the past few years dramatherapists are making contributions to the training of counsellors. This is important when the counsellor is able to see the situation in a different way, or should I say, 'yet another way', since the dramatic methods will allow new perspectives and experiences. It is encouraging to see that counsellors are using dramatherapy methods within their frame of reference, and that they have found certain techniques – especially those to do with the engagement of the client and the closure of the session, particularly valuable. Perhaps too, dramatherapists have helped counsellors to see their work also as a creative act. There was a time when the arts therapies were referred to as the creative therapies, but it is not only the arts therapies that are creative. All approaches that facilitate personal growth, insight, and change of any kind, must perforce involve creativity. We can be involved in a creative act or a piece of creative thinking, without necessarily involving an art form, though it is interesting to note how often we use the art form as a metaphor to understand something in counselling. For example we will say, 'put me in the picture', 'could you tell me about the scene again', 'am I tuning in to how you feel', 'it feels as if there is no movement'.

Just as counsellors assist the dramatherapists in both their personal and professional lives, so too dramatherapists can be useful to counsellors, both in their practice and in the way they perceive their work.

The theatre of counselling

When clients arrive for a counselling session, they are bringing to us a particular piece of their lives. It may be the 'piece' that is stuck or frozen, or that the client 'doesn't know what to say'. How similar this is to the actor who has forgotten the lines, and how important the prompter is at this point. How does the counsellor 'prompt' the client?

The counsellor may reflect the status quo thus, 'it feels very difficult', or 'it is always hard . . . to start' or '. . . to find the right words' or '. . . to wonder why you are here'. They may draw an analogy in reference to people not having 'to perform' or 'say the right lines' or 'if this scene feels too hard just now we can look at another one'. I find that a theatre analogy in my opening remarks can help by reassuring people that I understand that 'they feel under the spotlight' or 'centre stage' or 'have lost their script'. These are ways in which we may encourage expression from people who are struggling.

However, what about the person who will not stop talking, where our 'interruptive' skills are not having an effect, and we sense that the entire life is being poured forth, either for the first time or as a way of avoiding the 'real issues'. In either situation, we really need to call upon the capacity of theatre to condense space and time in the 'living present'. I invite you to see what happens when you say to someone, having first acknowledged how big a story they have to tell, 'let's imagine that what you are saying to me is a play in the theatre – which scene, right now, is the important one for me to listen to?'

It is remarkable how most people make this step into the metaphor of theatre and find it helpful. Obviously there has to be conviction or a client may feel they are not being taken seriously or that they are being 'too dramatic' (of course you may very well feel that they are 'over the top' and what better way to deal with that, than a paradoxical intervention of allowing it to be a piece of theatre!).

If there is a step into theatre and drama metaphor, and this obviously comes into the whole range of counselling skills such as summary, paraphrase and metaphor, it enables the counsellor to expand the frame of reference and paradoxically to focus more clearly. It is as if we can use both the wide-angle lens and the zoom at one and the same time.

Useful dramatherapy skills for counsellors

Sculpting

This may be sculpting of large or small objects, people themselves or chairs, used to represent the dynamics of a situation. Sculpting is comparable to 'freeze frame' when we hold a moment in the action. The advantage of objects is that they can be moved in different ways, as when you invite a client to create 'my life now' using small objects such as toys, stones, and so on. After they have explored the sculpt, move on with a question such as, 'how would you like this sculpt to look' or 'has this sculpt looked different in the past', or 'what would you like to change in your life'. Sculpts are useful in diagnostic interviews in enabling counsellors to see the clients' views of their life, and helping clients to express what is often too hard to put into words. Sculpting used by the dramatherapist is a projective technique which establishes 'dramatic reality'. People are creating small scenes in the theatre of their lives.

Role play

One of the greatest fears about role play is that people feel they must get off their chairs and look silly, whereas it is perfectly possible to use role methods sitting exactly where we are. When a client says, 'and then he said in a really angry voice . . .', I may ask them to create 'the voice' or 'the posture' or 'the gesture' of the person being talked about. Clients will say, 'If only I could really look her straight in the face and say, "get off my back".' It is straightforward to incorporate such an intervention within the counselling session, without feeling one has to set up a full-blown dramatic scene.

Letter writing

Letters can help when clients want to try out various types of communication to people close to them; either to distance themselves or to try to bring themselves closer. Writing an imaginary letter to the person within the counselling can help people to clarify what they *really* want to happen. Clients will say, 'If only I could tell her . . .' or 'There is so much I need to say . . .'. And there are times when people express these needs towards people who have died as well as those who are still living.

These three techniques, all of which can be elaborated in many ways, do not involve counsellor or client moving out of their chairs. Any dramatherapy literature has many additional techniques that can be used within the counselling session.

In order to facilitate the counselling process I have various things in my room such as a range of fertility statues, globes, lots of small toys, pictures of doors. The door pictures are particularly helpful when people are 'stuck' and talk about doors being slammed in their faces. I have a very large range of postcards and photographs – landscapes, families, trees and so on – that can be used at the appropriate moment. We could think of them as the 'props' of the counsellor-dramatherapist.

Summary

In this chapter I have attempted to commence a dialogue between dramatherapy and counselling and to show that in practice and in training they can enhance each other. I have suggested that the dramatic metaphor can be very useful to clients and that there are basic techniques to be used within a counselling framework.

Finally it is my hope that there will be greater dialogue between the various arts therapies, counselling and other interventionary disciplines, especially with the move forward into Europe. There is much to be learned from each other's professions and methods.

Further reading

Davis, R. (1995) *Scenes of Madness: a Psychiatrist at the Theatre*. London: Routledge.
Jennings, S. (1990) *Dramatherapy with Families, Groups and Individuals*. London: Jessica Kingsley.
Jennings, S. (ed.) (1994) *Infertility Counselling*. Oxford: Blackwell Science.
Jennings, S. (1995) *Theatre, Ritual and Transformation: the Senoi Temiars*. London: Routledge.

Discussion issues

1 Are there plays or novels or poetry that help you to make connections with the themes of your clients? Try free-associating about characters that appear in a recent play you have seen or book that you have read.
2 What devices do you use as a prompter, for yourself or your client, when one or both of you are stuck?
3 Write down any associations you have with the word 'performance'. Connect this with feelings about 'drama', 'theatre' and your life and work.
4 A client with fertility issues says 'my womb is like a garden where nothing will grow'; how might you respond using metaphor?

Dramatherapy training: There are currently seven postgraduate training programmes at universities in the UK, approved by the Department of Health for practitioner qualification. The courses vary in length from two to four years. The course run by the Institute of Dramatherapy at the Roehampton Institute (University of Surrey) is a four-year modular training with a mandatory requirement for three years personal therapy, of which at least a year must be individual counselling or psychotherapy. There are two MA programmes in the UK and several Diploma and Masters programmes overseas. For detailed information write to the British Association for Dramatherapists, 5 Sunnydale Villas, Durlston Road, Swanage, Dorset BH19 2HY.

19

Psychodrama

Marcia Karp

A little girl asked her mother, 'What's life?' The mother replied, 'Life is what happens to you while you're waiting to grow up.'

Psychodrama has been defined as a way of practising living without being punished for making mistakes. That is to say, practising growing up while you are doing it. The action that takes place in a group is a way of looking at one's life as it moves. It is a way of looking at what happened and what didn't happen in a given situation. All scenes take place in the present, even though a person may want to enact something from the past or something in the future. The group enacts a portion of life as if on a video seen through the eyes of the protagonist or subject of the session. The personal representation of truth by the protagonist can be eye-opening for someone else watching, who may see themselves reflected in the struggle to express what is real. J.L. Moreno, who founded psychodrama in Vienna in the early 1900s, described it, psychodrama, as 'a scientific exploration of truth through dramatic methods'. Moreno (1953) had observed that thus far there was science without religion and religion without science. He felt the way forward was in a combination: 'A truly therapeutic procedure cannot have less an objective than the whole of mankind' (p. 3).

Psychodrama was designed as a method of group psychotherapy. Moreno had great trust in the group. When he asked 'Who shall survive?', I think he felt the survivors will be those who both use and cherish their own creativity and spontaneity and that that these people will survive in a group. He used to say, 'If God ever comes back, He'll come back as a group.' In a group we can experience many things:

- We are not alone.
- We can feel normalized.
- We go back to the constellation into which we were born – the family group.
- The group can share the weight of emotional truth.
- The very form of this sharing, each person differently, may be liberating.
- To be emotionally or physically held by a group member who is not previously enmeshed in the story can be therapeutic.

The tools of psychodrama

The tools set out for the method of psychodrama are as follows:

This chapter was first published as 'An introduction to psychodrama', in *Counselling, Journal of the British Association for Counselling*, vol. 6, no. 4, 294–8 (1995).

1 A director
2 The group
3 A protagonist
4 Auxiliary egos
5 A stage

1 The director

In most therapies this is the therapist, facilitator or group leader. The director is a trained person who helps guide the action. The director is a co-producer of the drama, taking clues from the perceptions of the person seeking help. The following are some of the director's tasks.

- The director builds sufficient cohesion and a constructive working group climate.
- The director stimulates individual group members sufficiently and warms them up to action.
- The director considers group dynamics and measures group interaction at the beginning of a session.
- The director guides the appropriate selection of a protagonist and takes care of others in the group who were considered but not chosen to be a subject of the session.
- The director makes a treatment contract for the session which is an action-preparation negotiated with the protagonist.
- The director establishes a therapeutic alliance.
- The director prepares the action-space or stage on which the therapeutic drama takes place.
- By intervening, the director gives the protagonist sufficient freedom to select the focus of exploration.
- The director identifies the non-verbal messages of the protagonist as well as the verbal.
- The director anchors each scene setting in appropriate time and place.
- The director helps put auxiliary egos into role.
- The director identifies central issues in the enactment and helps the protagonist show the group what happened rather than talk about it.
- The director uses psychodramatic techniques such as role reversal to move the action from the periphery of the problem to the core of the issue.
- The core of the issue may involve a catharsis of emotion, insight catharsis, catharsis of laughter or catharsis of integration which the director maximizes appropriately.
- The director sufficiently creates safety for the protagonist and the group.
- The director ensures confidentiality in the group and physical safety.
- The director ensures that the psychodrama is a group process and not one-to-one therapy in a group.
- The director creates sufficient closure where the protagonist and group integrate the material presented in the session.
- The protagonist is helped to re-enter the group after the session.

- The director facilitates role feedback from group members who played auxiliary roles in the session.
- The director allows catharsis and integration of group members who identify with the protagonist and can share from their own experience.
- The director protects the protagonist from distorted responses or analysis of the group and adheres to each member sharing similar experiences or moments when they were most involved in the session.
- The director shares from his/her life history.

2 The group

The average size psychodrama group is ten to fifteen people: I have seen groups of as few as three and as many as 400. The emotional material in large groups seems to transcend the numbers and often people feel the group shrinks in size and are astounded that in a group of twenty-five they are able spontaneously to be themselves.

There are many societal roles represented in any given group. If, for example, the protagonist is an alcoholic, there may be a mother, sibling, partner or therapist in the group who, in the sharing, can present their own view of what happened to them. This feedback from other roles in relation to the problem enacted, can be invaluable insight for the protagonist. The socially investigative dimension of the problem is better researched in the session when many roles are represented. One of the aspects of psychodrama which sets it apart from other groups is the multiplicity of roles that are represented by each person in the group. We each play a staggering variety of roles in one day, parent, son or daughter, professional, friend, lover, citizen, boss, student, not to mention all the somatic roles, such as sleeper, eater, crier. Separate from the many roles we play in our own lives, we may be asked to play a role for someone else in the group – a dying mother, for example. If the person selected to play the dying mother has previously been seen as the group scapegoat, the role structure can change drastically in a psychodrama group, allowing a positive alliance to form between the protagonist and the person playing the dying mother; an alliance which previously did not exist. This constant change of role structure in a group disallows the role rigidity that may occur in other groups. The role repertoire is expanded by each group member playing a different kind of role from that which he or she may be seen to play in the group. A member of the group with low self-esteem may be stretched to play a courageous role, surprising both themselves and the group at the release of creativity hidden behind problematic learned behaviour. This glimpse of courage motivates the player to produce more and encourages group members to relate to them in a different way, and to consider that perhaps there is more to give than meets the eye.

3 The protagonist

I used to work in a public theatre in New York at 78th and Broadway called the Moreno Institute. Seven nights a week there was a public audience, a circular wooden stage and a director. A person seated in the front, middle or back of the theatre, a professor, housewife or carpenter could be a subject of the psychodrama session which they had chosen to attend.

Human beings have problems. Normosis, a word coined by Moreno meaning the struggle to be normal, confounds the best of us. Though psychodrama was designed to help psychotics, it has evolved into a therapy of relationships for everyone. The protagonist, meaning the first in action, is a representative voice of the group through which other group members can do their own work. The protagonist simply states an aspect of life he or she wants to work on; my fear of death, my relationships with my daughter, my authority problem at work. The director, with the protagonist, sets out to create scenes that give examples of the problem in the present, looking at possible behaviour patterns, seeing the problem as it exists in the past and trying to resolve the problem by establishing the core or roots of the issue so that future behaviour contains a more adequate approach. The spontaneity that is sought is defined as a fresh response to an old situation or an adequate response to a new situation. The idea of throwing away the 'script' was crucial to the conceptualization of psychodrama as an action method. The protagonist has a chance to review the life script that he or she is using, which may have been handed down for good reason but fails to be adequate for present life requirements. A person who was handed a script not to cry may no longer feel that serves them in their present-day functioning. One who has never grieved for the loss of a parent because they bought the 'brave script' may feel the relief of letting go of tears with a new definition of brave – one who has the courage to face what really exists within. That 'courage to be' may not have been within the role repertoire of one's parents, but within this new family group bravery may have a new climate in which the warm air promulgates seeds of self-expression that have lain dormant for years.

4   The auxiliary ego

In the first group I joined there was a psychiatric nurse for whom I formed an immediate dislike. While she was protagonist she was asked to choose someone in the group who could understand her inner thoughts and could help her express what she was not able to say. She chose me. I was astonished at her choice but found, once I stood next to her, and we worked as a team trying to explore her inner truth, I could understand her very well and I stopped disliking her. She also taught me how much of me was in her and introduced me to the reality that the people we dislike usually have behaviour that strikes close to home, therefore we are warding off the very thing we cannot deal with in ourselves.

The auxiliary ego is anyone in the group who plays a role representing a significant other in the life of the protagonist. This may be a role external to the protagonist, such as a family member of colleague at work. It may be an internal role such as one's fearful self, child self or one's inner voice, as in the role of what is called the double. The double helps express that which is not being expressed, with or without words. Because Moreno felt that the royal route to the psyche is not the word but non-verbal expression, the auxiliary ego can hold, by gesture, posture or distance, those unspoken secrets in relation to the protagonist.

I once was a double for a man who was having a quite normal dinner conversation with his wife of twenty years. He was telling her he did not like to eat liver and clenched his fist as he spoke. As his double, I also clenched my fist and went a step further. I slammed my fist down on the table and said, 'I've had enough of not being understood, I want a divorce.' He looked at me, shocked, and said to her, 'So do I!' It was the non-verbal clue that spoke the truth, not his words. His body conveyed the truth while his words masked it. He then chose to express his actual feelings.

The auxiliary ego who plays a dying parent may reach out with arms to say goodbye to the protagonist caught in a web of unexpressed emotion. Those very arms may represent years of love that was unexpressed. If the protagonist reverses roles and is able to speak or show what has not been said all those years, the role reversal can release spontaneity that was dammed or blocked in his or her own role as child. Often people are more spontaneous in the role of someone else than in their own role. Role reversal is the engine that drives the psychodrama. The role of significant other in the group is modelled by the protagonist and a group member then moves in to play that role. Through crucial role reversals, where learning is the greatest, the protagonist experiences a shift in role boundary by playing another person. The person being the auxiliary ego holds the role that has been set and creates within it, as they imagine the person in that role would play it. The role is played through the perception of the protagonist.

5 The stage

Psychodrama is based on life itself. The space a person lives in is reproduced on the stage. If a conversation took place in the kitchen, we set out the table and chairs and give imaginative space to a window, sink, door, fridge, etc. Constructing the reality of an individual's space helps the person to really be there and warms them up to produce the feelings that do or do not exist in that space. When someone remembers a conversation that took place at the table, in childhood, it is important to have the people in the scene played by members of the group. We can often learn more by looking in this way at a person's living space than we can in months of interview. I once was invited into a created space of a young man's apartment. He walked in by lifting his feet usually high as if carefully tiptoeing. I asked why. He said, 'I throw my old milk cartons on the floor, they are everywhere.' That spoke of isolation, not many visitors, a lack of care for the smell and look. An important clue to his alienation was his living space. Our task then was to look at why he had no friends and why he became a recluse. His words up until then belied his reality, but showing the 'stage' upon which he lived gave us a truer reality.

The phases of psychodrama

Every psychodrama has three phases:

1 Warm-up
2 Enactment
3 Sharing

1 Warm-up

The warm-up serves to produce an atmosphere of creative possibility. This first phase weaves a basket of safety in which the individual can begin to trust the director, the group and the method. When the room has its arms around you it is possible to be that which you thought you could not, to express that which seemed impossible to express.

There are many ways to warm up a group. Moreno did it by 'encountering' everyone and getting people to talk easily to each other. A theme was selected or a person who had a theme was accepted by the group as their protagonist. Another way is for the director to select a protagonist, one whom he or she thinks is ready to work. Another alternative is through a creative group exercise from which the subject of the session emerges. This is called a protagonist-centred warm-up. In a self-nomination warm-up people can put themselves forward to be the subject and either the group or the director can decide. These suggestions are ways of protagonist selection which come from the warm-up whilst the warm-up itself makes it possible for people to feel freer to trust the group, feel the cohesion and safety in the group and to present their problems in an atmosphere of love and caring.

2 Enactment

In this part of the drama the director and protagonist move the work forward from the periphery of the problem to the core. Psychodrama means literally action of the mind and it brings out the internal drama, so that the drama within becomes the drama outside oneself. The director uses the group members to play auxiliary egos who are significant people represented in the drama. The original psychodrama stage was three tiered, concentric circles. The first level was for the audience; the second for soliloquy and represented the space outside the heat of the drama; and the top level was for the drama to be enacted. The design was for the work to go from the periphery to the core of a problem. Enactment in most psychodramatic sessions takes place in a designated stage area. During the drama other group members do not sit in that space unless they are playing a role. The stage has a ritual-space feeling about it once the drama begins. That is to say, the event that is meant to take place in that space takes place only there. Psychodrama which is attempted within the group space with no designated stage area often falls flat because there are no boundaries spatially or methodologically.

3 Sharing

As described in the director section, sharing is a time for group catharsis and integration. It was meant as a 'love-back' rather than a feedback, discouraging analysis of the event and encouraging identifications. Points of most involvement by individual group members are identified and each member finds out how he or she is like the protagonist. Often, as in Greek drama, the audience member is purged by watching the enactment of another's life story. The sharing is meant to capture this learning process and allow group members to purge themselves of emotions or insights gained. It is also aimed at normalizing the protagonist's experience by hearing how others are similarly involved at different levels of the same process. Sometimes the effectiveness of the overall session can be measured by the depth of the sharing session. A further function of the sharing is a cooldown, a way of re-entering our individual realities after the group enactment.

For directors in training, an added part of the session is called processing: this is where clear rationale, theoretical assumption and a contract are discussed as part of the directing. The technical aspects are reviewed by the director, trainer and group members. How the director got from scene to scene, how aspects could be maximized, what worked and why, what could have been done differently are generally discussed as feedback for the trainee director and self and peer assessment are invaluable.

Power and cautions

There are many cautions regarding the use of psychodrama and many of the individual techniques. First and foremost, it is important to have a purpose for using a specific technique, for using a technique without purpose and forethought, can be dangerous for the protagonist. Some techniques may be too powerful for a particular individual, some may be too esoteric and some too frightening.

It is important to be aware of the ease with which an individual can be opened up using these techniques, as well as the difficulty and necessity in achieving closure, and the psychodramatist must be careful not to provide a fantasy happy ending for a session when the reality base is not present.

These are scenes that require extreme sensitivity in their enactment. We are faced daily with issues like abortion, rape, incest and sexual molestation. In order to accomplish what is necessary for the protagonist and still keep him/her intact we must use care and discretion (Goldman and Morrison, 1984).

Training

Psychodrama training is a postgraduate training for mental health professionals. It usually takes a minimum of two to three years after initial professional training. Psychodramatists have their own therapy and supervision as well as a primary

Marcia Karp

Figure 19.1   *A model of the therapeutic aspects in psychodrama*

trainer who follows their clinical and theoretical progress. Because psychodrama is a powerful therapeutic tool only those trained in its use should be using it.

Effectiveness

A large body of literature has been published on therapeutic factors in group psychotherapy (Bloch and Crouch, 1985). In 1958, Corsini and Rosenburg reviewed over 300 articles on group psychotherapy and made three broad categories to discuss the accounts: (1) emotional; (2) cognitive; and (3) actional.

Yalom (1975) found that interpersonal learning together with catharsis, cohesiveness and insight were the factors most valued by subjects. Kellermann (1992) found in two studies that insight, catharsis and interpersonal relations are therapeutic factors central to psychodramatic group psychotherapy.

Gretl Leutz, a German psychodramatist, suggests that making a conflict tangible, concrete and visible, also makes it dispensable and thus the person can change (Leutz, 1985). Thus making a process that is unconscious conscious helps the person gain control of their own behaviour.

Kellermann (1992) offers the model in Figure 19.1 illustrating the aspects of psychodrama which facilitate therapeutic progress.

The outcome of psychodrama

Some professionals who have never experienced psychodrama for any substantial length of time are afraid of it as a therapeutic method. Many tend to over-dramatize its process and emphasize its presumed dangers. Others exaggerate its virtues in a naive, superficial manner which violates the most elementary precepts of social psychology. Both groups are unaware of the relatively recent attempts that have been made to investigate scientifically psychodrama's therapeutic potentials.

Such controlled studies have shown that, employed by reasonably trained professionals with awareness of its limits, psychodrama can make a contribution either on its own or as an adjunct to any of the manifold branches of psycho-therapy, whether these be behaviouristic, psychoanalytic or existential-humanistic (Kellermann, 1992).

Who can use it?

Psychodrama may be helpful to a wide variety of people, cutting across categories, individual and social problem areas and a spectrum of behaviour disorders. 'Psychodrama can help the normal client solve actual conflicts, the neurotic client to uncover infantile conflicts, the psychotic to regain reality by means of concrete action and the narcissistic or borderline person in the process of separation and individuation' (Leutz, 1985). Leutz, myself and others have used psychodrama successfully with some people who had psychosomatic disorders. Psychodrama can be helpful only to those who are able and motivated. The ability to participate in the imagining process of role playing without losing touch with outer reality seems to be a minimal requirement for participation. Furthermore, participants must be able to:

- experience surges of feelings without loss of impulse control;
- have some capacity to establish relationships;
- have minimal tolerance for anxiety and frustration (ego strength);
- have some psychological mindedness;
- have a capacity for adaptive regression (Kellermann, 1992).

I have used psychodrama effectively in one-to-one work and in couples therapy. A single session usually has limited goals and is focused on a specific concrete issue. Psychodrama may therefore be characterized as a brief method of psycho-therapy, sharing many of the circumstantial characteristics of crisis-orientated and focused therapy.

References

Bloch, S. and Crouch, E. (1985) *Therapeutic Factors in Group Psychotherapy*. Oxford: Oxford University Press.

Corsini, R. and Rosenburg, B. (1958) 'Mechanisms of group psychotherapy, processes and dynamics', *Journal of Abnormal and Social Psychology*, 51: 406–10.

Goldman, E. and Morrison, D. (1984) *Psychodrama: Experience and Process*. Desmoines, Iowa: Kendall Hunt.

Kellermann, P. (1992) *Focus on Psychodrama*. London: Jessica Kingsley.

Leutz, G. (1985) 'What is effective psychodrama?' in *Mettre Sa Vie en Scène*. Paris: Epi.

Leveton, E. (1979) *Psychodrama for the Timid Clinician*. New York: Springer.

Moreno, J.L. (1953) *Who Shall Survive?* New York: Beacon House.

Yalom, I. (1975) *The Theory and Practice of Group Psychotherapy*. New York: Basic Books.

Further reading

Holmes, P. and Karp, M. (1992) *Psychodrama: Inspiration and Techniques.* London: Routledge.

Holmes, P., Karp, M. and Watson, M. (1994) *Psychodrama since Moreno.* London: Routledge.

Discussion issues

1 The struggle to be normal (normosis) confounds the best of us. What do you think this means and what is your experience, both personally and in your work with clients, of this struggle.

2 Imagine that you have chosen to be a protagonist in a psychodrama group. Which aspect of your life would you work on in the group. Which of your 'scripts' would you want to throw away?

3 Because psychodrama is a powerful therapeutic tool only those trained in it should be using it. Comment upon the value of psychodrama and the possible dangers which need to be avoided, if it is to be used responsibly.

4 Do you consider that psychodrama can be used as an adjunct to other approaches? Which approaches, and for what reasons?

PART TWO

COUNSELLING CONTEXTS AND PRACTICE

Introduction to Part Two

The shape and composition of this section – and of the Reader as a whole – are prescribed by topics representing the interests and experience of journal authors, which cover a cross-section of the counselling field but do not necessarily present a comprehensive view of it. Thus Part Two presents a diverse selection of journal writings from 1981 to 1995 covering a variety of counselling contexts. The word context is used to include the different client groups with whom authors have worked, set against the background of the social, cultural and organizational settings in which that work has developed. Contributions also describe particular aspects of practice which have been developed as the activity which we call counselling has expanded into more areas of society and human life.

The choice of inter-cultural therapy and counselling emphasizes the growing importance of the changes in attitudes and the extent of re-learning required for our gradual transmigration into a society which is capable of accommodating all its constituent cultural groups. Inter-cultural therapy seeks to address, confirm and embrace the reality of difference within a counselling setting. Aisha Dupont-Joshua's chapter is particularly concerned with psychodynamic counselling and therapy and mainly, though not exclusively, with the experiences of people from black minority groups. Ian Owen's piece considers the person-centred approach in a wider cultural setting and it may be a temptation to hope that the philosophy behind Carl Rogers' practice might lend itself more flexibly to working with difference. The reality is that whatever our counselling approach there are still too many occasions upon which we deal with social and cultural difference inadequately, clumsily or with cruel indifference. 'Racism is a complex and highly charged issue and there are no simple solutions', as Aisha Dupont-Joshua tells us. It is undoubtedly an issue which life currently, and in the future, compels us to address actively, despite the pain and hard work which that entails for our clients and ourselves. It is crucial to counter the curse of racism, but equally important not to underestimate the difficulty of changing our attitudes, even when we have worked hard to become aware of them.

We still have much to do to create an inter-cultural society within the world of counselling and this is perhaps our first contribution towards creating an inter-cultural society in general.

That wise understanding which underpins the practical application of psycho-analytic thinking is contained in two articles which demonstrate the strength of this approach at its best. Goldi Romm is the founder of the Centre of Analytical Psychotherapy and her work first appeared in a 1982 issue of the journal which addressed the theme of loneliness and aloneness. She provides a sympathetically discerning awareness of the tensions between individuals and the groups to which they would belong, in one of our rare articles on group work. Julia Segal applies a Kleinian understanding of the emotional aspects of disability and illness, through the uncovering and acknowledgement of the place of phantasy in giving a lan-guage which can make sense of everyday experiences, particularly in counselling or brief psychotherapy with those who are chronically ill. Her comment that 'it is important to avoid succumbing to the temptation to take control by replacing the experience of not knowing with the illusion of knowing', is a salutary reminder to all of us, whatever our theoretical orientation.

In addressing the controversial matter of the effects of drug therapy on per-sonality and, as a result, on counselling process and outcomes, Diane Hammersley and Linda Beeley advise counsellors to consider making the question of client's drug intake part of their assessment procedure before the start of counselling. This suggestion is made because of the implications of the effects of different drugs upon assessment itself, the level of therapy which may be most helpful, choice of intervention, possible outcomes of counselling and liaison with others involved in the drug therapy. The increasing use of drugs for leisure may also have effects on counselling which need some careful consideration.

The next group of chapters sandwich two accounts from the early 1980s within two from 1994. Counselling and homelessness would not have been readily linked in the early 1980s and neither had such a high media profile as they have today. Anne Bentley gives an insight into her counselling with homeless people who visit the well-established Social Care Unit of the church of St Martin-in-the-Fields in Trafalgar Square. She highlights some of the dissonances she and her clients experienced in integrating counselling and homelessness, generated by the very real struggles of those coping with the practical efforts of sustaining physical existence, who cannot afford what appears to be the luxury of acknowledging the effects of emotion which counselling requires.

In 1981 a special issue of the BAC journal focused on Counselling and the Disabled, and two accounts on this theme provide a historical perspective. Margaret Morgan describes her work with families and Mary Godden writes about her early experiences of people living in a residential setting. If we were to publish a similar issue now, it is likely that we would refer to counselling people with disabilities, in recognition of the fact that it is not the whole person who is disabled, and this is one example of the changes in our understanding since the 1980s. The Spastics Society, for which Margaret Morgan worked for many years is now called Scope and offers help for people with cerebral palsy, a further indication of our attempts as a society to replace damaging and disabling labels. The word 'spastic' was used as a standard term of abuse in our schools for far too long. It is perhaps an encouraging sign of the greater medical sophistication and acceptance abroad in society, which now enables Scope to use the term cerebral palsy in its title.

These early pieces are balanced by a recent perspective from Hillary Ratna of the Westminster Pastoral Foundation who encourages a wider recognition of the needs and difficulties of people who are deaf or hard of hearing and seek counselling help. There is some useful information about the new courses to provide counsellors with the additional skills which will help them to work in this context.

Homelessness, disability and hearing difficulties can severely isolate and reduce the self-esteem and confidence of those for whom they are a major influence on life. These chapters all have echoes of the loneliness and aloneness featured in Goldi Romm's piece and they may usefully be read in parallel.

Those who regularly read newspapers or watch television can be forgiven for gaining the impression that we live in an increasingly violent world, one in which much human behaviour appears to be more unacceptably out of control than we remember or imagine from the past. This impression is given some basis in reality by a triad of contributions which are a reminder that counselling is not necessarily undertaken in the middle of life's road, but is also used as a source of help both for those clients whose problems or behaviour take them to the edge of society, and perhaps indirectly, their victims. Peter Reynolds and Tricia Allison bring us up to date on their 1989 journal article on criminal assault at work and underline some of the problems of responding to violence and crime within organizations.

Working with violent individuals of either sex is not straightforward and therapy can be further complicated when the act of violence is used as an anxiety-reducing mechanism, becoming as habitual as handwashing rituals in a client imprisoned within an obsessional compulsive disorder. Adam Jukes' writing, and that of Tony Waring and Jim Wilson, both introduce the use of a psychosexual group work approach with men who have battered their partners. These are two realistic descriptions of the stubbornly difficult nature of work with this client group which show how it is fraught with problems for the facilitators.

Whilst help following trauma has been recognized historically for several hundred years, within limited areas which seemingly exclude fighting for one's country, post-traumatic stress disorder has been a psychiatrically recognized diagnosis only since the 1980s. It is perhaps the combination of medical recognition and the effects of the publicity following major national disasters such as those at Bradford and Sheffield football grounds and the maritime tragedy of Zeebrugge which has given impetus to the organization of counselling resources for those traumatized by such events. In 1988 Colin Weaver wrote in a personal way of the consequences of his experiences helping to meet the needs of victims of the accident to the ferry *Herald of Free Enterprise* at Zeebrugge. Suzanna Rose describes the concept, symptoms and treatment of PTSD in a hospital setting in the 1990s, a resource which has probably built on the experiences of people like Colin Weaver and his team years earlier.

Counselling as a discrete activity is increasingly accepted, taught and practised in a diverse variety of settings as we approach the end of the twentieth century. The use of interpersonal skills as an integral part of the work of other helping professions is also increasingly accepted, taught and practised. In his address to the consultation day of the Project 2000 Interpersonal Skills in Nurse Training in 1990, Philip Burnard gave a detailed picture of this latter development and of the obstacles, misunderstandings and objections that can arise from its introduction. Sue Coles delineates her struggles with the integration of counselling skills within her work as an occupational therapist, and it is interesting to note that her way of resolving the contradictions she encountered was to move further in the direction of counselling. The conscious use of counselling and interpersonal skills within the context of other helping professions is one in which it seems crucial to acknowledge to address the role conflict which is so often inherent in such use.

Antony Grey was secretary of the Homosexual Law Reform Society and was director of the Albany Trust (the pioneering counselling agency for sexual minorities) until 1977. In 1984 he wrote for the journal about his views on the challenge of AIDS, as an active member of BAC's executive committee. Caz Lack's writing arises from the beginning of her involvement in gay bereavement counselling in 1990. Scott Berry's 1995 account of his work with those who are learning to live with an HIV-positive diagnosis is, of course, primarily focusing on this particular life-threatening illness. However, the client responses and experiences he describes parallel the distress of those learning to live with other life-and-death illnesses, so that counsellors not working directly in the HIV/AIDS field may find his examples helpful. This author has worked in both Britain and Australia so his observations stretch across the world, as does the illness on which his work has been built. These three chapters exemplify some of the changes in thinking and attitudes which have accompanied the higher profile accorded to HIV/AIDS and the increasing support offered to its victims in the past decade.

In 1993 the film world challenged our gender expectations with *The Crying Game* and the film of Virginia Woolf's novel *Orlando*. A similar challenge within our own journal that year came from Jed Bland's description of the life style of dual-role transvestites and his thinking on the counselling needs of this particular minority group. Information which helps counsellors to understand the human condition of transvestism is not readily available in counselling literature. As transvestism becomes less hidden, transvestites are more likely to seek counselling help.

Peter Dale's major contribution makes a careful exploration of the implications of counselling adults who were abused as children, based on a major model for sexual abuse treatments from the Institute for the Community as Extended Family in San Jose, California. In 1995 BAC gave written evidence to the National Commission of Enquiry into the Prevention of Child Abuse, sponsored by the National Society for the Prevention of Cruelty to Children (NSPCC), which reported in spring 1996. The report on this evidence in *Counselling*, vol. 16, no. 2, May 1995, makes clear and unequivocal comments on the contribution which counsellors can make in the area of child abuse, in addition to pointing out the areas of conflict which accompany the involvement of counsellors in this field.

The majority of the articles selected address aspects of individual counselling and generally consider that it is a force for good. In presenting her case for couple therapy in the final chapter of Part Two, Daphne Boddington reminds us how powerfully the ripple effects of individual counselling can spread negatively as well as positively into close relationships and suggests her remedy.

If someone knowing nothing about counselling, or imagining, as people still do, that it is about tea and sympathy or an exercise in self-indulgence, were to read this section of the Reader, they might wonder why anyone would choose to work in an activity so full of sadness and threat, uncertainty and conflict. Whilst it is true that much counselling work is based in revealing and helping people to cope with their problems and their pains, it is also true that if counsellors are to survive they need an element of optimism. Helen Keller, who after graduating became a writer and supporter of people with disabilities, was herself deprived of sight and hearing before the age of two. In 1903 she wrote a book entitled *Optimism*, in which she said 'although the world is full of suffering, it is full also of the overcoming of it'. Perhaps it is sharing in the courage of our clients in the overcoming of it that enables counsellors to maintain their optimism.

20

Inter-Cultural Therapy

Aisha Dupont-Joshua

As both a black woman of mixed race living in a white host society, and a counsellor, working with the ideas of inter-cultural therapy has become an essential part of my perception of how I relate to the world. This has given me understanding and a willingness to work with the emotional problems facing black and other ethnic minorities living in Western white societies. My training and subsequent friendship with the late Jafar Kareem gave me some tools and a vocation to work with the problems of living in a multi-cultural society; and my involvement with Nafsiyat Inter-Cultural Therapy Centre, of which Jafar was the founder, has given me a sense of professional belonging which I had been unable to find in other white counselling groups. I would like to share with this professional readership some of the ideas of inter-cultural therapy, which have added to my picture of human experience.

Cultural diversity

In today's multi-cultural society, the need for counsellors and therapists to develop an awareness and understanding of cultural diversity becomes increasingly important. Modes of communication, relating and concepts of emotional distress vary vastly between cultures, and since counselling and psychotherapy as healing processes are now becoming more widely available to black and other ethnic minorities, so practitioners need help to extend their perceptions of the counselling relationship. Sometimes even the term 'counselling' may be changed for a more acceptable substitute – an Indian colleague felt that the term 'discussions' could be more acceptable in the Indian community. An Afro-Carribean practitioner sometimes uses the term 'advice' with her clients because they find this more empowering, and though she is not giving advice, she is willing to adapt her vocabulary for better communication.

Recognition and the willingness to work with cultural diversity form an integral part of inter-cultural therapy. This applies to concepts of family structure – the extended or the nuclear family; ideas of child-rearing – single parents, parental couples or multiple parent figures. A vivid example was used by Jafar Kareem, who described an experience with a Nigerian client of noble birth. The client became stuck when asked to describe his relationship with his mother. After a missed appointment, he came back and declared that he was unable to do this as he had been fed by nine pairs of breasts. Returning to concepts of the family

This chapter was first published in *Counselling, Journal of the British Association for Counselling*, vol. 5, no. 3, pp. 203–5 (1994).

structure, perhaps the most important is the relationship of the individual to the family – wherein lies the conflict between the individual's loyalty to themselves, to the family and to the community. All these issues reflect cultural diversity and affect people's perceptions of themselves.

The concept of cultural diversity requires an acknowledgement of, an acceptance of and a learning to work with, difference – be it race, religion, language, economic situation, class and gender. However, if we look at Western psychotherapy as largely based on European models of thought with their emphasis for example on the nuclear family, then a shift of perception is required, with a willingness to understand different cultural backgrounds and the need for anthropology and sociology within counselling training.

Cultural interpretation of behaviour

Kleinman (1976), a medical anthropologist, puts forward the idea that the health, illness and health-care related aspects of societies are expressed as cultural systems. He believes that health-care systems should be viewed as other cultural symbolic systems, such as kinship and religion, which are built out of meanings, values and behavioural norms.

Emotional behaviour needs to be understood in the client's cultural context, with less of a eurocentric viewpoint. A relevant example to consider here would be the number of people of Afro-Carribean descent admitted into British psychiatric hospitals in recent years, suffering from schizophrenia – which outweigh white British admissions by three to one. Why should this be? Are Afro-Carribeans more prone to schizophrenia? Or is mental distress, due to many extremely difficult social factors, being interpreted as schizophrenia?

Gaines (1982) suggests the medical anthropological idea that the patient, the family and their culture, as well as that of the practitioner, need to be explained and understood, and that each is an equally important ingredient of the cultural construction of illness and treatment. If we refer back to the schizophrenia diagnosis mentioned previously, Gaines argues that the interventions of professional healers, may come not from 'professional' evaluation of behaviour, but from cultural criteria which are used to make sense of it.

An example of the interpretation of behaviour in the therapeutic context is the view taken of eye contact between therapist and client. In many Western therapeutic models this contact is considered essential to the relationship and avoidance of it is literally considered an avoidance. To many traditional Asian clients direct eye contact might be considered disrespectful, or in the case of women immodest. An Indian psychiatrist tells of being summoned to a hospital by a white colleague who was unable to proceed with an Indian client because of the lack of eye contact. Another example concerns the interpretation of gift giving between client and therapist – a white British colleague of mine mentioned that she did not know what to do when a Nigerian client brought her a gift, should she have refused it categorically as seduction as her training had taught her, or should this gesture be viewed in the client's cultural context?

We, as therapists, need to consider our own limitations, who we are as people, what we represent and the prejudices and biases we bring to the relationship, in order that we may learn not to impose our own cultural values. We could call this a respect of difference. The acknowledgement and management of difference can be very threatening, and it is often managed by denial and an attempt to make everyone the same, what I see as white middle-class assumptions. In inter-cultural work our aim is to encourage counsellors and therapists to think and talk about these issues, and perhaps to look at and work on our own prejudices and splits.

Jafar Kareem, in his chapter 'The Nafsiyat Inter-Cultural Therapy Centre' (Kareem and Littlewood, 1992), asks the question, 'What does it mean to communicate across cultures?' He states that there are racial differences in 'cultural' attributes such as concepts of personhood, respect or disrespect, independence, position of elders in the family, obligations to family and community – the very notion of moral traditions that combine to make a human being a social being rather than an isolated organism. He thought that an understanding of these aspects of human life is fundamental to the success of any therapy. The need for psychotherapists to take such matters into consideration in both their practice and training is now acknowledged and this is evidenced in the proposals on inter-cultural therapy made to the United Kingdom Standing Conference for Psychotherapy (in Kareem and Littlewood, 1992).

The impact of racism

Addressing the impact of racism forms another essential ingredient of inter-cultural therapy – acknowledging and working with the pain and emotional damage it causes. Racism is a complex and highly charged issue and there are no simple solutions. Living in a white host society, black and other ethnic minorities often receive the racist message, whether consciously or unconsciously, that they are inferior. Racism's message is that human beings are not equal. This message is extremely damaging to the individual's perception of themselves and their culture of origin. This theory is also, I believe, the origin of the practice of slavery; which also enabled much of the savagery of colonization to be so great that it destroyed the whole fabric of many peoples' lives, and the kernel of their spiritual existence and identity. As therapists we need to take on this knowledge as central to the issue of racism – we also need to look at the ingredients of racism which constitute basic feelings of envy, hate, jealousy, greed, competitiveness, anger, violence, suspicion, fear, ignorance and conditioning – feelings we all have inside us, that is perhaps why racism is so threatening.

The ideas of transference, counter-transference and pre-transference in racism may be appropriate here. Curry (1964) puts forward the concept of 'pre-transference', which he describes as the ideas, fantasies, and values ascribed to the black psychotherapist and their race which are held by the white patient long before the two meet for the first time in the consulting room. This pre-transference relates to being brought up in a society which holds negative views about black people, and is constituted of material from the past: fairy tales, images, myths and jokes. Jafar Kareem (1988) points out that there is always an expectancy and dependency throughout the process of therapy, suggesting that this dependency is greater when the patient comes from a very deprived background, and that the transference has already taken place before the treatment has started. He also feels that the therapist who has definite ideas about groups of people who are different from themselves, and who lives in a society which projects negative images about particular groups of people, has a pre-counter-transference towards the client from such groups. Another way of looking at the transference in racism is as the projection of our own 'bad' feelings on to another race or ethnic minority – which relates to the difficulty we have in acknowledging such suppressed feelings towards ourselves and owning our 'bad' bits.

Expanding perimeters

In working with the effects of racism the inter-cultural therapy approach is that emotional distress is not always seen as self-induced but can be caused by external factors, and we aim to look at the effect of the social factors on the inner psyche. It is our belief that it is not sufficient for therapy only to resolve the conflicts of childhood, nor that the individual is necessarily responsible for their social condition. Our work encompasses the inner experiences of the client, together with their total life experience – including their communal experience and life before their arrival on Western soil. Mr J. had been a head-master of a flourishing school in South Africa, and a respected member of his community, before he emigrated to England so that his family could escape the degradation of being black in the apartheid system. Forced to work a day and an evening job to cover the high costs of living in London with a large family, Mr J. eventually sought help for depression and chronic ill-health.

Inter-cultural therapy enhances existing practices of therapy – it is a form of dynamic psychotherapy that aims to take into account the whole being of the client – their inner life and their communal life experience. It is based on the relationship between client and therapist as in other therapies – and similarly in this relationship we emphasize acknowledging and working with difference. Jafar Kareem and Littlewood (1992) cite the example of Victoria, who, when consulting a white woman therapist because she had become depressed and feared that she was going mad, was made to feel that issues of race were essentially her problem. Whenever she tried to bring up anything relating to her feelings about being black, the therapist always interpreted that as a projection of her inner chaos into the outside world. Victoria felt misunderstood and angry that her pain and confusion about being in a black/white situation where she was made to feel powerless was unacknowledged. She finally sought help from the Nafsiyat Therapy Centre because she needed a therapist who could immediately recognize her pain in being powerless and black in a society which is racist. The problem with the first therapist was not that she was white, but that she was unable to look at the inter-related themes of race and powerlessness as problems of reality.

Psychotherapy and counselling have until recently often been a white middle-class prerogative, largely for economic reasons, but also perhaps because black and other ethnic minority people were thought of by some as psychologically unsuitable. We are now breaking these social boundaries, both in theory and in practice, and stress the need for practitioners to look at their own limitations, and to look at what they might be unconsciously projecting on to black clients.

Jafar Kareem and Littlewood (1992) suggest that there is a double-edged argument going on between minority groups and white psychotherapists, with a great deal of hostility towards psychotherapy from the former because it is seen essentially as a 'Western', middle-class' form of treatment. When white psychotherapists reciprocate by arguing that minority groups are not suitable for psychotherapy, this dynamic of suspicion is maintained from both sides, with a mirroring effect. One of the major reasons for the distrust expressed by black clients is the inevitable imbalance of power that exists between therapist and client. This imbalance of power is a mirror image of the experience of powerlessness that black and ethnic minority clients feel in daily life situations, and they do not want this same situation to operate in a therapeutic encounter. This experience of powerlessness, especially for black clients, is a potent element in the therapeutic situation and one that must be addressed if work is to proceed.

Lennox Thomas (1992), current director of Nafsiyat Inter-cultural Therapy Centre, asks the potent questions 'What makes the dealings in a consulting room between a white therapist and a black patient "different"? What are the processes which the therapist needs to go through to disentangle themselves from the structural racism of the society in which they live and were raised?'

Conclusion

The idea of inter-cultural therapy is to make the psychotherapeutic healing process available to black and other ethnic minorities – to expand the limitations of the field. Its essence is in its humanity, the respect of each other in our difference, in language, history and traditions, and this approach enlarges our concepts of human experience and is mutually enriching.

Inter-cultural training and counselling groups

Nafsiyat Inter-Cultural Therapy Centre together with University College, London, run a three-year MSc in Inter-Cultural Therapy. For further information write to Roland Littlewood, Dept. of Anthropology, University College London, Gower St, London WC1E 6RT

The British Association of Inter-Cultural Therapists, for practitioners in the field, meets at Nafsiyat Inter-Cultural Therapy Centre. It is a forum for the discussion and presentation of cultural and racial issues within the counselling context. For further details contact Bernadette Hawks, Tel: 0181 509 0936.

The BAC has its own RACE division (Race and Cultural Education in counselling), which seeks to encourage the development of training methods, to organize and encourage the provision of workshops and conferences, and to develop a greater understanding of the problems created by racism. Divisional membership runs concurrently with BAC membership and enquiries should be addressed to the RACE division, BAC, Rugby, or Membership Secretary Bente Samuel, Tel: 01252 792808.

London University, Birbeck College, Extra Mural Dept., Counselling Section runs a six-month course in 'The Dynamics of Race and Culture'. This is for professionals in health and social services, psychologists, psychotherapists and counsellors. For further details contact: Nathalie Gallaway, Tel: 0171 631 6626.

Regent's College runs courses on 'Race, Ethnicity and Culture' and 'Cross Cultural Counselling and Psychotherapy'. Contact Anna David or June Roberts, Tel: 0171 487 7406.

The Inner City Centre (which is an offshoot of the Lincoln Centre for Psychotherapy) runs a course on 'Counselling Within the Context of Race and Ethnicity'. This is for Asians and people of African descent and lasts 18 months. Contact Steven Maynard, Tel: 0181 556 8494.

Goldsmiths College is starting a post-graduate certificate in Inter-Cultural Therapy. Contact: The Art and Psychotherapy Unit, Tel: 0171 919 7237.

Eric Ferron and Angela Hobbart run a black and white mixed therapy group, in the London area, which works on racial and cultural issues in individuals' lives. Contact Eric Ferron, Tel: 0181 764 9179.

References

Curry, A. (1964) 'Myth, transference and the black psychotherapist', *International Review of Psychoanalysis*.

Gaines, A.D. (1982) 'Cultural definitions, behaviour and the person in American psychiatry', in A.J. Marsella and G. White (eds), *Cultural Concepts of Mental Health and Therapy*. Dordrecht: Reidel Publishing.

Kareem, J. (1988) 'Outside in . . . inside out . . . some considerations in inter-cultural psychotherapy', *Social Work Practice*, November.

Kareem, J. and Littlewood, R. (eds) (1992) *Intercultural Therapy – Themes, Interpretations and Practice*. Oxford: Blackwell Scientific.

Kleinman, A. (1976) *Concepts and a Model for the Comparison of Medical Systems as Cultural Systems: Concepts of Health and Disease*. Berkeley: University of California Press.

Thomas, L. (1992) 'Racism and psychotherapy', in J. Kareem and R. Littlewood (eds), *Intercultural Therapy*. Oxford: Blackwell Scientific.

Further reading on race, culture and psychotherapy

Bochner, S. (1982) *Cultures in Contact – Studies in Cross-Cultural Interactions*. Oxford: Pergamon Press.

d'Ardenne, P. and Mahtani, A. (1989) *Transcultural Counselling in Action* (Counselling in Action Series). London: Sage.

Dennis, D. (1984) *Black History for Beginners*. New York: Writers and Readers Publishing.

Fryer, P. (1984) *Staying Power. The History of Black People in Britain.* London: Pluto Press.

Helman, C. (1990) *Culture, Health and Illness,* 2nd edn. Oxford: Butterworth-Heinemann.

Ho, M.K. (1987) *Family Therapy with Ethnic Minorities.* London: Sage.

Littlewood, R. and Lipsedge, M. (1982) *Aliens and Alienists.* Harmondsworth: Penguin.

Discussion issues

1 Would you say that Western psychotherapy and counselling have their basis in European models of thought, or in something more universal? Would you suggest any changes?

2 What are the processes which a counsellor/therapist needs to undergo to disentangle themselves from structural racism?

3 How do you work with difference in a creative way, e.g. when there is a black/while situation with either client or counsellor? Look at what assumptions might be made, perhaps denial or transference issues in the relationship.

4 What does it mean to communicate across cultures? What understanding does a counsellor need to have of a client's cultural and social being?

21

The Person-Centred Approach in a Cultural Context

Ian R. Owen

Person-centred therapy has led the way in producing non-directive counselling and psychotherapy. The aim of this chapter is to investigate ways in which the person-centred approach can be extended and bettered, so counselling practice can take into account new areas which are not mentioned in mainstream counselling literature. Year by year the clarification and development of guiding ideas, and the feedback of research and practice, come to enrich counselling which evolves step by step. The major point of the person-centred approach is to set aside any notion of counsellors as aloof professionals and requests them to be natural, honest and earnest in trying to reach out towards clients. Merry (1990) has emphasized person-centred therapy as a way of being with clients, rather than the application of technique: a statement which opposes the natural way of person-centred relating to the use of counselling skills. Person-centred therapy is seen as the release of innate qualities within counsellors, yet it is also a set of skills that can be taught and encouraged. This opposition of skills and natural capabilities is commented on at the end of this chapter.

This paper takes its lead from the writings of Carl Rogers, who tried to balance the need for intellectual rigour with the need for a psychological therapy that acknowledged innate human qualities (Rogers, 1965, 1974). In particular there is one paper in which Rogers (1990) touches on the subject of cultural relativism, and this is part of the ground which will be covered here. Below, the nature of meeting with clients is considered and it is suggested that all counselling is a cross-cultural event. The stages followed are:

1   The need for counsellors to be aware of the full qualities of clients, and the importance of the social and physical contexts in counselling.
2   The use of key ideas from social anthropology to focus awareness on the cultural and subcultural differences in the lives of counsellors and clients. These issues point to the topics of identity and the different assumptions of appropriate behaviour within any culture.
3   A brief analysis of some assumptions in counselling is attempted, including the assumption that the *treatment* given to clients is appropriate to them.

This chapter was first published in *Counselling, Journal of the British Association for Counselling*, vol. 1, no. 3, pp. 92–4 (1990).

Relationships exist within contexts

The anthropologist Hall points out that communication has other components to it apart from speech and non-verbal behaviour in the present moment (Hall, 1977). There are three aspects to communication which create the social action and reaction of a relationship. First, the *communication code* is the explicit medium used for the transmission of information between the parties involved. Communication codes are speech, pauses in speech, proxemics (the study of space between people) and kinesics (the study of gestures). However, to understand a message its context needs to be known.

Internal contexts are internal to both senders and receivers, and are their internal frames of reference. This context is comprised of the psyche, beliefs, experiences, attitudes, culture and ideas of causation about misfortune and suffering. Counsellors' internal contexts include their training, state of mind and beliefs about the efficacy of counselling, previous experience of clients and the range of problems worked with. Clients' internal contexts include how they present their suffering to counsellors, their personal explanations of their suffering and their understanding of counselling. Counselling is subjectively affected by mood as it occurs between counsellor and client, be it happy, confident, or anxious and preoccupied. The internal contexts which counsellors have include the influence of their specific training school and ideas of psychological health.

External contexts are the physical or social settings in which therapy takes place. For instance, Langs (1988) has written on the importance of creating a basic sense of safety and trustworthiness by having consistent boundaries such as set times for therapy, a set fee, and ensuring confidentiality. Rowan (1988) has written on the importance of the external context, for instance, where the counselling room says a great deal about the owner's status, education, theoretical orientation and therapeutic style. This setting may have additional symbols such as books, diplomas in frames hanging on the wall, cushions on the floor, or notes on the counsellor's desk. All of these items intimate something about the nature of the process taking place. Other external contexts in which counselling takes place include hospitals, universities, schools or drop-in centres. This all contributes to the effect whereby the same counsellor working in different physical settings could be viewed differently.

Defining culture

But first an excursion into the relevance of culture as a context for practitioners. Leach defines culture as: 'That complex whole which includes knowledge, belief, art, morals, law, custom and other capabilities and habits acquired by man as a member of society' (1982, pp. 38–9). Keesing defines it as 'systems of shared ideas, systems of concepts and rules and meanings that underlie and are expressed in the ways that humans live' (1981, p. 68). Culture is a set of implicit and explicit, conscious and unconscious guidelines which people inherit as members of a particular family, religion, profession or other social group. Culture tells people how to view the world and make sense of it. It gives cohesion to a group and shows people how to behave and misbehave, and provides a way of transmitting these guidelines to the next generation, or newcomers to a group. A culture teaches its members how to live in their shared world and how to perceive that world in the same way, thereby providing a sense of identity and cohesiveness. Personal identity is culturally created and culture influences the current lived states of illness and health. As a concomitant of this, no one is without prejudices based on their own cultural beliefs about morals, values, social, religious, economic, educational, political, ethnic or sexual criteria. This is particularly true in class-bound Britain. We all have culture and an upbringing, and the values and beliefs we have limit us. If we did not have values or beliefs we would be indifferent to everything.

Culture touches every part of people's lives. The people whom you know face-to-face, and whom you have personally known, play an influential role in shaping your beliefs. Culture is found in a shared heritage, in a certain place, in words, history, education, rituals and an established class system. It is also present in the learned behaviour and emotional expression of a group. Thus, the knowledge and ability to respond appropriately to others is gained from the group to which a person belongs. A group's categories of good and bad, their ethics, roles, power and status, all add up to make a description of their culture.

Social anthropology, the study of culture and social networks, holds many relevant insights for counsellors who are willing to study it. For instance, the group which influences you may be a series of individuals or a tightly knit club. To think culturally is not to emphasize individuality, but to concentrate on the group dimension. 'Positive' cultural thinking is having an awareness of probable areas of difference between yourself and clients. It is also the case that cultural thinking can be used negatively in stereotyping, where a person's individuality may be lost. Culture can be studied by agglomerating individuals into groups: for instance, men and women, young and old, urban and suburban, counsellors and clients. Different groups can be distinguished by their mode of dress, daily life, diet, spiritual beliefs, myths and explanatory models of all kinds, which include their health beliefs and ideas of human nature. After children are born their every experience is taught and shaped by culture.

The creation and maintenance of culturally held beliefs are the social networks of a group of people, because an individual's social network is the essence of their being in a world with others. However, there is a certain tension between a group and an individual. Individuals want to belong to others. Yet to do so may involve having to suppress part of their personal nature in order to conform, due to a desire to be like others. Therefore, agreement with others often gets the upper hand over personal values, as the effects of peer group pressure show.

Example of medical anthropology

Medical anthropology is the study of healing and health beliefs in different cultures of the world. Its purpose is not only to record the health practices of people who live in desolate areas or in impoverished countries, it is useful in the development of counselling and the client-centred approach. Medical anthropology analyses the life experiences of health and illness in the contexts of cultural meanings and beliefs throughout the world. For instance, Helman (1990) provides an introduction to the scope of medical anthropology. Littlewood (1987) gives an alternative theory of psychopathology from a cross-cultural viewpoint, an overview which also applies to counselling and psychotherapy.

In the West, one of the main cultures people belong to is that of their job or profession (Mars, 1994). Clear examples of job cultures which are well known are the police, nursing and teaching. In all professions there are certain implicit and explicit right and wrong ways of behaving. Only people with certain personalities find it most natural to fit into a specific human environment such as the job culture of a specific profession. As regards counselling, counsellors take on the beliefs and values of their training schools. The risk in becoming enculturated is that the cultural view people have blinds them to what can be seen. Such shortcomings are inevitable to a degree. The possibility of this mutual misunderstanding between individuals from different cultures makes a need to create cross-cultural communication in counselling.

Emic/etic divide in counselling

Problems arise when cultural beliefs and assumptions lead to a culture clash when each party's hidden rules conflict. In cross-cultural confrontation each party can accuse the other of being irrational. I would like to define rational and irrational in the following way: if something is rational then you agree with it, if something is irrational then you do not agree with it.

Anthropologists have three key concepts to help to describe the difference between insight into oneself and empathic knowledge of other people. An *etic* viewpoint is one which construes other persons, culture or the world, in such a way as to fit information about them on to one's own predetermined concepts. This contrasts with the understanding clients and cultures have of themselves, which anthropology calls an *emic* viewpoint. To get an emic understanding of another's cultural view requires counsellors to step out from their own internal context. The word *ethnocentric* can also be used to describe how cultures clash. An ethnocentric clash is one where the opinions of one group predominate over the opinions of other groups. Ethnocentricity is the holding of culture-bound views and the belief that one's own cultural bias is the only possible truth. Examples of ethnocentrism are racism, sexism and other forms of bias (Young, 1990). Differences between emic and etic viewpoints in counselling can also be summarized as follows:

emic/client-centred	*etic/counsellor-centred*
I am in two minds about it	Cognitive dissonance
It's my nerves	Stress
I am stupid and ugly	Low self-esteem

I just can't cope	Inadequate personality
I'm alright really	Denial
I don't know why I come here	Resistance
They make me angry	Blamer not taking responsibility

Medical anthropology considers the concepts that healers have, and their understandings of the suffering of clients, which it calls 'disease'. Diseases are often assumed to be abstract things or independent entities that have a recurring identity. They may be assumed to be universal in form, progress and content. The symptoms, prognosis and treatment are considered to be similar, regardless of the individual or cultural group in which they occur. Taking these notions and applying them to counselling we can see that counsellors' notions of 'disease' are contrasted with clients' experience of 'illness' (Eisenberg, 1977). One writer uses 'illness' to mean 'what the patient [client] feels when he goes to the doctor' (counsellor) and disease is 'what he has on the way home from the doctor's [counsellor's] office', (Cassell, 1976, p. 42). Illness can be defined as the subjective response of clients to suffering. It is made up of how clients have learned how to perceive the origin and significance of their suffering, and how they should or should not behave in relation to those around them, and remedy their suffering.

The whole of this debate demonstrates that counselling is another cultural product alongside many other forms of social life. Counsellors have actions which are stylized ways of responding and constructs which are ways of understanding and working out clients' needs according to a preconceived scheme. For example, you will never actually see a false self, critical parent or super-ego. These constructs belong to counsellors. With the above discussion in place, it is now possible to regard counselling in the following manner: *Because client and counsellor each belong to their own culture, all counselling is cross-cultural counselling.* When clients come for counselling they are being interpreted according to a counselling theory. Counselling concentrates on the assumptions used when clients make understandings, but perhaps counselling should look first at the assumptions within its own practice. Elsewhere I have criticized the cultural assumptions which I feel are implicit in humanistic approaches (Owen, 1991).

Brief analysis of counselling assumptions

1   Counselling is appropriate for all clients. For clients to have appropriate care means that there has been a consideration of the various styles of relating and the possibilities that are available. For counsellors to be able to deliver an appropriate approach requires them to choose a specific way of relating. For instance, there may be cases when counselling is not appropriate for those who find it too disturbing, or are unable to integrate the new information on themselves and their perceptions of others. There may also be cases when the needs of clients are too great to be met.

2   Counsellors do no harm. Prior to the writings and research of Robert Langs (1988) there had been an absence of critical thought about the possibility that

counselling and psychotherapy could be harmful to clients. It cannot be assumed that everything that happens within the bounds of a counselling relationship is helpful and freeing for clients. It is generally the case that after the selection of suitable trainees and thorough practice, clients teach counsellors how to be more effective, accurately empathic and skilful.

3 Interpersonal communication is relatively problem-free. Following the above, the cultural assumptions of counselling inevitably come into conflict with the assumptions of clients. Using the example of clients who come once or twice for therapy and never come again, what happens during such brief therapy? It might be the case that sometimes clients' needs have not been met. Or, clients perceive counsellors as being unable to meet their needs.

An example may make these issues more vivid. A young Pakistan-born Muslim woman is referred to you by her GP. She speaks in a broad Yorkshire accent. Her marriage has broken up and she wants to be with her baby. In a great rapidity of words she tells you that her mother-in-law is keeping her child and when she was two years old she was possessed by spirits. She currently cannot sit still, cry or sleep. She fears she has had a curse put on her. Her GP asks you whether she is manic. What do you reply? Do you break confidentiality? Do you keep on seeing her? What are the underlying factors to determine appropriate care for her? This is a complicated problem because three sets of cultural assumptions are in collision. The doctor assumes that it is acceptable to consult with a counsellor about treatment. The client may have too high a degree of distress to be helped by counselling alone.

4 Counsellors and clients should have experiences in common. It is often stated that for there to be an ease of understanding between counsellors and clients that it is preferable, or even necessary, for each to share some aspect of cultural background such as race, gender or sexual orientation. If this assumption were taken to an extreme there would be no counselling at all, for no two people have precisely the same background experiences as described by reference to age, gender, class, religious or political views and the like. Surely it is the case that those counsellors with a wide life experience can make empathic relationships with clients with whom they have little in common, and this ability is what makes them effective counsellors.

Implications for person-centred practice

If person-centred therapy has the aim of providing appropriate care for each client, then this care is appropriate according to the individual's personality, cultural group, educational, moral, political, sexual, family, religious and other relevant considerations. The provision of appropriate care in this revised person-centred approach takes into account both internal and external contexts as counsellors take full responsibility to prepare a total healing encounter suitable for each client. According to this redefinition of person-centred therapy, counsellors need to design a therapeutic structure in which each case takes into account the individuality and cultural context of each client. To create appropriate care, I believe counsellors need to have a good appreciation of clients' understanding. Person-centred counsellors need to be culturally sensitive in the service of clients. What is in the spirit of the person-centred approach is to regard both the cultural background and the uniqueness of clients.

If the intention of person-centred counsellors is to give appropriate care, what do we have to offer clients that might not be acceptable to them? One implication is to do with the naming of clients' problems and the possible labelling of clients. Using theory to name a problem of living can either be a useful practice for counsellor needs, or, it can also be a damning of clients by giving them a bad name. In using theory to guide practice, it is suggested that counsellors need to vary their interpersonal style and be aware of the assumptions and justifications that are used in counselling. I suggest that in order to provide appropriate care, at times counsellors need to try to step outside of their own view of the world, and into the views of clients.

When counsellors from the world of caring and sharing, self-responsibility and professional status meet clients from a world of pain, inability and indecision, the consequence will be difficulties in communication and understanding. For person-centred counsellors to evolve their practice while staying true to being with clients in a person-centred way, then the assumptions and justifications buried within their own theory and practice need to be brought out and discussed. I would say that a major implication of person-centred work is to be flexible in interpersonal style with clients. Also, counsellors need to note how their opinions differ from those of their clients, due to their inevitably different cultural identities. This is a step towards creating more appropriate, more person-centred counselling in the service of particular clients. Therefore, once person-centred counsellors are attending to the world-views of clients, they are working with specific experiences and understandings of illness and felt-inability.

If all counselling is cross-cultural, then effectiveness in cross-cultural communication with clients is a major concern. A paradox for person-centred therapy is that counsellors are their natural selves while playing a role within the person-centred discipline. I suggest that we are naturally and automatically a little different with each client and that this is an uneasy resolution to both being natural and working in a person-centred manner. This chapter has been aimed at increasing the awareness of the centrality of empathy and the difficulties involved in achieving it.

References

Cassell, E.J. (1976) *The Healer's Art: a New Approach to the Doctor–Patient Relationship.* New York: Lippincott.

Eisenberg, L. (1977) 'Disease and illness distinctions between professional and popular ideas of sickness', *Culture, Medicine and Psychiatry*, 1: 9–23.

Hall, E.T. (1977) *Beyond Culture.* New York: Anchor Books.

Helman, C. (1990) *Culture, Health and Illness*, 2nd edn. Oxford: Butterworth-Heinemann.

Keesing, R.M. (1981) *Cultural Anthropology: a Contemporary Perspective.* New York: Holt, Rinehart and Winston.

Langs, R. (1988) *A Primer of Psychotherapy*. New York: Gardner Press.

Leach, E. (1982) *Social Anthropology*. Glasgow: Fontana.

Littlewood, R. (1987) 'The butterfly and the serpent', *Culture, Medicine and Psychiatry*, 11: 289–335.

Mars, G. (1994) *Cheats at Work: an Anthropology of Workplace Crime*. London: Dartmouth.

Merry, T. (1990) 'Client-centred therapy: some trends and some troubles', *Counselling*, 1(1): 17–18.

Owen, I.R. (1991) 'The application of some ideas from anthropology to counseling, therapy and cross-cultural counseling', in E.L. Herr and J. McFadden (eds) *Challenges of Cultural and Racial Diversity to Counseling*. Alexandria, VA: American Association for Counseling Development. pp. 37–40.

Rogers, C.R. (1965) *Client-Centred Therapy: Its Current Practice, Implications and Theory*. London: Constable.

Rogers, C.R. (1974) *On Becoming a Person*. London: Constable.

Rogers, C.R. (1990) 'Do we need "a" reality?', in H. Kirschenbaum and V.L. Henderson (eds), *The Carl Rogers Reader*. London: Constable. pp. 420–9.

Rowan, J. (1988) 'The psychology of furniture', *Counselling*, 64: 21–4.

Young, I.M. (1990) 'Abjection and oppression: dynamics of unconscious racism, sexism and homophobia', in A.B. Dallery, C.E. Scott and P.H. Roberts (eds) *Crises in Continental Philosophy*. New York: SUNY Press. pp. 201–13.

Discussion issues

1 Define counsellor culture in regard to the assumptions of the four major styles of different practice – humanistic, cognitive, behavioural and psychodynamic.

2 Is it possible for counsellors and clients of different cultures to work effectively with each other? If so, what needs to take place?

3 To what extent can a person of one culture understand those of another? What limits this understanding? What limits empathy?

4 What should counsellors value and aim towards when working with clients of different background so that the therapeutic encounters may be more person-centred, rather than concentrating on counsellor assumptions?

5 Are all counselling theories and all persons ethnocentric? Can you not be ethnocentric?

22

Loneliness and Aloneness in Groups

Goldi Romm

Whatever the distinctions in meaning between the words 'loneliness' and 'aloneness' it would appear at first sight that both feelings are inappropriate to a good group experience, whether of a structured, therapeutic kind, or that of an informal meeting between a few people. Most people's preconceptions about groups tend to revolve around quite other connotations of communality, and sharing, the breaking down of barriers and the fostering of communication between members. For the idea expressed above to have any meaning, we must look more carefully at the distinctions implied between the two words. 'Loneliness', being rather a homely word is in some ways the more difficult to define: it is a familiar state of being to most people, and implies an alienation from the rest of the world that is so painful that much of life is spent, however unsuccessfully, in trying to avoid it. It does not depend on the presence of absence of other people, as the many variations on the 'lonely crowd' theme underline, but rather denotes a kind of bleak insufficiency whether in solitude or in company. It is therefore quite possible, though not desirable or pleasant, to be lonely in a group.

The idea of aloneness, on the other hand, lacks the negative connotations of bleakness and insufficiency; indeed, it implies a certain self-sufficiency. Though probably less painful than loneliness, it seems for this reason equally inappropriate to the group experience unless we make sense of it by relating it back to its origins in childhood, and refer to Winnicott's essay 'The capacity to be alone' (1958). In this he states that 'this capacity is one of the most important signs of maturity in emotional development', and has its origins, paradoxically, in the 'experience . . . of being alone, as an infant and small child, in the presence of mother'. Strangely, he does not elaborate much on this basic formulation (italicized by him), but explains what he means by reference to the corpus of his own work and to that of Melanie Klein: 'The capacity to be alone depends on the existence of a good object in the psychic reality of the individual.' This will be of particular importance when we look at the specific difficulties of schizoid personalities in groups; but for individuals who have received 'good enough' mothering, who have been neither over-impinged upon nor neglected in infancy, this capacity will have been developed by the reliable presence of the mother, in a way that enables the child to keep present the image of her even in her absence. Winnicott distinguishes between the positive strength the child derives from this, and the defensive withdrawal characteristic of schizoid states.

Obviously the individual who carries around the 'good internal object' of the mother in adult life, will find no great difficulty in coping with both solitude and

This chapter was first published in *Counselling, Journal of the British Association for Counselling*, no. 41, pp. 6–10 (1982).

the presence of others. Winnicott claims that 'the individual who has developed the capacity to be alone is constantly able to rediscover the personal impulse, and the personal impulse is not wasted because the state of being alone is something which (though paradoxically) always implies that someone else is there'. This has important implications for the behaviour of individuals in groups: it means that some will be able to 'experience id-impulses in the context of ego-relatedness', and not be frightened off by their intensity, whereas others, less secure with their internal objects, will shy away from such experiences into isolation or paranoia. It is precisely these latter individuals for whom groups are often counter-indicated in the psychiatric profession.

It should be said at this point that the word 'group' is being used here in its technical sense, as a specific 'coming together' for therapeutic or analytic purposes; but I take it as read that, although formal groups do often produce some rather peculiar and seemingly untypical behaviour, they reflect in intensified form enough of ordinary life to have real implications for 'normal' group behaviour. So just as a person with schizoid or paranoid tendencies will experience difficulties in ordinary social life, so will they be experienced, possibly in accentuated form, within the framework of the formal group. But if a group has the function of a corrective experience, as Foulkes (1948) contended, such disorders can be brought within its therapeutic orbit: 'The neurotic position, in its very nature, is highly individualistic. It is group-destructive in essence, for it is genetically the result of an incompatibility between the individual and his group'. Foulkes here uses the term 'neurotic' more for simplicity's sake than to draw distinctions with the psychotic clientele. The position he refers to is commonly held to have its origins in the three-person relationship of the Oedipal triangle, while the schizoid or paranoid disorders are considered to stem from the two-person relationship of the infant and the mother. The problems encountered by this second group are likely to be less susceptible to verbalization, since they have their origins in the pre-verbal phase, and the patients to be more withdrawn from personal relationships, than in a neurotic group.

In considering loneliness and aloneness in groups, we need to look at the specific problems encountered by the two broad diagnostic groupings mentioned above, though it would probably be more realistic to see them as points along a spectrum than as two distinct categories. (For whereas an individual psychotherapist can modify interventions, as Balint suggests, according to the specific level reached by the patient (the verbal or pre-verbal), because there are only two people involved, the group psychotherapist must structure the group from the beginning according to the predominant style of the membership.) From schizoid patients in a group then it is common to hear of a distressing sense of 'cut-offness', the 'plate-glass' feeling; they will describe a compulsion to withdraw, and an inner deadness which makes contact with others meaningless or threatening. The paranoid defences of such patients will lead them, in Kleinian terms, to project their bad internal objects on to the group, with the result that they end up feeling depleted or suffocated; they may describe a fear of having their productions 'gobbled up', in the same way that as infants they feared the devouring retaliation of the mother. It makes no difference that the group is a plurality: as Klein pointed out, the bad internal object is often fragmented, and can assume terrifying dimensions as a persecutory horde. The frightening vigour of Kleinian terminology may seem somewhat exaggerated in this context, but I have found it to be extraordinarily accurate in reflecting the reported feelings of schizoid or mildly paranoid patients in a group. In milder language, Winnicott (1972) describes how difficult it is for the child who was dominated by his (narcissistic) mother's mood to get into the group mood, as he has 'too strong a need to defend his own individuality'. As an adult such a child therefore withdraws, in order to preserve its very existence – for the schizoid individual 'exists by not being found' (Winnicott, 1955). This explains the resentment, often amounting to a sense of persecution, felt by some group members when attention is focused on them; what is intended as well-meaning concern is experienced as an attempt to break down the fragile defences the individual has erected to protect his even more fragile ego.

All this suggests that the widespread reluctance in therapeutic circles to treat such patients in a group may be justified. But, just as it took many years for individual psychotherapy to develop techniques and parameters appropriate to the non-neurotic patient (largely through the work of Fairbairn, Guntrip and Winnicott in the UK and Kohut and Kernberg in the States), so it is now more widely accepted that, with certain modifications in style, group therapy has something to offer this diagnostic group.

One such modification is to reduce the usual size of the group from eight or ten to five or six; this diminishes the tendency to paranoia, as it is easier to retain emotional contact of a realistic kind with a smaller group without retreating into fantasy. The interconnectedness thus fostered will work towards breaking down the defences originally erected to protect the ego against such dangerous connections. In line with the modification in structure of the group, some adaptation of the style of leadership must take place: ambiguous and metaphorical statements should be avoided as should the distant and cryptic persona of the leader, designed to foster the emergence of unconscious assumptions in neurotic groups. The leader should work towards reinforcing a sense of reality, and this is best achieved by warmth and concreteness, aimed at encouraging the group members to share their own reality with the rest of the group. In short, there should be no attempt to foster individual fantasy, which would further isolate each person from the rest, nor encourage the formation of a group fantasy, which would reinforce the fear of contamination and engulfment that is already present in such a membership. In this way the autistic tendencies of the schizoid patient can be counteracted, and a positive and even pleasurable experience of being in a group can be substituted for its frightening and isolating predecessors. For it must be remembered that, for many such patients, the mere fact of sitting in a room with other people is an unpleasant experience, rich in possibilities of destructiveness based on infantile fears of the family group. If, by dint of the 'corrective experience' of a series of comfortable and trustable group encounters, such fantasies lose their potency, some of the loneliness they engender may be mitigated, and this not only for the duration of the group. In time the fantasy of the group as good internal object will replace the bad internal object of the past. One client, who suffered greatly from loneliness and was also afraid of sleeping alone, sleeping only fitfully if there was no one else in the house, expressed it in this way: 'I'm almost ready to take the group home with me tonight.' She was about to substitute her loneliness for aloneness in its positive sense, though nothing in her external environment had changed.

It is time now to reconsider the differences between the two diagnostic groups. Guntrip (1968) has stated that, while the depressive individual fears the loss of the object, the schizoid fears the loss of the self. The main aim of groups could therefore be seen as countering the sense of loss of relationship caused by anger and guilt in the depressive, and the sense of loss of self caused by paranoia and withdrawal in the schizoid patient; ultimately the deep loneliness that is a consequence of both conditions. Foulkes (1964) brings together both aims in his concept of the work of 'translation' that is done in groups: 'The process of therapy in a group is intrinsically linked with the study and development of communication processes . . . Neurotic and psychotic disturbances are always linked with blockage in the system of communication, of socialisation of the patient, and the aim of analysis is precisely to translate the autistic symptom into a problem that can be verbalised'. A successful group will therefore work towards reducing not only the 'deviant' or disturbed behaviour of the individual, but also the sense of loneliness and differentness which accompanies such behaviour. The stipulation that all significant interactions should take place within the group's formal structure is of great importance here, because the healing and modifying process depends very much on the emotion being experienced in the presence of those to whom it related, in a framework of tolerance and freedom from valuations. This concept closely resembles Alice Miller's ideas on mirroring, in which the mother's close reflection of the infant's mood enables the baby to experience pain in her presence, thus rendering the repression of pain unnecessary: 'A child can only experience his feelings when there is somebody there who accepts him fully, understands and supports him' (Miller, 1981). The group as a transference phenomenon serves a similar purpose: just as it reproduces the mother's function in developing the capacity to be alone, it reproduces her function of encouraging the true experiencing of feeling. We have seen that it is because of the necessary avoidance of such experiencing that the schizoid individual feels so empty of emotion and unconnected with people. Similarly, if neurotic patients can learn to express anger in the group without being rejected for destructiveness, and express a sense of inadequacy without being derided for weakness, they will eventually be freed from the crippling isolation imposed on them by the turbulence of their emotions, and be able both to make and sustain the relationships they crave.

I should like in conclusion to extend some of these thoughts to the wider area of social life and living patterns, bearing in mind the original distinction between being withdrawn and lonely, and being alone in the presence of someone else. It is often held, and held in particular against those who experience difficulties with the demands of present-day society, that the ultimate indication of independence is the capacity to live alone. Anyone who has tried to set up communal living schemes with, for example, ex-psychiatric patients, will have grown accustomed to the question, from social workers as well as housing directors: 'Yes, but when will these people be *really* independent?' – meaning, when will they be able to live alone. In a sense, Winnicott's distinction could be taken to indicate that, while the capacity to be alone stems from the experience of being alone in the presence of the mother, its ultimate manifestation lies in the capacity to live alone. But in another sense, this is irrelevant: the capacity to be alone does not, when fully developed, depend on the presence or absence of others. Nevertheless, if this capacity has not been developed, it may be helpful to choose a facilitating environment of group-living to foster it; once this has been achieved, it is up to the individual to choose whether solitude or communality is the preferred lifestyle. Until that point, however, the presence of others in the same house, and the sharing of some basic facilities, can provide the nurturing environment that many people have lacked from childhood onwards. It can also, of course, lead to interpersonal conflict, but at least this conflict exists in the real world and has some chance of resolution, rather than being hopelessly re-enacted in the psyche of the individual. In this way the group, far from undermining the individual's capacity for independence, actually fosters the 'capacity to be alone' on which true independence and freedom from loneliness rest.

References

Foulkes, S.H. (1948) *Introduction to Group Analytic Psychotherapy.* London: Heinemann.
Foulkes, S.H. (1964) *Therapeutic Group Analysis.* London: George Allen and Unwin.
Guntrip, H. (1968) *Schizoid Phenomena, Object Relations and the Self.* London: Hogarth.
Kohut, H. (1977) *The Restoration of Self.* New York: International University Press.
Miller, A. (1981) *Prisoners of Childhood* (trans. Ruth Ward). New York. Published in paperback as *The Drama of the Gifted Child* (1984). London: Virago.
Winnicott, D.W. (1955) 'Aggression in relation to emotional development', paper published in *Deprivation and Delinquency* (1984). London: Tavistock.
Winnicott, D.W. (1958) 'The capacity to be alone', in *Collected Papers.* London: Tavistock.
Winnicott, D.W. (1972) *Holding and Interpretation: Fragment of an Analysis.* London: Karnac Books.

Discussion issues

1 'The capacity to be alone is one of the most important signs of maturity in emotional development.' Discuss this view on the basis of your own experience.

2 'Loneliness is a familiar state of being to most people and implies an alienation from the rest of the world that is so painful that much of life is spent, however unsuccessfully, in trying to avoid it.' What are the implications of this human situation for the counsellor/client relationship and the work of counselling?

continued

3 Outline your own recollections of a successful group experience in which you were enabled to verbalize a problem. What were the helpful characteristics of the group?

4 When might a therapeutic group be more enabling for a client than one-to-one counselling? If you had such a client how would you refer them to a group and what issues would you both need to deal with?

23

Use of the Concept of Unconscious Phantasy in Understanding Reactions to Chronic Illness

Julia Segal

Klein's concept of unconscious phantasy

Melanie Klein's concept of unconscious phantasy arose out of her work as a psychoanalyst closely following Freud. Her work with young children enabled her to understand some of the earliest levels of psychic functioning and also gave her a language in which to speak of it to others. This language enabled both her and her followers to increase our understanding not only of normal mental life, but also of the psychoses (Segal, 1992).

Klein found that she could talk to young children about the ways they perceived the world, using very simple concepts. It seemed to make sense to them when she recognized and spoke of phantasies in which people and parts of people, and the feelings and impulses connected with them, were pushed into or out of the child's body and its parents' bodies. She found children had unconscious phantasies of their parents inside them doing things both to the child and to each other. Some of these phantasies are not very far from consciousness: people easily recognize phantasies of the 'mother in your head' – the one who *really* understands you, or the one who criticizes everything you do, while the mother 'out there' is quite different (Segal, 1985).

Klein found that our perception of the world, both internal and external, is structured by these phantasies. For example, we see our parents in a sense *through* phantasies we have about them. Phantasies work as a kind of perceptual template which we lay over reality. We may or may not perceive the discrepancies between our phantasies and the real world. The phantasies themselves are shaped by the experiences we have had of the real world, but these experiences and the phantasies themselves are determined to a large extent by our emotional state at the time. The presence and behaviour of other people affects our perceptions and the consequent phantasies in many ways analysts have begun to explore.

Phantasies, then, give us ready-made, automatic assumptions with which to handle the world we live in. Some of them are very realistic; some are quite unrealistic. For example, our phantasies about our bodies in some ways will normally be fairly accurate: we do not need to think when running upstairs; we

This chapter was first published as 'The use of the concept of unconscious phantasy in understanding reactions to chronic illness', in *Counselling, Journal of the British Association for Counselling*, vol. 2, no. 4, pp. 146–9 (1991). It was originally presented as a paper to a group of Belgian psychiatrists and neurologists.

have good predictive phantasies which guide the movement of our feet. We may really have a good idea, without thinking much about it, how a member of the family would react to a particular request.

On the other hand, some phantasies are quite untrue:

More than one young woman has talked in counselling of the belief that having multiple sclerosis herself, she actually prevented other members of the family having it. One was afraid of even verbalizing her desire to 'wish it onto' a more fortunate but unpleasant cousin. The phantasy, that 'if I say it, it will come true' is a powerful determinant of behaviour for some people. Others are aware of it as an unrealistic phantasy they can laugh at.

The role of phantasy is important in understanding how people react to significant changes, such as the diagnosis of a chronic illness, or the presence of a new disability of some kind. It seems to take a long time for our basic phantasies about the world to change to fit changed reality. The process of change may involve feelings of falling apart; of furious anger; of fear of madness and of being unable to cope. These feelings may not be connected consciously with the change itself.

In order to modify the phantasies involved there must be conscious attention paid to the need for change in each affected situation. This cannot be maintained constantly and it seems that the phantasies change over time in a piecemeal way. Denial in one area may last a lot longer than denial in another, depending to some extent on how often a particular phantasy or expectation is activated, as well as on how emotionally charged it is. For example, changes in ways of eating may be accepted far sooner than changes in ways of relating to friends who are seldom seen. The tendency to slip back to using existing phantasies is always there in a situation which has not been experienced with the disability before, as well as in situations where the loss is most emotionally significant. Over a period of two years most of the phantasies determining daily behaviour seem to become adjusted to the new situation in one way or another.

Klein, after Freud, showed the importance of grief and mourning as processes in which phantasies change to fit closer to reality (Klein, 1940). Mourning gives an opportunity to distinguish between losses in the real world and phantasies of loss which are unrealistic. Some basic life-determining phantasies may be uncovered and found wanting: this can bring an increased maturity. An example of this would be where the phantasy of living forever is forced to change.

Fears of disintegration and abandonment are aroused by any significant loss. Feelings about internal loved objects are vulnerable at this point, and the sense of being internally supported liable to give way. The existence of a real external loved and supportive person can help to reduce these anxieties. Their presence may also help other phantasies involved to be brought into the open, confronted with reality and so modified.

A couple came to see me because the wife wanted me to make her husband talk to her. Since ataxia had affected his control over all his movements their relationship had steadily deteriorated. I asked the husband what the ataxia meant to him, and he said – as if I was stupid to ask such an obvious question – that it had lost him 'everything'. Sitting with this it gradually became clear that he had lost neither his job nor his wife and family. He was responsible at work for a large computer system. However, he felt he understood it really only when he could 'press the buttons' himself, which he could no longer do. This physical contact was terribly important to him. He was a man who used words only defensively; we now saw that he experienced and expressed real contact through his hands. As we talked of this his wife laughed and said that in their sexual relationship too, he had been very good at 'pressing the buttons', but he had never been much good at talking. The damage caused to their relationship by the ataxia was now seen by both of them more accurately and some of the sense of persecution both had felt disappeared. They went away to learn from a physiotherapist how to kiss again.

Klein made it clear how avoidance of grieving processes has serious consequences. Her work showed how important it is to trust in people's ability to face reality and to mourn. Any kind of lying or dissimulation undermines the sense of security and raises anxieties. This is partly because, as Klein showed, idealization is a defence against persecution: the pretence is erected not against reality but against phantasies which are worse than reality. The counsellor who assists in a cover-up and so fails to help someone make their fears more realistic is leaving them alone with unnecessary fears.

A young man was talking of his father and how useless his father was compared with himself. It occurred to me that he was ignoring the fact that his father had a wife and child which the young man himself seemed highly unlikely to do. I had the thought 'Why disturb his illusion; if it makes him feel better to feel superior to his father, why not let him?' I could not let him: I had agreed to work with him on his relationships with people. It was only after I had shown him how he cut off all recognition of his father's achievements that he told me of what he considered his real grievance against his father; he had stopped him showing his grief for the death of a teacher he loved when he was a child. He had never stopped feeling a lump in this throat since then, and in fact this showed. After this the shape of his face changed and he found a girlfriend. It seemed he had felt that admitting his father was right in any way would have meant saying he was right to stop the crying.

Loss, as I have already said, involves changing phantasies to take into account the new reality. Failure to do this work leaves us trying to live in a world in which our automatic assumptions are inadequate, prey to violent shocks as our expectations fail us.

Mourning however, is painful and difficult and it makes people angry. Sometimes the anger is expressed in refusal to make the necessary changes; people obstinately maintain quite untenable beliefs. This has all kinds of implications for relationships with other people and for the ability to think straight.

One man was insisting against all the evidence that he could still keep his business going in spite of his illness. His wife asked the counsellor to make him more realistic. She wanted the counsellor, she said, to make him see he was completely useless and unable to do anything.

Clearly neither was able to think realistically: each felt persecuted by the other's attitude and was erecting a defensive idealization against it. They seemed to be working on the basis of a phantasy whereby each carries or holds a set of beliefs or attitudes for the other in order to externalize a conflict which would otherwise be internal; in this way they were avoiding the work of mourning.

Often it helps families to realize that a considerable amount of obstinate denial is normal for two years or so. People seem to expect these things to change far more quickly than they do.

It is clear that a serious loss involves all kinds of anxieties being raised. There may be fear of a very primitive disintegration resulting from failure of a defensive system which depended on some aspect of life now lost.

Two young women with multiple sclerosis told me that their greatest loss was being active; one had played tennis all the time and one just 'was always doing something'. For both of these resting and inactivity was terrifying; what came into their minds when they were not doing things were quite frightening thoughts. One had terrible thoughts of hatred towards her mother: the other had been fending off thoughts of being useless and hopeless all her life.

The work these two had to do to modify their phantasy-world as a result of the multiple sclerosis was considerable. They had to find alternative means of dealing with these frightening anxieties; either continuing to deny them, or facing and modifying them.

They both found it helpful to have the situation described to them in these terms. They could feel that their activity prevented these thoughts from taking shape and they could recognize the anger and fear involved in having to make yet another change as a result of their multiple sclerosis. Talking of it in this way gave it a shape which restored a sense of potential control which the multiple sclerosis had undermined.

Klein's theories are expressible in the very ordinary language of everyday experience; this may make them unpalatable to French academics, but the British appreciate the extreme practicality of her concepts. They make sense of everyday experiences which previously were inexpressible, in a way which can be used with children or adults; with people who have a highly developed use of language or very limited language. This makes them particularly useful for those of us who work with people from all walks of life.

Using this very basic language, enormously complex theories have been built up. Here is not the time or place to look at the advances which have been made in the understanding of psychoses by Klein's followers such as Herbert Rosenfeld, Hanna Segal and Wilfred Bion. Here I would simply like to emphasize their use. Staff working with ex-mental hospital patients in various settings have found Kleinian interpretations of their experiences extremely enlightening. Ideas of attacks on thought, on sanity, on peace of mind and on communication have helped such staff to observe and clarify some of the disturbing experiences they were having which seriously threatened not only their work, but also their sense of themselves as good people (Segal, 1992, p. 125ff.).

Specific phantasies relevant to chronic illnesses

Kleinian ideas of particular relevance for my own work with people with multiple sclerosis include not only interrelations between past and present experiences but also phantasies about the body; perception; symbolism; grief and communication both within the psyche and between people.

Klein and her co-workers discovered that violent and aggressive phantasies are extremely common and that alongside these are powerfully loving and reparative phantasies which are vital for a healthy work- and love-life. She agreed with Ernest Jones that the subjects of the infant's phantasy-life are primarily its own body and sexual functioning, and the bodies and sexual functioning of members of the close family. She found phantasies of damage being done to these bodies and phantasies of the damage being repaired in both the internal and the external world (Klein, 1940).

Illnesses and disabilities are often interpreted as confirming some of the disturbing phantasies people have about themselves, their own bodies and the bodies of those they love. The sense that their bodies are really damaged may be interpreted in terms of these pre-existing phantasies. Some people feel their illness has been inflicted on them, perhaps as a punishment, perhaps to show the world their faith in God. They may find it difficult to separate out the real damage from primitive phantasies about damage to their insides.

Many people seem to interpret being 'bad' physically, in terms of their illness, as being 'bad' morally. Both Freud and Klein pointed out the strong relationship between the ego and the body: my own observations have shown me how clearly a sense of one's own goodness and worth seems to depend on physical health.

It is not simply one's own health which affects people.

One man said to his wife: 'I can mend the electrics, I can lay carpets, I can do the carpentry, but it all seems useless if I can't mend you.'

Sexuality is often disturbed in one way or another when one partner has a chronic illness. Klein found that men see their sexuality as potentially a source of cure and reparation; where it fails to make or keep their wife healthy, they may be thrown back on very disturbing phantasies in which it is a source of danger and damage. The belief that sexuality is dangerous to an ill person is common and it can be important to examine it to see how much it corresponds to reality.

In general, the symbolism involved in reactions to a chronic illness can be explored. I ask people what the illness means to them.

One young woman told me how her illness had stopped her working, how it had made her fall out with particular members of the family and make friends with others; and how difficult it was that diagnosis followed so soon on the death of her father. After a time she also told me how she sometimes sat in the corner withdrawn and depressed. She emphasized how close she was to her father; she now told me how he too had been depressed and withdrawn; how he had been unable to hold a job; how he had disliked certain members of the family and liked others. The similarity was striking and I remarked how the effects of the multiple sclerosis she had described were exactly ones which would make her just like her father. I pointed out that often people tried to overcome the loss of a parent by becoming them, as a way of avoiding having to know they had lost them. It seemed she did these things attributing them to the multiple sclerosis, when perhaps they were most attributable to her attempt to deny the loss of her father. This seemed to make sense to her, and her behaviour and relationships changed considerably.

This is not the only instance where it seemed that the multiple sclerosis some-how stood for a damaged internal parent. Another young woman talked of the fear of losing her job, and how important it was in her relationship with her father; it seemed with her too that the multiple sclerosis stood for an internal father. Often people have bad relations with one or both parents, and counselling which confronts this seems to be helpful. Multiple sclerosis attacks the spine, the 'backbone', which gives internal support, and allows people to stand up in society. With such people it seems that helping them to grieve over the relationship with their parent enables them to re-establish a sense of being supported. This in turn helps them to distinguish between losses which are a necessary part of the multiple sclerosis and losses which are not. Losing a job may not be necessary, nor may falling out with particular members of the family, or determining never to marry or have children.

There are other consequences of the multiple sclerosis diagnosis which are common and which can be usefully understood in terms of the phantasies involved.

It is common for people to withdraw from social life as a result of their diagnosis. They say things like 'I can't bear people who know me to see me like this'. They may be happy going out in the street in a wheelchair in places where nobody knows them, but near home they prefer to stay hidden. This kind of statement bears examination.

A young man who had gone to live in solitude as a result of the diagnosis of multiple sclerosis talked of his dislike of allowing his friends to see him like this. It turned out that he was afraid that if he saw them in their fancy cars, with their girl friends and houses which he felt he could never have, he would say something horrible to them and they would never want to speak to him again. He preferred never to see them rather than to do that. It was clear that it was his own envy and jealousy which he feared. We sat with this. As he left I asked him how he felt about the session and he said 'It's funny, I thought I was a nice bloke, but it's good . . .'

Melanie Klein drew attention to the role of envy as a powerfully destructive force attacking good and healthy development in many different ways (Klein, 1957). Later Kleinians have also pointed out how one part of the psyche can envy or be jealous of another and so attack it (e.g. Rosenfeld, 1971). Envy can attack (as in this case) relationships, creativity, goodness and sanity in particular. Recognition and acknowledgement of these processes can help bring about important changes. Once the young man was aware that his motivations arose from a 'bad' self rather than a 'good' self as he had imagined, he was able to see how much he was preventing himself from living a fuller life. With more sense of being in control he was able to alter his life style considerably. He moved and took a job and his social isolation ended.

Bion's understanding of the sense of isolation is more fundamental; the attacks on internal communication represented by denial in any form may leave the individual with a sense of being cut off which is not just an unrealistic phantasy but has some real representation in the internal world (Bion, 1955). Attempts to cut off unwanted feelings must leave part of the personality isolated from the rest; the sense of isolation may then replace the other unwanted feelings. Where counselling or psychotherapy can help people to face parts of their personality, rather than avoid them and cut them off, the sense of isolation too may be prevented.

The cutting off of bad feelings is bound to affect relationships. People are sensitive to being kept out of secret parts of the mind and the rejection involved may be very painful. It is common for people to 'protect' each other by withholding information, in particular about negative states of mind, in the belief that 'they have enough to cope with as it is'. They fear that the person they love will feel their own misery or upset or anger as an unbearable burden. This prevents real mutual support.

With a chronic illness anxieties are raised and the sense of persecution is raised. Klein formulated the concepts of the paranoid–schizoid position in which splitting and persecution rule, and the depressive position in which integration, guilt and depressive anxieties are more powerful (Segal, 1992). Under pressure, paranoid–schizoid anxieties are more likely to come to the fore, and the more mature depressive mechanism to be overtaken. The sense that people can cope with guilt, sadness, and loss depends on the mechanisms and states of mind accompanying the depressive position; in the paranoid–schizoid position these feelings are simply perceived as discomfort to be done away with. This reversion to a more primitive and destructive way of dealing with feelings may have serious consequences for relationships (Segal, 1985).

How people succeed or fail in modifying their anxieties depends upon the support, input and receptivity of those around them. Bion spelt out the 'containing' aspect of parental figures, who can take in the infant's fears and pain and transform them into bearable and usable feelings, language or symbols (Bion, 1961). On this relationship depends the reality-sense; the closeness or otherwise of phantasies to reality; the benign and supportive or malignant and destructive state of what are felt to be internal objects (that is, people or parts of people 'inside'). The counsellor or psychotherapist can clearly function as a 'good container' if she or he succeeds in taking in and transforming some of the client's fears.

I want to look now briefly at the role of a counsellor or psychotherapist.

We can distinguish two ways in which the counsellor can help modify phantasies and transform anxieties. The first is simple and straightforward. It involves helping clients to recognize their own experience and to redefine it as normal and bearable. Someone may come to the counsellor frightened because they are experiencing terrible feelings of being unable to cope; of wanting to cry; of losing control. The counsellor can help them to tease out what some of their feelings are. The counsellor's recognition of these states and acceptance of them as normal in the circumstances seems to help people regain some sense of control over the situation.

All of this is fairly simple and for many people it is enough. But there are some people where the counsellor or psychotherapist may find themselves behaving slightly differently. Sometimes it happens that people tell me things which evoke feelings in me quite different from those they are apparently experiencing.

A young woman told me of her relationship with her mother, who had multiple sclerosis. She said it was a very good relationship; she was the favourite and she had a role in the family of keeping people cheerful. She had not done very well at school, but she had never wanted to. She had a relationship with a young man who depended on her for everything; that was alright, her parents weren't very happy about it but they let her do anything she wanted. By the end of the session I was feeling absolutely exhausted and quite afraid. I was not sure I was able to do my job; was I good enough? Shouldn't I find someone else to do it rather than me?

I considered the reality of this, and in fact ultimately did find someone else to take this young woman on. But I also looked at the possibility that these feelings were some kind of non-verbal communication from the woman of feelings she could not bear to perceive herself. They seemed quite out of proportion to what she had said she felt.

Bion, amongst other Kleinian analysts, helped us to see how people sometimes evoke in others feelings they cannot bear to experience in themselves (Joseph, 1987). In phantasy they may put their bad mental state into another person. How those around react to these feelings is of enormous importance. If they are taken as a communication of an experience which can be shared, there is great potential for change and development. If they are simply thrown back accusingly, there is great potential for feelings of persecution.

With this client, the communicative aspect of these counter-transference feelings was confirmed over the next few weeks. My sense of an impossible task reflected her powerful phantasies that she was keeping her mother alive single-handed. My feelings that someone else should be doing my job seemed to reflect her unconscious conviction that the task was too much for her and someone else should be doing it. Uncovering and verbalizing these phantasies was enough to throw a new doubt on them and so to modify them.

Use of the feelings arising in the counsellor or therapist has to be considered very carefully. They need to be taken seriously both as a perception of reality – I did need to pass her on – and as a communication from the client. Where they can be used successfully as a communication, as in this case, the client can begin to work with aspects of herself she previously did not recognize. She learnt to grieve and to recognize that she did want to depend on someone, not just herself. This was a very painful discovery for both of us because it showed up a real loss in her life; she did not feel she had had a dependable mother because of the multiple sclerosis. The immediate result was that she recognized difficulties in her relation with her boyfriend as well as her parents. It was hard to hold on to the fact that ultimately this would improve her life; at the time it felt frightening.

It is always a worry to me when I use this kind of experience in my counselling. I am always very careful to seek evidence in the client's actual material which shows that the feelings I have may indeed be not only attributable to my own state of mind; even then I will couch my exploration in terms which the client can reject if she so wishes. It is important to avoid succumbing to the temptation to take control by replacing the experience of not knowing with the illusion of knowing.

Sometimes it is important just to sit with a client while feelings of despair and misery, fury and hopelessness are experienced by both of us. The temptation to transform experience into explanatory words which actually miss the full impact is to be avoided. It seems that just sharing bad feelings may be important at times. Bion gives us some understanding of the value of this process.

Conclusion

Klein's concept of unconscious phantasy and the work of later analysts using her ideas has led to a rich source of ideas for helping people examine and understand their feelings, thoughts and behaviour. Here I have tried to sketch in some of the ideas I find useful in my own work.

The concept of phantasy gives us a language which can make sense of everyday experiences. I have described some of the specific phantasies relevant to chronic illnesses; such as those affecting illness and sexuality; the sense of isolation; grief and mourning; and relationship problems. I have shown some of the ways in which counselling or brief psychotherapy for people with a chronic illness can affect their phantasies and consequently not only their experience of the illness but also their relationships.

Further reading

Bion, W.R. (1955/1971) 'Language and the schizophrenic', in M. Klein et al. (eds) *New Directions in Psychoanalysis*. London: Tavistock Publications.

Bion, W.R. (1961) 'A theory of thinking', in E. Bott Spillins (ed.) *Melanie Klein Today*, Vol. 1. London: Routledge and the Institute of Psychoanalysis.

Joseph, B. (1987) 'Projective identification – some clinical aspects', in E. Bott Spillins (ed.) *Melanie Klein Today*, Vol. 1. London: Routledge and the Institute of Psychoanalysis.

Klein, M. (1940) 'Mourning and its relation to manic-depressive states', in *The Writings of Melanie Klein*, Vol. 1. London: Hogarth Press and the Institute of Psychoanalysis.

Klein, M. (1957) 'Envy and gratitude', in *The Writings of Melanie Klein*, Vol. 3. London: Hogarth Press and the Institute of Psychoanalysis.

Rosenfeld (1971) 'A clinical approach to the psychoanalytic theory of the life and death instincts', in E. Bott Spillins (ed.) *Melanie Klein Today*, Vol. 1. London: Routledge and the Institute of Psychoanalysis.

Segal, H.M. (1973) *Introduction to The Work of Melanie Klein*, 2nd edn. London: Hogarth Press and the Institute of Psychoanalysis.

Segal, J.C. (1985) *Phantasy in Everyday Life*. Harmondsworth: Penguin (reprinted in 1991); London: Karnac (1995).

Segal, J.C. (1986) *Emotional Reactions to MS*. MSRC publication. (Available from Multiple Sclerosis Resources Centre, 4a Chapel Hill, Stansted, Essex CM24 8AG. Tel: 01279 817101).

Segal, J.C. (1989) 'Counselling people with disabilities/chronic illnesses', in Windy Dryden, Ray Woolfe and David Charles-Edwards (eds) *Handbook of Counselling in Britain*. London: Tavistock/Routledge.

Segal, J.C. (1992) *Melanie Klein: Key Figures in Counselling and Psychotherapy*. London: Sage.

Segal, J.C. and Simkins, J. (1996) *My Mum Needs Me. Helping Children with Ill or Disabled Parents*. London: Jessica Kingsley.

Discussion issues

1 How do you think you would feel if you were diagnosed with a chronic illness?

2 What would be your greatest fear if you had a disabling disease? Do others share this fear or not?

3 What experiences of illness or disability do you draw upon to understand others' experiences? What have you learnt from these? How do these lessons compare with others' lessons from their experience?

4 Would you expect to be lovable if you had a serious disability or illness? How do others' reactions compare with yours?

24

The Effects of Medication on Counselling

Diane Hammersley and Linda Beeley

It can be enormously frustrating for a counsellor to get 'stuck'; very often it is not long before the client feels it too. There are clients who constantly work on issues but do not seem able to get in touch with their feelings. Some do well in sessions but fail to transfer what insight they gain into real life. Others understand the problem and their feelings about it but are unable to make changes in their behaviour. However you deal with it; examining your own part; discussing it with your supervisor; confronting what is being avoided or exploring the process, there may be occasions when the problem remains unresolved. There are many ways of approaching this difficulty; for instance Paul Ware's theory of personality adaptations 'Doors to Therapy' (1983) can have dramatic results. However it is possible that outside factors are affecting the counselling, of which the most important might be the medication which the client is taking (Hammersley, 1995).

Implications of medication for the client

Clients who come for counselling are sometimes receiving psychotropic drugs for social and psychological problems. These include benzodiazepines (tranquillizers and sleeping tablets), antidepressants and antipsychotic drugs used in small doses for anxiety and other non-psychotic conditions. We are not referring to drugs used to treat psychotic conditions. The client on medication of whom we are thinking has at some time probably sought help with physical symptoms of stress, feelings of depression or with the thought that 'something might be wrong with them'. Accepting a prescription from the GP implies a medical view of the problem and a treatment for the symptoms rather than the problem itself.

Many people have greatly exaggerated expectations of what drugs can do, assuming that if drugs have been prescribed they are necessary, will continue to work and are part of the 'cure'. Clients are often unaware of the disadvantages of taking them for emotional problems. In the short term drugs often do relieve symptoms of tension, worry, crying and distress but it is just these symptoms which are the means of access to the underlying problem. Drugs can limit the person's ability to think (Golombok et al., 1988), feel and act but it is necessary for people to be in touch with their symptoms in order to work on and resolve them. For example, clients coming off benzodiazepines frequently have to deal with unresolved bereavements and forgotten sexual abuse in childhood which they cannot begin to do until they are almost drug-free (Priest and Montgomery, 1988).

This chapter was first published in *Counselling, Journal of the British Association for Counselling*, vol. 3, no. 3, pp. 162–4 (1992).

Drugs have side-effects and the client may wrongly think that these are part of the underlying problem.

Implications for the therapist

Therapy is essentially about defining and working through problems which underlie symptoms and to do this the client needs to be able to think clearly, to have access to feelings and the skills to do things differently. Above all, the client needs the symptoms because they act as a focus for the problem and its expression and as a 'thermometer' of change. Clients also need to be able to tell when they are 'getting to the bottom of things'.

Drugs remove the symptoms which motivate the client to deal with the underlying problem. They are one way of removing symptoms but they leave the cause of the symptoms unresolved. Lying awake at night going over the past or anticipating the future may be 'cured' by taking sleeping tablets; however, experiencing the worrying alerts the client to changes that need to be made. The re-experience of emotional pain may be necessary to work through past traumas. Clients need also to experience fully the relationship with the counsellor and the interactions that occur between them.

One implicit assumption in counselling is that the client has internal resources to take responsibility for finding real solutions. Conveying this belief to the client is undermined if you accept the drug use without question. Progress may be attributed to the drug rather than to the client's own efforts. Deciding to come off is the first step towards the client accepting responsibility and changing their view of themselves from being 'unable to cope' to being 'willing to find new ways to cope'. Counselling and drugs are therefore often incompatible approaches.

Effects of drugs

Benzodiazepines

What they are used for

Current recommendations on prescribing are that benzodiazepines should be used 'for the short-term relief (two to four weeks only) of anxiety that is severe, disabling or subjecting the individual to unacceptable distress, occurring alone or in association with insomnia or short-term psychosomatic, organic or psychotic illness. They should be used to treat insomnia only when it is severe, disabling, or subjecting the individual to extreme distress' (Committee on Safety of Medicines 1988). However in practice they seem to be frequently prescribed inappropriately for emotional distress, relationship difficulties, bereavement, depression, panic attacks, phobias and obsessions. Inevitably, this leads to their long-term use. They are also frequently used long term for insomnia, particularly for elderly people.

They are also prescribed for physical illness which is thought to be stress related; for example, irritable bowel syndrome, heart conditions, frequent headaches and as a muscle relaxant. Often such people will have had many medical investigations and may be taking other medication.

Unwanted effects

There are many possible side-effects which can mimic a variety of common complaints and are often not recognized (Ashton, 1984; *British National Formulary*, 1995). Some people never experience them but the chance of them occurring increases with long-term use.

Physical:

Nausea	Headache
Vomiting	Blurred vision
Constipation	Tinnitus
Diarrhoea	Dizziness
Irritable bowel syndrome	Vertigo
Rashes	Unsteadiness
Aches and pains	Numbness and tingling
Low blood pressure	Tiredness/drowsiness
Loss of libido	Lethargy
Impotence	Insomnia

Psychological:

Anxiety	Poor concentration
Depression	Poor memory
Agoraphobia	Confusion
Panic attacks	Irritability
Tension	Aggressive outbursts
Emotional numbness	Disinhibition
Social withdrawal	Obsessions

Long-term effects

People who have taken benzodiazepines for longer than six months may experience cognitive, affective and behavioural problems (Golombok et al., 1988). They may, for example, complain of their mind being in constant turmoil and find it difficult to think constructively. They have a tendency to interpret events negatively, always expecting the worst, blaming themselves and seeing themselves as failures. Affectively they seem cut-off, unable to experience or express feelings and have lost their sense of humour and the ability to have fun. Sexual activity has often disappeared. The agoraphobia shows itself in fear of going out or being left in the house alone and avoidance of large gatherings or even family visits. All activity is reduced, especially leisure activities and creative pursuits. Nurturing is directed at other people frequently at the expense of self. Some of these changes may be part of the problem presented to the counsellor.

Dependence

Benzodiazepine dependence has both physical and psychological components (Edwards et al., 1990). With clients who have been taking these drugs for several months or at high doses, there is the possibility that if the drug is stopped they will experience withdrawal symptoms, although it is not possible to predict this with any certainty. However, the possibility should not be ignored. In addition the person may have irrational beliefs about what the drug does for them and feel that they can not cope without it. This reliance on an external solution can inhibit the client's chance of identifying and developing their own internal strategies. The counsellor's efforts to draw on the client's internal resources may be thwarted by the continual return to the established pattern of seeking external solutions. An important decision in treatment is necessarily whether drug withdrawal is to be a part of the therapeutic approach.

Antidepressants

Antidepressants may be helpful when people are profoundly depressed, totally dysfunctional and therapeutically inaccessible. In less depressed people who are accessible to a counselling approach, antidepressants may have little effect and can sometimes make the depression worse. Antidepressants do not lead to the same distortions in thinking, feeling and behaviour as do the benzodiazepines and are less likely to cause therapeutic inaccessibility. However removing the symptoms of depression leaves the client without the signposts to the underlying problem. Since clients can make therapeutic gains while on antidepressants, continuing them is more compatible with counselling than continuing benzodiazepines, but they will need to be withdrawn for therapy to be completed. Resolution of problems cannot be assumed until drugs have been withdrawn and repressed material has been allowed to come to the surface. Gains will then belong to the client and will not be ascribed to the drugs.

As with benzodiazepines there can be both physical and psychological dependence and withdrawal effects can occur when the drug is stopped. These are less frequent and less severe than with the benzodiazepines and rarely present a problem. Antidepressant withdrawal is described in more detail by Dilsaver (1989).

Antipsychotics

Antipsychotic drugs are increasingly used in low doses as an alternative to benzodiazepines for the treatment of anxiety and other emotional distress. Although such doses do not produce the profound effects seen in people on higher doses, they nevertheless have side-effects which can interfere with counselling. These clients often seem very cut-off and therapeutically inaccessible. They may be unable to retain gains made in therapy or recall the work of previous sessions. Again, use of drugs perpetuates the tendency to rely on external means of coping and makes it difficult to attribute improvement to the client's efforts rather than to the drug. Some of the side-effects of antipsychotic drugs can mimic psychological symptoms such as anxiety, tension and depression, causing confusion for the counsellor.

Dependence and withdrawal symptoms are not usually a problem although even after low doses psychological symptoms can occur which do require the attention of the counsellor. Gradually re-experiencing reality, horrific nightmares and the return of emotion can be frightening and the client may need a lot of support.

Assessment

The significance of prescribed medication should be considered at the beginning of counselling because it will affect the decisions to be made about the scope and depth of the therapy. The counsellor will also need to consider whether or not coming off drugs will be part of the contract. However assessment is done, consideration of prescribed drugs should always be included.

Since drugs affect people's thinking, feeling and behaviour, the client's presentation and problems at the first contact may reflect this. Distortions in thinking, difficulty in expressing or controlling feelings, manner and dress may be indications of the drug's effects.

The wider context

In addition to taking a personal history, considerations relevant to the medical and psychological history could also be noted. These would include past and current drug use, including those which are bought over the counter. In considering dependence it is important to consider all addictive behaviour, including alcohol use, smoking, gambling and eating disorders. The client needs also to be seen in the wider setting of the family; the taking of drugs by one member might, for instance, be the way the whole family copes with its problems.

Rapport

In considering whether to accept the client for counselling, the counsellor will be assessing the potential for forming a therapeutic alliance. Clients taking psychotropic drugs may seem to have less insight, be less willing to explore feelings and take responsibility for themselves. They may appear to be poorly motivated, expressing reluctance to travel, join a group, take time off work or commit themselves to regular sessions. This may be a reflection of their ambivalence about their drug use, so rather than dismissing a client as unready for counselling, it might be productive for the counsellor to work with this ambivalence for a while.

The contract

If clients are taking drugs they will already have been offered and accepted help and it is important to explore their view of this. Taking drugs is a way of handing over responsibility and this may still be what they seek. It is crucial to make clear to the client that work at depth is not possible while psychotropic drugs are being taken. If withdrawal is part of the contract, the client needs to know how long it will take, and in the case of benzodiazepines this is frequently underestimated.

Withdrawing drugs

Withdrawal of prescribed drugs in counselling requires specialist knowledge described elsewhere (Hamlin and Hammersley, 1989). It is essential that drugs are always withdrawn gradually and at the client's own pace. Pressure to withdraw is usually counter-productive and the client has the right to make an informed decision. We advise that drugs are usually withdrawn in this order: antipsychotics, benzodiazepines, antidepressants. If prescribed drugs are being withdrawn it is important to monitor other drug use and particularly to note increases in alcohol consumption. Problem drinking should be dealt with first. If this is not the time to come off drugs, particularly benzodiazepines, the counsellor should consider whether it is appropriate to embark on counselling for the underlying problems. The door can be left open.

Counselling clients withdrawing from benzodiazepines requires a more intrusive therapeutic style than many counsellors are accustomed to, because of the client's inaccessibility. It is important to address distorted thinking, emotional numbness and passivity and so a wide variety of therapeutic approaches is necessary. Therapy and withdrawal are best integrated, with the depth of therapy increasing as withdrawal proceeds. The counsellor will need to respond to the intermittent resurfacing of repressed material, and be prepared for this to be delayed for some months after withdrawal is complete.

Liaison

It is important that counsellors see their role in relation to the prescriber clearly and deal with the problems that may arise when care is shared. Conflicting advice undermines the client's determination to withdraw from drugs and seek real solutions to problems. The medical view of emotional problems may focus on the removal of symptoms and the avoidance of pain, which 'rescues' people from the need to face their real difficulties. The counselling task is to encourage the client to experience the pain and work through it.

When working with clients on prescribed drugs, it is both courteous and desirable to inform the prescriber of their counselling and to work cooperatively whenever possible. It is tempting while liaising with the prescriber to reach agreements in which the client takes no part. Encouraging the client to take a responsible part in the liaison and decision-making is empowering for the client and respects the equality of the counsellor and prescriber. Doctors are under pressure not to prescribe benzodiazepines long term but this may be necessary for people who are already dependent. Clients who do not want to come off may need an advocate who recognizes that the client is the best person to judge this and can support this decision. The decision to stay on is never final.

Conclusion

Clients who get 'stuck', unable to resolve their problem, may drop out of therapy or hang on waiting for a resolution which does not occur. If this 'stuckness' is due to the drugs they are taking, it sometimes resolves itself when they reduce or stop their drugs. It is at this point that the part that the drugs play in inhibiting resolution becomes apparent. Because the client's drug use has important implications for assessment, level of therapy, choice of intervention, possible outcome and liaison, counsellors are well advised to consider drugs in their assessment. Will drug withdrawal be part of the therapy? If it is, it should be done first. If it is not, then it is important to help the client to set realistic goals.

This is the case whatever style of therapy is used and whether the setting is medical or non-medical. It is simplistic to assume that medical practitioners and counsellors have separate areas of competence. In the same way that doctors are enthusiastically embracing some of the skills of counselling, counsellors need not regard drugs as outside their field of operation or competence.

References

Ashton, H. (1984) 'Benzodiazepine withdrawal: an unfinished story', *British Medical Journal*, 288: 1135–40.

British National Formulary (1995) No. 28. The Pharmaceutical Press.

Committee on Safety of Medicines (1988) *Current Problems*, No. 21.

Dilsaver, S.C. (1989) 'Antidepressant withdrawal syndromes: phenomenology and pathophysiology', *Acta Psychiatrica Scandinavica* 79: 113–17.

Edwards, J.G., Cantopher, T. and Olivieri, S. (1990) 'Benzodiazepine dependence and the problems of withdrawal', *Postgraduate Medical Journal*, 66: S27–S35.

Golombok, S., Moodley, P. and Lader, M. (1988) 'Cognitive impairment in long-term benzodiazepine users', *Psychological Medicine*, 18: 365–74.

Hamlin, M.A. and Hammersley, D.E. (1989) 'Managing benzodiazepine withdrawal', in G. Bennett (ed.), *Treating Drug Abusers*. London: Tavistock/Routledge.

Hammersley, D.E. (1995) *Counselling People on Prescribed Drugs*. London: Sage.

Priest, R.G. and Montgomery, S.A. (1988) 'Benzodiazepines and dependence: a College statement', *Bulletin of the Royal College of Psychiatrists*, 12: 107–8.

Ware, P. (1983) 'Personality adaptations (doors to therapy)', *Transactional Analysis Journal*, 13(1): 11–19.

Discussion issues

1 What criteria would you use to decide whether to accept a client on medication for counselling?
2 What might lead you to suspect that your client was taking medication?
3 What drug side-effects might be confused with psychological problems?
4 How would you work with a client dependent on medication?

25

Counselling and Homelessness

Anne Bentley

Homelessness is a national problem that has risen rapidly over the past thirty years. It is difficult to define, address and work with. Anyone wishing to do so is faced with a complex picture of 'the ceaseless interplay of demographic, social and economic forces' (Greve and Currie, 1991) and their emotional toll on the individuals affected.

There are many categories of homelessness and as such no agreement as to how many people are homeless. It is known however that between 1962 and 1989 the number of households living in temporary accommodation rose from 5,000 to 36,000 (Greve and Currie, 1991). Single people make up a large part of the population of 'hidden homeless' in Britain. Faced with the certainty of a dispiritingly long wait for council housing, they share accommodation with relatives, friends or casual acquaintances, occupy squats and other forms of temporary accommodation, much of it substandard or squalid. They form a high proportion of the residents of hostels, houses in multiple occupation and bed-and-breakfast hotels. The National Federation of Housing Associations in 1989 made a 'conservative estimate' of 125,000 single people in London either homeless, or on the margins of homelessness in temporary accommodation (Greve and Currie, 1991). The increased visibility of people begging on the streets, at rail and tube stations, sleeping in shop doorways, or selling 'The Big Issue' highlight a cause for concern.

Homelessness of whatever category therefore appears to be growing. This article focuses on a neglected area of research, that of counselling and homeless people. I examine the meaning of 'homelessness' in a psychological sense and the distinguishing features of this client group. Drawing on my counselling work with those affected by homelessness at St Martin-in-the-Fields Social Care Unit, I try to show that for the literally 'roofless' open-ended counselling is not the most appropriate form of supportive service. When offered, however, as part of a resettlement process an important 'place' for long-term counselling is created. In this situation the focus of my counselling centres upon the nurturing of trust, safety and continuity in the relationship, to support and maintain the parallel commitment to a resettled way of life and to a process of developing emotional resources to sustain it in a more fulfilling way.

The meaning of homelessness

The term homeless applies to more than just those sleeping rough in Britain. To be homeless is to be insecure, to have no permanent claim to individual space, no

This chapter was first published as 'Counselling and homelessness', in *Counselling, Journal of the British Association for Counselling*, vol. 5, no. 2, pp. 132–4 (1994).

sense of being able to build on the emotional foundation a sense of home provides. As one of my clients at St Martin's stated:

'A home is more than just a place to stay, it's about stability and relationships.'

The effect of homelessness on the self and psychological development is profound in terms of the individual's ability to recognize and meet basic living requirements. Rogers and Stevens (1967) suggest that an infant values experiences that positively contribute towards life enhancement, one of these being 'security, and the holding and caressing which seem to communicate security'.

An infant's locus of evaluation is within themself. Over time and exposure to others' regulation of behaviour and their feelings, 'the individual relinquishes the locus of evaluation which was his in infancy and places it in others' (Rogers and Stevens, 1967).

In this way we 'accumulate the introjected value patterns by which we live'. In relation to homelessness I contend that these individuals have lost touch with the profound awareness of their individual 'organismic self' (Rogers and Stevens, 1967) and the valuing of security that this self would have. They are unable to meet and value one of the basic human needs, that Maslow (1962) calls 'instinctoid', such as shelter.

Maslow believes in a needs hierarchy, with humans having to meet four basic ordered needs before self-actualization or supreme human development needs can be satisfied. These needs are: physiological, safety, belonging and love, and esteem. Together, all four are instinctoid and failure to satisfy the need for security impedes growth toward 'self-actualization' and 'one's personal idiosyncratic potentialities' remain unfulfilled. In terms of valuing basic need provision, Maslow's (1962) and Rogers and Stevens' (1967) understandings seem to suggest that long-term homeless without the ability to take care of basic 'instinctoid' needs, are deaf to the inner prompting of their individual human emotional requirements. Consequently, before emotional needs can be addressed through counselling, satisfaction of physiological and safety needs must have occurred. This was in keeping with my counselling experience at St Martin's. Without adequate food and clothing, physical security and stability, clients were unable to use counselling constructively.

Integrating this into a humanistic conception of the individual who has lost touch with 'the ground of his being' (Mearns and Thorne, 1988), the homeless are bereft as they have found themselves in a position outside mainstream society. By not having a place in either a literal or non-literal sense, they can be perceived as rejected and discarded. Homeless people may have lost a sense of how to meet the expectations society places on them and face adapting to a life with different values and expectations. Janiel (1987) states: 'Life goes on and daily life becomes modified in response to the absence of home and related issues.' This 'modification' consists of finding a way of being in a different world.

Stuart McDonald, a homeless man featured in a Channel Four Television programme 'A–Z: Letters from the Homeless' in April 1993, said homeless life is characterized by 'Lack of money, lack of friends, lack of anywhere to go, lack of any contacts with "normality". You don't have any friends as such, just people you know who are homeless themselves.'

Stuart speaks of the perpetually violent atmosphere which occurs because 'the way you're living is very brutalizing and you just fall into that sort of set up'.

Homeless life is characterized by what it lacks. The focus moves away from the future, and becomes fixed upon day-to-day survival. It features 'a deprived family background, educational failure, poor health, unemployment and low income' (Greve and Currie, 1991), though, of course, some of these characteristics will be exacerbated by the experience of homelessness itself.

From a psychodynamic perspective, the powerlessness, frustration and visible deprivation of a homeless person demonstrate an inability to influence positively their external environment and can be seen as the symptom of an internal, psychological conflict. This, in turn, can be viewed in terms of a powerless ego unable to influence some instinctive id demands which are repressed and as Freud (1964) describes, 'may break through into the ego and into consciousness in the form of unrecognizable and distorted substitutes and create what we call symptoms'.

As the homeless person, for whatever reason, is unable to ensure their physical containment in accommodation, their poor 'ego strength' or coping ability means that they are similarly unable to contain their instinctive id demands. The counselling task then becomes to strengthen and develop existing coping mechanisms as a basis for later more in-depth work. I would argue that with such clients, psychodynamic work that does not incorporate person-centred approaches to relationship building may not be the most appropriate form of early therapeutic intervention.

Can counselling really help?

Successful counselling work at St Martin's has involved working with recently resettled people, supporting them in adapting to life with a roof over their heads. Counselling has been offered with little success to clients actually sleeping rough. Schutt and Garrett (1992) point out:

> Working with homeless persons is more than just a job: it is reaching out to people in extreme crisis; it is creating a bond to restore stability, it . . . involves the most delicate interpersonal problems and the least tractable interorganizational conflicts – it involves being there after others have left.

The roofless clients who expressed an interest in having counselling were unable to sustain commitment for more than two or three sessions, often returning later however when faced with a crisis. This raises the question can 'street homeless' clients internalize counsellor 'kindness'? It is my belief that a life based on uncertainty, characterized by a concern for immediate survival, renders the commitment for counselling impossible. Instability and a history of unsustained, often traumatic interpersonal relationships makes it difficult to have the confidence to trust the counselling process. The roofless client who comes to counselling is acknowledging the existence of impeding emotional difficulties or a lapse in coping ability, but is unable to do more than that whilst day-to-day life is spent attempting to meet needs for food, places to wash, visiting DSS offices and protection. There is a difficulty in investing trust in the counsellor in a life devoid of 'significant others'. This client group had an ability to experience the nurturing authority of the counsellor in the counselling session. But there it ended, each session a glass of water for a mouth that would soon go dry.

An explanation may be provided by looking at the motives that caused this client group to seek help in the first place. Generally, the kinds of problems experienced by roofless clients were situational in nature such as a partner's sexual infidelity, theft, or being the target of outside aggression, all of which interfered with the process of life. Given this, I would propose crisis counselling, focusing on building upon the client's strengths and maintaining functional defences to help the client through the situation. In-depth work which may bring the client into contact with painful unconscious feelings could overwhelm the client and undermine coping ability. It is worth remembering that the roofless client does not have the privacy of accommodation to return to after counselling. I believe that this may have accounted for the poor attendance of roofless clients to open-ended counselling. However my attempts established me as a trustworthy person who could be returned to in times of crisis. Helping roofless clients to acquire the skills of crisis management may help them to progress beyond living from crisis to crisis. It may later enable them to make use of more brief, focused work, but the extent of psychological damage renders the fulfilment of such hopes a long-term objective.

Hence preoccupation with immediate needs and crises makes commitment for counselling difficult, which would suggest that for counselling to be successful clients should at least be in some kind of secure accommodation and be free from basic immediate needs. This corresponds to American data on homeless alcoholics and the mentally ill, highlighting the high drop-out rates for those receiving treatment without housing. When treatment was provided in conjunction with housing, drop-out rates plummeted (Rosenheck et al., 1992).

This is illustrated in the case of Joe, who visited St Martin's Welfare Service for counselling. His history involved long periods spent in different cities travelling to where he could find work as a plasterer, returning home frequently to his mother in Newcastle for holidays. Whilst living for a spell in London his mother became seriously ill. Joe gathered his belongings and vacated his house, pushing the keys back through the letter box. Joe's arrival at home produced arguments with his brother who had assumed Joe's role as eldest son and was supervising his mother's care. The tension and arguments reached the point where Joe's mother asked him to leave without realizing that he had no place to return to. Upon his return to London the local authorities refused to accept Joe's request for housing assistance as he came under the category of 'intentionally' homeless. Joe then slept out on the streets until he was accessed by an outreach team who provided hostel accommodation and eventually resettlement into a shared flat. Joe learnt in the hostel that his mother had died whilst he had been sleeping rough and that he had missed the funeral. It was at this point that Joe requested counselling for 'depression'. I saw him weekly and used the sessions to explore the impact of the losses of family home and refuge, his mother and contact with his immediate family.

Counselling Joe was very challenging as he was unused to thinking introspectively and found it difficult to examine the causes of his depression and to realize the extent of his loss. He was insecure in his accommodation, having problems with his alcoholic, criminally inclined flatmate and with noise and abuse from his neighbours. Progress was slow as I tried to provide Joe with 'unconditional positive regard' in the face of his sensation of being a burden and constantly blaming himself for not being present at his mother's funeral. After nine sessions, Joe didn't return for four weeks and made no response to my letter. When he reappeared, he explained that, unable to bear the living situation at his flat, he had once again packed a bag, put the keys through the letter box and slept on the streets before presenting himself at his former hostel, where staff, appreciative of his difficulties, helped him to find a new flat which he moved into three weeks later.

Joe was unable to use counselling whilst actually homeless; as he said to me, 'I didn't want to think about anything. I just wanted to get through the day'. He was unable to reach out for help. The impact of the loss of his family relationships meant that there was nobody to go back to. His sense of self was hinged on the security of his mother and home in Newcastle. Rejection by his family underlined his sense of helplessness and inability to influence his own life positively.

An encouraging factor was that the sessions preceding Joe's homelessness had established me as someone he could come back to, someone who would accept and help him.

Having found that counselling is more likely to be successful when integrated with housing services, my role requires an understanding that simply being placed in accommodation does not alter the emotional and social deprivation from which the homeless crisis arose. Being given a house does not mean that psychologically you are no longer homeless. In fact removing the pressure of responding to immediate needs can give space for other emotional ones to resurface. When provided with secure physical and therapeutic space, clients can learn to recognize, name and work on satisfying emotional needs, leading to the abandonment of those traditional ways of coping that may have once enabled them to survive street life but are no longer necessary for and in fact impede, successful resettlement.

This occurred with Ben who had become homeless as a result of his alcoholism and violence towards his wife which led to his divorce. Fiercely independent and full of self-blame he steered away from approaching agencies for help, claiming benefit and living in a government hostel. One day when accompanying his friend to St Martin's Welfare Service, he accepted a housing appointment. The success of his housing interview prompted him to work on his alcoholism and when eventually rehoused he had curtailed his drinking considerably. When resettled he was referred for counselling by the Housing Department whereupon he disclosed his unhappiness with his accommodation. He was poor, isolated, lonely and experiencing problems with noisy neighbours. His expressed reason for coming to counselling was because 'otherwise I won't talk to anyone from one end of the week to the next'. For much of each session he would express his hatred of relying on others, particularly the DSS and local council. He had requested a housing transfer and was convinced that his request was being ignored. He felt his satisfaction was continually being frustrated, by the council, by his noisy neigh-bours, by his housing worker who he felt was not doing enough, by his former street friends who continually called, and by the poverty which confined him. He continually punctuated his speech with phrases like 'I bet you're sick of me', or, 'you don't have to listen to this. Do you want me to go now?' and would mask his vulnerability by cruelly mocking himself. He felt himself to be too intelligent to be what he termed 'an arsehole' and to go back to street life and drink, but was without the resources to live satisfactorily.

With Ben my focus was on remaining constant in my regard for him and belief in his potential and remaining with him in his frustration and despair. On our fourth meeting he came to the session looking vibrant and alive, he was charged with an aggressive feeling that filled the room. He announced that he had 'given up', he'd begun drinking and had spent some of his time on the streets with his former companions, and felt free of the pressures to master his life. He announced that I'd never have to see him again. When I explained that I wished to continue seeing him, he repeated that he wouldn't be needing counselling. He returned two weeks later and revealed that my not rejecting him when he had exposed some of his less attractive features had impressed him and helped him to avoid going back to a full-time homeless life. He had picked up a sense of being valued and it had affected his behaviour.

Conclusion

Homelessness is a serious cause for concern in Britain. On a variety of statistical definitions, homelessness has increased significantly over the past thirty years (Greve and Currie, 1991). The associated emotional problems that homelessness highlights suggest that counselling may have a role to play in addressing these issues.

Counselling at St Martin's shows that clients already either rehoused or involved in a resettlement process are able to make best use of counselling, as opposed to 'roofless' clients who are not able to maintain the commitment for counselling. The cases of Joe and Ben illustrate some key features of working with a resettled client group. Disruptions to continuity occurred and it took time to establish 'uncon-ditional positive regard', which was difficult for this client group to accept. Coun-selling those affected by homelessness can be a slow process and the counsellor faces client's feelings of helplessness, low self-esteem and insecurity. When the counsellor communicates support, nurture and faith, clients made able to internalize the counsellor's kindness and respect are in a position to discover the necessary inner resources for a resettled way of life.

References

Freud, S. (1964) *The Question of Lay Analysis*. New York: Anchor Books.
Greve, J. and Currie, E. (1991) *Homelessness in Britain*. York: Joseph Rowntree Foundation.

Janiel, R. (1987) 'The situation of homelessness', in *The Homeless in Contemporary Society*. Newbury Park, CA: Sage.

Maslow, A. (1962) *Toward a Psychology of Being*. New York: Van Nostrand.

Mearns, D. and Thorne, B. (1988) *Person-Centred Counselling*. London: Sage.

Rogers, C. and Stevens, B. (1967) *Person to Person: the Problem of Being Human*. New York: Souvenir Press.

Rosenheck, R., Gallup, P., Leda, G., Gorchow, D. and Errera, F. (1992) 'Counselling and case managing', in R. Schutt and G. Garrett (eds), *Responding to the Homeless. Policy and Practice*. New York: Plenum.

Schutt, R. and Garrett, G. (eds) (1992) *Responding to the Homeless. Policy and Practice*. New York: Plenum.

Discussion issues

1 Can you suggest any adaptations which counsellors using particular counselling approaches may need to adopt for successful work with this client group?

2 What measures would you use when deciding whether to terminate counselling?

3 How would you decide when a client was emotionally secure enough and ready to move on to more in-depth psychological work?

4 Are there any specific demands on the counsellor working with this client group? If so, what are the support needs of the counsellor?

26

Counselling People with a Disability

Mary Godden

Counselling people with a disability has to take account of a number of special difficulties, the major ones being that the client with a disability simply does not have the freedom of choice that is available to the able-bodied person and that in many cases communication is difficult as a result of both speech and body language being affected by the disability. In a residential setting there are a number of extra constraints and when I first went into a unit for young disabled people I felt daunted by them. In the event I have found it most rewarding and full of opportunities for creative work, some of which I have only begun to look at.

The Unit has fifteen residents with severe physical disabilities between the ages of eighteen and fifty-nine and is part of the Community Nursing Service. Approximately twenty other men and women with disabilities come in regularly as day patients and there are always a few short-stay patients there for a few weeks to give them or the people who care for them a rest and a change. The causes of the patients' disabilities are various and include multiple sclerosis, congenital conditions and accidents. The residents sleep in four-bedded rooms and there are a few highly prized single rooms, while a large common room caters for all daytime activities and meals. When entering the Unit, the atmosphere is one of informality, activity and friendliness. The occupational and art therapists are busy, as are those patients who are able to use their hands, and there are a lot of smiles. But the smiles hide a good deal of frustration and unhappiness. 'Problems of rejection, withdrawal, sulking, temper tantrums and depression are common' the consultant physician has written – he could have added bereavement and loss, sexual frustration, envy, rage and fear.

When he and the senior nursing officers, aware of the emotional needs of the patients, asked me to go into the Unit for one morning a week to offer counselling to them I wondered how I would set about it, since it was clear that my usual way of working, a completely private hour with one person on a weekly basis, would not be possible or even appropriate. The constraints on time and privacy made this kind of service an impossibility but I hoped an opportunity was there to find a new way of working. Many of the residents are confined to bed and although they are moved into the day-room when possible, there was not room for a bed in the small side-room which was all the Sister could make available to me. The lack of personal privacy also militates against patients making use of what *is* available: able-bodied persons can privately make their own arrangements to see a counsellor and no one need know unless they choose to tell them. In the Unit if anyone wants to talk to

This chapter was first published as 'Counselling disabled people in a residential setting. Constraints and opportunities: a personal view', in *Counselling, Journal of the British Association for Counselling*, no. 38, pp. 13–16 (1981).

me it is immediately public knowledge. Not only can it be seen but it can often be heard: I have winced more than once to hear a clear 'hospital voice' informing the world at large that *X* or *Y* is to see Mrs Godden. (Incidentally, to persuade people (patients or staff) to use my first name is a continuing battle.)

Recognizing the constraints, I decided that 'informal counselling' would be what I would offer, making it clear that if anyone asked for regular counselling in a totally private environment this would be arranged if possible. Every week I talk to a few of the patients, acknowledging them all as I pass and trying to be sensitive to whether they wish to talk to me or not. A new experience for me was that I had to be ready to be rejected and rebuffed. I am used to people asking me for help and in this situation I have to offer it and risk being refused.

In the eighteen months since I started in the Unit two patients have asked for secluded and regular counselling in the side-room and another asked for regular sessions when confined to bed in her room for a long time. Others have made use of regular sessions in the day-room either to work through some painful feelings or to talk over some specific problem. There is a lot of activity around us but there is very often an opportunity to talk with someone regularly for half an hour or so if they wish. At the beginning I went to every individual and explained why I was coming in which was not easy since they knew nothing of counselling and many of them thought I was from the local Council and could deal with bath rails and supplementary benefits. But they do understand now and rarely intrude when I am talking with someone. They clearly respect one another's privacy in an environment where it does not exist to any great degree. I realized this recently when a resident said to me 'You are a very private person, aren't you?' and added 'You're very unobtrusive in what you do'. In my counselling room I aim to be unobtrusive but out amongst people in day-to-day life I am not particularly 'reserved' so I was interested in what this patient had observed and appreciated.

I have come to realize that the greatest opportunity for me in this work is to stand beside some of the most powerless people in our society, and I find it both rewarding and frustrating. It is good to be able to help by listening and accepting, but it is frustrating being unable to do anything about their lack of power. It can be a great relief to them to have an opportunity to express their feelings to someone who does not try to 'jolly them along' (which in effect is to deny or minimize their pain) and without upsetting or depressing their fellow patients or upsetting the staff. They are afraid both of making the staff cross with them and of making what they consider are unreasonable demands on the very people who demonstrate the most care and concern for them.

Probably the largest part of my work is giving people an opportunity to unload their frustration – this may be anger against the physical disability itself; about apparently uncaring parents or children; about the irritating behaviour of fellow patients or about what they perceive as thoughtlessness or unkindness on the part of the staff. I cannot know if there has been any real unkindness or thought-lessness or whether some incident or remark has been exaggerated in the mind of the patient. Sometimes I long to tell someone about an injustice but I never do – it is essential that I do not pass on anything the patients tell me. If I do, they will never tell me anything else and will keep their worries, real or imagined, to themselves and it is to avoid that that I am there. In many ways mine is a lonely job – I cannot really get to know the staff because everything is so public and it is essential that the patients see me as their counsellor and can trust in the confidentiality.

I believe it is helpful for the patients simply to 'dump' painful feelings on me and they do this in quite unexpected ways. Probably the most insensitive remark I have yet made to a patient was to comment on the daffodils shining in the sun outside and to say 'It's nice to see spring coming again'. 'Is it?', he replied, and this led to some painful but useful sharing. On a recent occasion a man bitterly said to me as I walked past, 'It's all right for you'. I stopped and asked what he meant. Both his feet had had to be amputated some months ago and many people encourage him and tell him how well he is doing, learning to walk on his new man-made feet. He himself frequently tells me how well he is doing and how many steps he is taking. On this day he revealed the other side and I listened.

I find the rewards of the work very great but they are often fleeting. Long-term work is not possible in the face of impending death (the final constraint) but the opportunity to lighten the load a little is always there. I remember a woman who became very depressed and wanted to do nothing other than to 'run away' though she was unable even to leave her bed. She could at that time just use her hands a little and after two or three weeks of talking things through she said, with some determination, 'Now I *will* try and finish that picture'. She never did take up painting again as her condition deteriorated rapidly and she died soon after, but for that short time her depression lifted. Two other people I did a lot of work with are now dead and both were helped by having an opportunity to share some personal fears in their last weeks. The opportunity of enriching one's experience is present in this work as in any other counselling – to travel with one woman through her terror of dying and to reach serenity with her was a privilege and an experience I shall never forget.

There are a lot of dedicated voluntary helpers in the Unit – they write letters, play Scrabble, admire the handicrafts, run the sweet trolley, and take the patients shopping where possible. I do not do these things, but I have cut fingernails and held cigarettes to the lips of people too weak to do it for themselves. That is not primarily what I'm there for and I have to explain my presence from time to time to new patients. 'I haven't got any problems' is the most frequent immediate response and I accept that. One or two of the residents tell me every time I appear what a very nice place it is to live in, and how they like it there – and I accept that as true and do not probe for the dark side. But my offer does sink in and from time to time someone will share fears of distress or a specific problem that has come up either in the Unit or at home. Very often it has got quite out of proportion and is causing great distress simply for want of someone with whom to talk it through.

One of the greatest constraints on me as a counsellor arises in connection with other workers in the Unit and at the same time I realize that some of the greatest opportunities for increasing the understanding of the part that a counselling approach can play in caring for disabled people lie here as well. Before I joined the Unit I attended a large staff meeting about patient care but was not given the opportunity to talk about what counselling is. In retrospect, that opportunity should not have been missed and one of my tasks now is to try and find another. The nurse's real concern for the patient can sometimes inhibit useful work. I remember one occasion when a woman I had been talking with regularly at last allowed herself to weep for a great loss without feeling she had to apologize for 'making a fuss' – and along came a genuinely caring nurse who said 'Oh, come along, Betty, you know how it upsets me to see you cry'. A valuable moment of grieving was thus lost, but because I am working in the open community the nurses will never know if I am passing the time of day with a patient or really getting into something important.

Other incidents are more difficult to cope with – on one occasion when I was talking with a dying patient, an orderly came in to vacuum the room. I had had this problem before and ignored it but this time I asked if I could just have five minutes to finish off – 'I've got to go off duty soon' she said and switched the machine on. On another occasion a member of the domestic staff came through the 'quiet area' where I was sitting with a patient, to use the telephone – she did manage 'excuse me' as she walked right between us and pushed his wheelchair round out of the way with him helpless in it. Should I have taken it up afterwards? If I did and made a member of staff angry, who would she take it out on? Not on me in any way that would matter, but possibly on my client in some way, and I couldn't risk that.

The very layout of the building is an impediment and a constraint. That telephone call may well have been an urgent one and there is no other instrument available to domestic staff. A side-room was made available to me for counselling – it was not for several months that I discovered that when I am using the room the domestic staff have to have their mid-morning coffee standing up in the kitchen. They have their frustrations too!

The constraints are not only in the setting but in the work itself. The thought processes of a disabled person can be affected by a disease or head injury in ways that are not immediately apparent but counselling does give an opportunity to help such people as well as those whose minds remain acute. Counselling is sometimes said to offer choice, change and confusion reduction. There is little choice for many people with disabilities, and not much change, but sometimes a listening ear and some support in the confusion can be a comfort. There are many difficulties but for me they are far outweighed by the opportunities for rewarding work in passing moments or in longer sessions, in reaching, valuing, getting to know, learning from, and sometimes helping the real person so sadly locked up in physical disability.

Brief update

It has been an interesting experience to read what I wrote about a particular part of my counselling work fifteen years ago. I decided not to change to the past tense for, although I no longer work in the Unit, on re-reading the article I found myself back there very vividly as if it were indeed just last week.

In the years since 1981 people with a disability have become more vocal about their needs and society has become more aware, with changes such as wheelchair access being more widespread. Language has also changed. I know that people being cared for by the Community Nursing Service, of which the Unit is a part, are now referred to as clients and trust that readers will appreciate both the significance of that change and the complications that totally altering my terminology would have caused. I have used 'resident' where it applies but 'visitor' would not appropriately describe those who come in to be cared for on a short-term or daily basis. I trust that my occasional use of the word 'patient' will not cause offence.

There have been many changes but even today I am still aware of how frequently people with a disability are discounted or passed over and of how difficult it can be for them to voice their frustrations and disappointments. Despite the physical constraints, however, I believe that good counselling (particularly the elements of respect, empathy and a willingness to listen to whatever the client wants to talk about) can be of great benefit.

Discussion issues

1 How can professionals help people with disabilities to feel that their experience and views are relevant and valid?
2 What are the different losses likely to be felt most by those who have been disabled from birth, those who have developed a progressive disabling disease and those who have suffered physical trauma as the result of an accident or act of violence?
3 Severe physical disability does not mean the client has no sexual feelings. What might be their difficulties?
4 It seems to be very easy for able-bodied people to assume they know how a person with a disability feels and sometimes for sympathy to get in the way of empathy. How would you try to ensure that you explored the *client's* answers to the previous two questions?

27

Counselling Skills for Professionals Working with People with Disabilities and their Families

Margaret R. Morgan

Inevitably, a wide range of people with specialist skills and differing experience are involved with babies, children, adolescents and adults with disabilities, and also with their families. As the assessment of needs becomes more sophisticated an increasing number of professional workers are likely to be involved. These may well include doctors, health visitors, nurses, therapists, social workers, psychologists, teachers, careers advisers, job placement officers, employers, staff in day centres, care and other staff in residential settings, social security officers, ministers of religion, lawyers and many others. In addition a wide range of voluntary supporters with similar, or very different, skills and experience may also be available.

The involvement of professionals can be very varied and at many different levels; it may be on a once only or an intermittent or long-term basis; it may be statutorily required or it may be by request or on demand. The range of support, help and advice includes: diagnosis and prognosis, assessment of special needs, treatment (which may include surgery and may be painful and unpleasant), therapy of all types, personal care, teaching, direct action, contacts made on the client's behalf, provision of information and direct services, advocacy, listening and emotional support.

It is generally accepted that most professionals need specialized training and experience, together with a range of skills and information both within their own field and around it. In some professional training courses there is specific teaching about how to listen and to 'tune in' to clients and about the skills of counselling in general. In others specific teaching in this area of communication does not feature largely or even at all. As a result, some professionals will understand and practise counselling skills, others will not.

Many disabled clients and their parents do, however, have more insight and experience into some aspects of their lives than the professionals who are advising them. For instance, an adult with cerebral palsy may well understand more about the actual personal functioning of his or her own body than the doctor; a parent may know more about the strain of coping with a crying baby than a social worker. In some situations it may be very difficult for clients to express their views about their own situations or to contribute the knowledge that they know they

This chapter was first published in *Counselling, Journal of the British Association for Counselling*, no. 38, pp. 5–8 (1981).

have, and the professional may leave very little time or opportunity for any real dialogue to take place.

It is not easy, either, for clients to intervene in what appear to be very specialized recommendations or decisions and as a result many professionals are in a position of considerable power and authority. The recommendations they make frequently affect the provision, withholding or withdrawing of a wide range of services and financial support to disabled people and their families. These can include the type of school a child will attend, the provision of adaptations at home, the issue of a parking badge, the payment of specific allowances and grants, the securing of a job, or suitable housing, or a residential placement. Many clients do, in fact, expect positive help and advice and some want direct action to be taken on their behalf. There is frequently misunderstanding about what Local Authority Social Services Departments, in particular, can offer and evidence from several recent studies undertaken in Social Services Departments indicates that there are discrepancies between the expectations of the clients and the services that the professionals can provide. This gap has, of course, widened since the Care in the Community legislation was passed. It is no longer considered either feasible or appropriate for the state to provide care from 'the cradle to the grave', though who makes the decision about what, when and to whom services are offered is currently unclear. This makes the client's role even more tenuous and real counselling almost impossible.

A quotation from a book published in 1980, *A Difference in the Family: Life with a Disabled Child* by Helen Featherstone, is very appropriate in this context:

> The relationship between parents of disabled children and professionals is imbalanced. An individual family needs a professional far more than the professional needs them. The professional, particularly if he (*sic*) is a doctor, enjoys a higher status than the parent. (Parenthood, alas, confers negative status; only professional training or irrelevant social factors raise the parent to the professional's level.) In consequence of these asymmetries of need and prestige, the professional wields far more power than the parent.

Parents' vulnerability has at least three undesirable consequences. First, it reduces the incentives for certain sorts of professional learning. If a practitioner values a client's good opinion and patronage, he will search for signs of approval or disapproval and modify his performance accordingly.

Secondly, parents' relative impotence allows institutions to treat them as patients. Professionals expect passive acquiescence rather than active participation from powerless clients. As Roth and Gliedman (quoted in Featherstone, 1980) astutely observe, the pathological model that informs so much professional thinking about disability places parents in a double-bind; 'Either submit to professional dominance (and be operationally defined as a patient), or stand up for one's rights and risk being labeled emotionally mal-adjusted (and therefore patient-like)'.

Finally, professionals who encounter little effective resistance to their claims to dominance often come to confuse their technical expertise with a broader moral authority. Forgetting the role that values play in most child-rearing decisions. forgetting the fundamental uncertainty in which professionals as well as parents operate, they come to see themselves as arbiters rather than advisers; they expect parents to follow their recommendations on a wide variety of matters not directly related to their special training.

Consider, for example, the old practice of recommending institutionalization for children born with Down's syndrome. Clearly the paediatrician's clinical experience with similar children both inside and outside of institutions ought to be considered pertinent, but the issue is at bottom moral rather than technical.

The power of parent groups has grown in recent years. Their collective action has forced some changes in social policy and in specific institutional practices. But the relationship between parent and professional remains tipped in the professional's favour. Our policies and assumptions must shift, making parent satisfaction important to the careers of doctors and teachers, if we are to see important changes.

Other imbalances in relationships often arise because many people in the 'caring' professions instinctively want to give practical help to those with whom they are working. With disabled people this helping often moves into 'taking over' and 'doing for' instead of finding ways to enable the person with the disablement to function for him or herself. The concept of reciprocity, give and take, and the recognition of the importance of positive contributions from disabled people themselves are very often completely overlooked.

Conflicts in professional roles and areas of responsibility can also create difficulties and misunderstandings and there are, clearly, times when engaging in counselling may be neither appropriate nor possible. For instance, a teacher cannot easily interrupt a class to deal with the personal problems of one child. On the other hand, an occupational therapist who is visiting a disabled couple to discuss a practical aid may find herself involved in listening to a personal problem because this is the major preoccupation of the couple at that time. The vital skill is in assessing which particular component of helping the patient or client needs now.

In order to gain the maximum benefit from any discussion between a professional and a client there needs to be an understanding that there is a willingness to engage in counselling on the part of both the professional and the client. There are often, however, special problems inherent in the situation. The client may have communication problems or be inarticulate or inexperienced in talking on a personal basis with anyone outside – or even inside – his or her family. The professional is frequently heavily engaged, with limited time available and a number of other patients/clients to see, while the disabled person may have an abundance of uncommitted time but may feel guilty about taking up, or even wasting, the time of a busy professional.

It is particularly difficult for some professionals to find ways of communicating satisfactorily with those who have speech or hearing problems or who have learning disabilities, yet these clients have a right to express their views and to make their own contribution to any discussions about their needs and problems. This type of counselling can be time-consuming and difficult, but it is most important to recognize the needs of those who have communication problems and to try to find ways round them.

An understanding of the importance of counselling skills when working with disabled clients is vital and special training may well be necessary. Some people, whatever their profession or occupation, are 'natural' counsellors whether they have received training or not and many volunteers who have these special gifts, including disabled people and parents, are very valuable sources of help and support in this field. Some professionals, on the other hand, find counselling an inappropriate and unnatural way of working and some are unlikely to change their methods, however much information and training may be available.

Opportunities for personal counselling are often lacking in residential and day-care settings and it is not always clear which members of staff should have special skills in this field. Frank discussion with disabled people about how they see their needs might well help to clarify the situation and to identify which members of staff might be involved in a particular residential setting or day centre.

There is still a great deal to be done in encouraging professionals in many disciplines to reconsider their attitudes towards disabled people as patients/clients and the need to explore the relevance of the counselling framework and practices in all areas of work with people with disabilities and their families is as urgent as ever it was.

Reference

Featherstone, H. (1980) *A Difference in the Family: Life with a Disabled Child.* New York: Basic Books; London: Harper and Row.

Discussion issues

1 Do 'case conferences' help in identifying which of the many professionals involved with one family/client is best suited to offer counselling?
2 What training and experience would be helpful to those working with people who have disabilities which make communication difficult?
3 How can one ensure privacy and confidentiality to someone who needs a carer/facilitator to be 'on hand'? What do you do when a parent insists on being present?
4 Are people with disabilities, or parents with a disabled child, 'natural' counsellors? How valuable are self-help groups in dealing with personal problems?

28

Counselling Deaf and Hard of Hearing Clients

Hillary Ratna

In Britain, one person out of six has a hearing loss, yet issues related to deafness are seldom addressed by counsellors. Deaf people, like hearing people, often have problems that counselling might help them to resolve – if only they could find the right counsellor! Unfortunately, there are not enough deaf counsellors to go round, which is why a hearing counsellor may be assigned to, or approached by, a deaf client. In order to be helpful, the counsellor will require more than counselling training and experience; some deaf awareness is needed.

This chapter is written from a hearing person's point of view, in order to share with other hearing counsellors information I did not have when I first started working with deaf people. Since then I have taught counselling skills to deaf students, started to learn Sign Language and taken on my first deaf clients. It has been a time of rich learning for me.

I would like to pass on some of what I have learned in the hope that other hearing counsellors, who perhaps have had little or no contact with deaf and hard of hearing people, might be interested in working with them. The chapter is not aimed primarily at deaf counsellors, who will already be familiar with deaf issues.

Defining deafness

How do we define deafness? An audiologist would describe a deaf person as having a particular decibel loss across a continuum from mild to profound. Typically, they would refer to people in the profound range as **deaf** and to those with moderate losses as *hard of hearing*.

Onset, or the age when deafness occurs, is another variable used to describe the deaf person. Someone who is born deaf or loses his or her hearing before the age of three, before what some researchers consider the 'critical period' for spoken language development, is called *prelingually deaf*. Those who lose their hearing later in childhood or adulthood are called *postlingually deaf*. Both the degree of deafness and the time of onset will determine whether or not the person has intelligible speech. These terms are considered by some deaf people to be discriminatory labels, as they define deaf people in hearing/speaking terms.

A sociologist or linguist, on the other hand, would identify a deaf person as a member of the Deaf community, which one joins by accepting their values, such as

This chapter was first published in *Counselling, Journal of the British Association for Counselling*, vol. 5, no. 2, pp. 128–31 (1994).

the use of BSL (British Sign Language), identifying with other deaf people, and having shared experiences of surviving in the hearing world. This is often symbolized by referring to someone as Deaf, with a capital 'D', meaning culturally deaf, as opposed to 'deaf' with a small 'd', which denotes a loss of hearing. Thus, in terms of identity, the range of hearing loss is not as important as accepting the values of the community (Vernon and Andrews, 1990). The capital 'D' also denotes a level of political awareness, recognizing deaf people's oppression by the hearing majority as a human rights issue.

A profoundly deaf person might not be culturally Deaf, having rejected the Deaf community and chosen to interact only with hearing people. This is successful to varying degrees, as it often means isolation. For instance, Roy, a profoundly deaf student, has been brought up by his hearing, professional parents to speak and lipread, and to pursue higher education with the help of notetakers and extra one-to-one tuition. He mixes mainly with other (hearing) people in his scientific field, though he has few close friends. He does not belong to any deaf clubs, does not know sign language and has no interest in learning it. As far as he is concerned, the 'Deaf world' does not exist; he would like to be thought of as a scientist who happens to be deaf. Roy spends a lot of time on his own; he suffers from depression and at times feels terribly lonely. His parents think he has 'overcome his disability' very well.

More common than Roy's experience would be that of people who have lost their hearing later in life, having always identified with hearing culture until that time. These people are referred to as **deafened**. For them, loss would be a major issue to work through. They often suffer from loss of confidence as their hearing diminishes, feel ill at ease in social situations and suffer from increasing isolation and anxiety or depression. They may not have had enough emotional or practical support in order to adjust to the change in their life situation. There would also be the complex question of identity. This is the group most likely to seek counselling from a hearing professional.

In contrast, Sandra, a hard of hearing woman, has chosen to be part of the Deaf community. She says, 'communication is so much easier than in situations where hearing people are all talking at once and it's difficult to follow a conversation'. Having Deaf parents, Sandra is fluent in sign language and feels comfortable in the Deaf world, as do some hearing children of Deaf parents. She is a trainee social worker and active in campaigns for Deaf rights, so she attends many social and political events where deaf people meet. Sandra says that she tried for years to assimilate into the hearing world, and that she is far happier now that she has stopped trying to think and behave like a hearing person. She found that counselling helped her to sort out important identity issues.

Finding a counsellor

For many deaf clients, a deaf counsellor would be ideal: someone who would speak their language fluently, understand Deaf culture from the inside and know what it's like to be deaf. But although there are now counsellor training courses for deaf people in London, Derby and Manchester, this is a new development and there are not many trained deaf counsellors available (training for deaf counsellors is a topic for another article). So, a hearing counsellor may be the only option.

There are also reasons why a deaf person might actively choose a hearing counsellor, if s/he felt that communication would not be too great a problem. The Deaf world is small, and boundaries take on even greater importance than they do in the hearing world. A deaf counsellor may know the client's family, have friends in common or they may have worked together in the past. So a hearing counsellor may feel safer to the client because the relationship could be kept entirely separate and private.

Another reason why a deaf client might choose a hearing counsellor is because of internalized oppression, leading to a belief that a deaf counsellor could not possibly be as good as a hearing one. This is linked to negative self-image and images of deafness which the deaf person could easily have acquired as they were growing up, if their family and teachers were negative about deaf people's capabilities. This is similar to a Black person's preferring a white counsellor, because they lack faith in a Black professional's ability to help them, due to their own internalized racism (Thomas, 1992).

The counsellor's attitude

Before meeting a prospective deaf client for the first time, there are questions which you, as a counsellor, should consider:

What is your own attitude towards deafness?
Do you know any deaf people?
Do you think of deafness as a disability?

If you do consider it a disability, then you need to be aware that to some deaf people it is not, and they find it insulting to be considered disabled. They may see themselves as part of a cultural and linguistic minority group, with its own identity, language, pride (like Gay Pride or Black Power). This means being 'Deaf' with a capital 'D', which is a cultural identity. Not surprisingly, deaf people are extremely sensitive to arrogance on the part of hearing people or any condescension. The most important thing about you as a hearing person and would-be helper is your *attitude*. At first I did not understand what deaf people meant by, 'She has a good attitude' or 'They have a bad attitude'. Now I understand that a bad attitude is one which is prejudiced or patronizing. It is based on the assumption that to be hearing is superior to being deaf. A good attitude, on the other hand, means treating deaf people with respect, as equals, and recognizing that their difficulties stem less from being deaf than from the way they are treated by hearing society.

For deafened people, the situation is totally different. They usually do regard their deafness as a disability and a serious one at that. Having been used to a hearing way of life, they find their loss overwhelming at times. The Link Centre in Eastbourne has been set up specially to help people through the crisis of sudden hearing loss, which comes as a shock not only to them but to their families.

If mental health is defined as 'feelings of well-being, dependent on a positive self concept' (Bart, 1971), then helping a deaf client towards a positive self-concept may well be the counsellor's main task. This cannot be achieved if the counsellor is ill-informed or prejudiced. So you will need some background information. Oliver Sachs' book *Seeing Voices* (1990) is a good place to start. Well written and accessible, it is an excellent introduction to the subject of deafness and provides a bibliography for further reference.

Deaf people are marginalized and often excluded from mainstream culture, due to lack of access to information of all kinds. Think of having no input from the radio or cinema, and little from television. Subtitling on TV is a fairly recent development, and even now less than 50% of programmes are subtitled. This means being excluded, for example, from popular music, humour, and current events. Yes, there are the newspapers, but many deaf people have difficulty with the written word. Feeling an outsider is not exclusive to deaf people, but an experience they share with other marginalized groups, such as people of colour, women, Jews, gays, people with disabilities and others. Oppression and exclusion can lead to low self-esteem and low achievement in the areas of education, employment and personal satisfaction. Relationships can be affected. So there are many issues a deaf client might bring to counselling that have to do with the experience of being deaf.

Communication

Communication is one of the most important issues in the deaf world. It is important to know that deaf people have their own language; in this country it is British Sign Language (BSL). It is not a system of mime and gestures, nor does it parallel spoken English. It is a complete language, with its own grammar and vocabulary, using not just the hands, but the arms, face, and sometimes the whole upper body. A sign can correspond to a single word or a whole phrase. Finger-spelling is incorporated in BSL. Although Sign is the natural and spontaneous mode of communication for deaf people, many have learned to sign only as adults, having attended 'oral' schools where signing was punished and repressed. Deaf children have been stopped from signing and their hearing parents advised not to learn sign language, in the mistaken belief that speech is more important and that signing inhibits learning speech. In fact, the reverse is true; children who learn to sign early have a greater facility for verbal language. The ban on signing and insistence on 'oralism' has caused many emotional problems in itself and is a subject of ongoing controversy.

Before I knew any deaf people I imagined that they found it easy to communicate in writing and that they probably did a great deal of reading. This is not always true. Because of the education system and the way speech was emphasized at the expense of everything else, many profoundly deaf people find reading and writing extremely difficult. Imagine learning to read and write a language you have never heard, such as Icelandic, for example. If a person thinks in sign language, they will use a different word order and grammar in writing. For them, English is a foreign language, so written communication is a last resort.

Lipreading

Paradoxically, the ban on signing also means that some deaf adults have to rely on speech, which may or may not be easily understood, and on lipreading. They may choose to use this method of communication because English is their first language, the one they had to speak at home and learned in school. People with partial deafness, are also more likely to use English as their first language. They may or may not know how to sign. Lipreading is often misrepresented; tales abound of someone who can 'lipread a Russian spy 100 feet away in a dimly lit restaurant' but this is nonsense. Lipreading is in fact very difficult. The best lipreaders can actually lipread only about 25% of what the speaker says, in a quiet one-to-one situation, with good lighting. The rest is inspired guesswork, from context. Lipreading is difficult because of the 42 phonemes (sounds) that make up the English language, two-thirds are invisible or look just like some other sounds formed on the lips. This creates tremendous ambiguity for the lipreader. 'I love you' looks like 'I'll have a few'. Misunderstandings can easily arise! Other obstacles include a beard or moustache, a cigarette or something else in the mouth, a hand covering the mouth, etc.

Lipreading is a skill which some people have and many have not. It has nothing to do with intelligence. People who are losing their hearing can attend lipreading classes (if they are accessible and affordable), but it takes a good deal of practice. If a deaf or hard of hearing client chooses this method of communication, then a hearing counsellor will have to remember to speak clearly, without moving the head about or covering the mouth, and to avoid long, convoluted interventions. It can be quite a good exercise in focusing and learning to be succinct. One has to think twice before making a comment.

It is also important to think about the placing of chairs and the lighting in the room where you will see your deaf client. They will need to be able to see you clearly, and you may have to sit closer than you are used to doing. It is important not to have the lighting source behind you, casting a shadow on to your face.

Common problems deaf clients bring to counselling

One common theme is isolation. Ninety per cent of deaf children are born to hearing parents. Growing up in a hearing family can mean the child is excluded from conversations, jokes and secrets. It can be a lonely life, with minimal communication. An estimated 81% of the parents of deaf children never learn how to communicate with them! When they go to school with other deaf children, they learn to sign if they are lucky and begin to flourish in terms of self-expression. But school can be a very mixed experience. What happened to many deaf adults as children was that they were sent away to boarding school at a very young age, sometimes as young as two years old, still in nappies. Of course, they had no idea what was happening; they had no idea why they were suddenly abandoned. It felt like a terrible punishment. The fear, grief and distress are still there, just below the surface for many deaf adults.

For others, who went to mainstream schools or PHUs (partially hearing units), school meant boredom, because of being left out in class, and isolation or fear in the playground, where they faced teasing and bullying simply because they were deaf.

Another common experience is abuse: physical, emotional and sexual. Children with disabilities are considered five times more likely to be abused than other children (Kennedy, 1991) and it is estimated that as many as 50% of deaf children suffer some form of abuse. This can happen at home or at school, where adults in authority feel confident that the children they mistreat will not be able to tell. Whom could they turn to? There is a serious lack of services, counselling and protection for deaf children, which has been brought to public notice by the Keep Deaf Children Safe campaign. Deaf adults suffer the consequences of abuse, such as low self-esteem, a weak sense of identity, and relationship difficulties. Trust is a painful issue.

Deaf people often feel frustrated because of obstacles put in their path by a hearing society that has no deaf awareness. Anger may come out in counselling sessions about being taken advantage of in various ways, discriminated against at work, treated badly or with condescension. Most deaf people have not been educated to the level of which they are capable; they may not have had the opportunity to use their talents until late in life, if at all. They are not being paranoid; it is true that discrimination against deaf people exists, just as it does where race, religion, gender and ethnicity are concerned. Because of this discrimination and lack of opportunity, deaf people are frequently stuck in low-paying jobs, which means that money is short. Counselling is a luxury many cannot afford, unless fees are very low. Counsellors who work privately may have to look again at their 'sliding scale'; it may have to 'slide' lower than usual, which can be a real test of commitment on the counsellor's part.

The counsellor's response

Probably the most important quality a counsellor can bring to the relationship with a deaf client is empathy. An understanding of issues around difference and discrimination is essential, and a counsellor who has faced these issues for her/himself will be able to offer a more genuine empathic response to the client. Because of the way that deaf experience is discounted in the hearing world, it is most important for the deaf client to feel understood and validated as a person who is struggling with oppression.

Personally, I find that my experiences as a woman, as a foreigner in Britain and as a person of Jewish background were most relevant and helpful in relating to my deaf clients. I was able to understand the frustration of being stereotyped and misunderstood, and of being bombarded with the majority view of reality.

In working with clients who have lost their hearing as adults, an understanding of bereavement and loss issues is essential. They may have had limited support from family and overstretched health-care professionals, focusing more on the practical than the emotional side of their adjustment.

As far as counselling approaches or techniques are concerned, clarity of language and of ideas is most important. Deaf clients may be unfamiliar with counselling jargon like 'separation' or 'exploring an issue' or idiomatic expressions like 'not to put too fine a point on it'. It is best to be short and clear in making interventions; if the client does not understand a comment or question, re-phrase it, rather than repeating the same words.

A hard of hearing client will also value clear communication, as it will give her/him the opportunity to relax and concentrate on the content of the session. For people who are hard of hearing, the focus will depend on how much hearing loss they have and when this happened. They may feel very much 'between two worlds' – hearing and deaf – uncertain of their place in either. For instance, they may not know sign language and feel left out in Deaf circles, while at the same time finding it hard to follow spoken conversation, so that mixing in the hearing world is a struggle. Issues of identity will have to be explored in a supportive way.

The importance of non-verbal approaches to therapy with deaf clients is only beginning to be recognized. Corker (1994) describes the value of image-making, drama and movement in working with deaf people. It means using their powerful visual ability to convey what may be difficult in words. One does not have to be a trained art therapist, for example, to use drawings and images in working therapeutically, although it does require careful thought and preparation. Insights and feelings can be expressed vividly through images, not replacing the verbal approach to counselling, but supplementing it.

Conclusion

Taking a step into the deaf world can be fascinating and challenging; at times uncomfortable. Deafness challenges the very essence of communication which is central to counselling. So many of one's preconceived ideas are tested, forcing the counsellor to explore new ways of working, especially thinking and communicating more clearly. It also gives the counsellor a completely new perspective on everyday life; awareness of how we rely on our sensory perceptions increases, and concepts of mainstream culture that we assume we share are changed dramatically. One very rewarding aspect of working with deaf clients is how seriously they will take the work you do together and how much they will achieve, once they feel understood and validated. It is possible to witness and support real change.

Note on training

Westminster Pastoral Foundation in London and the University of Manchester offer training in counselling for deaf students. BAC Rugby has a list of Counsellors with signing ability and a sub-committee (DISC) dealing with disability issues.

References

Bart, P. (1971) 'Depression in middle-aged women', in *Women in Sexist Society*. New York: Basic Books.

Corker, M. (1994) *Counselling – the Deaf Challenge*. London: Jessica Kingsley.

Denmark, J.C. (1994) *Deafness and Mental Health*. London: Jessica Kingsley.

Elliott, H., Glass, L. and Evans, J.W. (eds) (1987) *Mental Health Assessment of Deaf Clients: a Practical Manual*. London: Taylor and Francis.

Kennedy, M. (1991) 'No more secrets – the abuse of deaf children', *Deafness Journal* (Spring).

Sachs, O. (1990) *Seeing Voices*. London: Picador.

Schein, J.D. (1989) *At Home Among Strangers*. Washington, DC: Gallaudet University Press.

Thomas, L. (1992) 'Racism and psychotherapy: working with racism in the consulting room: an analytical view', in J. Kareem and R. Littlewood (eds), *Intercultural Therapy*. Oxford: Blackwell.

Vernon, M. and Andrews, J.F. (1990) *The Psychology of Deafness*. London: Longman.

Discussion issues

1 What is your attitude towards disability? What is your attitude towards deafness, i.e. do you think of it as a disability?

2 What practical issues would you have to sort out in counselling a deaf or hard of hearing client? How would you facilitate communication?

3 What would you expect to face when working with someone who is losing their hearing? How do you imagine this would be different from other losses?

4 What non-verbal approaches could you imagine using with a deaf client? How would you prepare yourself for this and find out more?

29

Criminal Assault at Work

Peter Reynolds and Tricia Allison

As professional counsellors, over the past few years, both with the Post Office and elsewhere, we have become increasingly involved with, and concerned about, the incidence of criminal assault at work. Direct work with clients too often reveals a story of neglect and mismanagement. Indeed, in some cases, the policies and procedures of the employer appear to work contrary to the needs of individual victims involved. Furthermore, the main focus of organizational activity is usually directed towards prevention of assault with little attention being paid to helping in the aftermath. Obviously, such efforts are to be praised, but it is a fact that even the best preventative methods will not prove 100% effective, people still get hurt and both they and their employer lose out.

The purpose of this chapter, therefore, is threefold:

1   To review the current levels of criminal violence at work.
2   Drawing from casework, to examine the impact of violence on individuals together with current organizational responses.
3   To propose alternative strategies for action which should prove more consistent with both individual and organizational needs.

Estimating the size of the problem

Obvious candidates for violent assault are staff whose work involves handling money and valuables. Indeed, hardly a day passes without some newspaper reporting a bank, shop, building society or post office being involved in a raid. Usually violence is threatened, increasingly it is inflicted. The types of weapons used range from pick-axe handles, baseball bats and axes to ammonia sprays, shotguns and other more sophisticated firearms. However, although well publicized, this category of assault constitutes only a tiny proportion of cases of violence in the workplace. The largest group of employees who are affected by violence are those who provide a public service. Unfortunately, beyond this it is virtually impossible to obtain an accurate picture of the level of assault at work. In a survey in July 1987 the Labour Research Department found that of 210 workplaces surveyed, 45% indicated that violence had occurred, but less than half of these had any system of monitoring the incidents. Nevertheless, it should be noted that more than two-thirds felt that the general level of abuse and violence

This chapter was first published as 'Criminal assault at work: effects, responses and alternative organizational strategies', in *Counselling, Journal of the British Association for Counselling*, no. 67, pp. 15–23 (1989).

had increased over the past five years. To complicate matters still further, in large organizations where incidents are reported, the information tends to be confidential and not available to outsiders.

Given the absence of concrete data, evidence must be constructed from other more inferential sources. These would indicate a general upward trend. The numbers of agencies and networks such as Victim Support bears testimony to an awareness of both the growth of violent crime and its impact on individuals. Police statistics similarly reflect significant increases. Clearly, a sizeable proportion of these happen to ordinary people whilst they are carrying out their everyday work. Furthermore, even if an assault takes place outside of work, it will still have an impact back on the workplace through reduced individual performance, sickness absence and, occasionally, ill-health retirement.

A study from the Belgian Post Office indicates that there is always some level of psychological reaction to traumatic incidents at work (Jortay and Hallot, 1986). Obviously, the degree of effect is determined by a variety of factors, both individual and situational. However, the report goes on to point out that older women tend to be more affected than older men and, in turn, older men are affected more than younger men. Also, from an organizational point of view, sickness absence was incurred by 60% of victims as a direct result of being involved in the event.

Individual impact

The effects of involvement in any traumatic incident (whether as victim or observer) vary enormously from one person to the next. Although the level of physical injury from an assault may be considerable (or, by contrast, negligible), the psychological consequences can be devastating. The research history into this type of problem has evolved from studies of post-traumatic stress; initially studies concentrated on 'shell-shock' victims in the aftermath of the First World War and, more recently, ex-Vietnam combat soldiers and Second World War veterans who were exposed to excessive fear of combat situations (American Psychiatric Association, 1980). Also in the past few years attention has been given to:

- Hostages in aircraft hijackings.
- Police officers following major disasters (such as the Bradford Football Club fire) and following shooting incidents.
- Both victims and helpers following major catastrophes.
- Victims of violent crime (e.g. criminal assault and rape).

In most cases, reactions have been described in terms of post-traumatic stress disorder (PTSD). This has now been defined clinically and depends on recognizing a particular cluster of symptoms (Green et al., 1985); these include:

1 Having experienced an exceptionally stressful event which could be diagnosed as the basis of the problem.
2 Re-experiencing the traumatic situation; this might occur in a number of ways:
   (a) Recurrent painful and intrusive recollections of the event.

    (b) Repeated dreams and nightmares.

    (c) A dissociative state (fortunately very rare), lasting anything from a few minutes to several days. The victim acts as though reliving the original situation once more. This tends to be triggered by either something in the environment or by an intrusive thought.

3 Numbing of responses to, or involvement with, the external world:

    (a) Feeling detached from all things occurring in the environment.

    (b) Being unable to enjoy things which previously gave a pleasure.

    (c) Being unable to feel close to others (either emotionally or sexually)

4 A variety of other symptoms, of which at least two must not have been present before the trauma:

    (a) Being hyper-alert or having an exaggerated startle response.

    (b) Suffering initial, middle or terminal sleep disturbance.

    (c) Experiencing guilt at surviving when others may have perished, or guilt over the actions needed in order to survive.

    (d) Having a memory impairment and/or difficulty concentrating.

    (e) Avoiding situations likely to lead to recall of the event.

    (f) Suffering an intensification of symptoms when exposed to events, situations or activities which resemble or symbolize the original trauma.

The victim may also suffer depression or anxiety, occasionally in an extreme form. Furthermore, he/she may become irritable and have aggressive outbursts with little or no provocation. The extent to which an individual may present these symptoms can vary from mild changes in behaviour, to the disruption of almost every aspect of daily life. For example, from our casework, one client will now only use a side door to obtain access to her premises (the assault took place at the front door); and at the other extreme, a client who finally sought help some four years after the incident, by which time he was alcohol-dependent, in extreme financial distress, about to be dismissed from his job, and heading towards the divorce courts. However, although the clinical definition of PTSD appears comprehensive, in our experience, clients who have suffered violent assault at work often present other additional symptoms.

Suicidal thoughts

Although perhaps not a representative sample, 35% of assault victims from the authors' casework had suicidal thoughts; 8% were classed as very high risk (i.e. were actively thinking about suicide and had both the means to carry it out and a plan of action, and/or had already attempted suicide).

Hyper-sensitive to all reported crime

In our experience, all clients who were assault victims became hyper-alert to crimes reported in both the press and on TV and radio. In a sense it often appeared as though they were trying their best not to miss a reported case. Also as indicated in the PTSD definition, after finding a reference to violence, the symptoms intensified.

Sense of failure

Frequently victims reported a sense of failure – of having let either themselves, their colleagues, their family or their employer down. They believed that 'if only' they had done things differently then the incident might not have happened. Coupled with this was usually a loss of self-esteem together with a desire to hide away from people.

Difficulty holding normal conversations

Occasionally victims experienced difficulty holding a conversation. They lost track of what they were saying and jumped from one subject to another. From the counsellor's point of view, the ability to listen and pick up all the different threads of the dialogue was frequently put to the test.

Marked deterioration where cases involved criminal proceedings and/or compensatory interviews

Several examples from our caseload also involved both criminal proceedings and/or stressful interviews to determine levels of disability/suffering and award appropriate levels of compensation. In every case there has been a significant deterioration in the client's progress. Typically this occurred if the police required the client to attend an identification parade. Also, whilst giving evidence at a trial against the assailant posed a very real problem, the deterioration in recovery actually started at the point that the victim received the summons to attend the trial.

Deterioration similarly occurred with notification and attendance at DSS or insurance company medical reviews to assess the level of disability incurred. Furthermore, it is important to note that medical review panels are quite capable of overlooking anything other than the degree of physical injury sustained. For example, in one particular case the initial DSS assessment of disability was 3% (for superficial bruising and a laceration). Following appeal (which was held some 12 months later) and together with intervention by the client's GP and the counsellor involved, the case was reassessed at 60% disability! Needless to say, the client's sense of outrage and injustice created serious complications for his recovery.

Deterioration around the anniversary

As in cases of bereavement, many clients experience difficulties around the first and subsequent anniversaries. Even though the counsellor may have completed immediate work within a few months, it is worthwhile to re-establish contact around the time of the anniversary.

However, unfortunately, the whole thrust of diagnostic and medical approaches to PTSD often overlooks any wider impact which may have taken place. Again, in our experience, this principally includes the following aspects.

Impact on other relationships

The behavioural changes which accompany PTSD usually affect all other relationships in a client's life, particularly their spouse/partner, children, friends and colleagues at work. It is not uncommon for all of these relationships to deteriorate (sometimes irreparably) in the months following an assault. Indeed, we would argue that, wherever possible, it is important for the counsellor to become involved in the wider network of the client's relationships, in particular with their spouse/partner.

Organizational impact

From an organizational point of view, assault often involves reduced levels of performance in the period immediately following the incident. Frequently the victim will incur some period of sickness absence (in our experience ranging from a couple of days to two or more years). In exceptional cases the individual may even require early or ill-health retirement in order to recover.

In all cases of absence, the individual's normal workload must be carried out by others. In turn, this may mean that others have to work beyond normal hours and often at premium rates of pay. In short, assault costs a company a great deal more than either the material goods or money lost.

Organizational responses

Normal organizational responses to employees who have been involved in an assault frequently serve to complicate rehabilitation and recovery. At the level of individuals in companies we continue to be astonished at the lack of understanding of the potential impact of an assault. For example, recently one of us had cause to confront an armchair observer who heard about (and ridiculed) two employees who were suffering post-traumatic stress. Although they were locked inside a vehicle without windows at the time of the incident, the assailants attempted to gain entry using sledge-hammers and an axe. Perhaps the reader's imagination can conjure something of the degree of terror for the occupants inside the vehicle. Surely realistic simulation is not required?

Although individual responses are sometimes disappointing, perhaps the greater issue is embedded in the policies and procedures which are invoked by the organization. This is probably illustrated by looking at a typical pattern of response following an incident.

If the victim received physical wounds he/she is likely to be taken to a local hospital casualty department for treatment. Wounds will be treated and, depending on severity, the victim may be either discharged or detained. At some point during the examination, they are usually joined by their partner/spouse. Both are likely to be in shock and not aware of what has happened, or is happening. Hospital staff are more likely to be stretched to the limit and not available for anything other than immediate treatment of physical wounds.

Whether injury is involved or not, at the earliest opportunity the police will wish to go over the story (usually more than once) in order to take a statement. In the majority of cases this will be carried out at a police station. Victims of criminal assaults at work often report that police interviews are more akin to interrogations than questioning. In part, the police approach must be influenced by the fact that in some instances employees are involved with the claim. Furthermore, the mental state of the victim will influence their perception of any interview which probes to establish 'facts' at interrogation. Evidence from our caseload indicates this will take at least two hours and frequently considerably longer. When complete, the victim is usually released and returned home. Organizational responses generally start from this point.

In large organizations where incidents are monitored, the first contact from the employer is likely to be the company's internal audit section (or their equivalent). The purpose of this contact will be to establish if company procedure was followed. Again the tenor of the interview will be interrogatory; victims report that they felt as if they were guilty until they could prove their own innocence. In instances where policy was not followed (even with minor transgressions) internal disciplinary procedure is often withheld until the victim returns to work. On return to work a disciplinary hearing is convened at the earliest juncture and 'justice' administered.

Following interview by audit (or its equivalent), organizational contact is likely to be minimal. Colleagues and workmates will stay away for fear of not knowing what to say, but use the excuse that they wanted him/her to have a chance to 'get over it', or they 'didn't want to remind them'. Equally, by this time, management are likely to be involved with other more immediate problems.

NB: It should be emphasized that none of these groups act out of malice towards the victim. They actually do care about the individual who suffered the assault. In principle, they are intensely concerned that the victim recovers and returns to normal; yet in practice their actions are more likely to inhibit rehabilitation and recovery. For the victim their actions are often interpreted as neglect; 'they don't give a damn' is the often-repeated phrase which rings in the counsellor's ears.

Indeed, in some organizations contact is prohibited by policy. Following an assault, some organizations specifically instruct staff not to make contact with the victim for fear of prejudicing any further enquiry.

Although there are many variations, the basis organizational theme remains intact. Largely victims suffer alone and feel neglected and, as a consequence, individual recovery is inhibited and the cost for the parent organization inflated accordingly.

Alternative organizational strategies

Obviously, any acceptable proposal for alternative strategies will vary from one organization to another, depending on the sophistication of management information systems and the resources available. Furthermore, the authors also believe that any alternative proposal must be congruent with the research describing PTSD.

Green et al. (1985) have developed a working model of the disorder to help clinical work and empirical investigation (see Figure 29.1). Both individual perceptions and coping behaviours can be affected by preparation beforehand; equally social support following an assault can be enhanced and extended.

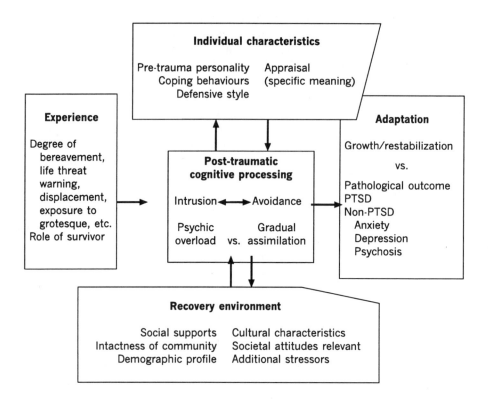

Figure 29.1 *A working model of post-traumatic processing (Green et al., 1985)*

Within an organizational setting all of these activities can become complementary parts of an assault procedure. In essence, a good procedure should address two issues; preparation beforehand and response afterwards. Let us look at each in turn.

1 Preparation beforehand

Preparation beforehand has a dual purpose; first, to set up an expectation that assault can and does happen and, secondly, to provide a degree of physical safety and psychological security. In some respects these are conflicting aims yet both are important.

Experience seems to indicate that if individuals are aware that an assault is likely to take place, the psychological suffering afterwards is reduced. By contrast, when an assault occurs unexpectedly, the degree of suffering tends to be greater. The belief that one should not talk about assault to avoid unnecessary concern is misguided. If particular groups in an organization are at risk then they should be aware of the fact. Furthermore, simply telling groups that they are at risk is rarely sufficient, the message needs regular reinforcement to be effective. We should take heed of comments made by clients that because none of their colleagues had ever been injured, they believed that violent assault was something which only took place in London and other big cities. As a consequence, when they were involved, the incidents came as a complete surprise.

Physical and psychological security is engendered primarily by a procedure or drill which individuals follow automatically whenever at risk. Obviously, the exact steps in the drill will differ from one company to another. However, the main purpose should be to minimize individual risk. Again, as with all other preparatory action, it should be rehearsed and reinforced regularly.

A second but no less important aspect of safety is the provision of adequate physical protection. This is a vast subject and beyond the scope of this discussion. Furthermore, it is more in the province of the security expert than that of the counsellor. However, it is important to be aware of this aspect of assault, and ensure that whatever mode of protection is selected is also written into any procedure.

2 Response afterwards

Whilst most companies have some form of procedure, rules or guidelines for the provision of employee protection, few have coordinated policies for supporting staff after an incident. Indeed, for clients this is often their greatest criticism. However, it is possible to develop simple guidelines which will provide psychological support for the individual and, in the process, help to minimize sickness absence and organizational cost. Again, the detail of any guidelines will vary from one company to another depending on the resources available, but in essence they should establish clearly and unequivocally that the company is concerned about the individual. At a secondary level, they should also help the individual overcome the trauma as quickly as possible and return to normal life. Both of these aims can be achieved quite simply by two broad stages of action:

Stage I   As soon as possible following the assault (and certainly within two to three days) the victim should be visited by some representative of the company who was not involved in the incident (often a supervisor, more senior manager or personnel officer). The purpose of such visit is simply to show concern, give the individual an opportunity to talk, and provide essential support which may not be available elsewhere.

Similarly, it is useful if colleagues from work are encouraged to make contact. In our experience, colleagues who are prepared to offer occasional dialogue with the victim provide real help in facilitating a victim's return to work. If no dialogue has been maintained throughout any period of absence, the first day back at work is a very real obstacle.

During the early days following an incident it is also helpful if the most senior manager possible can make an opportunity to visit the victim (or family). In some respects this type of contact is similar to a royal visit following a disaster. Clearly, a royal presence is of no practical use in a disaster situation, but it is of immense psychological value. The same is true with incidents within a company; involvement by the Chairman, Managing Director or Senior Director is of immense psychological value.

Stage II Around one to two weeks after the incident further contact should be made by someone who can demonstrate well-developed counselling skills. By this stage it is likely that the victim's family will be fed up with hearing about the incident and, in turn, the victim may start to withdraw into him- or herself.

In essence, the helper should be able to recognize and respond to normal reactions to trauma. He/she must be able to create a relationship where the victim can be honest and able to verbalize their feelings. Furthermore, they must also have the authority to decide if further contact or more specialist counselling help is appropriate.

In many organizations which are prone to assault, it is likely that this second stage of action will fall to the local personnel officer. However, although counselling is now formalized within the Institute of Personnel Management's Code of Professional Conduct, perhaps further training for those involved would be of value. It is easy to forget employees who suffer the effects of assault and assume their needs will be satisfied by medical specialists. Unfortunately, experience is demonstrating that whilst immediate physical wounds are treated, the less obvious psychological damage is ignored. For the company which cares to look, the costs are evident.

References

American Psychiatric Association (1980) *Diagnostic and Statistical Manual*, Edition III. Washington, DC: APA.

Green, B.L., Wilson, J.P. and Lindy, J.D. (1985) 'Conceptualizing post traumatic disorder: a psychosocial framework', in C.R. Figley (ed.), *Trauma and Its Wake: the Study of Treatment of Post Traumatic Stress Disorder*. New York: Brunner/Mazel.

Jortay, A. and Hallot, R. (1986) 'A study on health consequences following hold-up against Belgian post office'. Paper presented at the 1986 ICOMH Conference, Houthalen, Belgium.

Labour Research Department (1987) Bargaining Report, July 1987.

Brief update

Although some progress has been made since 1989, violence and crime at work is still a topic which few organizations are prepared to discuss openly. As a consequence, estimating the size of the problem is still difficult. Recent figures (in the public domain) tend to be industry-wide rather than related to specific organizations. Two notable examples include:

- The British Retail Consortium reported that in 1992/3 14,000 employees were subjected to physical violence, a further 106,000 to threats of violence and nearly 300,000 more suffered verbal abuse at work (Burrows and Speed, 1994)
- The Banking, Insurance and Finance Union (1992) commissioned a survey of banks and building society robberies. They discovered that in 1991 a total of 1,633 robberies took place, nearly all involving a weapon or threat of violence. In London the number of attacks doubled in one year, throughout the rest of the country doubling took two years.

Furthermore, all commentators and researchers point out that these figures are merely the tip of the iceberg; many incidents go unreported. It is also generally agreed that abuse, violence and crime now affect a huge range of different organizations, from large multi-national giants to the shop on the street corner, and the effects on individual employees are equally debilitating.

Among the more important recent developments, the following are worth highlighting:

- The Health and Safety Executive have developed guidelines on dealing with crime at work for the Finance Sector and, more recently, the Retail Sector.
- The BMA are currently developing guidelines for helping GPs deal with violence and abuse during the course of their work.
- Victim Support have set up a National Training Team specifically to help employers tackle violence and crime at work.

In 1989, the main thrust of our argument involved 'preparation of staff beforehand' and 'responding afterwards'. We would still argue that these two topics are just as relevant today. However, we would now propose that they are integrated into a broader, more comprehensive strategy which takes account of helping staff deal with aggression and abuse at work as well as violence and crime (see Figure 29.2).

Although space does not permit detailed discussion of this model, the following points are worth noting:

1 Effective strategic action must start by establishing the frequency and type of incidents which affect a particular organization. All organizations which have carried out such a survey have found the problem to be significantly worse than they expected.
2 We now include a separate sequence of actions for addressing aggression and abuse. As a general rule, the incidence of aggression and abuse will be far higher than for incidents involving overt violence. Also, given appropriate staff training, many aggressive incidents can be either prevented altogether or successfully defused.
3 The sequence of actions for dealing with violence and crime refines and expands the ideas we proposed in 1989.

A more detailed discussion of this model and its application in a number of organizations can be found in Reynolds (1994).

Although many developments have taken place since 1989, much more work is still needed. Furthermore, as far as victims are concerned, action is needed now. The responsibility for supporting victims of violence and crime at work must remain with the employer. However, it seems to us that employees who suffer unnecessarily because of a workplace incident pay a very high price for (what should have been) a normal day at work. Being ignored afterwards compounds their plight still further.

Peter Reynolds and Tricia Allison

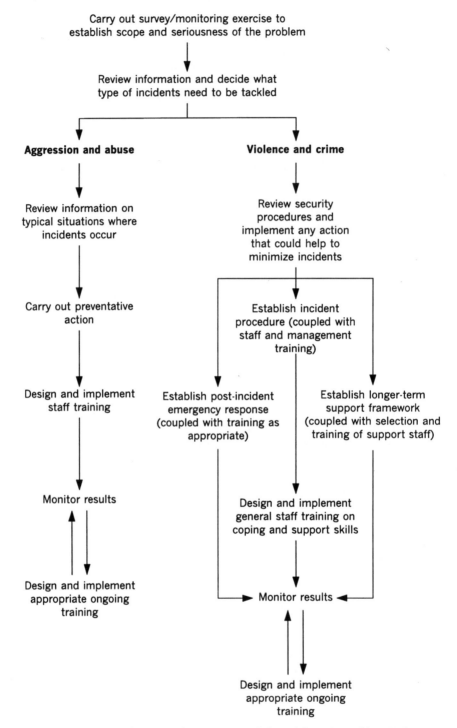

Figure 29.2 *A strategy for comprehensive action (adapted from Reynolds, 1994)*

252

References

Banking, Insurance and Finance Union (1992) *The Hidden Cost.* (Survey of bank and building society robberies.) BIFU.

Burrows, J. and Speed, M. (1994) *Retail Crime Costs: 1992/93 Survey.* British Retail Consortium.

Reynolds, P. (1994) *Dealing with Crime and Aggression at Work: a Handbook for Organizational Action.* London: McGraw Hill.

Discussion issues

1   What particular difficulties could arise when providing support for victims in a commercial setting:
    (a) for the counsellor?
    (b) for the client?
    How can these be overcome?

2   Discuss the relative advantages and disadvantages of an 'in-house' victim support network as opposed to providing support through an external agency? On balance which approach would you prefer?

3   How wide is an organization's responsibility for providing victim support? Who should be included, for example, employees, an employee's immediate family, customers or members of the general public who may become involved in an incident (either directly as hostages or indirectly as witnesses)? Where would you draw the line?

4   How would you deal with the dilemma of providing feedback to an employer/organization about the effects of aggression and violence at work whilst at the same time maintaining client confidentiality?

30

Working with Men who are Violent to Women

Adam Jukes

The Men's Centre in London is a specialist counselling service for men who are abusive to women. We run programmes which are primarily dedicated to stopping men being physically violent to women. We describe our programmes as psycho-educational rather than psychotherapeutic. The evidence is conclusive that the vast majority of men who abuse women are not sick. Although our work in the programmes is informed by psychodynamics, our understanding of abusiveness is derived from the politics of gender. In the circumstances, we do not regard treatment as an appropriate intervention.

Acceptance into the programme is preceded by some individual counselling sessions to prepare the man for group work and to introduce him to the basic structures he will be expected to follow during his six months in the programme. During these sessions we attempt to assess whether he is suffering from any pathology; in particular we refer on those who are sociopathic or schizophrenic. We accept alcohol and drug abusers provided they are willing to enter a specialist programme to deal with this problem. Another crucial issue for assessment is the degree of lethality. Our work is dedicated to making women safe. If there are grounds for it, we might make it a condition that the man lives apart from his partner during the programme.

Working with men who are violent to women is a complex and challenging enterprise. It would take a series of articles to cover the issues the Centre had to deal with before offering programmes and those that have arisen since we did so. The Centre has now been running programmes for almost a year and we learn something new with every one. It is an exciting and challenging time for us as novel clinical and organizational issues emerge and engage our attention. In this chapter I set out by imagining that I was addressing an audience of professional counsellors who are contemplating setting up a service for violent men. I asked myself what it was that I wish we had known before setting out. It may help the reader to understand what follows if he or she understands that the Centre is committed to a pro-feminist analysis of male violence.

It would have been nice if someone had actually told us how to work with male abusers. It's all very well having an intervention model which you've spent eighteen months elaborating, it's quite another matter when you're sitting there with seven anxious strangers and you're profoundly doubtful that group dynamics experiences and skills are of any value. We knew that we would be working with men who lack motivation. A probation officer friend commented that most of them would have been 'sentenced to change'. We thought we had gauged the

This chapter was first published in *Counselling, Journal of the British Association for Counselling*, vol. 1, no. 4, pp. 124–6 (1990).

likely level of resistance. We were much mistaken. We expected denial and minimization and even some mendacity; the scale, content and manner of it belie calm
description. I wish we could have known beforehand that it is not possible to work
from a position of trust with batterers. One example, drawn from many, will
illustrate how we learned this.

We had been telephoned by the partner of one of our clients. She informed us
that he had seriously battered her twice since the last group meeting. As is routine
for us, we asked how she felt about our confronting him with this knowledge. Our
clients know that we monitor with their partners but not how or when. She told us
that if he knew she had told us, he would feel 'betrayed' and would certainly
batter her for it and may even leave the programme. We agreed not to confront
him directly with our knowledge. In the following two meetings, we challenged
him hard about the details of his daily life with her in recent weeks. He steadfastly
maintained that everything was 'alright at home'.

It's impossible to know what might have happened if we'd known what a
political minefield we were stepping into and what the implications were, of
becoming politically aware. We were all clinicians from varying psychodynamic
backgrounds. We all had some ideological axe to grind and quickly discovered
them to be blunt, even useless, instruments until they were given a massive
underpinning of feminist understanding and bias.

One consequence of our naivety was that it never occurred to us to question the
wisdom of programmes for batterers. Are they necessary or justified was not a
question when the idea first began to germinate. What is the difference between
random social violence and marital battering? They are both crimes but nobody
suggests treatment as an alternative for the vast majority of crimes. What makes
battering any different? This is a complex issue which took us many months of
soul searching. One consequence is that we do not regard our programmes as
therapy. They may be therapeutic but they are designed to be psycho-educational.
This may seem a trivial point but it is crucial to the public perception of our
understanding of battering and other forms of abuse. We do not see it as symp-
tomatic of individual pathology, but as an expression of the ideology of sexism
which underpins the Patriarchy and structures masculinity and feminity so that
women are regarded as being responsible and therefore appropriate targets for
male sadism. We are committed to challenging the orthodox family systems or
Freudian models of male abusiveness which apportion blame to the victim. In
addition, we are firmly committed to encouraging the enforcement of the law and
the use of custodial sentencing for battering. We believe that this is essential for
the message it gives about society's attitudes to male violence to women. It is
important that men learn that it is criminal and that women learn it is not
necessary to endure this insupportable behaviour.

If we had been less politically naive, or more willing to sacrifice our therapeutic
omnipotence, we might have realized more quickly than we did that the batterer is
not our client, but his victim is. It is her we are engaged in helping. We might have
saved a number of batterings if we had been more alert to the consequences of our
intervention for the woman. Not that anything we did caused a battering, as far as
we can tell, but there were things we might have done to prevent a battering and

out of ignorance, didn't. A simple example is that from the outset we could have encouraged men to leave the relationship whilst they are in the programme. Where the perpetrator stays in the home we are unwittingly in danger of using the victim as an experimental subject in a violence study.

Although our opinions were mixed about it because of our different backgrounds, we had never officially intended to be concerned with men's growth. We did not see men as victims but as perpetrators. Increasingly, our mixed feelings have dissolved. We realize that we are not in the business of helping men to become more authentic or self-realized or to resolve transference neuroses. None of our clients is sick or disturbed unless our screening breaks down; they all suffer from the same complaint – masculinity. There is little room in our programmes for tender loving care and no room at all for unconditional positive regard. There is a great deal of room for tough caring. It is all too easy to take at face value a man's accounts of his partner's behaviour and to feel sympathy with his plight as a victim. This is a smokescreen. What we are actually dealing with is his sadism and cruelty. Once he has begun to take responsibility for this and is struggling to renounce his abusiveness, we allow time for exploration of his own pain. To do so before genuine work on his nastiness results in phony self-pitying remorse and sentimentality. We discovered from incidents such as described, that it is not possible to believe a batterer in our programmes. We now monitor with the victim what he tells us and we try at all times to empower her. At all times, her safety is our greatest concern.

In retrospect, it would have been very helpful if we could have predicted how likeable our clients would turn out to be. We all want to be liked, therapists included. Work with batterers is not for you, if the need to be liked is paramount. Maintaining victim empathy in the work, and using constructive anger and disapproval, is not easy if your social adaptations to please and be liked are very strong. It is also impossible in the short term to establish an abuser's trust in our benign intentions when they know that we are committed to monitoring with the victim.

It is often said that batterers lack social skills or are isolated and lonely. As far as we can tell, this is not more true of them than it is of men in general. The strength of the male bonding which occurs in our groups has to be experienced and it takes real courage to confront it. Unlike an analytic group, we encourage contact outside the group for the purpose of providing support. This has to be tightly defined and bounded or it can develop into a source of resistance. Male bonding is sexist. The problem for male facilitators is that we are short-sighted and even at times, blind. The pressure to be one of the boys is intense. Although we learned that we had to establish structures within the Centre for the staff to deal with our own sexism and misogyny, we learned late.

During the early weeks of our project, it constantly surprised me to discover how much I am like our clients. I discovered that I have the same expectations and attitudes with women. Okay, I don't use physical violence to get my own way but male facilitators quickly realized that we not only benefit from batterers' and rapists' abuse, we all have our own ways of being abusive. Women's fear of going out alone, and therefore being effective prisoners without the protection and support of a man is a direct result of random acts of rape. Women's knowledge of men's capacity for violence, or verbal and emotional abuse often directly witnessed during childhood, is an effective internalized control during later life. Women learn not to contradict men, to submit to men's control and devote themselves to meeting men's expectations. They know they can expect abuse if they do not. In these ways, even the 'New-Man' benefits from other men's abusiveness. Without a commitment to dealing with our own abusiveness, it would be the height of hypocrisy to work as we do.

A major resistance to learning was our therapeutic optimism (omnipotence?) about what is possible. We were mostly used to working with transference and with the security, trust and power this implies. In Centre groups, the transference is much more explicitly negative if our confrontations are effective. As facilitators we cannot afford to trust the client if we want to ensure the safety of women and there is no equivalent power, at least with non-statutory clients. It should hardly come as a surprise that abusers can become abusive when confronted. We have learned to lower our expectations of the programme and are rapidly coming around to the position that it is not possible to be a man and not be abusive. This follows from our experience of needing to widen the definition of what constitutes abuse. It is effectively a waste of time to draw up a list of the triggers than men use to initiate a battering. The only trigger is that a woman is incapable of being a totally submissive, telepathic princess.

We are long past surprise at how the most seemingly innocent behaviour can be used with abusive intent or underpin the attitudes which make the violence possible. One instance comes to mind. It concerned a man of 35, John, an otherwise charming and likeable working-class man who lacked psychological sophistication. He had been non-violent for eight months and it was generally thought he had made a firm decision about remaining this way. The group was focusing on his need to be in control of the family finances and how this is abusive and oppressive of women. After insisting that this was how his wife wanted it (a common justification for abuse) he was asked why he refused to countenance giving up this power. His spontaneous response was utterly without guile. 'Well, I would if I could be sure she'd do it the way I liked!' In a rare moment of genuine humour the group exploded into laughter. After initial confusion, John saw the joke and joined in. We had begun with the idea of physical violence being part of a continuum of controls which men use to get our own way with women and maintain power over them. It gets clearer with experience that it is not possible to isolate violence from all these other methods. This is what abusers and we as men, do; we isolate and deny violence. Men who are not physically violent are as prone to abuse as those who are. For heuristic reasons we have begun to adopt the position that men who are not violent are probably living with a woman whose internalized controls are powerful enough to obviate the man's need for it. It is just as abusive for a man to isolate a woman by constantly and subtly under- mining her friends and attempting to isolate her and enforce her dependency on him, as it is for him to batter her. Many women report that these forms of abuse are more damaging because they make her crazy and leave no scars. Who decides what television programmes will be watched in your home? Who has control of the car keys? Who decides where to go for holidays? Who always has the last word? Who decides what is 'reasonable' behaviour in an argument or discussion? Who decides when is the best time to talk about things?

The denial of responsibility is the major issue for any anti-violence or anti-abuse programme, including sexual abuse. It is not uncommon for a man to deny any knowledge of his violence by claiming that he blacked out during an attack. It is remarkable how often we discover that conscious self-awareness returned when his partner became totally passive and submissive, either because she was unconscious or playing possum. Patient work has always revealed that the perpetrator actually remembers the attack even if his memory has gaps. Breaking down the denial, either of the violence or responsibility for it, is hard work. It can only be achieved through a high level of confrontation and challenge. When denial is broken down, we can begin to work on the behavioural, cognitive, attitudinal and emotional distortions which underpin it. Almost invariably, the first line of defence is the denial of responsibility through excuses and justification. The most common justification is that 'she deserves it'; the most common excuse is 'I lost control'.

Any intervention strategy will fail if it fails to break down this denial so that abusers realize that they have to live with the knowledge of their violence in the same way that an alcoholic lives – a day at a time. This is necessary for a number of reasons. First, because ambivalence is never resolved and, secondly, we live in a society which encourages men to be violent and abusive to women. Any day of the week it is possible to turn on the television and see rape or violence to women as entertainment. Women are objectified in imagery in every respect. They are used as enticements to the sale of products. They are usually either sexy or servicing or both. Additionally, definitions of men which emphasize that they are expected to be in charge, always wear the trousers, are endemic. They will work to undermine whatever a man might learn in our programme.

When we began to plan working with abusers, we were a mixed sex group. We always intended to have male and female co-facilitators. We wanted to provide a model of equality and cooperation between the sexes. We also felt that a woman's presence would undermine the insidious male bonding which occurs between group members and male leaders. This proved a heavy burden for the female leaders. Eventually we evolved a rule that the woman would always get the support of the male co-leader. Only a woman can determine what is sexist when we are working at the boundaries of acceptable, patriarchally defined, social behaviour. In spite of all our efforts, relations between men and women have become strained almost to breaking point in some cases and beyond in others. That this has also happened between some men is perhaps testimony to the difficult nature of this work and the impact of the client group on the staff.

I wish I had known just what it was going to mean for my life and work when I founded the Centre. It is not possible for a man to do this sort of work without being profoundly influenced by it. This influence is extensive, from my perception of myself, my relationship with my partner and other women, and my perception of my work as an analytic therapist. Gender sensitivity means meeting people first and gender second. It means a commitment to examining my expectations of women and to dealing with them as equals. I would be lying if I said this is easy. Underpinning these changes is an entirely new perception of our society and culture, of women's place in it and how they are given that place. In fact there is hardly an aspect of my life which is not affected in some way. Given the scale of the problem and the scales before men's eyes, this is perhaps understandable and appropriate.

In fact this is probably what I wish could have been known. This work cannot be divorced from our most fundamental perceptions of our identity. Batterers are no different from me. It is not possible for a man to adopt and maintain a scientific or therapeutic attitude to male abuse of women and to distance himself from the client. There is no such animal as a neutral or value-free model, nor an intervention which does not communicate some implicit understanding of the roots of violence and who is responsible for it. We at the Centre are in no doubt. We men are responsible for our violence and abuse and for our passive and active collusion in the sexism which it expresses and encourages.

Bibliography

Adams, D. (1986) *The Continuum of Male Controls Over Women*. Boston, MA: Emerge.

Dobash, R. and Dobash, E. (1978) 'Wives, the "appropriate" victims of marital violence', *Victimology*, vol. 3–4.

Dobash, R. and Dobash, E. (1980) *Violence Against Wives*. London: Open Books.

Finkelhor, D. (1986) *A Sourcebook on Child Sexual Abuse*. London: Sage.

Hanmer, J. and Maynard, M. (eds) (1988) *Women, Violence and Social Control*. London: B.S.A.

Jukes, A.E. (1990) *Violence, Helplessness, Vulnerability and Male Sexuality*. London: The Men's Centre.

Jukes, A.E. (1994) *Men Who Hate Women*. London: Free Association Books.

Macleod, M. and Saraga, E. (1988) 'Challenging the orthodoxy – towards a feminist theory and practice', *Feminist Review*, no. 28.

Mitchell, J. (1986) 'The question of femininity', in G. Kohen (ed.), *The British School of Psychoanalysis – the Independent Tradition*. London: Free Association Books.

Discussion issues

1 Why do you think the groups described are designated psycho-educational rather than psychotherapeutic? What are the differences between the two approaches?

2 What are the difficulties in working with client untruthfulness? Do you know when clients are being mendacious? How important is it that clients tell the truth in counselling?

3 There is little room in our programmes for tender loving care and no room at all for unconditional positive regard. There is a great deal of room for tough caring. Does this surprise you? What is your reaction to this approach and why do you feel the way you do?

4 What do you think might be the effects and dangers of working with groups such as those described? What do you learn from the author's experience?

31

The Management of Denial in a Group Programme for Domestic Violence

Tony Waring and Jim Wilson

The well-documented tendency for men who have battered their partners to deny the occurrence or the severity of their actions is often seen as a barrier to progress in work with these men. Some workers have claimed that it is important to make the men acknowledge in full their actions and their responsibility for them (see Chapter 30). However, when confronted with this demand, many men will choose to withdraw from the programme and any potential gains will be lost. This article seeks to explore the idea of denial and to question the role which it is argued to play in group work with batterers. Our argument is heavily based upon the experiences which the authors have had with MOVE, a self-help group formed in Bolton in 1988.

The group

The MOVE group is run by ex-offenders, with the assistance of the first author, a professional psychologist. From the first, the sessions were designed to be open-ended. A man can join the group at the time during its cycle when he needs its services, rather than having to wait until a new, closed group is scheduled to start. Each session starts with each member reviewing his past week and homework exercises. This is followed by a training session designed to teach members a specific self-management skill which they are encouraged to practise during the following weeks as part of their homework activities. Any man attending the group for the first time would therefore gain something from the skills session without needing to know what went on in the preceding weeks. The result is that at any one time the group contains a couple of facilitators who are ex-offenders, some men who have been through the whole programme one or more times and some new members who are just starting on the programme.

The group adopts throughout a psycho-educational approach, believing that its function is to teach men a set of acquirable skills which they have either not learned before, or have failed to use in domestic situations. These skills include the recognition of anger signals, awareness of repressive cultural and social attitudes towards women, as well as empathy, assertion, negotiation and communication skills. Full details of the course can be found in the MOVE handbook (Waring and Wilson, 1990).

This chapter was first published in *Counselling, Journal of the British Association for Counselling*, vol. 3, no. 1, pp. 37–9 (1992).

In the context of this group it has been found that difficulties caused by denial are minimal. We would like to suggest that there are a number of reasons for this.

1   Non-confrontation

Miller (1983) has pointed out that denial is a product of the interaction between the therapist and the client. If the therapist insists that the client has done something reprehensible, the client due to all kinds of social and personal pressures will attempt to deny the behaviour or explain it away. That is to say, the therapist has induced the client to deny his behaviour.

The men who attend MOVE sessions are not required to 'confess their sins' in detail, either publicly or individually. It is accepted that they know that some part of their behaviour is wrong. The psycho-educational approach, in contrast to some psychoanalytic models, does not require confession but seeks to develop an awareness that there are better ways of resolving domestic conflicts and that such ways can be learned. Thus, the central part of a MOVE session will teach ways of avoiding conflicts and violence.

The review of homework encourages men to discuss their successes in using these techniques. Men will much more readily report for instance, 'I used time out to avoid a row and it worked' and importantly will add, 'Before coming to the group I would probably have battered her'. Such information concentrates on the essential business of learning to control the behaviour and does not dwell on details of what the man did, or would have done by way of violent behaviour. Also, when given in an open group setting, it gives hope and guidance to new members. It signals that they also can learn to change, without having to admit the gory details of their violence. The group thus minimizes the amount of denial which it could otherwise induce.

2   Power relations

To admit to another person that one has offended is to yield a significant amount of power to that other person, in this case the facilitator of the group. Not surprisingly, men resist this. The more the facilitator insists that such admissions should be made, the more he is overtly using this power and is modelling inappropriate behaviour for the member to copy. Also, *their relationship* will not start on the basis of equality, a situation which is indefensible in the context of trying to teach men to treat others as equals.

By contrast, the use of past offenders in the process of drawing the client into the group avoids this. The new member knows that the person he is talking to has committed the same offence and is thus 'no better and no worse' than himself. One might argue that a group leader who, not having battered, seeks to equate himself with his client through some intellectual process of political empathy ('All men are potential batterers, therefore I am a batterer') risks losing credibility. He creates another form of superiority, based upon his intellectual processes. It would seem a more honest use of self-disclosure for such a leader to acknowledge that he has no idea what it is like to be a batterer.

3 Adoption of an overt political position

While it is clearly the function of men's groups which work in this area to promote positive attitudes to women's rights, we would question the assumption that they should be overtly pro-feminist. If men are made aware that one of the functions of the group is to make them 'feminists', they are likely to reject that demand and, more importantly, deny the relevance of all that the group can provide for them.

It is, of course, necessary for men to be made aware of the ways in which macho and masculine attitudes affect their thinking and their behaviour towards women. However, there is a contrast between the approach which seeks to alter attitudes on the assumption that changes in behaviour will follow, and the approach which seeks to alter behaviour on the grounds that changes in attitude will follow. We favour the latter.

Ultimately, in a democratic society and within client-centred traditions of counselling, the decision about attitudes and political beliefs rests with the client alone. Any attempt to brainwash him into abandoning what he is entitled to believe (however wrongheaded he is!) will exacerbate a man's tendency to deny his actions and his need to alter his behaviour. By contrast, if he is helped to acquire skills which allow him to develop more cooperative and less controlling behaviour, he may find it less easy or necessary to maintain sexist attitudes. Equally important is the proposition that if the new behaviours work and are maintained, the gains for his partner are made even though he may not have overtly changed his sexist attitudes and talk.

4 Positive regard

If the man is pressured into revealing all of the details of each violent act, there will be an adverse effect on the capacity of the therapist to show unconditional regard. The psychologist author, being a non-offender, finds that when specific details are revealed about violent acts this does create a potential rift between himself and the group member involved. To some extent this problem can be resolved by differentiating between the person and his act. It is possible to show unconditional regard for the client, especially if he has chosen to learn to change his ways, while still heavily disapproving of his violent behaviour. If this distinction is made clear to him, the client may not feel that it is necessary to minimize his misdemeanours in order to retain the support of the group facilitator.

5 Acknowledgement of responsibility

This is very clearly a prerequisite for major changes in the batterer's behaviour. But at the outset, for him to accept responsibility for his violence runs against all of the beliefs which he has been allowed to develop to explain away his acts, many of which have been provided for him by previous generations of social scientists! One might argue that it is better to develop his awareness of his responsibility through means which do not immediately challenge these convenient beliefs.

Thus, if a man sees that he has used a technique by which he has avoided the use of violence, then he can be made aware of his choice. It can be made obvious that he has chosen a non-violent solution this time, so clearly he has made violent choices in the past. Then he can more readily accept *the argument that* the responsibility for such choices does lie with him.

6 Control

When he comes to a group, the batterer has learned that threatening his partner with violence whenever things don't go his way is an efficient way of running his life. To deprive him of that well-learned and effective piece of behaviour is highly threatening. If at the outset the man is told that he will have to give up these means of control, he may become very anxious. How is he going to run his life without these means? Unless he is solidly reassured that there are alternative behaviours through which he can maintain some control within his relationship (albeit not total control), he will again tend to deny his problem, thinking perhaps that 'it isn't as bad as all that!' Certainly he may not perceive it as being as bad as becoming some kind of wimp.

The solution is to put the positive aspects of the alternative way of life into the frame at the outset. What he is being asked to accept is that his new skills will be added on to those which he already has and can eventually replace his old habits. This is achieved through experienced members of this open group demonstrating to new members that there is an acceptable style of life after changing these old habits and that cooperation and negotiation do work.

7 Personal self-awareness

Men coming into the MOVE group are required to fill in a questionnaire indicating the extent of the violence and the nature of their beliefs. This is somewhat parallel to an initial interview which could, as indicated above, alienate the individual. However, the results of this questionnaire are for the man himself. They only require him to judge himself. There is no comment on the score by the group leaders. If a man has fudged issues, he knows about that himself. The next time he looks at that questionnaire, he is able to see the extent of that fudging and to see that it is neither necessary nor productive. In that later context, he has no need for denial.

8 Male bonding

It has been argued that male bonding could act against the intentions of domestic violence programmes. This would seem to be more likely, the more that men in the group are placed under threats, such as those outlined above, by their group facilitators, especially if those leaders emphasize their status or superior knowledge. It certainly would be possible for a group which has no old hands in it to argue that the facilitator is wrong and that their partners do invite violence, etc.

By contrast, if the old hands provide a group culture in which they have spent time supporting each other in the cause of positive change, the bonding will only include the new member when he conforms to the group's belief in the need for appropriate changes in attitude and the acquisition of new skills. If male bonding is a powerful mechanism, then it should be possible to recruit it to assist change rather than regard it as a threat. Indeed, it could be said that where men are attempting to move against the macho attitudes of their community they will need that male support in every way.

Conclusion

While it would be rash to assume that denial plays no part in the group processes used by MOVE, we believe that the use of the above methods does substantially reduce the damage which it can do. Clearly, what we propose in the above remarks, is not that a man should get away totally without revealing, acknowledging and taking responsibility for his violence. He will not get far if he does. Rather it is to suggest that denial may be subverted through a *low-key approach to the self-disclosure of violent behaviour* and that later changes in the batterer would render it less necessary for him to use denial as a defence mechanism. Certainly, the current MOVE members have all expressed the sentiment that had they been challenged to talk in detail about their own acts of violence from the first, they would have been much less likely to have continued attending.

References

Miller, W.R. (1983) 'Motivational interviewing with problem drinkers', *Behavioural Psychotherapy*, 11: 147–72.

Waring, A.J.G. and Wilson, J. (1990) *Be Safe: a Self-help Manual for Domestic Violence*. Bolton: MOVE. (Contact address via first author: A.J.G. Waring, MA, MSc., Dept of Psychology, Bolton Institute of Higher Education, Deane Rd, Bolton, Lancs BL3 5AB. Tel: 01204 528851, ext. 3150.

Discussion issues

1 What do you consider to be the strengths and weaknesses of 'open' groups which new members can join at any time, and 'closed' groups which are restricted to those who join the group at the start?

2   Some seek to alter attitudes on the assumption that changes in behaviour will follow: others seek to alter behaviour on the grounds that changes in attitude will follow. Which of these approaches do you favour and for what reasons?

3   In what ways might a psycho-educational group such as MOVE be better able to help men who are violent to their partners and children than one-to-one counselling?

4   How might you discover which particular aspects and experiences of your own life induce denial in you?

32

Counselling in a Disaster

Colin Weaver

On 5 March 1987 I was a Training Staff Development Officer working for Kent County Council and my part-time activities included work with CRUSE and counselling within the National Health Service. On 6 March the *Herald of Free Enterprise* ferry 'fell over' outside Zeebrugge Harbour and literally thousands of lives were affected, including mine. In this short account I hope to share just a part of what has happened regarding the counselling which has taken place since then. I am sure all the other aspects of the disaster will be documented elsewhere.

On 13 March I was asked to start counselling staff at the Townsend Thoresen headquarters, some of whom had been working almost non-stop for a week. Also in the building were Social Services staff, police, representatives of the various church organizations, Red Cross, etc., and their task was mainly directed to the immediate needs of those involved, i.e. identification of bodies, tracing relatives, supporting survivors and next-of-kin, arranging transport and accommodation, etc.

A sign, 'Counselling Room', was placed on the door and I started by seeing some senior staff. I felt a tremendous burden that first evening in that if the first few people I saw gained something by coming, then I hoped that 'counselling' would gain some credibility within the company. Even at that time I felt that all my training and experience would need to come together if I was to survive I knew not what.

It soon became clear that the counselling room was a safe place for staff to come and cry and share their anguish about what had happened to the *Herald*, their friends, their work colleagues and the reputation of the Company. The macho sailors needed permission to cry and the office staff, who had been typing endless lists of dead, missing, next-of-kin and identified bodies couldn't understand why they were so upset because 'they hadn't been there on the night of the 6th'.

The day after the counselling started a colleague, whom I had worked with in CRUSE, joined me and for a few days we interviewed mainly together. Her reason for this was to gain experience, mine was to support her. The reality, I guess, was that we needed each other's support to cope with the deep psychological pain which was being shared with us as the people we were seeing started to include survivors, other *Herald* crew who were off duty on 6 March and next-of-kin.

So what were we doing in the first few days? What can you say to a man who was on a day out, went to get some duty frees and within 60 seconds lost his mother, wife, daughter and grandson? What can you say to the man who was

This chapter was first published as 'Counselling in a disaster: a personal experience', in *Counselling, Journal of the British Association for Counselling*, no. 63, pp. 13–17 (1988).

inside the ship some days afterwards checking its condition when the body of a colleague and friend floated up to the surface right in front of him. Looking back, what we actually did was to show that we cared, we held people who were crying uncontrollably, we cried at times with them and the enormity of the task ahead loomed larger the more people we saw. Derek Nuttall, Director of CRUSE, described the early days as hand-holding time, and his description was very appropriate.

Again, in retrospect, what did we do with our own feelings after hours of emotional battering? It seemed that we supported each other. I used my wife to a certain extent but at the same time I was very aware that I could only tell her a certain amount, otherwise she would have been overwhelmed. One real problem at this time was that there were so few people either in Dover or elsewhere who could begin to understand the difficulties of our task and for us to share with. As the days passed other counsellors joined us and I felt a heavy responsibility in knowing what they would be subjected to as more and more extremely distressed people were referred to us. I took a conscious decision to keep us quite separate from the other helping activities and organizations in the hope that as time passed we would be able to consolidate the counselling service, which we were able to do.

On Wednesday 18 March, twelve days after the disaster, a meeting was held in Dover and it was agreed that the Social Services Department would be co-ordinating agency for all the collection of data which was being accumulated by the different agencies involved, and work on compiling a computerized data-base started immediately.

On 26 March the Herald Assistance Unit came into being and two teams were formed, one to work with those affected in the South East area of Kent, the Home Team, and the Away Team who would work the rest of the country. These included a number of part-time staff, CRUSE counsellors, psychiatric nurses, social workers, psychologists and other counsellors. The tasks of the two teams were quite different. The Away Team started to make contact with next-of-kin and survivors to assess their need for help and endeavour to put them into contact with helping agencies in their own area. The task of the Home Team was to offer a counselling service to those affected in the South East area, mainly Dover, Deal and Folkestone where the majority of the families of the deceased crew lived and also the crew survivors. In theory we were also responsible for all Townsend Thoresen staff affected, some 4,000 odd, although in practice many of these folk did not need counselling and were helped by their families, friends and other agencies.

A system was set up to provide a duty counsellor for clients visiting or tele-phoning the Unit during office hours. When the office was closed a telephone switching arrangement put calls through to a counsellor on call at home so that a 24-hour telephone service was available.

Acting on advice from Bradford following their own fire disaster, we adopted a pro-active approach. In other words we sent out letters to next-of-kin, followed some time after to survivors to say that we were going to visit unless we heard from them to the contrary. I am not sure about this approach and review and research will indicate whether it was the right move for the majority of those contacted.

While this was happening we were also debriefing rescuers and carers involved in the initial rescue operations. Police, Red Cross, Social Service staff, Church representatives, Townsend Thoresen staff and many others would 'just drop in' to see how we were and, with careful or should I say sensitive manoeuvring, many of them would end up in a counselling room pouring out feelings which were so necessary for them to share on their road to their own recovery from the trauma they had suffered.

During the setting up of the Unit we were continuing to see more and more new clients and they tended to fall into two main categories, those who were bereaved and those who were suffering from post-traumatic stress. Some of these clients went on to develop a full post-traumatic stress disorder. (Experiencing a major traumatic event will often result in the development of psychological and/or physical symptoms which can be extremely distressing. The recognition that certain psychological symptoms are characteristic of the after-effects of a traumatic experience led to the formulation of a specific mental disorder by American mental health workers. It is called 'post-traumatic stress disorder', and is defined by certain criteria in the *Diagnostic and Statistical Manual*, 3rd edition (DMS III) of the American Psychiatric Association.)

One of our hopes in setting up the Unit was to provide a safe caring environment where people could come and just be, share pain, share experiences and receive counselling appropriate to their needs on their recovery continuum.

So what did it feel like for me working with my clients? A chance remark compelled me to write the following on 13 June, thirteen weeks into the disaster. I share this with you.

Feelings are for sharing

These few comments came about with a chance remark made in a supermarket. What was the chance remark you will be asking? Well, it was that feelings had been expressed about the Herald Assistance Unit being seen as an elitist place. After hearing such a remark, I thought I would jot down some feelings about working with the horror of violent death, the loss, the bereavement and the trauma experienced by survivors who would never really 'get over it'.

It's not elitist, it's just very different; there hasn't been a unit quite like it before in this country. Not all the people involved will survive, and I don't just mean clients, although I am sure suicide will take some of them out of their pain. Some workers at the Unit will be able to work there longer than others; put that way it's not so frightening. What's that to do with people being professional you ask? We should be able to stand back and be objective, introducing an evaluative and effectiveness measuring system by now. We have a problem in this, because the effects of a disaster on people are difficult to evaluate, and each disaster is very different from the last or the next one.

So what happens to carers who are involved with a disaster? We are short on certainties at the moment because it's early days, but one thing is for sure, we shall never be quite the same again. Perhaps I should only speak for myself and say I will never be quite the same again. My Department needs to take care of those involved and I hope they take care of me when our task comes to an end.

The press are still coming and going as are the television crews, which I suppose gives an elitist limelight impression, but really they are an intrusion, often into our pain as we intrude into others' pain. So what is the work really like to do? No book or expert on disasters can tell you how to do it, but I can share with you the following.

It is a sunny morning outside but in the counselling room my first client is a male survivor who thought that he was 'getting over it', but now he feels he might be going mad. He starts by talking about what is happening to him as he can't stand being alone now. The nights are the worst because if it is dark he can still hear the screaming of people drowning, the prayers of others and he can still feel the bodies of those already dead knocking up against him in the water. He felt very alone then in the middle of a disaster and he can't stand being alone now. He can just manage to drive his car but he has to have the radio turned up so that he is not alone. He relives his story which he needs to do over and over again and he talks for an hour and a half. When he leaves he says he feels better for talking about it but can't see why.

Some of the feelings of horror stay with me so I go and find a colleague to share it with and it feels easier to cope! I then have half an hour before my next client, so I go for a walk along the prom. What luxury you might say, but it's not really. It helps to see the ferries coming and going again. It's difficult to believe that on 6 March a ferry fell over and 188 people were killed and the lives of thousands of other people were affected, including mine.

My next client is a widow. Well, that's the name society has given her and she can't accept it, not yet anyway. She sits sobbing, showing her pain, a person in deep distress, sharing pain which her family are unable to cope with because they are bereaved themselves. Her husband suffered a violent death. When she has gone I sit a while acknowledging my own feelings and shed a few tears; I guess it's what bereavement work is about, our own losses, and our own mortality. No I don't think we are elitists, but we are certainly different. It's a good place to work but at times a very painful place, made tenable only by colleagues, family and friends who can share and give support.

The delay in raising the wreck, and the recovery of the bodies contained, did cause much more suffering for those who waited. When the *Herald* was righted many clients wanted to know if they should view the bodies of their loved ones, impossible for us to advise on and the stance we took, feeling it to be the right one, was, 'if you feel you ought to then do it', and this proved, to be helpful to many of them. Some other agencies advised people not to and I feel this may delay long-term resolution for some clients. I am sure those worst off were the clients whose loved ones were not found in the wreck and those counselling these people suffered along with them.

Due to the Inquest being delayed, feelings about it started to build up not only with the clients but also with the Unit's staff. We worked very closely with the Coroner's Officers and endeavoured to make the attendance at the Inquest less harrowing for the clients and in doing so came under considerable pressure ourselves. As it turned out the Inquest was long and harrowing for all concerned.

What then of the pressure on me during this time? My physical health deteriorated, with minor upsets including a succession of boils under the arms, flu, stomach upset, food poisoning and disturbed sleep patterns to mention a few. Emotionally I became more and more exhausted, physically I was extremely tired and I longed for a rest. My wife and family were very supportive and my sincere thanks also go to Dr Lynn Franchino who supervised me on a regular basis and without this help I would have become a 'victim' myself. I took three weeks out and life came back into perspective. I could give more to my family and on returning to duty I felt new enthusiasm to support my team and the Unit in general. Our counselling now consists of bereavement work with families and we soon learnt that this meant next-of-kin plus the extended family, friends, work colleagues, including the whole community of Townsend Thoresen staff and staff of other ferry companies. We run groups for a whole range of different clients including parents with dependent children, survivors, older parents who lost children, survivors' wives, many of whom felt isolated because their partners find difficulty in sharing with them the events of 6 March, Townsend Thoresen staff, who acted as carers over in Zeebrugge on mortuary duty and worked with relatives; and so it goes on.

The next hurdles for all those involved will be Christmas and the first anniversary of the disaster.

According to the *Shorter Oxford Dictionary* a disaster is defined as anything ruinous or distressing that befalls; a sudden or great misfortune or mishap; a calamity. Personally, I can vouch for all of that, but it has been, and still is, a privilege to work at the Herald Assistance Unit.

Brief update

Since the article was published in 1988 much has been learnt on helping people in the aftermath of a major disaster. It was following the Zeebrugge accident that post-traumatic stress was taken more seriously in the United Kingdom.

In 1995 PTSD is often incorrectly described but more understanding is developing. Since 1987 I have been involved in debriefing clients involved in many different major incidents whose needs prior to that time would not have been recognized.

Also associated with this increase in understanding of trauma has come more awareness of the effect on carers. A wide group of helpers involved can themselves become traumatized and end up victims unless appropriate care and understanding is provided. This can also have serious effects on the family relationships of the carers.

After many years it is now being recognized that many professionals whose job involves working with trauma – police, fire, ambulance and medical staff, and others – can become traumatized even though they are expected to cope as part of their 'normal duties'. Again, adequate support is essential to prevent secondary traumatization occurring.

A mention must be made of the need for debriefers to be adequately trained. Debriefing requires the facilitator to know not only how to conduct a formal debriefing session but knowledge of the possible effects of the exercise on the recipients. Equally important is the need for debriefers to be able to handle on an emotional level the horror of the material which victims will need to share in the exercise if it is to help them to the maximum.

Further reading

Newburn, Tim (ed.) (1993) *Working with Disaster*. London: Longman.
Parkinson, Frank (1993) *Post-Trauma Stress*. London: Sheldon Press.
Raphael, Beverley (1986) *When Disaster Strikes*. London: Hutchinson.

Discussion issues

1 Research and discuss the main differences between a counselling interview and a debriefing exercise.
2 Discuss some of the ways in which the families of the carers involved in post-disaster work might be affected.
3 What are your own feelings at the prospect of becoming involved in the aftermath of a major incident?
4 How might the concepts of PTS debriefing be applied to more conventional aspects of counselling clients?

33

Counselling Following Trauma

Suzanna Rose

The word 'trauma' comes from the Greek meaning a wound or a piercing. We usually associate a wound with physical injury to the body but we know that the mind can also be wounded and the psyche pierced. Freud emphasized the principle of a 'protective shield', a metaphorical construct which he suggested was necessary to keep out external stimuli that might otherwise overwhelm the ego (Freud, 1964). A catastrophic event can by its suddenness and violence break throughout this protective shield, overwhelming the ego and causing disturbance to the psyche. The consequence of an extensive breach in the protective shield against stimuli is termed traumatic neurosis by Freud (1955). He also wrote, 'with an increase of stimulus too powerful to be dealt with or worked off in the normal way, the result is permanent disturbances in the manner in which the energy operates'. Nowadays we recognize that one of the damaging consequences can be post-traumatic stress disorder (PTSD).

Post-traumatic stress disorder

The psychiatric diagnosis of post-traumatic stress disorder was only created in 1980 and revised in 1987 and 1994 (DSM-IV). Although mentioned for the first time in International Classification of Diseases ICD-10 (WHO, 1992), historically it has been recognized at least since the time of Samuel Pepys (Daly, 1983). We now know that disasters carry a risk to mental health. This has been reviewed by, amongst others, Gist and Lubin (1989), Raphael (1986) and Lysand (1988).

One of the essential elements within the concept of PTSD is that the person has experienced or witnessed an event which involved a threat of harm to themselves or others and that the response was one of fear, helplessness or horror. This experience is statistically more likely to be the result of crime or accident, rather than a disaster. Although one could dispute what events might fulfil this criterion, the more common catastrophes such as the sudden destruction of one's home by fire or involvement in a serious road accident certainly would do so. Recent evidence has been concerned with a complex form of PTSD found in survivors of prolonged, repeated trauma (Herman, 1992), but in this article we are looking predominantly at survivors of relatively circumscribed traumatic events.

This chapter was first published in *Counselling, Journal of the British Association for Counselling*, vol. 5, no. 2, pp. 10–12 (1994).

The three main clusters of symptoms of PTSD involve:

1   Persistent re-experiencing of the trauma. The event may be experienced in the form of distressing recollections, flashbacks and nightmares associated with high levels of anxiety.
2   Avoidance of stimuli associated with the incident. Given the distressing nature of memories of the event, the person may try to avoid any reminders of the trauma and shut out all feelings associated with it. In addition the person may lose interest in activities previously enjoyed and feel emotionally numb and estranged from others.
3   Increased arousal. The third group of symptoms is associated with continued heightened arousal and reflects a state of constant preparedness for danger. The person may have difficulty in sleeping and concentrating, they may be hypervigilant and easily startled, irritability is common and many experience strong physiological reactions when reminded of the event.

Symptoms of intrusion and avoidance often alternate and the severity of symptoms may also vary over time. The increased use of alcohol or drugs may be a complicating factor. Symptoms of PTSD may emerge days after the trauma or after several weeks or months. In a small proportion of clients the symptoms may first appear more than six months after the event and this is described as delayed-onset PTSD.

Other effects of trauma

It is important to realize that PTSD is only one type of psychological response to trauma and Horowitz (1973) describes four different experiences of individuals after traumatic stress which would indicate intervention:

1   an acute stress reaction;
2   a more chronic stress reaction;
3   distress caused by activation of latent disorder by the traumatic event;
4   personality changes as a consequence of the event.

This formulation makes it clear that individuals have different treatment needs following a traumatic event and it should be noted that individuals may suffer these reactions at different stages following their trauma. Victims may suffer from bereavement reactions, grief and anxiety disorders. Those affected by physical injury, especially burns, may be especially prone to long-term psychological disorder (Roca et al., 1992). Traumatic stress can also affect those who work with catastrophe, such as police and fire and rescue personnel and for these staff, critical incident debriefing as part of a traumatic management programme has an important place in reducing symptoms and possibly preventing PTSD (Mitchell, 1993).

PTSD in the community

One of the complexities of working in this area is the lack of general information. There have been no British studies researching the level of PTSD within the community, but an American study has shown a lifetime prevalence of 1.3% for the disorder (Davidson et al., 1991). This is similar to the rate of schizophrenia in the population. Some evidence comes from research following large-scale disasters. Raphael (1986) suggests that 15–20% of those directly involved in a disaster will experience chronic levels of anxiety which will remain high for periods of longer than two years following the incident. Six months following the release of hostages just prior to the Gulf War in 1991, 25% of the men studied remained so disturbed that they required further help (Easton and Turner, 1991). Sadly, the difficulties are further compounded by evidence that many victims suffering from PTSD are failing to be diagnosed (Davidson and Smith, 1990). As counsellors then we are likely to come across sufferers from PTSD in our caseloads.

Most of us experience an acute stress reaction in the first few weeks following catastrophe. This normal response can cause distress and pain but the issues are often processed quite quickly, sometimes with the help of a counsellor. So it is worth remembering that the majority of those involved with a traumatic incident will not go on to develop the distressing and disruptive symptoms of PTSD. At present it is not known why some people are able to cope with the event, while others are not able to resolve the issues. The research debate continues between those who find that the amount of trauma is critical (Shore et al., 1986) and those who find that personality type is of primary significance (McFarlane, 1988). It seems possible that aspects of both are important. We do know however that there are sections of the population who are particularly vulnerable, such as children (Yule, 1991) and those with a previous psychiatric history (Palinkas and Coben, 1987).

It seems that one of the powerful features of this condition is its ability to construct a denial which spreads to all areas of contact. This can be seen in the way the individual client fails to acknowledge his/her problems and how the unique transference can disrupt therapeutic sessions in a most powerful way (Lindy, 1989). This denial may cause a failure of diagnosis and there is also evidence that the concept and distress of PTSD are denied by some organizations who have responsibility for emergency planning in the UK (Adshead et al., 1993). Experience has shown that many people suffering from PTSD do not consult health care professionals although they are suffering from chronic anxiety and emotional distress.

The value of a diagnosis

Unlike general counselling, it seems that making a specific diagnosis can be extremely helpful for clients suffering from PTSD. There is a lack of public awareness of the condition and consequently some sufferers experience acute isolation, think they are going 'mad' and often find great relief in the realization that their symptoms are a clearly recongized condition. Some clients have been suffering from undiagnosed PTSD for many years.

Diagnosis is also important in a medico-legal setting for compensation where the person is badly affected and perhaps unable to work. From a research point of view there is much that remains unknown about this condition and there is reason to think that knowledge gained in this area could give us important clues to the aetiological processes in other areas of mental health (Raphael et al., 1989). In the setting of a traumatic stress clinic, diagnosis is obtained by a personal assessment interview and also by use of various psychological instruments, such as the Impact of Events Scale (Horowitz et al., 1979) and the General Health Questionnaire (Goldberg and Hillier, 1979). Diagnosis is also helpful for the counsellor. Working with this client group appears to require a more active style of intervention and not all counsellors will feel able to work with explicit trauma. A precise diagnosis can aid referral and clarify treatment for counsellor and client.

Treatment

The treatment of PTSD is not easy and can be gruelling for both client and counsellor. At present the thrust of progress in the area comes from cognitive-behavioural-based therapies but these are not immediately suitable for every client. The basic skills of counselling are of course vital and the formation of a therapeutic bond essential. But counselling for PTSD is more focused and structured than other forms of therapy. The importance of proper initial diagnosis and assessment has been previously mentioned but counsellors also need a thorough understanding of PTSD as well as the parallel issues of possible grief reaction, alcohol abuse and depression.

Part of the assessment process is the telling of the event, examining both the thoughts and feelings associated with the trauma. Many clients will say that they thought they were going to die during the traumatic event and 'out of body' reactions are not uncommon. For some people it is the first time they have been able to fully explore their feelings surrounding the trauma. Listening to appalling incidents can be damaging for the counsellor and working in this area requires the counsellor to make a special point of self-care. Supervision, on-going therapy and a sensible time-table are all important. After disclosure a treatment plan needs to be discussed with the client and specific goals identified. It has to be accepted that life can never be the same as before the incident. Most people realize this and there is loss here that needs to be worked through.

It seems that exposure to the event can be extremely helpful to the client and aids integration of the experience of the event into the psyche. Some sufferers of PTSD are able at the outset to move into a formalized cognitive-behavioural programme with set 'homework' using exposure techniques. Others find it extremely difficult to even speak of the event to start with. Often asking a client to write his/her life story with emphasis on the trauma is helpful, empowering and less threatening than desensitization techniques. Desensitization can involve the client making a tape of the event in session and then listening daily to this tape at home and recording the levels of anxiety aroused. This powerful method of exposure is not suitable for all clients and can indeed increase distress if used inappropriately. In time, focused informed counselling can greatly help many clients but it should be remembered that chronic PTSD is a serious mental disorder and there are those who will carry the effect of their trauma all their lives to the extent of a permanent personality change. The composite case history below gives an example of treatment.

Case history

Jill is aged 30 and has a daughter aged six. She is separated, lives in a suburb of London where she works part-time as a clerk in an insurance office and her daughter attends primary school nearby. Nine months ago while Jill was ironing she heard a noise coming from upstairs and discovered an intruder taking items from her dressing table. When she came into the room he attacked her and punched her in the face, neck and chest. Although she did not lose consciousness she thought she was going to die. Eventually her attacker left the house empty-handed leaving Jill on the floor. Crawling down the stairs she summoned help and was in hospital for two days following the attack. She had seven stitches to her head and neck and suffered from four fractured ribs and extensive bruising. She was referred to the specialist NHS traumatic stress clinic by her GP six months after being attacked. Jill had moved house as soon as possible after being attacked and this had resulted in her daughter having to change schools. She was referred because she continued to suffer nightmares about the event and although she had moved house she found it increasingly difficult to feel settled and comfortable in her new home. She felt she was overprotecting and becoming more and more irritable with her daughter. Jill was drinking a half a bottle of vodka a day, something she had not done before the event. Her work performance was slipping because her concentration span was reduced and she had received a formal warning from her employers about this. On assessment Jill was found to be suffering from chronic PTSD with related alcohol abuse. She was suffering from intrusive thoughts about the event. During the day she would constantly imagine that she was reliving the attack and at night she frequently woke up after vivid nightmares of the event. She avoided any reminders of the trauma and had been unable since the event to buy and read a daily paper for fear it would contain reports of violence. She found it impossible to watch any TV programme related to crime. Treatment started with a full description of the event to the counsellor and focused work on the specific symptoms that were causing Jill distress. Following the second session she was asked to start writing her life history with specific reference to the attack. At first she found this very difficult but facing the anxiety that this provoked led to a feeling of empowerment and a reduction of symptoms eventually. It emerged that she had not come to terms with the sudden death of her father seven years ago and that she still tried to avoid thinking about this. She became able to examine past coping mechanisms which had contained a large measure of avoidance, and acknowledge that this tactic was not helpful to her at the moment. Later in treatment she was able to return to her old house with a friend and visit the site of the crime again, allowing herself to relive the event with all its attendant anxiety and loss. In total Jill attended for counselling for fourteen 50-minute sessions. These were weekly at first but became monthly towards the end.

Conclusion

PTSD is a serious mental health condition and features of its clinical presentation, aetiology and complexities parallel any major psychiatric disorder (Choy and De Bosset, 1992). In this short article it is impossible to do more than outline the issue. Counselling is concerned with support, empathy and generalized care and treatment. Although it may not be appropriate for counsellors without specific training in traumatology to undertake specialized intervention themselves, it is important that all counsellors are able to recognize PTSD and there is a need for training in this area. At present there is a very limited specialist NHS service for those with PTSD in the UK but there are signs that this may be changing. Given increased recognition and interest in this condition trauma victims who develop PTSD should at least begin to be able to expect informed treatment.

References

Adshead, G., Canterbury, R. and Rose, S. (1993) 'Current provision for the management of psycho-social morbidity following disaster in England', Report submitted to the Department of Health. London: Institute of Psychiatry.

American Psychiatric Association (1994) *Diagnostic Statistical Manual* (DSM-IV). Washington, DC: APA.

Choy, T. and De Bosset, F. (1992) 'Post-traumatic stress disorder: an overview', *Canadian Journal of Psychiatry*, 37: 578–83.

Daly, R.J. (1983) 'Samuel Pepys and post-traumatic disorder', *British Journal of Psychiatry*, 143: 64–8.

Davidson, J., Hughes, D., Blazer, D. and George, L. (1991) 'Post-traumatic stress disorder in the community: an epidemiological study', *Psychological Medicine*, 21: 713–21.

Davidson, J. and Smith, R. (1990) 'Traumatic experiences in psychiatric outpatients', *Journal of Traumatic Stress*, 3: 459–74.

Disasters Working Party (1991) *Disasters: Coping for a Caring Response*. London: HMSO.

Easton, J.A. and Turner, S.W. (1991) 'Detention of British citizens as hostages in the Gulf – health, psychological and family consequences', *British Medical Journal*, 313: 1231–4.

Freud, S. (1955) *Beyond the Pleasure Principle*, Standard Edition, vol. 18. London: Hogarth Press.

Freud, S. (1964) 'Introduction to Psychoanalysis and War Neuroses, including appendix', *Memorandum on the Electrical Treatment of War Neurotics*, Standard Edition, vol. 27. London: Hogarth Press.

Gist, R. and Lubin, B. (eds) (1989) *Psychosocial Aspects of Disaster*. New York: Wiley.

Goldberg, D. and Hillier, V.F. (1979) 'A scale version of the General Health Questionnaire', *Psychological Medicine*, 9: 139–45.

Herman, J. (1992) 'Complex PTSD: a syndrome in survivors of prolonged and repeated trauma', *Journal of Traumatic Stress* 5(3): 377–91.

Horovitz, M. (1973) 'Phase orientated treatment of stress response syndromes', *American Journal of Psychotherapy*, 27: 506–15.

Horovitz, M. (1976) *Stress Response Syndromes*. New York: Jason Aronson.

Horovitz, M., Wilner, N. and Alvarez, W. (1979) 'Impact of events scale: a measure of subjective stress', *Psychosomatic Medicine*, 41: 209–18.

Lindy, J.D. (1989) 'PTSD: phenomenology, dynamics and transference', *Journal of the American Academy of Psychoanalysis*, 17(3): 397–413.

Lysand, M. (ed.) (1988) *Mental Health Response to Mass Emergencies: Theory and Practice*. New York: Brunner/Mazel.

McFarlane, A.C. (1988) 'The aetiology of post-traumatic stress disorders following a natural disaster', *British Journal of Psychiatry*, 152: 116–21.

Mitchell, J.T. (1993) *Comprehensive Traumatic Stress Management in the Emergency Department*. Emergency Nurses Association Monograph Series, vol. 1, 8, USA.

Palinkas, L.A. and Coben, P. (1987) 'Psychiatric disorders among United States Marines wounded in action in Vietnam', *Journal of Nervous Mental Diseases*, 175: 291–300.

Raphael, B. (1986) *When Disaster Strikes – a Handbook for Caring Professions*. London: Hutchinson Education.

Raphael, B., Lundin, T. and Weisaeth, L. (1989) 'A research method for the study of psychological and psychiatric aspects of disaster', *Acta Psychiatrica Scandinavica*, 80: 1–75.

Roca, R.P., Spence, R.J. and Munster, A.M. (1992) 'Post-traumatic adaption and distress among adult burn survivors', *American Journal of Psychiatry*, 149(9): 1234–8.

Shore, J.H., Tatum, E.L. and Vollmer, W.M. (1986) 'Psychiatric reactions to disaster: the Mount St Helens experience', *American Journal of Psychiatry*, 43: 590–5.

World Health Organisation (1992) *The ICD-10, Classification of Mental and Behavioural Disorders*. London: HMSO.

Yule, W. (1991) 'Children in shipping disasters', *Journal of Royal Society of Medicine*, 84(1): 12–15.

Acknowledgement

The author acknowledges the help of Ian Cooper in writing the original article.

Discussion issues

1 Why do you think there is increasing interest in counselling following trauma?

2 Listening to appalling incidents can be damaging for the counsellor. What are the possible long-term effects on the counsellor working with this group of clients? How can these possibly damaging effects be minimized?

3 What is the difference between a post-traumatic stress disorder and an acute stress reaction?

4 On the whole, counselling is concerned with supportive care, empathy and generalized treatment. When, how and to whom would you refer a client who is suffering from chronic PTSD?

34

Interpersonal Skills in Nursing

Philip Burnard

The topics of interpersonal skills and interpersonal skills training are important ones. The particular issues that I will be addressing are these:

1   What *are* interpersonal skills?
2   How do nurses view their own interpersonal skills?
3   Why are interpersonal skills needed in nursing?
4   How do we teach them?
5   What are some of the problems associated with interpersonal skills training in nursing?

Project 2000 has presented us with an opportunity and with a challenge. The opportunity is to revise and organize our nursing programmes in new, interesting and appropriate ways, acknowledging, in full, the recognized need to train and educate nurses in all aspects of care – including the interpersonal dimension. The challenge is to avoid dishing up more of the same. My real worry is that some Project 2000 courses will end up being reorganized versions of present training schemes. The names will change but the content will linger on.

If we are to include full interpersonal skills training programmes in our new nursing courses, it is important to identify what skills are involved. A short list of necessary skills might include the following.

First, basic counselling skills, including listening, attending, skilful use of questions, reflection, empathy building and so forth. It might be useful to distinguish, while we are at it, between counselling skills as those skills that help others to discover their own solutions to their own problems and counselling as a form of ticking off. It is notable that the term counselling has become synonymous with some sort of disciplinary procedure in some quarters. The week before last, I was reassured by a ward sister that a student that she was finding difficult would no longer be so. She said to me: 'Don't worry, Mr Burnard, I've given her a bloody good counselling!'

The skills associated with counselling people with emotional problems and with difficulties in living turn out to be almost exactly similar to the skills needed in *any* therapeutic setting. Just as counsellors need to be effective listeners and skilled in the processes of reflection, empathy building and helping people to identify and cope with their problems, so do *all nurses* require such skills (Burnard, 1994).

This chapter is a transcript of 'Stating the case: Interpersonal Skills in Nursing', an address made by Philip Burnard at the consultation day on 2 March 1990 for Project 2000 Interpersonal Skills in Nurse Training and was first published in *Counselling, Journal of the British Association for Counselling*, vol. 1, no. 4, pp. 114–16 (1990).

Secondly, assertiveness skills, so that we can not only make our own case heard but make the case of our patients heard too.

Thirdly, group facilitation skills. These have a wide range of application from clinical meetings of various sorts to organizing therapeutic groups, support groups and so on.

Fourthly, skills in coping with other people's emotions. It seems essential that we can not only help people to express their emotions but also that we can cope when they do.

Fifthly, telephone skills. A considerable amount of hospital and community communication takes place down the telephone. And yet you only have to overhear a couple of conversations to realize that many nurses are not particularly skilled in this direction. I suspect that for many, telephone skills are not high on the list of priorities. Perhaps they should be.

Sixthly, skills in caring for yourself. Though much is written about 'caring for the carers', it often doesn't get translated into practice. Recently I was approached by some clinical staff from a large general hospital to help with the setting up of a staff support group. No sooner had this approach been made than a senior nurse told me that there would be no such group as 'nurses don't need these sorts of things'. And this was in late 1989.

Finally, in this short list, we need skills in supervising and caring for others. If we are to train nurses in developing effective interpersonal skills, we must make sure that we can help them to develop support systems that will encourage them to *use* those skills. We also need to be able to make sure that the process of becoming more involved in other people's lives does not make for burnout and emotional exhaustion. Co-counselling and small peer groups, to name but two, are media for structuring the supervision relationship.

These are some of the basic skills that can help to make the difference between a skilled nurse and a therapeutic one. If we really do want to expand the role of the nurse, this therapeutic dimension must be addressed. I know, too, that the issue *is* being addressed and that up and down the UK many nurse educators are making sure that interpersonal skills are a high priority in new nursing programmes. In psychiatric nursing, the 1982 syllabus (ENB, 1982) also did much to bring to the fore the need for specific skills. I think the real bonus with Project 2000 is that, because it calls for a total rewriting of curricula, it also gives us the chance to write systematic interpersonal skills training courses.

Nurses' perceptions of their own interpersonal skills

How, then, do nurses currently view their own interpersonal skills? In this section, I want to discuss, briefly, the findings of three research projects that Paul Morrison and I carried out at the University of Wales College of Medicine.

First of all, we asked a small group of professional nurses the question 'What is an interpersonally skilled person?' (Burnard and Morrison, 1989a). We asked them to address this question through the use of Kelly's repertory grid system which allows for the development of a wide range of different and personal views of the topic in hand. I won't go into the nuts and bolts of using repertory grids here. Suffice it to say that what emerged was a distinct sense that what those professional nurses noted most about the interpersonally skilled person was her *personal qualities*. Not her skills or her ability to ask questions or reflect or develop empathy but *what she was like as a person*. This is an interesting finding, given the current emphasis on skills training. In our study, very few people allude to particular skills: the personality and warmth of the nurse were much more important.

These findings, to some degree, further support Rogers' notion of the necessary and sufficient conditions for therapeutic change: warmth, empathy and positive regard (Rogers, 1957). In the end, it may once more be a case of 'it ain't what you do it's the way that you do it'. If this *is* the case, then we are left with an interesting conundrum when we try to teach interpersonal skills. I have a nagging feeling that there is a 'Factor X' in interpersonal relationships. I suspect that you can train people up to the nines with all sorts of therapeutic skills but unless they have this almost indefinable 'Factor X', much of it will be of no avail. Just as it is true that you can send people off to train as teachers but there can be no guarantee that they will *necessarily* inspire their students on return.

This, then, was one piece of research. The finding was that this particular group of professional nurses rated *personal qualities* above *skills* when it came to addressing the question 'What is an interpersonally skilled person?'

The second study aimed to identify nurses' perceptions of their own interpersonal skills (Burnard and Morrison, 1988; Morrison and Burnard, 1989). We used John Heron's Six Category Intervention Analysis (Heron, 1989) which will be familiar to many of you. Essentially, the analysis offers six ways of identifying therapeutic interventions in counselling, therapy, education, caring or *any* relationship where one person seeks help from another. Again, I don't intend to go into the details of the procedures that we used nor into details of the Category Analysis itself. All I want to do here is to flag up the findings.

Our sample was of nearly 200 nurses, both trained and in training and from both general and psychiatric nursing. What we found was that most nurses saw themselves as being most skilled in offering other people information and advice and in supporting other people. They were generally ambivalent about their ability to encourage others to talk more about their problems. They generally felt that they lacked skills in helping with other people's feelings and were *least* skilled in the area of confrontation.

These findings were so marked in the first round of the study that we modified the method of data collection to see whether the results were an artefact of the instrument or of the research approach. We had very similar results with the second approach. In both cases, at the extremes, nurses identified themselves as being good at giving advice and information and not so good at coping with emotion and confrontation. Further, we found no particular difference between general nurses and psychiatric and, of greater concern, no particular difference between the perceptions of student nurses and trained nurses. This suggests that even though nurses are getting more training in interpersonal skills than before, that training does not necessarily make a difference to the performance of the trained nurse.

The third study was of nurses' tendency towards client-centredness in their approach to nursing. The client-centred approach, best described by Carl Rogers (1952), is fairly widely discussed as an appropriate one for use in the caring professions. Essentially, Rogers argued that people did not need to be *told* how to put their lives right but, more appropriately, that they nearly always had the inner resources to discover their own path through their problems. The task of the counsellor, facilitator, or (in this case) the nurse, was to create the conditions for this self-renewal to take place.

In our study, we invited 140 nurses of various sorts of complete the Nelson-Jones and Patterson Counselling Attitude Questionnaire – a 72-item instrument which claims to identify the tendency towards a client-centred attitude (Burnard and Morrison, 1989b). Our sample included staff nurses, SENs, health visitors, district nurses, practice nurses and community psychiatric nurses. With some notable exceptions, very few of those nurses showed any great tendency towards client-centredness. Instead, the tendency was more towards prescription and advice-giving.

One particularly useful spin-off from this study was that we found the Nelson-Jones and Patterson questionnaire an extremely valuable method of conveying the principles of the client-centred approach through extensive discussion of the questionnaire with the various groups, following completion. It occurred to me that I often teach the *skills* that go with the approach but often skimp on the *theory*. As always, it is important that sound theory should inform practice.

Having said all that, I confess that I have doubts about the applicability of the client-centred model across the board, and this may have been reflected in our findings. Whilst the approach is of great value to the 'worried well', I am less sure that those who are unfortunate enough to be labelled 'psychotic' or 'schizophrenic' are best served by such an approach. Also, I am slowly coming to appreciate that sometimes a more confronting and challenging approach can be effective. Perhaps we shouldn't become blinkered by one approach or one ideology, for, in the end, Rogers' approach involves an act of faith. That act of faith is the belief that people *are* able to find their way through. What happens when they are *not*? We need to face the bleaker question too.

On the other hand, the Rogerian, client-centred method does offer a non-invasive and reasonably easily taught approach to helping others. After all, Rogers himself trained nearly 5,000 volunteer counsellors in the client-centred approach through very short workshops after the Second World War, to help returning troops. The specific skills of Rogerian counselling remain relatively simple.

Why do nurses need interpersonal skills?

On, then, to reasons for teaching interpersonal skills in nursing. Many of these will be self-evident. We need to enable nurses to communicate more effectively about their patients, their colleagues and themselves. This latter aspect often gets lost.

Many of us are not very good at talking about ourselves. As a result, *our* needs and wants, get lost.

We need to teach interpersonal skills, too, to enable people to cope with the more difficult aspects of patient care: those of spiritually, sexuality and meaning, for example. Often, I suspect, we shy away from these topics not because we do not know very much about them but because we do not know *how* to talk about them.

One thing is sure. We must be *committed* to the need for interpersonal skills training, otherwise we will find it hard to keep it a top priority when it comes to developing curricula. Somehow, more academic and theoretical courses have a habit of taking precedence in curriculum planning meetings.

Teaching interpersonal skills

How do we teach interpersonal skills? Of recent years, two particular approaches have been popular. First, the micro-skills training approach in which counselling and interpersonal skills have been broken down into manageable parts, practised through role play and skills rehearsal and then used all-of-a-piece. This approach works fairly well, though in my experience there are two problems that seem to recur. First, the process of training is often rushed, so that skills development is not particularly thorough. Secondly, the micro-skills are often not packaged back together sufficiently to enable students to see the *whole* of the process. Also, the whole thing can become a little mechanical with a greater emphasis on technical proficiency than on personal warmth and genuiness. Rogers (1975) back in the 1970s and MacKay, Carver and Hughes most recently (1990), have all stressed that personal attributes are always more important than technical skills in therapeutic relationships.

The experiential approach, calling as it does on people's previous life experience, is the other current approach. This has been my main research interest over the past five years (Burnard, 1989). One particular issue that I think needs to be clarified here is the degree to which experiential learning can be teased our from the general theory of humanistic psychology. It should not have to be necessary to have to accept all of the principles of humanistic psychology in order to use experiential learning methods. I sometimes worry that the previous dogma of Freudian psychodynamic theory which used to pervade counselling and psychotherapeutic practice has been replaced by a new dogma of humanistic psychology. This is not to throw humanistic psychology out on its ear, but merely to acknowledge that there are very many approaches to helping people and that not all of them come from one approach to psychology.

Problems in interpersonal skills training

This leads nicely on to problems in interpersonal skills training. To try to get straight to the heart of the matter, the issue seems to be: *do interpersonal skills training methods work?* In the past few years I have been interviewing a number of student nurses and a number of nurse educators about interpersonal skills training of the experiential learning type. What is beginning to become evident is that the two groups of people have rather different views about interpersonal skills training.

On the one hand, nurse educators generally feel that experiential learning methods enhance self-awareness and therapeutic skills. On the other, many of the students feel less enthusiastic about them and claim that they learn many of their interpersonal skills in the clinical setting. Plainly, nurse educators are out-numbered: there are far more clinical nurses affecting the way that students think and act than there are tutors.

An answer to all this may lie in the notion of not only teaching interpersonal skills in classroom and workshop settings but out there in the real world of clinical work. I really do not know. Part of me knows that I have benefited a lot from workshops and more 'formal' training but part of me also knows that the glow that I inevitably experienced when I left those workshops did not last. I had to compromise. I also had to modify my therapeutic practice in the light of what I found in the real world away from the supportive and even collusive atmosphere of the workshop. One of the real problems of the workshop setting is that, nearly always, interpersonal skills are practised with other, like-minded people – people like yourselves! In the real world, however, we practise not necessarily with like-minded people but with people in whatever situation they present themselves. Also, there is the transfer of learning problem. A number of people in my study told me that they found workshops on interpersonal skills training interesting and useful, but that the skills they learned were often forgotten once they returned to the clinical setting. Clearly, supervision and teaching at the 'coalface' remains a priority.

The other issue that I find difficult is the question of *authenticity*. Something strange often happens in the hot-house atmosphere of the workshop. People adopt particular expressions or phrases that they hear workshop facilitators using. This leads to a curious and rather stilted use of certain expressions that mark out the counsellor or humanistic therapist. One that I find very difficult to cope with is 'may I share something with you . . .'.

Now it is clearly important to learn to use certain skills and to use them effectively. I am less certain that this means becoming something of a clone of other counsellors, facilitators and trainers. We need, somehow, to find our own voice: to adapt interpersonal skills to suit *us*. If we are to remain authentic, it must be this way round. We must be *ourselves* first and trained in skills *second*. After all, think what we are trying to achieve in the therapeutic setting. We are trying to help clients or patients to be *themselves*. And yet, too often, that is exactly what *we* are not being! It is the ability to maintain this sort of balance that lies at the heart of interpersonal skills training. Exactly how it is to be achieved is a much more thorny question.

The other thing that must happen, if interpersonal skills training is to succeed is that we must offer adequate and effective supervision for those people learning those skills. If we do not, there are at least two possibilities. One is that students will find the whole process of exercising interpersonal skills too emotionally exhausting and give up. The second is that the organizational culture will swallow up the person trying out new skills and force that person to return to old and routine ways of relating to people. If we can offer support on both the personal and the educational level, we are much more likely to succeed in our training goals (Hawkins and Shohet, 1989). Another thing that I am less certain about, is whether we should be offering *therapy* to students. Whilst many psychotherapy courses make it mandatory that those in training be in therapy, it must be borne in mind that we are not training psychotherapists: we are training nurses.

One other thing that strikes me from my research is the need to think about the *slope* at which experiential learning methods are introduced. It is easy to bowl people over with experiential methods. Many of the students in my study said that they found many experiential learning activities embarrassing. I feel that it is important that we introduce activities that involve self-disclosure and sharing of self gradually and gently. Also, I think that these interactive sessions should also be backed up by the appropriate *theoretical* sessions to ensure that students have a thorough grounding in the *theory* behind interpersonal activity as well as developing the *skills*. In my study, I met a number of students who claimed that they were coming up to their final examinations and were very nervous because they had learnt all sorts of skills but didn't feel that they had enough knowledge to answer exam questions. Somehow, we have to achieve a balance.

The way forward

What, then, of the way forward? I would like to raise a series of suggestions for discussion with regard to the issue of interpersonal skills training in nursing.

First, it is important that we organize clearly structured training courses that progressively develop a wide range of skills. Some of the students I have spoken to have complained that either (a) they were often asked to repeat the same series of listening exercises over and over again or (b) that interpersonal skills training sessions became unstructured discussion groups with the tutor seeming to offer no direction and no overall plan. Planning, structure and development seem to me to be important facets of the whole process.

Secondly, I think we need to find effective ways of assessing people's interpersonal skills. Many nurse teachers learned to teach interpersonal skills at short workshops. The assessment and evaluation methods used at such workshops tend to focus only on self and peer evaluation of a short-term sort. We need to think about other sorts of assessment methods that can encourage students to develop their skills over a longish time span. On the one hand, this is necessary if we are to encourage people to grow in their skills. On the other hand, it is also necessary if we are to be able to show the national boards that we can train people up to a certain level.

Thirdly, we need to combine both theory and practice. It is not sufficient to teach people to listen and to reflect – though this is an excellent start. We need also to offer them a range of theories and research findings to augment and justify the skills we are teaching.

Fourthly, we need to be committed to further research in the field of interpersonal skills. If we are to develop the case for interpersonal skills to be a vital component of any nurse training course, we must develop the knowledge base. A knowledge base centred on research is nearly always going to be preferable to a purely theoretical one. There has always been plenty of rhetoric in the interpersonal field: let's ensure that the real world is a match for it!

References

Burnard, P. (1989) *Teaching Interpersonal Skills: a Handbook of Experiential Learning for Health Professionals*. London: Chapman & Hall.

Burnard, P. (1994) *Counselling Skills for Health Professionals*, 2nd edn. London: Chapman & Hall.

Burnard, P. and Morrison, P. (1988) 'Nurses' perceptions of their interpersonal skills: a descriptive study using six category intervention analysis', *Nurse Education Today*, 8: 266–72.

Burnard, P. and Morrison, P. (1989a) 'What is an interpersonally skilled person?: A repertory grid account of professional nurses' views', *Nurse Education Today*, 9(6): 384–91.

Burnard, P. and Morrison, P. (1989b) 'Client-centred approach', *Nursing Times*, 85(15): 60–1.

ENB (1982) *Syllabus of Training: Professional Register – Part 3: (Registered Mental Nurse)*. English and Welsh National Boards for Nursing, Midwifery and Health Visiting, London and Cardiff.

Hawkins, P. and Shohet, R. (1989) *Supervision in the Helping Profession*. Milton Keynes: Open University Press.

Heron, J. (1989) *Six Category Intervention Analysis*, 3rd edn. Guildford: University of Surrey, Human Potential Resource Group.

MacKay, R.C., Carver, E.J. and Hughes, J.R. (1990) *Empathy in the Helping Relationship*. New York: Springer.

Morrison, P. and Burnard, P. (1989) 'Students' and trained nurses' perceptions of their own interpersonal skills: a report and comparison', *Journal of Advanced Nursing*, 14: 321–9.

Rogers, C.R. (1952) *Client-Centred Therapy*. London: Constable.

Rogers, CR. (1957) 'The necessary and sufficient conditions of therapeutic personality change', *Journal of Consulting Psychology*, 21: 95–104.

Rogers, C.R. (1975) *A Way of Being*. Boston, MA: Houghton Mifflin.

Discussion issues

1 What *are* interpersonal skills?
2 How do you view your own interpersonal skills?
3 How might interpersonal skills be taught?
4 What problems might there be with teaching interpersonal skills?

35

Counselling in Occupational Therapy

Sue Coles

I recently took the opportunity to re-evaluate the role of counselling in my work as a domiciliary Occupational Therapist for Wiltshire Social Services, as a result of completing a two-year part-time counselling diploma at Bristol University.

As a domiciliary OT I visit physically handicapped clients in their own homes at their request, to assess problems arising from their disability. Clients range from children to elderly people, with physical, mental health and mental handicap problems. Anybody can make a referral to Social Services requesting an OT visit. There are waiting lists because of the large number of requests for help; priority is given to someone living alone or who cannot manage a basic activity of daily living such as using the toilet or feeding.

What happens on the initial visit?

I contact the client to make an appointment for an initial visit convenient to us both. During this visit I will carry out an assessment based on the presenting request, including medical background; social and home circumstances (i.e. layout of the house); mobility (including all transfers to bed, chair, toilet, bath); personal activities (i.e. feeding, washing, dressing); domestic activities and leisure. I teach alternative ways of carrying out everyday activities to help the person to become as independent as they want to be and where appropriate I provide equipment and adapt their home to this end. I work with the client, carer and the family to establish helpful routines of caring. The client chooses which areas to pursue; I may make suggestions as to alternative choices.

An initial visit usually lasts about an hour. Any longer overloads us both and so I will continue any unfinished business on the next visit. The initial visit is usually about practicalities as the client and I get to know each other. In OT training we learnt the phrase 'establish a therapeutic relationship'; in reality it was something that either happened or not. Now I know more about the mechanics of establishing trust as an OT visiting the client in his or her own home.

I become involved in his or her intimate and personal activities quickly, sometimes involving touch. For instance I may help a client wash and dress before lifting them with a hoist into a wheelchair. This seems to break down barriers and clients often share intimate feelings. It seems natural to explore such feelings when expressed by the client. Discussing future needs may bring up fears of increasing

---

This chapter was first published in *Counselling, Journal of the British Association for Counselling*, vol. 2, no. 4, pp. 135–6 (1991).

helplessness, particularly where someone has a deteriorating condition. It feels appropriate to deal with such as they come up.

The focus of my work

The counselling course helped me clarify the focus of my work. I am clear now that the focus should be the clients' needs and what they want to do about them. As an OT I had been trained to assess the situation, decide on the appropriate action and motivate the client to implement it. I had to be the 'expert'. I am more comfortable as an adviser with specialist knowledge that is available on the client's request. My focus has changed from my performance in how well I am doing to understanding the client and helping him or her to do what they feel is important. I now admit when I don't know something and I give the client space to make his or her own decisions about what the problem is and what they want to do about it. I can allow a client responsibility for his or her own life.

People with disabilities often say they feel helpless, their physical dependency on other people robbing them of power over their own lives. As professionals we often take the opportunity of decision-making away from them as if we were taking over their lives. I aim to bring 'choice points' to their notice and allow them to decide what they want to explore. I no longer have the conflict of trying to motivate someone to do something that they do not feel responsible for. There are limits to the client's ability to choose. Beyond the boundaries of capability and independence, there are constraints of time and budget for equipment and adaptations available. When I reach such a limit I feel able to discuss this with the client.

Case study showing constraints: Colin

Colin, who is twenty, recently had a road traffic accident. This left him paraplegic, dependent on a wheelchair for independent mobility. To enable him to be discharged home to live with his family, their house needed to be adapted to allow space for wheelchair circulation and a stairlift installed to allow Colin upstairs. Under the new Disabled Facilities Grant scheme they were assessed for their eligibility for such a grant. Unfortunately the financial assessment carried out by the environmental health officer took into account the income of all the family living in that house and did not allow for outgoings such as mortgage, etc. Their total income meant they would have to pay for the first £8,000 of the adaptation. The total adaptation was estimated to cost approximately £2,500, thus they would get no financial help towards it.

His parents were very angry about this. I felt powerless as this was the first time under the new legislation that a client who needed help had been turned down. It was also at a vulnerable stage in our relationship as they had not known me long enough to establish trust.

I shared my frustration with the new scheme with them and my feelings of responsibility as I had not realized that they might be turned down and had not prepared them for this. Through meeting regularly with them while Colin was still in hospital, I was able to support and advise them as to alternative options. Their expressing anger at the lack of financial help led on to their expressing their anger at the accident itself and Colin's loss. I was unable to meet Colin until he was discharged home as I could not spare the time to visit the hospital, which was not nearby. This meant that a lot of the decisions were made in his absence. A local charity stepped in and fund-raised to pay for the adaptation and Colin has come home.

Case study: Brenda, a client-centred approach

Brenda had been tentatively diagnosed as having multiple sclerosis. However, another doctor took over her case, diagnosed ME instead of MS and then arranged for her to see a psychiatrist. Brenda's permission was not sought for this. He felt her illness may have a hysterical base. Brenda was naturally upset and confused, clinging to the diagnosis of MS to make some sense of her illness. Her husband, who was more concerned with the day-to-day running of their home and the care of their daughter was also present. Although his main concerns were the practical arrangements, I decided to focus on Brenda's need to be heard non-judgementally. The person-centred approach helped me to understand her world and stay with her. I felt that my communication of unconditional acceptance enabled her to express painful feelings. It seemed as if the disagreement over diagnosis was invalidating her illness and feelings. After her feelings had been heard she was able to move on to more practical issues surrounding her care.

Case study: John, using Egan's 3-stage model

I find Egan's (1986) model of helping useful as an overview of the process. I use the Stage 1 skills exploring the present situation and establishing trust through accurate reflecting, paraphrasing and summarizing, allowing the client to feel heard.

John had Motor Neurone Disease and whilst I was talking with him and his wife he burst into tears. His wife told him not to be so silly, but I said I was willing to explore what was upsetting him. His wife walked out of the room and in her absence we agreed to meet for six sessions to explore his feelings of helplessness. His wife agreed to this. Stage 1 skills helped him identify that his physical dependency on his wife and her brusque handling of him was putting strain on their marriage. He was able to choose and experience what he wanted to say to his wife by using the Gestalt empty chair technique. By choosing the preferred scenario and committing himself to action, he was able to communicate his feelings of isolation and fear to his wife.

Disability and physical dependency of one partner on another can put immense strain on a marriage. I visited a couple, the husband had MS, who were unable to talk to each other without ending up in a pattern of arguments. In a counselling session I felt that the wife was not hearing her husband, stopping him from expressing his negative feelings and always encouraging him to be positive about his illness. I shared my feelings which they agreed were accurate and we practised good listening skills of her reflecting what her husband said to her before replying to him. He was able to tell her how helpless and angry he felt at her making his decisions for him and arranging things behind his back. She shared that she was trying to protect him and a useful talk together followed.

Case study: Malcom

I was asked to see Malcom by the nursing staff on his ward as he was being difficult and refusing treatment. I was working as a counsellor for an MS society and I visited Malcom in hospital where he was receiving treatment for pressure sores. His MS confines him to a wheelchair. We established how helpless he feels when the nurses handled him without asking his permission or including him. He felt 'treated like a piece of machinery not a person'. Over several visits we spoke about his wish to be out of hospital and to have a girlfriend. The content of these sessions was confused, moving backward and forward, and I found Egan's stages helpful to maintain an overview of what was going on. I thought he would say anything to keep me visiting on the pretext to other patients and staff that I was his girlfriend, and I shared my discomfort. In confronting him with this, we were able to move on to his admitting that he often did this with young female nurses, fantasizing that they were caring for him because they loved him rather than because it was their role. He expressed his jealousy towards the male nurses who bantered with his chosen nurse, and other such feelings. I wondered as Malcom was referred to me by the nurses whether he wanted counselling and when he admitted that he did not we looked at what he did want. His main aim was to get a girlfriend and be as 'normal' as possible and I put him in contact with the local MS society branch for social contact outside the hospital.

Using Gestalt

I find Gestalt helpful in bringing into focus the here and now when clients get stuck in the past. The 'moving on' skills of the empty chair technique are useful. In my personal experience I had a choking sensation following the death of John, an MND client. I received the news that he had died unexpectedly by a written message handed to me in a busy reception office. I wanted to mourn him but there was no time or place for this in a Social Services office. I suppressed the feeling and could not bring it up, hence the choking feelings. Using the empty chair I was able to say goodbye and cry for him. I know I was also crying for myself and the feelings around my grandfather's unexpected death.

Using life span development

The counselling course helped me broaden my horizons in ways of looking at life. Life span development as put forward by Sugarman (1986) helped me realize that many of the issues and concerns brought to therapists by elderly people are common to those brought by disabled clients. They are experiencing a continuation of losses that may be experienced by any of us in earlier life. The life span development concept helps foster the attitude that we all have issues in common at different stages of our lives, that we share common ground which breaks down the 'them and us' barrier that sometimes separates clients and therapists.

My frustration is having the potential but not the opportunity to help. Clients' practical needs have to take priority as it is essential to make someone as physically safe as they want to be. I am limited as to the amount of time I can spend with clients and if I give priority to someone's emotional needs through counselling, I am reducing the amount of time available to other people. Thus it is rare for me to set up counselling sessions. I become confused wearing the two hats of OT and counsellor as to my priorities. In the end I am employed as an OT and pass on clients' needs to other social workers or rarely to counsellors through RELATE. Disabled peoples' needs are often neglected because a worker may not have the time or the skills required. The disabled person may not have the income to visit a private counsellor or the physical access to one when travelling or the layout of the building makes it impossible.

Disabled persons' need for counselling is very often neglected. People often do not ask for help unless they know it is available. Perhaps schemes could be established to train clients and volunteers as counsellors, to supplement the counselling skills of the professionals. Such schemes would need adequate support and supervision for those involved in the counselling. If such support is neglected, burn-out of the individual may result.

I gained enormously from the Diploma in Counselling Course and recommend that all health-care workers have some form of counselling included in their training. There is a lot of scope in looking at the role of counselling for health-care workers and the needs of disabled clients for counselling support.

References

Egan, G. (1986) *The Skilled Helper. A Systematic Approach to Helping.* Monterey, CA: Brooks Cole.
Rogers, C. (1951) *Client-Centred Therapy*, 3rd edn. London: Constable.
Sugarman, L. (1986) *Life-span Development. Concepts, Theories and Interventions.* London and New York: Methuen.

Brief update

Since writing this article in 1991 I have progressed in my own process as a counsellor, after acknowledging that in my role as an OT working for Wiltshire

Social Services, counselling my clients was not seen as a priority and the time was not available for this. This was hard to accept as I believe that quality of life is more than physical safety and comfort. We are happiest when growing, not stuck and helpless, and counselling enables the growing process.

Subsequently I became an OT and counsellor in a day hospital for people dependent on alcohol, discovering that people who have experienced and survived illness or crisis are strong because of it and may be able to support and counsel others. This led to work supervising and training people in recovery from alcohol dependency and volunteer counsellors to counsel people with alcohol problems, through Advice and Counselling for Alcohol and Drugs. I also work with young people through counselling at Bristol University Student Counselling Services and supervise at Off the Record. Adolescence can be a potential and chaotic time where losses of childhood and expectations of adulthood can be a heavy burden.

My experience is that no matter which organization I am working for the person-centred approach can give people the time, attention and respect to enable them to understand and accept their losses and move on to looking at what they want out of life.

My training and supervision are based on person-centred theory with Egan's skills model and other active and experiential strategies. Whether we are counsellor or client, supervisor or supervisee, trainer or trainee depends on what stage we are at in our own journey and we will be all of these things at some time. My aim is to break down the barriers of 'us and them' that can arise in the helping professions. We all can be experts on ourselves and find our own strengths and knowledge if we want to. This seems to be the starting point for all my work; what does this person want, rather than what do other people want for him or her?

Discussion issues

1 What differences do you think it might make to a counselling relationship when a client is referred for counselling by someone else, rather than being self-referred?

2 What range of feelings do you experience when a client who has been referred to you seems (a) compliant or (b) hostile and reluctant to engage in counselling? What do you do in these situations?

3 Would you liaise with a person referring a client? When and in what ways would you do that?

4 Have you experience of a dual-role conflict such as OT/counsellor? What are the difficulties you encountered or that you think might be problematic in such a situation?

36

The Challenge of AIDS

Antony Grey

The problem

The advent of AIDS – Acquired Immune Deficiency Syndrome – brings a public health crisis the full extent of which will only become apparent over the next four or five years. Since AIDS surfaced in the United States in 1981, almost 40% of its victims have died and very few of those still alive have good prospects of recovery. Once AIDS is diagnosed, the patient's likely life span is about two years.

AIDS is a collapse of the body's immune defence systems against a variety of lethal illnesses, for which otherwise effective remedies no longer function in the case of an AIDS subject. Two usually rare diseases have occurred in many AIDS cases. These are Kaposi's sarcoma – a form of skin cancer – and *Pneumocystis carinii* pneumonia – a parasitic infection of the lungs. There are no clear-cut early symptoms peculiar to AIDS; a subject may have the syndrome for many months, and even years, before it is recognized.

The nature of the causative agent has not yet been identified, nor precisely how it is transmitted, although it is clearly connected with the blood and almost certainly results from intimate body contact involving exchange of body fluids. It is thought that the incubation period may be as long as up to four years – a fact with frightening possibilities in terms of the potential reservoir of as yet undetected infection.

The implications of this situation are extremely worrying and serious, not only for those groups so far predominantly affected (notably promiscuous male homosexuals, intravenous drug users and haemophiliacs) but also for the population at large, because established patterns of sexual behaviour make it inevitable that without an effective prophylactic and in the absence of any adequate screening procedure increasing numbers of people are becoming at risk as each day goes by. The epidemic pattern in the USA so far suggests that AIDS is spreading with geometrical progression, and is likely to escalate in a steady rising curve for the foreseeable future, unless some effective prevention and/or cure is found.

As yet, the medical profession remains largely helpless and widely ignorant. AIDS has sparked off primitive fears, even amongst professional health workers. Some hospital staff have refused normal nursing to AIDS patients, and in Britain a leading pathologist refused to carry out a post-mortem on a man who he thought might have died from AIDS.

The need for skilled, supportive and accurately informed counselling, not only

This chapter was first published in *Counselling, Journal of the British Association for Counselling*, no. 47, pp. 20–2 (1984).

for AIDS sufferers themselves but also for their spouses, lovers, relatives and friends, is already apparent. Agencies such as Gay Switchboard have been receiving hundreds of calls from worried people who think they may have been in contact with AIDS subjects. It is not just the relatively few who already have, or whose lives are directly affected by, AIDS, but the larger number who are destined to develop it in the near future and the hundreds or even thousands of people who are already suffering from 'AIDS panic', who need supportive counselling. The counsellors involved in this work will need even greater amounts of personal inner strength to handle the often extreme stress involved in this situation than is called for in most counselling encounters. Fear of early death caused by an unknown, invisible and as yet incurable agent is very frightening and demoralizing. How are we best to prepare ourselves to respond to this challenge?

Needs of counsellors

I believe that counsellors who are likely to be confronted with AIDS sufferers, their friends, or those who fear they may be at risk from AIDS, will require a special combination of counselling skills, practical knowledge and personal psychological preparation. The skills need to be primarily in supportive, reality-based techniques which, without being unnecessarily pessimistic, recognize the deep-seated fears and do not discount the anguish or raise false hopes. Awareness of and openness to clients' life-situations and their sexual and personal relationship needs must be combined with the ability to sustain them in terminal illness and bereavement.

There are some factors likely to be present in many AIDS cases which will make them even more stressful for both clients and counsellors than some other situations involving terminal illness. While it should be emphasized that AIDS is unlikely to stay confined to specific groups such as homosexuals and drug addicts (it is not a 'gay plague', but a sexually transmitted condition), it has so far been largely affecting men who have had a variety of homosexual partners. Many of those at risk may well not have been open about their homosexuality to their families and friends. Some will be married. The revelation of their double life, coming about as the result of a fatal illness, is bound to cause traumatic shock to their families. Yet it is the support of their nearest and dearest which is so essential to them in this crisis; and it will be of primary importance for counsellors involved with people with AIDS to ensure that their anxieties about their relatives' reactions, and the relatives' own shock and grief, is handled as sensitively and constructively as can be.

Nor will it be easy for counsellors themselves to confront and clarify their own attitudes and feelings about the behaviour which has led to AIDS. To condemn promiscuity, and tell those at risk to 'find a steady partner and settle down', is much too glib in the present social situation with which homosexual people and others leading unorthodox lives are faced. Yet until effective treatments and cure for AIDS are found – and, better still, a prophylactic – a lifestyle of sexual activities (whether homosexual or heterosexual) habitually involving a variety of partners will now carry a clear risk of early death. It is no use pointing this out in a 'moralizing' way, and I would hope that no competent counsellor would do so;

but the counselling process may well involve assisting the client to develop an equally (hopefully, a more) rewarding life style which combines prudence for oneself and others with sexual and emotional satisfaction.

Openness

Outside the counselling situation, there is a clear need for all humane and concerned persons to work for changes in personal and social attitudes so as to minimize the risks which AIDS presents. There is an urgent need for more openness about personal and sexual needs and relationships throughout society. At present we have the worst of all worlds – a press and public attitude to sexuality that is at once both sensational and trivializing, and consequent secretiveness on the part of thousands of people who don't feel that they can safely disclose their sexual needs and lives. The mounting backlash against a largely spurious 'permissiveness' is itself militating against community health. At present, nearly everybody finds it hard to be honest about their sexuality (not infrequently, even with themselves). We are all to some degree sexual humbugs. The weakest aspect of veneral disease containment is contact tracing, which is all too often rendered difficult or even impossible because infected people either don't tell the full truth about their activities, or else don't have the necessary information (such as partners' names and addresses).

With the arrival of AIDS, such information may well be a matter of life and death. It is therefore essential that greater sexual frankness should become not only more possible, but usual. This will require a huge transformation in society's official mores and practices, which we as counsellors must work towards so as to promote the open, less diseased – and let us hope soon once again AIDS-free – society most people would prefer to live in.

Further reading

Kessler, Jeanne (1983) *Gay Men's Health: a Guide to the AID Syndrome and other Sexually Transmitted Diseases*. New York: Harper and Row.

Brief update

The article I wrote for *Counselling* was a first attempt to familiarize counsellors with the newly emerging phenomenon of AIDS. Rather than revising it, I would prefer to let it stand as a historical reference point, and to add a few comments on issues which with hindsight call for another perspective.

'The nature of the causative agent' (paragraph 3) is now generally accepted as being HIV – the human immunodeficiency virus – transmitted through blood, semen and possibly other body fluids. The incubation period is now known to be far longer than four years (paragraph 3) in many cases – as long as fifteen or twenty years has been accepted as a serious possibility. This fact, coupled with the probability that early treatment prolongs the infected person's life, makes the central importance of testing to identify the presence of the virus even more essential. Such testing requires sensitive counselling, before and after.

While AIDS in the United Kingdom has not spread with the rapidity which was originally feared, we should not allow this welcome fact to lull us into false security – especially over the potential risks of an escalation of heterosexual AIDS if 'safe sex' precautions are not practised by everyone, and not just by the so-called 'high risk' groups.

Complacency is also dangerous on a generational basis. Safe sex education is not a once-for-all task, but has to be repeated for each new wave of adolescents and young people of all sexual orientations as they are becoming sexually active.

The medical profession (paragraph 5) are far better educated about AIDS now than they were a decade ago. But there are still far too many primitive fears around among professional health workers.

Counselling is a key resource in dealing with AIDS – not only for the patients, but also for their families, lovers and friends, and for those who are treating and caring for them. Some excellent education and training courses now exist, but there is still far too much ignorance and sheer ineptness on the part of some health workers. (I recently heard of a friend who was shattered to be told he was HIV-positive without even knowing that his blood had been tested for the virus: this is totally unethical!)

Promiscuity (paragraph 9) is no longer regarded as a primary danger if 'safer sex' is practised. This information is repugnant to puritan moralists; their objections to accurate information on this score merely reinforce the old adage that 'the British vice is not buggery, but humbuggery'.

In some respects, public attitudes to sexual issues are even more unbalanced and hysterical in the mid-1990s than they were in the 1980s. When will we British grow up? I have discussed all this in my book, *Speaking of Sex* (London: Cassell, 1993).

There is now a huge literature on AIDS – most of it helpful.

Discussion issues

1 What might be your personal and professional concerns on discovering that one of your clients is an AIDS sufferer? How would you deal with those concerns?

2 Are there any particular counselling approaches which you consider may be most suitable for people with AIDS? Which are they and why do you think they may be helpful?

3 Do you agree that there are thousands of people who don't feel that they can safely disclose their sexual needs and lives? Have you found that this is a dilemma in counselling? How can counsellors use their skills to put clients at their ease in talking about sex?

4 What issues would you expect to be raised by someone who had been tested for HIV without their prior consent? How would you counsel them, and how would you address the professional aspects?

37

Gay Bereavement Counselling

Caz Lack

THERE IS NOTHING REMOTELY 'GAY' ABOUT BEING BEREAVED
THIS STUDY IS DEDICATED TO ALL THOSE GAY INDIVIDUALS WHO HAVE LOST
THEIR PARTNERS
APRIL, 1989

AND IN MEMORY OF BERNARD WILLIAMS, FOUNDER MEMBER OF THE LESBIAN
AND GAY BEREAVEMENT PROJECT WHO DIED IN SEPTEMBER 1994

It seems certain that about 5% of the population is homosexual. Some may have many 'casual' relationships but most will settle into a partnership which is as stable as most marriages. As with heterosexual couples the relationship may be monogamous or open and may be for life or a shorter period. There will not often be children but some couples will be caring for children from previous marriages or, very occasionally, from a donor pregnancy.

The death of the one will leave the other as bereft as any widow or widower and there are problems not experienced by those bereaved by the death of a husband or wife.

There is lack of recognition. Many such relationships are discreet or even secret. The couple pass as flatmates or 'just good friends' and, even when neighbours have guessed or even had a quiet giggle about them, they will not respond to the loss as they would for a husband or wife. They will not write those little notes which mean so much, or offer to help.

The funeral service, which is ordinarily so important for grief work, can be a disaster. Often the blood relatives will have made the arrangements and the bereaved partner may be excluded from the service altogether or, if attending, may be left to sit at the back, shrouded in his or her personal grief, away from the expressions of sympathy directed to the chief mourners at the front.

Even when the bereaved partner is treated as chief mourner there can be problems. Some ministers of religion have negative feelings about homosexual love and may express these in the funeral. This can be openly as in prayers that the deceased may be forgiven the deviant life style, or by ignoring the partner, not mentioning his or her name in the service, or by coolness after the service.

All too often, same-sex couples fail to make valid wills and bereaved partners may suffer a further loss when they have to move out of the shared home. Frequently tenancies or leases are in one partner's name and the survivor has no rights to remain. Only a few councils will accept that same-sex survivors have the same rights as widows or widowers (Cave, 1983).

This chapter was first published as 'The "I" becomes "We" . . . then the "We" becomes "One"', in *Counselling, Journal of the British Association for Counselling*, vol. 1, no. 4, pp. 120–3 (1990).

Although much has been written and published about the subject of bereavement, there is very little mentioned about gay bereavement. With issues surrounding HIV/AIDS and the realization that homosexuality is a real part of society, gay bereavement is an area that needs to be explored and highlighted, so that society can understand and possibly remedy the indifference, the lack of care, thought or consideration which is experienced by homosexuals who may be HIV-positive, or have AIDS, or who have suffered the loss of a partner.

I am going to explore several areas of gay bereavement. The first area being bereavement issues in general, then those issues specifically related to gay bereavement which will be enhanced by the presentation of case studies. Secondly, I will view family grief in AIDS, the chosen gay family and counselling survivors of AIDS. The third and final area will involve the support services that are available to survivors of AIDS and bereaved partners.

Bereavement

Mourning the loss of a loved one is a painful experience. It involves dealing with emotional, physical and spiritual experiences which may lead the individual to feel disorientated, depressed, immobile and suicidal. For the gay bereaved there are additional problems which complicate the grieving process.

Jackson (1974) describes grief as follows: 'Grief is the intense emotion that floods life when a person's inner security system is shattered by an acute loss, usually the death of someone important in his or her life.' The pain at the loss of a significant other may be intensified by acute reactions such as headaches, insomnia, loss of appetite and a sense of panic. Furthermore, as Jackson continues, 'Grief is the silent, knife-like terror and sadness that comes a hundred times a day, when you start to speak to someone who is no longer there.'

The bereavement process is not linear. According to Parkes (1972) the following stages of grief may recur: alarm, searching, mitigation, guilt, anger and gaining a new identity. The process of mourning is layered. When the layers come off, previously discarded layers may be 'worn' again. For example, a person who felt numb during the first few days of mourning may re-experience that feeling on anniversaries of the death.

Mental health professionals and health-care providers in the last decade have witnessed a surge of literature outlining the need for grief counselling, diagnostic considerations, treatment plans and supporting case histories. The majority of the literature currently addresses the loss of a relative, e.g. a parent, spouse, sibling or child. Clinicians have previously been provided with guidelines to help clients through the grieving process when the deceased and the survivors are heterosexual.

Gay bereavement

There is a scarcity of literature dealing with the grieving process of gay persons who encounter the cruelty of society's antihomosexual stigma while simultaneously mourning the loss of a lover or 'spouse'.

A stigma is often attached to any survivor who has lost a significant other. Parkes (1972) characterized this stigma as: 'a change in attitude that takes place in society when a person dies. Every widow discovers that people who were previously friendly and approachable become embarrassed and strained in her presence.' Goffman (1963) defines stigma as 'the situation of the individual who is disqualified from full social acceptance'. Furthermore, he outlined three categories of stigma including homosexuality under 'blemishes of individual characteristics', because society conditions its members to feel apprehensive towards those who lead alternative life styles; it is more difficult for gay men and women to receive support while they mourn their loss. Society does not sanction intimate, same-sex relationships, yet it is the lack of sanction for this type of relationship that prolongs the grieving process. Hence the gay bereaved experience a double stigma, and reactions to these added stresses vary widely.

The following are case presentations which illuminate the particular concerns and unique situations that the bereaved gay experience.

Allan, a man in his late twenties, began counselling therapy after a recent move to San Francisco from a northern town. He found work, but accepted a lower pay scale than he had been earning as an insurance broker in the rural town. His lover had committed suicide three months previous to his move, just prior to Christmas. His lover had been under investigation by the school district, not due to sexual activity, but in regard to comments he reportedly made to staff and students and he had been fired from his job as a teacher in a junior high school. Allan's lover committed suicide while visiting his parents on the East Coast. Allan stayed in California for the holidays. His reaction to the suicide was shock and withdrawal. He went to his lover's funeral, but was unable to engage his lover's family in a level of communication in which he could safely express his grief. He left his job upon his return from the funeral. Additionally, he stopped attending a gay people's group in which he and his lover had previously participated, because seeing the members of this group and hearing their concerns generated by the firing of his former mate restimulated memories of his lover and intensified his suffering and he therefore withdrew.

His unexpressed grief made him too vulnerable in the group setting. He had not been aware of the stigma attached to him because he was mourning someone. His awareness of the 'mourner's stigma' from other gay persons did not occur to him until he entered therapy four months later.

There are several considerations which merit further note from this case. One issue is concerned with self-disclosure. Once one's mate is dead, the gay survivor, like any other bereaved person, may be subject to investigations by doctors, the police, and the coroner, thus running the risk of being exposed suddenly or unexpectedly to potential anti-gay stigma.

The deceased's relatives, especially those who were not aware of the deceased's life style, may desire further questioning. This infringes upon the survivor's privacy, creating an emotional conflict regarding self-disclosure and adding stress to the bereaved's situation. If there is not even a minimal social support network, the survivor is more likely to move, escape or embark upon a major life change rather than cope with the added stresses.

Additionally, emotional problems associated with concealment of a social stigma may be highlighted during the mourning process. Men in particular have had to suppress their urge to cry at a lover's funeral. Thus, a typical conflict to anticipate would be whether or not to appear in public at this time. Moreover, by withholding emotions, the survivor may say he or she is 'just a friend of the deceased'. When concealing the truth about their sexuality, many gay people attempt to pass off their intimate relationships as 'flatmates' or 'friends'. Hence, the depth of emotional pain during the grieving process may be intensified, self-esteem further damaged and guilt feelings channelled into self-destructive behaviour.

Brian, a sixty-year-old man, did not experience the full weight of social stigma until his lover died. As a couple, they experienced a comfortable social acceptance for twenty-five years among their heterosexual friends and neighbours in a middle-class suburb as well as their business-executive and gay friends. The deceased had been wealthy and socially prominent. Over the years they had become recognized and accepted invitations as a couple. After the funeral, the friends that Brian thought were his, began to ignore him. Similarly to being a widow, he was ostracized from his social network, not invited to dinners as he had been before his 'spouse's' death. His telephone calls were not returned, he felt acutely despondent, 'gave up' and withdrew from most of his friends. His only contact was the minimal amount he needed to maintain his pet store business. For over a year he was in a state of chronic depression. No longer a partner in a couple, his presence, like that of a widow, created awkwardness amongst his previous social friends and acquaintances. Brian was avoided, not simply for being gay, but also because he reminded others of the impermanence of life. Feeling the onus attached to his homosexuality and resenting rejection, his grief and difficulties in instigating new social contacts that would validate his positive gay identity, caused him to become depressed.

Brian's lover and partner in life died shortly before a cruise they had planned to take together. In an attempt to console himself, Brian went on the trip with a new acquaintance, a man thirty-five years younger, who was an alcoholic. His expectations of the young man's affection and caring were never realized, and he soon discovered that the young man could not fulfil his longing to be loved again. Such attempts to duplicate the lost relationship by the survivor are self-destructive, a sabotage to prevent the unloading of deep feelings of loss and resolution of grief. Brian did not enter counselling therapy until he re-experienced the shock on the anniversary of his lover's death one year later and again encountered the deep depression, insomnia and physical weakness he first experienced at his lover's death.

Guilt is one of the anticipated reactions the bereaved experience after the death of a loved one. For gay people the 'if only I had done' type of guilt may be exacerbated by the guilt about their sexual preferences. Guilt may take on many forms following a lover's death, conflicts regarding one's sexuality may resurface. A lover's death, particularly if it was a suicide, may restimulate old self-doubts, feelings and insecurities about being gay (Clark, 1977).

Another pertinent consideration in grief counselling with gays is the survivor's social network. The more dependent the survivor has been in the relationship, the more likely it is that the after-effects of the shock and far-reaching episodes will be acute and longer lasting.

If a person can reach out to other gay people and transform feelings of loss, anger, guilt and loneliness into feelings of self-regard and self-interest, it will be easier for that person to be validated in his or her social identity. Particularly for gay people, the social network functions as the mainstay of support and self-expression during times of identity reformation and provides resources during a personal loss. Without churches, families or a work environment where deep feelings can be expressed safely, the social network is the counsellor's focus for intervention and healing.

Usually, friends of someone who dies are only excused from work to attend funeral services, whilst persons related by marriage are often granted an extended leave of absence if requested. In the case where sexual identity is concealed, a request for an extended period of time off may raise suspicions or simply be denied to 'a friend' of the deceased. Also, when the deceased is a same-sex friend, the gay survivor's fluctuations in mood and other grief reactions can irritate co-workers who do not empathize with the depth of feeling which the survivor needs to express. When counselling the gay bereaved, ways to allow the opportunity for the expression of grief should be encouraged.

The lack of resources designed for gay people create an even more difficult situation. When one is gay and lives in a community where homosexuality is not considered a human right, where does one seek solace? She or he cannot go to a priest because gays are considered sinners. Gays are not able to go to a doctor, lawyer or work supervisor for fear of exposure, loss of a job or status in the community. Nor can they expect to get support from their families for fear of rejection. The likelihood of going to one's family is very rare.

Family grief and AIDS

Many families must face a double adjustment to the death of a son. They may have to cope with the realization that their son or daughter was gay, but in the situation of a son who has died as a result of an AIDS-related illness it can create immense conflict and trauma for parents. The level of denial in such families was probably high already if the sexual identity of the son is undisclosed before the diagnosis (Shearer and McKusick, 1988). Thus the counsellor includes helping parents to confront the psychological pain caused by the loss of this defence.

In many cases, once these conflicts are resolved, parents can approach the memory of their son with more love and support of their feelings. Any painful event is better dealt with openly. Protracted grief can have a secretive and depressing, but special and private aspect, one which usually dissipates when someone else is brought into the grief process.

Many men after leaving the family home develop a new 'chosen family' of significant friends. These friends usually rally round at the bedside of the person with AIDS providing social, financial and life management support. In a smooth process after death, the network and the nuclear family can help each other with their grieving. One mother, after having come from the midwest of America to her son's community for his memorial service, looked out from the podium at the many faces of his friends and said 'It certainly proves the feeling I have had for years that my son was loved and lovable to be here among his friends and to feel the love and support you have shown me this week.'

In some cases, families do not cross these boundaries, creating ritual and personal grief processes that exclude friends of the gay man. Whereas this may honour the philosophical or spiritual needs of the family, it can also be alienating.

If the family does not recognize the viability of their gay son's life style or the rights of his chosen partner to grieve and to decisions regarding the estate, conflict can result. This situation is often extremely volatile, given the stress of all involved as well as the emotional and financial stakes. It may be necessary at this time for a counsellor to mediate conflicts and, if alleviating confrontation, smooth the transition process and cushion feelings of anger and guilt in the family.

Like war, AIDS takes young people from their families. One mother confided 'It's not supposed to happen this way; he was supposed to bury me!'

Becoming closer to a dying son may awaken a parent's own reaction to the approach of death. If helped by the counselling process to integrate the experience, there is a profound wisdom to be learned by families who do suffer this loss, that the dying is over. Characteristically, loneliness, memories and heartache abound. It is a time of transition when survivors reassess their beliefs and relationships to the rest of the world.

During this time survivors often feel tearful, angry at the least provocation, misunderstood by those who have not also suffered loss, and even guilty for no good reason.

Many survivors of lovers who died from AIDS are young people who have never before experienced mortal loss, making their pain all the more confusing. It is not uncommon to hear the bereaved say 'I am going crazy'. The counsellor can offer simple validation of the bizarre nature of the client's experience with the reassurance that, yes it is an enormous tragedy to lose a loved one to AIDS.

Counselling survivors of AIDS

During clinical work with six surviving male lovers of men who died from AIDS common characteristics were found that may be helpful to a counsellor approaching therapy of bereavement in gay men (AIDS Health Project, 1985).

First, these men were experiencing bereavement in a community which is itself becoming expert in the stages of bereavement, including denial. Each man seen for counselling complained that his friends were getting tired of hearing him talk about his lover. All of them described pressure from their associates to conduct their grief in various appropriate fashions.

At the beginning of counselling therapy with these men, it was necessary to encourage them to use however much time they needed to talk about, think about, have erotic fantasies about, or cry about the loss of their lovers, exclusive of any time restrictions. This permission alone seemed to help the process because it counteracted whatever need the gay man's friends may have had to bury the process of bereavement soon after the funeral.

After the death the lovers became much more aware of their own possible susceptibility to AIDS, a fear of contagion that they suspended in order to remain close to their dying friends. Moreover, they were acutely aware of what AIDS looks like and were quite fearful of contracting it or passing it on to anyone else. Consequently, sexual repression and anxiety attacks about contagion occurred in the men treated.

The survivor often felt stigmatized by his association with the victim. On becoming aware that he was seropositive with the HIV antibody, one man expressed guilt that he had possibly transmitted HIV to his lover. Simple extensions of understanding and compassion appeared to help soften feelings of alienation and to help lessen the person's horror of his own contagiousness. Since the disease required exhausting schedules before their lovers' death, these men will have been too busy to worry about dating and safe sex. They may need good advice at this time with reassurances that they are capable of being close to men physically without exposure to, or transmission of, the HIV virus.

In this instance, denial may lend some saving grace. Among the men in this small sample, those who denied causality between their lover's illness and their own susceptibility to HIV adapted more quickly. They were more likely to become engaged in new relationships and less likely to have fears about contamination, even while being cautious about transmission.

In this population, research results that link bereavement and depression to suppression of immune functions are particularly relevant. For the counsellor, the question arises of how much depression and dysphoria should be encouraged as clients work through feelings about their lover's death. This is a dynamic question that usually must be related to each individual's coping style and personality factors. Fortunately it is most often answered by the clients themselves as they move naturally between the constituent phases of denial and acceptance.

Those who were primarily responsible for the day-to-day care of their lovers had a much more difficult time emotionally afterwards, particularly if they had conflicts with their lover's families about the care. These men were caught in a stance of protective vigilance at the moment of their lover's death, a tension-filled position which made relaxation very difficult.

A rigid idealization of the dead lover can occur, making new boyfriends unwelcome. At the same time that these bereaved clients longed for the closeness and support they gave to their dying partners, they also automatically compared them with the idealized image of their partners. This tendency only served to heighten their loneliness. In the last stages of his life the person with AIDS and his lover return to a stage where intimacy is extremely important and 'ego boundaries' are loose. Problems arise when the lover dies during this stage and leaves behind a fiercely devoted widower.

As most relationships progress, a working balance of autonomy and dependence is negotiated and maintained. Because of the inordinate dependence of those suffering from terminal AIDS, the youthfulness of the men it attacks, and the untimely interruption to intimacy that a lover's death brings, those who are left behind have sacrificed their autonomy but later need to regain it. Unlike a relationship which ends because of incompatibility, here it is difficult to mobilize anger at the departed partner as a means of resecuring one's sense of well-being and peace. In the special instance of bereavement, a therapist can help the partner finish the dialogue of the relationship and prepare to move on.

Finally, those who got involved with volunteers in an AIDS organization recovered more quickly after their lovers had died. Some reported that they found within these groups other men who had similar stories to tell. Since the loss of friends and lovers to AIDS has increasingly become a community-wide occurrence, a great deal of wisdom and support is available alongside the great amount of pain the community experiences.

Summary

This chapter is intended to sensitize the general public, and specifically counsellors, to the particular concerns of the gay bereaved.

Counsellors need to be aware of and accept homosexual and lesbian life styles as well as being knowledgeable about the grieving process before engaging in a therapeutic relationship with gay bereaved individuals.

The counsellor needs to be aware of the client's reactions to the stigma of being gay, as well as to the stigma of being a mourner, and help the client distinguish these feelings. Moreover, as previously mentioned, delayed grief reactions on anniversaries or some other special date in the former relationship are not uncommon. Hence the counsellor and client as a team might explore individualized strategies or rituals to acknowledge these events and thereby enhance the mourning process. For example, one of the important grief processes is to help the client establish their own personal strategies which symbolize commemoration and 'letting go'. Examples of such strategies include completion of a photo album, creation of a poem, dance, painting; the establishment of a specific time for a private conversation with the deceased, or the lighting of a candle. Such strategies are not unusual if one considers religious rituals for the acknowledgement of the deceased. (In the Jewish religion, a special candle is lit on the anniversary date of a death of a family member.)

A nurturing therapeutic relationship will often lead to great rewards for the counsellor and client. Both will observe the patient's progress from a stage of intense pining and pain to a renewed awareness of strengths, growing sense of identity and deeper engagement in a social network of friends and intimates. Finally, resolution of mourning may be accompanied by less guilt, greater self-esteem and stronger coping mechanisms to meet life's challenges.

Helpful organizations

The Terrence Higgins Trust and Body Positive Group

Both organizations are largely voluntary. The Trust provides 'buddy' support and assistance for clients who are unwell and also runs counselling groups where antibody-positive individuals can meet to learn more about AIDS and to talk to others with the same condition.

The Trust provides a 'carers support group' for the partners and loved ones of people who have AIDS.

The Medical Committee of the Terrence Higgins Trust provide documents for the public explaining exactly what AIDS is, and the meaning of being HIV-positive and also advises on how to reduce the risk of transmitting the virus.

The London Lighthouse Project

The Lighthouse was founded in 1988 and sets out to provide a continuum of care from initial diagnosis through to providing residential accommodation and respite care in the terminal stages. The Lighthouse also provides counselling, daycare, groupwork and training.

The purpose of the residential unit is to build a community amongst those affected by HIV and AIDS over the whole period of their illness, 'a home base' so that people can look forward to dying in familiar and friendly surroundings. The Lighthouse is situated in West London.

The Lesbian and Gay Bereavement Project

Dudley Cave and his partner Bernard Williams set up the Gay Bereavement Project which operates on a shoestring income of gifts and grants mainly from gay organizations and individuals and which offers a round-the-clock telephone counselling service. It is made up of a small group of people who are all comfortable with their own gayness and are suitably trained in bereavement work.

The project encourages gay women and men to prepare for the inevitable day when one partner will die; to arrange for joint ownership and to write wills. Too few realize that without a valid will, a same-sex partner cannot inherit and all will go to blood relatives or to the state.

A church or synagogue may be quite good at looking after its widowed members, but even the more liberal elements of Christianity or Judaism, for example, can find it hard to offer support to bereaved gay people. Trying to overcome this problem, the Gay Bereavement Project has been building up a list of 'sympathetic' priests, ministers and rabbis who are prepared to conduct a funeral in accordance with the wishes of the bereaved person and who can offer continuing support.

The Lesbian and Gay Bereavement Project also works to educate the caring professionals to the existence of gay bereavement, and to help people who care to recognize it. This is going to be of enormous value to the area of hospice work which is working towards accepting patients with AIDS and therefore involved with the partners and their inevitable bereavement. AIDS may just open up an area of need which has been largely ignored. In the next few years, the bereavement project is likely to be hearing from more young men who have been bereaved by AIDS.

The project welcomes calls from lesbians and gay men who have been bereaved or are preparing for a bereavement, whether or not related to HIV, as well as from parents, brothers and sisters, children, other family members, friends, neighbours, colleagues and carers (in whatever capacity).

Useful contacts

Lesbian and Gay Switchboard – 24-hour information and helpline
Tel: 0171 837 7324

The Terence Higgins Trust – information and support about HIV and AIDS
Helpline: 0171 242 1010; Legal line: 0171 405 2381

GLAD (Gay and Lesbian Legal Advice)
Helpline: 0171 831 3535

CRUSE – national organization providing bereavement counselling
Helpline: 0181 332 7227; HQ: 0181 940 4818

The Red Admiral Project – free, confidential counselling service for those affected
by HIV and AIDS
Tel: 0171 835 1495

The London Lighthouse – provides care, counselling and training
Tel: 0171 792 1200

References

AIDS Health Project (1985) *Working with AIDS: a Resource Guide for Mental Health Professionals*. AIDS Health Project, Box 0884, San Francisco, California.

Cave, D. (1983) 'Bereavement and the unmarried partner', *Bereavement Care* (CRUSE), Summer.

Clark, D. (1977) *Loving Someone Gay*. Millbrae: Celestial Arts.

Goffman, E. (1963) *Stigma*. Englewood Cliffs, NJ: Prentice Hall.

Jackson, E.N. (1974) *Concerning Death: a Guide for the Living*. Boston, MA: Beacon Press.

Parkes, C.M. (1972) *Bereavement: Studies of Grief in Adult Life*. New York: International Universities Press.

Shearer, P. and McKusick, L. (1988) 'Counselling survivors of AIDS', *Bereavement Care* (CRUSE) 7(2): Summer.

Discussion issues

1 What do you think are the likely consequences for lesbians and gay men of the lack of recognition of their relationship and their exclusion from public grief processes in their bereavement?
2 What are the physical and psychological effects of stigmatization?
3 How might you help a client expressing self-doubt, in particular regarding sexuality and identity?
4 What do you regard as the most important issues in dealing with conflict in your own life and in helping clients to work with it in their own situations?

38

Learning to Live with Life-Threatening Illness

Scott Berry

> As a society transplants itself from the old to the new world, the delicate and carefully maintained balance between the two systems of the psyche – between consciousness and the unconscious – is disturbed. Ego consciousness, which had become sophisticated and dominant, is suddenly reined in by the unconscious, which becomes stronger and more demanding in the new psycho-cultural situation. (Tacey, 1993)

There has been much material written about the psychological response to bereavement which focuses on those who survive the death of a loved one or, alternatively, on those who are about to die. In HIV counselling this material can be of use in working with people affected by HIV but only some of this material is useful in working with those who are living with the virus. The AIDS epidemic is forcing HIV practitioners to transform traditional bereavement theory. It may even demand an exploration beyond these theories and a focus on very different experiences of loss and change. Perhaps this is a good thing since it means practitioners need to pay close attention to HIV-positive clients and their individual responses. It also means that clients are teaching therapists about their needs and how to meet them.

For example, people diagnosed HIV-positive may continue to live for more than a decade with the notion that they may get ill or die. In fact, within the HIV community there is a continuing debate about whether HIV really does lead to AIDS. Questions of death and mourning may play a less specific role in practice but the question 'How do I live with this?' will be common. This question has led me to search for theoretical material that resonates with the experiences of my client group. As a counsellor who integrates both psychodynamic and humanistic theoretical ideas my study of theory in relation to these issues has been wide.

In this search I have been moved by the article 'The Australian Psyche' by David Tacey (1993) and his argument that what occurs in transplanted colonial societies is a kind of psychic shake-up. This rang a bell because some newly diagnosed clients speak of feeling as if diagnosis has transported them to a new world where all the surroundings are different: the buildings, the flora and fauna have changed and there are no maps to guide them. Exploring this metaphorical landscape can give valuable insight into such an individual's emotional state.

This article suggests that what can occur in HIV diagnosis is a similar psychic shake-up to that described by Tacey. Specifically, the initial response to diagnosis

This chapter was first published as 'Learning to live with life-threatening illness: some ideas on HIV diagnosis', in *Counselling, Journal of the British Association for Counselling*, vol. 6, no. 1, pp. 44–7 (1995).

can be likened in some cases to a psychic explosion, in which one's identity, what we call our 'self', feels as if it is destroyed and something akin to Bowlby's (1993) 'Disorganization and Despair' takes its place. The old map is ineffective and psychic 'Reorganization' can only occur through changing that map and, therefore, transforming identity. What emerges in post-diagnosis may feel like a partially new self with different needs, values and ideals.

Grieving in relation to HIV diagnosis

> In what . . . does the work which mourning performs consist? . . . Each single one of the memories and expectations in which the libido is bound to the object is brought up and hypercathected, and detachment of the libido is accomplished in respect of it. (Freud, 1991)

Most practitioners would agree that there is no singular standard response to HIV diagnosis. Each individual's response is unique and personal and the goal of the helper is to respect that. However, the grief process for some who are diagnosed HIV-positive is often a long-term prospect.

For these people, living with the grief of diagnosis means living with the idea that illness or death may strike at any time. To explain how this feels in initial diagnosis some clients refer to themselves as 'a walking time bomb'. Suddenly the perception of the body has changed and this has a dramatic effect on the newly diagnosed.

The quotation from Sigmund Freud (1991) above seems to support the notion that diagnosis may feel like moving from an 'old to a new world'. He suggests that the bereaved need to undergo a process of remembering and letting go of all their experiences related to the deceased. What Freud suggests of the bereaved, can be applied to the diagnosed, that people living with HIV re-experience and detach from their HIV-negative identity. Every new situation, every memory and expectation is re-evaluated and transformed because of diagnosis.

People living with HIV encounter the same familiar events and situations but, as some clients communicate, nothing seems familiar any more. The familiar situations beg new questions and demand new answers. For instance, 'How do I feel about dying?' may not previously have been a high-priority question in the lives of some who are newly diagnosed. Changes occur in attitudes to family, friends, vocation and dreams for the future.

It feels significant that some of what is described here could be compared to elements of what we have come to understand as the 'mid-life' process: feeling dissatisfied with parts of our lives we were previously contented with, needing to look deeply into ourselves and a desire to put some valuable meaning to our lives can all be an important part of working through HIV diagnosis.

There may be more personal adjustments to be made, for example, attitudes towards sexuality, a person's own body (e.g. glandular and immune systems), a person's own body fluids, especially semen, vaginal secretions, blood and saliva, undergo dramatic re-constellation.

Freud's comments imply that this transformation is an almost systematic and ordered process. Nothing could be further from the truth! The path to acknowledging and working through this material is often trodden in the midst of extreme emotional catharsis. The notion of 'psychic explosion' applied to Freud's observation helps to understand what he may have meant when writing *Mourning and Melancholia*.

Some ideas on the unconscious in HIV diagnosis

Is it possible that the themes involved in diagnosis parallel those inherent in our early life experiences? Diagnosis brings with it the fear of death and physical harm; it plunges us into the themes of transformation and survival.

The newly diagnosed find themselves in a new life, in a body with seemingly new limitations, where life values have changed; they also find themselves feeling powerful emotions which they have little control over. Many of my clients feel powerless over their situation and wish to return to an HIV-negative diagnosis.

This may be similar to the process of birth itself where we are delivered from one landscape into another and our bodies, removed from embryonic fluid, have new limitations. Inherent in birth are the themes of transformation and survival and the threat of death or physical harm is ever present throughout the birth procedure.

Infants experience extremely powerful emotions and may feel powerless over their situation. They may wish to return to the womb where everything was warm, where there was no harsh light and no hunger. Questions confronting the newly diagnosed may also parallel those of early life: 'How will I survive?', 'Can I survive?', 'Who will help me?', 'Am I alone?' The need for others is paramount as a theme in both these life experiences.

Perhaps the most striking parallel that can be made between early life themes and those of diagnosis is the notion of an 'emerging self'. The newly diagnosed are involved in a process of understanding who they may now be in the world and reorganizing themselves within this new internal and external environment. By its very nature, early life experience is about a similar process. Infants, involved in developing internal psychic structures in order to survive, are also evaluating the external world and those in it, in order to develop a firm notion of self.

It may be that what in pre-diagnosis remained unconsciously repressed, in post-diagnosis becomes irrepressible. Material that had been buried deep within the id is suddenly located much closer to ego-consciousness due to the psychic explosion brought about by diagnosis. Thus the initial response to diagnosis can be charged with emotions from earlier life.

This has enormous implications for HIV-positive people as it means that deeply disturbing feelings and experiences from the past can have a powerful impact in the present. A person with the potential for psychological disturbance or, with missing links in childhood development, may be affected by this after diagnosis.

Implications for practice

> ... the same principle ... [of good mothering] ... underlies the analyst's attitude towards his analysands. Every interpretation ... and every reconstruction, consists of two phases: first, the analysand must realise that he has been understood; only as a second step will the analyst demonstrate to the analysand the specific factors that explain the psychological content he had first grasped empathically. (Kohut, 1977)

Whilst people with HIV may be actively involved in the process of integrating the implications of their health status many newly diagnosed people are simply trying to hold their lives together. Most seem to have a great capacity to do this whilst experiencing extreme emotional fragility and sensitivity. This can last from a couple of hours to several months.

It is important to exercise a high level of awareness within these sessions and have an understanding and acceptance of the different communities affected by HIV in order to provide a safe environment. Allowing the client to be themselves helps to create a situation similar to Winnicott's 'facilitating environment' where 'non-purposive activity' or play is at least a viable option. If counsellees are experiencing emotions that are coloured by those of early life they need to express these without harm or judgement. Rogers' core conditions are an imperative in this work.

In working with the idea that the experience of diagnosis may be charged with emotions from early life Kohut's (1977) notion of 'transmuting' seems of real value. Kohut theorized transmuting as the necessary empathic mirroring of mother to child and expressed its importance in the analytic encounter. It was the need of a number of clients for empathic mirroring that first alerted me to the idea that the response to diagnosis may be charged with early life emotions.

In this crisis some clients can feel intensely alone and isolated if adequate understanding and warmth is not provided. These clients may often ask questions, needing reassurance that the counsellor understands and accepts them. The sometimes intense confusion may cause the counsellee to doubt that they are even making sense. In this intense emotional state the newly diagnosed may be extremely aware if the counsellor is distracted in any way, or if they are not bodily or verbally providing the acknowledgement needed.

Projective identification may play a role in the initial encounter with a newly diagnosed person. Specifically, questions may transfer a large amount of emotional energy from the client: 'Why is this happening to me?' and 'How do I keep on living?' At such cathartic emotional points, when the client simply needs to be held, some counsellors find that the fantasy 'I am a container for some of these feelings' helps both client and therapist bear the initial shock. In some cases there may be a shared fantasy between them that the sessions somehow hold the client's pain.

Kohut suggests that being understood is more important for a child than actually having its needs met and proposes that the same is true for the client in the counselling relationship. Perhaps meeting the client's need in this situation would be taking away the diagnosis. Unfortunately that is impossible. However, Kohut gives the hope that by accurately understanding the counsellee, and communicating that understanding, the client may feel a great sense of relief and comfort. Those with a personal experience of HIV may be even better at communicating such understanding.

Jim's experience

Jim originally came to see me after being diagnosed only three days earlier. In the session that appears below he was three months into diagnosis and was feeling extremely emotional and fragile. Jim was finding it difficult to understand and express his feelings so we agreed to some extra sessions for the purpose of helping him explore them. During the last few of these we had the following dialogue (C = Client/P = Psychotherapist).

C: I just don't know what's going on. I think I want to be alone but when I am I can't stand it. I think I want to be with people but when I am I can't connect. I find it hard to start things and when I do I can't finish them.

P: What does that feel like?

C: Well it makes me angry! Like there is a big hurricane inside me I guess . . . and it's ripping through my life and breaking everything up.

P: So it's like a big hurricane ripping through your life?

C: No . . . no that isn't right either. (*Silence*) I don't know.

P: It feels important that I understand what's happening for you now. (*Pause*) I'd like to suggest we do an experiment.

C: (*laughs*) OK.

P: Let's go over and sit by the window. (*We move our chairs to the window.*) I wonder what would be happening outside this window if it were to reflect your feelings? What would it look like?

C: Well there'd be a hurricane.

P: A hurricane.

C: But not just that because I don't always feel like that. Sometimes I feel good.

P: So how would that look outside this window?

C: Well the hurricane would be in that corner and everything would be being trashed by it. The people there wouldn't know where to turn or where to go. But on the other side it would be sunny.

P: So over this side it would be sunny?

C: Yes . . . and there'd be like a holiday resort and people lying around on deck chairs drinking martinis (*laughter*). Here there would be a tidal wave and people being drowned by it.

P: So people would be drowning. Dying?

C: Yes. (*Long silence*) Over here there'd be snow and sleet and over here an earthquake.

P: Would there be people there?

C: Yes. In the earthquake.

P: What would be happening to them?

C: They'd be getting crushed by buildings and eaten up by the earth.

P: (*pause*) Would you put yourself in this picture?

C: Oh god. I'd put myself in outer space if only I bloody could. (*Jim begins to cry.*)

Jim and I moved on to exploring what emotions these images represented. As we focused on each landscape, he expressed some feelings about it and became more capable of understanding those feelings. Jim became less fearful about some of his feelings and therefore more capable of caring for himself. A new language developed between us. He would come in to sessions and say 'Today I feel I'm in a hurricane', 'Today it's like the earthquake' or 'I'm drinking martinis in the sun today'. Jim was moving towards charting his own map depicting the new world of HIV diagnosis.

Interpreting metaphorical images within sessions is one way of attempting to understand the internal space of the newly diagnosed. I have found that exploring metaphorical landscape with clients can help move them into awareness and expression of their feelings. A client may use weather, natural disasters, or city-scapes to describe their feelings. A client who describes an Arctic environment (a landscape which is 'frozen over'), or a client who cannot place themselves within the environment they have created, may be in Kubler-Ross's (1982) stage of Denial/Isolation or Bowlby's (1993) phase of Numbing.

A client who describes an idyllic landscape which is being rocked by an earth-quake may be communicating that the very foundation of their being feels under threat – perhaps they are moving from Numbing into Disorganization and Despair. Whatever the landscape described, understanding, and conveying that understanding to clients, seems to help a great deal. A strong here-and-now relationship can be established which helps to hold clients through what is an extremely difficult time.

Conclusion

Elizabeth Kubler-Ross (1982) has given a great gift in her 'Stages of Dying' which provides a guide for understanding the psychic process of those with terminal illness. Bowlby (1993), and others, have provided us with the 'Phases of Mourning' which help to explain the emotional process of those in bereavement. While these theories may play a valuable part in working with people with HIV they go only part of the way to explaining the psychic process of those with life-threatening illness.

When a person is diagnosed with a terminal illness it usually means there is little chance of long-term survival. People with life-threatening illness have a disease with only the potential to threaten life and may find themselves living with their diagnosis for a long period of time. Thus, the concern with the established grief theories in relation to this is their focus on death. It means practitioners are working without a model that helps us understand how we live with life-threatening illness.

This article proposes 'psychic explosion' as a way of perceiving the process of HIV diagnosis. Perhaps after this initial explosion something akin to a mid-life process occurs for some HIV-positive people. Both these notions provide the possibility of re-evaluation, new life and hope. They suggest that diagnosis need not be a tragic death sentence but may lead to working through old hurts, repressed psychological disturbance and may help those with life-threatening illness find new ways of living. They have the benefit of fitting easily into Bowlby's (1993) 'Phases of Mourning' whilst making these more specific to those who are diagnosed with life-threatening illness.

Having worked through diagnosis and the implications of death, some HIV-positive people say that life feels more valuable and meaningful after diagnosis than before. They say they feel more self-regard and have a greater sense of their own dignity, integrity and right to be alive. Many make dramatic and creative changes in their lives. Although the experience of diagnosis is painful it has also reaped many rewards. This is an image of HIV-positive people that is far from the victim role. These people have gone on living and found, out of a seemingly hopeless predicament, real hope and value in life.

The fact is that people with life-threatening illness are giving us the answer to the question 'How do I live with this?' with each new day they continue to live their lives. We need only look and listen to understand how they are doing so.

References

Bowlby, J. (1993) *The Making and Breaking of Affectional Bonds*. London: Routledge.
Freud, S. (1991) *Mourning and Melancholia*. London: Penguin Freud Library.
Kohut, H. (1977) *The Restoration of Self*. New York: International University Press.
Kubler-Ross, E. (1982) *On Death and Dying*. London: Tavistock.
Tacey, D.J. (1993) 'The Australian Psyche', *Psychological Perspectives*, issue no. 38.

Discussion issues

1 How do you feel about the idea of working with people living with HIV/AIDS? Is it important to explore how it may feel to work with people who are experiencing intense emotions about living will illness and the idea of death? Have you explored these themes in your own life?

2 What are your feelings about working with the different communities of people living with HIV/AIDS? What work do you need to do to help you to understand your own values in relation to sex, gay men and women, non-gay-identified men who have sex with men, prostitution and injecting drug-use?

3 What do you think and how do you feel about HIV-positive people having sex? Some countries have made it illegal for HIV-positive people to have sex, whilst others expect that positive people will either reveal their status beforehand or always practise safe sex. Whatever your values, consider how they might impact on your HIV-positive clients.

4 Do you consider that the spread of AIDS is forcing HIV practitioners to transform traditional bereavement theory? What are the implications of this view for counselling practice?

39

The Dual-Role Transvestite
Jed Bland

Question: What is the difference between a feminist and a transvestite?
Answer: Both challenge existing assumptions about gender, the one consciously, the other driven unthinkingly to do so.

What is it about gender that affects people so deeply? Why has it become a straitjacket oppressing both women and men, too often leading to suicide? Why is there so little professional help?

A counsellor, who was trying to be helpful, said, 'Why shouldn't you wear what you like?' rather than 'Why shouldn't you have what feelings you like?' In a television programme about wives and their cross-dressing husbands someone said, 'It's a matter for negotiation'. To most people negotiation is not a word that implies feelings.

Since my article was first published in 1993, a number of phenomena have appeared. In a television advertisement, a beautiful girl gets into a taxi and, as it travels along the road, she pulls out a razor and begins shaving. Though people like Annie Lennox and David Bowie may have had serious intent, 'gender bending' has become material for commercial exploitation. Like sex it has become a saleable commodity. While it is portrayed as a game, like the pantomime dame and the drag act, we can laugh at it, but the moment we meet someone who is serious we feel very threatened.

Another common theme in the media is the glamorous high-flying executive who 'used to be a man'. Meanwhile cross-dressers appear on talk shows where the interviewer struggles with his, or her, own negative feelings. It is known that one presenter who conducted a show in a very professional way is privately disgusted by the whole idea.

These people, usually men, are the public face of a widely varying and little understood group of people who are the subject of this article – the dual role transvestites (Bancroft, 1989). They extend from the stereotype of people who 'cross-dress for sexual gratification' (to quote my dictionary) to the other stereotype of the transexual, the 'woman in a man's body' (and vice versa).

They spend part of their lives as normal heterosexual males, and part of it dressing and 'passing' as women, without actually wanting to 'change sex' or to have sexual relations with other men. For many people their transvestism was, and is, a serious issue and a frequent source of great emotional distress and confusion.

Because most transvestites remain hidden from view, the only evidence available is from those who feel able to give an account of their past and those who are

---

This chapter is based on an article first published as 'The dual role transvestite: a unique form of identity', in *Counselling, Journal of the British Association for Counselling*, vol. 4, no. 2, pp. 112–16 (1993).

engaged in helping work within the sub-culture. Usually, transvestism is described as a 'condition', which has overtones of a medical or psychiatric disability. My feeling is that it is a natural, even self-therapeutic reaction to social pressures. The problem is not the cross-dressing, but the guilt associated with it. In fact I am not alone in suggesting that it is a natural outcome of Western culture. It follows that for those who feel the need for help, counselling is more likely to be of value than medicines or behaviour therapy. Clearly if we could change society many of the problems brought to counsellors would disappear. That can only be a long-term solution in which many counsellors might find themselves 'signing on'. Meanwhile anyone who comes for help deserves to be heard.

Gender identity and gender role

Throughout the feminist, gay, psychiatric and psychological literature, the words sex and gender are used very imprecisely. A very good textbook account of the psychological development of gender identity is given in Gross (1987), but for brevity I will outline my own definitions. It is also necessary to explain why transvestites (and transsexuals) are not necessarily homosexual, just as people who have a 'normal' gender identity are not necessarily heterosexual.

The sex of a person is defined by their chromosomes, XX or XY. Though there are variants, my concern here is not with physically intersexed people. In practice the new-born baby is given a label – boy or girl – by the midwife. It is as unscientific as that and it usually works.

Different authors use the term gender-identity in different ways. Some use the term to imply that it is something babies are born with – that they somehow 'know' they are boys or girls. There is some evidence that certain sexually dimorphic behaviours are innate, such as reacting differently to others of the same or opposite sex. There are also such things as the maternal bond and the recently 'discovered' paternal instinct.

It is equally accepted that babies have unique individual precursors of personality. Let us suggest then that natal gender identity is a locus. It is one that does not start from a point – birth – and travel to one of two other points – masculinity or femininity. The end points are somewhere in a probability distribution. As the child grows it learns that certain expressions of its personality are appropriate to its sexual label, others are not. It attempts to become acceptably masculine, or feminine, though it is easier for a girl to be a 'tomboy', than for a boy to be a 'sissy'.

Money and Ehrhardt (1972) defined *Gender Identity/Role (G I/R)* to describe the child's negotiation between its personality, as masculine and feminine, and the stereotype offered to it, or imposed on it. In other words, 'who' it is and 'who' it 'ought' to be. The result is what Bem (1993) calls a *Gender Schema*. Schemas are the way the mind is said to organize memories, conscious and forgotten, into networks and structures, in this case relative to gender perceptions, so as to determine attitudes, behaviours and reactions ideally in the most efficient way.

To the author then sex is functional and gender is cognitive. Sex is described in verbs such as 'to procreate'. Gender is described in adjectives, like Bem's 'Fluffy Women and Chesty Men'.

To put it another way, there is a new buzzword – the 'third gender' (sometimes, wrongly, the 'third sex'). *There is no such thing.* By definition, there can be only two genders – masculine and feminine. But masculinity and femininity are themselves social constructs – the stereotypes of individual cultures. Bem (1993) criticizes the attempts to dignify them with scientific respectability by those who misused Binet's work to develop the IQ, which measures people's ability to pass intelligence tests. Is the attempt to introduce a third gender simply to prop up an increasingly unsupportable dichotomy? Why only three? Why not as many as we like?

Different societies, social classes, sub-groups and families may offer different gender roles and they may be offered with different levels of pressure to conform. Moreover what is important is not the individual stereotype itself, but the individual child's perception of it.

The third gender then is a composite. In negotiating a compromise between our individual personality and our individual stereotype, we adopt our own personal 'third gender'. Generally, we find a compromise that feels comfortable. It is perhaps those whose composite is a fragile construction who find the issues most threatening. For some people the composite is unstable and eventually gender identity problems appear with the need to express the hidden parts of their personalities.

This is why transvestism is connected to self-expression, rather than sexual preference. Gender has become disconnected from the simple motivation for men and women to find partners whose company they can endure for long enough to nurture a family.

Early development

In their early years few transvestites exhibit cross-gender behaviour openly. Most know that it is something to keep quiet, and if they acquire any cross-gender clothes, become expert in hiding them. Few report any trauma and there seems to be no one ascertainable cause. Most report a perfectly normal childhood, but this has to be a subjective impression since it is the only childhood they have known. It may simply mean that they have not noticed any problems or they have hidden them.

It seems that between the ages of three and about six there is a period of experimentation, as a child sets out to find out what the gender-concept means. Nursery nurses often speak of little boys who select little girls' clothes in dressing-up games. It is emphasized that Gender Identity Disorder in childhood relates to a *persistent* preference on the part of a boy for female stereotyped toys and feminine behaviour. It is recognized that there are some few children who can never adapt themselves to their assigned role; there is, for example, a paediatric gender identity clinic at St George's Hospital in London.

Many transvestites say they started 'dressing' around the age of seven. This age in everyone seems to coincide with some sort of life change. When I was young it was the age when boys started wearing long trousers, and it corresponds with Kohlberg's age of gender constancy. However, most men can remember when they felt the pressure to grow up. A whole range of feelings may be suppressed, rather than being assigned a suitable place in the personality. The more feelings and attributes are perceived by the social group to be unmanly, the more they will be suppressed as the boy is absorbed into boyhood society.

Typically the blame is laid at the mother's door and she often goes through agonies of guilt. Conclusions drawn by psychologists in the past, together with society attitudes have entrenched this idea in folklore, but it is becoming increasingly apparent that fathers are important too.

Gender-role stereotyping can be a feature of the family, but it can also be a feature of the peer group and the social environment. The peer group inevitably reflects the values of the local community so that even if the parents are non-authoritarian, it is likely that the sex-role behaviours of the majority will be imposed on those few whose parents have not imposed this behaviour. Boys' society in general enforces gender roles. Boys are 'different', girls are 'sissy' – and one must not be 'girlish'. Either the child in the minority will try to conform with the group, with a variable degree of success, or reject it altogether.

Some people can be themselves and not be worried too much by what people have told them in their infancy. Most people are happy to be as they 'naturally' are; they have no problems with their 'self'. They have the flexibility to adapt the role model as they need to. Others, in childhood, have constructed gender schemas that tried too hard to comply with the gender role, and were unable to achieve a comfortable compromise between it and their gender identity. They cannot modify their gender schema because of feelings of need to comply with one or other, rigidly defined role. Unable to settle in a middle ground they have to switch from one role to the other from time to time.

One could also conceive the idea of a man who becomes a stiff, stern, rather remote person or a tough 'man's man', strong as cast iron. I use the analogy deliberately; cast iron is strong, but brittle. Such a person may have problems peculiarly his own and would certainly create problems for his partner and family.

The place of fantasy

During teenage, cross-dressing is often an extremely erotic experience and many begin during these years rather than earlier. Perhaps negative attitudes to sexual fantasy and fetishism may encourage the progress to full transvestism. The enjoyment of all the senses, of touch and smell, in the wearing of strange and exotic clothes and fabrics, scent and personal adornment is the right of all human beings. There may be a need for admiration in a shy and retiring person. Scenarios of exhibitionism, narcissism, submission, in not wanting to be the leader all the time, may be enacted as sexual releases in a safe environment.

Humans seem well constructed to use their imaginative abilities to strive to overcome emotional hurts. The energy which drives and shapes childhood experiences into well-organized sexual scripts may stem from this need to overcome adversity, to avoid anxiety, and to replace pain and sadness with pleasure and delight. (Docter, 1988)

Sexual fantasies may be an important feature of life, releasing the stress of sexual control (as opposed to suppression) with other emotional stresses incorporated into the fantasy. Thus the person may at times fantasize a 'normal' heterosexual relationship and at others, a fantasy scenario.

The fantasy becomes a fetish when it becomes an obsession. If emotional fulfilment is not achieved, or the same scenario is endlessly repeated, the fantasy may assume undue importance, or other means may be adopted, such as putting the fantasy into practice. The fantasy that something might happen may turn into the belief that it can happen.

However, while many transvestites continue to enjoy the erotic aspects of cross-dressing and may extend it into unashamed fetishism, for others there appears a need to experience the feeling of being a woman in an everyday role. The sexual scenario does not continue to fulfil the emotional need, so they become content to spend periods 'being a woman'. Indeed many have a perfectly acceptable and fulfilled sex life, yet still feel the need to dress. There is a need to identify with actually being female and the feeling of identification may itself produce feelings of guilt.

Feelings of guilt

Even teenage cross-dressing may not be simply an erotic act. All teenagers are struggling to establish themselves as people in an unfamiliar adult world. In the process they have problems that are outside their parents' experience, and they struggle on alone. One may doubt the validity of Farrell's statistics in his book *The Myth of Male Power* (1993), yet he asserts that as boys attempt the process of becoming men their suicide rate rises by 25,000 per cent. Even if it does not involve cross-dressing it can still be perceived as a problem of gender.

Middle age too is a period of change, as fathers become grandfathers. I have met couples who were very worried that while the husband was becoming less assertive, the wife was becoming more so. To an extent this can be attributed to changes in body chemistry, yet if the children have left home, the husband has no longer to fight for a living and his wife can relax and look forward to being herself. Perhaps this is why so many men who may have been cross-dressing in secret 'come out' at this age.

Many transvestites accept their non-conformity very quickly, though they often say that they went through a considerable internal struggle to do so. They have become able to accept themselves as 'men who like to wear dresses' and set out to enjoy themselves. Meanwhile they also enjoy their masculine life style, often approaching it with a vitality that might be enhanced by the opportunity to relax from it occasionally. There is a feeling that transvestites often adopt stereotypically masculine careers, lorry drivers and builders, in the armed forces and the judicial system. I once met an ex-prize fighter. The Bulloughs (1993) suggest the transvestite's alternative female persona actually protects his male identity.

For many, however, there are years of guilt and secrecy. Some secret transvestites are literally paranoid about discovery and go to the most amazing lengths to hide their activities. Their cross-dressing may be unsuspected for years, by even their closest family. While dressing, they imagine that people can see through curtains and through walls. They jump at every creak of the floorboards. Afterwards they worry whether they have removed the make-up properly, or if they have remembered to put everything away. The release of cross-dressing is replaced by the fear of discovery, plus the guilt and secrecy.

A feedback system may be set up where guilt feelings conflict with the urge to dress, followed by a session of relief-dressing, followed by a reaction in becoming over-masculine, followed by yet more guilt. The need becomes an obsession, distracting from everyday life. Efforts to control, like 'wardrobe burning', fail repeatedly. Transvestites may attempt other escapes, through alcohol, drugs, tranquillizers, workaholism. In the face of direct confrontation they deny the problem, even the physical fact of the cross-dressing.

I have an often repeated maxim, which is that the first aim of counselling is not to help the transvestite 'stop dressing', but to give him the *power to choose*, whether or not to 'dress'. The opportunity to express his feelings more freely means that the compulsion to dress is reduced, along with the obsession. Transvestites who have already 'come out' have unthinkingly followed this process by giving themselves, not only permission to dress, but permission to be 'different' and permission to explore feelings.

Implications for counselling and counsellors

My theme is that the dual-role transvestite is a quite distinct form of identity, different from the gay cross-dresser and the transsexual, even though in real life there is considerable blurring. Many transvestites go through a transsexual phase; most go through a fetishistic one.

Often transvestites do not dress as 'real women', but incorporate the form of significant stereotypes from their pasts, usually teenage. Purnell (1994) describes a rather extreme client, who alternated between 'two fantasy persona, one a Lee Marvin type, a loner, a very masculine cowboy type; the other a Debbie Reynolds "sixties girl"'. He was in great distress, with the two characters 'at war . . . in his head'.

A classic reason often given for transvestism is that the boy was coddled by his mother, or that she really wanted a girl, or that when little he was dressed up as a girl. But the baby might have needed more nursing for a variety of reasons. There could be any number of reasons for his 'femininity' – an assertive mother, a distant or very macho father, a period of separation and so on, not to mention the biological argument.

Transvestism in fact turns out to be a complex phenomenon. One could build explanations based on the Jungian persona and archetypes. Freudians may see an imperfect resolution of the Oedipus conflict. For Freud, being human was individual people's endless conflict between the ego, and their biology expressed through the id. Becoming a man or a woman was based on the experience of having genitals. By rewriting Freud, Bland (1994) has visualized ways in which men may incorporate features of womanhood as a defence mechanism against their attraction to women.

For Jung, becoming masculine or feminine was primarily a cultural process – the individual persona constructed from the archetypes handed down through the generations. One could suggest that the transvestite has been unable to incorporate an effective anima within his persona. It has to be expressed as a different persona, often with large components of the archetype.

In the past professional help focused on behaviour therapy, tending to give transvestites an aversion for therapists. It was claimed that cross-dressing ceased for up to two years, without symptom-substitution. From talking to transvestites in later years, some referred to subsequent periods of acute depression. Others said that they stopped therapy because they were 'getting to like the electric shocks' – a classical sexual scenario of converting painful experiences into pleasurable ones. Haslam et al. (1994) suggest that it simply reinforces the pressures that lead to the transvestism in the first place.

Unlike a psychiatrist, the benefit a counsellor brings is total acceptance of the person, instead of standing outside (and too often above). Purnell (1994) says of her client: 'Nobody had before walked in his moccasins, or his high heels.'

To do so, however, counsellors need to confront their own social learning at a very fundamental level, whether as a 'gay' or a 'straight' person, and have to put their very identities to one side. Gender is the last great taboo. To confront it in one's self is a heady and a liberating experience.

This barrier may be why people say to me 'I prefer to talk to you, because you understand'. Yet because I am openly a transvestite many people, especially partners, may feel they may be 'drawn in'. They would certainly prefer to approach an agency clearly outside the cross-gender community, if they could find one.

First steps to help

I am not a practising counsellor, and probably never will be. The original article was written because I felt that it was time somebody wrote something. I have always been available for people to talk on the phone and, for a while, helped with the Trans-Net phoneline when we used to have Community Service Advertisements on Central and Yorkshire television.

For many callers it was the first time that they had spoken of their secret to someone else. Whatever they told us, we accepted their feelings totally and without judgement, even some of the abusive calls! It was not all doom and gloom, however!

I also used to meet people as an Area Officer for the Beaumont Society and always felt that I should do so in male clothes. The meeting would be difficult enough for the person without my being in a dress, and the reaction nearly every time was relief that I do, after all, look like an ordinary bloke. The person's thoughts, at these first meetings, were obviously 'Why am I here? Do I really want to do this?'

They were of course already members of the Society and so had 'come out' to that extent. There are meetings all over the country, which offer strictly social facilities. Anyone attending with deliberate sexual intent (either enacting erotic fantasies, or finding a partner) would be shown the door. It is not compulsory to wear a dress. Some meetings are in community centres or public houses whilst others, which are held in quiet private homes, may be better for the newcomer. Membership of one of the national organizations that produce regular newsletters provides a network of communication for shared experience, without the transvestite having to expose himself by going to a meeting.

However not all people can receive mail at home, which raises the ethics of counselling one partner without the knowledge of the other. The responsibility rests entirely with the client, yet there is some risk of an irate wife accusing the counsellor of encouraging her husband in his fantasy, delusion, perversion or worse.

The counselling situation provides more time and space to approach issues than the phoneline. The immediate and lasting benefit is that the client is able to share thoughts and feelings for the first time. Issues from the past may be explored and plans made for the future. If he wishes to explain himself to his wife, he has the opportunity to work out how to explain it to himself and to become comfortable with the idea.

The treatment of the subject by the media is often problematical. Even in response to talk-shows, the client may suggest that the people involved do not feel the way he does. If he attends a meeting, this could well be something to discuss. Often the client has a very feminine and probably unrealistic image of himself as a woman. The established members will, through past years, have accustomed themselves to the idea that they will never fully 'pass', so they may put over an aura of 'men in dresses'.

My central theme here is the transvestite, but there is much discussion about whether various factors are encouraging people to see themselves as transsexual. Only about 20% of those who attend gender identity clinics go on to full reassignment. Others find a compromise. Although it is a psychiatric route, there is still a need for counselling support – if not for the person, certainly for his family. Appointments at the gender identity clinic (GIC) are usually three months apart. Often transsexuals look for parallel local support in their day-to-day lives, both before and after the operation. Once again, networking is helpful, and membership of the Gender Trust is particularly valuable in this respect, since conformity to a predetermined stereotype is not a prerequisite.

Wives and partners

When (and if) the client should tell his wife is a thorny subject, and much depends on his reasons for doing so. His wife, of course, is suddenly confronted with a problem that he has been working on for years.

The central issue must be that the wife, who has found herself in a situation not of her making or choice, has the same right as her husband to have her feelings acknowledged. There are many couples who have incorporated this new dimension into their marriage, after a great deal of work by both partners. They have, from time to time, appeared in the media, which may have taken some of the threat out of the situation. However this may have led Agony Aunts in some daily papers to take an androcentric view that, like good little wives, they should go along with it.

Instead of the horror of finding her husband likes to wear a dress, the theme for helplines such as the Women of the Beaumont Society is nowadays that, having given tentative agreement, a wife finds herself being swept away. Suddenly she finds that her husband is pottering around the house in a dress at the slightest opportunity. Far from taking a 'feminine' approach, his attitude is the typically male one − 'like it or lump it'.

The wife whose husband suddenly announces that he is transsexual is in a dreadful position. The best scenario, in a situation where there are no good options, may be a 'clean break' divorce. An alternative for an older couple may be for the two to live together as 'best friends', but it does not alter the fact that she has lost a husband. Their sex life may have been non-existent, but she would have chosen to accept it. The taking of hormones by her husband leaves her without even that choice.

If there are children, they may accept the situation, and welcome Daddy as their new Mummy, but where does that leave the original Mummy? Not only does she not have a husband, but she no longer has a role in the family.

Yet a good, supportive social network, ideally including the family, is important for a satisfactory outcome, especially for the transsexual. Both transsexual and transvestite families have found answers based on mutual support, rather than mutual recrimination.

Social meetings provide surroundings where counsellors can be 'present' for people. The trust created may mean that the person may ask for a contract in more formal surroundings. The OASIS group is a good example of a total support network for transvestites, transsexuals, wives and families, run by a female social worker (Ross, 1994).

Moving forward

The foregoing should not lead the reader to underestimate the distress of many people with gender problems. Some have enormous problems in trying to make some sense out of their lives (Tully, 1992).

For transsexuals, progress to gender confirmation is long and hard. It involves hours of electrolysis, learning new behaviours and speech patterns, powerful medication and major surgery. Clearly it is no whim and, in terms of quality of life, it has the best prognosis of any area of mental health, if competent care is provided. The majority of transsexuals are rational and intelligent people and, given the chance to be 'themselves', go on to make a great success of their lives.

Meanwhile, freed of the day-long obsession, transvestites may also approach their working and family lives with new vitality. They may temper their more chauvinistic attitudes within the family, while not becoming less 'manly'. Their wives may also find the opportunity to find new expressions of self.

Often the transvestite settles down, with a new outlook on life, slipping into something comfortable to relax, just as his wife can. Both may dress up for a special occasion, like the weekends around the country where the transvestite groups may take over a complete hotel. Such transvestites take the attitude that, if society will accept their eccentricity, they will try not to give offence, and will try to behave responsibly.

As Gross puts it: 'Men and women are naturally different, but perhaps not as different as we think', and there is a growing feeling among psychologists that 'the rigid division of society on the basis of gender is unhealthy'. In particular, Bem proposes an ideal where men and women would not be equal but, nevertheless, would be able to find within themselves the best of what we now label masculinity and femininity.

It is, of course, people that matter, not labels. In the end, the only criterion that counts is the achievement of an optimal quality of life. Things we learn so young cannot be easily unlearned and so it is not a simple matter of choice. If society should become less judgemental, people may be able to see their motivations with minds unclouded by guilt. The Dual Role Transvestite, as such, may disappear, either dressing in an innocent role play, or, from the start, living his life in a more gentle way, without being trapped in a lifetime that denies his feelings.

Contact addresses

The Beaumont Trust, BM CHARITY, London WC1N 3XX
Tel: 0171 730 7453 (Tues and Thurs 7–11 pm)

The Gender Trust, BM GENTRUST, London WC1N 3XX

References

Bancroft, J. (1989) *Human Sexuality and its Problems*, 2nd edn. Edinburgh: Churchill Livingstone. p. 312.

Bem, S.L. (1993) *The Lenses of Gender: Transforming the Debate on Sexual Inequality*. New Haven, CT: Yale University Press.

Bland, J. (1994) *Transvestism: Four Monographs*. Belper: The Derby TV/TS Group.

Bullough, V.L. and Bullough, B. (1993) *Cross Dressing, Sex and Gender*. Philadelphia: University of Pennsylvania Press.

Docter, R.F. (1988) *Transvestites and Transsexuals – Towards a Theory of Cross-Gender Behavior*. New York: Plenum Press.

Farrell, W. (1993) *The Myth of Male Power*. London: Fourth Estate.

Gross, R.D. (1987) *Psychology: the Science of Mind and Behaviour*. London: Hodder and Stoughton. ch. 22, p. 561.

Haslam, M.T. (ed.) (1994) *Transvestism: a Guide*, 2nd edn. London: Beaumont Trust.

Money, J. and Ehrhardt, A. (1972) *Man, Woman, Boy and Girl: the Differentiation and*

Dimorphism of Gender Identity from Conception to Maturity. Baltimore, MD: Johns Hopkins Press.

Purnell, A. (1994) Gender counselling and its problems, in A. Purnell (ed.), *GENDYS '94: Third International Gender Dysphoria Conference.* Belper, Derbyshire: GENDYS Conferences.

Ross, B. (1994) Provision of Care for Minority Groups: the Importance of Home-Based Support Networks within the Establishment, in A. Purnell (ed.), *GENDYS '94: Third International Gender Dysphoria Conference.* Belper, Derbyshire: GENDYS Conferences.

Tully, B. (1992) *Accounting for Transsexualism and Transhomosexuality.* London: Whiting and Birch.

Discussion issues

1 What were your counter-transferences when first reading the title of this article, then on reading the article itself? What do think they will be when you meet your first client?

2 How will you counter the accusation that you are encouraging someone in a perverted fantasy?

3 What do you think is the legal situation in counselling a juvenile client? What minimum age, if any, would you set?

4 'Gender is the last great taboo. To confront it in oneself is a heady and a liberating experience'. Comment.

40

Counselling Adults Abused as Children

Peter Dale

This chapter draws on my experiences over the past six years of providing individual counselling to adults abused as children, co-leading four long therapeutic groups, and supervising the individual counselling of colleagues and other professionals.

Another significant influence has been my involvement in an intensive ten-day training course relating to therapy with adults abused as children, at the Institute for the Community as Extended Family (ICEF) in San Jose in 1987. This centre, founded by Hank Giarreto in 1971, provides a major model for sexual abuse treatment programmes throughout the world.

I also use the terms 'counsellor' and 'therapist'; 'counselling' and 'therapy'; and 'he' and 'she', interchangeably.

The chapter falls into two main sections: a review of some of the major consequences of abuse as they may present in the counselling relationship; and discussion of three major areas of focus in the therapeutic process.

Consequences

Many of the consequences in later life for adults who were abused as children (aaac's) amount to the continuation of learned adaptive, coping and defence mechanisms which were developed as essential survival techniques at the time of the abuse but which are *maladaptive* in later life and adult relationships. Calof (1988), from a therapeutic perspective of Eriksonian hypnotherapy, comments how defensive responses and patterns of behaviour which occur in situations of high emotional arousal, such as the fear and terror often associated with abuse, and where there is little cognitive understanding of what was happening, tend to be imprinted or learned at a deeper and more profound area of the personality. As such the defensive processes may become an integral part of the developing personality, and the child may grow up into adulthood having little conception of the possibility of being without such traits.

However, invariably for aaac's who seek counselling, the process of therapeutic change involves a re-structuring of such habitual and deeply ingrained mechanisms which were necessary and adaptive for survival and existence as a child, but which are maladaptive and counter-productive in adult life especially with regard to the process of forming and sustaining intimate relationships with others. It is often

This chapter was first published as 'Individual counselling with adults abused as children: opportunities and difficulties in working with the consequences of abuse', in *Counselling, Journal of the British Association for Counselling*, vol. 3, no. 1, pp. 25–30 (1992).

precisely because of the protective value of these defences in childhood, and *because* they have become an integral aspect of the developing personality, that the recognition and achievement of the need to let go of them altogether can be such an awesome task. This may feel like giving up an old trusted part of oneself, and stepping naked into an unwelcoming and inhospitable world.

Many of the consequences experienced by aaac's are familiar at some point in their lives to most people and indeed few, if any, are exclusively specific to people who have been abused when they were children. Many of these consequences are experienced to a greater or lesser degree in response to life events of various forms, especially those involving loss and trauma. However, aaac's – particularly those who were subjected to severe, prolonged and multiple abuse – often will experience many of these phenomena quite intensely and chronically throughout their lives.

Some of the difficulties experienced by aaac's which present in the course of therapy are summarized under the following headings: Physical, Emotional, Cognitive, Social, and Sexual Consequences.

Physical consequences

A wide range of largely involuntary physical and psychosomatic conditions are known to be associated with childhood abuse. Emotional pain may be manifested or displaced in almost any form of physical pain, and victims do a number of things with their bodies to deal with this pain. One common physical response is of a *dissociation* between mind and body, so that the body is experienced as separate, 'out there', and indeed as an 'it'. During abuse, many victims acquire the defence mechanisms of taking themselves out of their bodies – 'to a safer place' – so that the mind remains free whilst the body only is being abused.

In some cases there may be permanent physical damage or handicaps as a direct consequence of the abusive trauma; in many other cases the physical sequelae are the results of involuntary somatic responses to the abuse. Combinations of the following are commonly reported: sleep disturbance, chronic muscle tensions, jaw/joint tensions, headaches, migraines, stomach aches, nausea/vomiting, eating disorders, genital-urinary problems, bowel problems, seizures, permanent or transient skin conditions, anxiety and panic attacks, phobias; and many others.

Calof (1988) emphasizes the often symbolic importance of the symptom, and the unconscious role it may have had as the Body's own defence and protection against abuse. He gives an example of a client who continued to suffer from repeated vaginal infections, where as a child her Body *had learned* that vaginal infections were a way of keeping the abuser away from her. Hence the symbolic communicative message of the symptom is likely to be an important area for exploration in the therapeutic process.

Other physical consequences of abuse may be seen within a grouping of more conscious, often compulsive, behaviours. Many aaac's *blame their bodies* for the abuse – for example for being attractive, or for being a certain gender, or for being sexually responsive – and this can lead to a range of physical self-punitive responses such as self-mutilation, substance abuse, and other addictive and compulsive behaviours. Compulsivity can often be seen as a distracting mechanism against intolerable emotional pain. Similarly, self-mutilation is often experienced as a *tension-relieving* act when the intolerable feeling cannot be distracted away, or sedated by addictive or compulsive activity.

Sadly, suicide may be the ultimate physical consequence for an unknown proportion of aaac's. However, on a note of considerable optimism regarding therapeutic effectiveness with aaac's who seek help, it was reported by Giaretto in 1987 that in the history of the ICEF Programme since 1971, there had been no known successful suicides of aaac's treated at ICEF (Giaretto, 1987, personal conversation).

Emotional consequences

The chronically abused child often suffers massive emotional damage as a result of the combination of trauma, inhibition of the formation of basic trust, the 'crazy' family dynamics and communication patterns, together with a disjointing of the child's naturally unfolding pace of emotional development.

Giaretto (1987) describes the development of victim characteristics in the following sequence: the occurrence of abuse involves an overstimulation of underdeveloped senses and anatomy. At the same time there is profound damage to the child's early sense of security – the feeling of the nest falling apart. The ego-centric developmental level of the child is such that it can only blame itself for the events. The injunction 'I am bad' develops, and is strongly reinforced by family processes. The child involuntarily responds to the developing emotional agony and pain by defence mechanisms of dissociation, sedation and distraction.

It is in this realm that parallel processes of further splitting in the personality are likely to occur, in addition to the separation of mind and body already described. Aspects of the child's emotional development become 'out of sync'. There may be inappropriately accelerated development – often in the child's sexual awareness, arousal and responsiveness; and in the adoption of inappropriate responsibilities for caretaking of others from an early age. Such examples of inappropriately accelerated development often have the consequence of depriving the child of a developmental stage of childishness – such children adopt adult mentalities, may become highly intuitive; and do not learn how to play.

Simultaneously, other aspects of emotional development may become arrested, or frozen at the point of trauma, with the particularly common consequence of early and profound damage to the ability to trust. Many aaac's report the experience of split-off 'parts' of themselves, usually including 'inner child' parts. Often there may be experience of several of these, of different ages. The degree of this may range from the normal human experience of 'parts of self' (usefully conceptualized in psychosynthesis as 'sub-personalities') to the formal psychiatric diagnosis of Multiple Personality Disorder. MPD is diagnosed with much greater frequency in the United States, and correlates highly with severe and chronic childhood abuse (DSM III-R, American Psychiatric Association, 1987).

Many aaac's also experience a wide range of difficulties with regard to the **experience of emotion**. This involves problems with the *recognition* of feelings, the *understanding* of feelings, and the *expression* of feelings. They may suffer because they have dissociated all feelings, and do not feel anything at all. Sometimes, the capacity to experience any pleasurable feeling is the cost of deadening the pain. Similarly, feeling may be experienced at a chronically low level, without moments of intensity, as if the volume was permanently turned down low. In the midst of this, the person may have unpredictable and frightening mood swings. These may be explosive and rageful, or depressive with sudden suicidal impulses.

Not surprisingly, in therapy, many aaac's talk of a common fear of being overwhelmed by emotion, and of fear of loss of control. A frequently occurring metaphor is of containing an 'unexploded bomb'. Life may involve a constant struggle to suppress the explosiveness of their emotions of anger, hatred, disgust, shame and guilt.

Many aaac's are tormented by ambivalent feelings towards their abusers, and this is particularly so for those who feel that they experienced some positive aspects to the relationship, despite the abuse. This is predominantly the case for people who were abused in the context of an initially affectionate relationship (where often the abuser was the major nurturer), as opposed to those who were abused in the context of rejection by the abuser.

Emotional consequences of abuse, involving inability and unwillingness to trust others, are especially damaging in later life with regard to difficulties in establishing and maintaining intimacy. Relationships constantly fail through inability to trust manifested by constant testing-out of others, provocation of rejection, and withdrawal.

Cognitive consequences

Being abused within a sexually abusing family involves a process which often amounts to systematic brainwashing in addition to the directly abusive incidents. The context and processes of the family constitute a coercive distorted belief system, and this deprives the child of a crucially important developmental component of beginning to explore and trust its own perceptions in relation to a largely consistent external reality. Abused children introject a set of inappropriate beliefs about themselves and the abuse from a very early stage. This often involves incorporation and identification with the parental abuser's authority with regard to regularly reinforced statements such as: 'All children do this', 'You are enjoying it', 'It's your fault', 'You are bad/worthless etc'.

Calof (1988) describes how these and other key injunctions are imprinted in the child's thought processes and belief systems at the time of abuse, which serve to enforce the child's compliance and prevent the child from telling others who may offer escape and protection. These injunctions involve the child introjecting beliefs and principles such as: Be loyal to the Family; Don't show pain; Don't ask for help; Stay in control; Don't think about yourself or your situation.

Such early programming, or injunctions, are embedded deep in the core of the developing personality, and all other life events and relationships come to be experienced and interpreted through this filter. The filter often involves constant internalized negative self-talk. As a consequence, victims invariably develop profound senses and 'scripts' of low self-esteem, poor self-image, self-blame and failure. It is of great significance in the counselling relationship that these introjected injunctions are all powerfully anti-therapeutic: in therapy, old 'tapes' may suddenly come into play to push the therapist away from significant areas.

As part of the necessary process of survival, cognitive defences are constructed which protect the victim as far as possible from these internal experiences, and which also enable the victim to sustain some level of belonging in family and social groups. There are a wide range of cognitive defence mechanisms. *Denial, minimization,* and *rationalization* of the abuse are very common responses, especially when the victim is still attached to and involved in the powerful processes and procedures of the family. These families can maintain their abusive and collusive processes for decades after the abused children have reached adulthood.

Dissociative defences are also common, including *forgetting* (psychogenic amnesia) where the mind cuts off from conscious awareness and recall of the entire abuse experience or key parts of it. Often, whole chunks of all childhood experiences will be lost as well and the victim may be puzzled by the great gaps in memory. Facilitation and management of returning memories is often a major area of work in the therapeutic process (Briere, 1989).

Splitting is also exacerbated in the cognitive processes. The victim may experience her or himself as a set of disconnected and fragmented parts, with little or no sense of a whole. These parts may have their own voices, and victims often have acute fears of going crazy when they cannot escape from the constant dialogues, arguments, commentaries, and sometimes overwhelming babble which they experience between the parts in their head. A major element of therapy may involve work to bring these dissociative responses under conscious ego control. This is done primarily through increasing awareness (through feedback) of their occurrence in therapy, and identifying particular trigger scenarios. Avoidance and diversion strategies can then be identified, together with re-orientation and 'grounding' techniques which can be acquired and practised in all life situations to minimize and hopefully eliminate such occurrences.

Social consequences

Many aaac's often live isolated and lonely lives, lacking the ability to form deeply intimate relationships or to sustain rewarding friendships. These difficulties may be related to poor social skills such as lack of empathy, ego-centricity and lack of ability in conflict-resolution; or related to problems of identity and mood such as over-adaptability in relationships, shallowness, withdrawal and suspiciousness. The poignant challenge and repetitive sense of failure often hangs around the dilemma of longing for contact, and the desperate avoidance of it.

Aaac's may experience a sense of separation and difference from 'ordinary' people, in the course of relating to others on a superficial basis. They may resemble 'lost souls' – individuals with no roots or sense of belonging. The 'Wall' is a frequently described metaphor for a defensive barrier which stops people getting close enough to recognize their vulnerability, and which also inhibits spontaneous contact with and responses towards others. Pink Floyd's epic 'The Wall' is a good creative expression of this.

Vulnerability and needs are denied or hidden because they signal overwhelming needs for affection, acceptance and recognition which at times are powerfully felt. Gil (1983) describes how some aaac's often alienate others by the sudden expression of the intensity of their needs, and frighten others by the prospect of a sudden dependency, over-attachment and demandingness.

Relationships with partners are often entered into either as an escape from the abusive situation at an early age, or on the basis of an immature and unrealistic expectation that the partner will be able to provide every satisfaction that has been missing from life, and to make up for all previous deprivation. Commonly, two aaac's are unconsciously attracted to each other, and gradually the magical expectations turn to mutual bitterness as the pattern of the relationship begins to repeat old cycles. In some cases this can escalate into violence and child abuse.

Other patterns involve one partner entering into the relationship on the ticket of being 'helper' or 'rescuer' to the abused partner. Unfortunately, it is rare that one person can 'make up' for the damage of serious abuse and deprivation. Frustrations develop, the abused adult may repeatedly provoke the 'accepting helper' to the limit. When this point is reached the 'helper' whose own needs have been denied for so long (this helper may be an undisclosed abused adult) may break down into an emotional crisis, or turn on the partner in a persecutory rage.

Other powerful complications can arise for the aaac who adopts the role of 'helping' others, unconsciously attempting to resolve his or her own emotional problems in this way. The process can involve the sedation of or distraction from one's own pain through exposure to others in similar or greater pain, and is common in the helping professions. It is distressing to see energetic professional 'helpers' burn-out into states of bitterness and cynicism when ultimately their personal difficulties are not resolved by the adoption of such a 'helping' role. On the other hand, aaac's who have addressed their own issues directly in therapy can and do make excellent therapists and counsellors.

Sexual consequences

It is reported by ICEF that as many as 90% of aaac's experience sexual problems (Giaretto, 1987). These may involve inhibitions in desire and difficulties in arousal; aversions; orgasmic dysfunction; damaging learned associations (e.g. sexual arousal only possible in the context of violence); sexual addictions (which may come to involve abusing others); and problems stemming from intense associated feelings, such as guilt (Maltz and Holman, 1987). The dissociative phenomena of 'flashbacks' is commonly reported in the context of sexual activity, and the current partner may be misperceived as the abuser. As with therapy for sexual problems in general, there is a good rate of 'spontaneous improvement' of the specific sexual difficulty as overall improvements in the quality of intimacy in relationships occurs. Hence, specific focus on sexual problems may be more likely to be addressed towards the end of the therapeutic relationship if still required, than at the beginning.

Opportunities and pitfalls in the therapeutic process

It may be helpful to briefly review some of these key issues under the headings of Initial sessions and Three key areas of focus during work.

Initial sessions

As in most counselling relationships, it is a good idea to use first sessions to clarify expectations and ground rules in order to establish a contract for the work. The dynamics of the referral will often provide useful information about the client's needs and stresses – for example, is the client voluntarily seeking help? If so, why now? Is there a crisis? Is the client being 'pushed' to get help at the instigation of another, e.g. a partner threatening to leave the relationship unless things change? What expectations does the client have about what changes are possible, and how quickly these may be expected to occur? What *support* is available to the client in the family and community?

Experience suggests that for many aaac's who enter therapy, change often involves a process of getting worse, before getting 'better'. Perhaps this is inevitable in therapeutic work which involves the return to conscious awareness of repressed painful memories and associated (dissociated) feelings. Sometimes there is a pattern of regular 'ups' and 'downs' in this process, maybe involving dramatic mood swings; hopefully with an overall tendency towards recovery and stability. It is important that clients are aware of this, and equally important that significant others in their lives understand and can tolerate such changes. One of the key positive prognostic indicators for aaac's in therapy is a relationship with a consistently understanding and supportive partner.

Sometimes it can be helpful to involve partners in the work, either through their own individual sessions, or sessions for the couple together.

Exploration of previous helping relationships can provide important information about the client's 'process', particularly around how such relationships were terminated. Often this leads into key themes, and also raises straight away the transference implications of these previous relationships, for the new therapeutic relationship which is beginning.

First sessions are best used for exploring and clarifying the potential therapeutic relationship – rather than for beginning abuse-related work as such. On occasions it may be appropriate to discourage clients from sharing a great deal of abuse-related material at this stage, focusing instead on the need to establish prior to this the necessary 'safe container' that this work requires. Some clients who 'splurge' a great deal of abuse-related material in first sessions, before boundaries of trust and confidence have been established, tend not to become therapeutically engaged. They may be incapacitated through shame and guilt reactions from returning for further sessions. They may have a history of 'dumping' such material on unsuspecting counsellors in first sessions, never to be seen again; possibly leaving the counsellor feeling somewhat abused. This may reflect an unconscious leaking of aggression and persecution from often otherwise passive 'victim' personalities.

Finally, as part of agreeing a contract, it is important to be clear – and firm – about the boundaries of the counselling relationship. For aaac's – of all clients who have suffered the damaging effects of invaded and permeable personal boundaries – it is vital (an absolute therapeutic necessity) that the boundaries of the therapeutic relationship are clearly defined and adhered to. This includes keeping to the time limits of sessions, and providing clear boundaries to 'out of session' availability especially with regard to crises. Agreements regarding confidentiality and exclusions (e.g. re child abuse or serious suicide threats), and the management of psychiatric crises may be required.

Three key areas of focus

Once the contact for the therapeutic relationship has been established, it is likely that the content of the work will involve – often simultaneously – three major areas: the therapeutic relationship; other current relationships; and 'telling the story'.

Therapeutic relationship

It is within this relationship that the potent therapeutic opportunities and pitfalls regarding trust issues predominantly lie. Powerful transference and counter-transference processes emerge. Because of the intensity of the damage to trust issues for the client as a consequence of the abuse, *testing-out* of the therapist consciously and unconsciously will inevitably be a major component within the dynamic of the therapeutic relationship. A counsellor who can recognize such transference and counter-transference issues whilst maintaining firm boundaries and tolerating the inevitable frustration of the client, provides a powerfully therapeutic ingredient.

If such processes cannot be recognized and appropriately contained by the counsellor, the client is likely to gain little benefit and may be further damaged by the experience. Many dangers stem from the potential intensity of the transference and counter-transference dynamics. For example, a client may develop a fantasy that the therapist can make up for all the deprivation and abuse she has suffered in her entire life. If the therapist, from the perspective of his or her own 'helping script' secretly shares a sense of such responsibility or omnipotence, then the therapeutic relationship is set for collusive disaster. It is not uncommon in such scenarios that ultimately the roles switch, with the client coming to 'persecute' the therapist, who in turn switches from 'rescuer' into the 'victim' position (a stance which sometimes underlies the superficial 'helping' role all the time).

Testing-out is a necessary part of the process of the client beginning to explore and deal with issues relating to damage to trust. This may involve covert and overt behaviour around issues such as levels of caring, the therapist's availability, containment and expression of feelings, potential rejection of the client, abandonment, disinterest, judgemental attitudes and disbelief. Clients may also test the counsellor's sexual boundaries.

Such exploration around issues of boundaries is a central part of the therapeutic process with aaac's; and if testing-out issues do not occur, then counsellors could usefully give thought as to what in the relationship is inhibiting this. All such behaviour and incidents – often superficially trivial – may provide vital material for 'here and now' exploration of significant themes and processes occurring in the relationship between therapist and client, with regard to both the actual, and the transference/counter-transference levels.

In this, the therapist also models for the client the usefulness of clear and direct communication in the exploration of themes in the therapeutic relationship. Clients may experience considerable anxiety about such exploration, and defensive patterns of projection, avoidance and acting-out are likely to become noticeable. However, the open acknowledgement and exploration of feelings of attachment and affection, differences and conflicts, serves ultimately to deepen the relationship, rather than to threaten it. This can be the core ingredient of therapy which provides a fundamental experience of a specific form of intimacy and learning, which the client can then develop outside of therapy in the search for reciprocal intimacy.

Other current relationships

Often, for periods during therapy, these issues may dominate sessions. If crises in key external relationships with significant others were not in existence at the point of seeking help, it is likely that they will occur at some point during the therapeutic process. Such crises – with partners, family of origin, own children, work and social relationships – invariably dominate the attention of the client. The counsellor needs to accept that for periods this is likely to be so, to see the process of crises and their resolution as a significant part of the therapy, and to use a broad range of skills to facilitate the client overcoming such crises in ways which are compatible with their personal goals. It is only during periods when the outside world of the client is not focused predominantly on interpersonal crises that specific abuse-related work on 'telling the story' can productively occur.

Significant issues with other current relationships are likely to occur in the following areas:

Partners Are they supportive or hostile to the work? Sometimes initially supportive partners become hostile when the emotional turmoil of the client increases, or when changes seen by the client as being positive are not viewed in a similar light by the partner. A common example of this is with female clients who gradually become more assertive, seeking changes in relationships which partners are uncomfortable with. Alternatively, it may be that the partner, no matter how supportive, has never been told about the abuse, or the extent of it. They then have to deal with their own feelings about their partner having concealed this from them for so long, together with the need to re-evaluate perceptions and relationships with the other family members involved.

Own children Many aaac's are distressed by difficulties they experience in relation to their own children. This may include feeling distant, lack of affection and physical aversions to the child. Some aaac's feel impelled to provide everything which was missing in their own deprived childhoods and then struggle with distressing feelings of envy and resentment of their children for receiving this, particularly for 'taking it for granted'. Such resentment may lead to significant parental inconsistencies in attitude and handling of the child, who in turn may become confused, developing behaviour disturbances characteristic of anxiety and insecurity.

Aaac's often are highly sensitive to the prospect of their own children being sexually abused, and may over-protect the child to a damaging degree. Alternatively, and more ominously, an unknown proportion of aaac's consciously, or unconsciously expose their children to potentially abusive situations; commonly by allowing the child contact with their own abuser. This psychological process of exposing one's own child to the same risk is a predominant issue in child protection work, and requires further research into the psychological mechanisms.

An even deeper level of anxiety may be present for some aaac's, involving their own fearful fantasies of sexually abusing their child. One member of our group spoke of how she was dedicated to childlessness because of her recurring fantasies that she would sexually abuse any child she might have. As with a number of specific themes in therapeutic work with aaac's, including the question as to whether a sexual relationship with the abuser is continuing, this is of such a level of taboo that it is unlikely to be volunteered unless specifically asked about by the counsellor.

Families of origin It is important in the early stages of work to establish how close in terms of geography and influence are the key members of the abusive family of origin. When such influences remain significant in either or both respects, then it can be very useful to have an initial focus, and task, on the client establishing and maintaining firmer boundaries between herself or himself and these powerful undermining others. The importance of this cannot be overstressed: the abusing family of origin in action is a far greater potent force upon the client than the therapist, no matter how skilful; and the influence of the abusive family of origin will inevitably be *anti-therapeutic*.

For the client, achieving small successes at this stage – for example by not continuing to allow any family member to visit her at any time but to enforce her own decisions about this; or by installing a telephone answering machine so that contact takes place only on her terms – can significantly develop confidence that her behaviour with powerful family members can change without disastrous consequences following. The impetus gained from this discovery, often can fuel motivation during the most painful periods of therapy.

Without this initial achievement in creating some space between the client's own personal world and that of the abusive family members, the client cannot be free (from enmeshment in the family system) to learn how to *reflect* on how the family dynamics operate, and her unknowing role in this. The developing ability to reflect on roles and processes is likely to become one of the major cognitive aspects of therapy; and the ability to learn and rehearse how to assertively communicate an unwillingness to continue with these, and to renegotiate alternative relationships (if desired) similarly may be a major 'action' part of the therapy.

Whilst periods of rapid progress and increased confidence often result from such work, it is common for this to be undermined by other internal emotional processes experienced by the client. Perhaps the most universal and potent of these is the periodic resurfacing of the desperate infantile yearning to be loved by one's parents. The surfacing poignancy of this primitive need in therapy can be bewildering in working with clients who otherwise appear to be doing 'ever so well', unless the reality of this powerful dynamic is recognized and accepted. The pull of this need may be heralded by unexpected and superficially incomprehensible behaviour on the part of the client.

This may involve an impulsive approach to her family – abandoning all of the boundary-setting work – which is met by a punitive rejection, in turn provoking a spiral into a depression which highlights the despair stemming from the yearning for love and acceptance. Anniversaries such as Christmas and Mother's Day often provoke such impulsiveness, which may also signify an underlying compulsive masochistic element, learned helplessness, or an inability to tolerate personal achievement. Sabotage of progress and success is a common habitual self-defeating phenomenon, which is likely to require challenging by the therapist.

Work around such yearnings is often a major part of the therapeutic process. It has enormous emotional potency which is likely to become significant within the therapist–client relationship. Such feelings and expectations may be transferred on to the therapist, who may also face the fury of resentment from the client for not responding in the fantasized way of supplying the antidote to all of the accumulated deprivations. Instead, the therapist should gently focus the client on the issue of reality: which is that no matter how ingeniously adaptive the client may be in 'performing' for her family in the hope of gaining acceptance, nourishing and consistent love is unlikely to be forthcoming from this source. Her parents are not going to significantly change at this stage of their lives. They are never going to be able to sufficiently love her.

Working towards this realization is one of the most painful stages in the therapeutic process, and a particularly vital one. It is not until the client can gradually 'let go' of the infantile yearning for love and acceptance from her parents, and 'let go' of the notion that denying her needs makes them go away, that the process of grieving the loss (of what one never had) can begin. Until this occurs, emotionally the aaac remains in a state of timeless limbo, caught in a wholly unresolved and unrecognized primitive grief reaction. Dealing with this loss provides the opportunity for clients to begin to experiment with allowing themselves to recognize and accept their needs, and to become open to the possibility of such needs being met, if only partially, through current or potential relationships elsewhere in their lives. Hence, an associated major focus of work will often need to take place around difficulties relating to *intimacy skills*.

Telling the story

'Telling the story' is a key component of therapy for aaac's, and often something about which intense ambivalence is felt. To what extent the story needs to be told in therapy will vary from each individual to individual, and it is invariably helpful to explore this, as in doing so the various powerful inhibitions in telling the story can be identified and addressed. These may relate to the first two areas of focus already considered: within the transference relationship the client may have real or fantasy anxieties which revolve around the major emotional consequences themes of shame and guilt. There may be an acute anxiety that the therapist will see the client as *bad*, and that disgust and rejection may follow. There may be an issue around the client feeling that he or she has to protect the counsellor from hearing unpleasant details. This may be particularly so if the client has picked up the counsellor's unease in this area, and inevitable if the counsellor has specifically shared such unease.

Approaching the task of telling the story may also trigger strong sensations relating to the realm of other current relationships. Often the dynamics of the abuser coercing and maintaining the child's silence involved powerful threats of one kind or another. Given the timeless quality of such messages, original fears and anxieties relating to such threats can return in an overwhelming way at the point in the therapy when the client is poised to talk about the abuse. Sudden and significant changes in mood may occur, suicidal thoughts and actions may occur or return, and the client may suddenly behave in a withdrawn or angry way with the counsellor. These can be very challenging and stressful times for the counsellor, who needs to pay a good deal of attention to counter-transference reactions, including the not-uncommon one of feeling like an abuser. The balance between the right amount of pushing, and recognizing that the time may not be right is always a fine one, and mirrors the intensity of the client's own ambivalence.

For other aaac's the difficulty may not lie so much in these areas, as in being unable to remember the details of the abuse, or in finding the right words and language to express it. Both of these problems are likely to be factors if the abuse took place at a very early age. Often in the course of therapy aaac's begin to remember events and details, and careful attention needs to be paid to the pacing of this with clients who report large memory gaps. The fear, and the danger, is of the client being overwhelmed by sudden surges into consciousness of deeply repressed material. Unexpected memories, such as the involvement of a mother in the abuse, can trigger powerful destabilizing reactions. It is worth bearing in mind that this can occur at any time during the therapeutic work, and may result in a psychiatric crisis.

The healing component involves telling the story with appropriate emotion, to a trusted other in a safe environment, with the experience of being accepted. Such expression – and containment – of feelings and memories can only occur productively within a healthy therapeutic relationship where substantial trust has developed through the testing by the client of boundaries which have proved to be supportive and secure. Ideally, there should be opportunity to do this work either in individual therapy or in group therapy, as some clients find one or the other more facilitating, helpful, and supportive.

Having accomplished this in whatever detail the client feels is necessary (it is wrong for counsellors to insist on every detail), the next challenge is for the client to be able to tell certain selected others in his or her relationships outside of counselling. Hence, the ICEF principle that 'every appropriate person told is a step towards healing and growth'. It is in this respect that aaac's often feel motivated to provide support to other aaac's in crisis, or post-therapy to be involved in valuable public education functions by speaking out publicly about their abuse – and their recovery.

References

American Psychiatric Association (1987) *Diagnostic and Statistical Manual* Edition III (Revised). Washington, DC: APA.
Briere, J. (1989) *Therapy for Adults Molested as Children*. New York: Springer.
Calof, D. (1988) 'Adult survivors of incest and child abuse', *Family Therapy Today*. p. 8.
Giaretto, H. (1987) USA Training Workshop at the Institute for the Community as Extended Family (ICEF), San Jose.
Gil, E. (1983) *Outgrowing the Pain*. Walnut Creek, CA: Launch Press.
Maltz, W. and Holman, B. (1987) *Incest and Sexuality*. Lexington, MA: Lexington Books.

Brief update

Since writing the original journal article and the booklet which followed (Dale, 1993) I have undertaken a research project involving in-depth interviews with more than fifty clients and therapists exploring the therapeutic process with adults who were abused as children (Dale, 1996). The major focus of the study includes: the process of being ready for therapy and becoming a client; establishing the therapeutic relationship; multidimensional experiencing within the therapeutic relationship; communication in the therapeutic relationship; therapists' self-disclosure; therapists who were abused as children; abuse and exploitation in therapy; working with memories of abuse; talking about the abuse in therapy; and clients' experiences of resolution and meaning.

The research illustrates the complexity of the therapeutic experience, which for many results in profound positive changes in lives and relationships. It also illuminates the potential for therapy to be an unhelpful and sometimes harmful experience which can replicate a childhood context of abuse, exploitation or lack of individual understanding. The extent of lack of felt individual understanding of some clients by therapists was surprising. This appeared to be connected with two therapist factors: those who were experienced as being self-centred or charismatic; those who applied a predetermined therapeutic model; or both.

Therapists who adopt an analytic stance of distance, non-responsiveness and who prolong silences, can be experienced by inexperienced clients as being painfully rejecting. This can trigger either a range of feelings which are often concealed or dissociation. Silence in sessions can be helpful – but it can also be the loneliest experience on earth. Many clients in this study felt that their therapists were not very good at recognizing the difference.

One of the disadvantages of the enormous public attention that child abuse has received in recent years has been a tendency to group children or adults who have been abused together as a homogeneous group to whom stereotypical 'treatment' responses have been developed and somewhat indiscriminately applied. Therapists who have adopted popular models of specific abuse therapy such as over-simplistic 'inner-child nurturing' and the promotion of constant catharsis, can constrict clients' experience, recovery and growth potential by imposing an 'abuse explains everything' perspective in which victim identities are reinforced.

References

Dale, P. (1993) *Counselling Adults who were Abused as Children*. Rugby: British Association for Counselling.

Dale, P. (1996) 'Clients' and therapists' perceptions of the psychotherapeutic process: a study of adults abused as children', PhD thesis, University of Brighton.

Discussion issues

1 'Silence in sessions can be helpful – but it can also be the loneliest experience on earth. Many clients in this study felt that their therapists were not very good at recognizing the difference.' Discuss how it might be possible to recognize the difference.

2 In what ways do you think that the counselling experience might replicate a childhood context of abuse, exploitation or lack of individual understanding?

3 Which of the expectations and ground rules suggested to establish a contract in the initial sessions of work with aaac's are suitable for counselling with other clients? Are there any that you would not consider using in your work? Why?

4 In what ways has this chapter enlarged your understanding of the structure and process of counselling?

41

The Case for Couple Therapy

Daphne Boddington

My concern here is with the growing number of counsellors trained to work with individuals but who have no experience or skills in couple or family work. It is possible that this has the effect of limiting them to a very linear, intrapsychic view of their clients' problems, tending to lay the blame within the individual's psychology rather than in interpersonal relationships experienced in their present life situations. David Bott has written two excellent articles in this journal, in 1990 (see Chapter 3) and in 1992, explaining how systems theory, with its emphasis on reciprocal interaction in relationships, can be used by an individual therapist to enhance his perspectives about a client's problems. I would like to suggest that more counsellors who are trained to work with individuals should consider undertaking a serious training in couple or family work, so that they themselves can offer a wider, and sometimes wiser, choice of help to clients who complain of failure in relationships. An experienced family therapist, Margaret Robinson (1991), in a recent and comprehensive study, 'Family Transformation through Divorce and Remarriage', pleads for a more systemic approach from those helping individuals with marriage difficulties. She points out how helpers can 'identify with one or other of the family members, and thus perhaps unwittingly take sides which may exacerbate the conflict and prove unhelpful in the long run'. Counsellors, who are experts in personal counselling techniques, are often insufficiently aware of the danger of their expertise being potentially unhelpful to some individuals who are living in the context of ongoing partnerships and family interaction.

When I started my private practice in the early 1980s I soon learnt the extent of my limitations as a personal counsellor. A mother of four young children asked for help for herself and her husband. He was staying away from the family house more and more for 'business' reasons and it had become a bone of contention. I saw them both separately and then worked with her husband for six months, alone. As the counsellor, I became the bearer of his secrets – his affairs, the flat he shared with his lover, his increasing guilt towards his wife and inability to communicate with her or to show her affection. All this had developed in the previous three years since his father's death and his resulting distress and retreat into depression. He had turned to these affairs rather than to his wife, to alleviate his grief. I helped him work through his grief and his attitude to his wife, whom he had come to see as a 'controlling mother'. He learnt to identify and express his confused feelings and he came to understand himself more fully. He trusted me. He returned home and tried to resume his relationship with the wife and family he

This chapter was first published as 'Limitations of personal counselling: the case for couple therapy', in *Counselling, Journal of the British Association for Counselling*, vol. 4, no. 1, pp. 33–5 (1993).

wanted to be with, only to find her resentful, controlling and lacking in under-standing. It was difficult for me to relate to her honestly, when she had no knowledge of his affairs. She was angry with me. 'I don't know what you have been talking about all this time, but we are no closer, maybe further apart than before we came to you.' How much wiser I would have been to have taken both into couple therapy, to have explored the issues together, to have helped them understand each other and together to have taken some steps towards greater closeness in their relationship. It was my concern about this case that prompted me to seek out training in couple therapy.

Dangers of individual counselling to the couple relationship

Intense individual therapy can produce, or increase, the stress in a marriage or a committed relationship. Individuals entering the process of counselling become acutely aware of their own needs and feelings. They are likely to be encouraged to embark on a journey to satisfy these needs in order to fulfil themselves. This may mean a long period of introspection, guided and supported by their counsellor. They may come to see their partner at home as a burden, who fails to understand and accommodate them, who becomes a handicap or an obstacle in their journey to self-fulfilment. Thus, they can become increasingly dissatisfied with the rela-tionship, viewing it as a partnership they have outgrown.

The partner may become painfully aware that he or she is left behind – excluded from this process – confused about the changes in the spouse and the relationship. The client has turned to the counsellor and found an extremely close, exclusive, caring rapport. A wife, who has stood by her husband while he underwent weekly sessions in order to become aware of his needs and feelings, said 'His counsellor took over my role as his confidant. He was asked by the counsellor not to share the content of the sessions with me.' This couple asked for couple therapy to sort out the confusions in their relationship since his individual sessions.

Some individual work with married partners can be helpful if it is limited and taken back into the couple sessions or shared with the concerned partner at home. For instance, when working with adult survivors of child abuse, some sessions alone with the victim can help her recall and give voice to the horrors that happened (Douglas et al., 1989). Then sessions with the couple can help them both understand the influence this has had on her and on their lives together. For example, I am seeing a couple where the wife has experienced two years of intensive counselling, in which she was taken back through memories of childhood abuse and violence. She became withdrawn and depressed, with regular nightmares and increasing self-destructive behaviour. Her husband became so concerned about her during this process that he phoned her therapist and asked to go to just one session to understand what was happening. His request was refused. He became exhausted with a demanding job, taking over much of the responsibility for their small girls and trying to comfort his wife through her wakeful nights. He lost confidence in his own ability to cope. She ended the therapy and one year later they decided to seek marital therapy. She said 'Counselling almost cost me the only good stable relationship of my life.' In their sessions they are together reviewing what they can both learn from her experiences. They believe they are salvaging their relationship. I believe it would have been preferable if some couple therapy had been used concurrently with her individual sessions.

Individual counselling can also result in a counsellor being drawn into an unhelpful alliance in an unhealthy family process, possibly even unknowingly helping to maintain it. The following is an example from my own excursions into long-term individual counselling. For two years I worked with the very needy wife of an alcoholic, trying to help her survive one crisis after another, while she worked out her ambivalent attitudes towards herself and her husband and struggled to protect their adolescent sons. Then one son developed acute behavioural problems and they all came to see me together as a family – having resisted for two years all my invitations to do so. Seeing them together, with very different family interactions from those described by the mother, I was forcibly made aware how misleading a one-sided perspective can be. Without seeing the family together, I could not observe how my client was repetitively escalating most tremendous rows, both with her husband and sometimes with her sons. She only described to me her own distress about hurtful things that had been said to her. It became apparent that this family urgently needed to learn more constructive ways of communicating with each other.

There are often situations where it is appropriate to work only with the individual, particularly those undergoing divorce, those with reluctant or un-co-operative partners and those with no ongoing relationship. However, with clients in long-term relationships, many issues brought to counselling can be successfully addressed in couple therapy. For example, depression, anxiety, stress, low sexual desire, jealousy, low self-esteem, lack of assertiveness and so on. A discussion of each person's past history may help both members of the partnership to understand some aspects of the origins of their problem but sometimes present interactions are causing, maintaining or even increasing such problems. In joint sessions these current interactions can often be altered.

Ways of engaging the partner

I will now describe the methods I have developed over recent years in my private practice. Most individuals are referred to me by GPs. At the end of the first session I often suggest that the partner joins us for subsequent appointments, particularly when:

1 some of the session is taken up with complaints about the partner or their relationship;
2 the individual's symptoms could be a reaction to stress in the relationship;
3 the client's distress could be alleviated by a more supportive marital relationship;
4 the client states it is difficult to talk to his or her partner at home and I suspect that unhelpful communication patterns may be aggravating the problems.

Often the referred individual agrees to ask the partner to come. Some need encouragement as they fear the partner will protest. I am surprised how often the partner is willing to join us. When reservations are expressed, I take special care to make them feel included in the next session. I might offer the partner an initial individual session so that I, as therapist, keep equal rapport with both of them.

When the partner fails to come, for varying reasons, the attempt often opens the way to do some marital work, even though only one attends the sessions. Then I will send back 'messages' to share and discuss or make suggestions for the two of them at home (Bennum, 1985). For instance, many couples need to be reminded and encouraged to spend regular time together, for talking, for relaxation, for fun or for sex. This cannot easily be addressed if I have failed to make any contact with the partner.

Advantages of couple therapy – for the therapist

There are many advantages of having both partners in the room. As therapist it is possible to:

1 learn both perspectives of the relationship instead of relying on the account of one partner only;
2 observe the relationship and so spot the difficulties in communication, e.g. mindreading, over-generalizations, negative criticisms, monologuing, etc. and help them have a different experience of communicating in the session;
3 foster problem-solving skills by encouraging them to make positive suggestions rather than backward-looking blaming;
4 increase mutual understanding and rapport between the couple, rather than the focus being upon the relationship of one partner with the counsellor.

It can be more effective when the therapist uses the decentred position (Crowe and Ridley, 1990) asking the couple to turn their chairs to face each other as they talk. Whilst encouraging them to keep their interaction proceeding along helpful lines, the therapist can remain sufficiently apart to hypothesize about the relationship and the next useful step in the therapeutic process.

Benefits of couple therapy for the clients

The advantages to the client include the following.

1 Not having to spend hours describing their relationship to the therapist. Instead, the therapist is there with them while they interact. Thus they benefit from the understanding gained from direct observation as described above.
2 Being helped to experience a different way of relating, in the session, thus providing an initial encouragement to try this again at home, particularly if they agree to do 'homework' tasks.

3 Developing a concept of mutuality or reciprocity in their relationship, decreasing 'blame giving' and 'labelling' which can be so destructive. Thus their interactions may be freed up and become more equal and balanced.

4 Help in adjusting to the individual's symptoms which may appear insurmountable; for example, schizophrenia, manic depression, some phobias and obsessions and many medical conditions. Educative help and problem-solving training in such families has been productive (Falloon and Liberman, 1983). Studies have shown how reducing Expressed Emotion (critical comments, hostility and face-to-face contact) in families of schizophrenic and depressed patients has significantly reduced their relapse rate (Leff and Vaughn, 1985). Family work can be a useful addition to individual treatment for these patients.

5 An avoidance of unhelpful 'therapist dependency'. The client no longer returns home feeling the counsellor is the only person in the world who understands him or her. If the joint work is going well this person will begin to benefit from understanding and being understood by the partner.

Case study: Tony and Joy

Tony and Joy came to see me together. Both of them were concerned about Joy's lack of desire for sex since the birth of their daughter three years before. They had been to a counsellor and Joy had seen him for twelve sessions. She still was refusing sex and Tony was annoyed he had not been included in matters that concerned him so intimately. I saw them over twelve months, initially every two weeks, increasing the intervals to three then four weeks. In these sessions they talked mainly with each other about many aspects of their sex life and their general relationship. They were honest about their frustrations and resentments, which enabled them to understand and help each other. They made requests of each other; for instance, Tony agreed to stop bringing work home and Joy agreed to buy herself some pretty skirts. Joy worked at valuing her own body. Tony, on discovering that she found him less attractive when he was discontented with his work, enrolled on a training for a new profession, which excited him greatly. They made a pact to have sex every Saturday evening and he promised not to press for it any other day of the week. Such was the relief to both of them, that when they left me they were enjoying sex twice a week and the relationship was no longer acrimonious.

Case study: Anne and Jack

Anne was referred to me by her GP for help with her depression. A few months previously her husband, Jack, had been dangerously ill and she had continued her job and visited him in hospital every day. Although he was recovering and very appreciative of all her love and care, she had become depressed and unable to continue with her work. During her first session she described how, throughout their marriage, they had many violent rows. Now she lived in dread of these arguments recurring as Jack regained strength. She also spoke about her own very low self-esteem since her early childhood. I suggested that it could be helpful to ask her husband to join us for some sessions. They came together six times and they discussed their problems with each other. They reviewed the rows, the parts they had each played in them and their differing reactions afterwards. They planned how to handle them differently in future. They forgave each other and reassured each other of their love. They also reviewed the legacy each carried from their past, particularly from the abuse Anne had received from her father and the trauma of Jack's first marriage. Both felt they had been heard and understood. Subsequently Jack's illness recurred and he died. Anne returned to me for grief counselling and several times she gratefully referred to the improvement in their relationship following these conversations together.

Conclusion

With the breakdown of supportive family life more and more people are turning to counselling for help and counselling courses are mushrooming. I suggest that these courses should include in their syllabus a careful consideration of the most appropriate way of working with each client in their own particular context. Should one see the individual or the couple or the family?

The publication by Jack Dominian and the team of researchers at One Plus One entitled *Marital Breakdown and the Health of the Nation* (1991) was written in response to the Government's Green Paper on the Health of the Nation. It sets out significant statistical evidence for the severe consequences of family stress and marital breakdown both to physical and to mental health. Most counselling training places much emphasis on attention to personal development, self-awareness, self-needs, self-fulfilment and self-potential. Such work can sometimes actually contribute to family breakdown. There is much need for more awareness of, and training in, couple and family therapy, and an emphasis on mutual awareness, compromise and forward-looking togetherness.

References

Bennum, I. (1985) 'Prediction and responsiveness in behavioural marital therapy', *Behavioural Psychotherapy*, 13: 186–201.

Bott, D. (1992) '"Can I help you help me change?" Systemic Intervention in an Integrated Model of Counselling', *Counselling*, 3(1).

Crowe, M. and Ridley, J. (1990) *Therapy with Couples – a Behavioural Systems Approach to Marital and Sexual Problems*. Oxford: Blackwell Scientific. pp. 114–22, 129–50.

Dominian, J. (1995) *Marriage: the Definitive Guide to What Makes a Marriage Work*. London: Heinemann.

Dominian, J., Mansfield, P., Dormor, D. and McAllister, F. (1991) *Marital Breakdown and the Health of the Nation*. A Response to the Government's Consultative Document for Health in England. Marriage & Partnership Research One Plus One, Abbey Litho Ltd.

Douglas, A.R., Matson, I.C. and Hunter, S. (1989) 'Sex therapy for women incestuously abused as children', *Sexual and Marital Therapy*, 4(2).

Falloon, I.R.H. and Liberman, R.P. (1983) 'Behavioural family interventions in the management of chronic schizophrenia', in W.R. McFarlane (ed.), *Family Therapy in Schizophrenia*. New York: Guilford Press.

Leff, J. and Vaughn, C. (1985) *Expressed Emotion in Families*. New York: Guilford Press.

Robinson, M. (1991) *Family Transformation through Divorce and Remarriage – a Systemic Approach*. London: Routledge. p. 184.

Discussion issues

1 When would you suggest that couple therapy might be more appropriate than individual counselling?

2 What would be the advantages of combining some separate individual sessions for both partners during couple work? Would there by any disadvantages?

3 Would one or two couple sessions early in counselling lead to wider awareness with individuals?

4 How could counselling courses include more emphasis on couple issues in their training? Would a module introducing couple therapy lead to wiser counsellors or to too many semi-trained couple therapists?

PART THREE

COUNSELLING ISSUES

Introduction to Part Three

On the face of it, counselling is a simple business. We all encounter problems in our everyday life and for many people the problems become too much to bear alone. The death of a dear one, the breakdown of a relationship, starting a new job, losing what seemed like a secure job, the strain of exams are all examples of the stresses people are facing. For some, there may not be a specific problem but they know they are not happy and want to understand why. At times such as these we might well seek out some help from a counsellor.

Counsellors use a range of communication skills to help people who do not want to face these problems alone. They aim to offer a relationship in which the client can feel safe enough to explore his or her situation with a view to making any changes which might lead to a life which feels more satisfying and resourceful.

So far, so good. But, of course, human relationships are never as simple as they seem. Carl Rogers, whose work is the reference point for many of the authors of this book, believed that the nature of the relationship between client and counsellor was the essence of counselling and therapy (Rogers and Stevens, 1967). He felt that if counsellors were able to create the kind of relationship in which the client felt valued and free to explore their thoughts and feelings, therapeutic success was likely to follow. He wrote about the different types of counselling in which he was engaged – from brief contacts with clients who came for practical advice to long-term intensive psychotherapy – 'I have come to the conclusion that one learning which applies to all of these experiences is that it is the quality of the personal relationship which matters most.'

This deceptively simple viewpoint raises a range of issues which this section of the book aims to reflect. The first chapter, for instance, is about another seemingly simple matter – furniture. John Rowan's concern is with the conditions under which counselling takes place, and he focuses on the way details of the environment can influence the outcome of the counselling work. Ray Woolfe, too, writes about an important influence on the counsellor; in charting his own journey he encourages us to consider the importance of counselling literature.

347

Dorothy Rowe and Verena Tschudin wrote in the early 1980s about how the emotional cost of meeting society's expectations may bring someone into counselling; Colin Feltham writes of the possible cost to the counsellor. He raises the issue of counsellor accountability and accreditation by asking how we can devise good practice guidelines while at the same time being our own most radical critics.

Peter Ross notes that conflicting evidence exists as to the costs and benefits of counselling and that we stand to gain a great deal from grappling with this issue. Carole Sutton takes the theme even further and presents a goal-attainment approach to the evaluation of counselling. The situation is complex because there are basic differences between practitioners as to what makes good counselling. Ron Wilgosh suggests that in an increasingly competitive market, brief therapy approaches will be more and more in demand; Kay Goddard answers with a spirited defence of taking time to provide a safe, unhurried environment where the client can safely re-experience hostile feelings of infancy. Each provides a coherent argument for their case.

The idea of accreditation has raised anxieties among practising and trainee counsellors. Alan Frankland counters these with a clear explanation of the system developed by BAC which he believes is a sound one. He concludes that our behaviour in conducting the discussions about the continuing development of accreditation will reflect the measure of maturity of our profession.

Working with an experienced colleague who helps us to explore, challenge and develop our work is one of the ways we manage the issue of accountability. However, even supervision raises issues for careful thought and discussion. It is, for instance, something which is only appropriate to Western culture; Pat Justice asks us to consider how supervision relates to families from ethnic minorities. Tim Bond raises ethical issues for consideration. David Smith, concerned with how to ensure we do it well, describes how communicative theory can provide a basis for monitoring the supervisee's perception of the supervisor. Moreover the word itself is questioned by David Williams, who proposes that 'supervision' does not accurately describe the intention behind the activity. Mentoring is a process often allied to supervision and counselling and A.G. Watts suggests we might consider how these relationships incorporate counselling components.

As counselling moves towards achieving the status and autonomy associated with a recognized profession, legal considerations take on a particular importance. Peter Jenkins guides us through some of the complexities and argues a case for including some legal knowledge in counselling training. Janice Russell highlights one of the problematic areas in her research into the possibility of sexual exploitation of clients by counsellors.

The rapid growth of technology, too, has its potential problems. Many counsellors and trainees using audio-tape recordings to monitor and increase their effectiveness. Ian Horton and Rowan Bayne explore some practical and ethical implications and lay out a set of guidelines for the use of tapes. Peter Ross describes the process of computerizing client records. He reassuringly comments that at the beginning of the change no one on the staff had ever touched a computer but at the time of writing all were enthusiasts. A matter rarely discussed is touched on by Barbara Traynor and Petrūska Clarkson. They explore the ethical and practical implications of the death of a psychotherapist, providing a checklist of issues to be considered.

Some of the basic concepts attached to the practice of counselling also raise issues for debate. Chris Scott, for instance, was writing in 1984 about empathy as a confused concept. Fergus Cairns describes the difficulties of getting to grips with transference and counter-transference within counselling. This theme is developed further by Jane Leslie in her exploration of transference in adolescents' relationship with the counsellor. Tony Merry raises some questions about the way that client-centred therapy might develop.

One issue we could not ignore in a Reader such as this is the regularly occurring debate in the counselling world focused on the differences between counselling and psychotherapy. Are there any? If so, what are they? Is one better/deeper/more difficult/more valuable/etc. than the other? Chapters by Alan Naylor-Smith and Ivan Ellingham end this section by raising this issue once again.

Reference

Rogers, Carl R. and Stevens, Barry (1967) *Person to Person*. New York: Souvenir Press.

42

The Psychology of Furniture

John Rowan

As a result of conversations with people on the BAC Accreditation Sub-committee, it seemed that something needed to be written about the conditions under which counselling was being conducted. It is of course the responsibility of each counsellor to make sure that he or she has a suitable place to conduct the necessary interviews. If he or she is given a totally unsuitable position, such as in a corridor (and this is not unknown), or a room with a window in the door such that passers-by can peer in, or a room with a good deal of intrusion by external sounds, this must be opposed and the relevant people informed that this is unacceptable. But there are some more subtle things too, and it seemed that some counsellors were quite unaware of the implications of the furniture in the rooms where they were counselling: for example, there seemed to be one or two counsellors who did their counselling in their bedrooms and saw nothing odd in this. It seemed, therefore, worthwhile to put together some observations on furniture more generally.

I first came across the importance of furniture in the early 1970s, when I found that an exercise which worked perfectly well when carried out in a room furnished with cushions did not work at all in a room furnished with chairs instead. I had already come across the essay by Paul Goodman (1962) which struck me as very good, and this reinforced my opinion that here was something of great importance. Later I did a number of workshops on body language and read up most of the available literature on this, and even ran a couple of workshops on the Psychology of Furniture.

One of the most interesting examples of how useful this approach can be came when I was working with the London Fire Brigade on their new appraisal system for firefighters wanting promotion. The officers in the Fire Brigade struck me as very practical, down-to-earth people, not very much interested in psychology or abstract theory of any kind. I was puzzled at first as to how to explain to them the difference between a normal interview with a subordinate, where some instruction is being given or some reprimand is being issued, and so forth, and an appraisal interview which is more like counselling. In an appraisal interview the ideal is to approach the person in the spirit of 'Let's look together at what you have been doing and see how you have been getting on.' This is much more like counselling than it is like giving orders or evaluating performance in a one-sided way. But I did not want to explain the whole theory of counselling or give them a complete training in counselling skills, because this did not seem appropriate or necessary.

This chapter was first published as 'Counselling and the psychology of furniture', in *Counselling, Journal of the British Association for Counselling*, no. 64, p. 21 (1988).

So what I did was to say that the basic difference between an appraisal interview and the normal kind of interview was that in the normal interview the parties sat opposite each other with a desk between them, while in an appraisal interview both parties sat on the same side of the desk, looking at the papers together, and discussing them side by side. This they were able to understand and do immediately, and the whole spirit of the interaction changed automatically with the change of physical position.

The success of this very simple manoeuvre persuaded me that furniture can be very powerful in creating certain expectations at a psychological level, without the parties necessarily being aware of how this is working.

Paul Goodman contrasts Freudian analysis, Sullivanian therapy, Reichian therapy and Gestalt therapy from the point of view of what furniture they employ and how they use it, and shows that each arrangement springs out of the theory of what has gone wrong in the client, and what is needed to put matters right. And he goes on to discuss architecture more generally in this light.

All this is, of course, only an illustration of the general point that what a person does very often speaks louder than anything the person says.

Counselling

When it comes to counselling, the standard arrangement which I have most often seen is two chairs, often high-backed chairs with wooden arms, at right angles to each other, and about two feet apart. Often there is a coffee table between the chairs, enabling a box of tissues, a diary or whatever to be placed handily for immediate use. This arrangement is so common because in many ways it is perfect. Let us look at its features one by one.

The angle. If chairs are placed opposite each other, so that counsellor and client are head on, there is a suggestion of opposition or attack. Where chairs are placed like this, there is often a desk or table between, to make the attack less likely. As Goodman points out, the desk or table conceals the genitals and makes the situation safer. It is particularly suitable for schizophrenics or people with extremely weak or immature egos – the desk lends an atmosphere of objectivity and practicality, where we are not going to discuss things like dreams or fantasies. But with the desk taken away, and the angle adjusted to ninety degrees, counsellor and client can look at each other or look away very easily, and this gives much more flexibility as to what can be talked about.

There is an interesting point here which Aaron Kipnis brings out, and which I have not seen elsewhere: he says that men's bodies are used to hunting side by side, an ancient habit. Perhaps women's bodies also have the ancient habit of facing one another and talking while weaving and grinding grain. In any case, men often experience their intimacy more shoulder to shoulder. For men, being face to face often implies conflict or competition with the other team.

Most therapy these days is conducted with the therapist facing the client, one-to-one. Women are generally comfortable with this arrangement. But many men are more likely to face the one person in a room they dislike, orienting themselves toward a potential conflict, whereas women are more likely to turn toward someone they like most, a potential relationship. (Kipnis, 1991, p. 265)

I do not know how much to make of this, but it seems worth thinking about.

The chair

The straighter the chair, the greater is the suggestion of rationality. The tubular chairs which I have seen used in the Tavistock Clinic are perhaps the limit of this. There is a very strong suggestion with a straight chair that one will not move out of one's chair, and one will not say anything that might cause anyone else to move. Arms to a chair give more support, and make it less likely that the client will sit with arms folded – a closed position which does not make for easy rapport. A softer chair offers a suggestion of more relaxation, and more possibility of being emotional, but still suggests a basic rationality, a need to be sensible rather than silly. Cushions on the floor give much more flexibility and a suggestion that it is all right to be childlike or even childish. And a couch or mattress lends itself to fantasy, dreams, deep regression and loss of conscious rational control. All these things are there in the situation, in the furniture, before anyone comes on the scene.

The distance

The studies of proxemics which have now been carried out by many people all over the world, and which are described in books like *Body Language* by Pease (1981), tell us that there are four basic zones around a person. There is the intimate zone (6–18 inches), the personal zone (18–48 inches), the social zone (4–12 feet) and the public zone (over 12 feet). Now it seems obvious that counselling is mostly appropriate to the personal zone, since this is the zone for talking to someone we know on a personal level and want to exchange personal information with. However, at certain points in counselling we may need to enter the intimate zone, where a definite emotional closeness can be experienced. So the ideal distance is just beyond the 18-inch limit, but in such a way that one can reach into or lean into the 18-inch zone when this is appropriate. In other words, the counsellor should be within reach of the client. I remember seeing on television a counsellor who sat on one side of his fireplace, while the client's chair was on the other side of the fireplace; this seems to me quite wrong on all counts. There is an illusion prevalent among some counsellors that any mistakes, anything that is wrong between counsellor and client, can be counselled away; but this sort of ever-present structural fault cannot be counselled away. It is not a question of interpreting it or dealing with it, it is a question of putting it right.

Equipment

If a box of tissues is prominently displayed, this gives permission, as it were, to the client to cry. It offers a silent witness to the fact that people often cry in this room, and that it is OK to cry. One counsellor told me that a box labelled 'Professional

Wipes' was remarked on favourably by one client, as presumably superior to someone's own label. Similarly all the other things which happen to be in the room can tell their own story. A clock can either be available to the client as well as to the counsellor, or turned so that only the counsellor can see it; there seems to be more of a power play about the clock which the client cannot see. It hardly needs to be said that a telephone should not be in the same room where counselling is done, and that if there is no way of eliminating it, it should not be answered during a session.

A cassette recorder for recording sessions is quite acceptable to the client if it is first acceptable to the counsellor (Russell et al., 1984). Windy Dryden (1991) has an excellent discussion of the problems which can arise with cassette recorders.

Premises

Taking all this into account, what are we now to say about the situation where the counsellor does counselling in the bedroom? What are the suggestions there? A bed is unlike a couch, massage table or mattress in that it clearly suggests that someone uses the room for sleeping. If it is a double bed, it also suggests that someone sleeps with someone else. A double bed has the further function of suggesting that this is a room occupied by a conventional heterosexual married couple, and many of the implications of this could be deleterious for a client who was gay or having problems of sexual identity or had feminist insights or feelings. Even if it is a single bed, there is a suggestion that it could be used for sex as well as for sleeping.

Now it is already well known that the very act of getting rapport in counselling is reminiscent of courtship and making friends (Rowan, 1983, Chapter 4). This can bring great difficulties for a new client, who may be overwhelmed by the warmth of this new setting. To bring a bed into such a situation seems likely to exaggerate these possibilities considerably, and to be crossing some invisible boundary. One would expect that there would be a greater number of clients not returning for a second interview in such circumstances. Another thing which could happen would be if the client did continue with the sessions, but also went to another counsellor, or some other form of treatment, at the same time as seeing the first (bedroom) counsellor: the crossing of one boundary (by the counsellor) can lead to the crossing of another boundary (by the client).

One would also expect a greater suppression of sexual feelings and sexual material generally in such a context. Transference matters could very easily be complicated and made more difficult and intense with a bed in the room, especially where transference was a central element in the type of counselling being offered.

Van Velden (1984) has suggested that furniture also has important implications for sexual politics. He points out that the average home is designed to underwrite and facilitate male dominance and female service roles, in a variety of ways. For example, the kitchen sink and the sink or handbasin placed in the bedroom are of different heights. They are both intended for the same purpose – to wash the hands or to wash things with the hands – so one might expect that they would be of the same height. But the top of the kitchen sink is always higher than the top of the bedroom sink: why should this be? It is because the sink in the bedroom is designed for emergency use as a receptacle into which men may urinate. It has to be low enough to make this possible. As van Velden says, buildings are designed and built by men to fulfil male needs and male standards, under rules and regulations created by men, so none of this should be surprising.

A further point is that a bedroom setting may suggest that other rooms in the house or flat are being used by other occupants. The client may even hear other occupants moving around or talking, switching on radios or vacuum cleaners, and so forth. And there may be an issue here about the counsellor being afraid to be alone with the client. Clients may pick this up as an avoidance of real one-to-one engagement. More generally, the issue here is whose interests are paramount – is the counselling setting for the client's benefit or for the counsellor's benefit? Obviously both sets of interests must be satisfied; the question is, what is the balance, and how is this balance seen by the client?

It seems, then, that counsellors would be well advised not to counsel in their bedrooms. But the same principle applies to other rooms too. The living room can suggest a whole life style, and therefore a set of expectations which will underlie everything the therapist says or does. Books on shelves may be particularly revealing about the counsellor and his or her interests, and books by the counsellor may be especially powerful in impressing the client with authority problems. There is a moving paragraph in Ernst and Goodison (1981) which I have quoted before, where the author says:

> The oppression lay in *who he was*, the questions *he didn't ask* and the material *I didn't present*. It lay in the way I felt when I arrived at his house on my bicycle and he drew up in his large car; the sense I had that he must see his wife and family and home as normal and my household as a sign of my abnormality. To be cured would be to be capable of living like him.

Now obviously there is nothing we can do about some of this sort of thing, but it is important to be aware of these issues and not to indulge in unnecessary obstacles to understanding. The client is always going to have some fantasies about the counsellor. The question is – how does our furniture feed those fantasies? Everything in the room is going to say something. And the more disturbed the client, the more important these issues may be. The trouble is that difficulties with the premises very seldom come out directly in the form of objections by the client – all the effects are indirect, though they often come up between the lines, as it were, in the choice of topics to discuss or the emphasis in the way they are talked about. We are very little aware, in most cases, of what our furniture is saying. To the extent that we can be more aware of these matters, it must have an effect on the excellence of our counselling.

References

Dryden, Windy (1991) *Dryden on Counselling*, vol. 3: *Training and Supervision*. London: Whurr. ch. 6.

Ernst, Sheila and Goodison, Lucy (1981) *In Our Own Hands*. London: The Women's Press.

Goodman, Paul (1962) 'Seating arrangements', in *Utopian Essays and Practical Proposals*. New York: Vintage Books.

Kipnis, Aaron (1991) *Knights without Armour*. Los Angeles: Tarcher.

Pease, Allan (1981) *Body Language*. London: Sheldon Press.

Rowan, John (1983) *The Reality Game*. London: Routledge and Kegan Paul.

Russell, Richard K. et al. (1984) 'Counsellor training and supervision: theory and research', in S.D. Brown and R.W. Lent (eds), *Handbook of Counselling Psychology*. New York: Wiley.

Van Velden, Frans (1984) *Environment and Sexual Violence*. Eindhoven: Turtle Editions.

Discussion issues

1 Name some issues connected with the furnishing of the counselling room which are not mentioned in the article.

2 If a room cannot be set aside for counselling alone, what considerations would come into the picture when trying to decide which of the existing rooms to use, and how it might be modified?

3 What are the advantages and disadvantages of having someone else on the premises, and of letting the client become aware of their existence?

4 How does the room setting affect you personally, (a) as a counsellor and (b) as a client? Do any particular times in the past come to mind when it did affect you in some way?

43

Finding Meaning in One's Reading: A Report on a Counsellor's Journey

Ray Woolfe

This chapter attempts to make sense of my personal and professional development through the process of looking for meaning in the books that have influenced me over the years. This task is facilitated by concepts such as 'the counsellor's journey' (Goldberg, 1986), while Skovholt and Ronnestad (1992) talk about 'the evolving professional' self and 'stages and themes in therapist and counsellor development'. The idea of an ongoing journey with different phases is valuable in offering shape to the detail which follows.

Goldberg emphasizes the importance of early family experiences in the decision to become a counsellor. These include an awareness of pain and distress, a rich inner life, and an early helping role within the family. As he puts it:

> many of us who choose to become psychotherapists do so with the hopeful prospect that we can experience and be an ascendent agent in personal relationships without some of the risks for hurt and disappointment that we experienced in our earlier attempts at love and friendship, particularly within our own families.

These factors are there in my biography and may partly explain why I have found this a particularly difficult piece to write, entailing as it does the personal and professional journey of a counsellor with all the life drama that this entails. Rippere and Williams (1985) refer to helpers as 'wounded healers' and the journey, can, therefore, be understood as one of seeking to heal these wounds.

In 1982, I co-authored a book entitled *Coping with Crisis* (Murgatroyd and Woolfe, 1982). I think that one of the reasons for writing this book is that crisis has featured as a major theme in my life, associated particularly with the birth of a severely mentally handicapped son. The more politically correct term 'severe learning difficulty' does not seem adequately to describe the enormous meaning of this event to me.

At the time of my worst despair, I was teaching social science at a university and sought some kind of meaning and understanding in the subject matter (which was supposedly about human beings) in order to help me to cope with the powerful and disturbing feelings which I was experiencing. Sadly I found little or nothing and it was at this point that I first became involved with counselling as a client and as a participant in personal development activities such as encounter groups. I began to go on courses and started to come across a broad sweep of humanistic literature on Gestalt, Transactional Analysis, transpersonal psychology, Zen Buddhism, yoga, co-counselling, personal construct analysis, psychodrama etc. I experienced a

This chapter was first published as 'Books that have influenced me', in *Counselling, Journal of the British Association for Counselling*, no. 68, pp. 33–6 (1989).

wonderful sense, at this stage, of having discovered an Aladdin's Cave of new ways of looking at the world. The word which best describes this discovery is 'ecstasy', a feeling which I have never quite experienced again in the same form.

I could list 1001 books that influenced me at this point. Ones which stand out in the memory are classics such as Fritz Perls' introduction to Gestalt therapy (Perls, Hefferline and Goodman, 1973), Assagioli's work on psychosynthesis (Assagioli, 1965) and Schutz's account of encounter groups, with the wonderful title *Joy* (Schutz, 1967). I note with interest that the sub-title of Schutz's book is *Expanding Human Awareness*, while Perls' book is sub-titled *Excitement and Growth in the Human Personality*. These titles seem to convey strongly the flavour of the personal journey on which I was engaged at that time.

I have always made a conscious effort to integrate new learning with old knowledge and in this process I found one of John Rowan's early books offered me an excellent and integrative map of the humanistic field (Rowan, 1976). Moreover, its title 'ordinary ecstasy' also spoke directly to my personal journey.

It was at this period that I came across the writings of Carl Rogers and, like so many people involved in counselling, I have been greatly influenced by his work. However, there is one piece which I have always found rather inspiring. In the first chapter of *Becoming a Person*, Rogers offers an autobiographical account of the development of his personal philosophy and professional thinking. He describes how he gradually came to think of himself as a clinical psychologist, 'a step I eased into, with relatively little clear cut conscious choice, rather just following the activities which interested me'. I find this statement confirming of my own experience, which in some small way parallels that of Rogers. I never seem to have made many conscious decisions about becoming a counsellor. I started off my university career as an economist and eventually moved into sociology. Somehow, this did not wholly satisfy my interests or meet my needs, so I started reading and studying subjects which engaged me connected with personal development and change and gradually found ways of incorporating these into my professional life. Two decades later, I think of myself as a counsellor and counselling psychologist. I never consciously planned it. It came about, just as Rogers describes it, as a result of doing the reading and the personal work that I wanted to do and trusting the process.

Out of this learning process emerged a greater understanding of my own background and the ways in which this had influenced my self-identity. As this awareness developed, I found that the work of R.D. Laing (see Laing, 1959) offered many insights about my own adolescent experiences within a family. In particular, it allowed me to see that my refusal to accept the values of my family of origin was linked to a refusal to accept the role of scapegoat. Rather than being a sign of madness, as family messages sometimes implied, it was a sign of personal strength and mental stability.

As I began to read further within the field of existential phenomenology, I began to apply the notion of reality as socially constructed to my own research and writing. I did some research in which I explored how the label 'maladjusted' (then in common usage) was employed within a local education authority. It demonstrated that the authority coped with an embarrassing situation in which more children were being ascertained as in need of special school places than there were places available, by an arbitrary process of allotting them different labels, thereby solving the problem by administrative fiat (see Woolfe, 1981). In this project, I was influenced by the work of Thomas Szasz (1961). There is a wonderful sentence in *The Myth of Mental Illness* in which he says that 'the question, what is mental illness? is shown to be inextricably tied to the question, 'what do psychiatrists do?' Replace the word psychiatrist by the word counsellor and there is much food for thought for counsellors.

My first full-time jobs were in youth work and teaching and in the latter capacity I taught at an LEA secondary-modern boarding school. A high number of the pupils wet their beds and displayed other symptoms of emotional problems. Although I did not realize it at the time, this had been my first contact with emotional disturbance. However, the experience was significant in another way. For the first time, I experienced something of the rigid authoritarianism of institutional life and began to ask the question, 'how do people survive in such awful circumstances?' Erving Goffman's *Asylums* offered a great deal of insight (Goffman, 1961).

However, the question came to be more explicitly addressed in my next job which specifically involved doing research on boarding schools. I can see now how unconscious forces were at work in the choice of this job and in a continuing interest in researching organizations. It was at this point that I came across the work of Jewish psychiatrists such as Bettelheim and Frankl, who had been incarcerated in German concentration camps during the Second World War. Frankl's work in particular made a big impression on me (Frankl, 1964). In *Man's Search for Meaning*, he describes how he lived out the central theme of existential thought: that life involves suffering, but survival involves finding meaning in the suffering. Frankl is fond of quoting Nietzsche's aphorism that 'he who has a why to live can bear with almost any how'. For example, at his worst moments when he considered suicide, Frankl found meaning in the fact that if he died, the memory of his murdered wife would die with him. His desire to keep her memory alive gave him the will to live.

Through his work, I began to find possible answers to some of the questions which my own life experience had posed, particularly relating to the meaning of having a handicapped child. An awareness gradually dawned that perhaps through the experience of relating to this person I had learned something about unconditional love, both giving and receiving. Here was one of Rogers' core conditions in action.

Although I have moved away from sociology as a central focus of my teaching and research, understanding the social and political context of counselling has always been of major importance for me (see Woolfe, 1983). In part this derives from my training as an academic sociologist and the imperative this imposes to examine individual behaviour within its social context. However, it also owes something to the one aspect of my upbringing which I still embrace, namely a commitment to some kind of socialist society. The feature of this belief which most strongly impinges on counselling is that individuals are not completely free agents and that our awareness and consciousness derives at least in part from our position within society.

I like the work of Erich Fromm (Fromm, 1942), who in his book *The Fear of Freedom* applied the psychoanalytical method in explaining the rise of authoritarianism in the 1930s. He argues that while democracy brings freedom, it also creates a society in which people feel isolated from their fellows; where relationships are impersonal and where insecurity replaces a sense of belonging. Fromm suggests that it is this sense of isolation that drives human beings towards a desire for submission to an authoritarian state.

A more contemporary structural analysis and critique of counselling has been provided by feminist writers. They have appreciated that the personal is political and that to understand the nature of relationships between men and women we have to understand the gendered, sexist nature of family and work roles. As long as fifty years ago Karen Horney pointed out that if women were envious of men this had less to do with penis envy and more to do with the fact that in economic terms they were vastly underprivileged in relation to men. She refers to the importance of 'cultural factors . . . the expression of a wish for all those qualities or privileges which in our culture are regarded as masculine, such as strength, courage independence, success, sexual freedom, right to choose a partner' (Horney, 1939, p. 108).

Since Horney's time, the concept of patriarchy has been widely employed to describe the social structure through which gender relations are defined and reproduced. Understanding this context is important not just in facilitating analysis or diagnosis, but in devising programmes of action. For example, what is the purpose of helping a woman, who is depressed by her family circumstances, to adjust back into a family system which in the long term simply acts to perpetuate her dependence or to reinforce her sense of powerlessness and depression? She is not so much depressed as oppressed. Seen in this way, the therapeutic focus shifts towards helping people to understand the relationship between emotional life and its social and economic context. The work of Eichenbaum and Orbach (1982) is particularly impressive in demonstrating that these ideas are capable of being put into practice within a therapeutic framework. They offer hope for the development of a more culturally aware form of counselling in the field of race.

The journey described in this paper has been full of false starts, of doubts and uncertainties and sometimes despair and disillusionment. At the same time, in the manner described by Skovholt and Ronnestad, it has also been marked by a growing sense of competence and by an increasing diversity of interests and creativity. This is reflected in the wide range of literature which has influenced me; socialist, feminist, existential, humanistic, and psychodynamic. My conclusion is that through the process of reflecting about one's reading both in the past and in the present, counsellors can gain insight into the personal and professional journey on which we are all engaged.

References

Assagioli, R. (1965) *Psychosynthesis*. Wellingborough: Crucible.

Eichenbaum, L. and Orbach, S. (1982) *Outside In, Inside Out. Women's Psychology: a Feminist Psychoanalytic Approach*. Harmondsworth: Penguin.

Frankl, V.E. (1964) *Man's Search for Meaning: an Introduction to Logotherapy*. London: Hodder and Stoughton.

Fromm, E. (1942) *The Fear of Freedom*. London: Routledge.

Goffman, E. (1961) *Asylums: Essays on the Social Situation of Mental Patients and Other Inmates*. New York: Anchor.

Goldberg, C. (1986) *On Becoming a Psychotherapist: the Journey of The Healer*. New York: Gardner Press.

Horney, K. (1939) *New Ways in Psychoanalysis*. London: Routledge and Kegan Paul.

Laing, R.D. (1959) *The Divided Self*. London: Tavistock.

Murgatroyd, S. and Woolfe, R. (1982) *Coping With Crisis: Understanding and Helping People in Need*. London: Harper and Row.

Perls, F.S., Hefferline, R.F. and Goodman, P. (1973) *Gestalt Therapy: Excitement and Growth in the Human Personality*. Harmondsworth: Pelican.

Rippere, V. and Williams, R. (eds) (1985) *Wounded Healers: Mental Health Workers' Experiences of Depression*. Chichester: Wiley.

Rogers, C.R. (1961) *On Becoming a Person: a Therapist's View of Psychotherapy*. London: Constable.

Rowan, J. (1976) *Ordinary Ecstasy: Humanistic Psychology in Action*. London: Routledge and Kegan Paul.

Schutz, W.C. (1967) *Joy: Expanding Human Awareness*. New York: Grove Press.

Skovholt, T.M. and Ronnestad, M.H. (1992) *The Evolving Professional Self: Stages and Themes in Therapist and Counselor Development*. Chichester: Wiley.

Szasz, T.S. (1961) *The Myth of Mental Illness*. New York: Harper and Row.

Woolfe, R. (1981) 'Maladjustment in the context of local authority decision-making', in L. Barton and S. Tomlinson (eds), *Special Education: Policy, Practices and Social Issues*. London: Harper and Row.

Woolfe, R. (1983) 'Counselling in a world of crisis: towards a sociology of counselling', *International Journal for the Advancement of Counselling*, 6: 167–76.

Discussion issues

1 What experiences in your family of origin were influential in the process of your becoming a counsellor?

2 What books influenced you in your youth and how do these relate to your experiences then?

3 Since you made the decision to become a counsellor, what book(s) have influenced you? To what extent do these reflect personal issues in your life?

4 As you have developed as a counsellor can you identify patterns in your reading? What do these say about your personal journey and search for meaning?

44

Guilt is a Useless Emotion

Verena Tschudin

Our value systems, the standards against which we judge ourselves, are not necessarily static. However, because society's values change need not mean that our personal standards change. But where society's values and our own do not coincide, we enter an area of possible guilt, not knowing right from wrong. How useful or otherwise is guilt?

Being human means for most people being indebted to something. What that something is to the individual determines how we behave. This sense of being in debt can variously be called: duty, allegiance, conscience, sacrifice. Therefore, how we respond to this debt is how we express the fact of being human. 'Utilization and celebration, satisfaction and exaltation' all express our positive interests in and need of being human. When they are expressed as 'oughts' they are likely to become guilt. Expressing oneself in terms of guilt is only one side of the story (see Heschel, 1973, pp. 257ff) but one which warrants looking at from time to time.

Guilt and nurses

The areas where guilt is encountered by nurses in their working day cover all the above – duty, allegiance, conscience and sacrifice. Consciously or unconsciously they are with us in all we do by the fact that we deal with human beings all the time.

In nursing we have chosen to serve other people, therefore it is our duty to serve them to the best of our ability. We owe an allegiance to the institution that trains and employs us. We carry out our work not only with understanding and ability, but with conscience, trying to alleviate suffering by all the means at our disposal. This can sometimes mean going beyond the call of 'duty' to the point where to alleviate suffering for someone else we are led to suffer ourselves, by sacrificing our free time, convenience and sometimes our health.

This is a tall order, and the duty of the institution to its employees is to minimize risk and demands of conscience and sacrifice and reduce areas of possible stress and fear. But the possible and the impossible will always cause conflict between 'personal desires and what authorities said is right and natural' (Tiefer, 1979, p. 17).

Fear

Negative feelings have many faces. The most powerful emotion for most people is fear – fear for their own safety. Fear can lead us to act instinctively or irrationally in self-defence.

This chapter was first published in *Counselling, Journal of the British Association for Counselling*, no. 45, pp. 5–12 (1983).

Fear and guilt can hold each other in a tight vicious circle. Fear of not having done right will lead to the guilt of should have done right. In the sense of this article this means usually fear of superiors or someone to whom one owes something. 'The style of leadership and the patterns of interaction . . . may be determined by basic fears . . . in those who have authority in the medical setting' (Nichols et al., 1981). The fear is *basic*, not clearly conscious and therefore not seen or acknowledged. The pattern of behaviour thus repeats itself downwards in the hierarchy.

Mistakes

Nursing is full of areas of possible mistakes, e.g. giving wrong medications, handling patients wrongly, physically and emotionally, not using equipment correctly. Most hospitals have elaborate disciplinary procedures, but this does not diminish the fear of making mistakes and the guilt engendered when a mistake has been made. Normally, a wrong asks for a punishment, but the punishment does not wipe out the guilt. In Kierkegaard's stark words, 'Guilt is something absolutely different and far more terrible than the consequences of sin' (quoted in Heschel, 1973, p. 248).

How much guilt remains after a mistake has been made depends largely on how 'the delicate business of reacting to mistakes' (Nichols et al., 1981) has been handled.

Emotional involvement

With the increasing use of the 'Nursing Process', nurses find themselves more and more emotionally involved with their patients. Hand in hand goes an increasing abandonment of uniforms in some sectors of nursing. The image of the 'professional nurse' is being blurred, both for patients and nurses. With less clear boundaries the amount of desirable involvement is also less clear, hence the sense of guilt is increased when this boundary is seemingly overstepped. Until there are guidelines and/or support systems for nurses in these increasing grey areas, the sense of not knowing where right and wrong begin and end can only increase.

Responsibility

Job descriptions normally carry designations of responsibility and accountability. But the higher up the job is in the nursing hierarchy, the less clearly circumscribed are these areas. 'Protection from the impact of specific responsibility for specific tasks is given by the fact that the formal structure and role system fail to define fully enough who is responsible for what and to whom' (Menzies, 1970). Generally speaking, each nurse is responsible for the work of the nurse directly junior to her. Where practical responsibility is not clearly defined, conscientious responsibility will lead to feelings of guilt quicker than to disciplinary action from a superior.

Responsibility is here seen to be towards those in higher authority. How those in that position use their authority towards those below themselves will obviously produce or fail to produce that much-prized attribute: loyalty. This is what every senior nurse prides herself with when it is present, and when it is lacking she will still distinguish between personal and professional loyalty.

When certain standards of behaviour are not achieved by the junior staff, when mistakes are made or duties not carried out correctly, those responsible should, however, out of *their* loyalty to junior colleagues, ask themselves if the shortfalls are 'due to poor rules (set by themselves) rather than the nurse's non-compliance with good rules' (Young, 1981).

Ethics and legality

For guilt to be able to exist in the first instance, it has to be referred to something indefinable by law, but desirable by society. The area of 'duty' within nursing can be circumscribed, but it will be understood and carried out differently by every nurse. Hence it must be in this area where guilt is most readily induced and felt. 'Wherever the words should, ought, prefer, desire, responsible, good, bad, right and wrong are heard or seen, a whole set of moral reactions are called into play' (Young, 1981, p. 142).

This of course covers the whole range of care, of patients and colleagues. Some of the major areas have been well debated in hospitals, other issues are still blurred. The responsibility towards and their behaviour *vis-à-vis* abortion, euthanasia, experimentation and transplantation involves nurses in ethical situations which in some instances are also governed by law (The Abortion Act 1967 and The Human Tissue Act 1961). Nurses therefore have the 'duty' to comply with the law, but their personal involvement, say with abortion, depends on their degree of active or passive participation.

Agents of change

Nurses are increasingly encouraged to be autonomous and not to accept a status quo simply because it exists. This is certainly desirable, but it does not necessarily make for easy cooperation. Where nurses do act on their own initiative, or challenge set behaviours, they tread on dangerous ground; they become lonely. It takes a nurse who is assertive without being aggressive to be an effective change agent.

But in large or small measure every nurse is, by her very work of caring, an agent of change. How to be perhaps sympathetic and long-suffering with a medical patient, and barking without biting with a surgical patient is an art. Nurses who are not well enough trained in the art, but who try all the same without measuring the consequences can do themselves and their patients damage which may not be easily repairable, but which can carry the heavy burden of guilt. 'Perhaps promoting nurses' assertiveness rather than aggressiveness may . . . cushion conflict' (Kurtzman, 1981).

Insight and experience

Another commonly experienced source of guilt has to do with actual care. The author's experience was in a setting where post-registration nurses were taught systematic care of the dying. Many of these students expressed guilt at not having known or learnt earlier how to care for dying patients correctly. Many of these nurses felt in retrospect that they had unwittingly and unnecessarily made some patients and families suffer. Objectively these nurses could not have known or done otherwise, but subjectively they felt guilt. This experience is surely not only restricted to dying patients and must be more common than openly acknowledged.

Feelings of guilt come much more easily than they disappear again. Virtual torment can be caused by behaviour which may have been innocent at the time, but which through a different value-system has been called into question. It is not necessarily that one system is right and the other wrong, it is surely only in greater awareness and understanding of one's own set of beliefs and boundaries that guilt can be understood and/or reduced.

Guilt and patients

As the beliefs and behaviours differ with each individual, so also the reactions to beliefs and behaviours towards the self and towards others differ. Generally, the standards we apply to ourselves are far stricter than those which we apply to others. It is a matter of pride that we apply a rigorous standard to ourselves, but when we do not come up to that standard, guilt ensues – guilt which no one needs to know about or perhaps even guess or care about. We can repress the awfulness of the failure by feeling 'only' guilty about it. And guilt, like hostility, can then be a motivating force in our lives. But 'in all probability we shall learn some day that guilt feelings and a need for punishment play an important part in crises that are currently believed to be accidents. Illness is another way in which people punish themselves to alleviate guilt feelings' (Burton, 1977, p. 89)

Failure, guilt and illness

That patients do have guilt feelings is widely accepted, but what these feelings can do to a patient is virtually nowhere openly documented.

> . . . a patient thinks her cancer of the breast started when she was worrying about her daughter marrying a man unsuited to her. Feelings of guilt and misunderstanding were far more important than that she should be cured of her cancer. (Tschudin, 1982, p. 128)

It is generally accepted that cancer-sufferers fall into two groups – the fighters and the losers. It may be only speculation to think that 'the losers' are those who, faced with an illness, feel that the long-feared punishment has finally caught up with them and therefore it is no use to fight it. Guilt has had its use in warding off the hour of reckoning, but now it is here, guilt is useless, and there is no other viable defence mechanism available. If this is only a speculative statement, it is nevertheless one which is plausible. How useless is guilt?

Sexuality and guilt

Probably no other area causes so much guilt and misery than sexuality. A child discovered playing with his genitals gets his hands slapped, 'you naughty boy', and no further explanation is given because the parent is surprised and embarrassed. No wonder that all sexual activity from then on is likely to be seen as 'naughty'. Exactly what is meant by this is not clear, but it is not 'right', and the seed for uncertainty, fear and guilt is sown. When later on a patient suffers from a disease on his genital organs, fantasies about youthful misdeeds can play a major part.

A patient may not recall any such 'bad act' precisely, but suffering now from an illness of his or her sexual organs makes them think that it *must* have been something bad done in the past for which he or she is now paying. A great deal of soul-searching can go on for such a patient. When the punishment seemingly does not fit a 'crime', a fear of the punisher ensues and a consequent guilt at not having satiated this 'something', a guilt that the debt should have been recognized or paid.

Relationships

Most personal problems are problems of relationships. The worst problems normally occur in the family: we can choose our friends, we can to some extent choose our work colleagues, but we cannot choose our family. Hence the first reason for problems. By becoming ill a person will normally cause such problems to be highlighted. But these problems and the feelings they engender, do not stay outside the ward-door. Every nurse has been at the receiving end of pent-up emotions. Many an angry outburst from a patient conceals guilt, hurt pride and fear. When these emotions and feelings can be seen for what they are they lose their threat and patients and families and nurses may be able to see them in perspective.

The same cannot be said so easily when the patient is a child, but as nurses we deal also with the parents.

'It's my fault my boy has diabetes' (Burton, 1977, p. 188). This is a terrible dilemma and can become a 'focus of . . . guilt . . . because . . . both child and parents are likely to feel that they have failed' (Hooper and Roberts, 1973, p. 42). Guilt can be a powerfully motivating force here, but more likely for action than inaction as described above.

Dependence

The level of dependence on nurses varies of course with every patient. It is essentially the patient who has been admitted to hospital for the first time, perhaps following an emergency, who has not had to experience dependence before, who might find this distasteful and humiliating, but also comforting and helpful.

> Patients often resent their dependence; . . . envy nurses their health . . . are demanding, possessive and jealous. Patients, like nurses, find strong libidinal and erotic feelings stimulated by nursing care . . . (Menzies, 1970)

Between the resentment of dependence and the erotic feelings lie vast areas of personal contact between patient and nurse which can stimulate guilt. These areas can be all too easily overlooked or belittled, but they are as relevant for patients as for nurses, and indeed relatives, who may also envy nurses their intimate contact with 'their' patient.

If guilt feelings are to be reckoned with in the care of patients, they have to be much more widely acknowledged by nurses. The areas touched on are by no means exhaustive. With increasing knowledge of interpersonal behaviour needs also to go an increasing knowledge of the boundaries of that behaviour in terms of ethics and in terms of defence mechanisms.

Transference

Guilt and transference may not immediately and obviously be linked together. The two concepts are quite different. What they do have in common is that both happen, are real, but are very little reckoned with in nursing situations.

> Freud first used the term [transference] to describe how his patients used him as if he were the wonderful father, the loving mother or the hated authority to which they referred. (Altschul and Sinclair, 1981, p. 129)

It was pointed out above that patients often resent their dependence. As children they may have consciously or unconsciously resented their dependence on their parents. Now in a position they may not have wanted or chosen, they are again dependent, and the feelings which would normally belong to a parent now get transferred to a nurse. This may express itself in demanding, possessive or jealous behaviour.

Transference and counter-transference

Much the same process can happen with a nurse. Trying to help such a patient in any way can cause a nurse to regard this patient as if he were an ungrateful, spoilt child. What has happened is that a counter-transference has taken place from the nurse to the patient. This can be a very uncomfortable situation if it is not understood. The very fact that people become ill gives nurses their *raison d'être* as nurses, which puts them in a position of authority, and it is unsettling to have that authority challenged by 'childish' behaviour.

Guilt and counter-guilt

Just as transference calls forth a counter-transference, so guilt can off-set guilt in the other. If, for instance, the delicate business of handling mistakes is not handled appropriately, the person who made the mistake is certainly left with guilt, and so is the person who induced the guilt. But it is by no means only disciplinary procedures which produce guilt and counter-guilt. Any situations where value-judgements are made have this inherent possibility.

Destruction

Extreme guilt can lead to the point where a person does not function autonomously any more. Defence mechanisms have built up and taken over this function to the point where they interact like clockwork to maintain an apparent function.

Transference also could lead to the 'apparently fatalistic outlook ... that we cannot help behaving as we do because we merely repeat what we have learnt' (Altschul and Sinclair, 1981, p. 131).

Guilt and transference can therefore be used unconsciously as essentially destructive forces. However, it would take an emotionally immature person not to recognize that something is amiss. The fact of the realization, of the awareness, is the essential catharsis, the possible turning-point to the positive.

After having pointed out the possible hopeless situation, 'the important question is not whether [guilt, transference and] counter-transference occur, but what can the helper do about it?' (Brammer, 1973, p. 65). Obviously, they need to be seen for what they are; only then can something be done about them. For this to happen, a process of awareness needs to come into force. A willingness to learn, a willingness to acknowledge, i.e. bringing the unconscious into the conscious sphere, a willingness to change one's own behaviour accordingly, and a willingness to practise the new behaviour. In this way, rather than be a fatalistic treadmill, nurses can be their own and other people's agent of change.

The indebtedness referred to in the introduction to this paper can in this light be seen to be used actively for our own and other people's deeper understanding, rather than accepted passively as something that happens to us. From here we could also positively and actively use guilt for and to someone who might consider himself above duty, allegiance, conscience and sacrifice. It is up to each one of us how useful or useless an emotion guilt is.

References

Altschul, A. and Sinclair, H.C. (1981) *Psychology for Nurses*, 5th edn. London: Baillière Tindall.

Brammer, L.M. (1973) *The Helping Relationship*. Englewood Cliffs, NJ: Prentice Hall.

Burton, G. (1977) *Interpersonal Relations*. London: Tavistock.

Heschel, A.J. (1973) *A Passion for Truth*. New York: Farrar, Straus and Giroux.

Hooper, D. and Roberts, J. (1973) *Disordered Lives*. Rugby: National Marriage Guidance Council.

Kurtzman, C. (1982) 'Ethical issues in promoting autonomy in nursing students'. Paper delivered at the 1st International Conference on Nursing Law and Ethics, Jerusalem.

Menzies, I.E.P. (1970) *The Functioning of Social Systems as a Defence Against Anxiety*. Kent: Headley.

Nichols, K.A., Springford, V. and Searle, J. (1981) 'An investigation of distress and discontent in various types of nursing, *Journal of Advanced Nursing*, 6: 311–18.

Tiefer, L. (1979) *Human Sexuality*. London: Harper and Row.

Tschudin, V. (1982) *Counselling Skills for Nurses*. London: Baillière Tindall.

Young, A.P. (1981) *Legal Problems in Nursing Practice*. London: Harper and Row.

Brief update

On returning now to what I wrote, I realize the article made some sweeping statements and failed to follow through some arguments. Nevertheless, perhaps just because of its directness, it is also still valid. What is perhaps of more concern is that guilt among nurses is no better understood, generally, now than it was then. Indeed, with the changes and pressures of the present health-care system, guilt is ever more real and powerful. The guilt now hinges around issues of not being able to give adequate care because of lack of resources, be they financial, or of people and time.

A drawback of the article is that no mention is made of any 'helpful' guilt, such as Dryden (1994) describes. Dryden differentiates between guilt as 'an unconstructive emotion' and guilt as 'constructive remorse'. Perhaps in the light of Dryden's work, my title could now be better phrased as 'Is guilt only a useless emotion?'

Reference

Dryden, W. (1994) *Overcoming Guilt.* London: Sheldon Press.

Discussion issues

1 What is your own experience of guilt in helping situations?
2 Guilt can be described as 'useless' when it is nothing more than an 'unconstructive emotion'. But is 'useless' and 'unconstructive' the same?
3 What might be some ways of helping nurses to understand their patients' and clients' feelings of guilt?
4 How might nurses be helped to cope with their feelings of guilt and inadequacy and turn 'useless' emotions into 'constructive remorse'?

45

Depression and Happiness

Dorothy Rowe

What do human beings need to survive?

First, we need air, food, water and shelter. To some extent, in Britain at least, we have solved the problem of how to obtain these four necessities. But there is a fifth need which humans must satisfy if we are to survive: the need we have of other people. None of us can survive in isolation. From all the accounts we have of people who have been taken prisoner and subjected to torture we know that the one torture which affects even the strongest character is being isolated from all human contact. Such an experience produces strange and painful effects, and the longer the person is kept in isolation, the more serious and long-lasting the effects are. People have reported how, in a desperate attempt to meet their need for human contact, they have sought the company of their captors or have made friends with, i.e. humanized, a passing insect or an inquisitive rat. Of course, turning animals into human-like friends is a survival device used by many more people than isolated prisoners. This is why pets are so popular; many dog and cat lovers will tell you pets are more loyal than people.

Isolation and depression

This whole business of relating to people, or to pets as people, as a means of survival is a complicated business and not well understood. I want us to consider it in terms of the most common form of isolation – the prison of depression. Anyone who has been depressed can describe this experience in terms of a peculiar isolation, a sense of being completely alone, cut off from human contact, even though intellectually the depressed person is well aware that other people are around and available to be contacted. Depressed people will often describe this experience in an image, perhaps of being in a deep pit, or trapped in a dungeon, or abandoned on a desert island. The images all carry the same meaning; the person is alone in a prison, and serving an indeterminate sentence.

People who get depressed have a special way of seeing themselves and their world, which has the effect of cutting them off from their fellows. They suffer just as they would if deprived of adequate air, food, water and shelter; and if the isolation is sufficiently profound and long-lasting they die, either by their own hand or by an illness to which their weakened body has become vulnerable.

This chapter represents the text of an address given by Dorothy Rowe to the BAC Annual Conference at Reading University on 23–24 September 1983 and was first published as 'How can we survive?', in *Counselling, Journal of the British Association for Counselling*, no. 47, pp. 3–9 (1984).

Six beliefs of the depressed

The way in which people who become depressed view themselves and their world can be summarized as six beliefs which the person holds as absolute, unquestionable axiomatic truths.

1 No matter how good and nice I appear to be, I am bad, evil, unacceptable to myself and to other people.
2 Other people are such that I must fear, hate and envy them.
3 Life is terrible and death is worse.
4 Only bad things have happened to me in the past and only bad things will happen to me in the future.
5 Anger is evil.
6 Never forgive.

These beliefs relate together in various complex ways. Let us look at these beliefs in terms of their opposites and the implications these have for our survival.

Good and bad

When I speak of experiencing oneself as good or bad I am referring to the very basic sense we have of ourselves, which we rarely put into words. We are aware of existing, and in that awareness is a sense of goodness or badness. People who experience themselves as good do not think about this very often and so are often confounded by the enquiry 'Do you experience yourself as good or bad?' But people who experience themselves as bad are only too aware of this sense of badness. It is because they feel themselves to be so bad that they have to strive so hard to be good. They work hard in the service of others, they find it impossible to say no to a request for help, they strive to do everything perfectly and berate themselves for every little failure. People who experience themselves as good are able to stop working when they feel they have done enough or are tired or bored. They are able to refuse requests for help when they feel the request is unnecessary or unreasonable. They set themselves standards which are in their ability to reach and they treat themselves kindly when they fail. People who experience themselves as bad are forever ashamed of themselves. They feel they do not deserve to have a good life, or even to survive. They feel constantly guilty and are expecting punishment. Since in our culture good people show their goodness by accepting punishment (e.g. good children hold out their hands to be smacked, stay behind after school for detention, and good adults pay their fines) people who experience themselves as bad strive to be good by accepting the punishment which life may bring them. They may see not surviving as their punishment, just as they may see a bad marriage or physical illness as being the punishment which they deserve and not as a situation which should be avoided or ameliorated. But people who experience themselves as good feel that they have a right to live, to walk upon this earth and to share its space with other people. In conditions which threaten survival they feel that they are worth saving. Experiencing yourself as good means that, despite the troubles life may bring, you can live in harmony with yourself and with others.

People who experience themselves as being bad but who strive to be good are in constant fear of being found out and so being rejected. Sometimes they try to ward off what they see as an inevitable rejection by saying to a well-meaning friend or therapist, 'If you really knew what I was like you wouldn't like me.' If the friend or therapist persists in offering unconditional positive regard, then the person counters with, 'Whenever someone says they like me I know that person is either a fool or a liar.' When this is said to me in therapy I always ask which I am. I am invariably told that I am a fool, out of kindness no doubt and out of the certainty that one day I shall realize my mistake, see how disgustingly bad my client is and order him or her from my room with the admonition never to darken my door again. The client's challenge, 'If you really knew me you wouldn't like me' is the essence of therapy with a depressed person.

But if you experience yourself as basically good you do not get caught up worrying about whether people will like you. You accept that misunderstandings can occur, that some people might dislike you for peculiar reasons of their own; but you know that, as there is something inside you which is good and which will certainly not harm and may even benefit other people, most people will like you and want to share your company. You know too that some people love you and, since you have inspired that love, you can expect to inspire it in others. You do not find the affection of other people frightening because you do not find other people frightening.

We always assess other people in terms of ourselves. If we experience ourselves as bad then we have to worry whether other people are like us, essentially bad but pretending to be good. If they are, then they are dangerous. Of course, if other people are basically good, then they are equally dangerous, because they will certainly reject us the moment they discover how bad we are. Experiencing yourself as bad means trusting no one. However, if you experience yourself as good then you tend to see other people as good and you have no difficulty in trusting them. This can, in real life, lead you to make some tremendous mistakes and cause you great pain when you discover that there are some people who cannot be trusted, but usually such experiences lead you to think more carefully about trust and to see that we should not operate with generalized, pre-emptive rules like 'Trust everybody' or 'Trust nobody' but that we should try to identify the complexity of conditions in which people act in trustworthy or untrustworthy ways.

Understanding other people

Identifying the complexity of conditions in which people act as they do is part of the process of understanding other people. Understanding other people is a skill which we learn from infancy onwards, but if the learning of this skill is interfered with in our childhood we may never develop our understanding to the level needed in adult life to create satisfying relationships. One essential part of understanding other people is to look and to see clearly what is actually happening. We cannot do this if, before looking, we say to ourselves that we already know what that person is like, and then metaphorically cover our eyes with our hands so that we do not see anything which conflicts with our expectations.

Yet this is what has happened with so many of the people who experience themselves as being bad. Learning to experience oneself like this takes place early in childhood. When you were small and learning things from adults like 'You are a boy' or 'You are a girl' you were also being taught that 'You are a bad boy' or 'You are an unlovable girl' because these were the things which the adults around you were saying to you and about you. But often an even more profoundly affecting piece of learning takes place. Something happened, and we found ourselves being punished or betrayed by our parents. Immersed though we were in the pain of punishment or betrayal, we knew that we faced an even greater peril. The people who were inflicting the pain were the very people on whom we depended for our safety and survival. Did this mean that we had to conclude that the people whom we needed were bad people? Only a particularly strong and brave child could face this stark truth. What most of us did was to attempt to restore our sense of security by redefining who was bad. So we said, 'It is not my parents who are bad but me. I am bad and my good parents are punishing me.'

Such a decision to see one's parents as good despite evidence to the contrary not only forces the child to grow up believing an axiomatic truth of, 'I am bad' but it also establishes in the child the habit of not looking too closely at other people in case it leads to discoveries which undermine the child's sense of security. So the child stays fixated at the primitive level of assessing other people solely in terms of the way they can meet the child's own needs, i.e. whether they satisfy or deprive. Or the child may reach and stay at the slightly more advanced level of seeing people solely in terms of the roles they fill, and so in adult life he or she bases their relationships on judgements like, 'British is best', 'Blacks are lazy', 'I don't know what the youth of today are coming to'. Anyone who in adult life judges other people solely in terms of the roles they fill or the needs they meet soon has difficulty in relationships simply because other people fail to fulfil expectations. Wives fail to be all-nurturing mothers, while British, blacks, the youth of today and all other types of people fail to function in the way that their role demands. Such a person may deal with relationships totally unaware of the activities or even the existence of people around him except for those activities which actually impinge upon him. When such impinging does occur the person reacts with fear and anger. Some people, equally handicapped but not in sufficient control of their lives to reduce them to banal and predictable regularity, go through their lives in a state of anxious confusion and fearful impotence. I spent a great deal of my working life with these two types of people. The former is the spouse, usually the husband. The latter is the depressed patient, usually the wife. I try to teach them both ways of observing and assessing other people's behaviour which will enable them to understand other people and to react more appropriately to them, but I often feel that I would have greater success in teaching them the language of nuclear physics than the language of human behaviour.

Not being able to understand other people, we must fear them, and when we fear anyone for long enough we come to hate that person. Even when we are reasonably good at understanding other people, if we fear someone we do not allow ourselves to get close enough to understand him. When we don't understand another person it is very easy to come to envy him, simply because we don't see the difficulties which he is facing. Not understanding, it is very easy to see him going about his business without a care in the world and so come to envy him while feeling great pity for ourselves. Envy is bad enough, but with it comes its bitter twin, jealousy; we see someone else enjoying advantages and pleasures which we feel are rightly ours.

So, from learning to experience ourselves as bad we learn to fear others, to hate others, not to trust others, to view others with envy and jealousy, but not with understanding. We have to *learn* to experience ourselves as bad, for the feeling we have about ourselves when we enter the world is that we are good and that life is good. The supreme confidence of self-worth of the baby and infant can be carried forward in our hearts if the world around us will let us. If we are lucky the world around us will allow us to continue in our belief of our essential goodness, but it will not let us go on believing that we are omnipotent and will live forever.

Life and death

The young child discovers very early that not only is there death in this world but that death means, 'I shall die'. Discovering death, we have to give it a meaning. We puzzle over it, and discover there are only two possible meanings. Either death is the end of my identity or it is the doorway to another life. Each alternative has an implication for the way we need to live our lives. If my life and identity ends in death, then I need to make this, my only life, in some way satisfactory. If my death is a doorway to another life, then the rules of that other life, whatever it may be, affect the way I live my life now. Death shows us life and gives our life a purpose.

Many people say that they never think about death, and many more say that they think about it often but never talk about it. Yet even those who say that they never think about death can answer, 'How do you see your death, as the end of your identity or as a doorway to another life?' In my second book, *The Courage to Live*, I have described how every person has a set of religious or metaphysical or philosophical beliefs which, implicitly or explicitly, guide every decision and action. I found tremendous variety in the sets of beliefs which people hold, but whatever the beliefs, it is always easy to see whether the beliefs create in the person a feeling of optimism and courage or a feeling of pessimism and despair. It was not surprising to find that those people whose beliefs gave them optimism and courage were people who coped with their lives, while those people whose beliefs gave them pessimism and despair did not. For instance, many people said that they believed in God. Those who were coping with their lives spoke of a God who, at the very least, watched over them benignly and wished them well. But those who believed in God and were not coping with their lives believed in a malign and punitive God who would make sure that their lives turned out badly. Those people who were coping with life and who saw their life ending in death describe the satisfaction they would need in their life as something which was within their grasp, while those people who were not coping with life and who saw their life ending in death described how they had failed or how they were prevented from achieving the satisfactions which they saw as essential to their life.

Religious or philosophical beliefs

When we talk of the religious or philosophical beliefs on which we base our lives we are not talking of something in the abstract. Our beliefs determine what we see and do as we walk abroad and take our part in the life of the universe. If we believe that we are part of this universe, either as part of nature, of everything that is, or part of a *Grand Plan*, the origin of which lies in some transcendental power, then we feel joined in some way to everything else which exists. But if we feel that our life is meaningless or that in the *Grand Plan* we are rejected, then we feel a horrendous isolation. The world contains no being with whom we can form a connection, and we are doomed to a living death, a failure of survival more terrible than death itself.

There is no set of religious and philosophical beliefs which produces undiluted happiness and total certainty and security. All we can try to do is to formulate a set of beliefs which allows us to live with a modest degree of harmony and security. As we get older we find that we have to modify the beliefs we acquired in childhood, and to do this we have to review our lives and reconstrue our past.

The past and future

The philosopher Rom Harré drew an important distinction between the past and future in science and the past and future in language. In science the past is fixed. Things happened and what happened cannot be changed. But the future in science is open, indeterminate. In science we can talk of the future only in probabilities. In mixing oxygen and hydrogen, there is a certain probability that some amount of water will be created. But in language, the past is open to change and the future can be made certain. The past can be reconstrued. Those of us who are old enough to remember the Second World War will remember how during the war the Russians were our brave Allies. After the war they became, retrospectively, the Enemy. Now they are merely foreign. Where the future is concerned, that is something we can make completely fixed. We can make contracts, and then carry them out. Sometimes the contract we make is with other people, or we can make our contract with ourselves. We can promise ourselves that we will fail at the task we have set ourselves, or that we will not enjoy ourselves or that whatever happens to us we will know that it is a punishment and not a reward. By these means we can make sure that we can believe only bad things have happened in the past and only bad things will happen in the future. Alternatively, we can reconstrue our past and make it different. For example, instead of carrying a grudge against our mother we can say, 'I can see now that my mother did the best she could under difficult circumstances'. So, too, we can make our future pleasant by determining that matters, on the whole, will turn out well, and when they do not we should not be too disappointed for we shall be able to comfort ourselves with other things. In such a way we are able to connect ourselves to the people in our past and the people in our future.

Dealing with anger: forgiveness and love

Being able to reconstrue our past depends very much on how we are able to deal with our anger. Dealing with our anger depends very much on how we construe anger. If we construe anger as evil, as evidence of the badness within us, then we have made anger, our own and other people's, impossible to deal with. We try to repress our own anger and we run away from other people's anger. But if we construe anger as a natural human response to frustration, a force which can be used either destructively or constructively, then we are able to tolerate, and so modify our own anger and to accept, or to confront other people's anger. Doing this we neither turn on ourselves in guilt nor isolate ourselves from others in anger and unforgiveness, and so we maintain our relationships with others, despite the anger which such relationships sometimes create.

But what if we believe that we should never forgive? What if we believe that to forgive is to leave yourself open for further hurt? What if we believe that to forgive is to lose something of one's integrity or even something of one's identity? What if we have vowed never to forgive, but to seek revenge, even until death? What if we have made the seeking of revenge the whole purpose and meaning of our life? Then we have effectively cut ourselves off from other people in our present and in our past and in our future. And, of course, if we believe that it is wrong to forgive, then we must expect never to be forgiven. If we believe in God but not in forgiveness we cannot believe that God will forgive us, and whether we believe in God or not, we know that there is one person who will never forgive us and that is oneself.

But if we are to maintain relationships with other people and to live harmoniously with ourselves we must be able to forgive. Without forgiveness we can never be free to try again. Without forgiveness we can never love another person for what that person is, and loving a person for what that person is and not for what we want that person to be is the only kind of love which allows us to live freely without the demands and expectations which cripple and isolate us. Forgiveness and love are inseparable. We cannot have one without the other. We cannot live in relationships with others unless we can forgive others and forgive ourselves.

Basic truths

So, if we are to meet our fifth need, our need for other people, we need to hold as the basic truths of our lives the following beliefs:

1 Even though I make mistakes, I am basically good.
2 By understanding other people I can love them.
3 Life is acceptable and death is not to be feared.
4 I am reconciled to my past; I look to the future with hope.
5 Anger is human.
6 It is wise to forgive.

These are modest, tentative statements and not the absolute, pre-emptive beliefs which create the prison of depression. Living by such modest precepts we can live comfortably with ourselves and other people. Thus, despite what else happens to us, we have rich, fulfilling lives.

References

Harré, Rom (1983) Interview with Jonathan Miller, BBC TV.
Rowe, Dorothy (1983) *Depression: the Way Out of Your Prison*. London: Routledge.
Rowe, Dorothy (1987) *Beyond Fear*. London: HarperCollins.
Rowe, Dorothy (1989) *The Courage to Live* (formerly *The Construction of Life and Death*). London: HarperCollins.
Rowe, Dorothy (1991) *Breaking the Bonds*. London: HarperCollins.

Discussion issues

1 What is your approach to working with clients who are depressed?
2 Is it possible to 'learn the skill of understanding people'? How would you recognize that someone had that skill?
3 The author makes the point that it is important to face the fact of our death and give it meaning. Many people find this difficult and society does not really seem to encourage this view. What are your thoughts and feelings about your death? How might your response affect your work with clients?
4 Do you agree with the idea that in order to maintain relationships with others and live harmoniously with ourselves we must be able to forgive? How would you help a client to work through this process?

46

The Place of Counselling in the Universal Scheme of Suffering and Folly

Colin Feltham

As one of the 88% of questionnaire respondents who has never previously written an article for *Counselling*, I am moved to put my finger on the reason. It is not due to a lack of time, confidence or experience. It is due to a nagging feeling of wanting to say something fundamental about the nature of counselling and the whole helping enterprise, and to say it seriously rather than cynically.

For me, there are several sources of disquiet to do with counselling. When I receive my copy of *Counselling* and all the ads that accompany it, I feel a range of reactions. I see familiar names and I am weary at the ubiquitousness of the experts. I am suspicious of people who write articles for journals, who sit on committees and generally get themselves known. This is either because there is something ugly, ambitious and insincere about such behaviour, or because I resent their promoting themselves (because I am too timid to) or both.

There is also something faintly sickening about the burgeoning of specialisms within counselling. AIDS counselling is an obvious example, but there are plenty of others. I dislike and suspect this trend in the counselling world. I do not believe there are essentially different skills to be learnt in relation to AIDS, disability, racism or bereavement, and I think that creeping specialization is due more to economics and ambition than to necessity. I smell a bandwagon speciousness whenever I see ads for 'Advanced Cancer Counselling' or such-like. A fellow counsellor recently suggested to me that one way of getting on in counselling is to specialize, to write articles and do research on some micro-aspect of counselling. He intimated that in view of 'the competition' this was a necessary course to take. There is some personal bitterness mixed in with this, since the specialist training I had in student counselling has never landed me a single job interview (perhaps I lack the right contacts) and my six years of counselling offenders is barely recognized as professional (because I lack a CQSW).

I am aware that there is a need for watchfulness in the profession of counselling. Some people are more sincere than helpful, and some may be dangerous or ineffectual. I take it that BAC's accreditation scheme springs from protective motives. The scheme seems essentially worthy but questionable in detail. There is an emphasis on quantity rather than quality, on what the counsellor looks like 'on paper' rather than in person, and an unfortunate incitement to counsellors to enrol for more workshops, write more articles, etc! I suspect that counsellors will seek

---

This chapter was first published in *Counselling, Journal of the British Association for Counselling*, no. 60, pp. 6–8 (1987).

accreditation in order to legitimize themselves and to become part of 'the network'. BAC, whether it likes it or not, like other profession-protecting guilds, is a genteel mafia. I fully recognize that there is a mixture of good and bad in BAC's underlining of professionalism.

The issue has been raised before about the distinction between counselling and other helping activities. The word 'counsellor' is used to mean anything from sports coach or financial adviser, to psychotherapist. Psychiatrists, psychologists and psychoanalysts are at the most 'professional' (accredited and expensive) end of the market. Lay counsellors, befrienders, and so on, are at the other. Apparently counsellors-as-such are somewhere in the middle. Counselling is nebulous. It is possible to define and to analyse into different categories, but essentially it is an intimate activity that evades measurement. The measurements of psychiatrists are perhaps highly spurious and superfluous, and psychoanalysts remain above such considerations altogether. The only half-concrete piece of knowledge to come from years of research into counselling is that experienced counsellors do better than inexperienced. I have never heard a 'client' claim that counselling did not work but that psychotherapy did. I have heard a psychotherapist dismiss counselling as superficial and unskilled. And on my counselling training course psychoanalysis was mentioned only briefly and considered an anachronism and a hoax. So what is counselling and what is not? And why is there a need to distinguish? I suspect it comes not from the client's but from the counsellor's need to justify themselves and to form a professional identity (with economic self-protection). Whatever counselling is, the marketplace reality is that (in London, anyway) hourly rates charged by psychotherapists and psychoanalysts are always a few pounds higher than those of counsellors. And the fact that psychotherapists and counsellors do charge, and are backed by training and professional institutions, tends to create in some clients' minds the belief that help given by friends or volunteer counsellors is not of the same calibre as that on offer from the professionals.

Another point I want to make concerns the personal suitability of counsellors. Some of the counsellors I have known (and indeed some of the teachers and supervisors) have not been inspiring models of mental health. I have occasionally seen a new book on counselling appear, with a glowing blurb on the author, who I know in person to be highly-strung and (in my opinion) unsuitable as a counsellor. I know psychotherapists whose personal lives are an outright mess. The ability to master counselling theory and techniques and to talk about clients articulately in supervision is no indication of personal integrity and other qualities vital to good counselling. The requirement that trainees and practising counsellors be 'in therapy' or 'under supervision' is therefore understandable but logically faulty. The counselling industry is hierarchical like any other, and its institutions and personnel are self-perpetuating and self-protective. Institutions and supervisors need money and therefore need members and students, and therefore compromise (as do the members and students, who need endorsement). There is little room for radical reappraisals or open debate. Knowledge of how people deteriorate and recover is slow to grow because too many counsellors and others look to teachers and traditions (as well as to their own prejudices) instead of being profoundly open to their clients in an enquiring here-and-now manner. In my experience, analytically trained practitioners are perhaps the least enquiring, because of their allegiance to authority.

Counselling is a growth industry. One could speculate why (increasing urban alienation, loss of extended family, decline of religion, etc.), but the fact is there. 'Growth industry' means money, so it is attractive. Counselling involves few or no overheads, can be done from home, part-time; can be a 'nice little earner'. It is also fairly prestigious. It is nice to have people look up to you as if you know about the mysteries of human behaviour. I believe these are extremely common motivations. So-called 'reparation' is also of prime importance. The sick and guilty 'work through' and work-off their sickness and guilt by helping others. Then they write about it and secure a place in the profession's hall of fame.

I feel disloyal writing this and still cannot quite put my finger on my original point. Ours is (as the cliché goes) a complex and stressful world and people do suffer and need help. But our world is (as another cliché goes) a 'whole', and emphasis on one aspect can exaggerate or neglect others. The more we are involved in addressing unhappiness (or less than fully self-actualizing behaviour) at the personal level, the more we overlook the global (and vice versa). The more we professionalize counselling, the more we risk deluding ourselves and our clients. The more we identify with our working roles, the more we risk becoming absurd caricatures. The roles of client and counsellor are functional and temporary. The wish to be a counsellor is perhaps as unhealthy as the wish to be a client. Suffering, according to my reading of history and religion, is universal, as is folly. Counsellors are as riddled with pain and pain-avoidance strategies as anyone else. Religion has declined because it has become absurd, ritualistic, dogmatic, unliving, although its essence is vital and perennial. The compassion that must be at the root of genuinely helping others is equally open to distortion, reification and spurious parcelling. Compassion (rather than sentimentality) has an energy and intelligence of its own, I believe. It comes from beyond the place where any ambition-to-help begins.

In my terms, much of the activity known as counselling, and certainly the institutionalization of counselling, is steeped in human folly. Put differently, counselling, like religion, falls into the trap of egocentrically grasping and packaging an essentially good thing until it is unrecognizable. I almost lull myself into a complacent ending. 'I would welcome some debate on these points' I was about to write. But debate and criticism can be emptily schoolboyish. I would welcome some clarification of what I am only clumsily trying to say here. I cannot believe that I am alone in this sceptical position.

Brief update

I decided to leave my original text largely unchanged, in spite of some embarrassment at its raw style and subjective tone. I believe it captured the mood of many (I received quite a few supportive letters) and, in its questioning of accreditation and other professionalizing moves in the counselling field, it still represents a core of critical reservation among a significant section of counsellors.

Counselling is still in the process of moving awkwardly from an amateur vocation to a profession. I have myself become one of the published 'ubiquitous' and one of the accredited 'few'. However, I retain a critical perspective. I now consider professionalization with all its follies to be inevitable, but I hope that ours can become a healthily self-critical profession. We can perhaps devise guidelines for better professional practice and *simultaneously* be our own most radical critics. Much of what I was striving to articulate in this brief article has since been spelled out at greater length in Dryden and Feltham (1992), Feltham (1995; 1996) and Howard (1996).

References

Dryden, W. and Feltham, C. (eds) (1992) *Psychotherapy and Its Discontents*. Buckingham: Open University Press.

Feltham, C. (1995) *What Is Counselling? The Promise and Problem of the Talking Therapies*. London: Sage.

Feltham, C. (1996) 'Beyond denial, myth and superstition in the counselling profession', in R. Bayne, I. Horton and J. Bimrose (eds) *New Directions in Counselling*. London: Routledge.

Howard, A. (1996) *Challenges to Counselling and Therapy*. London: Macmillan.

Discussion issues

1 To what extent do you consider that the emerging profession of counselling has a shadow side?
2 What place should critiques of counselling have within counsellor training and continuing professional development?
3 How do you feel counsellors should be promoting themselves?
4 Do you agree with the author in his statement 'The more we professionalize counselling the more we risk deluding ourselves and our clients'?

47

Counselling and Accountability

Peter Ross

Accountability and culture

Not too many years ago, a gentleman's word was said to be his bond. Professionals could apparently be relied upon to act professionally out of a sense of obligation and good faith. There was something called 'honour'. My grandfather recently told me the story that when he was an academic at Leeds University he wrote a reference to the Home Office on behalf of a foreign academic whom he had never met. As my grandfather put it 'I knew he was alright, because, of course, he was a University man'. Today, such faith would seem to be naive at best. Times and assumptions move on, the old consensus breaks down, and society becomes a much more complex place.

In the past decade or so, right-of-centre ideas have taken hold all over the world. The market economy, with its dependence on the profit motive, has become central. Community ideas are demoted, personal aspiration promoted. Counselling has been part of this, with its emphasis on personal development and personal responsibility – though even assertion training has always also emphasized the integrity of standing up for the other. However, human motives are now widely seen as not totally trustworthy. As Higher Education becomes more widespread, professional fallibility becomes all too apparent. Hence the need for regulatory bodies, justification and accountability.

Counsellors cannot turn the clock back. Instead of defensive manoeuvring, we must make the best we can of the situation. Part of our response has been to accredit both individuals and courses. We must continue to deal positively and openly with notions of accountability, cost-effectiveness, cost–benefit analysis, performance indicators, and the like.

The purpose of this chapter is to elucidate some of these notions, and demonstrate how they apply to one university counselling service. I hope that this may enable others to helpfully compare and contrast their own situation, and mull over the many problems which arise.

Does counselling work?

The expressed purpose of accountability measures is to check on performance and improve it. When we are asked the most basic question 'Does counselling work?', we are immediately beset by problems of definition – not only of skills and labels

This chapter was first published in *Counselling, Journal of the British Association for Counselling*, no. 69, pp. 11–17 (1989).

for them – but by problems of role overlap. We use counselling skills in therapy, but also in everyday family and business life. This is why the article by Tim Bond 'Towards defining the role of counselling skills' (1989) is so important.

There is wide agreement, however, that when counselling skills are used for therapeutic purposes there is wide overlap with other psychological therapies. The evidence on whether any therapy or form of counselling 'works' or not, gives us no cause for smugness. In fact the evidence raises more questions than it answers – questions of fact, assumptive framework, and values.

Rowan and Walford (1987) help us greatly by pointing out that evidence from research is compromised by the ideology and value system which form the basic assumptions for that research. In practice, however, most of us are accountable to our own institutions and it is within the empirical research tradition of a contemporary British university that I have to fight my corner to justify both my own work and that of my service. The university has equally no choice but to fight within the ideological framework laid down for it by government, and so it is to this that I now turn.

The politics of performance indicators

Within the past two years, the government has imposed on universities the need to provide 'performance indicators'. These range from financial criteria to the proportion of graduates who obtain jobs within a specified time. The government has also refused to release money to the universities unless staff are appraised annually.

It is, of course, absurd to think that improvements in staff performance can compensate for huge reductions in university income. It becomes even more absurd when, following appraisal, weak areas are identified and finance requested to attend a training course to improve performance, only to be told that no resources are available. It is equally absurd to have a glowing evaluation, be told promotion is well deserved, but that no money is available for this. For these reasons, much appraisal simply breeds cynicism, in contrast to the best examples such as Marks and Spencer, which clearly work very well (Watson, 1987).

The literature abounds in examples of the absurdities of unchangeable performance indicators imposed from above. The tendency is to modify behaviour so that indicators are improved regardless of whether real improvement has occurred in the sense of furthering the objectives of the organization (Association of University Teachers, 1985). Fortunately, the scheme adopted by Reading University is one of self-appraisal as recommended by the British Psychological Society (Williams, 1987). This means we are able to propose our own performance criteria, and change them as required to maintain their relevance in a rapidly changing environment.

Self-appraisal and performance indicators

The implementation of self-appraisal followed by discussion with a line manager (in my case the Pro-Vice-Chancellor), gives a wonderful opportunity to do a good public relations job within an institution. The outcome can even be selectively quoted in annual reports and used to reinforce financial submissions.

The performance indicators we use are as follows:

1 All figures from our normal Annual Report – the number of clients seen, how often, which problems, sources of referral, client academic status, and so on.

2 The number of teaching hours, which in my case involves teaching Counselling Diploma students, trainee GPs and psychiatric nurses.

3 Lists of research published or in progress; other publications. In the last year this amounted to a research project on comparing overseas students' social problems with those of home students. This was specifically designed to help us target our resources more effectively. There was also a chapter in a book on hypnosis.

4 Administration: an account of reports on clients prepared for university committees – especially for examination and disciplinary purposes.

5 A list of submissions to the university on whatever is the 'issue of the month' – recently there have been reports on student incomes, overseas students and rape.

6 Supervision: this covers both my supervision of staff ('internal audit'), as well as supervision of me by an outside consultant ('external audit'). The feedback from staff, and the evaluation of the outside consultant are important measures to be quoted for public relations purposes – 'The level of expertise and experience you provide and your management of clients parallels the best clinicians in the National Health Service . . . your Department maximizes the benefit of the resources available to you . . .'

7 The Consultant Psychiatrist to whom we normally refer is also asked to evaluate. '. . . all referrals are entirely appropriate . . . you have taken considerable trouble to formulate problems before involving me . . . feedback from your clients indicates that the range of therapy that you offer is wide, wholly professional, and of great benefit to clients . . .'

8 Lists of committees attended: this is very important, because of the interaction with senior university decision-makers, talks to academics, staff departmental meetings, orientation programmes and so on.

9 Lists of external professional activities – and here BAC, ASC and BPS activities are important.

10 Attendance at training events and conferences.

11 Summary of client feedback. Over the years we have tried various ways to gather client views on how we are doing. At present we use five-point scales and are also looking at the possibility of using feedback from the referral agencies, such as GPs, tutors, wardens of hall and so on.

12 Finally, I write a review of the year – focused on my objectives for both self and service, and evaluate how they have been met.

My line manager changes every few years, though always a senior academic. With a quite different background, the line manager will usually have to be orientated to appreciate the subtleties of counselling evaluation. This is especially so as one indicator must check and balance another. It would be easy to increase the number of consultations per client by doing poor work, but client feedback and external supervision should check this.

External quality audit is now making an impact in universities (Cryer, 1993). University counselling services are to be assessed directly every three years but also indirectly every few months when the teaching quality of individual academic departments is assessed. The latter includes support systems. A joint project of the universities' staff development unit (part of the committee of Vice-Chancellors and Principals) and the heads of university counselling services (part of the Association for Student Counselling) has addressed standards as they apply to university counselling services (Ross, 1996).

Evidence and the empirical tradition

Regardless of the type of self-report measure we might use (Imber, 1975) or whether a supervisor says a counsellor has done a wonderful job – as per performance indicators – this is no indication whether or not the client would have done as well without counselling. However carefully the client or clients specify what will be happening if the counselling succeeds (Sutton, see Chapter 48), the same problem arises. Even more of a problem is that target complaints evolve during counselling. Even within families, where because of the system dynamics one would have expected more stability in this respect than with individual clients, several studies have found between 55% and 86% of clients report new target complaints during counselling (Sorensen et al., 1985). Even more unfortunate from a university counselling point of view is the fact that spontaneous remission is most likely to occur in a younger age group like ours and where fewer problems are chronic (Rachman and Wilson, 1980). We need to know how many of our clients would have got better on their own, and how long it would have taken. Eysenck in a series of publications suggested that two out of three neurotic illnesses would get better of their own accord in between one and two years. The best available arguments are set out in chapter 3 of Rachman and Wilson (1980) and the only comfort we can take in our own situation is that university students cannot wait that long to get better without wrecking their careers, so providing justification for our efforts, and that much recent development in cognitive and behavioural therapy provides rather better evidence for effectiveness compared with doing nothing. Even then the evidence is less than overwhelming. Smith et al. (1980) analysed nearly 500 evaluative studies of counselling and therapy and concluded that most forms of counselling and therapy are about 50% more likely to provide improvement than would occur without such intervention. This, however, is only from client self-report measures. Objective evaluation – from the therapist, counsellor, observer or from tests – is much less optimistic. The same study of studies showed no outcome difference between any form of counselling or therapy regardless of orientation, regardless of whether it was with groups or individuals, and regardless of presenting problem. The only exception is that behavioural methods were marginally – and only marginally – better with phobias and obsessions. A recent crucially important study (Prioleau et al., 1983) showed the comparative effectiveness of placebo treatments, some of which couldn't even be called psychological, against various forms of counselling and psychotherapy. I hope that I will not be reduced to arguing that even if no consultations take place, a counselling service is a good thing because the very knowledge that the counselling service exists (i.e. that 'a solution is knowable') and could be used, ensures that the client gets better quickly ('I put the Valium in my pocket, doctor, but didn't need it because it was there if it was needed'). McCord (1978) traced 250 clients who received Rogerian counselling plus social skills training, thirty years after termination of help. Although 80% of the Rogerian and social skills group had thought at the end of treatment that they had benefited a lot from it, the group had a worse health, criminal and employment record that did a matched 250-strong control group. In a re-evaluation of Eysenck's original data, McNeilly and Howard (1991) assert it proves psychotherapy accomplishes in about 15 sessions what spontaneous remission takes two years to do. All such studies are subject to many criticisms, but they are the best that we have at present and should engender a little humility in us all.

Cost-effectiveness

Much of the most interesting work on this area is American in origin. This is partly because insurance companies who pay for treatment are keen to get value for money and have this demonstrated to them. But it is also partly because Americans are rather more litigation conscious than we are – even to the point of a US counselling service being recently threatened with litigation for not applying the very latest researched methods rather than traditional ones. Despite the differences in culture, we ignore the trend at our peril. There is an increasing body of evidence which shows that for some kinds of problems and settings many of the major benefits of counselling and therapy can emerge in the first three, five or eight sessions of counselling and therapy (depending on which studies you read) and we need to be aware that sometimes benefits can be increasingly marginal after this (Barkham, 1989; Westlake, 1987).

Cost–benefit analysis

Krumboltz (1974), was one of the first to describe a useful broadly based account-ability model for counsellors, He suggested costing all counsellors activities and tried to cost, for example, the saving of a student from failure at study. There are numerous problems with such models. How do you weight unknown outcomes? What about the probabilities of positive or negative outcomes after a significant time lag? What if the Chaplain and friends also gave support? Millot (1981) took up the challenge. An economist by training, he devised several mathematical models and inputted data from actual cases. Though complex, and weightings being open to argument, he argues strongly that student services should not be cut back and provides detailed evidence of benefit to users, compared with non-users.

There is, however, an encouraging body of evidence from quite a different source. Over the past fifteen years many large American companies have employed counsellors to help employees whose performance at work is perceived to have deteriorated because of a personal problem. The parallel is of course tutor referral, or self-referral, of a student whose academic work is deteriorating. Even within the United Kingdom, many large companies either employ counsellors (most recently, the Trustee Savings Bank) or readily pay for and refer employees to outside agencies (for example, Digital). Such identification and referral programmes are usually labelled 'Employee Assistance Programmes'. About 80% of Fortune 500 companies run such schemes. Westlake (1987) reports that the University of Texas Health Science Center collated the cost–benefit analyses done by companies on these schemes. A few examples are worth quoting: United Airlines quotes a 16:1 ratio of benefit for every dollar spent. Equitable Life quotes 3:1, General Motors 2:1. Whatever the different method of calculation which accounts for the different ratios quoted, the fact is that such companies are convinced of the net benefit to themselves.

Some of the criteria which are both weighted and costed in the equations are level of absenteeism, sick leave, safety record, staff turnover, number of grievances reported, lost time on production, and number of disciplinary actions by management. It should be noted that counsellors are available to employees' immediate families too, on the grounds that the less worried the employee, the better the overall morale of the firm. That is to say, the firm is a more pleasant place to work in, for everybody, even if productivity does not actually improve and such factors can be given a weighting.

Westlake (1987) quotes General Motors as reporting lost time reduced by 40%, accidents cut by 50%, sickness benefits cut by 60%. Within AT&T where 'poor performance' was the referral criterion, 85% were no longer classified this way following counselling intervention. Bell Telephone reported a 77% improvement on the same criteria. It is interesting that the normal contract is for an average of 5 sessions, with the counsellor feeding back to the company only the broad type of problem being encountered. Few people could believe that so many major companies would continue with such programmes unless there was indeed a real return on investment, and we can learn much from their methods.

Problems in cost–benefit analysis

The most critical problem in devising any model is where to place boundaries. This problem was neatly illustrated for me a few years ago when members of the University Grants Committee came on an inspection visit and I had to give evidence on the functioning of the Counselling Service. In discussion, I gave research evidence that fewer drugs were prescribed by the university physicians where counselling was available, and pointed out the cost savings. They were unimpressed. This saving which they readily accepted as real, accrued to the National Health Service, not to the university. They were impressed by evidence that assertion training and social skills training prevented depression in university students and improved learning in seminars. They had no interest that evidence suggested the effects of the assertion training continued after graduation with accruing benefits to the National Health Service employee and employer alike. Could the answer be 'joint' funding – to share costs as well as benefits? But how? A related problem is how to assess feedback from counsellor to institution which results in structural changes – i.e. when a 'personal' presenting problem is diagnosed as a problem of institutional dynamics. Can anyone provide weightings for organizational change? A few days ago a student who graduated two years ago returned to visit and 'popped in' as she put it to see me. She had been meaning to write for months. I didn't even remember the one session she told me she had with me, but she came to say thank you. She told me she resented my gentle confrontation at the time and had damned me on the client feedback form. Now she saw the session as being one of the most important hours of her life. How do we model such time lags?

Music students tell me that our stress workshops permit some of them to play at concert level and go on doing so, which would otherwise have been impossible. How do we cost the difference between ordinary playing and concert playing? And should we do it from the listener's point of view or the player's point of view?

If a counselling outcome is nothing more than a subjective sense of increased satisfaction or happiness, should we weigh the equation for 'happiness'? And if so, how? And, of course, should we weigh only that portion of happiness within our accounting boundary and ignore the rest?

A few years ago if our social skills training had resulted in a student being more successful at job interview – and research shows that it can do so – we could not have counted it a benefit. But now that universities are judged on a 'proportion of graduates getting a job' indicator, we can count it. How do we deal with fashion trends? How much of our time can we afford to spend doing what we know to be of benefit to individuals even if that benefit is not yet recognized or not yet permitted to be recognized, by those to whom we are immediately accountable?

Conclusion

Much conflicting evidence exists as to the costs and benefits of counselling. Complex but nevertheless still inadequate models exist to compare costs and benefits. The weightings to be given to many factors would take the wisdom of Solomon. It is tempting to throw up one's hands in frustration and just get on with the everyday business of seeing clients. However, we can gain a great deal from being seen to grapple with these issues. This should not preclude us having faith to go on doing what we know to be right for as long as we can and for as many as we can, even if we do not have the methodology to prove it good beyond a significant doubt factor. Finally, let us not get too neurotic about accountability. Much of everyday life – including much of education and medicine – proceeds on faith and little else.

References

Association of University Teachers (1985) 'Performance Indicators – is anything new?', *AUT Bulletin*, Nov: 16–18.

Barkham, M. (1989) 'Towards designing a cost-effective Counselling Service: lessons from psychotherapy research and clinical psychology practice', *Counselling Section Review, The British Psychological Society*, 4(2): 24–9.

Bond, T. (1989) 'Towards defining the role of counselling skills', *Counselling*, 69: 11–17.

Cryer, P. (1993) *Preparing for Quality Audit and Assessment – Establishing a Quality Assurance System in Higher Education*. CVCP.

Imber, S.D. (1975) 'Patient direct self report techniques', in I.E. Waskow and M.B. Parloff (eds), *Psychotherapy Change Measures*. Rockville: National Institute of Mental Health. ch. 3.

Krumboltz, J.D. (1974) 'An accountability model for counsellors', *Personnel and Guidance Journal*, 53(10): 639–46.

McCord, J. (1978) 'A thirty year follow up of treatment effects', *American Psychologist*, 33: 284–9.

McNeilly, C.L. and Howard, K.I. (1991) 'The effects of psychotherapy: a re-evaluation based on dosage', *Psychotherapy Research*, 1(1): 74–8.

Millot, B. (1981) *Student Services: Rationale, Costs and Utilisation*. Stanford, CA: Institute for Research on Educational Finance and Governance, University of California.

Prioleau, L., Murdock, M. and Brody, N. (1983) 'An analysis of psychotherapy versus placebo studies', *Behavioural and Brain Sciences*, 6: 275–310.

Rachman, S.J. and Wilson, G.T. (1980) *The Effects of Psychological Therapy*, 2nd edn. Oxford: Pergamon Press. ch. 4.

Ross, P. (ed.) (1996) *Benchmarks for Quality Assurance Systems in University Counselling Services*. CVCP.

Rowan, J. and Walford, G. (1987) 'Ideology and values in counselling research', *Counselling Psychology Section Review, The British Psychological Society*, 2(1): 16–24.

Smith, M.L., Glass, G.U. and Miller, T.I. (1980) *The Benefits of Psychotherapy*. Baltimore, MD: Johns Hopkins University Press.

Sorensen, R.L., Gorusch, R.K. and Mintz, J. (1985) 'Moving targets: patients' changing complaints during psychotherapy', *Journal of Consulting and Clinical Psychology*, 53: 49–54.

Watson, A. (1987) 'The politics of appraisal', *AUT Bulletin*, September: 6–7.

Westlake, R. (1987) 'New futures: employee assistant programmes. Guidance and assessment review', *The British Psychological Society*, 3(4): 2–3.

Williams, R.S. (1987) *Staff Appraisal in Further and Higher Education*. The British Psychological Society, Working Party of the SAB.

Discussion issues

1 What performance indicators do you feel are most appropriate for the evaluation of your work as a counsellor?

2 What is your reaction to the information that the study quoted showed no outcome difference between any form of counselling or therapy regardless of orientation, regardless of whether it was with groups or individuals and regardless of the presenting problems?

3 What do you feel can be learnt from the American experience of counselling services in companies?

4 What are the counselling outcomes you are aiming for?

48

The Evaluation of Counselling

Carole Sutton

There exist a great many models of counselling: client-centred approaches, transactional analysis, rational-emotive approaches, and many others. There is a shortage of means of evaluating these and other models of counselling – particularly from the point of view of the client or customer. This chapter considers possible ways of evaluating counselling, and describes a goal-attainment approach being developed by Professor Martin Herbert and myself in which the *client* is the evaluator of the service offered.

Readers of this chapter will be aware of the wide range of 'models of counselling' which exist, and of the confusion which they can present both to people seeking counselling help and to those seeking counselling training. It was in 1979 that I quoted Patterson's comments upon the state of counselling and psychotherapy in 1977:

> Anything goes now in psychotherapy. The field is a mess . . . Every few months we have a new technique or approach being advocated in books and journal articles. But what is discouraging – and disturbing – is the lack of, or the inadequacy of, theory and concepts supporting the new methods or techniques; the ignoring, or ignorance of, the research . . . the evangelistic fervour with which many of the approaches are advocated . . . the failure to recognize that what is called counselling or psychotherapy can be for better or worse – that people can be hurt as well as helped! (Sutton, 1979)

I do not think that things have improved since that time. If anything, not only has the multiplicity of models increased, but those being trained in counselling are learning the particular model favoured by their trainers; this can bring major difficulties both for counselling trainees and for clients.

First, for counsellors: how does a student or trainee who has been taught, say, client-centred approaches, communicate with those using principles of, say, transactional analysis? How do counsellors versed in psychoanalytic theory communicate with social learning theorists? I suggest, with difficulty.

Secondly, and more importantly, for clients: does it *really* not matter whether a person seeking help finds himself or herself with a person trained in any of the different 'schools' of counselling? Are people really just as likely to be helped with their difficulties of living and relationships by *any* counsellor? The evidence, I suggest, from Truax and Carkhuff (1967), is to the contrary: people can indeed by harmed as well as helped.

It is time that we as counsellors and counselling trainers put our house in order.

This chapter was first published as 'The evaluation of counselling: a goal attainment approach' in *Counselling, Journal of the British Association for Counselling*, no. 60, pp. 14–20 (1987).

In the remainder of this chapter I wish to discuss three areas in turn.

1   To consider, briefly, research findings concerning helpful counselling, and to endorse them.
2   To describe the model of evaluating counselling which I have developed with Professor Martin Herbert.
3   To clarify that the model may be used with *any* theoretical orientation to counselling.

Research findings concerning helpful counselling

In the state of confusion which I have described earlier, perhaps one way out is do what any psychologist is trained to do: go to the literature. What *does* the research have to say about evaluated counselling – approaches which help rather than harm?

In my view the literature, particularly the extensive review published by Truax and Carkhuff (1967), suggests the value of a broad-based 'client-centred' approach, and that whatever else is offered, people seeking help should be met by counsellors who extend to them *accurate empathy, non-possessive warmth* and *genuineness*.

There has been discussion, e.g. Rachman and Wilson (1980), of the value of this 'therapeutic triad', but there are many who conclude with humanistic psychologists like Carl Rogers, Abraham Maslow and John Rowan that this approach to people contains something of enduring value. It is an approach which many believe will stand the test of time. It is, however, only the beginning.

Thereafter, then, what else? I have suggested elsewhere (Sutton, 1979), that a client-centred approach should be the foundation for counselling practice, but that in addition counsellors need a *repertoire* of additional areas of knowledge and skill upon which to draw. This is still my view.

How can we measure the usefulness of this repertoire? How can we judge our skills – with a view to improving them? In other words, how can we evaluate our work? We know of the hazards of subjective perception, of experimenter demand – effects, and even of the differential biases of independent evaluators. How then can we proceed? I suggest, *by inviting our clients to be the evaluator(s) of the service received.*

To do this without access to a full-scale research team seems at first sight impossible. However, since the Truax and Carkhuff publication in 1967, a major contribution has been made through the development of the work of Gerald Egan (1990); his model of 'the skilled helper', with its strong theoretical and evaluative base, is very impressive.

Surely we can go further than this however? Why should we not adopt an approach which, *from the outset*, builds in a simple means of evaluating the helpfulness of the service offered – by the clients themselves? It is this approach which Martin Herbert and I are developing and which I should now like to describe.

A model of evaluating counselling: the goal-attainment approach

Our thinking developed in this way. I am researching with Martin Herbert means of helping parents to cope with very young children, who, at the age of two and three, are already beyond the control of their parents. Such children are the cause of acute stress to their young and often isolated parents, and many are at risk of child abuse. We have devised a simple questionnaire where parents specify the areas of difficulty which the family is experiencing: sleep problems, aggressiveness, eating difficulties or parents' feelings of acute personal stress.

After an initial contact-making period, my practice is to agree with the parents what precisely will be happening *from their point of view* if, at the end of our period of work together, they think I have been able to help them. Such a goal might be, and often is, 'that David will sleep through the night, from 7.30 p.m. to 7.30 a.m., without disturbing his parents'. Another might be 'that Mrs Andrews will feel able to cope with her anxiety and stress'. These goals are written down.

We meet weekly, and as parents implement the suggestions I make – for example, practising daily relaxation – they tell me whether, against a scale which extends from –10, through 0 to +10, they think things have deteriorated, have remained the same or have improved. Our shared aim is to reach + 10. Mrs Andrews' view is of course subjective, but it is *her* subjectivity, not mine. Sometimes, because self-report *is* so subjective, it is possible to gain a separate view of any change, perhaps from another member of the family.

This is not the place to expand on the research work with parents; what I seek to do here is to draw people's attention to the value of this goal-attainment approach and its relevance to evaluating counselling.

It makes use of the ASPIRE sequence which is a process for practice in *any* setting from counselling to community development. The sequence enables us to work *with* people to consider their circumstances and needs and to negotiate and formulate plans with them so that they can take responsibility for their own lives but be supported in so doing.

ASPIRE is a mnemonic, composed of the first letters of other words (Sutton and Herbert, 1992). It is chosen because these letters represent stages in working with people which offer a useful reminder of the process at times when we may feel overwhelmed by information or events and need to find our bearings again.

AS   Assessment, while gathering information and developing relationships
P   Planning: negotiating and agreeing goals with the client(s)
I   Implementation (or Intervention, if you prefer) towards meeting those goals
RE   Review and Evaluation of the extent to which goals have been met.

Figures 48.1 and 48.2 show the process in diagrammatic form (Sutton, 1994). Let us consider each stage in turn:

(i)   Assessment, while developing supportive relationships
First of all time and space is given to establishing a relationship based upon the 'therapeutic triad' described above: accurate empathy, non-possessive

Stage 1	**AS Assessment**	1	Focus on the 'WHAT?' question. After gathering relevant information and recognizing individual perceptions and opinions: WHAT *do we see as the main problems/ concerns/issues/needs?*
		2	Focus on the 'WHICH?' question: WHICH *of the problems/concerns/issues/ needs require priority attention?*
		3	Focus on the 'WHO?' question: WHO *are the key people involved in the problems/concerns/issues/needs?*
		4	Focus on the 'WHY?' question: WHY *have the problems/concerns/issues/ needs arisen?* Try to reach a shared understanding of the difficulties
Stage 2	**P Planning**	5	Focus on the 'HOW?' question: HOW *as we together going to address the problems/concerns/issues/needs? What are our shared, realistic objectives?*
		6	*Negotiate a shared plan or agreement for reaching these objectives.* If appropriate, write this down, with copies for all those concerned
Stage 3	**I Implementation**	7	*Put the plan into action*
Stage 4	**RE Review and Evaluation**	8	*Review and monitor the working of the plan*
		9	*Evaluate the effectiveness of the plan.* How far have the objectives been achieved? If necessary, make a fresh assessment in a new cycle (*see* Figure 48.2)

Figure 48.1   *ASPIRE: a process for practice*

warmth and genuineness. This may take one session, but it may well take more, for the building of trust, as we all know, cannot be hurried. During this time, the counsellor may arrive at some preliminary views upon some of the areas of difficulty which the client is experiencing – but these are regarded as provisional. (It should be stressed that here it is assumed that particular features of a client's circumstances, such as psychotic features, will be recognized and dealt with as emergencies by a different route.)

There follow opportunities for exploring the client's circumstances and

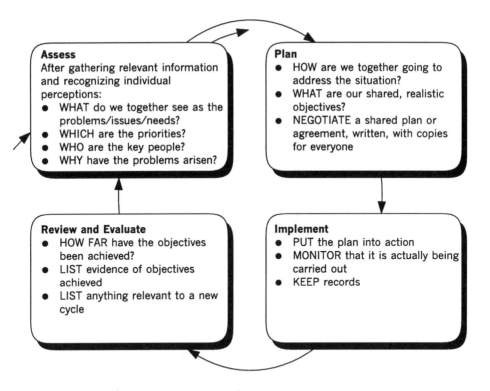

Figure 48.2 *The ASPIRE process as a cycle*

perceived difficulties. Here the approach of encouraging people to write a pen portrait of themselves and their difficulties – as written by an understanding friend – may help some. Others may need help in pinpointing just what their difficulties are: they may simply know that they feel 'awful' and do not know what to do about this.

(ii) *Planning: negotiating and agreeing goals with the client(s)*
Next, in the light of what has gone before, and following discussion of the most pressing difficulties *as the client perceives them*, a move can be made towards *agreeing the goals of work together and writing these down.* Such goals might read that by the end of our series of meetings: 'Mrs Jones shall feel able to cope with her anxiety' or 'Mr Davies shall be clearer in his mind about the important decision he has to make' or 'Mr and Mrs Roberts shall have reduced the number of rows they have weekly by 50%'.

We advocate a written agreement, which includes both a preliminary statement about the number of occasions on which counsellor and client intend to meet, as well as clear goals. Negotiating such an agreement has many advantages. It offers a *shared*, if preliminary, understanding of the focus of work together, and its goals; a helpful structure to a series of meetings, which can sometimes otherwise lose direction and clear purpose;

and a clarification of what an agency can and cannot offer. (Thus, if it becomes clear that a client is really wanting the counselling centre to find him a job, then this misconception can be gently corrected.) Finally, and most important, it offers a means of evaluation built in from the very beginning.

In view of the evidence of the usefulness of such contracts (e.g. from Rosenhan and Soligman, 1984), I would not now myself try to help someone by counselling without such an agreement, or at least, without agreeing that we were working towards writing such an agreement.

(iii) Implementation of plans – towards goals agreed with the client(s)
This stage may overlap with others, and characteristically features much of what might be called 'classical' counselling practice. It may be the time when the recognition of unspoken or unacknowledged feelings, the linking of past events with present difficulties, and the discussion of hitherto taboo subjects will occur. Please do not let it seem that we undervalue or disparage these crucial features of the counselling process. We do not. They are central and of the greatest importance. Sometimes the relief of sharing strong or unacknowledged feelings may of itself markedly reduce the misery or hopelessness with which people come. Sometimes there may be minimal relief because the difficulties have no solution.

In addition, however, it is at this stage that the repertoire of knowledge and skill which the counsellor possesses is vital.

We need every morsel of information and skill we can get: knowledge of practical resources from statutory and voluntary agencies; knowledge of organizations offering specialist skills, such as alcohol advice centres; knowledge of how people may pursue their welfare rights entitlement; skills of teaching relaxation and anxiety management – we need all these and more. For people do not come to counselling centres with neatly packaged difficulties responsive only to internal reflection and the gaining of insight. They come with personal tragedies overlaid with financial problems, with relationship difficulties exacerbated by disadvantages of housing and environment, and with private miseries compounded by mental and physical illness.

Thus it is at this stage that, if appropriate, possible courses of *action* can be discussed: the approach to a relevant agency to seek particular forms of help; the practising of relaxation; or the implementation of any of the particular forms of therapy in which the counsellor may have been trained, and which, to the best of their considered judgement and knowledge of the research, would be helpful to the client(s) concerned.

At every session in this stage, however, it is our practice to invite people to indicate on the −10 to + 10 scale which I described above, how they feel they are progressing towards the agreed goals. This can often be very salutary. What I perceive as 'progress' is not always felt to be so by the client. While sometimes my own feelings of pessimism are contradicted by the client's reporting a renewed feeling of confidence and of being able to cope. Progress or lack of progress over

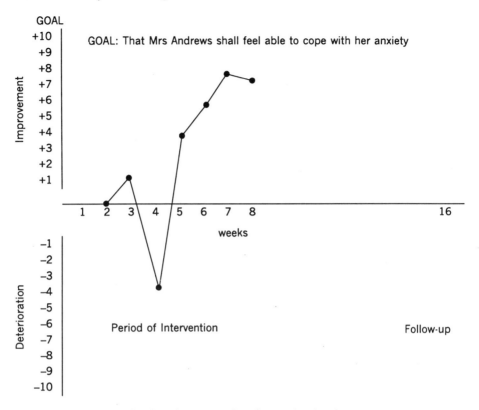

Figure 48.3 *An example of goal-setting and evaluation by the client*

the weeks for each goal can be displayed in a simple graph of the type shown in Figure 48.3.

(iv) *Review and Evaluation – of the extent to which goals have been achieved*
As the agreed number of meetings draws to an end, it will become apparent from the weekly feedback offered by the client whether or not the agreed goals are being, or have been, met. Where they have, this is the time for rejoicing and a shared feeling of satisfaction. Where they have not, then reappraisal is necessary. Questions to be considered will include:

- Would a further series of meetings be profitable?
- Have other matters emerged during counselling which the client did not feel able to disclose earlier, but which clearly need time and consideration?
- Would a specialist agency be able to offer further help?
- Would a change to a different counsellor be helpful?

If the answers to the above questions are Yes, then it is a fairly straightforward matter to negotiate a fresh agreement and to begin a further series of meetings with new or additional goals, or to arrange a referral to another counsellor or another agency. If the answers are No, and the evidence is that many of the original goals have been attained, then counsellor and client may say 'goodbye' – but with a clear understanding that a follow-up meeting at say, two or three months, will be arranged to see whether progress has been maintained. Such a follow-up meeting has many advantages and should be an integral part of the overall service provided.

Adapting the goal-attainment model to any theory of counselling

I hope it will be apparent from the above that using a model in which goals are negotiated at the outset in no way precludes the use of any particular theory of counselling or therapy. During the stage of intervention any theory at all which a counsellor feels is ethically appropriate to the needs of the client may be employed. *But it is employed in such a way that its helpfulness can be evaluated.*

In the intervention period then one might see counsellors employing not only ideas from client-centred therapy, principles of transactional analysis, rational-emotive therapy, Gestalt and behaviour therapy – but engaged also in the practicalities of giving information and putting people in touch with services. The goal-attainment approach is not yet another theory of counselling, it *is* a way of structuring intervention, and then of evaluating it.

The approach lends itself well to many of the difficulties brought to counsellors: stress-related problems, relationship worries, low self-esteem, periods of depression, family unhappiness and interpersonal tensions. It can be adapted to work with couples, groups or family systems, although clearly negotiating agreements and contracts with more than one person is a complex task, calling for specialized skills (Herbert, 1981). The approach is somewhat less appropriate and easy to adapt to people with severe illnesses, such as schizophrenia – although I anticipate that in such situations too the clarification of goals would be found helpful.

In the views of Martin Herbert and myself, its advantages however, are clear: first, it is *ethical*, in that it engages the client(s) from the outset in clarifying expectations and negotiating agreements; second, *it offers a structure* so that both counsellor and client have a framework within which their discussions may take place; third, it allows *evaluation by the client*, the person who has come for help, and who will know far better than the counsellor or any outside observer, whether he or she has found it.

References

Egan, G. (1990) *The Skilled Helper: a Model for Systematic Helping and Interpersonal Relating*. Monterey, CA: Brooks Cole.

Herbert, M. (1981) *Behavioural Treatment of Problem Children. A Practice Manual.* London: Academic Press.

Patterson, C. (1977) 'New approaches in counselling: healthy diversity or anti-therapeutic?' *British Journal of Guidance and Counselling*, 5(1): 19–25.

Rachman, S.J. and Wilson, G.T. (1980) *The Effects of Psychological Therapy*, 2nd edn. Oxford: Pergamon.

Rosenhan, D. and Seligman, M. (1984) *Abnormal Psychology*. New York: W.W. Norton.

Sutton, C. (1979) *Psychology for Counsellors and Social Workers*. London: Routledge and Kegan Paul.

Sutton, C. (1994) *Social Work, Community Work and Psychology*. Leicester: British Psychological Society.

Sutton, C. and Herbert, M. (1992) *Mental Health: a Client Support Resource Pack*. Windsor: NFER/Nelson.

Truax, R. and Carkhuff, C. (1967) *Towards Effective Counselling and Psychotherapy*. Chicago: Aldine.

Discussion issues

1 What are some counselling situations in which you had hitherto not considered using a goal-attainment approach, but where you now think the approach might be useful?

2 Are there any situations in which you consider a goal-attainment approach is entirely inappropriate? Why?

3 How would you respond to a person who had agreed to take a certain course of action (which he or she had identified as crucial) but then did not act upon the undertaking?

4 What are the advantages and disadvantages of arranging a follow-up meeting with a client?

49

How Can We See Where We're Going if We're Always Looking Backwards?

Ron Wilgosh

The commonly held view among therapists that they need to be informed of a client's history and thoroughly understand the problem has often been assumed a necessary part of the therapy process and considered a prerequisite to the problem's resolution. When practised it is a view that increases the potential for therapy becoming long-term. Although the therapist may consider this information to be both helpful and necessary to a successful outcome, in the author's experience clients, with increasing frequency, appear not to hold the same view. Instead they ask for help in moving forward without addressing their past or if, historically, they have learned that understanding causality is an essential component in resolving difficulties, with minimal education, they soon recognize that they have the ability to achieve the same results without the need to understand the problem's origin.

The prospect of therapy being a long-term process is one, research suggests, that clients are reluctant to countenance despite the therapist's conviction of its worth and necessity. It is also a prospect being challenged by the current political and economic climate where the financial consideration of long-term therapy is becoming increasingly paramount to the client, the funding agency, and consequently the therapist.

This chapter considers the effect of both the client's (often active) views of protracted therapy and those of the economic pressures to influence the course of therapy and examines how a brief counselling approach may be a viable therapeutic consideration that accommodates these factors.

When beliefs are taken to be truths

> The value of brief treatment modalities has to do with their challenge to the myth that psychotherapy must be of long duration in order to produce behavioural change. The notion that human beings are so rigid, so inflexible and so unyielding that they require a great deal of time to learn and change is an insult . . . . Sifneos (1990)

Therapy often has the potential to be brief but may be turned into something longer by the dictates of a theory. If we practise models that advocate the identification of a cause believing that the problem is, in fact, a symptom of something else then that is the direction, naturally, in which we will encourage the client to look.

This chapter was first published in *Counselling, Journal of the British Association for Counselling*, vol. 4, no. 2, pp. 98–101 (1993).

Although Freud (1960) had ultra-brief cures (he reports that he cured Gustav Mahler's sexual impotence in one session), because he was interested in a meaning or a cause, these brief outcomes were dismissed as flukes, a notion which confirms that we often find what we are looking for.

A client can sit before us and explain their problem as they see and experience it but if our training suggests that we look behind or beneath their explanation, we may miss the indications of a potentially brief resolution to the complaint. O'Hanlon (1989) suggests that 'if clients walk into a behaviourist's office they will leave with a behavioural problem. If clients choose a psychoanalyst's office they will leave with unresolved issues from childhood as the focus of the problem. If a client seeks help from a Jungian analyst, he or she is likely to get a problem that can be treated most effectively by examining symbolism in the client's dreams.'

The Freudian concept that problems in our present are rooted in and a consequence of repressed earlier experiences has become so widely accepted in our culture, that we immediately look in that direction for explanations. This retrospective search is further encouraged by the belief that change is unlikely to occur, and if it does it is unlikely to last, unless the origins of the complaint are identified. The idea that the problem, as perceived by the client, is not in fact the 'real' problem but is instead a manifestation of an unresolved conflict, necessitates the client's recourse to therapists who are skilled in helping them negotiate the labyrinth of their past. Traditionally this route to problem-solving involves a protracted journey spanning several months and sometimes years as the client is helped to give meaning to and develop an understanding of their experience.

Is therapy more theory-determined than client-determined?

Sifneos (1990) questions the conviction inherent in dynamic therapies that the process of therapy is necessarily a long and often painful journey, that problems are a long time in developing and therefore will take a long time to solve. He asserts that clients can achieve their desired change effectively and within a brief time span.

The view that complaint resolution can be achieved with expedience is also reflected in the works of Ferenczi (1920), Alexander and French (1946), Balint, Ornstein and Balint (1972) and Gillman (1965), who in fact considers 'regressive long-term therapy to be a disservice to any patient who views his or her functioning prior to the current problem as satisfactory'. Frequently clients are encouraged to question this satisfactory period of their life and to look for links, clues, or explanations, whether they want to follow that path or not, rather than to use their natural momentum and motivation to change by encouraging them to start behaving differently in the area of the complaint.

In America De Shazer (1985) studied the attendance rate of clients in therapy and found that regardless of the dictates of the model clients on average only attended six sessions of therapy. A second US study by Moshe Talmon (1990), a clinical psychologist, examined the practice of approximately 30 psychiatrists and social workers. He found the modal length of therapy was a single session and that

30% of all clients chose to come only once in a period of one year. He found that the therapist's theoretical orientation made no difference – 48% of a psychoanalyst's clients and 50% of a biologically orientated psychiatrist's clients were seen only once. Talmon found similar results in other studies; in one, 39% of 6,708 psychotherapy patients seen in one year had one session despite having insurance cover for the first ten visits. Pursuing this further he contacted 200 of his own clients who had attended one session only and found that 78% felt better or much better about the problem that prompted their treatment. Taking into account the tendency of clients to confirm what it is they think the interviewer wants to hear, blind interviews were carried out on a sample of Talmon's clients which showed essentially the same results. He further carried out a one-year project in which 60 single-session cases were seen, with a range of problems that involved panic attacks, domestic violence, depressive complaints and divorce difficulties. At follow-up 88% reported either much improvement or improvement since the session. Seventy-nine per cent thought that the single session had been sufficient.

As long ago as 1978 a research article by Koss and Butcher on brief psychotherapy found that although 'once viewed as a superficial and expedient treatment to be used only in "emergency" situations until long-term therapy could begin, brief psychotherapy is now considered to be a treatment of choice for most patients'. They summarized several factors that account for this emphasis on brief treatment methods:

1　It is now generally recognized that patients, when they enter psychological treatment, do not anticipate that their programme of treatment will be prolonged but believe that their problems will require a few sessions at the most . . . Indeed patients typically come to psychological treatment seeking specific and focal problem resolution, not for general personality 'overhauls' as assumed in the past.
2　Brief therapy methods, once thought to be appropriate only to less severe problems, have actually been shown to be effective with severe and chronic problems if treatment goals are kept reasonable.
3　Brief treatment methods have generally the same success rates as longer-term treatment programmes.

Professor Dryden's opinion (Palmer and Dryden, 1992) that the development of counselling services within the NHS would need to be cost-effective and that brief focused approaches are probably the way to achieve this, were reflected in Koss and Butcher's fourth factor:

4　Most insurance companies or prepaid health programmes recognize the benefits of brief therapy and limit the liability of payment for therapy in the case of psychological problems to a number of sessions that would fall within a brief treatment modality . . .

This latter point was echoed by O'Hanlon (1991) when he explained that some medical insurance companies in America are now only prepared to pay for therapy over a one-month span when previously they would do so over a twelve-month period. Mary Sykes Wylie (1992) cites instances of some US insurance companies now proposing financial cover for no more than 20 sessions of therapy in a client's lifetime.

Although these are examples from an American and predominantly fee-paying culture it would be naive of us to assume it cannot happen here. The political and economic climate in the UK is already beginning to influence the practice of therapy, with insurance companies becoming more vigilant about the amount of therapy they are prepared to pay for; fund-holding GP practices being cognizant of the range and cost of therapies available and clients themselves finding it difficult to commit themselves to day-treatment programmes opting instead, with increasing frequency, for sessional therapy because of employer pressure or job insecurity.

Practitioners are consequently finding it necessary to consider these factors and alter their practice accordingly: fortnightly sessions instead of weekly; terminating therapy after six or eight sessions when previously they may have offered three or four times as many, some may find themselves introducing more active and directive techniques into their practice.

One well-established psychodynamic unit known to the author, in order to remain competitive, now provides group therapy for clients offering a maximum of ten sessions when previously the unit's philosophy would have supported unlimited attendance.

Taking Koss and Butcher's finding that clients come to therapy seeking 'specific and focal problem resolution not . . . personality overhauls', should not we as therapists be guiding them forward towards a solution rather than backwards towards an explanation? 'Emphasis should be placed more on what the patient does in the present and will do in the future than on a mere understanding of why some long past event occurred . . .' (Erikson, in Haley, 1967).

Brief therapy in practice

Brief therapy approaches are well represented in the psychodynamic field as already cited here and also in the counselling field with cognitive-behavioural approaches and crisis intervention models. They are also represented in the area of family therapy, especially since the development of 'Brief Problem Focused Therapy' (Weakland et al., 1974). As Bott (1992) stated, although family therapy approaches view the problem as interactional in nature and therefore it is the systemic context of the problem that becomes the focus of attention, they are ideas that can be applied effectively in the field of counselling.

One such approach that is equally applicable to individuals, couples or families is solution-focused therapy. Although, like all models it does not claim to be a panacea for all ills, it is one the author has found helpful for clients across a broad range of psychiatric and emotional difficulties.

The model was developed by Steve De Shazer and the team at the Brief Family Therapy Centre in Milwaukee, USA in 1985. De Shazer was influenced by the work of the Mental Research Institute 'Brief Problem Focused Approach' and also by Milton Erikson, who effected changes in clients by working with their strengths and abilities instead of focusing on their pathology.

A solution-focused approach assumes, first, that change is constantly happening – 'stability is an illusion created by the memory of an instant', and secondly, that the therapist does not need to know where a client is travelling from on a journey in order to assist them in reaching their destination.

It is a method that focuses on people's competencies rather than their deficits, their strengths rather than their weaknesses and their possibilities rather than their limitations.

At the very least this model 'provides therapists with a way of questioning that enables their clients to think about solutions rather than illness and problems' (Wilgosh et al., 1992).

Although the structure of a first session interview using a solution-focused approach continues to adapt in keeping with research and client evaluation outcomes it is currently guided by the following format.

Socializing and joining

This stage simply refers to mutual introductions and engaging in a conversation with the client that may reflect their work, interests, etc.

It is also appropriate at this stage to explain any agency requirements and protocol such as form filling, the use of a one-way screen and team, or any other therapist/agency practices that the client will need to know about.

'What's brought you here today?'

Many clients will come to therapy naturally feeling plagued and dominated by their problem. Unless they are allowed an opportunity early in the session to discuss their reason for coming and in as much detail as they feel is necessary they will often continue to return to it to ensure that the therapist understands why they are there. 'What's brought you here?' allows the client time and space to inform the therapist about what the client believes he needs to know. The therapist's responsibility at this stage is to listen respectfully and avoid asking problem-focused questions that have the effect of encouraging the client to go unnecessarily further and deeper into the complaint. The therapist must also resist asking solution-oriented questions until the client indicates that he wants him to respond and take a more active role, at which point the therapist will ask the next question.

'What have you tried so far that has helped even in a small way?'

By asking this question the client is encouraged to reflect on strategies they are already utilizing and that are beneficial to them.

In our experience clients are generally doing something, however small, that is helpful in the area of the problem. Eliciting this information allows the therapist to enquire about how they knew this was the right thing to do, and how it helps. So very early in the session the therapist, by asking these questions, implicitly suggests that the client has some control over the complaint which is frequently contrary to the client's belief that they have no control over the course of the problem.

Their answers may reflect strategies generated by themselves or interventions made by previous professional contacts. Whichever it may be the therapist is discovering what already works or has worked. Successful behaviour can be repeated and unsuccessful behaviour can, of course, be ignored. In effect we avoid re-inventing the wheel.

'How can we help you with this?'

This question encourages the client to think carefully about what he expects from therapy and enables the therapist in turn to determine whether he can meet these expectations and whether they fall within the remit of his agency. Although some clients may not be able to answer this question initially we find that they are usually able to answer it later on in the session and it serves as a valuable way of keeping the session focused on realistic and obtainable goals. The therapist asking 'How will that help?' or 'What difference will that make?' in response to the client's answers has the effect of helping the client to further evaluate in full detail what it is that they want from therapy.

'Imagine that when you go to bed tonight and while you are asleep a miracle happens. The effect of this miracle is that the problems that brought you here are resolved, but you don't know this because you are still asleep. When you awake tomorrow morning what will be the first thing you notice that will tell you that this problem is resolved?'

This question is asked as early as respectfully possible in the session and has the effect of encouraging the client to build a picture of how they will be living their life when no longer influenced by the problem that they came with. The client's responses are further developed by asking 'How will that be helpful to you?' and by asking a full range of relationship questions, e.g. 'Who else will notice that this miracle has happened?' 'What will be different about them after the miracle?', etc. This allows the 'miracle' to be broadened and deepened in terms of the client's conceptual world.

The therapist remains in 'miracle land' for as long as possible, on the understanding that the longer the client can discuss solutions and break them down into relationship-based, observable small changes, the greater the potential for what Scott Miller describes as 'multiple end-points'. If the client can describe fifteen or twenty changes that constitute parts of a 'miracle' they are more likely to experience at least one of these between the first and second sessions than if they describe only one change. To this end the therapist invites the clients, if necessary, back to a description of the solution, if they go back to talking about issues in 'problem land', by asking a question like, 'After the miracle how will this be different?'

'Are there any parts of the miracle that are already happening?'

This question allows the client to describe exceptions to their problems, seeds of solutions, attempted solutions and pre-session change, i.e. changes the client initiated before coming to the first session of therapy, which he or she then of course builds on by amplifying these changes. 'How did you get yourself to do this?', 'What do you suppose needs to happen for this to happen more often?' We have found these 'miracle-generated' exceptions useful and meaningful to the client because they relate to pre-therapy changes and therefore reflect evidence of their own strengths, resources and competencies in the face of the problem.

Scaling questions

These questions are used to introduce a perception of the change that is occurring and also to measure the client's commitment to actively working on the complaint. Asking the client 'On the scale of nought to ten where nought was the problem at its worst and ten is how you would realistically like things to be in your life, where would you rate yourself today?' creates the opportunity for the therapist to respond in a number of ways, e.g.

1 'What will have to happen for you to move forward one step?', e.g. from three to four.
2 'How are you preventing yourself from slipping back?', e.g. from three to two.
3 'What did you do to get from nought to three in the first place?'

Each of these questions has the potential of enabling the client to identify personal strengths and achievements.

Asking the client 'On a scale of nought to ten, where nought is all you are prepared to do is hope and pray that this problem will go away, and ten is you will do anything that you think will be helpful in dealing with this problem, where are you today?' helps the therapist and the client to assess their motivation to change, thus putting anticipated change in a realistic frame as well as allowing the therapist to enquire of the client what would need to happen for their motivation to increase.

'Is there anything else that you think I need to know or that is important that you want to tell me?'

This question allows the client the opportunity to discuss anything that they consider relevant and that has not been discussed.

We strongly believe that no client should leave a therapy session feeling that they have not been allowed to talk about what is most important to them.

Discussion break

The therapist will take a break either to talk with his team or, if working alone, to collect his thoughts and formulate a message for the client that encapsulates everything they have talked about during the session.

This message includes:

- Validating and acknowledging – this involves reflecting back to the client what they have told us about how difficult or demanding their situation is in addition to the parts of the conversation that reflected strengths, resources, seeds of solution or what are already successful behaviours.
- A bridging statement – which simply explains the rationale behind the task, i.e. 'because you said that you gain more by fighting your panic attacks than by giving into them we would suggest . . .'
- The task – which uses the client's own words and may be vague, metaphorical, behavioural, instructional, supportive, etc., determined by their responses in the session.

The message is then shared with the client and they are asked if another meeting is appropriate and if so when they would like to return.

The purpose of this stage in a session is to continue reflecting the model's philosophy of directing the client to noticing areas of strength and competence in their lives and self-generated exceptions to the complaint.

Subsequent sessions will continue to focus on the step-by-step changes they are creating and helping them to identify how they will continue to maintain this change.

Although some of these techniques are easily applied, they have to be delivered within a setting of trust, warmth and genuineness to bring about change.

It is the author's experience, in using this approach over the past three years, that problem resolution frequently occurs in an average of five or six sessions and not uncommonly in one or two. It is a respectful model that believes the client is the expert on knowing about their complaint and as such the therapist will work with client-determined goals not therapist- or model-determined goals. Doing so results in the frequent opportunity for humour to enter the therapy session, clients are well engaged and resistance or antagonism towards therapy is eliminated.

Conclusion

It would appear that whichever model we choose to practise we do so with the knowledge that this practice will be influenced by the political and economic climate at the time and also by the client's covert and sometimes overt assertion that they want therapy to be brief and to be focused. Evidence seems to indicate that therapy, in an increasingly competitive market, will need to be provided more and more frequently over as short a time span as possible.

Solution-focused therapy, by promoting the client's own ability to resolve their difficulties without a need to explore either their history or a cause to the problem, provides a way of working that meets the client's expectations of therapy being both brief and focused. The potential brevity of the approach suggests that it will also become attractive in a therapy world where money is becoming a primary consideration.

It may be that getting from A (the complaint) to B (the solution to the complaint) need involve little more than moving in a straight line between the two without any prior exploration of – A (the patient and the complaint's history). Exploring everything that lies in and around the area of – A may get the client to B, but is it really necessary – or even the most helpful way of doing so?

A future-orientated approach that professes positive change within a brief time span and without having to interview retrospectively will naturally evoke scepticism. A view Mark Hubble (1992) may have anticipated when he wrote:

> Diehard believers in a pathology-based psychology will view the solution orientation as so much fluff and blather. No argument, no claims of effectiveness, even if supported by research, will persuade them that brief treatments recognize the complexity of human nature. But is therapy the appropriate forum for appreciating human complexity? These days, only a minority of our clients come in seeking personality reconstruction or an overhaul of their character. Most people want therapy to be short and are not terribly interested in hanging around our offices month after month as we satisfy our curiosity about the intricacy of the inner mind or family life. They're looking for immediate help with problems that confront them. The solution orientation gives people what they want: briefer therapy and a respectful relationship in which they aren't made to feel incompetent or mentally crippled.

With a degree of idealism and perhaps without fully acknowledging the merits of other brief approaches, he concludes:

> In an age when a sense of victimhood is epidemic, it is the ultimate form of therapeutic populism.

References

Alexander, F. and French, T.M. (1946) Cited by Koss and Butcher (1978).

Balint, M., Ornstein, P. and Balint, E. (1972) Cited by Koss and Butcher (1978).

Berg, I.K. (1991) *Family Preservation: a Brief Therapy Workbook*. London: B.T. Press.

Bott, D. (1992) '"Can I help you help me change?" Systemic intervention in an integrated model of counselling', *Counselling, Journal of the British Association of Counselling*, 3(1): 31–3.

De Shazer, S. (1985) *Keys to Solution in Brief Therapy*. New York: W.W. Norton.

De Shazer, S. (1988) *Clues: Investigating Solutions in Brief Therapy*. New York: W.W. Norton.

De Shazer, S. and Berg, I.K. (1990) 'From Problem to Solution'. Conference organized by Brief Therapy Practice, 10/11 May.

De Shazer, S., Berg, I.K., Lipchick, E., Nunnally, E., Molar, A., Gingerich, W. and Weiner-Davis, M. (1986) 'Brief therapy: focused solution development', *Family Process*, 25(2): 207–22.

Ferenczi, S. (1920) Cited by Koss and Butcher (1978).

Freud, S. (1960) *Letters of Sigmund Freud* (ed. by A. Freud). New York: Basic Books.

Gillman, R.D. (1965) Cited by Koss and Butcher (1978).

Haley, J. (ed.) (1967) 'Advanced techniques of hypnosis and therapy', in *Selected Papers of Milton H. Erickson, MD*. New York: Grune and Stratton.

Hubble, M. (1992) '"The search for strengths" – finding what's right in your clients. A review of M. Talmon "Single Session Therapy",' *Family Therapy Networker*, May/June: 89–91.

Koss, M.P. and Butcher, J.N. (1978) 'Research on brief psychotherapy', in S.L. Garfield and A.E. Bergin (eds) (1986), *Handbook of Psychotherapy and Behaviour Change*. New York: Wiley.

O'Hanlon, W. (1989) *In Search of Solutions: a New Direction in Psychotherapy*. New York: W.W. Norton.

O'Hanlon, W. (1991) 'Solution Oriented Brief Therapy'. Workshop organized by the Brief Therapy Practice. 14/15 November, London.

Palmer, S. and Dryden, W. (1992) '"In the Counsellor's Chair." Stephen Palmer interviews Windy Dryden', *Counselling, Journal of the British Association for Counselling*, 3(1): 10–12.

Sifneos, P. (1990) in J. Zeig and S. Gilligan (eds), *Brief Therapy: Myths, Methods and Metaphors*. New York: Brunner/Mazel.

Talmon, M. (1990) *Single-Session Therapy*. San Francisco: Jossey-Bass.

Weakland, J., Fisch, R., Watzlawick, P. and Bodin, A. (1974) 'Brief therapy: focused problem resolution', *Family Process*, 13: 141–68.

Weiner-Davis, M., De Shazer, S. and Gingerich, W. (1987) 'Building on pretreatment change to construct the therapeutic solution: an exploratory study', *Journal of Family and Marital Therapy*, 13(4): 359–63.

Wilgosh, R., Hawkes, D. and Marsh, I. (1991) 'Lifting the mist', *Context: a News Magazine of Family Therapy*, Summer, 11: 33–5.

Wilgosh, R., Hawkes, D. and Marsh, I. (1992) 'There are more things in heaven and earth', published as 'Focusing on solutions', *Nursing Times*, 88(31): 46–8.

Wylie, M.S. (1992) 'Toeing the bottom line', *Family Therapy Networker*, March/April: 30–9 and 74–5.

Discussion issues

1 How essential do you think it is to thoroughly understand a client's history?

2 Is there room for both long-term and brief therapy approaches? What do you see as the benefits and costs of each?

3 What is your reaction to the research finding quoted in the article that 'Brief treatment methods have generally the same success rates as longer-term treatment programmes'?

4 How far do you think market forces should determine the therapeutic service you offer?

50

In Defence of the Past: a Response to Ron Wilgosh

Kay Goddard

Whilst there is nothing intrinsically superficial about the utilization of appropriate short-term therapy, its strength may not, as Ron Wilgosh implies, lie in the abandonment of client history. If the 'Freudian concept, that problems in our present are rooted in . . . earlier experiences' had, as the author believes, 'become so widely accepted in our culture' then we might not be looking for short-term solutions based on disingenuous arguments.

The 'retrospective search', about which the author is so sceptical, has little to do with a clinical approach that delves headlong into a client's past. Freud's concept of repression, for example, was formulated from observation of his patient's present difficulties; the gaps, blocks and resistances that were revealed through language, and the specific ways in which they related themselves within the analysis. This was something concrete and alive, present as a dynamic force. He recognized that the past was re-experienced through the phenomenon of transference.

> What he [the patient] is showing us is the kernel of an intimate life history: he is reproducing it tangibly, as though it were actually happening, instead of remembering it. (Freud, 1962)

Far from subjecting clients to the dictates of a restrictive theory, psychodynamic therapy offers instead the possibility of intersubjective emotional understanding, the theory acting only as a guideline and a springboard for the emergence of subjective insight and strength. Of course this may sound remote and idealistic, at odds with the political and economic climate which so concerns the pragmatists, but we must be wary of looking for neat solutions in the interests of economic demand.

If, as Ron Wilgosh suggests, 'clients ask for help in moving forward without addressing the past' this may be very convenient for the economics of the NHS, but tends to overlook the important concept of resistance. We cannot easily think of ourselves as victims of childhood. The commonsense belief that psychical and emotional development run parallel with physical growth only adds to the difficulties that clients have in acknowledging infantile needs. The defences of idealization or indifference represent an unconscious attempt to ward off persecutory feelings or ideas of not being loved.

When idealization is carried over into adult relationships it results in lack of stability for, as Melanie Klein (1956) observes,

This chapter was first published in *Counselling, Journal of the British Association for Counselling*, vol. 4, no. 3, pp. 205–6 (1993).

Relationships tend to break down and then one loved object may have to be frequently exchanged for another; for no such person can fully come up to expectation. The forever idealized person is then often felt as a persecutor.

Thus idealization may be seen as the counterpart of persecution, indicating that the more the past is idealized or resisted the greater the pain it is likely to hold.

The forms of short-term therapy advocated by Wilgosh, where 'change is more easily noticed through observable action rather than in subtle changes of feeling states' is somewhat dependent on what the client might choose to tell us, rather than on what we might intuit from the telling. It is dangerous to disregard the urge of clients to comply and please. By focusing on behaviour rather than feeling there is also a danger that change is superficial, and that clients may develop a false sense of control, possibly being plunged into greater misery when one set of complaints is exchanged for another.

If Ferenczi (1955) and Balint (1968), amongst others, believe that 'complaint resolution can be achieved with expedience', neither of them ignores the relevance of early relationships and infantile trauma. In particular, Ferenczi's innovations lie in his adaptation of the classical therapeutic setting, and, most importantly, he was well aware of the dangers of overcompliance found within the therapeutic relationship. He discarded the notion of free association because of the client's 'fear of losing the analyst's friendship by disclosing certain facts or feelings' (1955) but at the same time he acknowledged that 'no therapy is complete if it has not penetrated to the traumatic level'. Likewise he recognized the need for self-scrutiny and the analysis of the analyst's own trauma: 'when we have gradually learned to take into account the weak points in our own personality, the number of fully analysed cases will increase' (1955). Certainly Ferenczi did not idealize psychoanalysis, but neither was he advocating a devaluation of the importance of the client's past which he recognized was re-experienced within the transference. What he sought to create was a setting in contrast with that which created the original trauma; it was non-judgemental, but that did not entail taking everything on face value, to the detriment of insight and understanding.

Neither did Balint turn his back on the client's past. His emphasis lay firmly on the role of the therapist being able to facilitate a new beginning. While it may appear, at first glance, that the present and future are all-important in this philosophy, there was at root a recognition that many problems originated in the client's earliest infancy. 'I put the emphasis on the lack of "fit" between the child and the people who represent his environment' (1968). Balint's focus was on a therapeutic provision; the creation of an environment where the client could safely re-experience the hostile feelings of infancy. This he believed was a pre-requisite for real change.

If therapy is about anything, it is about providing a safe, unhurried environment in which the client can experience often painful emotions without being judged or without sensing he/she needs to perform. Contrary to Wilgosh's premiss, it would appear that many clients do not demand that therapy sessions mirror the constraints of the outside world, with its emphasis on action, short-term solutions, cost-cutting ventures. We may, in the interests of 'a therapy world where money is becoming a primary consideration' prefer to believe that clients above all 'want therapy to be brief and to be focused', but too much structure merely enforces the idea that for change to be effective it must be outwardly rather than inwardly demonstrable. Of course it is both, but one wonders about the effects these short-term strategies have on obsessional clients or those who are hypomanic; problems that may not be revealed within four or five sessions, but problems that may be exacerbated within so short a time, nevertheless.

The findings of Talmon quoted by Wilgosh (see Chapter 49), are not particularly reassuring. If only half the referred clients attend only one session, the results of a blind interview no matter how apparently encouraging, do not measure important factors such as fear of stigma, fear of failure, etc. Other perhaps more relevant findings, based on psychotherapy research at the Tavistock, suggest that good results with severely disturbed clients were seldom obtained in less than 60 sessions (Clemental-Jones et al., 1990). In a review of 79 studies, Orlinsky and Howard (1986) found that longer treatments have better long-term results and that the training and experience of the therapist was a 'significant determinant of patient outcome'. Similarly, Lambert et al. (1986) concluded that 'psychodynamic therapy facilitates the remission of symptoms . . . the gains patients made, endure'. Such clients were fortunate that they did, in fact, have 'recourse to therapists skilled in helping them negotiate the labyrinth of their past'.

If Garfield is right in recognizing 'that patients, when they enter psychological treatment, do not anticipate that their programme will be prolonged but believe that their problems will require a few sessions at the most', this surely is more a reflection of the general lack of psychological insight and education and merely demonstrates the subtle introjection of a culture that places action above reflection and rates progress over process. In the interests of integrity, we ought not to take advantage of this lack of understanding, by giving clients what they expect; neither should we use it as a weapon, by making them feel ignorant and victimized. Instead we could see that to offer a challenge to his/her expectation is one way of empowering the client. The advocacy of an approach which shies away from the past and concentrates on goals, tasks and then claims to be respectful of the client's knowledge of their complaint, can hardly be called holistic.

It could be argued that reliance on formats which concentrate on short-term goals and over-directed sessions puts us in danger of infantilizing and patronizing our clients. The description of solution-focused therapy is reminiscent of a model of parenting that avoids painful contact with the underlying causes of complaints, offering instead a determined positivism that rates goal-attainment over understanding. It is not surprising that clients appear 'well-engaged and non-resistant'. There may, in fact, be nothing of substance to resist.

Wilgosh's argument in Chapter 49 seems driven by the notion that NHS counselling and psychotherapy have to be brief and goal-orientated if they are to exist at all. We must be careful not to impose this theory upon our clients, for it is this kind of short-term instrumentalism, and not psychoanalytic theory, that poses the greatest threat to effective treatment.

The history of the development of therapy, the knowledge that informs our practice, can no more be ignored in the interests of saving money, than can the personal histories of those in our care.

References

Balint, M. (1968) *The Basic Fault*. London and New York: Tavistock.

Clemental-Jones, Malan and Traver (1990) *British Journal of Psychotherapy*, 6(4).

Ferenczi, S. (1955) *Final Contributions to the Problems of Psychoanalysis*. London: Hogarth.

Freud, S. (1962) *Two Short Accounts of Psycho-Analysis*. London: Penguin Books.

Klein, M. (1956) 'A study of envy and gratitude', in *The Selected Melanie Klein*. London: Penguin Books (1986).

Lambert, Shapiro and Bergin, A.E. (1986) 'The effectiveness of psychotherapy', in S.L. Garfield and A.E. Bergin, (eds), *Handbook of Psychotherapy and Behaviour Change*. New York: Wiley.

Orlinsky and Howard (1986) 'Process on outcome in psychotherapy', in S.L. Garfield and A.E. Bergin (eds), *Handbook of Psychotherapy and Behaviour Change*. New York: Wiley.

Discussion issues

1 'The analyst, by analysing the transference, is analysing past and present at the same time' (Ruth Malcolm, *International Review of Psycho-Analysis*, vol. 13, p. 433, 1986). Discuss this statement in relation to this chapter.

2 In your own words, how do you recognize transference, and having recognized it, how can it be utilized in the 'here and now' of the counselling situation.

3 How far do you think there may be a collusive, defensive element at work in current attitudes regarding the preference for short-term counselling that does not address the past? Could a defensive posture be lurking under the rationale of market forces?

4 As there is little published research to prove the benefits or otherwise to be gained from personal therapy as an integral part of counsellor training, could you think of ways of measuring or quantifying the difference in effectiveness this experience might make?

51

Exploring Accreditation

Alan Frankland

I wrote this piece after the BAC Annual Conference in 1994, because I sensed there a real change of feeling about accreditation, with members coming to see themselves as the vanguard of a new (and to some extent new kind of) profession. Until that time accreditation had often triggered hostility and carping criticism of the motives and standards of those who created, developed and worked within the scheme. At last I felt a more widespread acknowledgement that we have something valuable, operated by sound people with honourable motives, which is inevitably imperfect, but which deserves to be supported as a flexible and worthwhile system of identification of mature professional practitioners.

Increasingly it seems that members are seeing BAC Accreditation as *our* scheme, operating criteria that *we* have agreed, against a background of definitions, standards and ethics *owned* by the Association as a whole. Here, I am to further clarify the system and its operation, aim to give readers a clear statement of the position as it stands at April 1996 and to raise some of the issues to which such a scheme needs to attend as it develops.

An initial overview

The somewhat complex criteria and processes of BAC Accreditation arise from the fact that counselling (like all other professional activities to some degree) cannot be adequately encompassed in quantifiable behavioural units, because much of the essence of counselling lies in *qualities* of the relationship and interaction between counsellor and client. The high level of complex, unquantifiable and even indefinable features of counselling activities leads inexorably to the conclusion that it is impossible to assess and predict effective professional functioning as a counsellor from a single type or set of observations; the attempt is like trying to draw a complex curve using only a ruler.

Like other accreditation systems, the BAC scheme has to *infer* professional commitment, capacity and standing from a number of different sources of evidence which vary in kind as well as in focus. These include:

- Induction
- Experience
- Probity
- Practice assessment

A shorter version of this chapter was first published as 'An invitation to accreditation', in *Counselling, Journal of the British Association for Counselling*, vol. 6, no. 1, pp. 55–9 (1995).

- Theoretical understanding
- Continuing development
- Use of supervision

Our system does *not* seek to appraise certain other areas which are seen as significant in some professions, e.g.:

- General education
- The capacity to work as a colleague
- Research capabilities

The focus here is very much on the actual work of counselling. We appear to have avoided hidden oppressive criteria (such as favouring male graduates from major public schools) but it must be admitted that there is no formal monitoring of our performance on such matters.

I take the view here that the diversity of the inferential base in our system is valuable, and should be protected against attempts to narrow the range and type of evidence that goes into the assessment of counselling professionals, because I have seen no evidence that the narrowing of the base will produce more accurate assessments.

Changing criteria

Healthy human systems, like healthy human beings, defend themselves from attack, but also try to learn from their experiences, and to adapt to new circumstances. After ten years in operation the accreditation system may be nearing the limit of its potential in its present form, and so a full review is now under way, to put in place revised criteria and a developed structure (following the agreement of the AGM), probably in 1996/7. Whatever then emerges must take account of the development of the United Kingdom Register of Counsellors and the potential for new counselling qualifications, whilst maintaining the standards that have now been widely accepted, and making the most of the experience of the past decade in developing and operating the present system.

The current system has not stagnated under the shadow of a potential review. After twelve months' preparation and following a brief debate at the 1994 AGM a new 'Middle Route' to accreditation was agreed by the membership. This removed the anomaly whereby an induction to professional practice by a *mixture* of extended experience and some course-based training was ruled ineligible under the old scheme, although each was valued separately. The new criterion has created a way in which both courses (substantial but less than 450 hours in total) and experience (again substantial but less than ten years in total) can be accorded the value they deserve in the accreditation system.

Because this is a significant change, and because the criteria for accreditation may sometimes seem like secret lore, it seems wise to publicize accreditation criteria as widely as possible. Potential applicants need a clear image of the requirements from early in their careers if they are to avoid the frustrations of following inappropriate training routes, or having inadequate or inappropriate supervision, etc. The 1994/5 criteria are printed in full in Figure 51.1.

Key issues of interpretation

Any rule system is subject to interpretation, and initial interpretations can themselves become rules subject to further interpretation. For a period, a few years ago, our system was moving defensively to tighter and tighter interpretations of the accreditation criteria; but following an important meeting in November 1993 we were able to re-establish the more flexible and enabling approach to applications that has been characteristic of the system at its best. It is no easy task for a committee to hold the tension between openness to individual differences and fairness to all; to walk the very narrow line between rigid adherence to the letter of the law and unduly broad interpretation of the spirit: we believe that our current interpretative framework assists us to do this.

What follows is an analysis of the 1994 criteria, which seeks to give some guidance to the current interpretative approach of the Individual Accreditation Group, and also to comment on potential areas for improvement or development that reflect my own thinking and which might stimulate yours.

Induction

This element of the system infers the probability of mature professional practice from evidence of a significant professional induction. In some professions this would be all that was required, although most also require a period of post-induction practice. Whilst many new professions start with a grandparent clause based primarily on prior professional longevity (a system that BAC Accreditation did not adopt), few, if any, have the radical possibilities for open access implied by our system which now can count training courses, development through sustained supervised practice (which could be seen as analogous to a kind of apprenticeship), or a combination of the two, towards proving eligibility of professional induction.

The completion of a Recognized Counsellor Training Course (1.i) produces few problems of interpretation; it is worth noting that this route is only available to those whose actual course was recognized – recognition is not retrospective on those who completed earlier versions of such a course. Completing a recognized course also goes some way to providing evidence related to other elements (see below) and, in consequence, those who have completed such a course have slightly less to do in making a submission for accreditation.

Those who have not undertaken a recognized course, but have other substantial training, demonstrate their professional induction by detailing their training to show that they have completed not less than 450 hours of counselling courses, divided into 200 hours of skills development and 250 hours of theory (very limited leeway on these figures is only used in the light of very considerable strengths elsewhere). Assessors need to be able to see that at least one part of the training claimed is a substantial course designed to prepare students for professional

These criteria apply only to counsellors working with individuals or couples. They do not apply to group counselling

There are **three** routes to Accreditation. The successful applicant will be one who prior to application:

1.i. Has completed a BAC Recognized Counsellor Training Course **and** has had at least 450 hours of counselling practice supervised in accordance with paragraph **2** below, over a minimum period of three years.

OR

Has undertaken a total of 450 hours of counselling training comprising two elements:

(a) 200 hours of skills development

(b) 250 hours of theory

and has had at least 450 hours of counselling practice supervised in accordance with paragraph **2** below, over a minimum period of three years.

OR

ii. Is claiming little formal (course-based) counselling training, but can provide evidence of seven years' experience in counselling as understood by BAC with a minimum of 150 practice hours per year under formal supervision, **and** has had at least 450 hours of subsequent counselling practice (supervised in accordance with paragraph **2** below), over three years. (NB: this is a **restatement** of the '**10 Year Clause**'.)

OR

iii. Can provide evidence of a combination of:

(a) some formal counselling training **and**

(b) several years of practice (of 150 hours minimum per year, under formal supervision). This *includes* a requirement for at least 450 hours of counselling practice supervised in accordance with paragraph **2** below, over three years.

75 hours of **completed** counsellor training = 1 unit

1 year of supervised practice = 1 unit

Together the total must add up to 10 units

Applicants claiming two or more training units must show a balance of theory and skills approximately in line with that stated in **1. i**.

In addition to the above the applicant is required to meet the following criteria:

2 Has an agreed formal arrangement for counselling supervision, as understood by BAC, of a minimum of one and a half hours monthly on the applicant's work, and a commitment to continue this for the period of the accreditation.

3 Gives evidence of serious commitment to ongoing professional and personal development such as regular participation in further training courses, study, personal therapy, etc.

4 Is a current individual member of BAC, and undertakes to remain so for the accreditation period.

5 Has a philosophy of counselling which integrates training, experience, further development and practice. Evidence of at least one core theoretical model should be demonstrated.

6 Demonstrates practice which adheres to the BAC Code of Ethics & Practice for Counsellors and undertakes to continue working within this Code.

Applicants are asked to give evidence of the above in the form of a written application including two case studies. Assessors will be looking for congruence between all parts of the application as well as checking that the above criteria have been and are being met.

Figure 51.1 *Accreditation criteria*

practice in counselling. It is unlikely that such a course could have less than 150 contact hours. Substantial pre-professional courses (Foundations, Introductory Certificates, Introductory Skills courses, etc.) may be counted when followed by a further substantial professional course, but cannot themselves be counted as the core course. Whilst it is possible to claim elements of other professional trainings and courses as elements of induction into counselling skills and values, they cannot be the core course (because their aim will not have been professional practice as a counsellor), nor is it likely that all the hours of such courses can be counted towards demonstrating eligibility for accreditation. Short courses, usually seen as less than 40 hours, are not normally seen as induction elements but as part of Continuing Professional Development (see below).

Courses are measured in programmed contact hours (including tutorials, and programmed peer learning situations) because they are the easiest to count and verify. Only completed/passed courses can be claimed.

The induction element of the '10 Year Clause' (1.ii) requires seven years of supervised practice of not less than 150 client hours per annum (three practice years, see below, are then added to make ten years overall). Whilst it will be important under other elements to see that some sense can be made of the pattern of the work undertaken, it is not essential that these are all consecutive years. It is, however, essential that the work took place under a regular pattern of formal supervision sufficient for the task (not necessarily precisely to the requirements of criterion 2) and that no less than 150 hours of counselling were completed in each twelve-month period.

The induction element of the new 'Middle Route' (1.iii) is calculated in units derived from courses, or from years of practice, in a way that is intended to be entirely analogous to 1.ii. The induction element of the Middle Route is make up of seven units either of supervised practice like those in 1.ii. or of completed training courses. (The remaining three units referred to in the criterion fulfil the professional experience element.) In assessing units derived from training, only completed courses of 75 hours or more can be counted. One unit may be counted for each 75 hours of class contact on a completed course.

Thus:

```
 75–149  hr = 1 unit
150–224  hr = 2 units
225–299  hr = 3 units
300–374  hr = 4 units
375–449  hr = 5 units
```

Candidates with 450 hours counselling training are usually able to apply under the Courses Route (1.i), but the calculation under 1.iii may exceptionally be continued up to 7 units where there is good reason to do so. Hours may be aggregated between courses, so long as no course to be counted falls below 75 hours. For example, three courses, one of 120 hours, one of 100 hours and one of 80 hours, may be counted equal to four courses each of 75 hours, both being equal to 4 units (so long as together they meet the 'balance criterion' of 1.i.). As in 1.ii. it is not a requirement that the units are acquired in a continuous process; breaks in practice for family or professional reasons are not unusual. Applicants may gain units for practice years and training courses in the same calendar period.

Two areas for improvement in relation to the induction criteria which seem sensible to me are the integration of the various routes into a unitized system (based on 1.iii), and the inclusion, as an essential, of a substantial period of personal counselling/therapy.

Professional practice experience

Once eligibility has been demonstrated through the completion of a suitable induction, candidates must show that they have completed a significant amount of professional practice. (In the current listing of criteria the Professional Practice element of the system is also contained under Criterion 1.) The key features of this element are 450 hours of client contact under the supervision requirements detailed by Criterion 2, over a period of three years. Under 1.ii. and 1.iii. the three years' practice do not have to be the three years immediately prior to application, but it is required that the level of practice in those years does not fall below 150 hours per annum. Candidates coming through 1.i. may acquire their 450 hours over more than three years. Applicants must be in current practice and will normally have been working (under Criterion 2 supervision) for at least the six months immediately prior to application with a workload equivalent to 150 client hours per annum. It is a condition of continuing accreditation, to which applicants assent, that they will work to this level throughout the period until re-accreditation.

Minor but important improvements here could be:

1 That *all* applicants will have to show their capacity to work at the level of 150 client hours per annum for three years prior to accreditation including at least the twelve months prior to the date of application.
2 That the professional practice experience of those coming through a course-based induction takes place during or after completion of at least their core training (at the moment this is not actually a requirement).

Probity

Criteria 4 and 6 (and arguably some aspects of 2 and 3 too, since supervision and continuing professional development can be discussed as ethical obligations) relate to issues of professional probity. Applicants are required to agree to be in membership of BAC (which implies acceptance of its codes, etc.) and to demonstrate practice that adheres to those codes. This is attested in the accreditation application in a number of ways: by signed undertakings, by demonstrating that the codes have been studied and understood (part of the supervisor's report), and by the provision of an appropriate reference. The diary and case studies that are part of the application procedure also indicate the nature of the applicant's practice, so the system here does not rely completely on the views/evidence of others, but asks assessors themselves to come to opinions on material supplied by the applicant. The accreditation system is set up so that the application of any member complained against in an official complaint to the Association cannot be processed until that matter is resolved.

Improvements I would advocate here would include giving a counsellor's agency (where they have one) or professional colleagues a greater stake in their application by changing the referee of the current system to a **proposer,** who (or which) would attest quite specifically to the applicant's suitability on ethical and professional grounds. It may be that those who have completed recognized courses should be proposed (once the practice and other requirements can be met) by their courses.

I think it is possible to argue that we need to be more rigorous in testing whether applicants are really *au fait* with the current standards and ethics of the Association. I also take the view that it is not appropriate for the Association to process the applications for accreditation of anyone involved in complaints procedures whether as complainant or complained against, since a successful application for accreditation whilst a complaint is under consideration may be seen as an endorsement of one or other party to the dispute. It is possible, during a complaints procedure, for the complainant to be ruled against on the grounds that they have entered the procedure on trivial or malicious grounds, which would also place a serious question mark over the probity of the accreditation applicant.

Practice assessment

In many systems of entry to recognition as a mature professional practitioner the practice element is subsumed under the induction (training) elements and those concerned with probity. The question asked about the practitioner being: have they shown that they can do the job effectively and with integrity?

Professional accreditation in counselling sets a higher level of effectiveness than that of a novice practitioner. In many cases an applicant's practice capacity is partly attested by their completion of a professional course which has required them to demonstrate effective, skilled performance of professional tasks, but because the standard is set higher than that of the novice practitioner we seek additional indicators of effectiveness for all applicants. At present, the system uses a minimum of two kinds of evidence to appraise applicants on this issue. The most important of these is the evidence provided by the third party closest to the applicant's work, their professional supervisor, who is asked to attest to the standards of work with clients. Secondly, standards are explored through the applicant's written accounts of at least one case study, more usually two. (Recognized Course applicants only complete one study.)

To me and many accreditation assessors it is clear that we are most open to criticism in relation to practice assessment, for we rely heavily on **report,** and insufficiently on direct observation (although there are also experienced assessors who oppose including more direct elements on economic, technical and ethical grounds). I believe evidence through reportage is valid and valuable but there is also widespread acceptance that inferring effectiveness from direct observation of practice as well would add strength to the credibility of our accreditation. One way to do this might be to collect consumers' views of the counsellor's effectiveness.

Taped sessions, interviews with applicants, role-played work and direct observation have all been suggested, but the problem remains of how to gain direct assess to a counsellor's work ethically and at a cost that can be afforded by all applicants (many of whom are not in paid practice). Every additional measure proposed must be carefully evaluated to ensure that its benefits are not outweighed by the inevitable increase in the time and cost of assessment. There are a number of current developments which **may** assist us in this area so long as we do not entertain for too long the reductionist fantasy that the objective observation of practice elements would in itself be sufficient to fulfil the assessment of this element, or even replace **all** the elements of the present system.

Theoretical understanding/clarity

Most systems of professional recognition define a body of knowledge that it is necessary for applicants to have grasped before they may be deemed to be ready for independent professional practice, but BAC has not done this. Our system acknowledges the breadth and diversity of potentially illuminating material, but stresses that the value of theoretical knowledge in relation to counselling lies in applicant's capacity to use what they have to inform what they do. Criterion 5 therefore does not set out a particular syllabus or curriculum, but (in keeping with many counselling traditions) looks to see how applicants make sense of their counselling, placing emphasis on conceptual congruence and a core theoretical model rather than a particular knowledge base.

Many potential applicants seem to be afraid that this element, attested through a personal philosophy statement and case studies, requires of them a set of academic skills that their particular pattern of training and development has not previously demanded. Obviously some facility for verbal expression in a coherent structure in written English is required, but the skills being tested here are not primarily academic (complex arguments referenced back to major authors, etc.), but associated with clarity of thought and the capacity to observe and reflect on self within some wider framework of analysis. These are more like the attributes required to write helpful case notes, or those used in presenting material in supervision.

There is no prescription or preferred theoretical formulation in the criteria. It is simply clear that there must be some core approach or harmonizing strand that is consonant with BAC codes of ethics and practice (i.e. it would be difficult to accept an applicant with a core model that denied the value of the client's view of themselves or their situation, however coherent and consistently argued, because BAC practice codes could not accept this as a basis for counselling).

As more and more quantitative and qualitative research enables us to see what it is that is helpful in human interactions it might be argued that a syllabus could be written that would define a core body of knowledge for the accredited counsellor. As an academic it might be expected that I would look forward to that day, but I do not. Whilst I think it of great importance to the vitality of our profession that we encourage individuals and courses to develop **clear** models and theoretical positions, I believe the profession is best served by syllabuses presenting the diversity of knowledge and belief that our present approach allows, for the Association has no monopoly on truth, and a fixed syllabus easily becomes rigid and unresponsive. I believe passionately, however, that accredited counsellors must be aware of the social context in which they work and of the principles of anti-oppressive practice, and I hope alterations to the criteria will rapidly phase in a requirement for such syllabus material and relevant assessments in theory and practice.

Continuing professional development

It may be that this element originally got into our criteria almost as an after-thought, but now we find that it puts us at the vanguard of professional associations who are increasingly clear that continuing development and updating are essential features of professional life. Our system emphatically marks this by making accreditation time-limited, requiring practitioners to put their record before their peers for re-appraisal every five years. Continuing Professional Development (CPD) is also assessed at the initial stage because evidence of such activities prior to accreditation seems a reasonable predictor of continuing development throughout a professional career.

Criterion 3 refers to both professional and personal development. Since BAC adheres to a broad model of counselling and therapy which places the person and personal relationships at the heart of our work, there is no problem in subsuming personal development under professional development (and to some degree vice versa) but it is helpful to see both words used in the criterion since that suggests that we are not just seeking evidence of 'output' (committee work, running courses etc.) but also of 'input' (course and conference attendances, reading programmes and personal counselling/therapy, etc.).

This is an area of continuing debate in committee: I would like to see the requirement for input and output made ever more explicit, and to invite members to indicate how they have made use of their personal experience over the years to enhance their professional effectiveness: other colleagues would find this intrusive. The question of how continuing professional development should be recorded or logged and the approval by BAC of CPD opportunities must also be tackled before long.

Supervision

Counselling and psychotherapy are, as far as I can tell, unique among professions in having, as a norm, the expectation of professional consultancy on an on-going basis. I hope that this will not always be so and that other professions that rely extensively on interpersonal interactions, like teaching and many aspects of medicine, will come to value consultative activity for every professional worker, as we do.

During the most defensive period of our work, Criterion 2 came to be read as a requirement that professional counselling experience (the 450 hours/last three years) must have been supervised to the equivalent of 18 hours of individual equivalent time per annum. It gradually became clear that this was not an appropriate interpretation (because it was using a time period that the criteria themselves did not mention) and that we were at risk of denying accreditation to thoroughly effective members who fell short of 18 hours by minutes per annum. This was plainly ridiculous.

Since the autumn of 1993 we have adopted an interpretation of this criterion which refers to supervision *for the months in which applicants work* (many student counsellors seeing no clients during August for example), and which looks for suitable and realistic arrangements to meet the criterion, rather than calculating minutiae, e.g. when supervisor and practitioner holidays failed to coincide, etc.

Our system continues to use the notion of 'individual equivalent' supervision because we believe that the ethical requirement is for presentation time (for the review and hence protection of clients), and whilst there are many general learning opportunities for the counsellor in supervision groups, specific attention to a practitioner's clients only takes place in individual or presentation time. Thus we seek an agreed formal arrangement for counselling supervision with a suitable individual (one who has clearly relevant experience and a clear understanding of counselling) either on an individual basis of not less than one and a half hours for every month in which counselling takes place, or its equivalent in a group, or some combination of both. Group equivalence is established by dividing the time available by the number of people in supervision in the group. Peer groups (without a designated leader or 'supervisor') are acceptable if they are properly contracted, and have the kind of membership that seems likely to provide the same qualities of maturity and independence that we would look for in other supervision arrangements.

There has been considerable discussion and apparent uncertainty about the use of line-managers as counselling supervisors/consultants. The Codes of Ethics and Practice are quite clear on this; B.3.3. states: 'The counselling supervisor role should be independent of the line manager role.' There are situations where this is difficult, which the code and the accreditation system acknowledge since B.3.3 goes on to say: 'where the counselling supervisor is also the line manager, the counsellor should also have access to independent consultative support.'

We interpret access here to be a formalized arrangement, agreed with the line manager and a suitably qualified/experienced independent consultant, whereby the practitioner can see the consultant at their own discretion. It is not a requirement that this has actually happened, although it might be hard to believe in the reality of an arrangement that is never activated.

A further feature of the system is the check that is made that supervision is not just a matter of formal attendance, or of using the supervisor as a substitute for the practitioner's own struggle with their work. Both through the supervisor's report and through case study 2 (that is intended to show the use of supervision), assessors have the opportunity to come to some understanding of what the practitioner is being offered and how they are making use of it. As with counselling practice, BAC does not prescribe any particular model of the supervision process, so what assessors are looking for is creative and reflexive consultation and a clear indication that the applicant has a concept of what their supervision is for (beyond meeting professional norms or accreditation requirements) and can put the time invested in supervision to the benefit of their clients.

I can foresee three positive alterations to current accreditation criteria and practice here. First, I think we need to make it ever more clear that although professional supervision has normative and formative elements, it is never appropriate for supervision to become 'remote therapy' where counsellors look to the supervisor to indicate the most appropriate course of action for them to take, or supervisors believe that they have the right or duty to prescribe counsellors' actions with their clients.

Secondly, I would like to see the system recognize that practitioners have different needs for supervision or consultative support varying on three dimensions – their experience as workers, the number of clients they are working with, and the impact the kind of work they do has on them. In my view the current provision under Criterion 2 is entirely suitable for someone who is well established and experienced, working with up to eight clients a week, with relatively few cases that they find really heavy or emotionally challenging. I am not sure what figure I would want to set for a newly qualified practitioner, carrying sixteen or eighteen client hours per week of whom at least half are survivors of sexual abuse, but I guess it would not be less than one and a half hours a week. I interpret the Codes of Ethics and Practice as proposing a ratio of supervision to practice and I think it desirable that the accreditation system should move to reflect this as soon as possible, whilst retaining the current Criterion 2 supervision as an absolute minimum.

Lastly, I expect to see us moving towards more rigorous prescription of the qualifications and standing of those who offer supervision to counsellors who are reaching towards professional standards. I think we are a long way off (because of the numbers) being able to insist that all supervisors are BAC Recognized, and some way off ensuring that at least they are all accredited counsellors, or equivalent professionals in very closely allied associations, but I am clear that that is where we should be going. I can think of few measures that would so effectively drive up standards both of practice and probity than improving the levels of supervision for counsellors, particularly between the period of their induction to the profession and their acceptance as mature practitioners.

Other features of our accreditation system

The remaining feature of our system that I want to discuss does not relate to the individual elements listed above, but calls for an overall assessment of the entire application. In other systems, the overview of an application is principally to allow for weakness in one area to be compensated by particular strengths in another or by a sound average profile. There are only a few areas for discretionary compensation in the BAC system, and reviewing the application as a whole is about testing for coherence or 'congruence between all parts of the application' as set out in the final paragraph of the criteria.

This sense of wholeness is quite crucial to the assessment. It is clearly a qualitative judgement, but it is *not* arbitrary. As an assessor works through the various items which are asked for as evidence for other elements of the system, they are also alert to discrepancies, not so much of fact (although these are important and can be vital in a system that relies so heavily on self-report), but discrepancies in attitudes and values, between what people say they do and how they describe a particular piece of work; between the training undertaken and the philosophy of practice that develops, etc.

It is not at all that we are saying that if you have done, for example, a person-centred course you must be a person-centred practitioner – the system is much more flexible than that, and we do not expect counsellors to be clones of their courses or to cease to develop once formal training finishes. What we are saying is that a mature professional practitioner will be able to reflect on their training and make sense (initially for themselves, but in their application, for others) of the position they have come to and how they arrived there, and will then be able to show that position in action through a case study. They will be able to produce an application that is consistent and congruent, noticing and explaining apparent discrepancies where they arise so that assessors are left with a coherent picture of their philosophy and practice.

The administration of the system

The Accreditation system is centrally administered by excellent paid staff at head office, but all the decision-making rests with some seventy unpaid peer assessors and convenors (all themselves accredited), who staff assessment panels and are responsible (through the Individual Accreditation Group) for the monitoring, maintenance and development of the scheme at a practical and policy level.

The various Accreditation and Recognition Schemes (currently Individual Accreditation, Re-accreditation, Courses Recognition and Supervisor Recognition – shortly expanding to include Pre-professional Course Recognition and Trainer Recognition) are individually responsible for ratifications and appeals and develop policy co-ordinated and ratified by the Accreditation and Recognition Committee. Each working group also has access to the Association's Professional Committee and Management Committee through the A&R Committee.

The operation of the accreditation system is a matter for executive decision by the Individual Accreditation Group – so elements of the system may change quite rapidly so long as changes are co-ordinated through the committee structure and all are satisfied that they do not result in de facto alterations to criteria or accreditation policy. It is widely agreed that developments in criteria should go through the committee structure to be put before the membership for approval at an AGM.

Members' applications are read by small teams/panels in four batches a year. Assessors are encouraged to approach applications in a facilitative but rigorous manner – to look for the positives in each application whilst maintaining the standards of which the Association has a right to be proud. This is a hard discipline and it takes a long time to read thoroughly even the most professionally presented forms.

Assessments of the application are fed through the team's convenor to the Individual Accreditation Group meetings where decisions are made. Three outcomes are possible:

- An application may be successful.
- An application may be deferred for further clarification or to give the applicant time to satisfy minor shortfalls.
- An application may be refused because the applicant is not practising counselling as understood by BAC; because they are not eligible (on the grounds of insufficient induction, experience, supervision, etc.); or because the applicant has failed to provide evidence to satisfy assessors on the more qualitative elements of the scheme.

Applicants who are unsuccessful receive a fairly detailed letter identifying all the grounds on which their application has been refused; they have a right of appeal on both matters of fact and interpretation. Where there are relatively minor clarifications, corrections or additions which may resolve the identified difficulties, the Chair of the Individual Accreditation Group may exercise the right to invite the applicant to re-submit their application, usually within six months.

Well over half of all applications are successful; many of those who have been unsuccessful in the past have not actually been eligible, but have applied nevertheless. An exploration like this should encourage more of those who are eligible to apply and help more of those who are not to identify shortfalls in advance and thus save their money and their feelings until they have significantly improved their changes of success.

It is hard to recruit assessors to this fascinating but time-consuming role, and there is increasing demand on the system, so it has recently been necessary to reduce the number of assessors on each panel: which is less than ideal. We are exploring the possibility of recruiting as assessors senior counsellors (perhaps Fellows of the association or other highly experienced members of the counselling community whose work and qualifications are approved by the association) who may not be accredited or re-accredited because they are retired or no longer carry a sufficient case load for accreditation, etc. but clearly have the expertise and experience to assist in the assessment process. This is a delicate and contentious issue, but such members may represent an under-used section of our constituency.

Conclusions

I believe I have shown that BAC has a remarkably open, multi-faceted system for the recognition of mature professional practitioners of which members can be proud. I think a detailed comparison with similar systems in other professions would show that while we are interested in satisfying many of the same kinds of criteria, we have retained flexibility and qualitative subtlety which I hope members will be willing to defend against narrow behavioural reductionism masquerading as the way, the truth and the light.

I have also tried to offer members a complete account of the accreditation criteria, and some elucidation of the current interpretative framework through which decisions are made. I have added a limited account of how applications are processed and offered a few critical discussion points and developmental ideas.

I hope those who read this will be better informed about the framework of Individual Accreditation and its procedures and thus less daunted by the process of preparation and application, and more able to engage in discussion of the issues and principles it involves.

I believe BAC has a sound system of accreditation already in operation. It must continue to improve, building on the standards established to become increasingly sensitive, accurate and fair, and being seen to be so. I believe that the way in which we conduct the discussions about the development of accreditation, the counselling register and eventually the question of combining registers and schemes to create the broad profession of counselling and psychotherapy, will be a measure of our maturity and a test of our belief in many of the central values of counselling such as openness and responsibility, courage, sensitivity and co-operation. I hope this exploration of accreditation will go some way to assisting you to take your place in the debate and developments to come.

Discussion issues

1 What are the purposes of professional accreditation – for the accredited individual and for the wider society?
2 What should the relationship be between academic qualifications, NVQs and accreditation?
3 Should accreditation criteria include a 'live' element and/or a requirement for experience as a client? How could this be done?
4 Is it really desirable that there should be different systems for the accreditation and registration of counsellors, counselling psychologists and (psycho)therapists?

52

The Communicative Approach to Supervision

David L. Smith

This chapter gives a brief account of a method of supervision developed by Robert Langs (Langs, 1992a, 1992b, 1994; Smith, 1991). As Lang's supervisory method is an intrinsic part of the *communicative approach* to psychoanalytic psychotherapy that he has developed over the past twenty years, I will first need to introduce the essentials of the communicative approach.

We all live within social systems. Social systems are governed implicitly or explicitly by *rules*. More critically, social systems are *defined* by rules. Psychotherapy and counselling are examples of rule-defined social interactions.

According to Langs, we all have an innate, unconscious model of a sound counselling relationship. More specifically, we unconsciously expect counsellors to abide by certain rules of social engagement. For instance, we unconsciously expect our counsellor to refrain from exploitative behaviour. According to Langs, clients continually unconsciously monitor their counsellors' behaviour against these apparently universal criteria.

Classical psychoanalysis and its offshoots have assumed that phantasy is the most significant manifestation of unconscious mental activity. According to communicative theory, our deep inbuilt capacity to unconsciously monitor and evaluate the real implications of our counsellors' behaviour is far more significant than the role (if any) of unconscious phantasy. *The unconscious is regarded as a highly sensitive organ of interpersonal perception.*

How can these claims be supported? Communicative theory holds that we express our profoundest and most incisive insights when we tell stories. Story-telling is an ancient social activity, perhaps extending right back to the beginnings of human culture. According to Langs, spontaneous story-telling is the special vehicle for unconscious expression. When clients switch to the narrative mode, when they concretely describe events which are apparently unrelated to what is going on in the consulting room, when they recount episodes that are specific and easily visualized, and when they refrain from speculation, self-analysis and generalizations they convey highly important information about what is going on in the 'here and now' of the counselling relationship. This information is never stated directly. The part of the mind that unconsciously monitors human interaction relates to the world in a *poetic* way, using vivid images and analogies to express its thoughts. We can only understand this 'poetry' by paying attention to

An earlier version of this chapter was first published in *Counselling, Journal of the British Association for Counselling*, no. 62, pp. 3–7 (1987).

its *themes*. Listen to the themes of your clients' stories. Do they involve deception, seduction or hurtfulness? I think that you will discover that most of the narratives you hear will express such negatively toned motifs. According to communicative theory, this happens because, although they usually wish to be helpful and altruistic, counsellors have a tendency to exploit their clients. This seems to be intrinsic to the counselling arrangement. There appears to be something about the privileged role of counsellor, combined with the vulnerability of those who approach them as clients, that activates the basic human need to use others to one's own advantage.

Here is an example. A client begins her counselling session by referring back to their previous meeting. She says:

> You were very confronting last week. It hurt, but it was good for me. I needed to be forced to face up to how I avoid making my life work. I was moved that you extended our session. I saw a programme about the torture of political prisoners last night. Did you see it? A woman was burned with red-hot pieces of metal, she screamed in agony, until she would comply with what they wanted from her.

Consciously, the client is happy to have been confronted by the counsellor, who also extended her session time. However, when she moves into the story-telling mode, the client presents narrative themes of someone being held prisoner and tortured until she complies. According to communicative theory, these themes probably express her evaluation of the counsellor's interventions. This should not be taken to imply that the client's stated opinions are ungenuine. It simply means that she, just like the rest of us, possesses deep, instinctual capacities for interpersonal perception of which she is unaware. There is nothing mystical or mysterious about this. All animals are able to automatically detect and interpret subtle social cues pertaining to threat, courtship, dominance and so on. The social world of human being is uniquely complex, and it is therefore hardly surprising that our perceptive capacities should be uniquely sophisticated.

From the counsellor's position, however, such 'unconscious messages' can be bitter pills to swallow. They are wonderfully confrontative and exposing, and usually uncannily accurate. Small wonder that many counsellors prefer to treat their clients' narratives purely on the manifest (surface) level or entirely in terms of the past.

Supervision is a process ostensibly intended to safeguard standards of practice. Supervisors are supposed to strive to ensure that clients receive a high-quality service. Traditionally there have been two distinct emphases in the practice of supervision. *Supervisor-centred* work involves the supervisor offering advice on how to proceed, offering diagnoses of the client or situation, proffering advice on strategic and tactical decisions, and so on. *Supervisee-centred* practice, on the other hand, attempts primarily to help the supervisee make up his or her mind about such matters, and is not always clearly distinguishable from a counselling relationship. The advent of communicative psychoanalysis has given rise to a third form of supervision: *client-centred supervision*. Here, the primary role of the supervisor is neither to offer advice not to provide support. *The supervisor's role is to translate the client's narrative images.* Each intervention made by the supervisee is evaluated neither on the basis of the supervisor's nor supervisee's sense of its 'rightness'. Interventions are evaluated on the basis of client's spontaneous narrative responses which embody his or her 'unconscious' supervision of the counsellor.

To offer a simple illustration, I recall the case of a counsellor working with a young man suffering from severe social anxiety. The counsellor presented the second interview to me for supervision. During the first portion of the interview, the counsellor deluged his client with questions. No sooner had the client responded to one question than the counsellor produced another one. At last, towards the middle of the session, the client was given the opportunity to express himself. The counsellor asked him, 'When did your feelings of anxiety begin?' The client replied:

> I don't really know . . . When I was about eight years old I used to have this terrifying dream that my father was trying to put me in a coffin and close the lid. I would struggle to get out, but he would push me back and slam the lid down.

The counsellor was quite pleased with this piece of disclosure. He believed that he had unearthed a crucial bit of information which threw new light on the client's difficulties. The client's social anxiety must stem from his problematic relationship with his father during childhood. I understood things differently. Once the client had moved into the story-telling mode, I regarded his account of the dream as a powerful portrayal of the counsellor's interventions. He seemed to be saying that his experience of the counsellor's incessant questioning was like that of being forced into a coffin and having the lid forced down on one. It was like experiencing the childhood nightmare all over again. He may feel that the counsellor is attempting to obliterate him. It may well be that the counsellor's behaviour was reminiscent of that of the client's father, although there was insufficient information to warrant coming to any conclusion about this.

I did not venture to offer the supervisee my own opinions about the technique of questioning, nor did I encourage him to speculate about this or other matters. I waited to hear the client's 'poetry' and attempted to show the counsellor how to make sense of it. I find this form of supervision to be an immensely rewarding experience. I can almost always rely on the client to provide the real supervision, and I marvel at its creativity and perceptiveness. Supervisees usually find the process rather unnerving, but come to develop an appreciation of the extent of their often hurtful impact on the client which, if tolerable, results in a heightened sense of humility.

References

Langs, R. (1992a) *Science, Systems and Psychoanalysis*. London: Karnac.
Langs, R. (1992b) *A Clinical Workbook for Psychotherapists*. London: Karnac.
Langs, R. (1994) *Doing Supervision and Being Supervised*. London: Karnac.
Smith, D. (1991) *Hidden Conversations: an Introduction to Communicative Psychoanalysis*. London: Routledge.

Discussion issues

1 Why might counsellors find it threatening to open themselves to clients' unconscious supervision?
2 Think of a story recently told to you by a client, or a story that you have recently told your counsellor. What might the story be saying about the counselling relationship?
3 How might we make use of unconscious wisdom in everyday life?
4 How might a sensitivity to clients' unconscious wisdom inform the way that you work?

53

Counselling-Supervision – Ethical Issues

Tim Bond

The expectation that practising counsellors who are members of the British Association for Counselling will have adequate counselling-supervision was first clearly stated in the 1984 version of the BAC's *Code of Ethics and Practice for Counsellors*:

> Counsellors monitor their counselling work through regular supervision by professionally competent supervisors . . . (p. 2, para. 3.3)

This view is repeated and elaborated in later versions of the code for counsellors.

It has been my impression, gained from discussions at conferences, that in 1984 this was accepted as an ideal to receive supervision but that a significant number of counsellors were having practical difficulties in obtaining supervision. The position seems to have changed over recent years. It is rare to find a counsellor who is a member of BAC working without supervision. Since 1984 not only has (i) supervision come to be viewed as essential to competent practice, but also (ii) the understanding of what constitutes supervision has developed in response to an increasing literature on the subject and through shared experience on supervision training courses. Both these trends have influenced the development of more recent statements about ethical standards.

Why is counselling-supervision considered to be essential for the practising counsellor?

It is useful to question norms from time to time, to discover whether they still serve any purpose or are merely habitual. The grounds for questioning the requirement for supervision are even stronger, because it is a norm that is not generally accepted outside the United Kingdom. David Mearns and Brian Thorne found it necessary to explain to a potential international readership that their 'emphasis on supervision reflects the counselling setting in Britain, where continued accreditation as a counsellor with the British Association for Counselling (BAC) requires life-long supervision, a condition which is not obligatory in most parts of America and Europe' (1988, p. 3).

In fact, supervision is a requirement of all practising counsellors who are members of BAC, and not just accredited practitioners, as acceptance of the Codes of Ethics and Practice is a condition of membership (see *Standing Orders*, BAC, 1987, p. 1). Therefore, it is worth considering why supervision has become so essential for the practising counsellor.

This chapter was first published in *Counselling, Journal of the British Association for Counselling*, vol. 1, no. 2, pp. 43–6 (1990).

1 Supervision provides a system of personal support for the counsellor. The importance of this is emphasized in BAC's Information Sheet on Supervision (1987):

> By its very nature, counselling makes considerable demands upon the counsellor. Supervision helps to overcome some of the difficulties this creates. A counsellor can become over-involved, or ignore some important point, or may be confused as to what is happening with a particular client. He may have undermining doubts about his own usefulness. (p. 1)

It is inevitable that working with the distress and difficulties of others can in turn affect the counsellor, and lead to a way of working which may not only be defensive of the counsellor's needs, but will prevent any healing for the client. Peter Hawkins and Robert Shohet in their *Supervision in the Helping Professions* (1989) conclude that: 'A good supervisory relationship is the best way we know to ensure that we stay open to ourselves and to our clients' (p. 157).

2 Counselling is a complex process which often demands that the counsellor is both immediately engaged in responding to the client, and simultaneously to the relationship with the client. It is difficult to hold on to these two seemingly contradictory activities at the same time without losing one or other perspective. Regaining the lost perspective is often facilitated by discussion in a confidential relationship with another. Also, most approaches to counselling involve the counsellor in working with intangible phenomena such as the therapeutic process and the relationship between counsellor and client. An opportunity to review these with another who is familiar with them can be invaluable, and expedite the counselling process.

3 Counselling-supervision provides a form of ongoing training which is as important for the experienced counsellor as for the less experienced. Counsellors never stop learning. The monitoring of their work involves a continual sifting of experience and reviewing of theory and practice.

4 The importance attached to supervision is confirmed by personal experience. Most counsellors find that counselling-supervision is enabling of their work with clients as well as personally rewarding in their increased understanding of themselves and the way they interact.

5 Counselling-supervision is the main means of monitoring the effectiveness of the counselling. This works at two levels. It provides a setting in which individual counsellors are facilitated in their evaluation of their work. It also operates at an organizational level because the cumulative effect of all the individual experiences of supervision pervades the culture within BAC. It assists the development of a culture in which there is an openness to new learning and personal re-evaluation, as well as an expectation that individual experience will be shared and disseminated. It seems to me that most of the time this culture predominates over the potential for personal defensiveness arising from BAC encompassing practitioners with different methods of working based on apparently conflicting assumptions. Certainly when a spirit of personal openness does predominate it is easier to engage in constructive work towards the advancement of counselling.

Arguments against the use of counselling-supervision are often based on pragmatic grounds. It is costly in time and often finance. There may be practical difficulties in obtaining adequate supervision in areas of the UK where counselling is relatively under-developed. This latter situation may require the adoption of temporary strategies to enable the tasks of supervision to take place in other ways. Some are concerned about the quality of the supervision. Poor-quality supervision may be destructive of the counsellor's practice. This point is so important that the BAC's *Code of Ethics and Practice for the Supervision of Counsellors* (1988) strongly encourages counsellors 'to make arrangements . . . to help them evaluate their supervision work' (p. 3, para. 3.4). Doubts about the requirement that supervision should be used throughout a counsellor's working life (and not simply during the training and early stages) are sufficiently significant to consider them separately.

Whatever the cost to the counsellor in terms of time and finance, and however problematic it proves to obtain adequate counselling-supervision, such arguments against supervision, which, at root, suggest that the value of supervision must be weighed against the cost, are unsustainable, for the value of satisfactory counselling-provision must be contrasted with the dangers associated with counselling monitored solely by the counsellor.

So far as I can tell, there are no sustainable arguments against the importance the BAC attaches to counselling-supervision. Some organizations undertaking similar work have relied on research as the means of monitoring the quality of practice. Whilst counsellors increasingly welcome research and use its findings to inform their own practice, research does not directly facilitate the process of monitoring the provision of counselling in the way that supervision can.

Why 'ongoing' counselling-supervision?

It is the ongoing nature of counselling-supervision throughout the working life of the counsellor that makes the British position different. Internationally, it is generally accepted that supervision is appropriate for trainees and less experienced counsellors, but there is a widely held view that this is a process one grows out of after training and a period of experience. The members of BAC have adopted a rather different position. This position is based on a view that being a counsellor does not exempt the counsellor from changing as a person over time. Indeed being a counsellor may facilitate change, and hence the need for continued self-monitoring remains relevant throughout the lifetime of the practising counsellor. Anyone who has been involved with counselling over many years will be aware of how there is an endless sifting and re-evaluating of theory, practice and the relationship between them. It is because of both the personal changes that take place in the counsellor and in the understanding of counselling that supervision needs to be ongoing.

Speaking personally as an experienced counsellor, I have found that as my capacity as a counsellor has developed, there has been a corresponding growth in the usefulness of supervision. This personal experience is not a sound basis for generalizing about what is appropriate for others, but it seems to me that when I have begun to lose interest in supervision it has been due either to a resistance or rigidity in me, or if this is not the case, that it may be an indication that I need to review my supervision arrangements and perhaps change them.

What is supervision?

It may seem strange to have considered why supervision is so essential before attempting to define what it is. However this to some extent parallels the process within BAC, in which the consensus about the importance of supervision has led to a pouring of energy into increasing our understanding of the supervisory process. The development of training courses in supervision and the many discussions that have taken place in conferences, as well as the widespread experience of the process of supervision within the membership, has produced a rich and developing understanding of the topic. Although there are no definitive publications on counselling-supervision, there are a growing number of useful publications.

A partial view of counselling-supervision can be found within the Codes of Ethics and Practice. It is not the function of these Codes to encapsulate the richness of this experience. Their role is to provide a basic structure of ethical principles within which a diversity of practice may flourish. They are also constrained by the need for brevity. The *Code of Ethics and Practice for the Supervision of Counsellors* (1988) provides an extended consideration of this topic, which has been condensed in the current Code for counsellors as a brief description of what is meant by counselling-supervision:

> Counselling-supervision/consultative support refers to a formal arrangement which enables counsellors to discuss their counselling regularly with one or more people who have an understanding of counselling-supervision/consultative support. Its purpose is to ensure the efficacy of the counsellor–client relationship. It is a confidential relationship. (BAC, 1993, Section B.3.2)

One theme that runs throughout the codes and the literature on supervision of all kinds is the importance of establishing a clear contract which clarifies the roles of the participants. This is the significance of the word 'formal' in the extract from the Code quoted above.

Is the requirement of ongoing supervision a matter of ethics or practice?

At first sight this may seem rather an obscure point, but with further consideration it seems to give some important insights which also have practical implications. Janice Russell, in unpublished correspondence with me in 1990, argued against supervision as an ethical requirement on the following grounds:

> ... The undertaking of counselling without supervision is bad practice rather than unethical. It seems to me that it can only be seen as unethical if the supervisor is expected

to ensure the ethical practice of the counsellor. While this may be so to some extent, the ultimate responsibility must surely be that of the counsellor to the Code, not to his or her supervisor. The second point is that I am not sure the supervisor is able to ensure the counsellor's ethical behaviour in the final analysis. And, more importantly, what a responsibility, or position of power! If I remember my Latin correctly, quis custodiet custodes? Is it – who ensures the ethical behaviour of the supervisors? If my interpretation is correct, we would be putting too much into the hands of too few.

There followed an informative discussion which disentangled two separate issues: what is the ethical principle behind the requirement of supervision; and who is responsible for the quality of the work with the client?

Consideration of the first point highlighted the ethical principle as the counsellor's commitment to ongoing monitoring of his/her work with clients. In other words, the responsibility for ensuring that supervision takes place rests on the counsellor by engaging in systematic counselling-supervision. Similarly, it is the counsellor's responsibility to ensure the adequacy of the supervision that is provided. In the ideal arrangement, the supervisor should be familiar with both counselling and counselling-supervision, but if this proved to be impossible, a counsellor could still go a long way to satisfying the ethical principle by using a supervisor who is experienced and trained in a field closely related to counselling. Observing the ethical principle as far as possible is clearly more desirable than abandoning both the ethics and the practice-related requirements.

Who is responsible for the work with the client?

There are two different views on this. The 'consultative model' envisages that the supervisor will be someone who is independent of the counselling and whose main role is to facilitate the counsellor's self-monitoring without taking direct responsibility for the work with the client. This form of supervision is commonly used in three different settings by counsellors working (i) independently, perhaps in private practice or as a member of the clergy; (ii) in organizations where the line manager has little counselling background; (iii) in organizations where the line manager has experience of counselling. In the first of these, the independence of the supervisor is a matter of necessity as there is no other way of obtaining supervision. In the second, it is the way the counsellor is most likely to receive informed and sensitive supervision. Some also favour this approach in the third situation. Separating the supervision from accountability to a line manager may create a less defensive relationship. This could be very important because the value of the supervision is in direct relationship to the openness of the counsellor. Brigid Proctor highlights the importance of the counsellor's openness in her exploration of the difficulty in discovering what actually happens between the counsellor and client:

> . . . it is a fantasy that as a supervisor I can gain access by demand to what is essentially a private relationship between counsellor and client, or worker and group. In reality, the work people do with other people is predominantly 'unsupervised'. What someone brings to supervision is selective and subject to 'presentation'. What is watched or heard direct (or on video or audio tape) is always partial and influenced by the watching or hearing. I can encourage my supervisee to give me more appropriate access to a practice. I cannot

control the courage, honesty, good will or perception which determine the presentation (or performance) she chooses to offer me. (Proctor, 1988, p. 26)

The alternative 'managerial model' envisages that the supervisor is also the line manager. This approach is used in some voluntary and statutory organizations. Typically, counsellors working within social services would receive this form of supervision. It is clearly the model favoured by Peter Hawkins and Robin Shohet in *Supervision in the Helping Professions.*

> It is our intention . . . to help the supervisor develop an integrated style of supervision. We are not only advocating integration of the educative, supportive and managerial roles, but also some supervisory approach which is relationship based. (1989, p. 5)

However, their assumption that the managerial model is the norm is a major limitation of this book for use by most counsellors who do not receive supervision within this model. The unquestioning enthusiasm for managerial supervision ignores the power issues and responsibilities which may confuse or inhibit effective supervision. An alternative arrangement has been developed in some situations which combines managerial and independent supervision. As early as 1979 it was reported that agencies in Switzerland had developed a practice of divided supervision. This involved the worker being administratively accountable to one person in an agency, the line manager, but supervised professionally by another whose services may be purchased from outside the agency. However, it has not been universally implemented for many reasons. At a pragmatic level, organizations find it easier to use internal resources, in this case the time of a supervisor, rather than to generate the revenue necessary to hire external supervisors. A divided provision of supervision also carries with it a risk that a harmful split may be fostered between the wider institutional needs and the professional requirements of the counsellor unless the supervisor is sensitive to this issue. If a split occurs, the client, counsellor, supervisor and organization are all potential victims should they fail to bridge the metaphorical chasm between them. The advantage to an organization in combining accountability to a manager with counselling-supervision is that it is readily understood and reflects the way in which the manager may have some responsibility for the counsellor–client relationship.

In 1989 it seemed that any attempt to make an absolute choice between 'consultative' and 'managerial' models rests on an impossible hope that there is a structural or organizational solution to the underlying ethical issues. Both approaches were well established historically within counselling. Since then views have moved towards the importance of maintaining a clear distinction between managerial and counselling-supervision. The level of personal openness required to enable counselling-supervision to work is discouraged when the supervisor is also a line manager with responsibilities for deciding about the allocation of resources, workload, promotion, disciplinary offences or the provider of references for other posts. Most line managers will have responsibilities for many of these activities. Therefore the counsellor will be cautious about admitting a sense of confusion, being troubled or blocked in counselling which is often the starting point for presenting cases for supervision. This level of caution is more appropriate to the line manager relationship but should be unnecessary in the relationship with the independent supervisor. In either method, a cooperative approach between the supervisor and counsellor is most likely to produce the quality of interaction necessary for supervision to work (Proctor, 1988, pp. 25–7). This approach will also increase the likelihood that any conflicts of interest will become creative tensions which inform the development of the organization.

We return to our original question: who is responsible for the work with the client? It is clear that there is no simple single answer. In the first instance it is the counsellor, and in some circumstances it may be only the counsellor. It is hard to envisage any circumstances in which the independent counselling-supervisor could or should take any direct responsibility for the counselling. In some circumstances, a line manager acting on behalf of an agency may share responsibility with the counsellor for the provision of adequate counselling. However, current experience suggests that even within agencies, the counsellor is usually viewed as being the person responsible for the counselling. The privacy of the counselling relationship makes this an appropriate view.

Two hypothetical scenarios have been posed to test the practicalities of who is responsible for the counselling. In the first, the client is dissatisfied with the counselling provided, what is his/her course of action? As the contract is normally between the counsellor and the client, it is appropriate (and often therapeutic) for any grievance to be dealt with between them. If this fails to resolve the issue, the client may wish to take the matter up with the agency, or the line manager (any), or use the Complaints Procedure within BAC. It is inappropriate that the client should have recourse to the supervisor as that role is facilitative rather than one of direct responsibility.

A second scenario was suggested by Julia Segal at the BAC Annual General Meeting in 1988 as a deficiency in the current *Code of Ethics and Practice for the Supervision of Counsellors*. What is the position of a supervisor who believes a counsellor is acting improperly or incompetently to such an extent that he or she ought to withdraw from counselling temporarily or permanently? Again in the first instance it is presumed that the supervisor and the counsellor will attempt to resolve the problem between them. If this fails the supervisor may have a number of options. These include withdrawing from the provision of supervision, with or without giving reasons in writing; the use of a mutually agreed arbitrator; the use of BAC's Complaints Procedure; and the possibility of direct contact with any line manager. It seems that, in most circumstances, direct contact by the supervisor with the client would represent such a blurring of boundaries of responsibility for the counselling that any positive intentions of the supervisor would be undermined.

Who is responsible for the supervisor–counsellor relationship?

In all circumstances, it is envisaged that the agreement to have a supervisor-counsellor relationship is a shared responsibility. The developmental model of supervision advocated by Stoltenberg and Delworth (1987) indicates that the responsibility for structuring the sessions and suggesting options will shift from the supervisor to the counsellor as the counsellor gains in experience and competence.

Conclusion

The article on which this chapter is based first appeared in order to establish some of the background to the thinking behind the Code for counsellors which was going through its consultative phase prior to being formally adopted later that year. A few references to the consultation process which was under way have been deleted because they are of little interest now that the Code has been adopted. However, it is an indication of the importance of counselling-supervision that it was the topic chosen to establish the basis for discussion of the proposed Code rather than new developments in the presentation of the responsibility of the counsellor or adjustments in the understanding of confidentiality. Counselling-supervision has remained paramount in ethical standards. Five years on it was the focus of a considerable amount of work by the standards and ethics committee of BAC during the consultative process of a new Code for the supervision of counsellors (BAC, 1994), which was formally adopted in September 1995.

If anything, counselling-supervision has become much more important within BAC and this standard has been adopted elsewhere. The use of counselling-supervision is likely to become an important component in the proposed National Vocational Qualifications in counselling and psychotherapy. The *Guidelines for the Professional Practice of Counselling Psychology* (Division of Counselling Psychology, 1995) requires regular supervision or consultative support from a suitably qualified co-professional (Section 2.1.2). Supervision will become an important criterion for entry on to the United Kingdom Register for Counsellors, which is likely to come into existence in 1996. It is worth noting that inadequate supervision is one of the more common reasons for applicants failing to satisfy the accreditation criteria for counsellors and this may be repeated when the Register becomes operational. The use of supervision in counselling has been so successful that other caring professions are experimenting with developing parallel procedures to support and develop staff working closely with distressed people.

All this bodes well for the future of counselling-supervision. It is well established as a method of professional support and development. However, this success is creating a quiet revolution in supervision which may be changing its character. The independent counselling-supervisor is much more likely to be asked to provide references for counsellors seeking to satisfy the requirements for professional recognition or employment. This may mean that the concept of supervision as a safe place for a counsellor to discuss personal vulnerability and doubts about his or her work is steadily being eroded. As the supervisor's evidence becomes more important in gaining professional status, the role starts to look much more analogous to the responsibilities of a line manager. Does this mean that there is a need to review the current antagonism to supervision being provided by line managers? It is too early to say, but it does indicate how fast the profession is developing.

What was considered a touchstone of good practice can become more questionable within as short a period as five years. As the issue is so important, it deserves careful consideration and public debate otherwise the increasing responsibilities of the supervisor in professional procedures will resolve the matter by default.

Counselling-supervision could become the victim of its own success and that would be a tragedy. It is more desirable that the future of counselling-supervision should be a matter of deliberate and public decision-making.

Another important development within counselling-supervision is the result of an increasing understanding of the legal requirements of confidentiality. It is a breach of confidence to discuss personally identifiable clients within supervision without the client's prior consent. It is much more legally defensible to discuss counselling in ways which protect the client's identity by a determination to maintain a client's anonymity (Bond, 1993, p. 127; Cohen, 1992). Counsellors regularly argue, quite correctly in my opinion, that a high degree of confidentiality is essential to their work. This view is only sustainable if we are as conscientious in the way we communicate within our profession as we are in communicating with others on the outside. The usual practice in counselling is to avoid communicating personally identifiable information about clients without their consent. This needs to be the usual standard within counselling-supervision.

The increasing interest in counselling-supervision has resulted in a steady flow of useful publications, some of which are listed below. Ideas about how to structure supervision and models of the process abound. However, there is a need for research into supervision. Most of the literature is based on careful analysis of the potential benefits of supervision. This needs to be increasingly balanced by studies of what actually occurs in supervision and its value to the participants and clients. The case for requiring counselling-supervision is based on the accumulated experience of many counsellors. Inevitably, there will be differences in the experience of so large a group of people working in diverse settings with a considerable variety of issues. Research could provide a better understanding of what takes place within supervision, and its value. If supervision is to retain its pre-eminence within the world of counselling, we need to know much more about what it entails, and its effectiveness.

References

Bond, Tim (1993) *Standards and Ethics for Counsellors in Action*. London: Sage.

British Association for Counselling (1984) *Code of Ethics and Practice for Counsellors*. Rugby: BAC.

British Association for Counselling (1987) *Supervision of Counselling*. Information Sheet A. Rugby: BAC.

British Association for Counselling (1988) *Code of Ethics and Practice for the Supervision of Counsellors*. Rugby: BAC.

British Association for Counselling (1989) *Standing Orders*. Rugby: BAC.

British Association for Counselling (1993) *Code of Ethics and Practice for Counsellors*. Rugby: BAC.

British Association for Counselling (1994) *Code of Ethics and Practice for the Supervision of Counsellors – Consultative Version*. Rugby: BAC.

Cohen, K. (1992) 'Some legal issues in counselling and psychotherapy', *British Journal of Guidance and Counselling*, 20(1): 10–26.

Division of Counselling Psychology (1995) *Guidelines for the Professional Practice of Counselling Psychology*. Leicester: British Psychological Society.

Hawkins, Peter and Shohet, Robin (1989) *Supervision in the Helping Professions*. Milton Keynes: Open University Press.

Mearns, David and Thorne, Brian (1988) *Person Centred Counselling in Action*. London: Sage.

Proctor, Brigid (1988) 'Supervision: a co-operative exercise in accountability', in Mary Marken and Malcolm Payne (eds), *Enabling and Ensuring Supervision in Practice*. National Youth Bureau UK.

Stoltenberg, Cal D. and Delworth, Ursula (1987) *Supervising Counsellors and Therapists – a Developmental Approach*. San Francisco, CA: Jossey-Bass.

Further reading

An understanding of the ethical issues involved in counselling-supervision is merely a shared framework, a metaphorical scaffolding, with which the supervisory relationship is constructed. The specific ways supervision is provided varies between different approaches to counselling and variations in settings. The following books represent a range of approaches relevant to counselling.

Feltham, C. and Dryden, W. (1994) *Developing Counselling Supervision*. London: Sage.

Foskett, J. and Lyall, D. (1988) *Helping the Helpers – Supervision and Pastoral Care*. London: SPCK.

Page, S. and Wosket, V. (1994) *Supervising the Counsellor – a Cyclical Model*. London: Routledge.

The last version of the *Code of Ethics and Practice for the Supervision of Counsellors* can be obtained directly from British Association for Counselling, 1 Regent Place, Rugby CV21 2PJ.

Discussion issues

1 How has your experience of being supervised varied between different voluntary or professional roles? Compare and contrast these experiences of counselling-supervision.
2 What issues would you want to prioritize if you were a counsellor going for your next supervision session?
3 What issues would you want to prioritize if you were providing supervision for a counsellor?
4 How do your current arrangements for supervision meet the requirements of your professional codes or guidelines?

54

Supervision: a New Word is Desperately Needed

David I. Williams

'A counsellor should not work without regular supervision' (British Association for Counselling, *Code of Ethics and Practice for the Supervision for Counsellors*, 1988). There has been much discussion as to the nature of supervision, with general agreement to its value, but what of the word itself? The 'word supervisor is an unfortunate one' (Murgatroyd, 1985), as I will try to show.

Supervision is the cornerstone of counselling. It is through the positive use of supervision structures that both the understanding of counsellors and counselling is able to advance. In mundane terms it is an insurance for the client, the counsellor, the agency, the Association and the public. It is an acknowledgement that the helper needs help and of the need for continual personal and professional development. It is a form of control, yet an opportunity for innovation and creativity. It allows counsellors to realize both their potential and their limitations and prevents counselling from becoming an isolated individual experience. All this is well known. It is the reason that BAC puts supervision at centre stage in its attempts to develop training and accreditation schemes.

What does the supervisor do? There is no one model of supervision. But it is evident that whatever the context, the supervisor and counsellor share a concern for counselling and strive to create a supportive relationship in which issues can be handled with trust. A good supervisor is ideally a teacher, a conscience, a friend and more – knowing when to support and when to push. What the supervisor does not do is to administer, boss, command, manage, manipulate, order, regulate, steer or sway the supervisee. Yet these are the primary meanings of the term in my dictionary. So the word *supervise* does not actually have the meaning for most people that counsellors want it to have. The use of the term in counselling derives from psychoanalysis, but are the uninitiated going to realize this, or see that it makes any difference? A supervisor in common usage is the boss, the person who is to be obeyed, the person who tells us what to do and is responsible for our actions. This way in which the word is generally understood is inappropriate to counselling supervision.

Even within counselling both meanings of the word are current. There are times when it does mean to control – as when an agency or employer has a line-management system. It is usual to distinguish between 'management supervision' (the boss model) and 'non-management supervision' (the 'consultative support' model). The BAC Code makes it very clear that although the task of a supervisor

---

This chapter was first published in *Counselling, Journal of the British Association for Counselling*, vol. 3, no. 2, p. 96 (1992).

includes monitoring and developing the work of the supervisee, this is a 'non-managerial' role and it is this work that needs a new, non-ambiguous word.

The revised Code (BAC, 1996) uses the term 'counselling supervision' throughout in an attempt to distinguish it from other forms of supervision (see *Counselling*, 1995, 6(3): 178–9).

Inconsistent code?

Unfortunately even the revised 1996 BAC Code is not entirely consistent in the role it prescribes for supervisors. For example, it asserts (Section B, clause 3.2.5) that 'The disclosure of confidential information . . . is permissible when relevant to . . . (a.) Recommendations concerning supervisees for professional purposes, e.g. references and assessments.' This is a managerial job if ever there was! How can the 'true' role of supervision occur in a situation where the supervisor is 'assessing' the work in order to report back to the superior or worse still to an examiner!! Also confidentiality may be broken in '(b.) Pursuit of disciplinary action involving supervisees in matters pertaining to ethics and practice.' Again this police-officer role is very much a management one and, I believe, incompatible with the supervisor's proper function. So even within the BAC there are definitional ambiguities.

What word would suffice? I wrote this piece at the University of Coimbra and so I have a fancy for the word *orientação*, but although the meaning in Portuguese is perfect, it loses in translation to the English word orientation. The French *secours* is worthy of attention. The derived *secourer* is ugly but the full *aide de secours* could be used. *Consultation* is another suggestion (Goddon, 1990), but I believe this has too many other connotations. The introduction of a hyphen to give *super-vision* (Carlisle, 1990) is very clear but could add to the confusion. My own favourite would be *mentor*. This is not an original suggestion, for it is used in similar contexts by other organizations. The term does have the immediate advantage that it conveys the right sort of message to clients and to the public, and it is sufficiently near the true meaning of 'non-managerial supervision' to allow it to be moulded to counsellors' needs. It also has a strong and worthy tradition in teaching and the evolution of ideas.

Maybe a completely new word is needed. My own attempts to devise an acronym from words like 'support' and 'listen' have not been successful. Perhaps BAC could organize a competition? – with the prize a place in posterity!

But however the word is arrived at, it is desperately needed. At the very least it would save each of us hundreds of hours in our counselling career and prevent the perennial struggle to explain yet again to a client, student, or employer that 'supervision does not mean supervision'!

References

British Association for Counselling (1988) and British Association for Counselling (1996) *Code of Ethics and Practice for the Supervision of Counsellors.* Rugby: BAC.

David I. Williams

Carlisle, J. (1990) 'Supervision', *Counselling*, 1(3): 78.
Goddon, M. (1990) 'Supervision', *Counselling*, 1(4): 110.
Murgatroyd, S. (1985) *Counselling and Helping*. Leicester: BPS/Methuen.

Discussion issues

1 What do you understand by 'non-managerial supervision'?
2 On what occasions might supervision be managerial?
3 Can all a counsellor's needs be met by a single supervisor?
4 Can you suggest a term to replace 'supervision'?

55

How Supervision Relates to Families from Ethnic Minorities

Pat Justice

My first encounter in this field was when I was asked by a Bangladeshi lady, or rather told, she needed to pray five times a day and would this be alright in our session. I quickly evaluated the situation and arranged sessions in between praying times and my little understanding of the needs of the ethnic communities began to become apparent.

That was in the early days, and I would like to share with you some of my thoughts on working in the borough of Tower Hamlets supervising people that I train in basic counselling skills who become Parent Adviser to families with children with special needs. Apart from supervising English people, the majority of those I supervise are Bangladeshi although I also have Vietnamese, Chinese, Afro-Caribbean, Indian and African Parent Advisers.

Ethnic awareness

Every family is individual as is every Parent Adviser and I have learnt a great deal from my supervisees. Between us we construct a plan for helping the families and also other professionals involved to understand their needs a little better.

The problem is not just one of language and the interpretation of it, but a need to understand their feelings, culture and situation. It is not just different religions we are talking about, we have that within our own community, but much more important is that I have had to attempt to understand a culture to enable me to supervise people as effectively as I can. I had to put aside my own feelings as a woman who believes in equal opportunities and equal rights and is fairly assertive in working with people to whom assertiveness is a word not even in their vocabulary. Bangladeshi women, for instance, are brought up not to speak and not to argue back with an elder or husband, and I would have to take this into consideration if I was not questioned about something I was perhaps querying about a family in a session. It may have been that I was not on the right track and questioning was required even though it did not come.

Setting up the contract

I thought that perhaps one of the easiest tasks of the supervision session would be in setting up the contract and the acknowledgement of this. However I had to

This chapter was first published in *Counselling, Journal of the British Association for Counselling,* vol. 1, no. 1, pp. 13–14 (1990).

understand feelings as to the time scale that exists in a Muslim context, which is not necessarily my own. Many of their practices are dictated by sunset and minutes become meaningless in this context. However, for my own personal reasons I had to get this across to my supervisees. They in turn were able to be helpful to their families as regards their time-keeping and their dates and appointments by becoming a role model. I therefore needed to have an idea of religious festivals, to know in advance how to plan ongoing training or sessions or events for families, as these are generally not well publicized (e.g. knowledge of 'fasting' times). These are the kind of issues I feel we must be aware of if we work with ethnic groups.

Considerations for focus

My Bangladeshi Parent Advisers are in many ways quite Anglicized, but work with families who still live in a very traditional way (e.g. some of the husbands have more than one wife). After the Parent Advisers have the father's approval and have gained the mother's trust, they share their feelings, and there is often a lot of unhappiness. For my supervisees it can be stressful when listening to and containing such information, especially when they know these mothers have to face the difficulties of coping with a handicapped child and/or many siblings with often very little support and husbands who may have another wife and family to support.

Contrary to the myth that there is always an extended family with ethnic groups, I have found this rarely to be the case. (More often than not marriages are arranged from afar and therefore women find themselves living here isolated with no family to turn to.) Having a child with special needs exacerbates this, as is often the case in our own society.

They bring to supervision dilemmas such as parents wanting their daughter with learning difficulties to get married in line with the more open and liberated attitudes that exist here and are planning arranged marriages with unknown husbands from Bangladesh. I have to listen extremely well to try to understand exactly what they are telling me, or whether it is their own prejudices and unconscious judgements coming into focus (e.g. they also have daughters). This also applies to women enquiring about abortion/sterilization and whether they are able to effectively work with such issues. Sometimes husbands will question their position and it can be very difficult to challenge them.

English is not always an easy language to understand, especially if it is not your mother tongue and direct interpretation can be misleading. So before we attempt to work on anything I always check out with them that I have understood correctly, even when my instinct says I already have! I have to give them confidence to challenge some of these traditional cultures without denying their importance.

Bangladeshi women work amongst professionals who in many ways expect 'English results' working in an English system. For them this is an added responsibility and I have been working on their assertiveness skills in challenging people who confront them in this manner. Covert racism abounds throughout and I feel we really do have to try to understand each other's cultures in order to avoid this. Just teaching them our own culture and patronizing theirs is certainly not the answer. One cannot question what I would do in a similar situation with a family from my own culture and it may not be appropriate anyway. Between us we have to devise ways of dealing with some of these complex issues.

Personal approach

One also has to take into consideration the problem of men talking to women and women not looking at men. When I supervise a Vietnamese male for instance, I have had to learn what is appropriate behaviour and what is not, even though I am seen as his supervisor. If I don't get this right, or attempt to, how can I expect any respect to be shown? On one hand I know they value my knowledge but on the other I don't want to be seen as the 'expert white professional'. Many beliefs are laid at my feet which can be highly contrary to mine and Western thinking in general. I must therefore carefully exclude any reflex reactions that might occur and look at how problems embodied within these beliefs can be explained and resolved within their own community and how the supervisee could deal with such matters. This of course is normal practice, but it allows the acknowledgement of the differences between the cultures we come from.

I therefore must have an awareness of:

1 The supervisee's expectation of me (sometimes they would like answers).
2 My knowledge and understanding of their culture and a willingness to learn about it.
3 The confidence that I must have in their ability to help in their style and language.
4 A recognition of where they might find support.

I sometimes relate a similar story from my own 'white' experience and pick out pieces that may be relevant. The supervisee also has pieces and between us we work on the 'jigsaw'. Often I feel we may use my skills in connecting but the picture on the finished article must be from their culture. The skill being in sorting and clarifying the correct pieces and not *'forcing'* pieces together because they *seem* to fit, the pressure coming from another professional wanting action (i.e. child needing an operation – parents refusing through lack of trust and understanding).

I have had to learn to stand back with my own anger about how some of these ethnic groups are still treated. I support very strongly my supervisees (Parent Advisers) with the counselling work they are doing as well as with their long-term goal in helping educate the white workers beside them as to a way forward. This definitely is not speaking for them but giving them the confidence and the skills to be able to speak for themselves on behalf of their own community. I also value them a great deal as a great resource for my own learning.

Future plans

We have started group supervision where possible in order to give mutual support and share some of their common anxieties. I am hoping they will take this on board themselves eventually with encouragement and ongoing training. Their ongoing training is vitally important as we look towards their needs (and those of their families) for the future.

I am hoping to involve more people from ethnic minorities on my counselling training courses as I feel in this way we can reach families far more effectively. One of my supervisees has gone on to participate in a supervisor's course and it is envisaged she will now supervise her own ethnic group more realistically than I can.

Attitudes are changing and progress is being made slowly. I relate a story from a recent supervision session. A Bangladeshi Parent Adviser was explaining the difficulties she had in convincing a family not to spoil and give into the child whose behaviour was becoming increasingly difficult. She used one of their prophet's sayings: '. . . *that charity was not giving a bag of wheat but teaching how to grow it properly for themselves . . . the reward from God is better if they showed love by education not by spoiling and protection.*' I feel there is a lesson to be learnt here for us all.

Bibliography

Cunningham, C. and Davis, H. (1986) *Working with Parents: Frameworks for Collaboration*. Milton Keynes: Open University Press.

Gulliford, F. (1984) 'A comparison study of the experiences and service needs of Bangladeshi and white families with severely mentally handicapped children', Unpublished dissertation for the Diploma in Clinical Psychology. Leicester: British Psychological Society.

Horn, E. (1982) 'A survey of referrals from Asian families to four social services area offices in Bradford', in J. Cheetham (ed.), *Social Work and Ethnicity*. London: Allen & Unwin.

Powell, M. and Perkins, E. (1984) 'Asian families with a pre-school handicapped child – a study', *Mental Handicap*, 12: 50–2.

Watson, E. (1984) 'Health of infants and use of health services by mothers of different ethnic groups in East London', *Community Medicine*, 6: 127–35.

Discussion issues

1 How important is it to have a supervisor from the same ethnic group?
2 What difficulties do you face when working with clients from a different culture?
3 What steps can/could you take to get a better understanding of minority groups?
4 Is the concept of counselling/supervision a purely 'Western' idea?

56

Mentoring

A.G. Watts

In North America there has in recent years been growing interest in the concept of 'mentoring'. The interest seems to have stemmed from the seminal study by Levinson et al. (1978) of forty men aged 35–45, which found that a relationship with a 'mentor' was 'one of the most complex, and developmentally important, a man can have in early adulthood' (p. 97). The nature of this relationship in its more developed forms was described in these terms:

> In the usual course, a young man initially experiences himself as a novice or apprentice to a more advanced, expert and authoritative adult. As the relationship evolves, he gains a fuller sense of his own authority and his capability for autonomous, responsible action. The balance of giving/receiving becomes more equal. The younger man increasingly has the experience of 'I am' as an adult, and their relationship becomes more mutual. This shift serves a crucial developmental function for the young man: it is part of the process by which he transcends the father–son, man–boy division of his childhood. (pp. 99–100)

The study also suggested that many men did not experience the benefits of mentorhood, and that this represented 'a waste of talent', a loss to the individuals involved, and an impediment to constructive social change' (p. 334). Subsequently, interest has grown in the role of mentors within work organizations in adapting the individual to the organization (Collin, 1979), and particularly in providing mentors for women on the assumption that – in confronting traditional limitations on their roles – they may be even more in need of such help (see Shapiro et al., 1978; Speizer, 1981).

This interest has led in turn to schemes designed to establish mentor relationships in colleges and in high schools (Borman and Colson, 1984). In some of these cases, the mentoring has consisted mainly of informal relationships set up between mentor and 'mentee' which are then allowed to develop in their own way (e.g. Lynch, 1980); in others, they have included 'internships' which provide opportunities for direct experience and/or observation. An example of the latter is the Executive High School Internships Program, in which high-school students serve as 'special assistants to distinguished leaders in government, business, law, the arts, health, education, communications, and other exciting fields' (Hirsch, 1974).

The concept of 'mentoring' *per se* is used in confusingly different ways by different American authors. It seems however to embody three main elements. The first is that of *modelling*. One of the basic ideas in social learning theory is that 'most human behaviour is learned observationally through modelling: from observing others, one forms an idea of how new behaviours are performed, and on later occasions this coded information serves as a guide for action' (Bandura,

This chapter was first published in *Counselling, Journal of the British Association for Counselling*, no. 57, pp. 4–7 (1986).

1977, p. 22). Many young people's ideas abut themselves and about their possible futures are influenced by the occupational role-models presented to them through their parents and family friends, through their contacts with working people, and through the images presented in films, on television, etc. By identifying with these role-models, they test out who they are and who they might become. Mentoring can be a particularly intensive form of such modelling.

The second element is that of *sponsorship*. Kanter (1977) identified a mentor as a sponsor or 'godfather' who utilized power on behalf of his protégés in three ways: (a) by being willing to fight for the person in question, (b) by helping the person to by-pass the hierarchy, and (c) by providing 'reflected power'. The emphasis here is on power-based patronage: on mentors taking their 'mentees' under their wings and 'opening doors' for them.

The third element is that of *guidance and counselling*. Even if mentors do not have power to exert on behalf on their 'mentees', or do not choose to use it, they can offer help by pointing out pitfalls to be avoided and short-cuts to be pursued, and by providing a sympathetic sounding-board for the mentee's thoughts and ideas.

Within Britain, North Westminster Community School in London has recently started to introduce a 'mentoring' scheme. The school has for some time had a list of over 50 'associates' – mostly retired governors and others who are happy to continue to be associated with the school. The idea is to extend this into a list of adults in the community who might be interested in forming a helping relationship with a particular student in need of help of some kind. An example is a black girl who was interested in becoming a lawyer but had no professional contacts and indeed virtually no contacts at all with white people outside school: the head effected an introduction between her and a local lawyer, in the hope that the contact might prove fruitful in various ways. Another notional example is students who do not have anywhere to do their homework at home and who might benefit from having a sympathetic adult willing to provide a space for them from time to time. The kinds of roles which a mentor could play seem very varied: a source of information and advice (as with the lawyer); a counsellor or friend who would simply provide someone to talk to; a source of support and encouragement; a source of resources (as with the homework facilities); a role model; a sponsor. The scheme is reviewed as an extension of the tutorial system, with the tutor in some respects 'sub-contracting' his or her pastoral relationship to the mentor – making the mentor, in a sense, a tutorial equivalent of a 'godparent' (a 'godtutor', perhaps?). The scheme is still in its early stages, and so far its development has been hampered by lack of referrals from tutors. The head, however, believes that it potentially represents a valuable way of 'breaking down age-layering' and of tapping the substantial resources within the community of adults willing to help young people.

Some of the same ideas have been built into other British schemes too. In the 'Capital Jobmate' scheme, for example, unemployed young people have been put in touch with a 'jobmate' who can provide them with help in coping with unemployment and in looking for employment. As an evaluation of the scheme put it:

Jobmates were ordinary people with experience of work and the search for it, experience which could be invaluable to the inexperienced unemployed youngster. More important than the knowledge of 'how', 'what', 'where', and 'when' in relation to jobs, though, could be the personal support that an adult could give a young person. Without self-confidence a young person's chances of finding a job were severely reduced. (Hicks and Parkinson, 1981, p. 10)

Another approach used with unemployed young people has been the concept of 'working coaches' developed by the Grubb Institute within the Transition to Working Life (TWL) project. Among the key ideas within this project have been the developmental value to young people of being able to meet adults on 'equal terms', and the particular value in this respect of relationships with 'ordinary competent working men and women on the shop-floor' who have practical experience of coping with the stresses and uncertainties of working, and can assist young people to realize their own potential (Grubb Institute of Behavioural Studies, 1981).

In both the 'jobmate' and the 'working coach' concepts, there is thus a strong emphasis on the value of contacts with 'ordinary' adults whose backgrounds bear directly on the kinds of tasks confronting young people, and with whom the formality and dependency of professional–client relationships can be avoided. There are, however, differences between the two approaches (Knasel et al., 1982). Jobmates form one-to-one relationships with their partners, whereas the support offered by working coaches is essentially a group process, conducted with access to professional support and advice. Moreover, in the case of the working coach much tighter boundaries are drawn around the relationship that is offered: the workshops meet at specific points each week within a given period, and are not intended to extend outside these times, whereas with jobmates the relationship is a much more open-ended one.

Counsellors tend to be preoccupied with the helping relationships they offer directly to clients. In some cases, however, the best form of help they can offer may be to facilitate relationships with others. This is particularly true in relation to young people, where the support offered by relationships with key adults can be of considerable benefit in facilitating maturation. Many young people will form such relationships for themselves. But in some cases structures need to be set up to enable the relationships to form and develop. Establishing such structures is, perhaps, a technique which more teachers and counsellors should seek to add to their repertoire.

References

Bandura, A. (1977) *Social Learning Theory*. Englewood Cliffs, NJ: Prentice-Hall.

Borman, C. and Colson, S. (1984) 'Mentoring – an effective career guidance technique', *Vocational Guidance Quarterly*, 32(3).

Collin, A. (1979) 'Notes on some typologies of managerial development and the role of mentor in the process of adaptation of the individual to the organisation', *Personal Review*, 8(4).

Grubb Institute of Behavioural Studies (1981) 'TWL Network in Practice, Part One: report and assessment of a research and action project with unemployed young people, 1978–1981'. London: Grubb Institute (mimeo).

Hicks, M.M. and Parkinson, R. (1981) *Helping Young People to Survive Unemployment: Capital Radio Jobmate Scheme*. Special Programmes Occasional Papers, no. 1. London: Manpower Services Commission.

Hirsch, S.P. (1974) '"Starting at the top": Executive High School Internships', *Educational Leadership*, vol. 32, November.

Kanter, R.M. (1977) *Men and Women of the Corporation*. New York: Basic Books.

Knasel, E.G., Watts, A.G. and Kidd, J.M. (1982) *The Benefit of Experience*. Special Programmes Research and Development Series, no. 5. London: Manpower Services Commission.

Levinson, D.J., Darrow, C.N., Klein, E.B., Levinson, M.H. and McKee, B. (1978) *The Seasons of a Man's Life*. New York: Knopf.

Lynch, S.M. (1980) 'The mentor link: bridging education and employment', *Journal of College Placement*, 41(1).

Shapiro, E.C., Haseltine, F.P. and Rowe, M.P. (1978) 'Moving up: role models, mentors, and the "patron system"', *Sloan Management Review*, Spring.

Speizer, J. (1981) 'Role models, mentors, and sponsors: the elusive concepts', *Journal of Women in Culture and Society*, 6(4).

Brief update

My article for *Counselling* was largely drawn from a report on work shadowing which I prepared for the School Curriculum Industry Partnership. This was subsequently published in full (Watts, 1986). It was for this reason that it particularly stresses examples that are relevant to schools. In practice, interest in mentoring is, of course, much more widely based. It has also continued to grow rapidly in the years since the article was initially written, particularly in the field of career development within organizations (Jackson, 1993). Most of the issues raised in my article, however, seem still to be pertinent, which is why I am pleased for it to be reprinted here.

References

Jackson, C. (1993) 'Mentoring: choices for individuals and organizations', *International Journal of Career Management*, 5(1): 10–16.

Watts, A.G. (1986) *Work Shadowing*. York: Longman/School Curriculum Development Committee.

Discussion issues

1 To what extent do mentoring relationships incorporate counselling components?

2 Are there circumstances in which counsellors might adopt mentoring roles in relation to their clients?

3 In what situations might counsellors seek to encourage and support others in forming mentoring relationships with clients?

4 What do you see as the future development of the mentoring process?

57

Counselling and the Law

Peter Jenkins

The counselling community is currently making a determined effort to achieve the status and autonomy associated with a recognized profession in the UK, as evidenced by the rapid growth of the British Association for Counselling (BAC), and the related activities of the British Psychological Society and the United Kingdom Council for Psychotherapy (UKCP). A key feature of the former's attempt to develop its standing as a professional body has been its recent adoption of codes of ethics, aimed to regulate the behaviour of its members and practitioners. These distinguish between those seen to be counsellors, and those using counselling skills in a wide variety of settings (BAC, 1989a, 1992). This article will consider some of the legal issues in relations both to counsellors and to those using counselling skills, whether on a private contractual basis, or on behalf of an organization.

What is perhaps surprising about the seriousness of this effort by counsellors is that it seems to understate a key element of the process of developing professional status, if compared with other semi-professional groups. While law and medicine both have a close and well-established relationship with regard to legislation, other occupational groups, more accurately described as semi-professions, such as nursing, teaching and social work, have all had to clarify the way in which their core activities interact with the law (Brazier, 1992; Brayne and Martin, 1995; Dimmond, 1995; Harris, 1993).

However, what was a noticeable former lacuna in counselling research and practice is rapidly being eroded. In the USA, legal aspects of therapy are so complex, they are now thought to be beyond the scope of a single book (Hopkins and Anderson, 1990; Meyer et al., 1988). The Californian earth tremors of litigation against therapists have now reached the UK, with growing concern about the legal vulnerability of therapists in the case of 'false memory syndrome' (Butler, 1994; Jenkins, in press). At a less alarmist and more pragmatic level, the attention given to legal issues in counselling practice has been manifest in the revised BAC *Code of Ethics and Practice for Counsellors* (1992), and in the clear acknowledgement given to the legal foundations of competent counselling practice by BAC's current chair (Bond, 1993, 1994). In addition, a growing number of articles have explored the relationship between legislation and the opportunities presented for counselling practice (Etherington, 1990; Jenkins, 1993; Marks, 1995; Owen, 1993; Robertson and Tudor, 1993).

This chapter was first published in *Counselling, Journal of the British Association for Counselling*, vol. 3, no. 3, pp. 165–7 (1992).

451

Possible functions of law in relation to counselling

Despite these developments, the possible objection to a focus on legal knowledge in counselling training or in professional discussion could well be that counselling is primarily concerned with developing therapeutic relationships, rather than with acquiring an apparently technical expertise. Furthermore, it could be argued, the range of settings in which counsellors and those using counselling skills operate is so wide and varied that it is impractical to consider the impact of the law in each occupational context – this really has to be the concern of the bodies offering training for the other semi-professional groups in this field, such as teaching, social work and nursing.

However, there are serious drawbacks involved in counselling's continuing to neglect legal aspects of its practice, as will hopefully be made clear below. In addition, some of the benefits which would accrue from considering counselling in relation to the law would include:

● setting counselling within a wider social frame;
● specifying the nature of counsellor liability;
● clarifying boundaries for counsellor/client behaviour;
● denoting clients' rights.

Setting counselling within a wider social frame

Counselling, as a process of intimate, purposeful human interaction, obviously does not take place in a social vacuum. The nature of the worker–client interaction will vary according to norms derived from culture, gender, role and counselling model adopted, amongst others. Legal systems will also have a bearing on key aspects of the dialogue, not least with regard to matters such as confidentiality. An example from the medical field confirms the varying legal status of confidentiality in international terms, in that whereas medical confidentiality is absolute and protected in the criminal law in other countries such as France and Belgium, the degree of legal protection in the UK is much more limited (Mason and McCall Smith, 1994). In the USA, the situation is different again: in one case, a Californian psychiatrist, George Caesar, was jailed in 1972 for contempt of court, for refusing to break confidentiality. In the cases of *Tarasoff* in 1974, and *Milano*, 1979, courts found against therapists who had failed to warn potential victims of the extreme danger posed to them by their current clients. As the court concluded in the former case: 'protective privilege ends where the public peril begins' (Austin et al., 1990).

The purpose of such an approach is not to attempt to turn counsellors into ersatz lawyers, or even into students of comparative law, but to sensitize them to the issues, and to explore the ways in which they are dealt with in different legal settings. The actual personal dilemmas of counselling practice will continue to revolve around recurring issues, such as liability, confidentiality and redress, regardless of the actual country in which they occur.

Specifying the nature of counsellor liability

The increasing numbers of cases brought against professionals, and the growing pressure for such workers to take out indemnifying insurance policies are merely two indicators of the importance of the issue of counsellor liability. At a minimum, it is necessary for counsellors to understand how the nature of their liability varies according to the context in which they practise.

Counsellors, as professionals, are under a duty of care to their clients, that is, a duty to exercise reasonable skill when performing their activities. Failure to do so can result in action being brought against them for damages in respect of a tort (civil wrong), or for a breach of contract (Cohen, 1992). As Lord Denning put it in a case of medical negligence in 1969, the standard applied was that a doctor 'was liable when he fell below the standard of a reasonably competent practitioner in his field so much that his conduct might be deserving of censure or inexcusable' (*Hucks* v. *Cole* [1968]; Harrop-Griffiths and Bennington, 1985, p. 42). This sets out the broad bench-mark that would be applied in such circumstances.

The potential danger areas for counsellors have been succinctly described in the context of the USA by L. Talbutt and D. Hummel, as 'falling below conduct appropriate to one's profession; failing to warn or take action when someone is in danger; taking advantage of the counselling relationship for personal gain; and advising beyond one's skill and training' (Talbutt and Hummel, 1982, p. 8). If a counsellor is working on the basis of a private contract with their client, then the action can be brought against them as individuals. If they are carrying out their activities for an employer, then liability will apply both to the individual and vicariously to the latter, on the basis of the principle established in the case of *Cassidy* v. *Ministry of Health* [1951] (Harrop-Griffiths and Bennington, 1985). In such situations, the personal liability of the individual social worker or medical practitioner may be expressly limited by law, 'unless the act was done in bad faith or without reasonable care'. Thus, under section 139 of the Mental Health Act 1983, with regard to actions against social workers or doctors by patients, 'civil proceedings require the permission of the High Court, criminal proceedings require the permission of the DPP' [now Crown Prosecution Service] (Anderson-Ford and Halsey, 1984, p. 82).

Clarifying boundaries for counsellor/client behaviour

The second application of law to counselling practice is in relation to clarifying the proper boundaries for counsellor/client behaviour. The eclectic nature of counselling practice requires an awareness of developments in the law which may not, at first sight, have immediate relevance for their own area of work. The best example of this situation is the effect of the *Gillick* judgment, ostensibly concerning the right of children to determine their own medical treatment under the age of 16, without necessarily obtaining parental consent, for example, for contraceptive advice. By implication, the principles underlying the *Gillick* judgment affirm the right of mature children to obtain confidential advice and counselling, independently of their parents' knowledge. As Lord Scarman put it, '. . . parental right yields to the child's right to make his own decisions when he reaches a sufficient understanding and intelligence to be capable of making up his own mind on the matter requiring decision' (*Gillick* v. *West Norfolk and Wisbech Area Health Authority* [1985]; *Childright*, 1989). While children's rights to be consulted about decisions made about them by professionals, such as social workers, are now firmly enshrined in the Children Act 1989, counselling working in a school setting sometimes seem unaware of the import of the *Gillick* judgment, and rely on the assumption that they can inform parents of sensitive matters, on the basis that they are acting *in loco parentis* (*Williams* v. *Eady* (1893)). Counsellors in this situation need to be aware of the legal parameters to their actions in order to be able to serve their clients effectively, and minimize their own vulnerability to challenge.

Confidentiality is a crucial area for exploring the way that legal obligations intersect with professional codes and ethics for counsellors. The foundation of this is the common law duty of confidence, which obliges an individual to keep secret all information imparted to them in a trusting relationship. The duty derives from the nature of the relationship, rather than from a contractual or employment relationship (Harris, 1990). A breach of confidentiality can be met by a restraining injunction, or by a claim for damages.

Counsellors are thus covered by this obligation, but the duty of confidentiality is not total, with a number of exceptions recognized by the courts, namely:

> where the law requires disclosure; to assist in the investigation or prosecution of a serious crime; to prevent a continuing and serious threat to health of either specific identifiable persons or the public at large; where disclosure is necessary in the performance of a public or statutory duty, and where it is necessary in the public interest. (d'Eca, 1990, p. 12)

Thus, for example, confidential information is seen to be held by the employing organization, such as a health authority, rather than residing with the individual doctor alone (Blom-Cooper et al., 1987). As BAC advice indicates, counsellors in England cannot claim professional privilege as a defence against revealing confidential information to a court of law, since this claim is only recognized for 'confidential communications made for the purpose of obtaining legal advice from professional advisers' (BAC, 1989b). Similarly, counsellor's files are not privileged in the latter sense. Under the Police and Criminal Evidence Act 1984, the police may gain access to such material, classified as 'protected' under the Act, on making an application to a circuit judge.

Normally, a counsellor's first duty is to their client. However, situations can arise where there is a conflict between the counsellor's professional role, and a wider duty to society. Such a conflict arose in the recent case of a person with a history of violence and mental illness, who applied for access to his birth records under section 51 of the Adoption Act 1976, with a view to obtaining information about his natural mother. When refused the records on the grounds that he posed a potential threat to his natural mother, he appealed. The Court of Appeal dismissed the appeal, on the grounds that 'a statutory duty was not to be enforced if there was a significant risk that to do so would facilitate crime resulting in danger to life' (*Guardian*, 1990). In this case, the counsellor's responsibility to the client was clearly outweighed by considerations of a wider nature, not least the conflict of duties under the law.

Denoting clients' rights

In the present political culture, the emphasis is on the rights of consumers, patients and clients. A grasp of the legal issues surrounding the counselling relationship can clarify the respective rights of counsellor and client. The structural imbalance of power in this situation, to the counsellor's advantage, has been noted by a recent critic, as have the opportunities for its abuse by practitioners (Jehu, 1994; Masson, 1989). Where the counsellor is self-employed, the boundaries of counsellor–client interaction are set by the law of contract, as an essentially private affair between two parties. The client's rights of redress are limited to legal action against the counsellor for damages, as outlined above.

Where the parameters of counselling practice are determined by statute, clients make a complaint against the employing authority. The provision for a complaints procedure is specified in legislation in the case of groups such as doctors, and social workers (Health Complaints Procedure Act 1985; Children Act 1989). The non-statutory position of counsellors is reflected in the lack of an intermediate level for redress other than professional sanction for professional misconduct, or recourse to legal proceedings (BAC, 1994).

One possible route for counselling to go down is for it to acquire the traits of a profession, i.e. legal recognition for its unique expertise, embodied in control over access to the profession via a registration process with its own internal disciplinary procedures for breaches of discipline and the code of ethics and behaviour. Accordingly, both BAC and the UKCP have recently instituted voluntary registers of practitioners.

Another possibility is for counselling to examine its relationship to the law in greater detail, to clarify situations where its practitioners are faced with real dilemmas, with serious consequences for counsellor and client alike. As a parallel, social workers, with a host of statutory duties to perform in relation to children, people with a mental illness, and other vulnerable groups, have been subject to severe criticism for the lax state of their competency in legal affairs (CCETSW, 1995). Given the complex and demanding nature of many of the situations faced by counsellors, whether as private practitioners, or as employees of larger organizations, it seems surprising that the guidelines for course recognition for counsellors do not specify a legal component (BAC, 1996).

Persistence of counselling dilemmas

This represents the strongest argument for closer attention to legal issues with regard to counselling practice – that counsellors will continue to encounter situations where they decide to take action, or not to take action, with often little more than an intuitive knowledge of their legal standing and liability. Witness the following examples:

> You are counselling a consultant anaesthetist over his problems caused by unresolved aggressive feelings. He discloses to you that he has deliberately caused the deaths of three patients, specially selected on the grounds of frailty and ill-health, by unobtrusively curtailing their oxygen supply in the course of long and complex operations. There is no immediate prospect of either the consultant responding to therapy, or of being detected in his behaviour.

The example is apparently so extreme as to be unrealistic – but the example is, in fact, genuine (Laing, 1986). The options open to the counsellor may appear to be obvious, even to one without legal training of the most rudimentary kind. Yet the question remains open as to how adequately those in counselling practice are equipped to deal competently with situations such as this which pose real ethical dilemmas with a legal dimension.

References

Anderson-Ford, D. and Halsey, M. (1984) *Mental Health Law and Practice for Social Workers*. London: Butterworths.

Austin, K., Moline, M.E. and Williams, G.T. (1990) *Confronting Malpractice: Legal and Ethical Dilemmas in Psychotherapy*. London: Sage.

Blom-Cooper, L. et al. (1987) *A Child in Mind: Protection of Children in a Responsible Society* (Report on Kimberley Carlisle). London Borough of Greenwich.

Bond, T. (1993) *Standards and Ethics for Counselling in Action*. London: Sage.

Bond, T. (1994) *Counselling, Confidentiality and the Law*. Information Guide, no. 1. Rugby: BAC.

Brayne, H. and Martin, G. (1995) *Law for Social Workers*, 4th edn. London: Blackstone.

Brazier, M. (1992) *Medicine, Patients and the Law*, 2nd edn. Harmondsworth: Penguin.

British Association for Counselling (1989a) *Code of Ethics and Practice for Counselling Skills*. Rugby: BAC.

British Association for Counselling (1989b) *Confidentiality and the Law*. Information sheet no. 1. (Reference from *Halsbury's Laws of England*, 4th edn, vol. 11, *Criminal Law*, para. 464.)

British Association for Counselling (1992) *Code of Ethics and Practice for Counsellors*. Rugby: BAC.

British Association for Counselling (1994) *Complaints Procedure*. Rugby: BAC.

British Association for Counselling (1996) *Recognition of Counsellor Training Courses*, 4th edn. Rugby: BAC.

Butler, K. (1994) 'You must remember this', *Guardian*, 23 July.

CCETSW (Central Council for Education and Training in Social Work) (1995) *Law for Social Workers in England and Wales*. London: CCETSW.

Childright (1989) no. 58, pp. 11–14; no. 59, pp. 19–20.

Cohen, K. (1992) 'Some legal issues in counselling and psychotherapy', *British Journal of Guidance and Counselling*, 20(1): 10–26.

d'Eca, C. (1990) 'Medico-legal aspects of AIDS', in D. Harris and R. Haigh (eds), *AIDS a Guide to the Law*. London: Routledge.

Dimmond, B. (1995) *Legal Aspects of Nursing*, 2nd edn. London: Prentice-Hall.

Etherington, K. (1990) 'The Disabled Person's Act 1986: the need for counselling', *Counselling*, 1(2): 51–2.

Guardian (1990) Law Report, 16 November.

Harris, D. (1990) 'AIDS and employment', in D. Harris and R. Haigh (eds), *AIDS: a Guide to the Law.* London: Routledge. (2nd edn 1995)

Harris, N. (1993) *Law and Education: Regulation, Consumerism and the Education System.* London: Sweet and Maxwell.

Harrop-Griffiths, H. and Bennington, J. (1985) *Professional Negligence,* 2nd edn. London: Fourmat.

Hopkins, B. and Anderson, B. (1990) *The Counselor and the Law.* Alexandria, VA: American Counseling Association.

Jehu, D. (1994) *Patients as Victims: Sexual Abuse in Psychotherapy and Counselling.* Chichester: Wiley.

Jenkins, P. (1993) 'Counselling and the Children Act 1989', *Counselling,* 4(4): 274–6.

Jenkins, P. (in press) 'False or recovered memories? The ethical and legal implications for therapists', *British Journal of Guidance and Counselling.*

Laing, R.D. (1986) *Wisdom, Madness and Folly.* London: Macmillan.

Marks, L. (1995) 'Adopted and at home in the world: a message for counsellors', *Counselling,* 6(1): 48–50.

Mason, J.K. and McCall Smith, R.A. (1994) *Law and Medical Ethics,* 4th edn. London: Butterworths.

Masson, J. (1989) *Against Therapy.* London: Collins.

Meyer, G., Landis, E. and Hays, J. (1988) *Law for the Psychotherapist.* New York: Landis.

Owen, I. (1993) 'Assessment for counselling and the psychiatric services', *Counselling,* 4(4): 287–9.

Robertson, G. and Tudor, K. (1993) 'Counselling in the context of community care', *Counselling,* 4(3): 188–90.

Talbutt, L. and Hummel, D. (1982) 'Legal and ethical issues impacting on counselors', *Counselling and Human Development,* 14(6): 1–12.

List of cases

Cassidy v. *Ministry of Health* [1951] 2 KB 343.
Gillick v. *West Norfolk and Wisbech Area Health Authority* [1985] 3 All ER 402.
Hucks, v. *Cole* [1968] 118 NLJ 469.
Williams v. *Eady* (1893) 10 TLR 41 CA.

Discussion issues

1 Why do counsellors often feel uncomfortable in dealing with legal issues concerning therapy?
2 What guidance on legal aspects of counselling do you have for your current work, e.g. regarding confidentiality, reporting child abuse, etc.?
3 What access do you have to advice or training on legal issues outside your sphere of competence?
4 How can clients' rights best be protected in therapy?

58

Breaking Boundaries

Janice Russell

While I was a member of the Brighton Women's Mental Health sub-committee, my attention was drawn to complaints from two separate sources of role-inappropriate sexual behaviour within the therapeutic relationship. This aroused considerable concern, and alongside other initiatives, I undertook a piece of exploratory research into this area. At a time when the BAC code of ethics was under revision, it seemed appropriate to offer a summary of the research findings as of interest and import to this body.

Issues of sexual exploitation within the therapeutic relationship are not new, and the first formal investigation of which I am aware took place during the reign of Louis XVI, who was concerned about the exploitative potential within the mesmeric relationship (Certok and de Saussure, 1979, pp. 10–11). In this century, Freud's contention that erotic attachment between patient and therapist is a product of transference (1979, p. 145) and should be seen as such has carried considerable weight. Additionally, most therapies have become increasingly professionalized and adhere to a code of ethics which take their cue partly from the medical mode and which specifically prohibit sexual contact between therapists and clients. Yet there seems to be little 'public' awareness that this is an area with unresolved issues, that sexual contact does occur within therapeutic relationships, and that for clients this may be experienced as devastating, enabling, or with various shades of confusion, distress and mixed reaction.

Two points need to be clarified regarding the terminology in this chapter. First, and reflecting the sociological orientation of this work, I have used the term 'therapist' to describe all those who are designated, by themselves and others, as psychotherapists, counsellors, psychiatrists, clinical psychologists, psychiatric social workers – all those 'mental health workers' who operate in one-to-one relationships. No doubt this would be contested by many of the professions involved. For this initial research, however, which may be seen as a broad-based trawling exercise, the point was that:

(a) All claim to have some degree of expertise in the field of mental health.
(b) All operate, in some sense, in one-to-one relationships in the belief that they may skilfully be able to help their clients develop a more satisfactory way of living.
(c) The nature of this relationship is seen as 'therapeutic' (healing), and relies to a large extent on a 'talking cure'.

This chapter was first published as 'Breaking boundaries: a research note', in *Counselling, Journal of the British Association for Counselling*, vol. 1, no. 2, pp. 47–9 (1990).

In these respects, then, all these professions may be said to share an underlying 'ideological' perspective which is derived from, and perpetuates, a treatment model for mental disease. In this sense they may all be said to be performing a common function in society. This is not to conflate these professions into one, or to obscure important theoretical and practical distinctions which inhere to them.

Secondly, the term 'role-inappropriate sexual behaviour' was chosen after some deliberation. On the one hand it reflects the fact that professions do have standards and modes of role-appropriate behaviour which must be conformed to and which are stated in codes of ethics. Within BAC, the 1984 code of ethics states categorically that: '*Engaging in sexual activity with a client whilst also engaging in a therapeutic relationship is unethical.*' (2.7).

In this sense the term 'role-inappropriate sexual behaviour' is reasonably straightforward, inasmuch as it would denote behaviour by the therapist which is in contravention of that code. On the other hand, life is rarely that simple. The interpretation of the code, any code, usually furnishes the opportunity for a few grey areas, and this is no exception. It is very difficult to delineate precisely what is ethical behaviour, and in this context it also begs the question of what is sexual – a look, a comment, a physical act? For me, whether behaviour is ethical must relate to the intention behind it, and to whose interests are being served. Still room for greyness, and we must bear in mind that it is not enough for a practitioner to know the intention behind an intervention, s/he must also be able to communicate this to the client and check that expectations are matched. My specific interest here, then, was to try to gain some understanding of the nature of the (failed) expectations of the clients, and of what, for them, constituted role-inappropriate sexual behaviour. In this respect, then, the term may be seen as a sensitizing concept. The ascription of meaning by the client is seen as a crucial factor in furthering our understanding as counsellors.

One of the concerns of some participants in the research was that the findings should be disseminated as widely as possible, and BAC is seen as one preferred avenue for this course of action. With the proviso that any (mis)interpretations are mine alone, these are some of the findings of this pilot study.

Method

The method of this research is, as stated, of an exploratory nature rather than hypothesis testing. The intentions were not to discover whether role-inappropriate sexual behaviour occurred, rather to discover how people who felt that they had experienced such behaviour identified and ascribed meaning to it. Thus I was not concerning myself with incidence, nor was I looking to gather a representative sample population. Rather I approached the question as a limited study informed by qualitative research methodology and theory (see Stanley and Wise, 1983).

I therefore advertised in a local newsletter (see Appendices) concerned with mental health projects in Brighton, and by word of mouth. This course of action produced twelve respondents, detailed below. Each respondent gave me a taped interview, and the interviews were very loosely structured. I invited participants to tell me whether their therapist was NHS or privately employed, how they had come to enter that particular therapeutic relationship, and then to tell me in their own words what they thought was relevant in their experience to this particular research. This was in keeping with affording subjectivity to participants. My own intervention was in one sense minimal, though this is not to say non-influential, as the interviewer's presence is clearly an integral part of the research process (1983, p. 158).

Responses

Of the twelve respondents, nine felt that they had had direct experience of sexual behaviour from or interaction with their therapists. These were seven women and two men. Eight of them identified the behaviour as role-inappropriate, while one woman had talked to me specifically to make the case that the intimate physical contact which she experienced with her therapist was a crucial and integral component of the therapeutic process. This respondent was concerned that my research would provoke a 'clamour' which would prohibit therapist–client physical contact.

Three other people gave me interviews; a social worker who had worked with a psychiatrist who was believed to be behaving inappropriately with adolescent girls; a therapist who had given an assessment interview to a practitioner who confessed the sexual abuse of clients; and a student on a counselling course who knew of an affair between a tutor and a student, the tutor also acting as counsellor to that student. These three interviews underlined the personal and professional dilemmas of those 'in the know' about possibly unethical practice, and how these dilemmas had been exacerbated by lack of professional awareness or discussion of the issues involved, as well as by conflicts over confidentiality.

Three people arranged to see me and then failed the appointment. Some people spoke to me informally, either knowing someone who 'it had happened to, or as practitioners who were interested in the dilemmas surrounding touch and sexual feelings, or expressing conflict over whether or not to have an affair with a client. This suggests that the problems under review are not confined to the small sample represented in this study.

Range of behaviours

The range of behaviours identified as role-inappropriate sexual behaviour was wide. It included episodes of kissing and hugging; lengthy affairs; offensive and inappropriate verbal responses and demeanour; inappropriate dress on the part of the therapist; denial on the part of the therapist that there was an erotic component within the relationship; ambiguous hugs; sexual intercourse; intimate physical contact as a diagnostic procedure. In some cases, the behaviour concerned took place after, or precipitated, the formal termination of the therapeutic relationship. It was generally seen as one point within a lengthier interactive process which was in some cases characterized by the breaking of other traditional boundaries.

Motive imputed to the behaviours again varied considerably. Some respondents voiced confusion about why the therapist acted as s/he did, while others had formed their own interpretation of the needs or motivations of the therapist:

'I can't say that it was lust, I can't say that is was fetish, I can't say that it was therapy.'

'I knew that he cared . . . I felt he was genuinely concerned . . . I was pushing him really . . . He was always very easily led.'

'This woman I take to be very lonely . . . She was full of love but love which didn't take into account my needs or feelings.'

'It seemed very evident that he enjoyed the power in the relationship.'

Identification of behaviour as inappropriate

For most of the respondents, behaviour had not been immediately identified as wholly inappropriate. Only one woman knew this immediately in the sense of gaining no positive sense of what had occurred but feeling only distress. This is not to say that other participants did not register any distress, rather that it was confused with other responses emanating from pleasure or a belief in the therapeutic potential:

'I was getting very distressed . . . I was in a therapeutic state.' (*sic*)

'It made me feel absolutely fantastic . . . and at the same time I was terrified.'

'I wanted that sort of contact . . . I was pretty naive . . . I knew that he shouldn't be doing what he was doing.'

The feeling that the behaviour was wrong often became the burden of the client who internalized guilt for what had happened. This was experienced as having powerful repercussions; one woman viewed her experience as an abuse which led to attempted suicide and others saw it as causing or perpetuating a variety of self-destructive feelings/behaviours.

It is notable at this point that the woman who found intimate physical contact to be both appropriate and constructive differed in three identifiable ways from the other respondents. First, she and her therapist were of the same gender; secondly, she was the only respondent who was still in the therapeutic relationship in question; and finally, she felt strongly that the physical contact, which was initiated at her request, was fulfilling her needs and not those of the therapist. Every stage of therapy was talked through together and negotiated, so that she understood the physical contact as a means to an end, and not an end in itself:

'I'm using her sexually, she's not using me . . . There's been clear boundaries and limitations from her, even when there wasn't from me fantasy wise.'

Janice Russell

Evaluation of the experience

As already indicated, the process of evaluation of the experience has been ongoing for most of the respondents, often accompanied by feelings of confusion, betrayal, guilt and hurt. All but one identified their experience as damaging in some way. Many participated in more therapy and use the language of therapy in their evaluative process, while some have located it within the wider scenario of sexual abuse, and one participant now questions the whole practice of therapy:

'I think I had an enormous transference to her . . . I see it as extremely damaging and incestually violating.'

'I found a therapist . . . she said "I think that's dreadful, it's just another form of sexual abuse" . . . it was wonderful because it . . . gave me the confidence to have my own response to it.'

'It's taken me a long time to make any sense of it, people who did know used to make it out to be a really big scandal . . . I couldn't relate to that . . . I wanted them to understand . . . I've never been able to fit it into any of the moulds that I'm supposed to fit it into . . . on the other hand I know . . . what a powerful position a [therapist] is in . . . and it's really a terrible abuse to go beyond what you're supposed to do . . . I'm not convinced that all therapy isn't some kind of an abuse . . . now I'm doing co-counselling I can see what's wrong with any kind of therapy . . . maybe it's just one of those things, my views of it will change as I go along.'

This last participant was keen not to be seen as a passive victim, and felt that in some ways she had gained from the therapeutic relationship. Other participants also insisted on the active role that they had taken in the whole process; to deny this is to invalidate in some way an aspect of their whole experience. This illustrates that evaluation is a complicated procedure within which experience cannot easily be labelled as either helpful or harmful, passive or active.

The therapist

It seemed important to emphasize from the outset that this research was not intended as a head-hunting exercise, and I asked for no information which might identify therapists. I was told however that those who were experienced as behaving role-inappropriately included those from the following schools; psychoanalysis, bioenergetics, primal therapy, Marriage Guidance, psychiatry, clinical psychology, psychosynthesis, client-centred counselling. To my knowledge, some at least were highly trained, members of professional organizations, and in supervision. Two were employed by the National Health Service, one was initially but later transferred his client to his private practice. At least three were involved in provision of training. Six were male, three female. With the exception of the therapeutic relationship which was experienced as wholly appropriate, all the dyads were mixed gender.

Complaint procedures

One of the participants in this research had taken the step of making an informal complaint to a Health Authority. Another had experienced a complaint being made by close relatives, without her consent. Neither was satisfied with how these were handled. One participant observed that he would not have been able to take advantage of a complaints procedure at the time. It seemed that the prevailing mood of the participants here was that there was no forum to which they could take their grievances with confidence. Informal discussions with counsellor colleagues also indicated some confusion about how and in what circumstances they may express concern about other therapists.

Concluding remarks

In the spirit of inquiry in which this research was undertaken, I propose no conclusion. I do have some suggestions of directions for further exploration and input which I will make with specific reference to BAC. These fall into three discrete yet interdependent areas.

One is within the provision of training and supervision. There is a case to be argued that practitioners and users of therapy need more education on this issue in two senses. One is in making issues of sexuality and of sexual attraction explicit in counselling skills training. The second is in keeping in touch with available literature on harmful therapeutic practice and on the effects of sexual abuse in a wider sense.[1] Underpinning these strategies, I would suggest that behaviour identified as inappropriate should be seen not in isolation but as indicative of an inappropriate relationship, and needs to be considered as an overt sign of the inability of the counsellor to offer effective, boundaried counselling at that time. As counsellors, it is important to recognize our own vulnerabilities and limitations, and boundary-keeping in all its guises is one useful focus for facilitating that process.

Secondly, the ethical dimension of the problem under review needs to be clearly acknowledged. I mentioned earlier that the 1984 code of ethics offers a clear directive. The revised consultative code under consideration, however, at present proposes a major shift, in removing the clause quoted above from the 'pure ethics' dimension, and in relocating its updated version within the code of practice:

> Counselling is a non-exploitative relationship in which counsellors should not exploit their clients financially, sexually, emotionally or in any other way. A physical sexual relationship between counsellor and client would usually be considered exploitative (B2.2.7).

The consultative code reflects an attempt to recognize the complexities of ethical stances and recognizes that it can only ever provide a framework built around an adherence to a clearly stated value system. The rephrasing of this particular clause is helpful in recognizing sexual exploitation as one form of power abuse. To see sexual exploitation as bad practice rather than as an ethical transgression is a radical departure, however. Although the two are linked, they may also be seen as discrete categories. For the problem under review here, my own preference would be to retain a clear prohibition on purely ethical grounds, thus making a statement which relates to an external morality.

Thirdly, there is perhaps some work to be done on liaising closely with user groups in order to negotiate and make available some clear guidelines for what to do when dissatisfaction arises within counselling. This is also true for practitioners; although there is guidance in the consultative code, there are a good many complexities which interweave with those raised over the counsellor's responsibility for confidentiality (Bond, 1988). My research led me to contemplate some difficult scenarios which had arisen for people; the client who tells the counsellor of (sexual) abuse by her/his previous therapist was more common than I had appreciated at the beginning of this research, and poses some difficult dilemmas. Perhaps discussion and exploration of these issues should be more widely available to counsellors and clients alike, with notions of advocacy being recognized as central.

Finally, any of these courses of action needs to be mindful of the wider social and political context within which we operate. Part of my study was to make a detailed review of the research in this area available from the States. One important, repeated finding was that 'offenders' are most likely to be male, trained, accredited and to have undergone their own personal therapy. Despite differences in the system there, this does seem to indicate, as do my limited findings, that there is a case to be made that although training and supervision may go some way to preventing abuse of clients, they are unlikely to be totally successful. Thus we need to see abusive practice not only as an individual aberration, but as a symptom of wider issues. I would suggest that we need to be aware of the power dynamics engendered within the counselling relationship, and to acknowledge that these may intensify as the counselling body goes through the professionalization process. We need also to challenge sexist and heterosexist attitudes and practices at both individual and institutional levels. BAC has gone some way over the years to show its awareness of these issues, but we must realize that they are far from resolved. Neither will they be while the public issue of abusive practice is seen only as private miseries. A degree of detachment may be necessary in examining our own practice.

These are but some of the strands of thought that this research produced for me, and space does not permit a fuller exploration. I will be interested to see what response it generates and hope it will be one part in a constructive process of examination.

The author acknowledges with thanks all who took part in the research and those who encouraged me in its coordination and writing-up.

References

Bond, Tim (1988) 'Confidentiality: the need for greater clarity in the code of ethics and practice', *Counselling*, no. 66, November.

Certok, L. and de Saussure, R. (1979) *The Therapeutic Revolution: from Mesmer to Freud*. New York: Bruner/Mazel.

Stanley, L. and Wise, S. (1983) *Breaking Out: Feminist Consciousness and Feminist Research*. London: Routledge and Kegan Paul.

Note

1 To my knowledge, there is no other research available in Britain on this area. (I would be pleased to hear of any that I've missed.) From the States, there is a work by K. Pope and J. Bouhoutsos (1986) *Sexual Intimacy Between Therapists and Clients.* This is firmly grounded in the clinical perspective. As part of this work, I made a critical survey of relevant research and offer a wider perspective to the problem, which will be offered for publication at a later date.

Appendix I

Research into sexual abuse/inappropriate role behaviour by mental health professionals

Last year, I began some research into clients' experience of role-inappropriate sexual behaviour by mental health workers (including counsellors, psychotherapists, psychiatric social workers, clinical psychologists and others). I will be completing this work by September 1990 and would like to renew my appeal for people to take part. Several people have participated so far, and the range of abusive/inappropriate behaviour is very wide; inappropriate behaviour can be subtle as well as overt, and is a complex phenomenon. My findings so far have reinforced my belief that this research is important, as the effects of role-inappropriate behaviour can be devastating, causing confusion and bewilderment. This can be particularly alarming where a client has suffered sexual abuse previously.

I would like to hear from anyone who feels that they have experienced role-inappropriate sexual behaviour from a mental health worker. All contact will of course be treated in the strictest confidence, and I am not looking to identify workers concerned; my interest is in the experience of the client and the identification of the problem. I am aware of how difficult it may feel to come forward, and am indebted to those who have already done so; I know it wasn't easy. When written up, the research will be available to Brighton mental health organizations, and sent to a counselling journal in the hope of having the issues considered seriously by professionals.

Appendix II

Research project: Sex in the therapeutic relationship

I am carrying our some research into clients' experience of sexual contact between mental health workers and themselves. I use the term 'mental health workers' to include counsellors, psychotherapists, psychiatrists, psychiatric social workers/nurses and others, indeed any worker who enters into a one-to-one relationship on a therapeutic basis. I would like to hear from anyone who has had such an experience.

I wish to emphasize that I will *not* be seeking to identify workers concerned; my interest is in the experience from the clients' point of view. I am aware that the issue is a very complex one, and that often the negative experience of a sexual relationship within therapy of any kind itself may inhibit people from being able to then trust another worker or talk about the experience at all. Nevertheless I hope that anyone reading this who would like to take part will feel able to do so, and assure you that all contact and information will be treated in strict confidence. I would like to meet for an interview in the first instance, with a possibility of a follow-up interview at a later date.

I am myself an experienced counsellor and am carrying out this research as a part of my MA at Sussex University. I am also working closely with the Women's sub-committee of the Brighton Mental Health Group; I hope that one of the uses of the research will be in identifying the experiences of abuse of the therapist's role which must be of concern to both users and workers in the mental health field. This seems to me to be very important and I hope people will feel able to come forward.

Janice Russell, BSc. Dip. S.W.

Footnote on 'Role-inappropriate Sexual Behaviour'

The author raises some important issues here which have already been exercising the minds of the BAC Standards and Ethics Sub-Committee.

(i) What is 'role-inappropriate sexual behaviour'?

The key question is what is 'inappropriate' in counselling? There appear to be two schools of thought on this. One favours a straightforward prohibition of sexual activity. This unequivocally covers penetrative sex and probably mutual masturbation, but is less clear so far as cuddling, kissing, verbal and mental activity are concerned.

The other approach concentrates on the underlying ethical principle that counselling is a non-exploitative relationship, including sexually. Some fear that this places too much reliance on the counsellor's view of what is exploitative in an area of life where self-delusion is commonplace.

(ii) What should the Code of Ethics and Practice say on this issue?

This is being actively considered in relation to the consultative code for counsellors. Janice Russell's point that there is an ethical issue as well as one of practice is accepted, and a statement will be included within the code of ethics. We have received letters arguing for different forms of wording. Some correspondents favour retaining a slightly modified form of the 1984 wording, 'Engaging in sexual activity with a client whilst also engaging in a counselling relationship is unethical' (Option 1). Another view favours a shorter version of the wording in the consultative code, 'Counselling is a non-exploitative relationship. Counsellors should not exploit their clients financially, sexually, emotionally or in any other way' (Option 2). Both versions have advantages and disadvantages. Some of these are explored within the article.

Tim Bond
Chair – Standards and Ethics Sub-Committee, 1990

Brief update

Following publication of this article in the journal, I received many letters from people wishing to talk to me about their own experiences in counselling which they had felt to be sexually exploitative. I followed these up with interviews, and subsequently wrote up my findings and a more thorough discussion of the subject in a book entitled *Out of Bounds: Sexual Exploitation in Counselling and Therapy* (1993). There has also been wider discussion of the subject within BAC, as counselling finds itself within a process of professionalization, and there have been amendments to the Code of Ethics. It is relevant to provide a very brief summary of some of the key points emerging.

First, further research served to confirm that for those people involved in my research, the experience of overt sexual relationship within the counselling dyad was almost unanimously experienced as exploitative and damaging. Specifically, it was possible to identify a range of effects which closely mirror those well documented as typical of the experience of sexual abuse, namely, confusion or disorganization, a loss of trust in self and others, guilt, anxiety, frustration, helplessness, anger, ambivalence, poor or distorted self-concept, isolation and desperation. These effects manifested behaviourally in a wide variety of ways. Those for whom the feelings of anger and isolation seemed paramount had found themselves behaving in ways which they identified as being destructive to self or others, sometimes being physically violent or suicidal.

Problems also arose in subsequent counselling, where it was, understandably, extremely difficult to trust in the helping process, given the previous violation of trust. Most people found it almost impossible to approach ethical committees of the professional organizations involved, suspecting them to be biased or sexist, or at times finding them bureaucratic and unfriendly. Those who did go through the process of reporting still felt frustrated when, even where complaints were upheld, professional bodies had no means of preventing exploitative counsellors from practising, being limited to withdrawing their membership of the professional organization.

A further issue increasingly emergent was the position of counsellors who trained with educational bodies who were perceived to be acting unethically with students. Some students had left a particular organization where tutors had been assessed as violating the code of ethics and professional practice by having or condoning sexual relationships between tutor and student. Other professionals I know express reservations about training institutions where the tutor acts as counsellor and/or supervisor to the student, and where professional and personal boundaries are blurred. For those who leave, they feel that their own training is contaminated and incomplete, yet it would be inappropriate to embark on another three-year course of study. Those who do not leave may struggle with feelings of collusion and a lack of value.

Such findings leave ongoing issues for the profession of counselling and for BAC. Much thought and hard work has been put into these issues, and there has been debate among the membership. The Code of Ethics has twice been revised since 1990, recommending a three-month 'cooling off' period between counsellor and client where sexual attraction is strong, and subsequently adding a clause which attempts to capture and allow for the complexities of human relationships by stating that

> The decision about any change(s) in relationship with former clients should take into account whether the issues and power dynamics present during the counselling relationship have been resolved and properly ended. (1993: 2.3.1–2.3.2: pp. 4–5)

As I have argued elsewhere (Russell, 1995), my personal view is that a clearer directive is necessary for the safety of clients and for the credibility of the profession. While being mindful of the pitfalls and the possible arrogance of prescribing which adults may have relationships with whom, it seems to me that in naming itself a profession, BAC already assumes a responsibility for guidelines to the relationship between counsellor and client, and that this should not be reneged where sexuality is involved. The danger here is that we collude in a view of sexuality as being an uncontrollable biological imperative. I would argue that informed choices can and should be made with the well-being of the client being paramount, and, importantly, being seen to be paramount. I would prefer to see at least a six-month gap imposed, on the grounds that this represents a grieving period which allows the client time to assess the emotional impact of their experience and of separation from the counselling relationship (Russell, 1993, 1995). It also allows the counsellor a period of supervised review and reflection. Within this period, it would be unethical for the counsellor to be in contact with the ex-client. Any further contact after this point must be under the control of the ex-client. Counsellors who choose to further a relationship after this period must be aware of the possible consequences to furthering a relationship at this point in terms of credibility, as must a profession which endorses this as a possibility.

The debate will and must continue, and this addendum is necessarily brief. User groups exist to help those who feel that they have been sexually exploited in counselling and therapy (see Russell, 1993), and much productive work has been done. We have further to go in trying to create user-friendly forums for people who have felt exploited, prior to the point where they decide to make a complaint. We may also need to reconsider whether there should be some measure of independent arbitration necessary to the complaints process. There is also potential for funded research into this area, to ensure maximum safety and support for all those involved.

Ultimately, the profession relies on the awareness and integrity of its members. I have already stated that there are issues of education and training which are central to this ethic. It is therefore perhaps pertinent to leave the reader with some points for personal consideration.

References

Russell, J. (1993) *Out of Bounds: Sexual Exploitation in Counselling and Therapy*. London: Sage.

Russell, J. (1995) 'Sexual exploitation in counselling and therapy', in R. Bayne et al. (eds), *New Directions in Counselling*. London: Routledge and Kegan Paul.

Discussion issues

1 At what stage in a counselling relationship would you consider that the power dynamics are resolved? How does this accord with the client's perception?

2 How would you react if you were strongly sexually attracted to your client?

3 It has been suggested that we should never be vain enough to take personally a client's sexual attraction to us as counsellors. What are your views on this? How would you interpret a client's feelings of anger towards you, or feelings of wanting to strike up a platonic friendship? Are there any differences between these and sexual feelings?

4 Where counsellors pursue a sexual relationship with a client or former client, it seems that the justification is in the reciprocation of the feelings. Does this then mean that the counsellor's feelings are the deciding factor? Whose needs are justified here?

59

Audio-tape Recordings in Counsellor Education and Training

Ian Horton and Rowan Bayne

Audio-tape recordings are increasingly used by both counsellors-in-training and experienced practitioners to monitor and increase their effectiveness. One outcome is that some of the agencies in which our students have worked as counsellors have enquired about our policy on audio-tape recording. Our response was to produce a handout for students which has been adapted for the main section of this chapter. We spell out a method of obtaining and using audio tapes, and touch on some of the practical and ethical issues involved.

There is very little in the literature on the use of audio tapes, particularly at the level of ethical and practical guidelines. Two perspectives are provided by Dryden (1983) and Jacobs (1993). Dryden (1983) discussed two obstacles to recording sessions for supervision: 'overconcern' for clients, which he argued tended to reflect the counsellor's own anxiety more than the client's, and technical problems with tape recorders, which he suggested challenging with a question like 'Imagine what it would be like to present an *audible* tape for supervision?' Jacobs (1993) discussed his reservations about the effects on clients of being asked for permission and about counsellors and supervisors becoming obsessional about the details of the counselling and therefore neglecting the essence of the overall relationship between the counsellor and client. However, like Dryden and Feltham (1992, pp. 13–15), we see the potential benefits of tapes as outweighing the problems.

Method (suggestions and guidelines)

1 Experiment with the best way to set up and use your tape recorder. If you can afford around £175, the new portable Marantz PMD 101 is excellent. It has a battery unit which is rechargeable overnight. However, good small recorders can now be bought quite cheaply, but most benefit from an additional external microphone. We have found the Realistic PZM useful. It is relatively cheap, inconspicuous – it doesn't look like a microphone – and records well. Good-quality 90-minute tapes and fresh batteries may also contribute. We suggest trying out your recording equipment with colleagues or friends beforehand. Recording colleagues as clients and being recorded by them with you as a

This chapter was first published as 'Some guidelines on the use of audio-tape recordings in counsellor education and training', in *Counselling, Journal of the British Association for Counselling*, vol. 5, no. 3, pp. 213–14 (1994).

client during supervised counsellor training, is an essential prerequisite of recording 'real' clients.

2   The most appropriate time to introduce the idea of tape recording to your client will vary. We suggest that, when you have chosen a time and have the equipment available and visible in the room, you may wish to assure your client that the tape recorder is off and actually demonstrate this by, for example, disconnecting the lead. Then the next step is to explain the purpose for which the recording will be used, who may listen to it with you (possibly including several people in a supervision group), where and how long it will be kept, boundaries of confidentiality and anonymity, and that the tape recording can be stopped at any point during the session.

Moreover, you need to point out that the client can change her or his mind about being taped, and about what happens to what has already been taped, at any point. We believe it can be helpful to *briefly* confirm that the client still agrees to the recording at the end of the session, although an alternative view is that to do so may increase their anxiety.

It is vital to listen very carefully for any doubts or anxiety in the client's response to your request for permission to tape record the session. Clients may say 'Yes, I don't mind but . . .'. Remember Perls' (1988) notion that everything said before a 'but' is bullshit, gently explore the 'but', and do not record if you sense the client has reservations. On the other hand, many clients feel fine about being tape recorded and some are pleased that what you are doing together is important enough for you to want to record it.

It is easy to convey your own unease to your client who may then become ambivalent or refuse for that reason. Many counsellors-in-training feel anxious about tape recording their work. It can feel like a threat to professional identity, skill or personal worth. One approach we have found helpful is to recommend to trainee counsellors that they record every skills training session from the start of the course but contract with themselves not to listen to the first two or three sessions. Then, when the counsellors feel more comfortable having the tape recorder on, they listen to a short section, and explore their feelings and experiences.

A similar procedure can be adopted when using audio-tape recording with colleagues prior to recording your work with clients.

3   Listen to the tape, if possible, within 48 hours of recording; Kagan (1984) has shown as part of his work on Interpersonal Process Recall (IPR) that within this period your emotions, feelings, thoughts, images, etc. in the session are more readily recalled or apparent for the first time. Notice what happens to you as you listen, what attracts your attention, where you get bored, anxious or critical of yourself and so on. The emphasis here is on you in the relationship with your client: what was going on within you? What thoughts/feelings/physical sensations, etc? What may have been going on within the client? What may have been going on between you and the client? (See the entries on supervision (p. 145) and IPR (p. 82) in Bayne et al., 1994).

4   Decide whether to listen through the whole tape or to a particular section, e.g. the first five minutes, the end, or any critical episodes or turning points.

471

5 Select an element to focus on, for example:
- Micro-skills analysis. What was your intention in saying what you said or did not say? What were you trying to achieve? What was the impact of the intervention? Did it achieve what you wanted? How useful was it? Which interventions did the client take up and develop? Which interventions were lost or ignored? What alternative or more effective interventions could you have used? Can you identify any other options?
- Frequency and style of interventions, e.g. silence, summaries.
- Significant words, emotions, feelings or meanings which you failed to hear at the time or did not respond to, e.g. the client's or your use of 'should', or the client's fervent expression of hate.
- Non-verbal information, e.g. changes in voice quality, laughing, sighing.
- Themes or patterns: contradictions in what the client says, or discrepancies, blind spots, conflicts, distortions, evasions, failure to own problems, etc. which you did not hear at the time (Egan, 1990). Consider whether it would have been appropriate to explore more deeply, or challenge, or hold as silent hypotheses.

6 Make notes on, or draw diagrams about, your reflections and what you have learned, but remember not to identify the client in writing, and to keep the notes, as well as of course the tape, in a safe place (Bond, 1993, Chapter 12).

7 Consider playing part of the tape with your supervisor or supervision group (see the entry on Supervision in Bayne et al., 1994).

Some ethical issues and suggestions

1 Work within the BAC Code of Ethics and Practice for Counsellors, paying particular attention (as far as practicable) to confidentiality and client anonymity (Bond, 1993, Chapter 9).

   We suggest writing on the tape label:
   - Date and number of session.
   - Your name or initials and client's initials or code letter or number.
   - Restrictions on who can listen to it.
   - Date to remove/destroy recording.

2 Check that you understand and strictly adhere to any agency or organizational policy or guidelines on using audio-tape recording. This will mean you cannot tape record your counselling in some agency settings.

3 Obtain your client's freely given and informed consent before tape recording. 'Informed consent' means that the client understands and accepts the purpose for which the recording will be used. 'Freely' means that the client has no reservations and has not been coerced in any way. Some clients conceal their objections in order to please, but we believe the counsellor's responsibility is to be clear and not to make decisions for the client.

4 Ownership of the tape is a difficult issue. Unless you are recording primarily for your clients and you have asked them to bring their own tape for that purpose, we take the view that the actual cassette tape belongs to you, but that

the content of the tape 'belongs' to the clients, both their words and the interventions you offer. Perhaps this point is more clearly expressed the other way round: the content of the audio tape does *not* belong to you, for you to use for your own purposes outside your working relationship with the client – unless of course, you have obtained the client's explicit permission to do so.

5 You may invite your client to listen to the tape – some clients find this very useful and welcome the opportunity – or your client may ask to do so. We recommend discussing this in detail, e.g. where, when, will anyone else hear the tape, possible reactions and outcomes, your concerns and fears, and where the tape will be kept. The desirable balance is between overconcern and a proper and ethical respect for the well-being of everyone involved (Bond, 1993, Chapter 10).

References

Bayne, R., Horton, I., Merry, T. and Noyes, E. (1994) *The Counsellor's Handbook*. London: Chapman and Hall.

Bond, T. (1993) *Standards and Ethics for Counselling in Action*. London: Sage.

Dryden, W. (1983) 'Supervision of audio-tapes in counselling: obstacles to trainee learning', *The Counsellor*, 3(8): 18–25.

Dryden, W. and Feltham, C. (1992) *Brief Counselling*. Buckingham: Open University Press.

Egan, G. (1990) *The Skilled Helper*, 4th edn. Monterey, CA: Brooks/Cole.

Jacobs, M. (1993) 'The use of audio tapes in counselling', in W. Dryden (ed.), *Questions and Answers on Counselling in Action*. London: Sage.

Kagan, N. (1984) 'Interpersonal process recall: basic methods and recent research', in D. Larsen (ed.), *Teaching Psychological Skills*. Monterey, CA: Brooks/Cole.

Perls, F.S. (1988) *Gestalt Therapy Verbatim*. New York: The Centre for Gestalt Development.

Discussion issues

1 What do you feel about the idea of tape recording some of your counselling sessions?

2 How do you respond to Dryden's (1983) assertion that counsellors 'overconcern' for clients has more to do with their own anxiety?

3 How would you explain to a client the purpose of making a tape recording? What would you actually say?

4 What do you think are the most important professional and ethical issues in tape recording counselling sessions?

60

Paperless Client Records

Peter Ross

In December 1989 the Research Committee of the Association for Student Counselling took a decision to investigate ways in which client records might be computerized. We were aware that some counselling services had been using a computer to produce figures for many years. Other services were just beginning to consider the matter. An unspoken assumption was that we could do sufficient preliminary research to come up with some recommendations for those new to the area. We hope that what follows will be a helpful point of departure, not only for those involved in student counselling but for those involved in other areas of counselling as well.

A case of necessity

Most counselling services do not need to computerize client records and never will. Size is the critical factor. A brief look at our experience at the Reading University Counselling Service may be helpful. For some years we had been aware of spending an inordinate amount of time extracting figures from our manual record system and of doing it less well that we would have liked. Numbers rose rapidly and resources decreased and we found ourselves under continuous pressure to reduce costs by improving efficiency. We see staff as well as students and we now have a catchment population of about 12,000, a full-time student population of about 8,600, and large numbers of part-time students. We will see about 450 individual clients this year and all the numbers are rising rapidly. Our experience suggests that when numbers get to about 400 clients served by three or more counsellors on several sites, it is definitely time to think about getting a computer. In December 1989, no one on our staff had ever touched a computer. Fear of the unknown would be too mild a description – terror was more like it. Yet now we're enthusiasts.

It was a happy coincidence that work for the ASC Research Committee and practical developments at Reading coincided. So it is possible to write this not just from theory, but informed by 'nitty gritty practice'.

Information for what?

Whether one has a filing cabinet or a computer it is important to be clear about what information needs to be collected. Why keep records at all? Those who spend

This chapter was first published as 'Computer databases: towards paperless client records', in *Counselling, Journal of the British Association for Counselling*, vol. 2, no. 4, pp. 137–9 (1991).

public money should be accountable for it. At the very least one ought to be able to produce an annual report, outlining the range of activities undertaken. However, the larger a counselling service, the greater the need for management information. At its most simple, this is the question of who is doing what . . . and where! Management information can also reveal whether a particular group of clients – say, overseas women – are attending the service in a proportion commensurate with the raw population. Within a university one academic department might provide clients out of all proportion to raw numbers; the organization ought to be aware of this. To plan for the future, it is first necessary to know exactly what one is doing right now. In recent years the ASC, other counselling bodies and numerous researchers have showered counselling services with requests for information on activities. Without this information no comparisons or attempts to identify 'best practice' can be made. Records also need to be kept to note a client's progress of lack of it, the number of 'no show' appointments and so on. With small numbers one can remember all this, but as numbers increase there is no possibility of doing so. Records are necessary to protect counsellors in case of client complaint or legal redress, as well as for research purposes, especially on process and outcome.

'Generations' of development

Three generations of computer development can be identified. In the first a service will tidy up manual records and enter information in bulk on to a computer at the end of a term or year. The computer then processes the information as asked and it becomes relatively easy to produce annual reports and even some management information. The computer is usually a mainframe and the service has relatively little control over the process. The software package is usually a statistical one. This means the questions which can be easily asked of it have to be pretty straightforward. Corless et al. (1984) give an overview of this stage of development. The University Counselling Services at Nottingham, Lancaster, Cambridge and Ulster have been pioneers in this respect. While a great improvement on manual records, the outcome is fairly rigid compared to the next generation. For the technically minded, Nottingham uses SPSSX (Statistical Package for the Social Sciences) on the ICL VME system. Lancaster have recently moved away from a mainframe system to using their own PC – an Opus PCV. They now employ an INGRES database rather than a statistical package. Cambridge have also just moved from mainframe to a PC within their own department – and IBM PS2 – and use an SPSS-PC with data entry feature.

A second-generation system is characterized by switching from a statistical package to a relational database, on an in-house PC, as at Lancaster. At Reading we had no experience of the first generation. We just plunged straight into a second-generation IBM Compatible system. We use a Victor V386A with 50mB hard disc, 50mB Add-Pak for easy backup and DataEase software. At present we put the facts on to the computer on a daily or weekly basis when we have a moment, but do not (yet) write in textual descriptions of our counselling. We keep this in parallel manual files. The database provides a text entry facility should we choose to use it. Some day, probably much in the future, we might just have sufficient confidence and courage to enter text immediately after seeing each client. We could then throw away all the paper records, so entering the third-generation phase. This would be at no extra capital cost and would reduce our running costs yet further.

Reading University is currently (April 1996) working on scanning documents into the computer (known as 'imaging technology') so bringing the paperless office ever closer! A scanner adds about £300 to the cost of a PC.

Costs

It is almost impossible to cost mainframe systems as the allocation of overheads requires an accountant to do some rather subtle juggling. Costing PC systems in much easier. The Reading basic system cost £1,700 (+ VAT) for the Victor – but the current cost is about £700. The Add-Pak which slips into a neat compartment in the front of the machine, making it much easier to use and back up, costs an extra £360 (+ VAT). Software prices vary widely, with high-quality databases costing from about £400 to £700 retail. Our DataEase package cost £40. Both PC and software prices quoted are very reduced prices for educational use only. New databases enter the market at a rapid pace. They sell by introducing new but often marginal features. DataEase is a product at the most sophisticated end of the market and at £40 had to be cost-effective. Data from it can be easily imported into or from other Databases should one change one's mind at a later date. DataEase is so versatile that not only does it easily run our medium-sized record system but also that of many Universities in the USA, even as big as Stanford. It is used widely in industry for stock control and sales and marketing applications. In addition, GP practices use it for patient records – for example, the Reading University medical practice. Although it is possible to find more sophisticated databases, it would be difficult to fault DataEase for overall cost-effectiveness for our purpose. The one fault it does have for our purposes is a very marginal one. Should one choose to go paperless, text entry has to take place in 'paragraphs' or blocks which means one cannot write very long text without an occasional line break.

However, line breaks could be an advantage in promoting clarity of thought. A counsellor would probably with to use frequent headings within Text, such as: hypotheses, formulation, process, homework, etc. These all count as both line breaks and 'field' boundaries – a 'field' being a unit of information the database can manipulate. Consequently it is possible to pick out a word within these boundaries and ask the database to report on how often the word, or combination of words, occurs across all records. This facility would be useful to counselling process researchers.

The only other cost one might incur is for a printer. These vary from about £200 for a dot matrix draft-quality printer, to vast sums of money for laser printers which produce perfect commercial-quality output. Most college counselling services will get along quite well with a dot matrix printer for most of the time. Most college computer centres provide laser printers for staff to bring a floppy disk along and produce their own high-quality output. The compromise solution is to consider the Hewlett Packard 500 – a bubble jet printer which costs about £130 (+ VAT). This gives as high a quality output as most people and services are ever likely to need.

The current (April 1996) most sensible buy to allow for flexibility and extension would cost about £1,300 (including VAT) but be ten times more powerful than the system described above and far easier to use. This would consist of a 486 processor with 8 mb RAM and 560 Mb hard disk complete with CR ROM drive. The software included in the price is more than adequate, being a Windows 95 operating system with Microsoft Office – an integrated suite of wordprocessor (Word for Windows), database (Access) and spreadsheet (Excel).

Database applications

A sophisticated relational database such as DataEase comes on a set of three floppy disks which are then installed on the computer hard disk. In essence, this gives a set of principles. It is now necessary to tailor the principles for a specific application, in this case the client record system. This is known as application programming. This is also where the fun starts.

Should one begin as an experienced computer user it would no doubt be possible to develop the application quickly. We had to begin by wading through four large instruction manuals and then experimenting on screen. Our greatest difficulty however was trying to decide exactly what we wanted out of the system. How easy or difficult it would be to put in and extract information would be a direct function of how we designed the system. We spent much of the summer of 1990 trying out different ideas and then scrapping them. Giving birth was exciting, frustrating, and occasionally downright painful when neither we nor an adviser could solve a problem. To cut a long story short, we designed our way out of the problems and went 'live' on 1 October 1990. We have refined it here and there since and have further minor changes in mind. However, we are delighted with our new system and find it so easy and quick to use that we do not even involve secretaries.

A new client records system

We have given the computer two screens and each screen is a 'form' to be filled in. The first screen we call Client Data and the second Consultations. Our clients register by filling in a paper form. It gives name, address, who referred, academic position, academic department, etc. This form provides us with everything we need for our Client Data screen. The computer cursor moves from one section of the screen to another, asking for the appropriate information. We have so designed it that no typing is required apart from name and some of the address. For the rest, the computer gives the counsellor 'choice fields'. For example, the computer asks: Who referred the client? Across the top of the screen appears all possible answers: 1 Self, 2 Doctor, 3 Tutor and so on. All the counsellor has to do is key in the number and the computer writes the word 'self' or 'doctor' on the screen.

The second screen form – Consultations – allows no typing at all, apart from filling in the date. All the rest is either filled in automatically by the computer (e.g. client number) or is again a choice field. The main choice fields cover which counsellor has seen the client, at which location, whether it was a routine appointment or an emergency and whether we referred on or involved anybody else. In addition the screen asks for the presenting problem (as defined by the client), diagnosed problem (3 allowed, as defined by the counsellor); working problem and time spent with client.

The consultation screen is designed to make it easy to enter each consultation as it takes place, but even easier to bulk enter say a dozen consultations for a particular client at the end of a term. This is because one can fill in a screen form for the first consultation, enter it in to the computer's memory and then change only, say, date and session number to re-enter all subsequent sessions. One does not have to 'clear' a screen and start again for each entry.

The screens are linked by the computer-generated client number so enquiries can be made of both at the same time. The screens are also so designed that entry of a number will provoke the computer to write on the screen the corresponding problem category. For example: 125 'Suicide – thoughts of' *or* 126 'Suicide – attempt'.

This may seem complex but with only a few hours' practice each counsellor took only 3 minutes to enter both screens. The examples show what we think is important information. One can easily increase or decrease the number of fields on the screen forms and hence increase or decrease entry/retrieval time at will. The beauty of the system is the virtual elimination of typing with choice fields ensuring accuracy. If one adds a document scanner life is even more simple.

Diagnostic categories

It is difficult to draw up a list of diagnostic categories. The most glaring difficulty is that different theoretical orientations can persuade one to see problems in a very different light. A second problem is that a typical young persons' counselling service sees large numbers of developmental problems rather than clinical ones. There is even less agreement among experts on how to categorize developmental problems than there is on how to categorize clinical ones. A third problem is that a counselling service of any size will have to face the necessity of getting all its counsellors to agree definitions so that when counsellor A records a client as 'mild reactive depression' and counsellor B records the same for a different client a month later, they mean the same thing. If they do not, the computer will be producing very hollow information.

A first reaction to these problems would obviously be to go to the literature for help, to see what other people are doing. Traditional British and American categories – devised over many years by psychiatrists in clinical practice – are so pathologically orientated as to be useless for a college counselling service. However a relatively new system, the Diagnostic and Statistical Manual of the American Psychiatric Association (universally known as DSM III-R) has some clinical and developmental material which initially seems helpful. It lists a label like 'panic disorder' and specifies that, for example, 8 out of a list of 12 possible features must be present to justify the label.

The University of Massachusetts Counselling Service tried this out in 1982 and it was judged not entirely appropriate due to the lack of adequate developmental categories. The system was amended by Hoffman and Weiss (1986) who produced an Inventory of Common Problems for college counselling services together with reliability and validity data. They also produced means and standard deviations for a large random sample of American college students. This system has been further amended by individual American college counselling services to suit their own local circumstances. The staff of the counselling service at Stanford University was kind enough to send us a recent paper (Martinez et al., 1990) which specified their own adaptation. This separates problems into developmental, environmental and clinical disorders. To give some idea of the content: 'Developmental' covers relationships, intrapersonal, transitions, sexuality and academic concerns; 'Environmental' covers housing, legal, childcare, abuse, and authority conflicts; 'Clinical Disorders' covers the obvious. We have adapted the system for our own use.

Last year we made a brief regional survey of diagnostic categories used in college counselling services. The result revealed a range from 6 to 42 items. The Reading University manual system used 27. Our new computerized system gives us 3 sections (as previously quoted) which break down to 19 groups (for example: depression) which break down to 144 individual codes. Although very simple to use, it remains to be seen how useful this is. An end-of-year assessment of both range and frequency of use of individual codes will shape modification. The Research Committee of the ASC has continued to work on the problem and is now (April 1996) field trialling a new generation system for university counselling services.

Asking questions of the computer

The beauty of a fully relational database is that the computer can relate every bit of information to every other bit. Simple questions can be asked; for example – How many clients have been seen? How many clients were seen by each counsellor at location x? More complex questions can also be asked: How many clients has each counsellor seen between dates (a) and (b) who were between the ages of (x) and (y), who came from the EEC, and whose initial presenting problem was stress? The question could be repeated with the last clause to read 'and whose diagnosed problem was stress?' or even 'and who discussed stress at any one consultation'. The combinations are endless, determined only by the information which one chooses to input during screen design. The DataEase program will, of course, do straightforward calculations.

However, asking unique questions takes time. A counselling service will normally have a requirement for asking a lot of routine questions: exactly the same questions, year after year for an annual report, for example. DataEase permits you to set up a 'report Menu' on screen. This means you need to work out for the computer only once exactly what files and parameters should be searched for your question. These are memorized by the computer under a menu heading. Subsequently you can ask the same question by just tapping in the number corresponding to the routine question.

Speed of response is determined by total memory and how the computer is asked to memorize particular items. However, the Victor system specified earlier will initially give answers on screen as quickly as questions can be asked, but may take up to 4 minutes to give an answer to a complex question when the files of several years have to be searched. Output speed to printer is determined by the quality of the printer.

Computer security

Most counselling services keep records in filing cabinets. They are fairly easy to break into if one is really determined. Computer files are guarded by normal building security and in addition passwords are required to enter the system. With DataEase, each counsellor can have a personal password for all files, for only their own files or for combinations at different specified levels of security. The passwords are scrambled in the computer's memory so even a 'break in' will not reveal them. It would be naive however to think that any system was totally secure.

Any university with a computer science department is producing students quite possibly capable of hacking into systems much more complex than those of a university central administration. Counsellors are therefore urged to think not just twice but a dozen times before abandoning a stand-alone counselling computer for a link to a university central administration one. Important ethical issues are of course involved, but there is a legal duty to care by ensuring 'reasonable' steps to maintain confidentiality. The standard which is judged 'reasonable' is likely to rise as general knowledge of computer systems arises.

Everyone who holds personal information on others within a computer database has to register under the Data Protection Act. Clients are entitled to see any information which is kept on them, but not that which is kept on anybody else. They can view it either on screen or in printout form.

Conclusions

Computer hardware and software is expensive, though prices are dropping all the time. Prices for both hardware and software are greatly reduced for educational use. Any counselling service in an educational setting should seek the advice of the 'educational sales' department of each manufacturer or take the advice of its computer centre which may have concluded special deals with suppliers on behalf of the institution. For this reason, no specific recommendations would be sensible with regard to equipment. However, a rough idea can be gained from the preceding text.

With regard to software, we can recommend without reservation a *fully relational* database. There are many on the market and each institution will have a favourite. Local expertise is invaluable as when the database has to be tailored for specific applications problems can arise. Each relational database has strengths and weaknesses ('selling points') which should be fully understood before purchase for a specific purpose.

This was intended as an *interim* report on the situation with regard to the known use of computer databases within ASC-associated counselling services.

By the 1993–4 academic year, 50% of the 'old' universities and 30% of the 'new' universities were using computers to track the work of their counselling services (ASC, 1995). Although most of the hardware is IBM-based and software Windows-based, no universal package has emerged. This may be possible when a long-term project, to devise ways of recording client problems, has been completed by the ASC Research Committee. This may well not be until 1998.

References

Association for Student Counselling (1995) *Survey of Student Counselling Services in Further and Higher Education 1993–4*. ASC Research Sub-Committee (limited circulation). Rugby: BAC.

Corless et al. (1994) 'The use of computerised records in a university student counselling service', *Counselling*, no. 49.

Hersh, J.B., Nazario, N.S. and Backus, D.A. (1983) 'DSM III and the College Mental Health Setting: the University of Massachusetts experience', *Journal of American College Health*, 31: 247–52.

Hoffman, J.A. and Weiss, B.A. (1986) 'New system for conceptualizing college students' problems: types and crises and the inventory of common problems', *Journal of American College Health*, 34: 259–66.

Martinez, A.M., Daher, D. and D'Andrea, V.J. (1990) 'Multilevel approaches to the evaluation of psychological services at university settings'. Cowell Student Health Centre, Stanford University (personal communication).

Acknowledgements

This article could not have been written without information and encouragement from numerous members of the ASC. In particular we would like to thank:

Isobel Derricourt and John Elder	Lancaster University Counselling Service
Liz Gleed	Cambridge University Counselling Service
Helen Henry	Nottingham University Counselling Service
Chris Hodgkinson	University of Ulster Counselling Service
Charlotte Siegel	Stanford University Counselling Service
Annette McGee	Dublin City University Counselling Service

They bear no responsibility for the finished product however.

Help

Information and advice can be obtained from Peter Ross, University Health Centre, 9 Northcourt Avenue, Reading RG2 7HE. Reading (01734) 874551.

He very much welcomes comments on the above and information on other systems.

Discussion issues

1 What is your view about the use of computer databases for keeping records?
2 What possible risk could there be in keeping computerized records?
3 What are the advantages of computerized records?
4 How do you think the use of computers might develop in the future?

61

What Happens if a Psychotherapist Dies?

Barbara Traynor and Petrūska Clarkson

The role of the psychotherapeutic executor

This chapter is intended for counsellors and psychotherapists, and concerns the ethics and practicalities involved in appointing a psychotherapeutic executor in the event of death, illness or becoming incompetent to practise. It explores our responsibilities towards ourselves and our clients in these circumstances. The original idea came from Petrūska Clarkson and is included in the Code of Professional Practice of Metanoia Psychotherapy Training Institute (1990).

The guidelines and examples given here are not prescriptive. One possible option is offered, which has been found effective. The authors hope to engender discussion in an important and neglected area.

We have examined the Code of Ethics and Practice for Counsellors of the British Association of Counselling (BAC, 1990), the International Transactional Analysis Association Statement of Ethics (ITAA, 1989) and the Code of Ethics of the Gestalt Psychotherapy Training Institute in the United Kingdom (GPTI, 1990). We think the ideas we express are implicit in the above codes but believe they should be made explicit.

There are four types of psychotherapist/client endings:

1 Client's planned termination
2 Client's unplanned termination
3 Psychotherapist's planned termination
4 Psychotherapist's unplanned termination

Ideally we can take time to discuss and prepare for termination, preferably when both client and psychotherapist are agreed (1). As psychotherapists, we sometimes have to deal with clients who terminate suddenly, or when we consider the time is not right in view of the presenting problems (2). When we are responsible for the termination, for example for a pregnancy or a move, we can plan withdrawal (3). However, whilst much is written about the first three examples, less is written about the last and that is the focus of this article.

The implications of our long-term responsibilities to our clients are complex. They may ask, 'What happens to me if anything happens to you?' A more suspicious client may be concerned about what happens to their notes. I, Barbara Traynor, have found that they are relieved that I have considered this eventuality, thereby acknowledging that I have a commitment to them that extends beyond the immediate.

This chapter was first published in *Counselling, Journal of the British Association for Counselling*, vol. 3, no. 1, pp. 23–4 (1992).

Most psychotherapy books or texts assume that the practitioner is always alive and well. But psychotherapy is a profession practised by a large number of older people. There are few young psychotherapists, and often people work beyond the statutory retirement age. It is therefore essential to plan for how the client is to deal with termination if for some reason the psychotherapist is no longer available.

In the event of the psychotherapist's unplanned termination of contract, there is a caretaking responsibility. Clients are precious human beings who entrust themselves to our care and may be in various stages of vulnerability. They confide in us, and their records and psychological processes should be safeguarded. It is appropriate professional practice to take responsibility for the client in these circumstances, and to ensure that arrangements are made that are mindful of their continuing psychological journey, and which protect confidentiality.

In a group practice, fellow psychotherapists can provide support, arrange referrals, etc. but we suggest that, no matter how small the practice, all counsellors and psychotherapists should write a 'Letter of Direction' to accompany their current legal will which includes instructions for the termination of their practice and appropriate care for clients, and inform their executors of the contents.

The appropriateness of informing the client about this arrangement and whether or not it is discussed, depends upon the individual client. For example, someone whose parents died when they were young may have problems making a therapeutic alliance. If they are concentrating on early issues, it may be important to bring this into focus. Another client might ask directly about it. Equally, if you have reason to believe that a client has deep-rooted or out-of-awareness fears about the death of another person it might be appropriate to discuss the issue. The act of making a will has to do with facing up to one's own death and dispensability. It is particularly important for psychotherapists to do this so that they can help clients to deal with issues of death, dying and mortality. In order to be able to leave, I need to ensure my affairs are in order. By bringing this into focus for the client, the therapist is, amongst other things, modelling self-support.

It would be preferable to choose as psychotherapeutic executor a fellow practitioner, someone who is not so close as to be emotionally bereft at one's loss but close enough to be familiar with one's way of working and sympathetic to the idiosyncrasies of the filing system. There is a considerable amount of work involved in the execution of these duties so it is important that a proviso for the psychotherapeutic executor to claim expenses from the estate is written into the letter of direction.

Practicalities

Outlined below are some of the issues I (B.T.) have covered.

1 Instructions to ensure that my psychotherapeutic executor and the two executors of my estate will contact each other.
2 Instructions about gaining access to my flat, study and records.

3   Information about where my files are kept.

My practice file contains names, addresses, phone numbers and GP details of my current clients. At the front of the file I have written a detailed explanation of the key. I have used coloured stickers to denote who is in my various groups, who is in training and in what discipline (e.g. Gestalt, TA or counselling) and who is seeing me for supervision. In this way I have ensured that clients can be referred appropriately.

Some clients have given me personal letters and material to 'hold' for them. Those are kept separately and clearly marked as they may wish to reclaim their property.

In order to ensure confidentiality, when a client leaves my practice I go through their notes, removing their names and material which will obviously identify them. I keep their notes in a plastic numbered envelope. A card index system is kept separately, so that I may relocate their notes should they return to my practice.

4   Instructions to the executor to destroy all past and current client notes and references. I give details of where my tapes are stored and instructions to wipe them all and retain them for use in the executor's practice.

5   Instructions as to disposal of photocopied material, articles, journals, books on child development, health, philosophy, psychology, psychotherapy and notes from workshops I have attended. Instructions to keep any books, notes, stationary for the executor's practice as she deems useful. Otherwise to offer them for sale as a charitable contribution to training bursaries.

6   Instructions to send my accounts, petty cash receipts, vouchers, etc. to my accountant for auditing; I give details of where they are filed.

7   An outlined procedure for the aftercare of my clients includes:
   • ringing all clients as soon as possible;
   • arranging for facilitator to take my groups and, where appropriate, to do bereavement work;
   • arranging for a facilitator to see individual clients and continue in bereavement process with them until they have either transferred or terminated, so that the transition can be appropriately dealt with.

Ethics

BAC stress the counsellor's responsibility for maintaining confidentiality includes personal information . . . 'which may result in identification of the client' (1990: B4.2, p. 7). GPTI's code of ethics states that 'All exchanges between client and Gestalt psychotherapist must be regarded as confidential' (1990: 2, p. 5). BAC requires that the counsellor 'should not counsel when their functioning is impaired due to personal or emotional difficulties, illness, disability, alcohol, drugs or for any other reason' (1990: 2.2.18, p. 5). GPTI states that 'The welfare of the individual client must be the therapist's first concern' (1990: 1, p. 5). ITAA combines a relevant statement on confidentiality and professional responsibility:

However, certain professional responsibilities continue beyond the termination of the contract. They include, but are not limited to, the following: (a) maintenance of agreed-upon confidentiality; (b) avoidance of any exploitation of the former relationship; (c) provision for any needed follow-up care. (1989: 8, p. 78)

They further state that:

If members of the ITAA become aware that personal conflicts or medical problems might interfere with their ability to carry out a contractual relationship, they must either terminate the contract in a professionally responsible manner, or ensure that the client has the full information needed to make a decision about remaining in the contractual relationship. (1989: 11, p. 78)

Although none of these ethical codes deals specifically with the issue of the psychotherapist's unplanned termination, it seems to us that this article reflects the spirit of their humanistic existential philosophy and follows good counselling and psychotherapy practice.

We look forward with interest to hearing the opinions of our colleagues.

References

British Association of Counselling (1990) *Code of Ethics and Practice for Counsellors.* Rugby: BAC.

Gestalt Psychotherapy Training Institute in the United Kingdom (1990) *Code of Ethics.* London: GPTI. p. 5.

International Transactional Analysis Association (1989) *Statement of Ethics.* USA: ITAA.

Metanoia Psychotherapy Training Institute (1990) *Code of Ethics and Professional Practice.* London: MPTI. p. 2.

Discussion issues

1 What would happen to your clients if something happened to you at this moment which precluded you working or making any necessary arrangements?

2 How do you imagine individual clients would react if you were to die?

3 If you were to die without having left adequate provision for clients to be contacted and referred appropriately, might this present a specific negative repetitive experience for any of your clients?

4 It has been said that record keeping from a liability perspective is a compilation of evidence of the adequacy of care a patient has received. Do your records reflect the quality of your work and would this be evident to a reader?

62

Empathy – Examination of a Crucial Concept

Chris Scott

Empathy – a confused concept

Historians of behavioural science might wish to debate the origins of empathy; an examination of the history and development of the concept can be found in Hunsdahl (1967). The earliest therapeutic use of the term seems to be by Rogers in his now classical paper (1957) where empathy was one of the 'necessary and sufficient conditions for personality change'. The issue of empathy as one of six *necessary and sufficient* conditions for positive personality change, coupled with his definition of empathy as being able to 'perceive the internal frame of reference of another with accuracy, and with the emotional components and meanings which pertain thereto, as if one were the other person, but without ever losing the "as if" condition' (Rogers, 1959, p. 210) has provided the basis for much subsequent theory, research and application in the counselling and psychotherapy field. Today, 27 years since Rogers' seminal paper, empathy is still one of the most commonly occurring concepts in the counselling literature. In that time, however, it is a concept that has been defined and redefined and undergone considerable change. Even before the end of the 1970s Hackney (1969) could document 21 definitions of empathy, some of which marked a radical departure from Rogers' definition. All this would be no more than a terminological quibble were it not of course for the fact that empathy had been identified (at least by Rogers) as crucial to successful therapeutic outcomes. The issue was not so much that it was *necessary* but that it was also considered *sufficient*. The concept had rapidly assumed the central importance of, say, that of 'social class' in sociology and just as the research into the relationship between class and social behaviour often proved at best inconclusive and at worst contradictory, so too was the evidence in respect of the necessity of empathy.

The importance of empathy in therapeutic outcomes had apparently been established by Truax and Carkhuff (1967). Gladstein however, in 1970, in a review of the literature on empathy concluded there was very little evidence to support the belief that empathy facilitated counselling outcomes. In a later review (1977) the same author came to a similar conclusion: 'despite the large number of theory, discussion, case, and process articles describing the positive relationship between empathy and counselling outcome the empirical evidence remains equivocal'.

How then can these disparate research findings be explained? Certainly one reason must be that the conceptual confusion surrounding empathy is such that

This chapter was first published in *Counselling, Journal of the British Association for Counselling,* no. 49, pp. 3–6 (1984).

researchers have not been studying the same phenomena. One fundamental prob-lem, and we can see it in Rogers' original definition of empathy, is that we are trying to measure an internal and unobservable state. Truax (1961), one of the early empathy researchers, tried to resolve this problem by defining empathy as 'sensitivity to current feelings and the verbal facility to communicate this under-standing'. This addition of the communication element in empathy was an elegant sleight of hand for it enabled Truax to work with some observable phenomenon he could measure.

However, whilst Rogers was well aware that the counsellor's empathy, if it were to be effective, had to be communicated to the client, he did not confuse the *state* of empathy with the *process* of its communication. Barrett-Lennard (1981) makes the distinction most dramatically when he suggests that for empathic under-standing to occur 'it would not be essential for the person being empathized with to actually be present'. Hackney (1978) concludes that empathy has undergone an evolutionary process that had altered its meaning and 'moved its locus from a internal state to an external process'. It has been a process fuelled by the growth of behaviourist psychology and the application of natural scientific method. Some-what ruefully, Hackney quotes Thorndike (1918), 'whatever exists at all exists in some amount'. Such a view it seems has underpinned the researcher's search for measures of empathy.

Empathy – confused measures

I have argued so far that much of the confusion surrounding empathy is a result of expanding the concept of empathy to incorporate the notion of empathy as a communication skills, and that this change has been largely prompted by the researcher's desire for quantification. These differing perspectives on empathy, first as the sensitivity of the counsellor to pick up accurately the internal feelings of the client, and secondly the ability to communicate that affective awareness are not the only ones. Another contrast frequently found in the literature is that between *affective* empathy (feeling the same way as another) and *cognitive* empathy (seeing the world as the other does). In many respects there is a close parallel between on the one hand affective empathy and what Rogers originally depicted as the state of empathy; and on the other cognitive empathy and what I call here empathic communication.

Whatever perspective is adopted, however, *measures* of empathy have com-pounded the confusion surrounding the concept largely as a result of focusing attention on the measurement of empathic *communication* at the expense of unobservable empathic experience.

As Feldstein and Gladstein (1980) suggest, most measures of empathy can be labelled as either objective or subjective. By objective they mean external inde-pendent judgements of actual counselling sessions made usually from short inter-view excerpts on video or audio material. Two such frequently used scales are those of Truax and Carkhuff. The observer judges rate on a 5-point (Carkhuff's Empathic Understanding Scale) or 9-point (Truax's Accurate Empathy Scale).

These two scales have met with considerable criticisms. Gladstein (1983) points to the problems of using audio tapes judged by independent raters; the training of the raters; and the inconsistencies between the stated definitions of empathy and actual measures. What we have essentially with both these scales are measures of empathic communication rather than empathic experience. Barrett-Lennard makes a similar point when he refers to several studies that show that 'raters achieve initially the same results when they only hear the statements of the responding or empathizing person as they do when they hear the statements of both people involved'. At the least this seems to suggest that even as a measure of empathic *communication* the scale is heavily dependent on the reflective verbal style and tacit knowledge of the empathizing communication as recognized by the raters; as a measure of empathic *experience* the scales must be seriously called into question. I am reminded here of a fable told by Pollner (1972). He tells of a sociologist from another planet visiting Earth with a research student. The student is to carry out fieldwork on Earth societies. Instead of his own report however he returns with copies of sociology journals, claiming they will tell all. The sociologist reproves his student: 'Can't you see,' he exclaims, 'that these records constitute data for analysis in the same way as do the societies themselves? For both rely on the tacit knowledge of their members and this knowledge defines the reality in ways that we must investigate'.

Conclusion

The importance of empathy in the counselling literature has not diminished over the years despite the considerable confusion surrounding the concept and a wealth of inconclusive data on its relationship to therapeutic outcome. Thus a much respected counsellor trainer, Nelson-Jones (1974), claimed that 'the central skill in the provision of a successful counselling relationship is empathic understanding'. By 1975 Rogers himself was arguing for empathy as not only one of three core conditions for successful therapeutic outcomes (along with congruence and respect) but as the central condition of his counselling approach, empathy as a 'very special way of being'. Refinements of the concept have proliferated; recently Egan (1975) argues for the importance of empathy in counsellor training and defines two types of empathy. His *'primary empathy'* and *'advanced accurate empathy'* parallels the distinction drawn here between Rogers' original definition and empathic communication. So too Carkhuff's (1969) notion of *'additive empathy'* refines the concept but does little to help us recognize it in practice.

What finally may we make of all this conceptual confusion and conflicting data? First, that empathy is a complex phenomenon and we might do better to think in terms of *types* of empathy, as explored in this paper. Secondly, we need to recognize clearly the *processual* nature of empathy and think in terms of relating types of empathy at different points in time in the counselling process (Barrett-Lennard's (1981) cyclical model is useful here). Thirdly, we must heed Hackney's warning (1969) and not assume that someone highly capable of empathic experience can necessarily communicate that experience to a helpee. More importantly perhaps, given the current emphasis on communicative skills training, we must beware of the possibility that someone with highly developed communicative skills may nevertheless 'lack even the most elemental sensitivities on which empathy is built' (Hackney, 1978, p. 38).

Finally, and this is a point addressed primarily to counsellor researchers, we need to recognize the fact that the nature of empathy does not easily lend itself to study by traditional scientific method. We need to look to more phenomenological, even ethnomethodological techniques for a guide here (*see* for example Garfinkel, 1967; Garfinkel and Sacks, 1970), otherwise problems and definitions simply pass one another by. To let Hackney have the last word, 'the use of Likert scales and other communication strategies to demonstrate the "product" (levels of empathy) is like using counting techniques to measure the level of love between two people. Such strategies simply miss the point.'

References

Barrett-Lennard, G.T. (1981) *Journal of Counselling Psychology*, 28: 91–100.

Carkhuff, R.R. (1969) *Helping and Human Relations*, vols 1, 2. New York: Holt, Rinehart and Winston.

Egan, G. (1975) *The Skilled Helper*. Monterey, CA: Brooks/Cole.

Feldstein, J.C. and Gladstein, G.A. (1980) *Measurement and Evaluation in Guidance*, 13: 49–57.

Garfinkel, H. (1967) *Studies in Ethnomethodology*. Englewood Cliffs, NJ: Prentice Hall.

Garfinkel, H. and Sacks, H. (1970) 'On formal structures of practical actions', in J. McKinney and E. Tiryakian (eds), *Theoretical Sociology*. New York: Appleton Century Crofts. pp. 337–66.

Gladstein, G.A. (1977) *Counselling Psychologist*, 6(4): 70–9.

Gladstein, G.A. (1983) 'Understanding empathy', *Journal of Counselling Psychology*, 30(4): 467–82.

Hackney, H.L. (1969) 'Construct reduction of counsellor empathy and positive regard'. Unpublished doctoral dissertation, University of Massachusetts.

Hackney, H.L. (1978) 'The evolution of empathy', *Personnel and Guidance Journal*, 57: 35–8.

Hunsdahl, J.B. (1967) 'Concerning Einfühlng', *Journal of the History of the Behavioural Sciences*, 3: 180–91.

Nelson-Jones, R. (1974) 'Some thoughts on counsellor training', *British Journal of Guidance on Counselling*, 2(2), reprinted in A.W. Bolger (1982) *Counselling in Britain – A reader*. London: Batsford.

Pollner, M. (1972) 'On the foundations of mundane reasoning'. Unpublished PhD dissertation, Santa Barbara. Quoted in Filmer, P. et al. (1972) *New Directions in Sociological Theory*.

Rogers, C.R. (1957) *Journal of Consulting Psychology*, 21: 95–103.

Rogers, C.R. (1959) in S. Koch (ed.), *Psychology: a Study of a Science*. New York: McGraw Hill. pp. 184–256.

Rogers, C.R. (1975) 'Empathic: an unappreciated way of being'. *Counselling Psychologist*, 21: 95–103.

Thorndike, E.L. (1918) in *Seventeenth Year Book of the National Society for the Study of Education*, part II, ch. 2.

Truax, C.B. (1961) 'A scale for the measurement of accurate empathy', *Psychiatric Institute Bulletin*, University of Wisconsin, 1(12).

Truax, C.B. and Carkhuff, R.R. (1967) *Toward Effective Counselling and Psychotherapy*. Chicago: Aldine.

Discussion issues

1 What is the difference between empathy and sympathy?
2 How would your client know that you are being empathic?
3 Are there any dangers of the use of empathy?
4 Can empathy be broken down into counselling competencies?

63

Transference and Counter-transference

Fergus Cairns

I have recently completed a diploma in counselling and supervision. The course was firmly in the humanistic tradition, operating on student-directed lines and was designed primarily for people such as youth workers or nurses who might use counselling as part of their work, but would tend to be using it in a short-term or *ad hoc* way.

I knew that clients could be resistant but I attributed resistance, in brief counselling at least, solely to a very rational distrust in the client. Clients had a right to draw their own boundaries and would take a considered if not necessarily dispassionate decision on which issues to look at and how deeply to go into them with any particular counsellor. The clients' resistance was their way of saying, 'This far and no further'.

Transference, as far as I understood it, was a special kind of resistance where, by idealizing or demonizing the counsellor as an all-wise or wicked parent, the client evaded the reality of the counselling relationship and the changes they wanted to make. I thought this was likely to be a problem only in in-depth psychotherapy where regression occurred. I was into problem-solving, not delving into the unconscious. Discussion with other students revealed that they too seemed to regard transference as a difficult phenomenon which trainee counsellors should steer clear of and leave to the psychoanalysts. There seemed to be a resistance to understanding the idea at all – 'What's being transferred? From where? To whom?' This started to intrigue me. I wanted to get this transference thing clear.

As for counter-transference, surely this was simpler. I knew counsellors could be angered, shocked, bored, seduced by clients, and I realized this could clash with maintaining unconditional positive regard. Such responses however could be 'neutralized' directly by rigorous self-knowledge. The more I looked at counter-transference, however, the more fuzzy it became, until it seemed to split into two totally opposite phenomena.

In an attempt to clarity my understanding, I decided to write about transference and counter-transference for a course assignment. This chapter is an edited version of my guide to transference and counter-transference for beginners, by a beginner.

Transference

Transference: the unconscious repeating of an earlier relationship in a current setting. It is strictly defined for psychoanalysis, where a transference edition of the original childhood

This chapter was first published as 'A beginner's guide to transference and counter-transference within counselling', in *Counselling, Journal of the British Association for Counselling*, vol. 5, no. 4, pp. 299–301 (1994).

neurosis is developed towards the therapist and overcome. But it applies in any thera-peutic setting – indeed any kind of setting where a difference in power is an issue. (Kovel, 1976, p. 341)

It seems that some of the resistance to looking at transference arises because, as originally used by Freud, it appears a one-sided notion, capable of abuse, and of perpetuating a view of the client as 'sick'. A client may be justly upset by prejudiced, ignorant or abusive treatment by his/her counsellor. It is only too easy for the counsellor to cling to a position of authority and put these feelings down to transference. 'I'm not racist/abusive' (they may say), 'it is you who interpret every intervention of mine as such because you view me as any white man/the father who abused you. Your view of me is part of your resistance.'

Kovel (1976), however, suggests that occurs in any relationship where power is involved. A power difference is *inevitably* part of a relationship that includes challenge, reframing, holding.

An alternative viewpoint is to see transference as a tool, a method of looking at any human relationship. It is an analysis of the way we unconsciously give, demand or withhold power from each other.

Transference – the client reacting to the counsellor

It is easier to explain transference by looking at it working in practice with an example from my own experience as a client.

I have had a bad week. I feel 'stuck' and have wasted my time by indulging in an addictive behaviour which I want to stop. Although we have been looking at this addiction in counselling I seem to get no nearer to controlling it and feel guilty and angry with myself.

In my counselling, instead of talking about the pattern, which is uppermost in my mind, I spend the whole session on another subject. In fact when my coun-sellor asks me about the behaviour I say it has not bothered me this week.

Rationally, it makes no sense to withhold from my counsellor information which would help him to help me. I *know* he is not there to judge me but to help me examine the 'stuckness'. So why do I lie? Because I *feel* guilty.

The guilt feeling arises because I think I have offended against my internal standards – laws of behaviour instilled in me by my father and other authorities in my childhood. Projecting the internal standards on to my counsellor – making him responsible for them – is easier than feeling helpless. I 'expect' my counsellor to fail me in the way my father did, which was to turn his back, to give up attempting to understand.

I have *transferred* my memories of my father's neglect of me into the here-and-now. This all occurs unconsciously at the time and is only revealed with hindsight after further sessions.

On a later occasion, when we do discuss the pattern, my counsellor gives me 'homework' – the classic suggestion to resist the addiction one day at a time. I fail in this task. I am at first depressed but then find myself angry with my counsellor. 'What's *wrong* with doing this, anyway?' I think. 'He's just conventional and can't cope with free spirits like me. He *would* tell me to stop, wouldn't he?' I catch myself thinking this, and realize it was the way I used to reassure myself that I was 'all right' as a confused, self-loathing teenager.

For the first time I begin to experience my anger against my distant, baffled, unhelpful father; the resultant mixture of rebellion and guilt I hold towards authority; and the way I use these feelings to avoid the responsibility for change.

The phrase 'He would, wouldn't he?' encapsulates the making of an assumption about another. The question then to ask is 'Why would he?' The answer may be 'Because he has this very good reason to do so'. If the answer is more like, 'Because that's just the sort of person he is', or 'Because that's what I think he thinks', then one may be fairly sure that transference is at work.

The above example shows:

- that by looking at transference a lot of information may come to light that may not be accessible by other counselling procedures;
- that helping a client catch such assumptions in the moment of their occurrence is one of the most valuable things a counsellor can do.

The counsellor's reaction to the client

A counsellor may experience strong feelings about a client for many reasons, apparently both rational and irrational. Because of the communication imbalance in counselling, where the client reveals far more of themselves than the counsellor, the counsellor may rightly think, 'X does so-and-so because that's the person s/he is', where 'the person s/he is' is the complex being who has revealed themselves in counselling.

If the counsellor, however, finds him/herself thinking 'X does so-and-so because that's the *sort of* person X is', s/he is already generalizing, making assumptions. This is not always acknowledged to be counter-transference, or properly analysed even when it is. To illustrate the various levels on which a counsellor can interpret their own counter-transference feelings, and the mistakes that can be made when they are misunderstood or defended against, I use a composite case which is a mixture of several of the first clients I saw at the counselling agency where I still work as a volunteer.

An example of unprocessed counter-transference

A. is a young man whose presenting issue is his current relationship. He has been involved for some time with another man, G., but says he now wants the relationship to end. The other man is putting him under heavy pressure to continue. A. says, 'I don't think I ever really wanted a relationship. It was all about proving I could attract someone.' He also says, however, that it has always been he who initiates sex in the relationship, and that 'it's always better with him than anyone else at the time but afterwards I can't wait to get rid of him.'

In the second session A. tells me that he allowed his friend G. to stay recently and they had sex – 'The inevitable happened.' Two nights later G. had followed A. home. 'I kept telling him to go away but he kept following so I punched his teeth in.'

I suddenly became aware of feeling intense anger towards A. My notes written immediately afterwards say: 'I didn't like A. very much when he was talking about this. I explained that I didn't think it was OK in general to put people's teeth out but I could see the frustration that led him to do it.'

With hindsight this is an obvious mistake. A. has not asked me to give him moral guidance, nor indeed to air my reactions. He dislikes himself and does not need a counsellor, of all people, to tell him he is 'Not OK'. He is, quite simply, trusting me enough to tell me who he is, someone who has abusive relationships. I have not even checked out how he feels about his own behaviour before coming in with my feelings. And I am not being congruent: I feel anger and it is at that moment not true to say that I understand his feelings.

A. comes for two more sessions but both times seems ill at ease and eventually does not return.

Four possible reactions

There are four possible ways a counsellor may react when s/he experiences strong feelings towards the client.

1 Diagnosis

The counsellor may make a 'diagnosis' or judgement of their client. I prefer the word 'diagnosis' both because 'judgement' carries too strong a flavour of moral condemnation and to point out that it is often easier for counsellors to retreat into a falsely 'objective' view of their client than to investigate their own counter-transference. The diagnosis may be accurate but even so it is a professional mask behind which the counsellor may feel more confident. It has emerged from the counselling relationship but is not going to be changed further by it. For instance, my notes say 'When A. was telling me about [hitting G.] he had an embarrassed smile partly because he was worrying about what I thought and partly because he was enjoying the reminiscence.' Was he? I did not ask *him* what the smile meant.

A counsellor who develops a fixed diagnosis of a passing or lasting aspect of their client will tend to try to enforce change rather than enable it. Something like this will happen: 'X needs to realize s/he is so-and-so. I must use skilful interpretations to get this across.' These interpretations may be helpful, but are more likely to be experienced as directions, and the counsellor risks reinforcing the client's transference, thus perpetuating an unequal, manipulative or defensive relationship.

Categorizing the client as a 'sort of' person – an angry person, a manipulative person, a seductive person – is a failure to allow the counselling relationship to develop, and the client to show themselves in all their rich dynamism and unpredictability. At worst it turns counselling into a battle of wills.

2 Prejudice and compensation

A counsellor with a degree more self-awareness may know that thoroughly 'unprofessional' feelings may lie behind their diagnosis or judgement. I *was* in touch with the degree of anger I experienced towards A. – of the raw material of what I eventually said. In my notes I wrote: 'I was thinking, "You little ****. First you seduce G., then you knock his teeth in."' This is an uncomfortable feeling for a counsellor who has been taught to treat their clients with unconditional positive regard.

One way in which counsellors may question their own diagnosis is by attempting to place themselves and their clients in a broader *social* context. I think this is an important and necessary step: for instance, as a gay man I am only too aware of the way in which the helping professions' definition of what constitutes mental health has followed, rather than shaped, society's views.

Sometimes counsellors think, 'Am I viewing this client from a privileged or resentful standpoint as a wo/man? A white/black person? A "professional", and so on? Am I ignorant of their background? I'll just have to try to be extra understanding and as unjudgemental as possible.' In A.'s case this was what I was doing when I said I understood his frustration. I was thinking, 'Well, I'm middle class, educated, from a secure nuclear family; he's working class, from a chaotic extended family; if that were me I guess that might make me enjoy the power I seem to have over this man.'

The problem with this sort of compensation is that not only is it incongruent, but clients are likely to find it unreal or patronizing, and to be patronizing is as discriminatory as to be hostile. The counsellor is not giving the client real feedback on how s/he is experienced. If this process goes on, the counsellor may become afraid to form real opinions on the client at all and the process will become mired in mutual helplessness. Nor is being 'extra understanding' much help to clients who will find that the other people in their lives do not make such allowances.

Neither of these responses actually honours the individuality of client and counsellor, or the unique relationship between them. To do so is to acknowledge counter-transference.

3 Counter-transference

In my particular reading I cannot find as succinct a definition of counter-transference as Kovel's description of transference. This is my definition.

> A situation where the counsellor finds him/herself experiencing feelings towards the client which upon examination seem either unrelated, or out of proportion, to the client or the content of the session.

This is a broader definition than the one of transference. The problem is that there seem to be two very different things meant by the term counter-transference.

Furthermore these two phenomena may occur at the same time, but it feels important to distinguish them. They are: (i) **active** or 'counter-active' transference, caused by unconscious material the counsellor is bringing to the counselling relationship, and (ii) **reactive** or 'counterpart' transference, where the counsellor becomes aware of his or her reaction to the unconscious or unexpressed material the client is bringing (Aveline, 1990, p. 322–4).

3a   Active counter-transference

Counsellors and therapists are human, and none is free of 'unfinished business'. Clients may 'push our buttons' and we have a responsibility to know at least the approximate location of those buttons.

I was certainly aware that A. posed counter-transference issues for me. Here is another section from my notes:

A. admits to a violent temper, especially 'When I go out drinking' (sounds familiar),

and then in square brackets, which I use to indicate an afterthought:

[What I *meant* to say is that it sounds that being drunk is a familiar experience for A. What I also realize I'm saying is that it sounds familiar to me: A. has a lot of D. in him.]

D. was a friend of mine; an alcoholic whose violent rages when drunk I had endured. At this point I could not tell whether my comparison of A. with D. was accurate or completely wide of the mark. It was an acknowledgement that those parallels were there, and that there were very personal and specific roots to my vision of the 'sort of' person A. was. I was sounding an alarm for myself which later, unfortunately, under pressure of a more forceful communication from A., I failed to hear.

Active counter-transference can be any strong emotion awoken in the counsellor; not just personal reactions that spring from the counsellor's individual development, but often perfectly justifiable reactions to prejudice or hostility from the client. It can be a struggle to remain open to the essential humanity of a client who is racist, sexist, homophobic, or discloses deeds of violence or abuse, while at the same time not colluding with their defences.

3b   Reactive counter-transference

A counsellor's reaction to such a client is not just a problem for the counsellor to handle, an internal balancing of emotions and skills. It is also likely to be a sign pointing at a problem of the client's. If so, the counsellor's reaction is partly an instance of one sort of 'reactive' counter-transference.

If the counsellor continues to experience feelings disproportionate to the apparent level of emotion in the counselling relationship, s/he may come to realize that in fact s/he is responding to the *hidden* anger, sadness, desire, etc. of the client. What do I mean by this?

First, it is the *complement* to the client's expressed feelings – the counsellor is witnessing the whole meaning of a communication of which the client can only afford to see a part. The counsellor is feeling 'what's missing'.

Secondly, the counsellor may also be feeling what other people feel when they encounter the client – sensing at first hand the client's particular sort of mis-alignment with other people.

Thirdly, as this misalignment tends to be caused by the client casting others into roles dictated by his/her past experience, the counsellor is also sensing the 'echo' of the client's transference – feeling themselves being squeezed into a mould the client has cast.

Lastly, the intensity of the emotion may be a clue that the client is playing the game called projective identification – getting other people to behave towards them in ways which are negative but familiar, and thereby relieving the client of the responsibility for the life they are living.

I did not fully understand all these implications at the time I met A. otherwise my thought might have been: 'I don't think my personal stuff about D. fully explains my anger with A. It was that *smile* that did it. He almost seems to invite an angry response. I wonder if his way at being angry at the world, or men, or the kind of man he thinks I am, is to get them to be angry back? That way he can be told he's no good, which is what he's used to hearing, and is more comfortable than daring to have hope for himself; but he can also get it to be someone else's fault.'

If I had fully analysed my counter-transference in this way, I would have simply noted it at that time, and used it possibly as an interpretive tool if A. became able to hear feedback on how he was experienced without regarding it as a judgement. But because I immediately acted on it, I stepped neatly into the role A. had prepared for me, as yet another in the line of people who confirmed his own opinion of himself.

My stuff or their stuff?

I make it look as if the distinction between active and reactive counter-transference is an easy one to make. On the contrary; I have found making the distinction between 'Their stuff' and 'My stuff' one of the most difficult and challenging lessons to learn on the way to becoming a counsellor.

References

Aveline, M. (1990) 'The training and supervision of individual therapists', in W. Dryden (ed.), *Individual Therapy: a Handbook*. Milton Keynes: Open University Press.
Kovel, J. (1976) *A Complete Guide to Therapy*. Harmondsworth: Pelican.

Discussion issues

1 What kind of relating by a client towards you might indicate that a transference response is involved? What might distinguish this from other ways of relating?
2 How might you respond to a client showing these responses?
3 A client evokes a strong emotional response in you. What questions would you ask yourself about your feelings?
4 How would you make use of these feelings within your counselling?

64

Transference in the Adolescent's Relationship with the Counsellor

Jane Leslie

In this chapter I explore the phenomenon of transference as it occurs in the client group with whom I work – adolescents – looking first at adolescence as a developmental stage, then examining the current understanding of transference in the client–counsellor relationship and the ways in which it may be interpreted and used by the counsellor. I draw on my own work experience to give examples of transference, not only of parental figures, but also of other figures of authority, lecturers or other professional carers.

Work setting

My work setting is a student advice and counselling centre in a large further education college. In presentations and publicity to students and staff emphasis is placed upon student self-referral, and as far as I can judge from contact with staff, parents and other professionals, the vast majority of students do come along to the centre of their own accord. In common with national trends the average age of students in the college increases each year, but still approximately 80% of my clients fall within the 17–21 age band and may therefore acceptably be labelled as 'late adolescents'. Clearly many of the students who arrive at the centre do not need counselling so much as practical advice on matters such as finance, accommodation, or course enrolment. However, approximately 20% of those who come are categorized for statistical purposes as having 'socio-emotional problems' either with their peer-group or, more commonly, with their family. Students in this group tend to return more frequently than others and for them a model of non-directive psychodynamic counselling seems appropriate. I rarely make explicit contracts but my experience suggests that many of the students in this group return three or four times over a short period, and then occasionally over a longer period to seek further support or practical help. Each year there is also a very small group of students who visit the office on a more regular basis throughout the year.

The conflicts of adolescence

In many ways the developmental theory of Erikson (1950) is a definitive view of the conflicts which face individuals at each stage of their life. He sees adolescence

This chapter was first published in *Counselling, Journal of the British Association for Counselling*, vol. 4, no. 3, pp. 202–4 (1993).

as a period in which an emerging sense of identity struggles with the role confusion caused by the internal and external pressure of changes which take place in the transition from childhood to adulthood, and broadly categorizes these changes as biological, social and psychological/emotional. On a biological level, the sudden and frequently unexpected changes in puberty throw the adolescent's self-image into confusion.

In his examination of Erikson's theory Lowe (1972) cites the teenagers' frequent use of mirrors and their written equivalent, diaries, as evidence of an obsession with appearance and image. Although for many students in further education puberty is long past, outlandish styles of dress and exaggerated or idiosyncratic gestures or speech still indicate uncertainty as to how to project their personality on to their radically changed body. Their uncertainty is compounded by the fact that on a psychological level radical changes are also taking place. The teenager moves from a childish concrete mode of thought to the adult abstract mode, tending to swing from one extreme to the other, until they are comfortable. The adolescent is often preoccupied with philosophy, ideology and morality and will spend hours in discussion with peers, testing out his, or her, view against theirs. In both the physical and psychological process a large peer-group is required to reflect all the different possible facets of the adolescent personality and image. As Lowe (1972) says: 'Kaleidoscopic personalities require multiple mirrors.'

In a similar way the adolescent seeks out a host of adult role models against whom to test out the possibilities for their adult self. Adults with whom the teenager comes into contact become the unwitting heroes and villains of the adolescents' world. Parents are the first objects of this process, idealized and then rejected as the teenager moves towards independence, but other significant adults, pop stars, TV personalities or even members of the individual's peer-group may become the object of a temporary crisis during the search for identity. On a social level, most teenagers are under pressure to choose and progress towards an adult career. Most students who enter further or higher education are free from this pressure as their education continues into their twenties. There is a price to pay, however, both in terms of higher expectations when they do enter work and in terms of their inability to take certain steps towards independence because they lack a realistic income. For every individual these years involve a reworking of childhood conflicts, but for those whose childhood has been in some way unsatisfactory the conflicts which now arise may be overwhelming.

Three themes of adolescence

Noonan (1983) analyses several themes around which adolescent conflict may occur. She sees the adolescent years as a period of loss of childhood and dependency and believes that in the transition to adulthood the teenager goes through a number of processes akin to mourning; he or she withdraws from their formerly stable world into a period of 'to-ing and fro-ing' between their past identity and their possible future one until the desirable parts of the past have been internalized and can be left behind. This process is accompanied by all the extreme emotion of bereavement. Noonan enumerates a number of areas where accommodation of past experience must take place. The first of these is relationships and the principal relationship to change is that of child and parent. The adolescent rebels and rejects parental values but, Noonan asserts, it is important that the parents remain firm in order that the teenager can adequately test and finally assimilate some parental values. In my experience the worst adolescent crises occur where a boundary-setting parent is absent, or rejects the rebellious teenager. A second area of assimilation of new values is that of responsibility and authority. The child accepts external responsibility and authority; the adolescent rebels against this and seeks independence; adults need to be sufficiently secure in their own value system to be able to take responsibility for their own actions and exercise some authority over themselves.

By the nature of the college and the courses it provides many of its students have already experienced one partial or total failure at GCSE or 'A' level, and many of my clients go on to fail again. The most frequent example of the responsibility and authority conflict occurs in the way students apportion responsibility for this failure; only the more mature students can make a realistic acknowledgement of their own shortcomings. Noonan also talks about a third area of crisis, where the change from child to adult in gradual stages has been replaced either by a desperate struggle to maintain childlike dependency or a complete rejection of remaining support and a bid for absolute autonomy. Faced with one of these problems the student may, for example, avoid all career or higher education decisions in an attempt to maintain the status quo, or opt out of college, rejecting all further opportunities in favour of immediate employment and independence. In all of these conflicts the role of the parent and other significant adults, or at any rate the teenager's perception of their role, is particularly important because of the adolescent's over-riding concern with the establishment of an independent identity. The rest of the article considers the transferences which arise from these relationships and their significance in the counselling relationship.

Transference

Transference is the process, first described by Freud, in which the client transfers to, or places upon, the counsellor the qualities (positive and negative) of another significant person in their life and behaves towards them as if they were that person. Thus, the unwitting counsellor may find him- or herself cast in the role of another important person in the student's life and come to realize that the student expects them to behave as if they held a series of values which are alien to them or had experienced things in the relationship which in reality have never occurred. Transference behaviour is completely unconscious on the part of the client and so the counsellor may find him- or herself at a loss to say where these unfounded assumptions about their values and behaviour have come from. The feeling of incongruity which they experience is often their first clue that transference is occurring.

Because the client relates to the counsellor as an authority figure who holds the knowledge and power to resolve their problems the transference which they bring to counselling sessions is generally one of a similar significant relationship in the past; for example, parent–child, or less frequently teacher–pupil, or social worker–client. Storr (1960) points out that by virtue of the fact that they are driven to seek counselling, clients may be expected to have had a bad experience, especially of the parent–child relationship, and therefore to bring a negative transference to the relationship. Particularly for adolescents, in a state of rebellion against their parents, a parental transference will evoke negative expectations of the counsellor. However, Storr also suggests that individuals have an instinctive understanding of what they need from a relationship, which in the absence of a satisfactory real figure gives them an idealized image of the significant other (generally parent) they would wish to have. From that idealized image they may also bring a positive transference to their relationship with the counsellor. Storr believes that the more isolated the client, the stronger the transference will be, and he also suggests that the transference will tend either towards dependence or towards independence and rebellion according to the needs and experience of the client.

Of course the phenomenon of transference is not confined to the counselling relationship. No individual comes to a new relationship devoid of expectations based on their past experiences of similar relationships, and many misunderstandings occur because of this. However, transference has a particular importance in the counselling situation, first because of the profound nature of the relationship formed, and secondly because of the significant part which working with the transference can play in resolving the client's difficulties. Freud tended to see the manifestations of transference as a series of separate phenomena, each of which had to be explicated and destroyed before a cure could be achieved. Thus he was inclined to see them as obstacles to treatment. Nowadays transference is viewed much more as a single phenomenon which colours all parts of the client–counsellor relationship and is seen more positively as an aid to treatment. Although the relationship from which the transference originates is often in reality defunct, it is of such significance to the client that it continues to be alive in the psyche and to influence their current view of the world. Where transference is sound in a client–counsellor relationship it is valued because it brings the counsellor into contact with the roots of the client's behaviour and often the origins of his or her problems. Thus it is important for the counsellor not to reject and challenge the first manifestations of transference but to stay with the situation until a fuller picture is seen. The counsellor may then work with the transference in two ways: first, as Storr suggests, having understood the nature of the client's transference the counsellor can use the relationship formed to replace the client's negative experience with a more positive and accepting one; then the client's negative transference will cease to have such a strong hold on their current behaviour. Secondly, when they have a clear understanding, the counsellor can begin to reflect the patterns of behaviour from which the transference originates back to the client and so offer them the insight to analyse and thereby change their own behaviour. It very often happens that a distortion based on transference in one relationship will be repeated elsewhere, in other similar relationships, and so the resolution of one set of problems assists towards the resolution of others.

Types of transference

I now examine some examples of the types of transference which have occurred in my experience as a counsellor of adolescents. The type of transference which occurs in such a relationship is dependent upon two factors. First on the type of expectation that the student has formed of the counsellor, either from their own introductory meeting in the induction period, from their friends' experience of me, or where the student is referred or advised to attend by a tutor, from the tutor's explanation of my work. The second, and probably more important factor where a transference is set up concerns the type of relationship which the student finds problematic or especially significant. Broadly speaking, the transferences set up seem to fall into two basic categories: parental and those based on lecturers or other significant authority figures, e.g. social workers or medical practitioners.

Parental transferences occur where the counsellor takes on for the client the role and value system of a parent. Negative transferences of this type seem to occur most often amongst the most disturbed minority of my clients. It appears that students who have experienced poor models of parenting, when they reach adolescence, are not simply trying to find a new synthesis of their identity in relation to their parents, but are struggling to reach any understanding at all. The transferences they set up often contain the assumption: 'You must think I'm inadequate/lazy/unmotivated' or more poignantly 'I have to prove to you that I'm not immature/uncaring/undeserving' – scripts which seem to be drawn from a dialogue with disappointed, disapproving or rejecting parents. However, it is often possible to hear from the same students a more encouraging strain which harks back to Storr's concept of the positive transference of the idealized image of a parent. The student states the negative assumption which his parents have made and follows it up by: 'But it's not like that, is it?' or 'But I'm all right really, aren't I?' Occasionally, the counsellor is also the object of a positive transference which has little relation to reality. Unfortunately, students with special needs who have received a great deal of special care have often also received from their parents and carers the message that they are particularly deserving. Arriving in a college department dedicated to integration they find themselves frustrated and seek the attention of the counsellor in order to remain 'special'. It is particularly hard for the counsellor to confront this transference whilst seeking to maintain a caring image.

Many of the students who have experienced poor parenting have also had contact with social workers, pastoral care teachers, educational psychologists and others, and because the counsellor in a college is perceived to have a similar role a transference of the relationship is set up. This seems to occur most often where the professional involved has been particularly powerful in a practical sense or particularly likeable (and therefore has been able to help the adolescent resolve some of the difficulties caused by poor parenting). The nature of the transference set up varies according to the relationship which the client had with the professional and according to the intervention they made and can be anything from extremely negative to extremely positive. No general rules can be made but perhaps a common strand is that adolescents who have been involved with the caring professions as children expect the counsellor to be all-powerful, and it is often a struggle to make them accept the counsellor's inability and often unwillingness to intervene on their behalf. In this context it seems important to mention the transference relationship between the counsellor and people who have been involved with such professionals as parents of child-clients. These are occasionally students but more often parents of problem students. They, sadly, become as secondary children themselves, disempowered in their role as parents and dependent on the counsellor for approval; this in contrast to parents with no such previous experience, who often question the counsellor's authority and expertise.

By contrast, any transference based on a lecturer–student relationship seems to have a far less profound effect on the clients involved. However, knowing the lecturers and subjects involved it is often interesting to see that the type of problem that the students bring and the way in which they expect to be counselled or advised varies according to their course and tutor.

Summary

I have set out to outline some of the developmental issues which, according to Erikson (1950) are particularly important in adolescence, and to examine our current understanding of transference within the client/counsellor relationship. On the basis of my experience I have tried to pick out some of the common themes which arise in the transference in an adolescent–counsellor relationship. I have become aware that the conflicts in relationships with parents and with other authority figures which are the origin of the transferences adolescents bring, whilst crucial to the development of identity in adolescence will nevertheless be repeated on transference relationships throughout adult life unless they are resolved. This underlines the importance to counselling work of the conflict marking developmental stages which Erikson (1950) outlined.

References

Erikson, E.H. (1950) *Childhood and Society*. Harmondsworth: Pelican.
Lowe, G.R. (1972) *The Growth of Personality*. Harmondsworth: Pelican.
Noonan, E. (1983) *Counselling Young People*. London: Methuen.
Storr, A. (1960) *The Integrity of the Personality*. Harmondsworth: Pelican.

Discussion issues

1 What issues do you think might be significant in deciding whether or not to make a formal counselling contract with an adolescent client?

2 Can you suggest examples of the type of interventions you might make in order to reflect a transference back to the client?

3 'Kaleidoscopic personalities require multiple mirrors.' In your experience how is this requirement manifested in the behaviour of adolescents?

4 Counter-transference is the process by which counsellors, on the basis of their own past experience, impose expectations on the client. What expectations might you as a counsellor have of an adolescent client?

65

Client-Centred Therapy: Trends and Troubles

Tony Merry

In February 1987, Carl Rogers died peacefully, surrounded by his friends and relatives. At the Memorial Service held later that year in London, people came from France, Germany, Ireland and from other European countries. Carl's work has had a major influence throughout the world, and his contributions to our understanding of the process of human change and growth are unparalleled.

One hope expressed at that service was that the person-centred approach would continue to grow and develop in the way Carl would have wanted. I think this is happening, and I am optimistic that more and more people will be touched by the spirit of person-centredness that lives on and is flourishing in the UK and elsewhere.

Although I am optimistic, I am troubled by two things. One is the way the term 'person-centred' is becoming widely used to describe situations which do not do justice to the spirit or the original meaning of that term – 'person-centred hypnotherapy', for example. The other, and the one on which I want to concentrate here, is the growing, but mistaken view, that client-centred therapy has no distinct and unique identity, but is simply a means of providing a psychological climate in which other techniques, methods and approaches can then be applied. This, to me, is the most troubling development (and it was going on even before Carl's death), which should not go unchallenged. I have read a number of articles recently which seem to point in this general direction. (An example is 'Feeling and meaning in client-centred therapy' by Jonathan Hales-Tooke that appeared in *Counselling* in 1989.)

I found a lot in these articles with which I could agree. Yes, client-centred therapy has grown and evolved in the last fifty years. Its theoretical formulations have been influenced, tested and extended by many writers and practitioners. The way Rogers wrote and spoke about client-centred therapy changed, though he was never shaken from his belief that it is the qualities of the therapeutic relationship that are growth-promoting, and not any particular technique or method. To that extent, and it's a very fundamental one, client-centred therapy has not changed.

I recognize that some of the terminology has altered, that this reflects differences in emphasis, and gives more accurate ways of reporting what client-centred therapists believe and actually do. What is difficult for me to accept, however, is that this leads to the conclusion that client-centred therapy has ceased to exist in anything like its original form, or that it has changed into a kind of 'eclectic' approach in which the core conditions of empathy, positive regard and congruence merely provide a background against which therapy proper can proceed.

This chapter was first published as 'Client-centred therapy: some trends and some troubles', in *Counselling, Journal of the British Association for Counselling*, vol. 1, no. 1, pp. 17–18 (1990).

Some articles, and Hales-Tooke's is an example here, assert that few therapists today 'use *only* client-centred therapy'. This is not my experience, and the term 'use *only* client-centred therapy' is, for me, quite revealing. I think of myself and my colleagues as client-centred, not as people who, among other things, use client-centred therapy. The 'Way of Being' that Rogers described is not something that can be put on and off like an overcoat. It fundamentally underpins everything we try to do in our relationships with our clients, and it points to a set of values and attitudes, not of standard behaviours, techniques or methods.

I have to ask myself, 'Why would I want to use another procedure, like the Gestalt empty chair, if I am a client-centred therapist?' Would it be to supplement the process, or to replace the client-centred process with a different one? It seems to me that as soon as you introduce a Gestalt empty chair, you are a Gestalt therapist. There is no such thing as a client-centred empty chair.

In an article in *Person-Centred Review*, J. Bozarth and B. Temaner Brodley (1986) identified three misunderstandings about client-centred therapy. All of them are important, but one is more relevant here:

> Client-Centred Psychotherapy is a way of establishing 'rapport' and an understanding of the client that provides an opportunity for the therapist to apply other approaches, techniques, and interventions.

This mistaken view seems to represent an ignorance or mistrust of the process of client-centred therapy. For me, and I think for very many other people, client-centred therapy has an identity and a discipline of its own. It is both an artistic and a scientific process. It is also a process of beauty and creativity. I find, more and more, that if I can create in my own way, the kind of relationship that Rogers so thoroughly described, then it is enough for therapy to proceed with purpose and deepening levels of awareness in my client and myself.

In the past if I felt stuck, or if I believed that my client should or could be moving faster, be different from the way he or she was, then I would be tempted to change the process by employing some technique or other (and I know plenty). I quickly learned that this was therapist-centred therapy. What was going on in me that urged me to provide an empty chair, or make some suggestion to 'help the client out'? What I found was *my* insecurity and *my* anxiety. It certainly did not belong to the client.

Bruce Meador (1986) put this well:

> There is also a sense in which Client-Centred Therapy may not satisfy some of the subtle needs of the therapist. It may have profound therapeutic moments. It can be extremely powerful, involving the therapist totally. But sometimes it is not, and we live in an impatient age. I am suggesting that Client-Centred Therapy may be sufficient for the therapeutic process, but not for the therapist's subtle need to jump into the process.

I am against the kind of 'eclectic' therapy that is a mixed salad of techniques and methods, especially when it masquerades under the title of client-centred therapy. What I would prefer is that therapists are adequately trained and prepared so that when the process becomes problematic they do not instantly reach for a technique or a game or a suggestion. Instead, I hope they have internalized a set of attitudes and values that are empowering and facilitative of their clients and themselves, and that they have become skilled at communicating those attitudes and values. I hope they have gained sufficient trust in the process and in their clients to discover ways forward for themselves. And I hope they trust themselves enough to be able to stay congruent and willing to remain engaged with their clients' frame of reference. This is the direction in which I see client-centred therapy continuing to move.

I cannot detect anything in Rogers' later writings to suggest that the complex set of meanings summarized by the term 'client-centred' or 'person-centred' underwent any radical changes. If anything, Rogers became more convinced that the major element of concern in the psychotherapeutic relationship was the distribution of power. The original term 'non-directive therapy' later gave way to the term 'client-centred' partly to underline the fact that this approach was first and foremost a means to access the personal power of the individual client in the change process.

The 'Formative Tendency' of which Rogers spoke (similar in many ways to Maslow's 'Actualizing Tendency') remains the wellspring of his personal power. All of the therapist's efforts are directed towards providing the kind of psychological climate in which this tendency can find expression. The core conditions – empathy, congruence and positive regard – are qualities exhibited and communicated by the therapist, and when they are experienced by the client to a significant degree the client will discover within her/himself the resources needed to effect personal change and reintegration.

This, put a little simply, forms the basis of client-centred theory, and by extension, the underlying theory of the whole of the person-centred approach. Interventions by the therapist, however well intentioned, run counter to client-centred theory if they determine or manipulate the client's behaviour, feeling state, sense of self or process of self-exploration away from what's going on *now* to what the therapist thinks *should* be going on now. This is not to say these things are necessarily no good, but to say they are not client-centred since the therapist has determined how time will be used, what means of expression will be used, and maybe even what 'theme' the client should explore. In other words, the therapist's expertise, technique and power have taken precedence over the client's personal power.

However, I believe client-centred therapy to be alive and well, growing and developing. For example, there are now several well-established training programmes in client-centred therapy in the UK, and throughout Europe and the USA. To my knowledge none of them trains people to use concepts from Gestalt, TA, psychodynamics, or anything else, though they might ensure that their participants are aware of competing and complementing approaches.

John Shlein (1988) put it nicely:

Therapists of other orientations now consider themselves sufficiently 'client centred' (warm, empathic, call their patients 'clients', and so on), so that as superficial effects spread, there seems to be less point in the distinctive identity. Still worse, there is the haemorrhage of meaning from the words 'person-centred'. What is that? It is only an 'approach' – not a defined practice or theory. 'Approach' signifies influence, not identity. Thus we have 'person-centred' Gestalt, and psycho-analytic therapy, even person-centred hypnosis, contradictory practices and philosophy.

Here's the danger that I believe is not well understood. I believe there is a possibility that therapists might start to trust their techniques more than they trust their clients. I fear that if client-centred therapists become 'eclectic', they might well turn into 'therapy-centred therapists'. (By this I mean the tendency continually to collect techniques, interventions, games and so on so that the therapist has a response to any and every situation that might occur with a client. Such therapists pride themselves on the range of such techniques at their command, and continually look for opportunities to exercise them. Of course, the possible range of human situations is infinite, so the search for a fully comprehensive repertoire of techniques is never ending.)

This would undermine, and eventually destroy, everything that Carl Rogers stood for. It would undermine the trust in the formative, directional tendency of people to move towards growth and change within the definable, facilitating relationship provided in client-centred therapy. It would undermine the fundamental feature of client-centred therapy that the approach is 'grounded in the therapist's attitude and the belief that the client is the only natural authority about him or herself' (Bozarth and Temaner Brodley, 1986, pp. 262–3).

Do I detect a movement towards a position that client-centred therapy, *of itself*, is not sufficient? Do some people see it as a generalized orientation rather than the creative and disciplined practice it now is? The vision, if I've got it right, of the client-centred therapist as a mobilizer of a pastiche of techniques does not sit easily with me. In this vision client-centred therapy loses its unique identity.

On the surface, to some, it may look attractive. As a therapist, why not do whatever you think needs to be done to get your client moving? Why not import all those techniques, ideas and formulations that other approaches seem to be based on? Why not? Because to do so would be to strike at the heart of the philosophy that has stood, tested again and again, for fifty years. It would move clients to the fringes of the therapeutic endeavour and replace them with concepts. What would be client-centred about this?

But what I see as a need for techniques and methods is understandable. When my students say, 'But what do I do when my client seems stuck?', they are voicing the fundamental dilemma of all therapists. And my response? It is to help them listen to and be with their clients, empathizing with them in their 'stuckness', trusting in them and themselves. It is to support them as they struggle alongside their clients, engaging with them and caring for them, but not taking away their opportunity to unstick themselves.

Of course, this answer cannot satisfy the natural need to be helpful, to solve the client's problem – to seem like a good therapist. How much easier it would be to say, 'Get them to relax. Ask them to visualize the feeling of being stuck, talk to it, ask it why it gets in the way. Ask them what other situations give rise to this feeling . . . and so on.' But this is not client-centred therapy. It is not trusting of the clients' ability to work through their own process in their own ways, in their own time.

The idea that Rogers provided us merely with a method for getting therapy started, and that what's really needed from then on is good, solid technique, is a mistake. If this is the direction in which client-centred therapy is moving, I shall mourn its passing.

But client-centred therapy does have an identity all of its own. It is the result of fifty years of research and experience. It has grown, developed and changed in that time, and will continue to do so, but it has never departed from the basic philosophical positions it holds regarding 'human nature' or the process of personal change, or that the client is the best and only expert.

Client-centred therapy will continue to change, but it will, I am sure, always retain its unique identity. It will continue to develop its artistry and its rigour, and will continue to challenge its own concepts and ideas as Carl Rogers so dearly wanted. I leave the last word with him:

> There is only one way in which a person-centred approach can avoid becoming narrow, dogmatic, and restrictive. That is through studies – simultaneously hard headed and tender minded – which open new vistas, bring new insights, challenge our hypotheses, enrich our theory, expand our knowledge, and involve us more deeply in an understanding of the phenomena of human change. (1986, pp. 258–9)

References

Bozarth, J. and Temaner Brodley, B. (1986) 'Client-centred psychotherapy – a statement', *Person-Centred Review*, 1(3).

Hales-Tooke, J. (1989) 'Feeling and meaning in client-centred therapy', *Counselling*, 67: 9–13.

Meador, B. (1986) 'Roundtable discussion', *Person-Centred Review*, 1(3).

Rogers, C. (1986) 'Carl Rogers on the development of the person-centred approach', *Person-Centred Review*, 1(3): 258–9.

Shlein, J. (1988) 'Roundtable discussion', *Person-Centred Review*, 3(3).

Discussion issues

1 What do you understand by Rogers' belief that it is the qualities of the therapeutic relationship that are growth-promoting and not any particular technique or method? Do you share that belief?

2 'There is a possibility that therapists might start to trust their techniques more than they trust their clients . . . they might turn into "therapy centred therapists".' Is this threat one which you sense, and for what reasons?

3 From your experience and understanding have you found it possible to trust the process of client-centred therapy or have you experienced insecurity or anxiety when the work becomes 'stuck'? What do you do if this happens?

4 Do you think that client-centred therapy has a unique identity, or is it merely a method for getting therapy started? How does your experience bear this out?

66

Counselling and Psychotherapy: Is There a Difference?

Alan Naylor-Smith

'It's increasingly difficult to define where that boundary line (i.e., between therapist and counsellor) is, and even if there is one.' So said Judith Baron, general manager of BAC, quoted in the *Guardian* on 5 May 1994. This chapter seeks to address the question of whether counselling and psychotherapy are two words for the same function or whether they describe different activities. It is an important question for BAC and for the Psychoanalytic and Psychodynamic section of the United Kingdom Council for Psychotherapy (UKCP). I am seeking to argue here that although the processes of counselling and psychotherapy overlap so that at times it is hard to distinguish one from another, the words do not express the same, and that to accept that there are differences is vital to the understanding of our respective crafts. I also seek to affirm the value and validity of both counselling and psychotherapy, and to express for counsellors of other traditions something of what makes the psychodynamic tradition distinctive; for it is with psychodynamic counselling and psychotherapy that I am concerned.

An analogy may help. The colour yellow changes to become blue through any number of variations of green. In the same way we can identify counselling that is focused on a particular problem as being at one end of our spectrum; in our analogy this is yellow. Psychodynamic counselling takes us further along the scale, yellow becoming green. Psychodynamic psychotherapy takes us further along; this is green, becoming at some times blue. But mostly we reserve blue for analysis, which is however beyond the scope of this chapter. I hope no one will seek to analyse my choice of colours; no significance is intended!

I am conscious that to argue that there is a difference and that there is overlap in this way is to restate the position so vigorously attacked by Brian Thorne in his paper at the 16th BAC Annual Training Conference on 3 September 1992. It may be true that in client-centred work the words are used interchangeably and that this is often true of cognitive therapies as well. I believe this leads to confusion. In the psychodynamic tradition the words express a difference that is real and useful. So I offer the following as a contribution to an ongoing debate.

I want to look at the art of counselling and of psychotherapy and to ask in what ways these arts may differ. I shall use the word practitioner rather than counsellor etc., so that having sought to distinguish between the different arts, I can then go on to ask the question: if there is a difference, then who is or should be doing what?

This chapter was first published in *Counselling, Journal of the British Association for Counselling*, vol. 5, no. 4, pp. 284–6 (1994).

Looking at the differences

1 The art of counselling

Some counselling can rightly be highly focused or task-orientated; for example, after a trauma or a bereavement a client may need space to express powerful feelings in an atmosphere of confidentiality and safety. It is the client's life 'out there' that is important, and the practitioner seeks to be with the client as these feelings are expressed and explored. The trauma or bereavement may well affect how the client relates to others; how he/she functions at work, or engages in or withdraws from social life. Staying with these problems as they are worked through requires patience, skill and focus, and the willingness to face painful and difficult feelings.

The practitioner may also see it as part of his/her task to provide a situation where the unconscious can be known; for example after a bereavement a client may need to acknowledge how difficult the relationship was at times, and how much disappointment there was in that relationship. Feelings of guilt and anger may need to be faced and whilst some of these feelings may be conscious, just awaiting expression, others may be repressed. Providing a safe place where feelings can be expressed and new situations faced is a vital task, but is, in my prism analogy, at one end of the spectrum. With the exploration of the unconscious we have moved; a touch of green is introduced into the yellow.

A further significant step is taken when it is acknowledged that the present trauma or bereavement may evoke previous similar experiences, so we find ourselves referring to the client's personal history. The past is explored as well as the presenting problem, and the impact of the one upon the other is noticed. We have moved further along our scale; yellow is becoming increasingly green.

A further step is taken with the realization that the client will begin to relate to the practitioner in ways that reflect the client's personal problems and psycho-pathology. Feelings that the client has about people and life will be transferred to the practitioner; for example, if the client feels that it is useless and dangerous to allow him- or herself to get close to another person, this feeling will be projected upon the practitioner. This will happen whether the practitioner is aware of it or not. Rightly used, this can give us insight into the nature of the client's problems. If not noticed or addressed it can destroy the effectiveness of our work. But again there is a gradation; we can use the insight from the transference to inform us about the nature of the client's difficulties; or we can bring our relationship into the sessions as a subject itself to be reflected upon.

With the exploration of the unconscious, the relating of the present problems to the past, and reflection upon the relationship of client and practitioner (the trans-ference relationship), this is now psychodynamic counselling. We are using all three parts of the 'triangle of insight' (Michael Jacobs, 1988; Malan, 1979, 1992). We are also in the area where the arts of counselling and of psychotherapy most overlap; we are in the green area of the prism.

In psychodynamic practice it is predicated that it is in the unconscious that the root cause of our client's problems lie. For example, the presenting problem may be loneliness. As this problem is explored it may emerge that the client feels that he or she has always been let down in life, and that therefore it is not actually worth getting close to another person. This despair will be noticed in the descriptions of relationships with others; it will also become apparent in the relationship of practitioner and client. The unconscious may contain many powerful and varied feelings, amongst them guilt and shame, strong irrational hates, deep rage or longings, or envy of others. In each case we will notice that it is these unconscious feelings that are causing havoc in our client's life. And in each case this same process needs to be worked through; the unconscious needs to become known; the feelings need to be felt and contained; the causes need to be understood; and while this process continues both client and feelings need holding within the therapeutic relationship both during the exploration, and as the client tries out new ways of relating.

In psychodynamic work the exploration of dreams and phantasies is an important route to coming to know the unconscious. Freud called dreams 'the royal road to the unconscious', for it is very often in dreams that new elements in our client's unconscious become clear. The transference will also get much attention, for it is in the transference relationship that our client's problems often show themselves clearly for the first time. If they are afraid of intimacy, they will keep us at arm's length. If they are afraid of abandonment, they will either cling to us or demolish the relationship with a raging denigration when it feels that we have let them down. All the tendencies that make our client's lives problematic at some point turn up in the transference, and so may hopefully be both understood and tackled. The practitioner will also notice his or her own counter-transference. The relationship of client and practitioner can produce powerful feelings in us as practitioners, such as sadness, anger, fear or boredom and we need to analyse these feelings. Some may belong to our own character; others may inform us of strong movements in our relationship with the client, which will need to be addressed as the therapy progresses.

What are we now involved in? Counselling or psychotherapy? What is clear is how far we have moved from where we began. The focus has changed; at the beginning of this article I described a process where it was life 'out there' that was the rightful focus of the work; now the focus is the unconscious, dreams, phantasy, the transference and counter-transference, and the relationship of all this to the client's personal history and to present problems. If the former is clearly counselling, then the latter is psychodynamic counselling or psychotherapy. What is clear is that what we are doing has changed. Here the art of counselling and of psychotherapy overlap.

2   The art of psychodynamic psychotherapy

We now move further along the prism. A feature of much psychotherapy is that it involves work with clients on a more frequent basis than once a week. This shift to a greater frequency greatly assists the change in emphasis described above. A number of further differences may be noticed.

First, with the greater frequency, less is happening between sessions in the life of the client. This tends to shift the focus of the sessions away from day-to-day crises;

these also usually decline as the 'central neurosis' is held in the therapeutic relationship; that is, as the feelings that have been buried in the unconscious begin to become known, the client is often less fearful or angry in everyday life, which therefore may begin to improve. There is now more time to stay with the 'central core' problems of the client.

Secondly, the client is given the security of knowing that the practitioner will be there for him/her on a frequent basis over a considerable period. This allows defences to be gradually brought down. For example, when in childhood there is fundamental failure in the primary care, children may have to become prematurely competent by looking after themselves, for they have learned that others are not to be trusted. This may lead to a reluctance in adulthood to risk any real intimacy. In these situations greater frequency of sessions is often needed to allow the client to let go of that militant self-reliance that blocks closeness with others. For others, without this greater frequency, areas of great distress cannot be contemplated or even known about.

Thirdly, and closely related to the above, greater frequency of sessions allows greater degrees of dependence and the experience of regression. This is not to say that dependence is to be encouraged; but we do need to allow it when appropriate. The exploring of the unconscious produces great anxiety; to hold that in the transference relationship does mean allowing the client to become dependent as these anxieties and conflicts are experienced and explored. The same is true of regression. Again we do not encourage regression, but as clients experience their unconscious selves, often they discover there a self that has been disowned as the result of feelings being experienced as a child that were too powerful and frightening to integrate. As clients get in touch with these feelings they may come to feel like a child in a very frightening world; the world indeed not of the present, but of the past, where they experienced those fundamental hurts, and where feelings then experienced towards the primary carers are now felt in the present and focused upon the practitioner. The practitioner needs to be able to tolerate and work within these powerful situations. We need to be at home with strong feelings of love and hate, of hope and despair, which we will experience in the transference relationship. Our own counter-transference feelings are also going to be equally powerful.

With more frequent sessions, more focus on the unconscious, on dreams and phantasy, and on the transference and counter-transference; and with the allowance of greater dependence and of regression, the work is now, in my view, clearly psychotherapy. In my analogy, yellow has moved through many shades of green, and now is nearing the blue. The blue would correspond with analysis; but there is not space to examine the similarities and differences between psychotherapy and analysis here.

Illustrating the differences

A male client with few if any real friends talks sadly about how he sat in his flat cuddling his cat. His cat is more friendly than the people among whom he lives, who could not care one bit. Now all practitioners would surely notice the great sadness and sense of disillusion, and to reflect this back, to communicate that the practitioner had heard, would surely be helpful. But perhaps too the cat represents the client's soft vulnerable part that longs to be cuddled and held. It may be that it is precisely because this part of him has never felt heard, accepted or held in a relationship that the client's problems continue, leading to the angry lashing out that was also a feature of this client's nature. Depending on the setting and the relationship of practitioner and client, this too might be reflected upon. With hurts going so deep, work with this client is clearly going to be long, difficult and emotionally costly for both practitioner and client. For it is certain that the longing to be heard, accepted and held is bound to become focused upon the practitioner, within the transference relationship. This means holding in that relationship great depths of anger, despair, hate, grief and envy. Much attention has therefore to be given to the transference, but even with this there is a marked tendency to 'act out'; that is, the feelings that are felt in the transference cannot be contained, and so the client expresses them by missing sessions or by focusing his rage in other relationships.

The client often presents as a competent intelligent person, but one who also at times lashes out in relationships with great ferocity. A way of understanding this is to say that it is the hurt inner child that at times causes this havoc. Who in treatment cares for this child? Much here depends upon the interpretation of the transference, but also upon the frequency of the sessions. With cognitive counselling, emphasis may be placed upon teaching the coping, competent self to manage life in a different way. This surely has validity. The difficulty may well be that the child sabotages any attempt at better life skills with that same ferocity noticed in other areas of his life. With psychodynamic counselling, the aim could be to come to know the inner child; to understand the hurts, and how these come to be expressed in present relationships; and to help the client care for that inner child in a more merciful way. Some of the compassion for that child would be mediated by the counsellor. Again this surely has validity. The difficulty may be the containing of the client as noticed above, and also that the integration this client so desperately needs could perhaps only take place within a setting that allowed greater degrees of dependence and regression. It is these conditions that psychotherapy would hope to provide, allowing the client to relinquish the care for that inner child much more into the care of the therapist, to grieve for the primary loss, and so hopefully to find that greater integration. The difficulty is the cost and length of time that such a treatment would require.

This leads to the difficult question of what type of help individual clients need. Some may need twice or more times a week work over a considerable period if their problems are to be resolved; others may benefit more from less intensive work. Here we need great honesty about our successes and failures if we are to learn and to be of maximum use to our clients.

Who does what?

The question now has to be, who is or should be doing what? I want to argue for flexibility and caution. The needs of the client come first. For some, weekly sessions over a short period provide the help they need. Psychotherapists should recognize this, and be prepared to provide this sort of help when appropriate. For others more concentrated work over a long period is required. Some counsellors because of the nature of their training are able to provide this. This should surely be encouraged. At the same time others should not attempt this type of work without further training.

For we also need caution. Any client/practitioner relationship has potential for good and for evil. The more intense that relationship is, the greater is the potential for good but also for harm. The vital need is for good training and supervision. And especially here I want to mention the practitioner's own therapy. The exploring of the unconscious involves great skill. A practitioner has to become used to listening to communications at many different levels. This is especially true of understanding the transference. Our own therapy makes us sensitive to the atmosphere in the room. It helps us to understand what may belong to us and our own psycho-pathology, and what is coming from the client. It also helps us to tolerate and understand the power of the feelings that are projected upon us, and how these may be explored between practitioner and client in a helpful way. It is surely a good rule that we should not work with clients on a more frequent basis than we have ourselves experienced in our own therapy. The necessary qualifications for intensive work include the ability to work in the transference; to analyse the counter-transference; and to be competent to cope with dependence and regression.

Conclusion

I have argued that there are valid differences between counselling and psycho-therapy. Surely our respective crafts and our clients are best served if we acknowl-edge these differences, and seek to respect and know our own and each other's strengths and weaknesses. The crafts are complementary. We need each other. If at this point I include psychoanalysis, it, due to the high cost and low availability, is only ever going to be possible for the few. Even were it more available, it would not be appropriate or the chosen form of help for many, but for some it is a life-saver. The same is true of psychotherapy, though this can seek to reach more. Counselling can help many more still. Of all the psychodynamic arts this is the one most available. It is used in social work departments, industry, schools, youth centres, surgeries and low-cost counselling centres. Its wide availability is one of its strengths.

Again we need each other in training, therapy and supervision. Many psycho-therapists go to analysts for their own therapy or supervision; in the same way, many counsellors come to psychotherapists for theirs. And, round the other way, counsellors have much to teach analysts and psychotherapists, in the variety of their work; the different clients they work with, and the settings in which they do that work; and in relationship to work that is focused, time-limited, or on a once-a-week basis.

My hope in writing this is that we can learn to respect our differences, value our own and each other's strengths, be realistic about our weaknesses, and learn to work together.

References

Jacobs, M. (1988) *Psychodynamic Counselling in Action*. London: Sage.

Malan, D. (1979) *Individual Psychotherapy and the Science of Psychodynamics*. London: Butterworth.

Malan, D. (1992) *Psychodynamics, Training and Outcome in Brief Psychotherapy*. London: Butterworth.

Discussion issues

1 At what point on the spectrum described in the chapter do you feel most comfortable working? What part does exploring the unconscious and analysing the transference and counter-transference play in your work?
2 Is working on a once-a-week basis a problem with some clients; if so with whom and why?
3 To what extent do dependence and regression play a part in your work? Do you see them as problems or essential elements of the counselling relationship?
4 How do you see your own development as a counsellor? To work in a more focused, problem-solving way, or to move along the spectrum towards working with dependence, regression, and analysing the transference and counter-transference? What new training might be necessary?

67

Person-Centred Counselling/Psychotherapy versus Psychodynamic Counselling and Psychotherapy

Ivan Ellingham

The most intensive and successful counseling is indistinguishable from intensive and successful psychotherapy. (Carl Rogers, 1942, p. 4)

Within the field of counselling/psychotherapy the debate smoulders on over whether the terms 'counselling' and 'psychotherapy' refer to the same or different activities. Two articles in *Counselling* which have recently stirred the embers on this issue are Brian Thorne's 'Counselling and psychotherapy: the quest for differences' (1992), and Alan Naylor-Smith's 'Counselling and psychotherapy: is there a difference?' (1994), published as Chapter 66 in the present volume.

Made plain by these two contributions is the way in which different schools of counselling/psychotherapy line up on opposite sides on this question – key protagonists being the person-centred school, to which Thorne belongs and which espouses sameness, versus the psychodynamic school, of which Naylor-Smith is a member and which claims fundamental difference. Thorne and Naylor-Smith each present arguments supportive of the position of their respective schools, Naylor-Smith's piece being in large measure a rejoinder to Thorne's article.

Now as it happens, ideas of my own have already surfaced in this latest bubbling of what is a long-standing debate, for in his 1992 article Thorne makes substantive reference to ideas I expressed in a paper written earlier that year entitled 'On the conceptual development of a person-centred paradigm of counselling/psychotherapy' (cf. Thorne, 1992, p. 247). Two conclusions which may be drawn from the title of this paper are:

1   That I am committed to the person-centred school both in terms of practice and theory – hence my predilection for the composite term 'counselling/ psychotherapy' ('c/p', for short) to indicate that I hold the person-centred position that 'counselling' and 'psychotherapy' are the same activity. (Throughout the present chapter my terminology – which will include the use of this composite term – seeks to reflect such a position.)
2   That I believe significant light can be shed on the endeavour to generate scientific understanding of the phenomenon of c/p through taking account of Thomas Kuhn's characterization of a 'paradigm' as the hallmark of understanding which is genuinely scientific.

This chapter was first published as 'Quest for a paradigm: person-centred counselling psychotherapy versus psychodynamic counselling and psychotherapy', in *Counselling, Journal of the British Association for Counselling*, vol. 6, no. 4, pp. 288–90.

On the basis, then, of my commitment to the person-centred approach and my faith in the illuminatory power of Kuhn's notion of a paradigm, what I here attempt is the further elaboration of ideas contained in my earlier paper, my aim being to point the way towards resolution of the dispute between the person-centred and psychodynamic schools over the sameness or difference of 'counselling' and 'psychotherapy'.

In part I of what follows I overview Kuhn's notion of a scientific paradigm. In part II, drawing upon Kuhn's ideas I set forth a number of conclusions apropos the dispute between the person-centred and psychodynamic schools over the proper definition of 'counselling' and 'psychotherapy'. In part III, I discuss some of my reasons for reaching these conclusions.

I On paradigms and would-be paradigms

The notion of a paradigm as the quintessential ingredient of a genuine science stems from Thomas Kuhn's formulation in *The Structure of Scientific Revolutions* (1970). Whilst difficult to define exactly, in broad terms a Kuhnian paradigm may be said to be the framework of thought to which all members of a particular scientific field own allegiance, the ideational 'Gestalt' by which they define the field's proper subject matter and legitimate methodological procedures. Included within the embrace of a paradigm, therefore, are not only a general world-view and overarching theoretical scheme, but ideas of varying degrees of refinement, ranging from tacit assumptions regarding practical methods, say, to one or two explicit concepts of a pivotal and powerful nature, e.g. Newton's concept of gravity and Darwin's concept of evolution.

The use of the term 'Gestalt' – German for 'form', 'pattern', 'whole' – is apt with respect to paradigms due to the influence on Kuhn's thinking of findings of the Gestalt psychologists. Kuhn is particularly indebted to the Gestaltists' demonstration of our ability to interpret the same visual 'facts' as conforming either to one overall pattern or to another, but not to both at the same time – as, for instance, when we 'see' the same marks on the page as either the face of a young woman, or that of an old 'hag'. The central tenet of Kuhn's interpretation of the history of science is thus that science advances not only through the patient accumulation of empirical findings, but by either/or revolutions of fundamental sense-making perspective, i.e. by ideational Gestalt-switches of the kind that took place in the shift in conceiving the sun at the centre of the planetary system and not the earth – namely, the Copernican 'revolution'.

A further significant feature of Kuhn's analysis concerns the manner of a paradigm's emergence. According to Kuhn, prior to a paradigm's birth within a particular field there exists 'a multiplicity of competing schools' espousing divergent frameworks of thought (1970, p. 163). Such 'initial divergences . . . disappear' though, says Kuhn, with the rise of a paradigm, an event which 'usually is caused by the triumph of one of the pre-paradigm schools' (p. 17). In the course of time, that is, the framework of thought of one of the schools develops to the point that it is generally recognized as providing a more precise and comprehensive explanatory scheme than its rivals. Kuhn's scenario is thus Darwinian: the fittest thrives, the not so fit wither away.

II Kuhnian conclusions

Kuhn's ideas have, I believe, special relevance for the field of c/p. They shed light, in my view, both on the current condition of the field as a whole and on the specific issues of the dispute between the person-centred and psychodynamic schools over the sameness or difference of 'counselling' and 'psychotherapy'. On such a basis, the conclusions I draw pertinent to this dispute are:

1   that what each of the two schools takes to be the proper definition of 'counselling' and 'psychotherapy' is indeed an integral function of that school's overall framework of thought;
2   that the incompatibility of the two schools' definitions of counselling and psychotherapy results from an underlying incompatibility between their respective frameworks of thought;
3   that the two schools are thus best viewed as competing pre-paradigm schools;
4   that examination of the central concepts of each school suggests that it is the person-centred framework of thought not the psychodynamic that is set to provide a more adequate base on which to ground a paradigm for the field of c/p – in which case the view that 'counselling' and 'psychotherapy' are the same activity will eventually become paradigmatic.

III Discussion

Here, with little space, I cannot go into great detail regarding these conclusions, but shall simply aim at indicating their general plausibility. To this end I take as my initial focus for discussion the psychodynamic argument of Alan Naylor-Smith (Chapter 66) 'that there are valid differences between counselling and psychotherapy' (pp. 512–18).

In 'Counselling and psychotherapy: is there a difference?' Naylor-Smith's entire case that 'counselling' and 'psychotherapy' are markedly different rests on the Freudian concepts of 'the unconscious' and 'transference', concepts central to the framework of psychodynamic thought as a whole. Baldly put, for Naylor-Smith the psychological practitioner who helps an individual resolve his or her psychological problems without delving into 'the unconscious' or utilizing 'transference' is a common-or-garden counsellor, someone who operates on the surface of the mind, i.e. in the region of 'consciousness'. By contrast, the mark of a psychotherapist, a 'psychodynamic' expert, is that s/he is able to venture deep into the client's unconscious and identify for the client the 'many powerful and varied feelings' buried there from the past (p. 513) – especially those feelings whose true tie is to significant others in the past, but which by way of 'transference' presently attach themselves to the person of the psychotherapist.

Even this brief overview I hope makes clear how crucial the two concepts of 'the unconscious' and 'transference' are to the psychodynamic case that 'counselling' and 'psychotherapy' are fundamentally different. Clear, too, given that 'the unconscious' and 'transference' are central to the entire psychodynamic framework, how questioning the validity of such a difference involves questioning the validity of the psychodynamic edifice *per se*. Dispense with the concepts of 'the unconscious' and 'transference' and not only does the psychodynamic case for a difference between 'counselling' and 'psychotherapy' become shaky, but the entire structure of psychodynamic thought begins to wobble.

And, of course, it is exactly this kind of comprehensive challenge that is mounted by adherents of the person-centred approach. For the person-centred view that 'counselling' and 'psychotherapy' are the same activity is based on a framework of thought which finds no place for the concepts of 'the unconscious' and 'transference' – from a person-centred perspective the two simply do not exist. Which is not to say that person-centred theorists deny the reality of the phenomena which psychodynamic practitioners categorize on the basis of 'the unconscious' and 'transference'.

Consider, then, some of the misgivings of person-centred theorists regarding the concepts of 'the unconscious' and 'transference' and the alternative concepts they employ.

From a person-centred perspective the crucial flaws intrinsic to the Freudian concepts of 'the unconscious' and 'transference' have to do with their being expressions of an outmoded, Newtonian world-view. Note, in this regard, the language used by Naylor-Smith to describe psychodynamic practice: how he speaks of 'the root cause of our client's problems' lying 'in the unconscious'; of 'the unconscious' containing 'powerful and varied feelings'; of these 'unconscious feelings . . . causing havoc in our client's life' (p. 514).

What such language makes plain is Naylor-Smith's reliance on Freud's conception 'of the mind in terms of a spatial arrangement of the unconscious and conscious states' (Malcolm, 1982, p. 29). Just as such a spatial model guided Freud in his writings on psychodynamic practice, so it continues to guide Naylor-Smith (cf. Malcolm, 1982). The basic picture of psychotherapy from a psychodynamic point of view is thus one in which mental phenomena (ideas, thoughts and feelings – conceived as psychical 'entities') get moved from one chamber of the mind ('the unconscious') to another ('consciousness'), after the fashion of bits of matter flowing from one chamber in a hydraulic system to another (cf. MacIntyre, 1958, p. 18). As Alasdair MacIntyre clarifies, instead of unchanging bits of matter being propelled by external physical forces what we have in such a Freudian model are unchanging bits of mental stuff being propelled by psychical forces: the placing of the mind within 'the "billiard ball" universe of Newtonian mechanics' (p. 17). Not only has Descartes' mental 'substance' become equated with his physical 'substance', but it is imagined as behaving in exactly the same mechanical manner.

In contrast to this psychodynamic Newtonian scheme, person-centred theory strives to make sense of the nature of c/p in the post-Newtonian terms of Einstein and Darwin. That is to say, in terms which view 'matter' as at root 'process', patterned activity, and nature in general as a field of evolving processes. As Carl Rogers, its originator, has testified therefore, the person-centred theory of therapy 'is a process formulation . . . a field theory' (1980a, p. 2160).

However, it is not Rogers but Eugene Gendlin who has contributed most to the person-centred conception of c/p in process terms. Gendlin too, among person-centred theorists, who has been most keenly aware of the radical difference between the person-centred process conception and the Newtonian rendition of Freud. Employing the term 'contents' to refer to psychological 'entities', Gendlin stresses that to adequately conceptualize the personal *growth* engendered by effective c/p, 'We will require "process" categories that attempt to distinguish, not contents, but different modes or dimensions of process' (1962, p. 32). 'Our concepts,' he elaborates, 'will have to follow a "process" model, rather than a Newtonian "content" model,' the psychodynamic version of which posits that '[w]hether they are "in" awareness or "in" the unconscious, the contents are viewed as already defined, fully formed and unaffected in their nature by "coming into" awareness' (pp. 32–3, 30).

Here it is not that Gendlin is unaware of the seeming reasonableness of the psychodynamic model, based as it is 'on the striking way in which the individual during psychotherapy becomes aware of what (so he now says) he has long felt but has not known that he felt' and 'realizes how powerfully these previously unaware experiences have affected his feelings and behaviour' (1964, p. 132). But rather a matter of how one explains this experience theoretically. Based on empirical research, person-centred theory posits that individuals do have available to them previous awareness of what they later become *fully* conscious of, such previous awareness being a 'gut-level' or 'bodily-felt' mode of apprehension – a vague, global sense of discomfort, say, at the edge of awareness (cf. Rogers, 1980a). Thus on the one hand continuity exists between earlier and later apprehension, and on the other constructive change takes place in the shift from a less to more evolved mode of apprehension.

The notion of increase in complexity allied to continuity, i.e. the notion of growth, has always been at the heart of person-centred theorizing regarding c/p – witness comparisons between the growth of plants and personal development (cf. Rogers, 1980b, p. 118). In person-centred terms, it is the stunting of the processes of growth within the person that results in psychological disturbance, stunting sensed in a gut-level manner and brought about through past failure to provide the individual with a psychologically nurturing ambience or 'field'. So viewed, the counsellor's task is to furnish the individual with such a field for the purpose of bringing to full flower that individual's personal potential. This remedial facilitative process has been termed 're-parenting', a term well chosen in so far as it highlights that the ideas and attitudes conveyed by everyday language are 'good enough' to create such a nurturing ambience; that continuity exists between ordinary relationships and the relationship of c/p; that no divide exists between 'counselling' and 'psychotherapy'; that scientistic notions such as 'the unconscious' and 'transference' are obfuscatory.

From a person-centred point of view, therefore, feelings which the client experiences in the moment are a product of the moment, of the active processes within the individual relative to the surrounding psychological field. In that the processes which make up the individual's world have been shaped and affected by the past, feelings engendered in the present may have degrees of similarity with feelings experienced in the past. But to say, as psychodynamic practitioners do, that the client has feelings from the past buried in his/her unconscious, that the therapist can know what these feelings are even though the client does not, that the feelings of hate and sexual love which the client has for the therapist are simply the re-surfacing of childhood feelings, that 'counselling' is different from 'psychotherapy' – all this is to employ concepts which are incapable of comprehending the process of growth and creative development which is the essence of c/p. It is to remain rooted in a paradigmatic vision which owes everything to Descartes and Newton and has yet to appreciate the revolution in thought inspired by Darwin and Einstein.

The resolution of the debate over differences between 'counselling' and 'psychotherapy' is at hand. It is simply a matter of facilitating the further articulation of a truth which mystics such as Carl Rogers have previously intuited at a gut level.

References

Ellingham, I.H. (1992) 'On the conceptual development of a person-centred paradigm for the field of counselling/psychotherapy.' Unpublished manuscript.

Gendlin, E.T. (1962) *Experiencing and the Creation of Meaning*. New York: Free Press.

Gendlin, E.T. (1964) 'A theory of personality change', in J.T. Hart and T.M. Tomlinson (eds), *New Directions in Client-Centred Therapy*. Boston, MA: Houghton Mifflin (1970).

Kuhn, T. (1970) *The Structure of Scientific Revolutions*, 2nd edn. Chicago: Chicago University Press.

MacIntyre, A.C. (1958) *The Unconscious*. London: Routledge and Kegan Paul.

Malcolm, J. (1982) *Psychoanalysis: the Impossible Profession*. London: Pan Books.

Rogers, C.R. (1942) *Counseling and Psychotherapy*. Boston, MA: Houghton Mifflin.

Rogers, C.R. (1980a) 'Client-centred psychotherapy', in H.I. Kaplan, B.J. Sadock and A.M. Freeman (eds), *Comprehensive Textbook of Psychiatry III*. Baltimore, MD: Williams & Wilkins.

Rogers, C.R. (1980b) *A Way of Being*. Boston, MA: Houghton Mifflin.

Thorne, B. (1992) 'Psychotherapy and counselling: the quest for differences', *Counselling*, 3(4): 244–8.

Discussion issues

1 Counsellors committed to a variety of approaches have been shown to provide clients with effective psychological help. As long as a counsellor is effective, would you say it matters as much as the writer suggests which theoretical approach a counsellor happens to be committed to?

2 The history of the field of counselling has seen the development of an increasing number of different theories and approaches. Do you think the author justified in holding that a unitary theory and unified approach to counselling will one day be achieved?

3 Most practising counsellors today describe themselves as 'eclectic'. That is to say that in their practice they make use of ideas and techniques from various counselling approaches, selected on the basis of which they consider best for their client. If you are eclectic in your practice, what are the grounds on which you decide what is best in this manner? If you base your decision on 'intuition', how do you ensure that you are not acting in terms of a personal whim?

4 Do you agree with the author that the issues of whether 'counselling' and 'psychotherapy' are the same or different can only be resolved through the development of a 'paradigm' of counselling/ psychotherapy?

Counselling and Psychotherapy: a reply by Alan Naylor-Smith

The dialogues between person-centred counselling and psychodynamic counselling, and between counselling and psychotherapy are important ones. Unfortunately the article by Ivan Ellingham does not in my opinion take the discussion much further.

First, he is not interested in dialogue but in dismissing. Psychodynamic psychotherapy makes up the largest section of the United Kingdom Council for Psychotherapy and 60% of the membership of BAC. If we are to find new paradigms we will find them surely by listening to and learning from each other, not by triumphalism.

Secondly, Ellingham misrepresents what I said in the article and then attacks this representation. I never said that those who do not utilize the transference are 'common-or-garden counsellors'; I value their work too much. Nor did I draw the distinction between counsellors and psychotherapists as rigidly as is stated; in contrast, I emphasized a great area where psychotherapy and psychodynamic counselling overlap. Nor do I believe that 'mental phenomena get moved from one chamber of the mind (the unconscious) to another (consciousness), after the fashion of bits of matter flowing from one chamber in a hydraulic system to another'. What a travesty! If Ellingham wishes to attack my article he should attack what I say, not what he thinks I may believe. In fact what I think is that events that are too disturbing or painful to be contained, felt or thought about are repressed in the mind, where they lurk exercising their baneful influence on people's lives in a manner similar to that described by Gendlin in Ellingham's article. For example, a deeply depressed mother may look with despair at her baby or child; the child reads in those eyes that he or she is no good, impossible and difficult to cope with. The occasions when this was experienced may be forgotten; but the feeling that he or she is no good tragically remains, harming the life of the individual. Feelings like this have their impact in the life of the client but are also carried into the relationship with the counsellor, that is, into the transference, and so can be understood in the here-and-now and addressed. It is this reality that all counsellors of whatever theoretical persuasion have to tangle with, and it is the debate about this that is so central to the person-centred/psychodynamic debate.

Then there is the psychotherapy/counselling debate that has to address the other topics I mentioned in my article, including frequency of sessions; the depth of distress that can be tolerated and therefore acknowledged by clients; the opportunity to give greater attention to the unconscious; and the place of dependence and regression. I hope the debate can move on, and that first we can learn to listen to each other.

Counselling and Psychotherapy: a reply to a reply by Ivan Ellingham

By way of response to Alan Naylor-Smith's response to my article, let me say that in addressing the questions of the relationship between counselling and psychotherapy and of the relationship between the person-centred and psychodynamic approaches to counselling/psychotherapy my fundamental concern is for clarity of thought, not triumphalism, as Naylor-Smith suggests. To resolve the questions concerned, it is my view that a coherent and unitary theoretical scheme of counselling/psychotherapy needs to be developed, one which rests on fecund and powerful key concepts. Such a resolution, in my view, will not come from the glossing over of basic conceptual differences between schools. To advance discussion, any dialogue/debate between schools must grapple honestly with such issues. It is on such a basis that I am interested in dialogue. It is the quality of ideas espoused by psychodynamic practitioners that command my respect not the number of individuals who espouse them. Contrary to what Naylor-Smith claims, I am not dismissive of psychodynamic ideas *per se*, but critical of them as being sound enough as a basis on which to ground a paradigm of counselling/psychotherapy.

Alan Naylor-Smith effectively accuses me of not listening to what he says in his article. In fact I believe I heard exactly his message for members of the person-centred approach. It is a message which accords with that of other psychodynamic writers, such as Sue Wheeler (*Counselling*, November 1995); namely, that the person-centred approach is 'an excellent foundation' and 'a good starting point' for counsellors, but that if one wishes to help people at a deep level one must comprehend both 'the unconscious' and 'transference', i.e. become a psychodynamic counsellor. As to who is the good listener, it doesn't appear to me that Naylor-Smith listened at all to the arguments of one of the articles to which he refers, that of Brian Thorne (*Counselling*, November 1992).

I am pleased, though, that Naylor-Smith's reply does clarify somewhat his conception of the psychotherapeutic process. Pleased that he essentially distances himself from Freud's hydraulic drive model – although I have to say that I have yet to be convinced that outside such an aquatic setting the psychodynamic concepts of 'the unconscious' and 'transference' are not simply dead fish. I wonder, however, if when he embraces Gendlin's views Naylor-Smith realizes that one of Gendlin's views is that 'the unconscious . . . is not really *unconscious* for it can be felt'.

Discussion points

1 Do you think that these protagonists accurately reflect the two approaches to counselling that they represent?
2 Have they accurately reflected each other's approaches?

Note

This debate continued in following issues of *Counselling*.

PART FOUR

COUNSELLING AND RESEARCH

Introduction to Part Four

The Relevance of Research for Counselling Practice was the focus of the special issue of *Counselling* in February 1994 and there are good reasons for making these articles more widely available in the *BAC Reader*. The guest editors for this issue, Sue Wheeler and John McLeod, invited accounts of the experience of doing research, the skills involved in carrying out research and the impact of research upon practice. The contributions reflect some of the richness and diversity of counselling research in Britain today.

Although counselling in the UK is now sufficiently established for us to step back and learn from experience, one of the difficulties in achieving the required detachment is that we are often so involved in and committed to our daily counselling work, that we can become deeply suspicious of the capacity of the outcomes of research to challenge our accepted practice and thinking. The chapter by Carolyn Hicks and Sue Wheeler addresses this challenge and Geraldine Shipton, a counsellor and trainer who worked with a researcher, shares very openly some of the difficulties and resistances which that collaboration engendered and their resolution.

Michèle Crouan illustrates how research informed practice in a voluntary counselling agency. She shows how the sometimes unexpected facts and information revealed by research can be used to change the well-meaning assumptions of a counselling service and lead to a more accessible allocation of resources to particular client groups. Peter Ross similarly illustrates how research findings impacted upon and were used to change both the practice of counselling and the structure of a university counselling service.

Counsellors considering items for their research agenda will find that John McLeod offers a wide-ranging consideration of some of the areas in which research may prove productive.

Although Gillian Thomas tells us that she is a practising counsellor first . . . she also wrote as a current researcher, whose chapter will resonate, as do the others in this section, with those who struggle with the dilemma of the perceived incompatibility between the process nature of counselling and the experimental nature of research.

By way of encouragement we include in this section a practical example of counsellor-initiated research in a GP Health Centre carried out by Peter Thomas. We would like to remind counsellors that BAC has a Research Sub-Committee which organizes an annual research conference and has produced a series of leaflets (obtainable from the BAC Publications Office) which summarize evaluation research into the effectiveness of counselling in various settings.

68

The Role of Research in the Professional Development of Counselling

Sue Wheeler and Carolyn Hicks

Over recent years there has been an increasing demand for open accountability within the welfare professions, together with a requirement to justify practice on proper empirical grounds. This has offered a serious challenge to many professional groups whose service has been based on time-honoured ritual and tradition. Consequently, there has been a significant shift towards research as one means by which practice can be rationalized, systematized and made more effective and efficient. Counselling, with its increasing prominence in both public and private sectors, has not been exempt from these pressures.

The 1993 BAC survey of its members' research activities reported that 20% of the respondents had at some time been actively involved in research and 14% had published their findings. The first BAC research conference held in 1995 was over-subscribed and attended by 80 enthusiastic research-minded counsellors. These figures confirm counselling research as a higher-profile activity than had been assumed by many of those involved in the profession. However, while these statistics may present an encouraging picture for counsellors committed to the role of research in their profession, this perspective may not be held by many for whom research represents an undermining of the core value system on which counselling is founded.

Research and counselling

Counselling relies on empathy, care, subjectivity and intuition as a routine part of the therapeutic process, while research is stereotypically perceived as being detached, objective and dispassionate. In this way, the two activities may be construed as being diametrically opposed. Thus, for some counsellors the whole issue of research, with its connotations of experimentation and quantification, is seen as being incompatible with the process of counselling and for that reason alone it is eschewed. It is crucial though for those counsellors opposed to research to address the real source of their opposition. For many, conducting research will necessitate the acquisition of new and alien skills, which had previously been deemed to be the province of academics. Research derived from health-care professionals has repeatedly demonstrated that resistance to research stems from a

This chapter was first published as 'Research: an essential foundation for counselling training and practice', in *Counselling, Journal of the British Association for Counselling*, vol. 5, no. 1, pp. 29–31 (1994).

deep-seated diffidence to undertake new activities, although the formal explanations for rejecting the research culture have typically been similar to those outlined by counsellors (e.g. Hicks, 1992, 1993, 1995). Fundamental changes to working practice always alter the status quo and generate a sense of threat within a workforce. It may be important for counsellors, then, to disentangle their affective reactions from the intellectual argument.

In a climate of increasing accountability and limited resources, it is critical for welfare and service agencies to prove their worth. While the reasons behind this requirement are primarily political and economic, the reality remains that any service, just to survive, must be as cost-effective as possible. That many counselling agencies are either within the public or voluntary sectors means that they are likely to experience a pronounced pressure on resources. Consequently counselling organizations, as with other welfare agencies, must be aware of issues of cost-effectiveness, through the rationalization of activities. If this is not to mean a wholesale cut in services, it is essential that the process of streamlining and rationalizing counselling should be based on information derived not from intuition and gut-feeling, but from objective observation of the facts. In other words, a scientific approach may be required if counselling is to optimize its practice and to survive in the current climate of welfare cuts.

Indeed, counselling may even have to justify its very existence, if the early damage from Eysenck's (1952) study is to be undone. This investigation challenged the counselling and psychotherapy professions with the conclusion that clients were more likely to recover from spontaneous remission than through psychotherapeutic intervention. Inevitably these results were potentially damaging to the professions in question and generated much further research. While Eysenck's study has since been criticized on a number of grounds (McNeilly and Howard, 1991), any research which investigates the effectiveness of counselling – despite the inherent methodological difficulties when relating it to outcome (Lambert and Bergin, 1994) – is likely to add to the knowledge-base of the profession. This has a further valuable function. One of the necessary criteria for an emerging profession is the development of a corpus of knowledge which is specific to that profession, based on empirically gathered data, coupled with experience. Therefore, if counselling wishes to continue its growth into a legitimate profession in its own right, it is imperative that it also derives its own research information base. However, this source of data should not be seen as one which is exclusively scientific. Empirical evidence about counselling should be gathered alongside documentation gained through insight, observation, personal experience and debate.

It is almost axiomatic that systematic evaluation of the most effective ways of organizing and delivering a counselling service at all levels to the variety of individuals who seek it is important to the profession. There are many questions as yet unanswered about the relative value of different counselling models and types of intervention. However, as counselling involves the dynamic interaction between individuals, it is highly unlikely that simple cause–effect relationships between intervention and outcome will be found. None the less, the capacity to predict which treatment procedures are most likely to produce best outcomes with particular client groups would be a valuable skill in a counsellor's repertoire. To achieve this objective, even if only in part, decision-making in counselling should be based not on *ad hoc* reactions but on empirical evidence gathered from scientifically derived data.

Cost-effectiveness

Central to all this is the issue of cost-effectiveness. While the discussion of finances alongside human welfare is anathema to many counsellors, the reality for many counselling organizations is one of having to meet increased demands for help with decreasing resources. Counsellors sometimes find it difficult to make hard-headed decisions (for example imposing a maximum number of sessions for all clients) that may impact negatively on some of their clients. However, these decisions are easier and more comfortable to make when there is a body of research evidence to guide and justify the decision. While the concept of evaluating human welfare in such objective terms may undoubtedly be distasteful to many practitioners, there is a positive aspect. Those studies concerned with assessing the value of counselling in the workplace have shown that the availability of a work-based counsellor can improve the well-being, both physical and psychological, of employees (e.g. the Post Office study, Cooper et al., 1990). Reduced absenteeism, sickness and stress-related problems have clear benefits for the individual as well as for the wider contexts of the organization, the welfare system and the economic state of the country.

Similarly, other studies have assessed the merits of a counselling service within health centres. While it is unwise to judge the effectiveness of counselling in General Practice solely in financial terms, some results have suggested a reduction in pharmacological interventions and hence costs when a counsellor is attached to a practice (e.g. Robson et al., 1984), and highlight the beneficial impact for patients, their families and GP fund-holders (Salinsky and Curtis Jenkins, 1994). These studies are constructive and valuable, both in the strategic planning of counselling services, as well as in the discharge of the therapeutic process, and illustrate clearly the potential impact research can have on the way in which counselling can be directed and organized. Examples such as these make a good case for an increase in research-based decision-making in counselling, and for counsellors to be equipped with a knowledge of research skills which allows them either to conduct their own research, or to evaluate that of others. This latter is essential if published findings are to be applied judiciously within a practice setting.

BAC Research Committee

The increasing acceptance of the need for more counselling-related research is confirmed by the existence of a research committee within the BAC whose specific remit is to encourage research and to provide advice and guidance to organizations and others on research issues, including ethical considerations. In addition, many training courses, and in particular those that are award-bearing and based in higher education, have a research training component within them. These courses often require a small piece of counselling research to be undertaken as part of the assessment process. Through the practical application of research theory to their own counselling practice, students develop their research skills, and moreover, enhance their ability to make informed appraisals of published findings. Consequently, training courses may be one essential forum for the development of research competencies within the counselling profession, and this, in turn, may increase the range of counselling research-based literature available to inform choice.

Undoubtedly, research as a core subject in training may ring alarm bells in students on these courses as well as in counsellors outside, given all the associations that research has with scientific rigour and laboratory experiments. Unswerving allegiance to formal scientific method is clearly inappropriate, unacceptable and unethical in a counselling context. However, this definition of research is a narrow and limiting one. At a general level, research involves asking questions about everyday events and finding answers to those questions in a systematic way. Translated into a counselling context, this means that practice should be continually challenged and evaluated using techniques of objective scientific enquiry. Only in this way can valid conclusions be drawn about how counselling can be delivered to optimal effect.

These challenges to existing practice can be made using a variety of methodologies, of both a qualitative and quantitative variety. While qualitative research tends to be more attractive for counsellors, only quantitative research can lead to predictions concerning best treatment procedures. Consequently, it may be that the balance needs to be redressed, with an increased emphasis on quantification and hypothesis-testing.

Research methods in counsellor training

This viewpoint governed the authors' thinking when designing the research methods module on a Master's Degree in Counselling. (See Table 68.1 for an outline of the module contents.)

As tutors on this degree course, the authors are well aware of students' anxiety and apprehension about the research element of the course. Although many are competent and experienced as counselling practitioners, they approach the research methods module with fear and trepidation, clutching calculators and statistical tables. For some the reality turns out to be as bad as they anticipated, but for others the experience raises many interesting and valuable questions.

A microcosm of the research debate

The statutory assignment for the research module is a piece of *experimental* research within the counselling domain and it is to this that the students have sometimes taken principal exception. Because this module represents a microcosm of the research debate in counselling as a whole, some of the objections and the counter-arguments, the reasons and resolutions may be worth considering in more detail.

Table 68.1 *Counselling and psychotherapy research methods module*

Objectives
To introduce students to some of the basic concepts involved in research design and data analysis
To give students the skills to be able to evaluate critically published research articles, and to carry out research projects of their own
To consider both quantitative and qualitative methods relevant to counselling research

Course content
Library orientation: index and abstract use, using library services
Computer literacy: literature search software, BIDS, CD ROM, etc.
Qualitative research: interview and survey methods, questionnaire design
Single case research design
Descriptive statistics: graphs, normal distribution, etc.
Inferential statistics: the principles of experimental and correlational designs, the experimental and null hypotheses
Related, unrelated and matched subject designs
Sources of error in research
Levels of measurements: probability, significance levels
Statistical tests: parametric and non-parametric statistical tests
Research reports: reading, planning and writing
Counselling: monitoring and evaluation, methods and models

One of the main problems for the first cohort of 20 experienced and highly competent students on the Master's degree course was the variety of their academic backgrounds. The majority of the participants possessed Arts degrees and consequently the concept of scientific research was alien and threatening. To undertake the assignment, they needed to learn a new set of skills, relevant jargon and concepts, many of which were associated with school subjects long rejected. Memories of a poor showing in 'O' level Maths seemed to flood back and impede concentration. Those students from a science background fared little better, but for reasons of purism and ideology. The problems of transferring scientific skills derived from the natural sciences with their predictable laws and phenomena into a human context was unacceptable for many students who felt that their own intuitive skills of enquiry were being compromised. One of the more successful ways of resolving these problems derived from customizing the research methods course, which involved ensuring that all the concepts, examples and topics were specifically tailored to be relevant to counselling. In this way the whole module became more meaningful to the participants, who saw that research methodologies were not immutable techniques, but merely a means of asking questions and eliciting answers.

Particular fears were expressed about the statistical analysis of research data. Most students had finished their mathematical education at age 16 with considerable relief and this, together with an abhorrence of using techniques of quantification within a subjective, dynamic counselling arena, conspired to generate difficulties. At the risk of offending the purists, it was continually emphasized that statistical analyses are simply a means by which sense can be made from a mass of numbers. As there was no inherent virtue in the long-hand computation of formulae within this research module, calculators and computers were used as part of the teaching medium. Students simply needed to know how to enter the data into a calculator and how to interpret the results; the theory and mechanics of statistical probability were reserved for devotees of the subject.

Wider concerns about research were also voiced. Many students were concerned about the relevance of any project they wanted to do. Influenced by media representations of research findings, many intending researchers in a wide variety of disciplines are deterred because of assumptions that to be useful, research has got to be large-scale and costly. Nothing could be further from the truth. Whilst not denying the value of the big project, there have been many important findings from small-scale, local initiatives which have the potential to influence counselling at a number of levels. Examples include a study of waiting-list time and non-attendance within Relate which has the potential to make a significant impact on the local agency's organizational structure, thereby limiting resource wastage while simultaneously responding more appropriately to client need (Hicks and Hickman, 1993). Other examples are given by Ross (1994), who investigated the impact of pre-counselling information given to clients in a university counselling service, the results of which were used to improve practice, and Crouan (1994) whose research led to a reorganization of a counselling service to make it more accessible to ethnic minority groups.

Ethical issues

Ethical issues were also a source of discomfort to many students on the course. The deliberate manipulation or interference with clients and their therapy to meet the requirements of experimental design is obviously unacceptable. Moreover, the conventional definition of the control group as a no-treatment group implies a withholding of therapy which is wholly unethical. It is, however, perfectly appropriate to compare clients from existing therapeutic settings in order to contrast counselling effectiveness. Similarly, a no-treatment control group can be selected from waiting-list clients – a practical solution to a difficult ethical problem. Ethical guidelines recently produced by the BAC Research Committee (BAC, 1995) provide a long-awaited and valuable resource to refer to when ethical issues are in doubt.

Diffidence as a prevailing emotion amongst students is commonly observed in groups attempting to respond to their profession's demand for research (Hicks, 1992; Erhard, 1995). A regular mentorship system was evolved to support these students through the theoretical and practical problems surrounding the course content and the assignment. Despite this almost universal emotion, the quality of the resulting projects has been gratifyingly high, and many students, including some who showed marked opposition at the start of the course, became more excited by the empirical methods used and their potential for the development of counselling. Projects undertaken for this assignment were quite small and had to be clearly focused. One student looked at the relationship with the counsellor (measured through the therapeutic alliance) depending on whether the counsellor/

client were of the same or different sex. Another looked at teenage pregnancies and the facilities available for counselling such young people. A third looked at the counselling competence of students on the course, in relation to their previous professional training and orientation.

Research – a foundation for practice

It is now important that national organizations take a lead to encourage research in all its forms as part of the counselling profession's overall development. Top-down directives and initiatives emphasizing the role of research as a means by which good practice can be enhanced and resources used with optimal effect are likely over time to foster an awareness and acceptance of research as essential to counselling as a whole. As this shift in viewpoint is effected, more counsellors will become familiar with basic research techniques, more research will be undertaken and published, and research reports will be read with an increased awareness and understanding. At the moment these skills are only possessed by a minority; to train the majority of counsellors, both individual and organizational strategies need to be employed. Institutes of higher education could start running free-standing courses in research methods, tailored to meet the needs of counsellors, with examples relevant to counselling practice. With the increasing pressure on universities and colleges to generate income, courses of this sort are likely to be a welcome innovation in the normal prospectus, particularly in departments concerned with continuing adult education.

For individuals, we hope that recent attention given to research issues (Wheeler and McLeod, 1994) will inspire counsellors, as well as increasing the publications specifically addressing counselling research (*see* McLeod, 1994; Sanders and Liptrot, 1994). Clearly, if counsellors are motivated to seek training in research methods they will become more familiar with research publications and will be able to make informed decisions about their own practice and even undertake their own research projects. Participants at the first BAC research counselling conference, held in February 1995, expressed the need for a Research Division of BAC and the importance of including Counselling Research at the annual national conference. If this were to be implemented, it would have a secondary pay-off in that groups of like-minded people could get together to offer advice, experience, mutual support and encouragement.

The road to research mindedness, research knowledge and experience can be tortuous and/or exciting. It is a road worth taking to help the discipline of counselling become more valued and recognized as a profession continually striving towards higher standards, quality of service and conscious of the need for monitoring and evaluation at all levels.

References

BAC (1993) *Membership Survey*. Mountain & Associates, Marketing Services Ltd, Keele/Rugby: BAC.

BAC (1995) *Ethical Guidelines for Monitoring, Evaluation and Research in Counselling.* Rugby: BAC.

Cooper, C.L., Sadri, G., Allison, T. and Reynolds, P. (1990) 'Stress counselling in the Post Office', *Counselling Psychology Quarterly*, 3(1): 3–11.

Crouan, M. (1994) 'The contribution of a research study towards improving a counselling service', *Counselling*, 5(1): 32–3.

Erhard, R. (1995) 'Research phobia of educational counsellors'. Paper presented to IRTAC Conference, Malta, April 1995.

Eysenck, H.J. (1952) 'The effects of psychotherapy: an evaluation', *Journal of Consulting Psychology*, 16: 319–24.

Gath, D. and Catalan, J. (1986) 'The treatment of emotional disorders in general practice. Psychological methods versus medication', *Journal of Psychosomatic Research*, 30: 381–6.

Hicks, C.M. (1992) 'Research in midwifery: are midwives their own worst enemies?', *Midwifery*, 8: 12–18.

Hicks, C.M. (1993) 'A survey of midwives' attitudes to, and involvement in, research: the first stage in identifying needs for a staff development programme', *Midwifery*, 9: 51–62.

Hicks, C.M. (1995) 'The shortfall in published research: a study of nurses' research and publication activities', *Journal of Advanced Nursing*, 21: 594–604.

Hicks, C.M. and Hickman, G. (1993) 'The impact of waiting list times on client attendance for relationship counselling', *British Journal of Guidance and Counselling*, 22(2): 175–82.

Lambert, M. and Bergin, A.E. (1994) 'The effectiveness of psychotherapy', in A.E. Bergin and S.L. Garfield (eds), *Handbook of Psychotherapy and Behaviour Change*, 4th edn. New York: Wiley.

Martin, E. and Martin, P.M.L. (1985) 'Changes in psychological diagnosis and prescription in a practice using a counsellor', *Family Practice*, 2(4): 241–3.

McLeod, J. (1994) *Doing Counselling Research*. London: Sage.

McNeilly, C.L. and Howard, K.I. (1991) 'The effects of psychotherapy. A re-evaluation based on dosage', *Psychotherapy Research*, 1(1): 74–8.

Robson, M.H., France, R. and Bland, R. (1984) 'A clinical psychologist in primary care. Controlled clinical and economic evaluation', *British Medical Journal*, 288: 1805–8.

Ross, P. (1994) 'The impact of research upon practice', *Counselling*, 5(1): 35–7.

Salinsky, J. and Curtis Jenkins, G. (1994) 'Counselling in general practice', *British Journal of General Practice*, May: 194–5.

Sanders, P. and Liptrot, D. (1994) *An Incomplete Guide to Inferential Statistics for Counsellors*. Manchester: PCCS Books.

Wheeler, S. and McLeod, J. (1994) 'Editorial – Special Edition of *Counselling* on the relevance of research for practice', *Counselling*, 5(1): 28.

Discussion issues

1 What research into counselling has directly affected your practice?

2 How could you evaluate your counselling practice with respect to quality and effectiveness?

3 What reservations do you have about counselling research?

4 What ethical considerations might you have when evaluating your own counselling practice?

69

Working with Resistance to Research

Geraldine Shipton

In their very useful book, Watkins and Schneider (1991) make the claim that two independent professions seem to have evolved: counselling researchers and counselling practitioners. They cite numerous studies which show that counsellors tend not to engage in research and, generally, hold negative views about research. This opinion would seem to be challenged by recent publication of practitioner-based research and methodological advice (*Counselling*, 1994; McLeod, 1994; Sanders and Liptrot, 1993.) In 1992, the Association of Student Counsellors convened a conference on research and evaluation which attracted 90 participants, mainly counsellors (Shipton and Smith, 1993). It is possible that counsellors are undergoing a transformation in their thinking or that they still hold the same kind of views but are being pressurized into participation in an activity which is antipathetic to them.

This chapter considers the issue of resistance and reluctance to carrying out research or evaluation. The terms 'evaluation' and 'research' are really quite distinct. The former is usually concerned with investigating the effectiveness of counselling practice in relation to a perceived standard whilst the latter seeks to discover new facts which are generalizable and which can be used to bring about a development of knowledge. For the purpose of this discussion the terms will be paired up, since they are both related to practical, explicit methods by which the counsellor explores and interprets information about counselling practice.

As an aside, it is pertinent to remember that the earliest attempts at researching the effectiveness of psychotherapeutic work did not begin with the efforts of Eysenck, towards whom we all perhaps have strong feelings, but with Otto Fenichel, the early collaborator of Freud (in fact, Freud wrote the Preface to Fenichel's account of his research project). The disinclination of other analytic contemporaries to follow Fenichel's example suggests that unwillingness to engage in research is not a new phenomenon.

Setting up the research project

The time-limited research project which is referred to in this study took place in a university counselling service where the author worked (Mathers et al., 1993). The project, which involved the use of pre- and post-counselling questionnaires, grew out of the counselling service's interest in auditing its own work and was developed with the help of a consultant research scientist. At no point was there a

This chapter was first published as 'Swords into ploughshares: working with resistance to research', in *Counselling, Journal of the British Association for Counselling*, vol. 5, no. 1, pp. 38–40 (1994).

suggestion that the research would be owned by anyone other than the researchers and the counselling service. The findings were not intended to be interpreted as 'performance indicators' (a management term that means quantifiable variables which are related to specific goals and objectives and which can be then be used to demonstrate how well a person performs in achieving those goals). Needless to say, the service had its own political as well as professional motives in setting up the project. The venture described here was freely chosen (at least on a conscious level!). In situations where counsellors might feel coerced into an activity which can be used to serve the interests of agencies that are not sympathetic to clients' needs, the notion of resistance takes on an altogether different meaning and may be an appropriate strategy.

Impressions and feelings

Counsellors who attempt to set up research or evaluation projects will recognize the kinds of feelings that are commonly aroused: for example, there may be anger or puzzlement that such enquiries should need to take place at all. Counsellors 'know' that they are often effective: clients attend repeatedly and don't complain, clients even recommend their friends to seek counselling when they are in trouble. Negative feedback is rare and some clients even pursue training in counselling because the experience has been of great personal value.

All of these impressions are founded on daily contact with clients and consideration of the process of counselling. The notion of substantiating the perceptions formed, in a systematic way, can be experienced as pointless or lacking in good faith. While this 'commonsense' view of evaluation is understandable, it may appear complacent and unprofessional to the general public or even defensive to managers. Lack of research interest may be combined with confusion about what is being researched: is it the counsellor, is it the 'method' he or she uses or is it the client who has to find a way of using the counsellor and his or her techniques? Furthermore, will the counsellor feel he or she can actually incorporate consequent new knowledge into her or his practice, anyway?

The results of comparing therapeutic methods are unclear (Stiles et al., 1986), although there seems to be some relation between counsellor effectiveness and the counsellor's preferred method of counselling. Studies (Schofield, 1964) show that young, attractive, verbal, intelligent and successful people are considered to make the best clients (especially by the therapists/counsellors themselves!). Counsellors' personal qualities have long since been seen as influential (Bergin and Garfield, 1971). One of the things counsellors need to know is how to do a better job more often and with a wider range of clients. Another factor often driving research and evaluation is the demand to be able to help increasing numbers of people over short periods of time.

At this particular point a healthy scepticism sneaks in: the research that already exists is often difficult to read, let alone, use. Articles are often written up in dense and technical formats which fail to appeal to most practitioners or, alternatively, case-studies are carefully and exquisitely elaborated only to shame the 'jobbing' counsellor. Such articles have a twofold effect: they put off readers and they put off would-be researchers.

Crises of identity and confidence

It may be hard for counsellors to feel they can genuinely change their ways of relating to clients, or indeed, other aspects of their practice. They, too, get 'stuck' and suffer from crises of identity and confidence. Like clients who would change if they knew how to do it on their own, counsellors need to be able to express their apprehensions before they can tap into their creative capacity to learn and develop. Just as in counselling or therapy we would help people look at their fears, as well as at the benefits of making changes, so too do we need to take seriously our own feelings and thoughts about research.

One supposed myth which seems to haunt counselling is that 'it' cannot be accurately portrayed or understood by any research methodology. Empirical studies are suspected of being unfriendly to counselling values, and even qualitative methods, which appear to offer more harmonious approaches to research than quantitative ones, can seem daunting to the uninitiated and bring with them their own set of ethical difficulties (Finch, 1984). Few counsellors are trained in any research methodology although several training courses are now including research options. Lack of experience and pressure on time both cause anxiety and self-doubt in counsellors who are contemplating research. Counselling is a stressful activity and evaluating the process generates a great deal of work. If counsellors cannot see direct evidence of how such an activity might be useful to them, they are making reasonable professional judgements in resisting involvement.

However, most evaluation projects patently offer the possibility of important feedback to the counsellor as well as clear evidence to clients and managers that the counsellor is taking self-evaluation seriously. Perhaps other aspects of self-doubt are triggered by the prospect, including fear that the counsellor is not as effective as he or she believes. There is always a risk of being 'found out' by the investigation of practice. Indeed, I wonder if this fear also unconsciously promotes the production of certain kinds of questionnaires and other research tools which bring forth only bland, equivocal information which is hard to make use of but which is not a threat to established traditions. If fear, whether of ineffectiveness or discredit, is a dominant factor in resistance, it needs to be treated with respect both as an emotion and as practical information. This means that counsellors must feel able to have control over what happens to data that is produced and some means by which they can then learn from the findings in order to implement appropriate changes in their working practice.

In some ways, feelings aroused by research are not unlike those which other impingements on the therapeutic relationship precipitate. Taping of sessions for use in supervision, for example, will provoke a range of responses in counsellors and clients, all of which will have significance and will need to be explored. A crucial option (Aveline, 1992) in taping sessions is to ensure the client has the right to switch off the tape at any time. In a similar vein, the counsellor who is embarking on research activities needs to feel confident he or she can determine the appropriateness of the activity. In practical terms this can be quite straightforward; for example, there may be a degree of counsellor anonymity built into a scheme or guidelines established about criteria for excluding certain clients from the research in order to satisfy particular ethical considerations.

Operation of the research project

Many of these points had been addressed before the setting up of the research project under discussion. None the less, the 'researching-counsellor' had to confront some powerful issues in a way which felt akin to 'culture shock', once the project went into operation. The issue of potential infantilization of clients was the first controversy which came into play with the research consultant, who was accustomed to running 'pure' research programmes, where every referred client was included in the project. The notion of handing out a questionnaire to a new client who might be in tears was felt to be objectionable by the counselling service and aroused a heated discussion. Eventually it became clear that the strong emotions aroused in the counsellor indicated a clash of values which had an important content: a student counselling service often provides the first point of contact for a client in a crisis. Most students are self-referred and normally are seen within a few weeks and, if necessary, the same day. To meet distress at a time of crisis with a request to fill in a questionnaire might well be deemed improper. The counsellors' misgivings were useful in initiating a debate which enabled a realistic research design to be made which fitted the ethics of our particular service.

Contemplating the resistance

A key factor which emerged in contemplating the resistance we experienced in our own service was the importance of ongoing discussion about the project as it was carried out. After only a few weeks we discovered that criteria other than the ones planned were being put into practice in the selection of clients to be included in the pilot project. We found that when participating members of staff were invited to record an identifiable reason for not handing out a questionnaire and were alerted to the possibility that we might include discussion of such categories in the research, questionnaires were then handed out as planned. Similarly, we had to specify how late a 'late arrival' meant before the client was excluded from the project, and whether English not being a first language was justifiable reason for non-participation. Time was needed for all of these concerns to emerge and to be discussed. The surprising aspect was that so many obstacles disappeared after being aired and recorded. It was as if the 'contract' between members of staff involved had to be worked on over a period of time and that a vital component of the project was a regular meeting of core workers. A meeting, it should be said, which included confrontation and conflict over ethical considerations and assumptions. In this respect, resistance and reluctance seem to be normative and to require a collaborative approach, much in the same way as Egan (1990) describes working with the reluctant client.

Protecting the clients?

Some of the thoughts aroused by the prospect of conducting a research project included the previously mentioned notion that nothing useful would emerge; that students would be unhappy and would object to it; that the students' union, their advocates, might complain; that students would experience the questionnaires as invasive and insensitive. These issues had to be returned to frequently and addressed clearly and honestly. In fact, very few students expressed doubts about the value of the questionnaires and most seemed very keen to take part. The students' union was contacted and was happy to see the project take place. Counsellors themselves became interested in the research and eager to make it a success. Overall, counsellors expressed far more anxiety about the project than did students. While the reasons for counsellors' views being, apparently, at odds with those of students are unclear, it may be that counsellors displaced some of their own fears on to students. Concerns about students being treated insensitively may have also related to their own feelings that their professionalism was in question. Counsellors are sometimes requested to prove their legitimacy as helpers in a way that other professionals may not be called upon to do, perhaps reinforcing a sense of potential threat against them.

Behaviours of resistance

One of the aspects of the project which was fascinating was the resistance or reluctance which was acted out rather than talked about. Right at the beginning of the project, in a 'trial run', clients were sometimes not given questionnaires because the counsellor 'forgot', yet at breaks and meetings, jokes about the research were always being made which showed it had not been forgotten. Arbitrary decisions, as mentioned earlier, would be made about who was to be involved and a whole 'other' project began to evolve organically, a bit like the garden which grows rampantly in summer unless you keep an eye on it! Whilst some unspoken objections had to be fathomed out and put into words so that they could be given due consideration, others had to be challenged immediately. Again, it was not unlike a therapeutic situation where some boundaries had to be maintained rigorously but with care and thoughtfulness. Ironically, timing was one boundary that the counsellor-researcher had to protect in two ways. First, against initial attempts to withstand handing our questionnaires on the grounds of insufficient time, and secondly, against what seemed like an attempted enticement on the part of the research consultant into making a commitment to extend the project into ongoing evaluation and research!

The role of the consultant to the project and of the co-researcher were also instrumental in addressing reluctance in the project. At times, the consultant occupied a similar role to that of a counselling supervisor who helped the researchers to voice their worries and find solutions to management difficulties. The counselling colleagues then would, at times, seem to fit a role like that of a client who was rather ambivalent and whose anxieties the researchers needed to discuss regularly in 'supervision'. Meetings to monitor progress and to deal with matters arising from the project were essential, as was the preparatory pilot run of the project to detect the most obvious difficulties. As can perhaps be surmised, the author's own ambivalence (and perhaps counter-resistance?) was often at the heart of the matter. The professional expertise of the consultant and the co-researcher, as well as their indispensable personal qualities, helped to clarify and resolve many issues.

Healthy resistance

In some ways, research seems to have become rather fashionable as a touchstone for what is right and proper or, conversely, an example of what is interfering and invasive to the integrity of professionals. In the current economic climate, many professionals, for example, health workers and teachers, are experiencing dramatic changes in their working practices which some feel affect their sense of professionalism. It seems likely that research and evaluation can be used to both defend against such moves as well as to justify them (Edwards, 1993). Similarly, resistance and reluctance can be seen as normative and healthy as well as inconvenient and unhelpful.

Where there is a risk of damaging the client or the counsellor by any intervention, it is wise to spend time unravelling the fears from the reality. Sometimes the fears are justified. One aspect which has not been mentioned, hitherto, is a fear of researcher-enthusiasm overriding sensitivity to client and counsellor feelings. Certainly, research-like activities can be exciting and induce the sort of fervour which many counsellors may recall from their first encounters with counselling or psychotherapy. Resistance to enthusiasm can be useful for the researcher as well as colleagues, if it prevents inappropriate intrusion or simply unmanageable workload. It may also be that unabashed intellectual curiosity is both a driving force and something that is embarrassing to acknowledge for some counsellors, who prefer to see themselves as motivated in a different way.

Conclusion

In conclusion, there appear to be many comparisons to be made between setting up a kind of contract with clients and engaging them in therapeutic work and setting up a research project with colleagues. Time and effort need to be dedicated to creating a solid framework for the research which allows resistance and reluctance to emerge and to be worked through, or to be taken into account in the operation of research activities. The skills required in setting up a research project are therefore not simply composed of new and unfamiliar techniques belonging to the world of research but encompass the ordinary routine strategies the counsellor uses to work with clients. Counsellor resistance to research can be both an act of professional self-assertion and a key to important issues which need addressing.

References

Aveline, M. (1992) 'The use of audio and videotape recordings of therapy sessions in the supervision and practice of dynamic psychotherapy', *British Journal of Psychotherapy*, 8(4): 347–58.

Bergin, A.E. and Garfield, S.L. (eds) (1971) *Handbook of Psychotherapy and Behaviour Change: an Empirical Analysis*. New York: Wiley.

Counselling (1994) Special Issue: The Relevance of Research for Practice. *Counselling*, 5(1).

Edwards, D. (1993) 'Why don't arts therapists do research?', in H. Payne (ed.), *Handbook of Inquiry in the Arts Therapies: One River, Many Currents*. London: Jessica Kingsley.

Egan, G. (1990) *The Skilled Helper: a Systematic Approach to Effective Helping*. Monterey, CA: Brookes/Cole.

Finch, J. (1984) '"It's great to have someone to talk to": ethics and politics of interviewing women', in C. Bell and H. Roberts (eds), *Social Researching: Politics, Problems, Practice*. London: Routledge.

Mathers, N., Shipton, G. and Shapiro, D. (1993) 'The impact of short term counselling on GHQ scores', *British Journal of Guidance and Counselling*, 21(3): 310–18.

McLeod, J. (1994) *Doing Counselling Research*. London: Sage.

Sanders, P. and Liptrot, D. (1993) *An Incomplete Guide to Basic Research Methods and Data Collection for Counsellors*. Manchester: PCCS Books.

Schofield, W. (1964) *Psychotherapy: the Purchase of Friendship*. Englewood Cliffs, NJ: Prentice-Hall.

Shipton, G. and Smith, E. (eds) (1993) *Perspectives on Evaluation and Research in Counselling*. Association for Student Counselling. Rugby: BAC.

Stiles, W.B., Shapiro, D.A. and Elliott, R. (1986) 'Are all psychotherapies equivalent?', *American Psychologist*, 41: 165–80.

Watkins, C.E. and Schneider, L.J. (1991) *Research in Counseling*. Hillsdale, NJ: Lawrence Erlbaum Associates.

Discussion issues

1 What are some of the advantages and disadvantages in setting up a project to evaluate counselling?

2 How would you present a client with the option of taking part in any aspect of research or evaluation?

3 What kind of data do you think would be:
   (a) essential information to collect about client usage of a coun-selling service?
   (b) desirable information to collect about client usage of a counselling service?

4 How do you imagine you would feel about your own effectiveness as a counsellor being studied?

70

The Contribution of a Research Study Towards Improving a Counselling Service

Michèle Crouan

> A lot of therapy shows an inadequate awareness of class issues – the so-called bread-and-butter issues of poverty, hunger, cold, homelessness, etc. – and fails to address issues like the cost, language, style and assumptions of therapy that effectively exclude most working-class people. (Trevithick, 1988, p. 65)

How often do you find yourself addressing such criticisms as these? How frequently are you in the position of trying to explain that, on the whole, counsellors tend not to be complacent about social inequalities, and they may not be all that comfortable with the apparently exclusive nature of much of counselling practice?

Whether we address these issues through personal reflection, or discuss them with others, they need serious consideration and, sometimes, action. Whilst I don't think I ever disregarded thoughts and niggling doubts about counselling in its social, cultural and economic context, I know that I had comforted myself with the fact that I was actively engaging in filling the gap – or at least I thought I was.

This chapter describes how my growing discomfort with the exclusivity of counselling prompted me to undertake a research project that is currently helping a large, voluntary counselling agency to become more accessible to people from diverse social, cultural and economic backgrounds.

How the study came about

For several years I had worked as a voluntary counsellor with this inner-city agency. One of its main aims is to offer an accessible, high-quality counselling service to anyone needing it from within a large geographical region, especially those who may be socially and economically disadvantaged. The agency's founders particularly wanted to alleviate some of the mental distress experienced by people living in the increasingly economically deprived inner-city. In order to be within reach of as many people as possible, clients are asked to donate what they can afford for their counselling, and no one is ever refused the service on the grounds that they cannot pay anything.

The combination of working 'for free' with a counselling agency that was genuinely available to people from all social and economic backgrounds helped me to feel mostly good, and at times quite saintly about what I was doing. That was until I moved house to a city where there was no equivalent counselling

This chapter was first published in *Counselling, Journal of the British Association for Counselling*, vol. 5, no. 1, pp. 32–4 (1994).

service. Although I continued to commute to the agency, suddenly the volume was turned-up on my questions and doubts about counselling and its social context.

New friends were openly challenging about what they saw as the elitism of counselling – it was great if you could afford it/could get somebody to mind the kids/were white, able-bodied and middle-class – but what if you weren't? I met, and continue to meet, a succession of people for whom one private counselling session will probably cost all of their income support. Statements I have heard so many counsellors make along the lines of, if someone *really* wants counselling they'll find the money for it, have a hollow ring to them.

I started to think about the many clients I had counselled in the agency and how, with a few exceptions, most of them had lived in the 'better-off' parts of the region, were in professional jobs and were white. At that time the agency could not accommodate wheelchair-users and even now can only offer its service to people with a fairly limited range of disabilities. I did not doubt the genuineness of the agency's altruistic intentions. However, if my clients were anything to go by, it seemed that its work may have gone somewhat off course. If the people I saw were typical of the agency's clients, some important questions needed to be asked about the absence of people from the more socially and economically disadvantaged areas of society, for whom the agency also existed, and for whom, to a large extent, it was primarily intended.

I was not alone in experiencing a growing awareness and concern about the agency's mono-cultural image. Several other workers, including voluntary counsellors, supervisors, trainers and trainees were also raising issues concerning equal opportunities and the need for general improvements in accessibility to, and within, the agency. Central to this developing awareness was a relatively recently appointed agency Director, who was both receptive to the questions and issues raised, and was herself committed to developing the organization's equal opportunities policies and practices.

All these issues, together with the fact that I had to undertake a piece of research for my MA in Counselling Studies, helped me find the focus for a study which has, so far, proved very worthwhile.

Doing the study

I wanted to find out exactly who was coming for counselling, in terms of clients' social, ethnic, geographical and economic backgrounds, and whether any of these factors influenced people's uptake of the counselling offered. It may seem strange that during its fourteen years of existence no one had ever tried to find out precisely whether or not the agency was being used by the full range of people for whom it was intended. However, contact with several other British counselling services was to reveal that this omission was by no means unusual.

Through studying a group of 97 new clients it was possible to find out whereabouts in the geographical region they lived and how many people were from minority ethnic groups. Whether or not they were home owners/buyers, or received any kind of state benefit was also noted, since this gave some indication of standard of living and income. Each of these pieces of information, when collated together, helped produce a picture of the general social, ethnic and economic backgrounds of the agency's clients.

In fact, the picture revealed a large group of relatively affluent white women living in the better-off parts of the region. Very few clients of either gender lived in the inner-city, and almost all were white. This was despite the region, and the inner-city in particular, containing large, long-established black and Chinese populations. The study also found that a relatively high number of clients withdrew from counselling within the first half-dozen sessions. None of the factors mentioned above seemed to influence clients' tendency to withdraw; similarly, there did not appear to be a connection between rate of withdrawal and the length of time a person had spent waiting for their first appointment. Clearly, this phenomenon needs further investigation (Crouan, 1992).

The fact that I can now summarize the study's influential findings in just one paragraph seems quite amazing considering the amount of work that went into it. Much of my job as researcher went into finding and reading other writers' work on the subject, and having numerous discussions with informed people about what I had read, wanted to do, or had found out. Trying to see things from as many angles as possible, and thinking/talking through the possible implications of every aspect of the research helped me find the most appropriate, pragmatic approach to getting the information I wanted and making some sense of it.

For me the opportunity to concentrate on a subject that I was really interested in, together with having a legitimate reason to indulge in such challenging discussions was one of the highlights of doing this study. I value that process immensely as one through which I learned a great deal, developed my ability of critical thinking, and gained self-confidence.

A major area of difficulty that I experienced, however, was having to wait and trust other people to collect key pieces of data for me, which was an essential part of the methodology I chose. Much of my 'hands on' experience of getting the information I needed involved laboriously searching through written records of application forms and appointments diaries myself. The task of actually getting the information from clients in the first place, and then accurately recording it, fell to two administrative staff who had face-to-face contact with all new clients.

The staff members were committed to improving the counselling service, and saw the information they were being asked to collect as beneficial to that process. The information they were collecting was so important, however, that the success of the entire research study depended on their goodwill and commitment to it. Every person who applied for counselling during the period of the study had to be asked the same questions, and each response needed to be recorded.

In a busy voluntary organization which was not known for having a smooth-running administrative service, and wherein the general goodwill overdraft was already fully extended, this required my engaging in a considerable act of faith. It also made it essential for me to have regular discussions with the staff concerned, so that I could keep track of how the data collection was going, check out whether there were any problems with it and offer appropriate support, as well as find out the staff's impressions of the information that was coming in. It was important to work with, not against the organization, as there was a substantial amount of wisdom around, and a lot of hard work was already going into just keeping the service going as well as improving it.

In fact, the whole process of researching the information went by with remarkably few difficulties. In addition to the undoubted willingness of the staff, I am quite sure that the Director's active and observable support for the study was a major influence on the smoothness of its passage.

How the research is leading to action

Once the research was completed it would have been easy to pass a copy of the final report to the agency and let it stand for itself. Tempting though this was, such low-key dissemination of the results would probably have meant that the study was forgotten about fairly quickly. It was important, however, that the research evidence and recommendations led to some form of positive action. With this in mind, in the year since I finished writing the report I have endeavoured to publicize and promote the study within the agency.

In addition to giving the Director a copy and discussing it with her, I also sent copies of the abstract to every chairperson of the many committees that exist within the agency. Whilst not agreeing with all of its contents, the Director has again lent her support to the completed study. She has circulated additional summaries to relevant committee members, recommending that they read the document in full, and ensuring that the research has been tabled on appropriate agendas for lengthy discussion.

The combination of promotional strategies and directorial support has led to the study provoking much thought and discussion about previously little-spoken-of issues. It has also been used effectively to support several new and important developments within the agency.

The main strength of the research lies in the fact that it has provided the evidence that was previously missing from efforts to improve certain aspects of the agency's practice. For example, the evidence that there were so few clients from minority ethnic groups has been used to support several ground-breaking initiatives. These include a successful bid to gain outside funding to subsidize fees for students from minority ethnic groups on the agency's counsellor training programme. Since at the moment all the counsellors are apparently white, this is a crucial step in making the organization more inviting and relevant to non-white clients.

In line with some of the main recommendations of the research, links have been established with local black and Chinese community organizations, and their representatives are advising the agency concerning anti-oppressive practice. Similarly, people from a wide range of cultural backgrounds have formed a working party to identify and monitor ways of improving all aspects of the agency's accessibility.

The study's findings and recommendations have also supported reviews of committee membership, with the intention and gradual achievement of bringing in appropriately qualified people from a variety of ethnic groups. This process began with the inclusion of a black woman on the most powerful committee in the organization's hierarchy. Whilst this may provoke accusations of tokenism, it is part of a genuine plan to involve more people from minority ethnic groups at this and all other levels of the organization.

The study's findings and recommendations have also been used to support a review of all written material and pictorial images used by the organization. This is to try to make such material more relevant to people from different ethnic and cultural groups. The review and replacement is a slow process and to a large extent depends on the cultural awareness of the staff, trainers and others who devise and use the materials.

Much of the work so far has concentrated on improving the image and accessibility of the agency. A further, vitally important issue highlighted by the research was the discovery that rather a lot of the agency's clients withdrew from counselling within the first six sessions. More research is intended to find out the reasons behind this phenomenon.

One very simple, but crucial way in which the research has improved practice within the organization relates to the recording of client's post codes. Before the research started, clients were asked to give their address, but not necessarily their post code, and the distribution of where, geographically, they came from was worked out using the health authority's districts. The system did not work well, because each district covered a large area, making it impossible to monitor precisely in which of the smaller, specific areas clients were living. For example, a client identified as living in District 1, could have lived anywhere, from the relative poverty of city centre tenements to the detached prestige homes in leafy suburbs five miles away.

As part of the research the agency started recording clients' post codes, and it immediately became possible to identify with much greater precision the parts of the region in which clients were living. Specific distribution patterns could be clearly and easily identified, and this has already been used to target areas where community links need to be developed, and information and advertising needs to be improved. Not surprisingly, recording clients' post codes has been adopted as a permanent part of agency protocol.

Information provided by the study is, therefore, being used to help direct efforts away from ineffective or counterproductive practices, towards those more likely to help the agency to meet its aims. It is also being used to support several new developments.

Of fundamental importance, however, is the fact that, a year after its completion, the research continues to stimulate discussion, thus helping to keep key issues in the forefront of individual and organizational awareness. In so doing it helps guard against the exclusivity and inadequate social awareness of which Trevithick (1988) suggests counsellors have a tendency to be guilty.

References

Crouan, M. (1992) 'So, who are our clients?'. Dissertation presented for MA in Counselling Studies, Keele University. Unpublished.

Trevithick, P. (1988) 'Unconsciousness raising with working class women', in S. Krzowski and P. Land (eds), *In Our Experience*. London: The Women's Press.

Brief update

Since I wrote the journal article three years ago, my research study has continued to play a definite, though increasingly background, role in developing the work of COMPASS, the Liverpool-based counselling agency which formed the arena of investigation.

Perhaps the most useful aspect of the study continues to be the fact that it actually exists. It is there as a tangible, historical record of COMPASS's achievements and limitations concerning the range of people who use its counselling service. This means that developments occurring in relevant areas of the organization can be measured against the data contained within the study, and many of the study's recommendations are still referred to as guidelines for action. When appropriate opportunities arise, the study's findings continue to be used to add factual substance to funding applications.

Much effort has been invested into developing the work which began as a result of the study, with the goal of increasing COMPASS's accessibility to black people taking the main focus so far. Whilst they are still grossly under-represented, the number of black people involved in all aspects of the organization has increased.

A great deal more work needs to be done before COMPASS is truly relevant, welcoming and accessible to people from a range of cultural and economic backgrounds. Until it is, my research study will continue to serve a useful purpose.

Discussion issues

1 Who are *your* clients? Do they reflect a range of cultural and economic backgrounds, or is your counselling service mostly used by people from one particular section of society? How do you know?

2 Counselling in Britain is sometimes criticized for being inaccessible to people who receive low incomes, are working-class, black or from other cultural minorities. Do you agree with this criticism? On what evidence do you base your answer?

3 How might you go about making a counselling service more inclusive of clients and counsellors from a wide range of cultural and economic backgrounds?

4 The usefulness of research findings is measured by their application. Discuss the ways in which this chapter illustrates this view.

71

The Impact of Research upon Practice

Peter Ross

There is a long university tradition which suggests that good teaching is a function of continuing research and scholarship. The latter keeps a teacher up to date and ensures a suitably critical view when reading published research. Knowing from experience just how difficult it is to be sure of 'the facts', but fascinated by the process of discovery, we convey to our students a mixture of enthusiasm and careful reservation. These are attitudes which the students will need in order to take their turn in advancing knowledge.

This article is written from the conviction that good counselling is underpinned by personal research and scholarship. Research and scholarship engender humility in us. This is a function of knowing just how fragile are the foundations of our profession. We then behave with real vulnerability in our relationships with clients. Indeed, our ethic demands that we do our best for the client, a best that can only be demonstrated by a concern for questioning assumptions and refining techniques and theories.

Many of us see everyday counselling as unique research with each unique client. We reflect upon our assumptions in regular supervision. But formal research tools and methods bring a systematic approach which test 'knowledge' in a quite different way which frequently can reveal very surprising aspects of a problem. If even one reader is encouraged to sharpen their perceptions and humble their assumptions about their own counselling by engaging in some personal research or scholarship as a result of this chapter, I will have succeeded in my objective. My method is to make myself vulnerable to the reader by describing the personal reasons behind my interest in a piece of research, by describing the research itself, and by describing its impact on my counselling practice and management of a counselling service.

Research

Research which makes an impact upon personal practice is likely to be done out of personal concern. I grew up in Ireland. From an early age I was aware of the importance of religious belief. The power of belief, for both good and evil, began to fascinate me. Contradictory conviction, however firmly held, could not be equally true. I was in awe of the power of whatever social and cultural processes could bring about such firmly held convictions. This was one of the reasons I read psychology as an undergraduate.

This chapter was first published in *Counselling, Journal of the British Association for Counselling*, vol. 5, no. 1, pp. 35–7 (1994).

As an undergraduate, I became interested in hypnosis. I studied the way belief and experience could be engineered and packaged (the induction) to produce hypnotic behaviour. Much later, as a Member of the British Society for Experimental and Clinical Hypnosis, I trained in the techniques of clinical hypnosis. I discovered that the most important skill was matching induction techniques to the unique personality and beliefs of the client.

With this background, it will come as no surprise that I became particularly interested in the early stages of psychotherapy, and the process therein. It was obvious from both experience and the literature that some client behaviours, such as early self-disclosure, were good indicators of rapid and positive outcome. I thought I might have a go at seeing whether explicit encouragement (an induction) prior to the start of therapy would lead to an increase in such client process variables. All I needed was a way of telling clients about psychotherapy and how to behave to get the best out of it!

Accordingly, I wrote four A4 pages ('the experimental induction') about psychotherapy, and arranged for the induction to be given to selected new clients before I saw them in the university setting in which I then worked. The induction reflected my then 'personal construct' phase of development as it described the client as 'man and scientist', contrasted a counsellor or therapist with a GP, and other prior helping figures, and made boundary issues and transference explicit. The research (Ross, 1982) used this experimental induction for one group of clients, a placebo induction about the history of psychotherapy for another group of clients, and no induction at all for a control group. Sessions with clients were taped, and six process variables judged by experienced raters. The task of training raters was not easy (Moras and Hill, 1991). As these process variables, and others, were crucial to the subsequent impact upon practice, it is worth elaborating them here. The first was 'agenda making', the extent to which clients set their own agenda (either explicitly or implicitly) and determine their own priorities. The second process variable was 'rules and roles' – the extent to which the client adopted a role and assumed rules of conduct appropriate for therapy, or questioned these, or was silent on the issue. Another variable – 'hypothesis making' – reflected the extent to which a client drew attention to any ideas, theories, models, guesses, or hypotheses he or she had about the nature, meaning, or cause of the problem. The remainder of the variables were 'client centred' type ones concerned with depth of involvement in reflection, dependence and independence of emotional expression, and so on.

A one-factor analysis of variance showed that the experimental induction did indeed influence client process. Perhaps I should not have been all that surprised. It was well known even then that normal behavioural responses to drugs were unlikely to occur if patients were not told what to expect (Penick and Hinkle, 1964) and that, in counselling, if the counsellor did not supply explicit expectations, clients would search for them in voice tone, facial expression, posture, etc., or just rely on imagination to fill the vacuum (Morris and O'Neal, 1975). However, the research outcome made a big impact on me.

I have to confess I am not sure why the latter was so. It probably had a good deal to do with it being my first serious piece of research. It was as if the power of research had been revealed to me. No doubt it also had a good deal to do with the experimental induction being so personal. I had gone through agonies of self-doubt and soul searching in writing the experimental induction. I felt it necessary to try to be personally transparent on paper for my clients.

The immediate impact on clinical practice

The most immediate impact of this research on my practice was that I tried to extend and refine what I had learnt by writing different inductions for different groups of clients. At the time, I worked in a university setting, in a local clinic attended by relatively uneducated poor people, and had a private practice largely attended by senior managers in the business community. In addition, I rapidly discovered the obvious: that when, after assessment, I intended to work long term with a client, a written induction inhibited the very transference phenomena which I wished to encourage and use. I therefore eliminated inductions, whether written or verbal, for the latter.

As I supervised others and listened to their audio tapes, I became very aware that many counsellors spend significant time over the first three or four sessions dealing with boundaries and expectations. The first few sessions often contain discussion on how to go about the counselling, who can set the agenda, and whether it is right to do one thing or another. No amount of good-quality feedback within any orientation seems to eliminate this: working in a very empathic way, a recent supervisee was met with – 'You seem to encourage me to be so introspective and self-indulgent you must be bad for me'! Since completing the research, I have made a point of highlighting for supervisees the importance of being alert to these process variables in the early sessions of counselling.

The longer-term impact on clinical practice

Shortly after completing the research described, university counselling services began to go through a resource squeeze. This still continues. Naturally enough, many a mind began to focus on effective short-term work with clients. Short-term work requires the counsellor to focus more actively than in long-term work, especially at the beginning. Apart from being very clear about working to a core objective, the counsellor must explicate as rapidly as possible a method of working, and agree it with the client – that means focusing on roles and rules. There is no doubt in my mind that doing the research mentioned facilitated my move from the dynamically based long-term work for which I had spent years in training, to more cognitively based short-term work. The research had assured me that focus on roles and rules, as well as other variables, really made a crucial difference to process.

I have already mentioned that one of the process variables examined by my research was 'hypothesis making'. As the raters and I listened to the audio tapes it became clear that frequently the client's view of what was necessary to produce the desired change was linked to the client's view, or lack of view, as to the cause of the problem. This drew my attention to the distinction between attributions as to cause and maintenance. As this distinction is so important to short-term work, some elaboration of the point is in order.

Much long-term psychodynamic work focuses on long-past parent–child relationships. The 'cause' may be said, for example, to be lack of appropriate boundary maintenance in the child/parent relationship, leading now to over-dependence on others. The 'cure' is to try to get the client to relate to self in a more adult way via relationship with the counsellor. In short-term cognitive work we also need such a cause attribution. However, in practice we go on to focus on what it is the client now says to him/herself to maintain the situation. We also focus on and contrast what he or she would or could or might say to him/herself if he or she were able to relate to him/herself directly in an adult ('rational') way. The counsellor has to take direct responsibility for urging this method on the client, and reassuring him/her that if tried it will be helpful. Once tried, the client usually experiences it as helpful. This validates the cause/maintenance attributions, downgrades the importance of the temporary counsellor reassurance, and upgrades the client's sense of control.

Equally, in, for example, 'person centred' work, the fact that a counsellor is taking infinite care and time in ensuring he or she understands every nuance of a client's feeling and thought, can lead to the client's self-talk developing along the lines: 'I am special, valuable, unique and worthy of my own serious attention and respect as well as that of the counsellor.' For the short-term counsellor, the issue is to find the most economic balance between the emotion-charged experiences needed to bring this about and the directly focused cognitions needed to do so. All in all, I believe my original research alerted me to focus more precisely upon such 'critical ingredients' than otherwise would have been the case.

The impact of personal research on counselling service management

My early interest in the power of religious beliefs, and my later professional interest in the power of beliefs in hypnotic and psychotherapeutic processes, was soon to extend to cultural systems. This has had an important impact on the way I manage a university counselling service.

Some 20/25% of the students at Reading University are from overseas. I am deeply involved with them. The Overseas Student Adviser is a member of my staff. I chair the committee which organizes the welcome programme for overseas students.

This part of the story all began when, within the space of a few months, two unconnected visits to my office by East African students found them disclosing to me that they suffered from 'bewitchment'. Clueless in how to deal with this, I found the minimal literature to be confused and confusing. Within a few months of this, I was invited to Uganda to do some consultancy work and took the opportunity to research 'bewitchment'. As an account of this research has been published (Ross and Lwanga, 1991) it will suffice to skim the surface here. Behaviour described by East Africans as a state of bewitchment is akin to an agitated depression. It is a function of being unable to resolve complex moral problems and the need to display to others the great effort being made to do so. It is attributed to ancestral spirits calling people to regain integrity and wholeness. These dead spirits are the guardians of the historical continuity of a family, clan or tribe. The spirits hurt the living until the living take such action as will satisfy the integrity of the collective historical identity of a family, clan or tribe.

The importance of the research was to make a little more explicit than before the nature of the process involved in building up behaviours labelled 'bewitchment'. In fact, they are remarkably similar to processes involved in building up behaviours labelled 'hypnotic' and many other kinds of deeply felt realities. The details are far less important than the subsequent impact upon me of engaging in this research. As before, I am not entirely clear about why the impact was large. But it has something to do with the level of personal engagement in the enterprise, rather than the research outcome. A good analogy from personal experience: it is the difference between navigating while on a centrally heated classroom exercise, and navigating on a yacht in the middle of a stormy night in a crowded sealane.

At any rate, the impact has been to sensitize me anew to the fragility of cultural processes and identities. It has also been to alert me to the potential of the rich and diverse mini-culture which a university counselling service could be, and my responsibility as head of such a service for bringing this about.

I have always felt the great importance of such a counselling service being an open culture. This is one where all are valued regardless of sex, culture and religion. But now there is an urgency to my explicit efforts to value the enrichment of differences rather than the security of sameness. For this reason, we now deliberately set out not only to have both male and female counsellors, but to have counsellors with different therapeutic orientations, from different cultures, and with different religious beliefs and none. No doubt there is a point at which diversity gets so great that it is no longer possible to hold the whole together for lack of bonds. So far this is not so, and we greatly enrich our mutual understanding. In doing so, I hope we also offer a genuine symbolic beacon of acceptance to a very diverse client population.

Conclusion

What, then, of the importance of research? I believe every counsellor has the potential to engage in some research or scholarship. I believe that doing so makes the counsellor much better at counselling than would otherwise be the case. Few of us have the time or finance to tackle the great issues of the day and get dramatically significant results. This hardly matters. It is the process of engaging in research which makes the impact. The more personal the research, the greater the personal impact. Can there be anyone out there who does not have personal concerns?

References

Moras, K. and Hill, C. (1991) 'Rater selection for psychotherapy process research: an evaluation of the state of the art', *Psychotherapy Research*, 1(2): 113–23.

Morris, L.A. and O'Neal, E.C. (1975) 'Judgements about a drug's effectiveness: the role of expectations in outcomes', *Drugs in Health Care*, 2: 179–86.

Penick, S.B. and Hinkle, L.E. (1964) 'The effect of expectation on response to phenmetrazine', *Psychosomatic Medicine*, 26: 369–73.

Ross, P. and Lwanga, J. (1991) 'Counselling the bewitched: an exercise in cross-cultural eschatology', *Counselling*, 2(1): 17–19.

Ross, Peter, J. (1982) 'The effects of a detailed written induction procedure upon certain aspects of process in individual psychotherapy with sophisticated patients'. MSc thesis, Department of Psychology, University of Warwick. Unpublished.

Discussion issues

1 Good counselling is underpinned by personal research and scholarship. Which areas of your own development as a counsellor need greater underpinning?

2 What do you consider to be the strengths of short-term counselling and what its drawbacks?

3 Which of your personal concerns about life issues or counselling issues would you choose to subject to the power of research?

4 Is it important for a counselling service to be an open culture? Why is such diversity to be recommended, or not, and what are the difficulties it may engender?

72

The Research Agenda for Counselling

John McLeod

The similarities and differences between counselling and psychotherapy have been widely debated, and remain a matter of controversy in some quarters (see Chapters 66 and 67). However, there would appear to be general agreement on the idea that, whatever differences might exist, there is a significant area of overlap between these activities. Counselling and psychotherapy employ the same theoretical models and techniques to help broadly similar sets of clients. This sense of counselling and psychotherapy being almost indistinguishable from each other in practice is also reflected in the types of research that have been carried out. For example, an inspection of the titles of articles published in counselling research journals such as *Journal of Counseling Psychology* and *Counselling Psychology Quarterly*, and psychotherapy research journals such as *Psychotherapy* or *Psychotherapy Research* reveals a high level of correspondence in topics and methods.

The parallels between counselling research and psychotherapy research are partly due to the substantial area of common ground between these disciplines, but are also a product of the domination of the field by psychotherapy researchers. Beutler and Crago (1991), in an international survey of psychotherapy research projects, found 41 research teams in 6 countries. Many of these teams were located in prestige, well-resourced psychiatric and medical establishments. The stream of publications from these groups have a strong influence on what topics are considered researchable and what methods are deemed appropriate. The majority of active researchers have been trained in these departments. But how relevant for counselling in Britain are most of these studies? How many counsellors actually read these research articles? I would suggest that it is essential to identify a set of research questions and priorities which are both meaningful and significant for counsellors, and that will make a difference to the quality of service offered to clients. There exist a wide range of research questions distinctive to counselling that have received only minimal consideration from psychotherapy researchers. Some of these will be briefly outlined below.

1 *The organization and management of counselling agencies.* Counselling in Britain is largely delivered through 'agencies', which can vary in size from large national organizations such as Relate, to small local collectives. Many counsellors have first-hand experience of the ways in which organizational factors can affect the counselling process. It is usually at an organizational level, in a committee or management meeting, that decisions are made about service delivery issues such as the number of sessions clients can receive, the

This chapter was first published in *Counselling, Journal of the British Association for Counselling*, vol. 5, no. 1, pp. 41–3 (1994).

type and amount of training and supervision available to counsellors, and the extent to which the agency makes an effort to enable access to disabled or culturally different clients. It is the organization that creates procedures for monitoring client satisfaction, or dealing with unethical conduct. Also, within counselling agencies, it is necessary to create an organizational culture that will enable the expression but also containment of strong feelings in both clients and workers. The interaction of these factors with service quality is a topic that has received scant attention in the research literature (although see Crandall and Allen, 1982; Lewis et al., 1992). Potentially, the identification of principles of good practice for the organization and management of counselling agencies could be of great benefit in improving standards.

2 *The training, support and supervision needs of voluntary, non-professional counsellors.* A psychotherapist is almost certainly someone who has undergone extensive training, and is paid for his or her work. By contrast, a great deal of counselling is carried out by lay people who receive only very limited training and supervision. The research literature on training and supervision consists almost entirely of studies of full-time, professional counsellors and therapists. Although there have been several pieces of research that have examined the effectiveness of non-professional counsellors (Hattie et al., 1984; and Strupp and Hadley, 1979) little is known about the specific training and supervision needs of this group of counsellors. For example, many counsellor training courses require that trainees participate in personal therapy. But how appropriate, relevant or cost-effective is personal therapy for non-professional counsellors who may be seeing only two or three clients each week? Many volunteer counselling agencies, for example rape crisis centres, deal with clients who are in extreme distress or who have not found professional therapists helpful. Workers in these agencies often find it difficult to cope with the intense demands of such clients, and may 'burn out' and leave (O'Sullivan, 1978). What can be done to offer effective support and supervision that would prevent this type of turnover of volunteer counsellors?

3 *The boundaries between counselling and other forms of work with clients.* Many counsellors work closely with members of other professions such as nursing, teaching or social work. Traditionally, studies of psychotherapy have focused on the dynamics and processes of 'pure' therapy. However, for many counsellors, who may work in highly imperfect counselling environments, a therapeutic space or frame must be painstakingly constructed. These counsellors face innumerable pressures arising from role conflict, incompatible aims, client assumptions and expectations, and the interpersonal ethos or culture of the settings in which they work. For example, a counsellor employed in General Practice will be expected to become a member of the primary care team (Corney and Jenkins, 1993). To resist such assimilation is to risk isolation and marginalization. To accept it involves facing difficult issues around boundaries and confidentiality. Counsellors in other settings, for example in student counselling (Bond, 1992) or employee counselling (Sugarman, 1992) encounter similar dilemmas. The situation is even more difficult and complex when the counsellor has other roles in relation to clients. The conventional

wisdom, handed down from psychotherapists, is not to engage in 'dual relationships' with clients (Pope, 1991). However, the reality for many people is that the only counselling available to them is to be obtained from their probation officer, teacher or priest. There is a significant contribution to be made from research that explores the ways in which counsellors can best manage such role conflicts, and the actual impact on clients of these situations.

4   *Evaluation of the processes and outcomes of telephone counselling.* The existing counselling and psychotherapy literature is almost wholly concerned with what happens in face-to-face work with clients. A vast amount of counselling, by contrast, is delivered through telephone helplines. On any single day, more people are in contact with Samaritans, Childline and other telephone counselling agencies than ever actually meet a counsellor in an office. Yet, although some research has been done (Stein and Lambert, 1984), not enough is known about counselling in which the relationship is mediated wholly through vocal cues.

5   *Evaluation of the use of self-help manuals or 'bibliotherapy'.* Many more people find insight and support through reading self-help books than ever make an appointment to see an actual counsellor. The impact of both practical manuals such as Anne Dickson's (1982) *A Woman in Your Own Right* and transformational texts such as *The Road Less Traveled* (Peck, 1978) or *The Drama of Being a Child* (Miller, 1987) has been immense. Some researchers have made a start in investigating the ways in which people make use of self-help books, either alone or in combination with counselling (Craighead et al., 1984). But again, as with telephone counselling, there is much to be learned about how best to design self-help manuals, the problems that are most amenable to self-help, and the dangers or limitations of this mode of help.

6   *Research into the nature and maintenance of ethical standards.* The work of Jeffrey Masson (1988) has drawn attention to the prevalence of exploitation and abuse of clients that occurs all around us. Much of the discussion of this topic has, for obvious reasons, been either descriptive (how often does it happen?) or judgemental in nature. Up to now, there has been very little systematic research into the conditions and processes that either facilitate or prevent unethical conduct (Miller and Thelen, 1987), or into the most effective means of rehabilitating clients and counsellors after an abuse has taken place. This is clearly a highly sensitive area for research. Yet, for example, material presented in case studies such as the one published by Bates and Brodsky (1989) can make a significant contribution towards the construction of a model of the process of therapeutic abuse.

7   *Adaptation of counselling methods, techniques and concepts to meet the needs of a more culturally diverse client population.* Counselling and psychotherapy have evolved as forms of interpersonal helping indigenous to Western secularized Judaeo-Christian urban-industrial societies (Cushman, 1992). There are few counsellors or therapists in Islamic cultures or in Africa or Japan. One of the great challenges for the profession as a whole is to make the transition from being a 'monocultural' activity. This is a challenge faced by many counsellors in Britain in their day-to-day work, particularly those working in ethnically

diverse inner cities. It seems highly likely that the future legitimacy of counselling as a service supported by public funds will depend on its ability to work with people in ways that make sense within their own cultural frames of reference. At present there is an absence of research into this area of practice (Ponterotto, 1988).

8 *The processes and outcome of short-term work with clients.* Many counsellors work with clients in settings where some, or even all, of their clients will attend for only one or two sessions. There has been a substantial amount of research into brief or time-limited counselling (Steenbarger, 1992), but this has been mainly carried out in institutes and clinics staffed by highly trained professional therapists, and in circumstances that enable careful assessment of client eligibility for short-term work so that, for example, unsuitable clients can be referred elsewhere (see Gustafson, 1986, for a discussion of some highly technically sophisticated models of brief therapy). These factors are seldom present in counselling agencies. There is a need, therefore, for research into the actual practice of time-limited counselling in action. Given the pressures from resource providers and funding agencies to reduce the number of sessions clients receive, how can counsellors develop means of working most effectively in a time-limited mode?

9 *Strategies for enabling the client or consumer's voice to be heard.* From the earliest work of Carl Rogers, much of counselling has been carried out in a spirit of 'client-centredness'. The political stance of many counsellors would be to emphasize empowerment and equality between client and counsellor, rather than the administration of detached professional expertise. Yet in practice it is no easy matter to create possibilities for clients to feed back to their counsellors their views about the service they have received. Relatively few counselling agencies have set up mechanisms for collecting information about client views, and there is little research on the client's experience (McLeod, 1990). However, the experience of the client is always different from that of the counsellor, sometimes in striking and unexpected ways, and the danger of not listening to the voices of clients is to lose touch with their needs.

The research agenda for counselling outlined in this paper does not have the aim of generating new discoveries at the cutting edge of theory or technique. The intention instead has been to identify a set of topics about which not enough is known, and from which might flow meaningful improvements to quality of service. These research questions are all closely allied to practice, and are consistent with the image of the 'reflective practitioner' or 'scientist-practitioner'. The values underlying these images reflect a commitment to linking the sensitive clinical wisdom and skill of the practitioner with the questioning, critical, systematic inquisitiveness of the scientist or scholar in ways that are beneficial to both science and practice.

It is crucial that counsellors do research that is meaningful to them. Most counsellors have a primary occupational identity as social worker, health professional, educator or clergy, and so bring into counselling the research traditions of these disciplines. Counselling can draw upon these traditions in pursuing its own distinctive research agenda. It is important to remember that the mainstream psychotherapy and counselling research literature largely reflects the output of American researchers, almost all of whom are trained to Doctoral level in psychology, with the emphasis very much on quantitative methods and statistics. There is no reason for counselling in Britain to follow this route, which has resulted in a growing gap between the interests of clinicians and the output of researchers (Cohen et al., 1986). There is a strong interdisciplinary current in British counselling (Thorne and Dryden, 1993), and a willingness in journal editors and academics to promote research that is applicable and relevant rather than merely methodologically rigorous. The task now is to find ways of enabling and encouraging counsellors to regard research, broadly conceived, as a normal counterpoint to practice.

References

Bates, C.M. and Brodsky, A.M. (1989) *Sex in the Therapy Hour: a Case of Professional Incest*. London: Guilford Press.

Beutler, L.E. and Crago, M. (eds) (1991) *Psychotherapy Research: an International Review of Programmatic Studies*. Washington, DC: American Psychological Association.

Bond, T. (1992) 'Ethical issues in counselling in education', *British Journal of Guidance and Counselling*, 20: 51–63.

Cohen, L.H., Sargent, M.H. and Sechrest, L.B. (1986) 'Use of psychotherapy research by professional psychologists', *American Psychologist*, 41: 198–206.

Corney, R. and Jenkins, R. (eds) (1993) *Counselling in General Practice*. London: Routledge.

Craighead, L.W., McNamara, K. and Horan, J.J. (1984) 'Perspectives on self-help and bibliography: you are what you read', in S.D. Brown and R.W. Lent (eds), *Handbook of Counselling Psychology*. New York: Wiley.

Crandall, R. and Allen, R. (1982) 'The organizational context of helping relationships', in T.A. Wills (ed.), *Basic Processes in Helping Relationships*. New York: Academic Press.

Cushman, P. (1992) 'Psychotherapy to 1992: a historically situated interpretation', in D.K. Freedheim (ed.), *History of Psychotherapy: a Century of Change*. Washington, DC: American Psychological Association.

Dickson, A. (1982) *A Woman in Your Own Right*. London: Quartet.

Gustafson, J.P. (1986) *The Complex Secret of Brief Psychotherapy*. New York: W.W. Norton.

Hattie, J.A., Sharpley, C.F. and Rogers, H.J. (1984) 'Comparative effectiveness of professional and para-professional helpers', *Psychological Bulletin*, 95: 534–41.

Lewis, J., Clark, D. and Morgan, D. (1992) *Whom God Hath Joined Together: the Work of Marriage Guidance*. London: Routledge.

McLeod, J. (1990) 'The client's experience of counselling: a review of the research literature', in D. Mearns and W. Dryden (eds), *Experiences of Counselling in Action*. London: Sage.

Masson, J. (1988) *Against Therapy: Emotional Tyranny and the Myth of Psychological Healing*. Glasgow: Collins.

Miller, A. (1987) *The Drama of Being a Child and the Search for the True Self*. London: Virago.

Miller, D.J. and Thelen, M.H. (1987) 'Confidentiality in psychotherapy: history, issues and research', *Psychotherapy*, 24, 704–11.

O'Sullivan, E. (1978) 'What has happened to rape crisis centres? A look at their structures, members and funding', *Victimology: an International Journal*, 3: 45–62.

Peck, M.S. (1978) *The Road Less Traveled: a New Psychology of Love, Traditional Values and Spiritual Growth*. New York: Simon and Schuster.

Ponterotto, J.G. (1988) 'Racial/ethical minority research in the *Journal of Counseling Psychology*: a content analysis and methodological critique', *Journal of Counseling Psychology*, 35: 410–18.

Pope, K.S. (1991) 'Dual relationships in psychotherapy', *Ethics and Behaviour*, 1: 21–34.

Steenbarger, B.N. (1992) 'Towards science–practice integration in brief counseling and therapy', *Counseling Psychologist*, 20: 403–50.

Stein, D.M. and Lambert, M.J. (1984) 'Telephone counseling and crisis intervention: a review', *American Journal of Community Psychology*, 12: 101–26.

Strupp, H.H. and Hadley, S.W. (1979) 'Specific vs nonspecific factors in psychotherapy: a controlled study of outcome', *Archives of General Psychiatry*, 36: 1125–36.

Sugarman, L. (1992) 'Ethical issues in counselling at work', *British Journal of Guidance and Counselling*, 20: 64–74.

Thorne, B. and Dryden, W. (eds) (1993) *Counselling – Interdisciplinary Perspectives*. Buckingham: Open University Press.

Discussion issues

1 Do you agree that the research agenda for counselling outlined in this chapter has identified the most significant priority areas? What research topics would you want to add to the agenda? What do you suggest that BAC or other professional bodies could or should do to promote these kinds of research?

2 If you are able to get access to a university library, take a look at the kinds of research that are published in key academic journals such as the *British Journal of Guidance and Counselling*, *Journal of Counseling Psychology* or *Psychotherapy*. How interesting or relevant did you find the articles in these journals?

3 If you work in a counselling agency, reflect on the systems that the agency operates for selecting, training and supervising counsellors, for assessing clients, and for gaining feedback from clients. What kind of evidence does the agency use in deciding whether these systems are operating effectively? How might research play a role in developing better systems?

4 Consider your own work as a counsellor, and the types of clients you meet. To what extent, and in what ways, does a knowledge of research findings make a positive contribution to this work? Are you satisfied with your relationship with research? What could you do to become more 'research-informed'?

73

A Counsellor First . . .

Gillian Thomas

I still remember the unpleasant shock I experienced when, reading an interview with the eminent researcher David Shapiro, I came across the comment, 'the thing I see myself as is a researcher first rather than a practitioner'. For me, a virgin researcher, the exact opposite was true. The thing I saw myself as was a counsellor first rather than a researcher, and it was disconcerting to realize that I saw things so fundamentally differently from such an expert in the field. Perhaps my route into research had something to do with it.

Although I have been involved in different aspects of counselling for nearly 20 years, it is only in the last seven years that I have seriously developed my interest. In 1986 I embarked upon a two-year part-time Certificate in Counselling course at my local university. As part of the final assignment I had to write a 6,000-word paper on a counselling issue of particular personal interest. The choice of topic presented me with no difficulties. For the past year I had been counselling people affected by ulcerative colitis and Crohn's disease (collectively known as inflammatory bowel disease or IBD) and, as a sufferer myself, my interest was both particular and personal. Having been a member of the executive committee of the National Association for Colitis and Crohn's Disease (NACC) for a number of years I was acutely aware that one of the issues constantly exercising the membership was the desire to talk to someone about the impact of having these unpleasant, debilitating chronic diseases. As both a counsellor and a patient I felt that I was uniquely placed to offer this service.

Getting established

Because the practice of counselling people specifically affected by IBD was new, and because I was offering something complementary to existing medical and surgical treatment of the conditions, I felt that it was important to locate the counselling where people with IBD were already being treated. Since the average GP's list has only two or three patients with IBD, this meant hospitals. So, with the encouragement of NACC, I approached the consultants in two nearby leading gastroenterology units with the suggestion that I offered a voluntary counselling service to people affected by IBD. The consultants were aware of my work with the national executive of NACC and were interested in what I was proposing. Their involvement was to prove to be of crucial importance in what later developed into a research project. Getting myself established within a hospital

This chapter was first published in *Counselling, Journal of the British Association for Counselling*, vol. 5, no. 1, pp. 44–6 (1994).

setting was not easy despite the mentorship of the consultants. From gaining the trust of the relevant social work departments to establishing a reliable system for taking phone messages from potential clients, it was a complex and at times frustrating venture. However that foundation of hard-earned lessons and successful relationships formed the bedrock upon which I eventually built the current research study.

Discovering the 'inner researcher'

I made my availability as a voluntary counsellor known through the *NACC Newsletter*, which went to every member of the association. Gradually, clients made contact and the work began. In the year during which I collected information for my final assignment paper, I began to see that issues emerging in the counselling sessions had not been reported elsewhere in the literature on IBD. It was also clear that it was both feasible and desirable (from both the clients' and the counsellor's viewpoint) to continue the service. In listening to the stories my clients told and the way in which they told them I was, like Kipling's Elephant's Child, filled with ''satiable curtiosity' (surely a vital characteristic for any researcher?). What was going on here? Was what people told me particular to inflammatory bowel disease, or to chronic disease in general? Were there common themes across these unique stories? What was the most pressing thing people needed to say? What did people require from me? At the end of the certificate course all these questions and many more were bubbling through my mind unanswered. These questions, which now form the basis of my current PhD research study, were the first stirrings of the embryonic researcher struggling to emerge from within me. I felt compelled to try to address some of them.

Ethical criteria

In my counselling I strive to practise a person-centred approach. Any research I undertook had therefore to be 'client-led' as this was the only possible way in which I felt I could do the work. This deep person-centred conviction ultimately had a profound effect upon the ethical stance that I evolved. My criterion was always, 'the client comes first'. This became the benchmark against which I measured any possible conflict between the needs of the research and the needs of the clients. Inevitably, this also played a part in forming the style of the research study.

In order to do the research in a hospital setting, I first had to satisfy the relevant Health Authority and University Research Ethics committees. These bodies are used to dealing with experimental medical research, which was reflected in the application forms I had to complete. However it was gratifying (as a qualitative researcher) and reassuring (as a patient) to recognize that the ethics committees' main concern was clearly the welfare of the patients involved in research studies. Their approach may have been rooted in a different discipline, but their 'patient concerns' and my 'person-centredness' were at heart the same thing. I needed to carefully explain and justify my proposed procedures, which in a number of cases ran counter to their recommendations. For example, the requirement for an external witness to the consent form, I felt would undermine the confidentiality which lay at the core of the counselling relationship. Similarly, the names and addresses of patients participating in medical research are usually known to more than just the main researcher. This again seemed unsuitable in a counselling research project involving one counsellor.

I felt strongly that with these issues and others there could be no compromise, otherwise I should be failing my clients (and myself). Fortunately the ethics committees were receptive to my ideas and accepted that, although my route was different, the end to which it led was one of which they approved. Having to closely argue and defend my case was daunting at the time but in fact ultimately helped me to define and delineate my own stance and to feel that the position I had arrived at was absolutely right for me.

Finding a methodology

The fact that the questions I wanted to answer arose from my practice, rather than from my reading about the subject, was a crucial point in choosing a research methodology. It was also important that these questions were based on clients' **experiences**, as relayed to me. These factors, together with the manner in which I framed the questions to myself, the very language in which I thought, were of enormous significance in identifying the methodology that best suited my style of work (Strauss and Corbin, 1990).

It is undeniable that the very act of researching a particular phenomenon causes that phenomenon to change. I felt that my aim should be to keep such changes to a minimum so that what emerged reflected what was important to the client, not what was required by the researcher. Concentrating on the clients meant that I had to have a methodology that was capable of reflecting the uniqueness of each individual and the myriad ways in which human nature adjusts and adapts in the face of ongoing adversity. I knew from personal experience that the life of a person affected by IBD is a life full of uncertainty. For me, the practice of counselling is also all about the ability to dwell in uncertainty. Therefore, if I wished to research the effect of counselling on the lives of IBD patients my methodology would have to allow for this. Only qualitative research methods could provide a flexible enough framework for this sort of investigation.

Within the constellation of research methodologies the one that seemed best suited to my personal approach was phenomenology – the study and description of a phenomenon in all its depth and richness (Becker, 1992). The phenomenon I wished to describe was what it was like to have IBD and what place counselling might play in helping people to adjust to it. Phenomenology also lays stress upon using people's own descriptions of situations to illuminate their experiences because **they** are the experts in the field (a concept familiar to counsellors) (Morse, 1989). I took this idea to its (to me) logical conclusion and used the clients' own individual statements regarding what they felt about their condition to form baselines for assessing the effect of counselling upon each person's problems and aims. This assessment was followed by up to 10 counselling sessions with each client, after which we completed a re-assessment. There was a follow-up assessment six months later. Using people's own words to describe their concerns and aspirations proved very popular with clients who felt that too often they had to modify the expression of their experiences in order to fit the assumptions and expectations of others. I felt that because of this they were denied the opportunity to explore and assimilate these experiences and often remained burdened by them. Simply being given the opportunity to name their worst fears and highest hopes was felt to be cathartic. Witnessing the dignity and courage of people, whilst being ever conscious of my twin responsibilities to do justice to them as clients and to the stories they told me as research material, was at times an awesome task. I was afforded many a wry smile at the thought that qualitative research is sometimes referred to as 'soft' research.

Personal supervision

Unlike quantitative research with its emphasis on objectivity, qualitative phenomenological research recognizes the centrality of the person of the researcher, in that the researcher is the means by which the story is transmitted (Rudestam and Newton, 1992). The qualitative researcher has to be as aware as possible of her or his own preconceptions and assumptions of the phenomenon being looked at, in order to try to lay them aside whilst conducting the investigation (Morse, 1992). Because of this factor, and because additionally I had my own experience of what it is like to have IBD, I felt that good supervision, both academically and for the counselling was vital. It was my incredible good fortune to find an academic supervisor with great experience in the field of counselling, and a counselling supervisor with great academic experience. This unique combination allowed me to move and think freely and comfortably in both worlds and to develop my feelings and ideas knowing that they would be received with understanding.

At times the work I was doing obviously raised pertinent personal issues for me. I was not immune from the anxieties my clients raised about having such an unpredictable condition. My plans for the future were also always made with the unspoken reservation, 'providing I'm not having a flare-up at the time'. The fear that medication would not hold the condition in check and that radical surgery might have to be performed, was mine as well as my clients. Weekly sessions with my counsellor allowed me to explore my own feelings on these matters and kept the experience of being a client fresh.

Data

The amount of data gathered in a qualitative study is huge, yet all of it is valuable and deserves to be treated with respect (Wolcott, 1990). These are people's life stories, freely offered and infinitely precious. I feel that in the counselling work done during this study the research element has at times been transcended and people have spoken deep and fundamental truths. I see the data as jointly owned by both counsellor and client, but with the client having the final say in what is ultimately used in the project. Therefore I sent clients the sections of the case note analysis that dealt with material concerning their own expression of their story, asking for their approval for its use. I also asked them to comment on how they now felt about their counselling. All the clients approached gave permission for the material to be used and spoke warmly of how the counselling had helped them.

In writing up the results of the study I inevitably had to compress the data into a manageable form. At first it felt difficult to 'group' or 'theme' clients' problems and aims – surely each client meant something different even when using the same word? However, gradually I managed to elucidate the common themes that linked the individual experiences. I had (almost) anticipated the vast amount of work required to sort the data but what I had **not** anticipated was the pain of reading straight through all the sets of client notes. Perhaps because I was looking for themes, rather than concentrating on individuals, what I experienced was the impact of the cumulative distress of the group unrelieved by each client's courage in adversity.

The richest (and to me most telling) part of the material lies in what clients have said about their experience of counselling when, at the end of our sessions together, I have invited them to reflect upon the counselling process. It appears that having someone to talk to outside the immediate family is highly valued. Clients also deem helpful the opportunity to explore previous events in their lives and the way in which these events might be influencing how they are handling their present circumstances. Feeling that they had permission to express strong emotions is deeply appreciated too. People with IBD who come for counselling seem instinctively to feel that the only way **out** of darkness is **through** it and that with an on-going condition that tends to relapse and remit, the darkness may have to be negotiated many times. The issues raised in the research appear to be extremely important for clients, counsellors and health professionals and I hope my work will be of value in informing the understanding of those who have IBD and those involved in their care.

Doing counselling research means merging the worlds of academia and counselling and this is not easy. Usually something has to give and often it is the counselling requirements. I feel that in qualitative phenomenological research I am able to merge those worlds in a way that does violence to neither of them, nor to myself. I hope that I have managed, creatively, to synthesize some of the best of both worlds. I will always be 'a counsellor first', even when I am being a researcher, but I believe that, paradoxically, it is in this way that I do my best research.

References

Becker, C.S. (1992) *Living and Relating – an Introduction to Phenomenology*. Newbury Park, CA: Sage.

Morse, J.M. (ed.) (1989) *Qualitative Nursing Research. A Contemporary Dialogue.* Rockville, MD: Aspen.
Morse, J.M. (ed.) (1992) 'Issues of methodology in qualitative inquiry', Special Issue, *Qualitative Health Research Journal*, 2(4).
Rudestam, K.E. and Newton, R.R. (1992) *Surviving your Dissertation.* Newbury Park, CA: Sage.
Strauss, A. and Corbin, J. (1990) *Basics of Qualitative Research.* Newbury Park, CA: Sage.
Wolcott, H.F. (1990) *Writing up Qualitative Research.* London: Sage.

Contact address

National Association for Colitis and Crohn's Disease (NACC),
PO Box 205, AL1 1NX
24-hour Answerphone: 01727 844296.

Discussion issues

Imagine that you are required to undertake a piece of research. Ask yourself the following questions:

1 What personal meaning does this research have for me?
2 How should I deal with the personal factor in the research?
3 What would be my attitude if the requirements of the research conflicted with my role as a counsellor?
4 Are there any circumstances in which I might abandon my role as a researcher in favour of my role as a counsellor?

74

Patients' Perceptions of Counselling within General Practice

Peter Thomas

Often in counselling research the potential consumer's voice is silent. Although there are not any precise figures available at present, the indications are that the uptake of counselling in general, and within general practice in particular, is growing.

Some general practitioners are now employing counsellors within doctor's surgeries and health centres. In July 1989 the BAC asked all 94 Family Practitioner Committees if they were employing counsellors in general practice: 52 responded to the questionnaire and, of those, 27 were currently using counsellors, with 30% being in the South-East and the rest of the country being evenly though sparsely spread. Of those who replied, 42% agreed to reimburse GPs 70% of the counsellor's salary. At present there is little information relating to how prospective clients would like to use this service. Little is known about the public's perception and expectations prior to entering a counselling relationship.

Often the first port of call in times of crisis and distress is the GP's surgery. As early as 1964 Balint was reporting that patients often attended the surgery with non-medical problems that were largely emotional and psychological in origin. In recent years there has been a marked shift from the old family-style 'one man band' doctor to the adoption of Primary Health Care Teams. These teams now often include counsellors who are employed part-time by the GPs and offer an alternative form of treatment for the psychological problems presented in general practice. The doctor might benefit by being able to communicate more easily with a counsellor on site and will receive direct feedback from referred patients. The counsellor might benefit from having a regular income, access to medical back-up and being part of a team and the patient might benefit for the reasons already stated. Seeing an 'in-house' counsellor might not attract the same stigma as a psychiatric referral.

The purpose of my study was firstly to discover whether or not patients perceive a personal need for counselling and where they normally go to have that need met. Secondly, what are the psychological and emotional problems that they perceive might benefit from counselling. Thirdly, to discover their present understanding of counselling and what their perception is of the work of a counsellor. Also to ask what preferences they have related to the sort of counsellor they would choose to see. Fourthly, to discover whether patients perceive the option of counselling in general practice as advantageous or not.

This chapter was first published as 'An exploration of patients' perceptions of counselling with particular reference to counselling within general practice', in *Counselling, Journal of the British Association for Counselling*, vol. 4, no. 1, pp. 24–30 (1993).

Method

Subjects

There were 100 subjects: 68 were female, 25 were male and 7 were not stated. The subjects varied in age from 18 years to 64 years, with a mean of 34.6 years.

The only material used was the questionnaire (see Appendix 1).

Procedure

The receptionist was briefed to hand out the questionnaire to the first 100 patients, aged between 18 and 64 years, entering the surgery to see the doctor. Each patient was requested to fill it in and return it to the receptionist prior to leaving the surgery. The completed questionnaires took 6 working days to collect.

Discussion

Patients' perceptions of their need for counselling

Forty-six per cent of respondents said that they had never felt like talking to an independent counsellor about a present or a past problem in the last three years. But 53% had felt the need to talk to someone outside of their family and friends during the past three years. One could argue that this is a strong indication of the need to employ counsellors within general practice. If one widened this figure to represent the practice as a whole it would indicate that over 2,000 patients in the practice may have felt like seeing the counsellor during the previous three years. This may be a dangerous assumption to make from such a small sample, but it does give a strong indication of the perceived client need for counselling in general practice. It would be interesting to know whether clients, if given a choice, would prefer to see a counsellor instead of their doctor.

The figure 53% seems quite high and may reflect the wording of the question to indicate 'past' as well as present problems. If counselling was available as an ongoing service one might expect to see a reduction in this figure over the years as those with 'past' problems seek help. Of course there is a big difference between 'feeling like talking' and actually taking the plunge to agree to see a counsellor.

Seventy per cent said they normally turn to friends and family when in need of personal support whilst 21% keep their problems to themselves. Even so 8% normally seek independent help from a professional person. This figure could include doctors, priests and other professionals who are not necessarily counsellors. Fifty per cent of the respondents who said they kept their problems to themselves were men, which is a high percentage as men only made up 25% of the sample, Only 2 men said they would normally seek independent help.

Asked why they might consider seeing a counsellor, 42% said to feel less stressed and more confident; 32% to feel less confused and try to think afresh; 14% wish to feel happier with themselves and the world; and 5% would wish to alter their present lifestyle.

Eighty-four per cent of respondents would prefer to be offered a referral to see the counsellor if they consulted their doctor feeling stressed, depressed or anxious, rather than be given a prescription for some tablets 4%, be given a sick certificate 6%, or be told to pull themselves together 3%. It would be interesting to know whether they would choose to see a counsellor in preference to seeing a doctor for emotional difficulties. This would obviously be of benefit to a busy GP and concurs with the study by Marsh and Barr (1975) who found that time-consuming patients reduce their demands on GPs and take fewer psychotropic drugs. Cocksedge (1989) suggests that the presence of the counsellor in the surgery may heighten the doctor's sensitivity to non-organic problems.

If most people would prefer to see a counsellor for these problems, having a counsellor on site could be a big advantage, and as De Groot stated in 1985, 'A general practitioner is more likely to make referrals to a counsellor known to him (*sic*) who works on the same premises'. Also, as Waydenfield and Waydenfield said in 1980, 'counselling may be coordinated with other forms of treatment'. So, although the question asked specifically for their preference there is no reason why more than one of the options could not be combined, e.g. a patient could be offered counselling as well as being given time off work. As one respondent said, 'I usually feel most stressed at having to work and run a home. A short break would give me time to myself for a while.'

Patients' perceptions of the problems that might benefit from counselling

Fifty-one per cent said they would be most likely to seek the help of a counsellor if they became depressed or anxious. The second highest group was bereavement and loss (16%), and this may reflect the growing awareness of bereavement counselling following the recent disasters at Bradford, Purley and King's Cross. Relationship difficulties came last (11%). This might reflect that those with relationship difficulties are less likely to visit their GP than those with anxiety or depression which may be viewed as having a medical origin. There are currently prescribable medications for the treatment of anxiety and depression whereas there is no pill that can be prescribed for relationship difficulties.

Patients' perceptions of counsellors and counselling

One of the major reasons for conducting this piece of research was to establish people's perceptions of counsellors and counselling. My silent assumption was that most people do not understand the role of a counsellor or what counselling involves. To test this I listed my definition of a counsellor, a psychiatrist and a psychologist and added on a person who listens and then advises. Only one person chose the psychiatrist definition and only one person chose the psychologist definition. Thirty-four per cent opted for the person who listens and gives advice and 59% chose my definition of a counsellor as a person who 'helps people accept and come to terms with their difficulties and identify ways of coping more effectively'. These figures seem encouraging but also mean that counsellors still have some way to go to shake off the perception of 'advice-givers'. The title 'counsellor' seems to be increasingly used by employers and agencies and often the employee has no professional counselling qualification, e.g. 'debt counsellors'; the title 'counsellor' remains ambiguous.

As to the purpose of counselling, 65% felt that it was to explore the problem and help increase self-understanding. The others were split between 'giving advice', 'creating a trusting and supportive relationship' and 'to make suggestions and offer concrete action plans'. Thirty-four per cent of respondents correctly identified all three questions about the role and purpose and clientele of counsellors.

When questioned on their biggest fear about seeing a counsellor, 33% responded that they did not know what would happen. This is certainly an area that counsellors could do something about. At present in the surgery prospective clients are offered a copy of the BAC publication *Counselling and Psychotherapy – Is it for Me?* to read prior to the assessment session. Eighteen per cent said they don't like the idea of talking to a stranger; 4% replied that friends and family might think they were mentally ill; 34% felt the biggest fear was not liking to admit that they couldn't cope. This could mean that some people still view seeing a counsellor as a weakness rather than a strength.

Patients' preferences of counsellor attributes and their referral system

This question produced some interesting results. Thirty-seven per cent stated that given a choice they would prefer to see a counsellor of the same sex and 26% would prefer someone who is about their age. Fourteen per cent would prefer a counsellor from a similar race and culture and 5% would prefer someone who is smart and attractive, Thirteen per cent stated that they had no preference at all, although this was not offered as a choice. The comment 'I don't care, professionalism is more important' reflects a few of the comments. Others were more specific, 'As long as the counsellor is sympathetic yet practical I would have no preference, although someone smart and attractive would most likely put me off.' One person felt that 'someone of a different cultural and sexual orientation may increase self-awareness and offer alternative cultural or sexual aspects.' A 40-year-old woman said 'someone whom I could trust, felt was warm and I was comfortable with. Perhaps I would feel insecure or couldn't open up to someone much younger than me'. Another respondent said that 'the ability of the counsellor to be open-minded and genuine towards my problems, not seeing an issue from only one point of view or value that he/she may hold themselves'. The high number of written responses to this question may well indicate that the counsellor's personal qualities are of varying importance to clients. Some people have no preference at all, whilst others feel that the counsellor's professional ability is the most important aspect. Others believe that the attitude and ability to be empathic is important and overrules other considerations such as age, sex or cultural background. However, the answers are split enough to indicate that some people would like a choice in whom they see. An expansion of this issue would be very useful, with further research into potential preferences of clients.

Of the 37% who preferred a counsellor of the same sex only 2 were male and 32 were female with a mean age of 33.5 years. It is not possible to know why such a high proportion of women would prefer a female counsellor but again this would be an interesting area of further study. It would also be interesting to know what issues these women feel that they would not like to talk to a male counsellor about. Another interesting observation is that this practice has two female doctors and no male doctors and that might be a reason for women joining the practice who feel more comfortable with women than men.

In response to question eleven 3% said they would not want to see anyone, 2% would prefer to pay to see a private counsellor of their choosing and 6% would like a referral to a hospital or outside agency. However, 85% said they would prefer to see the counsellor at their doctor's surgery. The high response rate could reflect the awesome esteem in which patients hold their GPs and the power that patients give to their doctors. Ninety-three per cent of patients said they would choose to see a counsellor if the GP suggested it to them. This figure seems very high and may have been influenced by the fact that the questionnaire is about counselling and in particular about counselling in general practice. There is a strong case here for the employment of counsellors in general practice and it gives a strong indicator that the client would prefer to see a counsellor within general practice rather than outside of it.

Advantages v. disadvantages of counselling in general practice

Thirty-four per cent said that the biggest advantage of having a counsellor attached to their surgery is that it is less frightening than going somewhere they don't know. A high proportion of these were women (27), compared to 6 men. Most patients in the practice are living in the locality and the doctor's surgery may seem a safer place to go for counselling than outside the locality. For women with young children needing to find child care facilities whilst in counselling, this may be a decisive factor in their uptake of the service. As the counsellor works in the surgery from 4pm to 6pm, during the dark evenings a local service may be an important factor for women. This area could be further explored.

The group that preferred a free service tended to be younger, with a mean age of 31.1 years and again the women outnumbered the men 11 to 2. The fact that this was the least chosen option might reflect a willingness for people to pay something towards the cost of their counselling, although again this would require further information. The issue of payment is an important one as some counsellors argue that paying something towards their counselling reflects an increased client commitment. At present the FHSA reimburse 70% of the counsellor's fees and the doctors within the practice pay 30% of the cost. It is difficult to draw any conclusions from the 19% who felt the biggest advantage was that it is more confidential because it begs the question – more confidential than what? Going to a hospital or finding a private therapist? The mean age of those who said it is someone whom the doctor trusts was older, at 38 years, than the mean age of 31.1 years. This could be that older people have more trust in their doctors than the younger generation or that they could have known their GP for longer and built up a more trusting relationship. Having a counsellor recommended by the GP reduces the dilemma of having to find a counsellor themselves. More than a third of the men chose this option (9 out of 25). One might conclude that this reflects that men have a greater trust in their doctor than women, but it may be that the other options were less attractive to men. Some men may not be so frightened of going elsewhere and more able to pay for counselling than women. Nine per cent of respondents commented that they felt there were no disadvantages of having a counsellor attached to the surgery.

One 27-year-old man commented that his fear of being seen by people who knew him was that 'the public associate "trick cyclists" with counsellors'. Sixteen per cent felt the biggest disadvantage was that they might be seen by someone they knew, and 16% felt it was less confidential. Forty-nine per cent were concerned that there was no choice as to whom they could see. Thirty-five out of the 44 whose sex was stated were women, which may relate back to some of the answers in question eight. Eighteen women who were concerned there was no choice also said they would prefer a female counsellor in question eight. Those practices which employ counsellors for ten hours a week or more might consider the value of having two part-time counsellors of different sexes. The answers may reflect that there are some issues that women would prefer to discuss with a female counsellor and this may affect their willingness to engage with a male counsellor in the first place.

Conclusion

In conclusion, this study would indicate there is great value to the consumer placed on the availability of counselling in general practice, and that prospective clients would like to be given more information regarding this service. There is some evidence to indicate that improved communication with the prospective client could save time and money by increasing the uptake of offered counselling and decreasing non-attendance at the initial assessment.

My study has asked the potential consumer for some of their perceptions about counselling in general and counselling in general practice in particular. It is by no means a large study but the 100 responses do allow some conclusions to be drawn. These results should be observed in the light of reflecting one general practice only and any conclusions made about counselling in general practice in general must be guarded. It is important to acknowledge that due to the random nature of the sample it is not known how many respondents have had any previous contact with the counselling world.

Despite the weakness of the study it does build on some of the existing work. In contrast to the Mayer and Timms study, I did not find that the biggest reason for seeking counselling is marital discord (34%); in my study only 11% chose relationship difficulties, whereas 51% said it would be if they became depressed or anxious. This might reflect the difference between asking patients in general practice and those seeking social workers.

This study cannot support the results of the Leverholme Project, who found that those who rejected the idea of counselling tended to be in the older age groups.

There is no evidence here to show that within the 18 to 65 age groups there is any difference (Ashurst and Ward, 1983).

Epperson's study' (1987) pointed to the need for more explicit pre-therapy information and my study builds on this finding that 28% would like some telephone contact with the counsellor prior to the initial assessment; and 56% would like the doctor to spend five minutes explaining their reasons for a counselling referral. Overall there was no firm preference as to how the counsellor should contact the client, although there is a clear indication that clients would value an explanation of how counselling might benefit them as a person. Thirty-three per cent of respondents felt unsure as to what would happen if they saw a counsellor and this is a group that all counsellors should take notice of. It would be useful to see more 'pre-therapy' research taken up in this country rather than having to rely on studies from the US. If Larsen's (1983) study was reflected in Britain that verbal client–counsellor contact prior to the initial assessment reduces the no-show rate by 10%, it should be of great interest to counsellors in all settings.

Further studies to look at the cost-effectiveness of counselling in general practice and the pros and cons of short-term therapy would be of benefit, especially with the recent introduction of budget-holding practices.

References

Ashurst, P.M. and Ward, D. (1983) 'An evaluation of counselling in general practice'. Leverholme Project.

Balint, M. (1964) *The Doctor, his Patient and the Illness.* London: Pitman.

Cocksedge, S. (1989) 'Counselling in general practice: a brief review of the literature', *Counselling in Medical Settings, Newsletter*, 21: 14–20.

De Groot, M. (1985) *Marriage Guidance Counsellors in Medical Settings.* Rugby: National Marriage Guidance Council.

Epperson et al. (1987) 'Issues of informed entry into Counselling', *Journal of Counselling Psychology*, 34(3): 266–75.

Irving, J. (1988) 'Counselling in general practice – the need for provision of formally structured and funded counsellor attachment schemes in primary care', *British Psychological Society Counselling Psychology Section Review*, 3: 4–15.

Larsen et al. (1983) 'Enhancing the utilization of outpatient mental health services', *Community Mental Health Journal*, 19(4): 305–20.

Marsh, G.N. and Barr, J. (1975) 'Marriage guidance counselling in a group practice', *Journal of the Royal College of General Practitioners*, 25: 73–5.

Mayer, J.E. and Timms, N. (1970) *The Client Speaks.* London: Routledge and Kegan.

McCleod, J. (1988) 'The Work of Counsellors in General Practice'. Occasional Paper 37, Royal College of General Practitioners.

Oldfield, S. (1983) *The Counselling Relationship.* London: Routledge and Kegan.

Gray, P. (1988) 'Counsellors in general practice', *Journal of the Royal College of General Practitioners*, 38(307): 50–1.

Rowland, N. et al. (1989) 'Can general practitioners counsel?', *Journal of the Royal College of General Practitioners*, 39: 118–20.

Waydenfield, D. and Waydenfield, S. (1980) 'Counselling in general practice', *Journal of the Royal College of General Practitioners*, 30: 671–7.

Wyld, K.L. (1981) 'Counselling in general practice – a review', *British Journal of Guidance and Counselling*, 9(2): 129–41.

Appendix 1   Questionnaire

FILL IN   AGE   SEX
FIRST

Please read each question carefully and *TICK ONE BOX ONLY*. There is not necessarily a right or wrong answer. It is important that you answer every question by putting a tick in the box that best represents your opinion.

EXAMPLE

Question   How many hours of television do you watch every week?

A. None
B. About 1–5 hours
C. About 5–10 hours
D. Over 10 hours

ANSWER   A ☐ B ☐ C ☐ D ☐

Comments:

QUESTIONNAIRE

QUESTION   During the past three years have you ever felt like talking to an
ONE   independent counsellor about a present or a past problem?

A. Never
B. Once
C. Twice
D. More than twice

ANSWER   A ☐ B ☐ C ☐ D ☐

Comments:

QUESTION   When I feel in need of help or personal support I normally:-
TWO

A. Seek independent help from a professional person
B. Speak to a member of my family
C. Speak to one of my friends
D. I keep my problems to myself

ANSWER   A ☐ B ☐ C ☐ D ☐

Comments:

QUESTION   I would be most likely to seek the help of a counsellor if:-
THREE

A. I became depressed or anxious
B. I was having relationship difficulties
C. I suffered a bereavement or loss
D. I would never seek counselling help

ANSWER   A ☐ B ☐ C ☐ D ☐

Comments:

QUESTION *FOUR*	The place where I feel most stressed is:-

    A. At home
    B. At work
    C. Whilst travelling
    D. I never feel stressed

ANSWER   A ☐ B ☐ C ☐ D ☐

Comments:

QUESTION
FIVE   A counsellor is someone who:-

    A. Helps people accept and come to terms with their difficulties and identify ways of coping more effectively
    B. Uses tests to assess a person's problems and then decides on the therapy best suited to each individual
    C. Listens to people's problems and then advises them on the best course of action
    D. Is a trained Doctor who is concerned with the diagnosis and treatment of mental disorders

ANSWER   A ☐ B ☐ C ☐ D ☐

Comments:

QUESTION
SIX   Counsellors mostly see people who:-

    A. Are mentally ill
    B. Are weak and unable to cope on their own
    C. Are in need of support
    D. Need advice

ANSWER   A ☐ B ☐ C ☐ D ☐

Comments:

QUESTION
SEVEN   The purpose of counselling is to:-

    A. Give advice
    B. Create a trusting and supportive relationship
    C. Make suggestions and offer concrete action plans
    D. Explore the problem and help increase self-understanding

ANSWER   A ☐ B ☐ C ☐ D ☐

Comments:

QUESTION
EIGHT   Given a choice I would prefer to see a counsellor who is:-

    A. About my own age
    B. The same sex as me
    C. From a similar race and culture
    D. Smart and attractive

ANSWER   A ☐ B ☐ C ☐ D ☐

Comments:

QUESTION NINE   If I decided to seek counselling it would be because I wanted to:-

A. Feel less confused and try to think afresh
B. Feel happier with myself and the world
C. Feel less stressed and more confident
D. Alter my present lifestyle

ANSWER   A ☐ B ☐ C ☐ D ☐

Comments:

QUESTION TEN   If you consulted your Doctor because you felt stressed, depressed or anxious, would you prefer to:-

A. Be given a prescription for some tablets
B. Be given a sick certificate
C. Be offered a referral to see the counsellor
D. Be told to pull yourself together

ANSWER   A ☐ B ☐ C ☐ D ☐

Comments:

QUESTION ELEVEN   If your Doctor suggested that you see a counsellor would you prefer:-

A. Not to see anyone
B. To pay to see a private counsellor of your choosing
C. See the counsellor at my Doctor's Surgery
D. To be referred to the Hospital or outside agency

ANSWER   A ☐ B ☐ C ☐ D ☐

Comments:

QUESTION TWELVE   If you agreed to take up the offer of counselling at the Doctor's Surgery would you prefer:-

A. To make an appointment with the receptionist
B. To arrange an appointment with the counsellor by telephone
C. That the counsellor sent you an appointment in the post
D. No preference

ANSWER   A ☐ B ☐ C ☐ D ☐

Comments:

QUESTION THIRTEEN   The biggest advantage of having a counsellor attached to my Doctor's Surgery is that:-

A. It is someone who my Doctor trusts
B. It is more confidential
C. It is a free service
D. It is less frightening than going somewhere I don't know

ANSWER   A ☐ B ☐ C ☐ D ☐

Comments:

QUESTION FOURTEEN The biggest disadvantage of having a counsellor attached to my Doctor's surgery that:-

    A. I might be seen by people I know
    B. I would prefer to pay for my counselling
    C. It is less confidential
    D. There is no choice as to who I see

ANSWER A ☐ B ☐ C ☐ D ☐

Comments:

QUESTION FIFTEEN The biggest fear I have about seeing a counsellor is:-

    A. I don't know what would happen
    B. I don't like the idea of talking to a stranger
    C. Friends and family might think I was mentally ill
    D. I don't like admitting that I cannot cope

ANSWER A ☐ B ☐ C ☐ D ☐

Comments:

QUESTION SIXTEEN I would be much more likely to agree to see a counsellor if:-

    A. I was given a handout explaining what counselling is
    B. I could speak to the counsellor on the telephone before committing myself
    C. The Doctor spent five minutes explaining to me how they think it might benefit me
    D. There was less social stigma attached to it

ANSWER A ☐ B ☐ C ☐ D ☐

Comments:

Thank you very much for taking the time to fill in this questionnaire. Please check that you have answered every question and that you have only ticked one box for each answer.

Please hand the completed form back to the receptionist before leaving the Surgery.

Appendix 2 Results

One hundred and five questionnaires were handed out randomly. One questionnaire was discarded as the subject was aged 15 years. Two questionnaires were returned empty, and two were discarded as they were incorrectly filled in. Hence, the total sample was 100 subjects.

Most of the incorrectly answered questions came into two main categories. First, the question was not answered at all. Secondly, subjects sometimes ticked more than one box.

Patients' perceptions within general practice

Question One

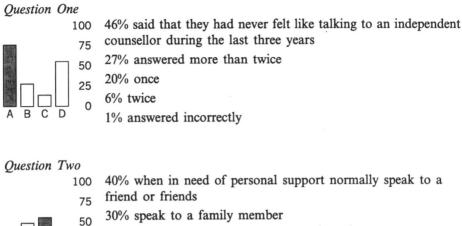

46% said that they had never felt like talking to an independent counsellor during the last three years

27% answered more than twice

20% once

6% twice

1% answered incorrectly

Question Two

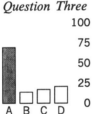

40% when in need of personal support normally speak to a friend or friends

30% speak to a family member

21% keep their problems to themselves

8% seek independent professional help

1% answered incorrectly

Question Three

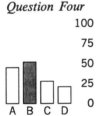

51% would be most likely to seek counselling help for anxiety and depression

17% would never seek help

11% for relationship difficulties

16% for a bereavement or loss

5% answered incorrectly

Question Four

39% fell most stressed at work

34% at home

15% whilst travelling

9% never feel stressed

3% answered incorrectly

Question Five

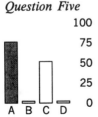

59% correctly identified the role of a counsellor

34% chose an adviser

1% a psychologist

1% a psychiatrist

5% answered incorrectly

Question Six

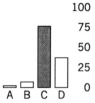

100
75
50
25
0

A B C D

66% believed that counsellors mostly see people who are in need of support

30% chose those needing advice

2% weak people who cannot cope

1% the mentally ill

1% answered incorrectly

Question Seven

100
75
50
25
0

A B C D

65% said that the purpose of counselling is to explore the problem and increasing self-understanding

12% to give advice

10% to create a trusting and supporting relationship

9% to make suggestions and offer concrete action plans

4% answered incorrectly

Question Eight

100
75
50
25
0

A B C D

37% would prefer to see a counsellor who was the same sex

26% who was about their age

14% from a similar race and culture

5% who was smart and attractive

13% wrote in the comments section that they had no preference

5% answered incorrectly

Question Nine

100
75
50
25
0

A B C D

42% would seek counselling to feel less stressed and more confident

32% to feel less confused and to think afresh

14% to feel happier with themselves and the world

5% to alter their present lifestyles

7% answered incorrectly

Question Ten

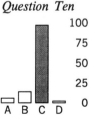

100
75
50
25
0

A B C D

84% would prefer to see a counsellor if they were stressed, depressed or anxious,

6% would like a sick certificate

4% would prefer some tablets

3% would like to be told to pull themselves together

3% answered incorrectly

Question Eleven

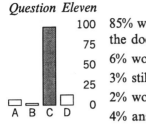

85% would prefer to see the counsellor in the doctor's surgery if the doctor recommended counselling

6% would prefer a hospital referral or outside agency

3% still wouldn't see anyone

2% would prefer to choose a private therapist

4% answered incorrectly

Question Twelve

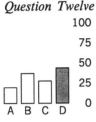

37% stated no preference how the counsellor contacted them

28% preferred to speak to the counsellor by telephone

20% were happy to have an appointment sent to them

14% were happy to make an appointment with the receptionist

1% answered incorrectly

Question Thirteen

34% felt the biggest advantage to having an attached counsellor was that it was less frightening than going elsewhere

28% felt it was seeing someone their doctor trusted

19% felt it was more confidential

14% felt that it was a free service

5% answered incorrectly

Question Fourteen

49% felt the biggest disadvantage to having an attached coun-sellor was the lack of choice

16% felt it would be less confidential

16% were concerned they might be seen by people they knew

1% would prefer to pay

9% felt there were no disadvantages

9% answered incorrectly

Question Fifteen

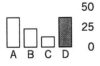

34% said their biggest fear about seeing a counsellor was not liking to admit they couldn't cope

33% felt they didn't know what would happen

18% do not like the idea of talking to a stranger

4% were worrying friends and family might think they were mentally ill

11% answered incorrectly

Peter Thomas

Question Sixteen

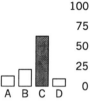

56% said they would be more likely to agree to see a counsellor if the doctor spent five minutes explaining how it might benefit them

13% if they could speak to the counsellor on the telephone first

9% would prefer a handout

7% if there was less social stigma about coming

15% answered incorrectly

Brief update

Since the completion of this study new developments are happening all over the country. A lot of positive work has been achieved by the Counselling in Primary Care Trust, both in promoting counselling in general practice and in guiding relevant research and training opportunities. A set of *Guidelines for the Employment of Counsellors in General Practice* has now been published by BAC and is increasingly being used by health commissions who are responsible for funding the employment of counsellors.

Twenty-five per cent of all general practices in England and Wales now employ counsellors. A far more professional approach is being adopted with concern for training, payment and supervision.

However, the client's voice is still rarely heard.

Reference

British Association for Counselling (1993) *Guidelines for the Employment of Counsellors in General Practice*. Rugby: BAC.

Discussion issues

1 Who would benefit from an increased understanding of patients' perceptions of counselling?
2 What are the possible benefits and drawbacks of a client-led service?
3 What are the advantages and disadvantages of counselling in general practice?
4 How could you measure the cost-effectiveness of counselling in general practice?

PART FIVE

THE LAST WORD

Introduction to Part Five

Though not quite the book of revelations, our final section considers those future developments, changes and trends anticipated by several widely experienced educators, trainers, practitioners, writers and administrators currently active in the world of counselling in Britain.

The good ship BAC Enterprise is taken on a trip round the galaxy by Michael Reddy, who presented 'The Counselling Firmament' as a paper at the BAC Annual Conference in 1992. In August 1994 Windy Dryden, Britain's own first professor of counselling, offered a trend-spotter's guide to counselling and counsellor training in an inimitable personal view.

The roundtable 'New Directions in Counselling' is a collection of contributions from seven notables in the field who were asked to offer their thoughts on counselling trends. Ray Woolfe, Brian Thorne, Michael Jacobs and Diana Whitmore espouse differing counselling approaches as practitioners and although collectively they represent counsellor training and education, it is a challenge to trace the similarities and differences in their points of view. Judith Baron and Fiona Palmer Barnes focus our thoughts on the British Association for Counselling whilst David Lane directs our attention to the social policies and economics of liaison with our European neighbours. Their thoughts make succinct, varied and challenging reading.

Judith Baron has the last word, as general secretary of BAC, in her account of the past, present and future of our association.

The *BAC Counselling Reader* has concerned itself, as counselling concerns itself, with the effects of history, the very real and pressing concerns of the present and directions for the future.

75

The Counselling Firmament: a Short Trip Round the Galaxy

Michael Reddy

This paper wrote itself and eventually came up with a slightly different title from the one planned. What happened was that it kept making unexpected excursions along new dimensions of the counselling universe and discovered vantage points which are round the corner from our usual world-view. If it weren't too contrived I would move around the auditorium and take a new microphone for each of the major segments, simply to illustrate how discontinuous each viewpoint can be.

The galactic image also brings out how much movement, even turbulence, there is in the current counselling world, and of course it underlines the matter of perspective. I remember my personal indignation when I discovered the Milky Way (which I thought has been provided for us all as a private spectacle) was the central reality, of which our entire solar system was a mere fringe ornament.

Well, there are over *two million* workers throughout the UK whose job formally involves them in counselling – in counselling, please note, not in something we may loftily deign to call counselling skills – but in counselling. On the other hand, BAC has only some 10,000 members and about 600 of them are accredited. Could we too be a fringe ornament in counselling's Milky Way?

This naturally prompts some satellite questions such as: Is the good ship BAC Enterprise on course? Are we due for a quick burn of the boosters? Is Captain Bell steering us close enough to the true centre of the universe? Could BAC disappear down a time–space warp? . . . Or is our role to be simply a beacon? And what if everyone is looking the other way?

First sighting: Europe

You can start a circular tour from anywhere, but I noticed Europe in the original programme announcement . . .

Last year Emmy van Deurzen-Smith, standing on this very spot, woke us up to manoeuvres and machinations (my words, not hers), pressure groups and vested interests within the European Community which *could* result in our being deprived of the right to the title of counsellor. (An awful lot of what she said then still calls for urgent attention.) It was and is still possible that psychotherapy could occupy

This chapter represents the text of a paper delivered at the BAC Annual Conference, September 1992 and was first published in *Counselling, Journal of the British Association for Counselling*, vol. 4, no. 1, pp. 47–50 (1993).

so much of the significant areas of the counselling map that our own remnant would be altogether diminished and entirely the wrong shape.

Alternatively, counselling (therapeutic counselling?) could become one among many modes of psychotherapy and share a common map.

Well, the EAP (European Association for Psychotherapy), formed in April of this year, is the latest on this particular scene. Its members will form a powerful lobby within the EC but have decided on a slow start. The danger has receded, I am glad to say. Or rather, sorry to say, because it has only receded, as one of our more popular European generals said, *'pour mieux sauter'*. I would hate this lull to convince the Europhobes among us that the problem has gone away for ever and that masterly inaction will carry the day once again.

BAC, Politics and BAC

The European Association for Psychotherapy will be back. They will succeed. They have begun their work in collaborative and constructive fashion amid the complexity of the European scene. You will enjoy a glimpse of that complexity tomorrow morning if you are attending Konstantin Veitinghoff-Scheel's workshop. The Association has foresworn in-fighting, it has postponed for the moment any premature attempt at harmonization. Rather each member will help the others, as a starting point, to define each one's separate uniqueness.

In Britain we have been protected from some of this complexity just because we have BAC. There is nothing like BAC in the rest of Europe. No one has taken the profession of counselling as such as far as we have. But we can't let that delude us that everyone else will recognize the same goal posts or even want to play on the same pitch.

When the Europe bus returns (doubtless via the Channel Tunnel) we must have a ticket. Maybe it will be a train and we will have a carriage to ourselves. I say that because another association is in the making, backed strongly by BAC, called the European Association for Counselling. This in itself is a key strategic move – hopefully in keeping with a total strategy. Do we know what that is?

One of my happier conclusions from a lifetime in counselling is that psychotherapists and counsellors, when they put their minds to it, make good institutions. There seems to be a tendency for good honest folk to rise to the top.

The UK Standing Conference for Psychotherapy is case in point. It originated in the mid-seventies in the desire of one rather narrowly based sector of the psychotherapy world to be VAT-exempt and thus protect their already quite useful fees. The scope of the Standing Conference has however been steadily widened (to the point when the originating group departed in disgust) up to the present day where it represents an extremely catholic (small 'c') kirk, while gathering strength as a serious player on the UK political scene.

I mean political. Counselling can no longer float free in the real world. Politics, economics and professionalism now tango on the same floor, and we counsellors don't have too many trained reflexes in such company. We may discover some stiff muscles in the process but when it comes to the Last Waltz we need BAC still on its feet. In concrete terms that means we have to be very sure who we are and what we stand for. We know who we are, don't we? I think we do but whether we are conveying this in a way which natives on distant shores can understand – or even 10 miles outside Rugby – is another question.

I am going to lace this paper with the occasional mountain-top utterance and I can feel the first one coming on . . .

We need to define ourselves more tightly in everyday language.

Second sighting: Our new paymasters

The big advance in counselling in the UK – the definitive step – will be via workplace counselling. Why? Because that is where the serious money will come from, i.e., from employers.

As if it was not distasteful enough to bring politics into it, here comes business and commerce. There are reasons: I will discuss three.

First, **healthcare** is going to loom ever larger on the national agenda. We will never be able to afford the NHS we want or believe we need. *Nobody* can pay for the ever-increasing options which medicine will always discover. Nobody ever will – not to mention the millions more who will live longer. Did you know there are more people alive at the present time than the sum total of all those who have lived throughout human history?

Healthcare costs naturally escalate. Rationing of healthcare is perhaps the most unpleasant consequence of this revolution. Increasingly people die and suffer who shouldn't. No health service of any kind – not just the NHS – will ever be able to keep up, and that is not a political statement. It makes no difference which political party is in power. Private healthcare and private health insurance will play an ever-growing role, and provide an increasing proportion of the cash, simply to bridge an ever-widening gap.

Employers in particular will continue to pay for an ever-larger slice of the cake, and will see counselling as an important ingredient in protecting what everyone tells them (and many of them know) are their greatest asset, namely people – and also in keeping total healthcare costs down. There will, however, be no sentimentality in this process. 'Managed Care' will be the new slogan and employers will look harder and harder at what they get for their shilling. Quality, qualifications and money-back guarantees will be in their minds when they buy – including counselling. Are you ready for that – money-back guarantees?

So, it's basically good news, then! BAC has looked after us well, took the high ground in terms of accreditation long ago. It's true. You may detect traces of irony but I would like it to be clear that it is not at BAC's expense. The accomplishments of BAC over the last two decades are formidable. If anything BAC has done all too well for us. If the irony is at anyone's expense it is at mine and yours. We are just as much likely to be out of touch, complacent, in a rut, as those running BAC.

What we need to know most, however, is this: is BAC's hand strong enough to do what it needs to do next? Is it a big enough player on the national scene? Does it need more capital, more time, more workers? Will it ask for what it needs? You know what we counsellors are like when it comes to asking for what we need. Only this afternoon we were asked, with apparent trepidation I suspect, for another measly £5, which I believe to be a pinprick compared with the funding BAC really needs to make the next quantum leap on our behalf.

Second reason, **Employee Assistance Programmes** – Hurricane EAP. Those of us who scan the western approaches with rheumy eye and have wearily watched a variety of initials heave in view on the transatlantic horizon – TA, NLP, TM, TQM, JIT and so on – will have noticed EAPs increasingly on the agenda. Let me say briefly that an EAP is a systematic way of delivering counselling and other forms of assistance to an entire workforce.

The arrival of Employee Assistance Programmes has given counselling a high profile, such that even without formal EAPs, counselling uptake will rise steadily. BAC accreditation may indeed have gained high profile as a benchmark but the system creaks in the context of workplace counselling. Some of its limitations are highlighted by the fact that so few people (relatively speaking) think it worthwhile to apply for accreditation and that quite a few potential and enthusiastic candidates are recommended not to. If ever the moment were ripe for a review of the whole system it is now. Not to go back to square one – too much has been achieved – but to take a second step.

Third, the **outplacement** industry (that is, firms whose 'consultants' help redundant employees find new jobs) is here to stay. A great deal of money has already been thrown at it, and the rising trend in unemployment has greatly consolidated its position. But career counselling as such, in good times and bad, will be its permanent legacy. All outplacement firms will be quick to rechristen themselves 'career counsellors' (the process is well under way). 'In-placement' is a nice catchy way to announce the shift in emphasis. And as employers ask ever more searching questions about quality, the outplacement career counselling firms will be ever more anxious to establish standards and credentials above and beyond what has been the traditional baseline – grey hair.

I think another *ex cathedra* pronouncement is brewing. Yes, here it comes . . . Lapidary Statement, Number Two:

The argument for a revision of the BAC Accreditation system is increasingly pressing.

I am thinking of parallel systems rather than two-tier, focused in different arenas, rather than on different levels. It may even be possible to devise a switching system to allow individual practitioners to change tracks. It would be an enormous bonus to me in my own work if I could fish in the same pool for clinically aware personnel officers and organization-smart counsellors.

Third sighting: the IPM (Institute of Personnel Management)

We are now very much in a different part of the galaxy

Within the outplacement industry, attempts were made in the past to exclude the cowboys, by a number of firms such as the John Wayne Company and Clint

Eastwood Associates using codes of ethics and practice which would keep the market in the 'right' (i.e., their own) hands.

Then, a few months ago, the IPM itself [Institute of Personnel Management – now the Institute of Personnel and Development – Ed.] took charge of and stamped its authority and its prestige on this process through its newly constituted Career Counselling and Outplacement Forum along with its definitive Code. In one stroke IPM has moved centre stage in the counselling movement. It will not be long before it seeks to consolidate that role in a number of other ways, which will include positioning statements on behalf of its 47,000 members, very many of whom are engaged in workplace counselling (not just career counselling) on a daily basis – and many of whom will increasingly see value in some form of recognition for their counselling practice and responsibilities.

The Career Counselling and Outplacement Forum Code of Ethics and Practice includes some brief paragraphs on qualifications for individual practitioners. It is clear that IPM intends its own membership criteria to play a significant role in this qualifying process. It will also cross-reference to the accreditation procedures of other organizations. It refers explicitly to the British Psychological Society, but not to BAC. Have we missed the boat? Are we talking to these people? Well we are, as a matter of fact, thanks to the Association for Counselling at Work. This Association, every bit as much as BAC itself, is in need of your support – where are you, out there? Can we have that again! ACW needs your support.

I can feel another oracular ecstasy coming on. I can promise it will be the last . . . Lapidary Statement, Number Three:

The centre of gravity of the counselling universe is moving inexorably to the workplace.

Fourth sighting: EAPA, BPS, the Lead Body

Still not sure? There are some people over here I'd like you to meet . . .

The **EAPA** (Employee Assistance Professionals Association) is only about a year old in the UK. It is part of an international organization but each 'chapter' is autonomous. The UK association is highly proactive and is taking a strong interest in standards, both in terms of providers – a Trade Association of EAP firms – and for individual practitioners – a Professional Association for EAP counsellors, consultants and managers.

EAPA is not in competition with BAC in terms of accreditation. Rather, it too will seek to cross-reference its standards with those of institutions such as BAC. It might however want to define supplementary parameters for EAP counsellors, not to contest the adequacy of a counsellor's basic competence but to assess the ability of counsellors to work in a particular environment. To be involved in workplace counselling one has to grapple at first hand with issues outside the counselling session itself; the implications of the three-cornered contract between counsellor, client and paying customer have to be worked out in sometimes tedious detail; and even some of one's most cherished beliefs may be put under pressure.

Or perhaps you prefer the view from over here . . .

In relatively recent times the **BPS** (British Psychological Society) formed a Special Interest Group – not a new Section let alone a lofty Division, of which there are only a handful – for Counselling Psychology. In an incredibly short time its 1,300 members have come to dwarf all other subsets within BPS – bar one, I believe – and are hell-bent on becoming a fully fledged Division (within a year or so) [*now a reality*, Ed.] and thus gaining Chartered status. It has just announced its accreditation procedures for a Diploma in Counselling Psychology and will hold its first exams in 1993. The outline criteria bear a strong resemblance (as one would expect) to those for BAC accreditation. The Society is negotiating with the CNAA and the Open University with a view to converting its Diplomas into postgraduate degrees. These people are really motoring. Are we talking to them? We haven't missed another boat have we?

Talking about boats, there is another one leaving shortly . . .

The single factor which will have the most impact on the practice of counselling in the UK, and which is already producing cross-currents the like of which we have never seen, is the **Lead Body for Advice, Guidance and Counselling**. This is one (of 187) such bodies, government-inspired and entirely within an industrial context, which will change the face of work and, in this case, all work defined as counselling, for decades. That is, if there is to be only one Lead Body in which counsellors have an investment. Maybe we need two? It is a momentous challenge for BAC and an enormous opportunity. The process is irreversible – but nothing is yet fixed. The Feasibility Study is complete, a Lead Body is at an advanced stage of formation. By the time this is in print, it will be a fact.

Everything is still to play for. You will note that BAC – far from being caught napping – has offered you a chance, at tomorrow's Plenary, to hear and talk to Julie Janes, who conducted the Feasibility Study on behalf of the Department of Employment.

Once more we face pressure to define ourselves more stringently. We are to situate ourselves in a world, and therefore on a map, which includes guidance, advice, befriending, counselling, counselling skills and psychotherapy. We are to seek to locate ourselves on a continuum – or even within a multi-level spectrum (where perhaps our tendency has been to claim discontinuity), to be part of a universe which we may have thought we dominated. To be only a part of a National Vocational Qualification system. If you have not noticed NVQs before, you soon will.

Quick reference

Let me briefly review where we have got to.

First, I have introduced six separate constituencies, half a dozen quite different starting points in counselling space: the European Association for Psychotherapy, the UK Standing Conference for Psychotherapy, the Institute of Personnel Management, the Employee Assistance Professionals Association, the Counselling Psychology Division of the British Psychological Society and the new Lead Body for Advice, Guidance and Counselling. All are heavenly bodies with varying amounts of gravitational pull. Their orbits interact with BAC's.

Secondly, I have suggested three ways in which BAC might respond to a new situation: by tightening the very definition of what we do, by reviewing and overhauling the accreditation process, and by responding to the new emphasis on workplace counselling. I will finish by saying just a little more about two of these.

The definition of counselling

By 'tightening the definition' of counselling I have in mind the verbal definition but also something more fundamental. There is something quintessentially paradoxical about counselling, as a profession, even in its very conception.

Here we are, a healthy and thriving group, bound and determined to exact recognition from the general public as a viable and worthy profession. A profession means in the last analysis that only its qualified members can perform its proper actions or at least perform them properly – or at a level measurably superior to other people, or with legal sanction.

Yet counselling is something which occurs spontaneously in nature.

People are counselling each other all the time, wanting counselling from each other, offering counselling to each other – all the time. If counselling is a profession at all, it certainly isn't a new one. It is a very old one. Is it that separate from merely being human that we can justify our claim to be a profession? The burden of proof may still be on us to define what it is we do differently (or what is different about what we do), what it is precisely we do to certain, externally verifiable, standards, do so uniquely, or so uniquely well that others may not claim to do likewise. Does our present definition of counselling do that for us?

> *'The task of counselling is to give the client an opportunity to discover and clarify ways of living more resourcefully and towards greater well-being.'*

Now I'm afraid my Uncle Jack could not in the end be here, but I know what he would say to that. The dialogue is in fact quite familiar to me. It goes like this (Jack was born north of the Ribble by the way):

> 'Here's our Michael, Jack.'
> 'Come in lad, tek thee clogs off . . . etc.'
> 'Our Michael's a counsellor now.'
> 'IZAWO?'
> (I'll spell it for you – I-Z-A-W-O. The 't' is silent as in Wodehouse. It means: He's a what?)
> 'He's a counsellor.'
> 'What's that then?'
> 'Well, he offers his clients the opportunity to explore, discover and clarify ways of living more resourcefully and towards greater well-being.'
> (I can't go on. It's too painful.)

The trouble is that our definition is about 'being' rather than doing; about a particular stance in a relationship, rather than any discernible separate expertise. The definition is about being human, isn't it? Well that's no small accomplishment, of course. But is it enough to allow us to carve out a separate profession? On a commercial basis is it enough to attract funds from potential users? Is it enough to protect our domain from potential competitors? Would it sustain a serious marketing initiative?

Put it another way. There is no reason why *every* form of psychotherapy (psychiatry and psychoanalysis included) should not make an examination in the core conditions a prerequisite for everything else – for their individual areas of expertise, intervention, methods, tools and conceptual armoury. The question for us then would be: what is our particular area of expertise? Or are we just good at what everyone else takes for granted? We all know that stupid story about that stupid emperor who wandered around quite naked and allowed himself to be kidded by others who admired his raiment. That couldn't be us, could it?

There is another aspect to the problem: adjectival counselling. Even in some relatively sophisticated circles telling someone you are a counsellor arouses a wary reaction. But tell them you are a debt counsellor or an AIDS counsellor or a marriage counsellor or an alcohol counsellor or a career counsellor and they are relieved. They know what you are talking about. You are accepted as knowing something – something extra, something special.

But what does the non-adjectival counsellor know? Knows a bit about all of them, knows nothing about any of them?

Workplace counselling

The true centre of gravity in the counselling galaxy is the workplace. Not 'will be' but 'is'.

So this is the best news yet, right! Here we are in Boom City with the only counselling shop in town.

There are only two slight shadows. One lies with our clients. The jury is still out on counselling. The 30 million or so working men and women in heart-of-oak UK are not yet wholly convinced. Uncle Jack has not quite got the message.

Not to mention, of course, that we may no longer have the only shop in town and that our competitors may be more adept at selling counselling, in commercial terms, in the name even (and heaven forbid) of monstrosities such as performance management.

The second shadow lies with us, and it is mirror image of the first. We are poor self-publicists. We talk our own language not theirs. No wonder Uncle Jack and heart-of-oak UK is wary of us, why they can't situate us alongside medicine, social work, education and the other necessities of life. We are not only poor self-publicists but proud of it. We shudder at the idea that we might be a 'market commodity'. Our role model is the Wizard of Oz. To get to see the Wizard you had to cross six continents and face unimaginable dangers. And when you got there all he did was point out you were already wearing the magic shoes to transport you back home. (What a therapist! That's real counselling!) Although, come to think of it, he must have had a good PR agent too. Everybody knew where he was and how to find him.

The earth is shaking, our centre of gravity has already shifted. Are we ready to move with it? If we counsellors aren't prepared to move centre stage it will be wasted effort for BAC to get there before us. If the great body of counsellors continues to harbour natural suspicion of organizations it will be no use asking ACW to be our new flagship. Can you imagine that – ACW our flagship! Our public face! Our Whitehall lobby!

Come to that, is ACW ready for it? It has changed its name, it has moved up a couple of gears under the new leadership. Can it now shed its native diffidence? It is hard to shed the habits of a lifetime and the old CAWD was rather bashful and retiring. It was a relief to see that the new ACW now takes it as its mission to go beyond counselling skills and promote *counselling* and *counselling services* in the workplace. If all we can do is promote counselling *skills* we may as well all go home.

Conclusion

We can't say that BAC faces only 'x' number of options because that would pre-empt the debate. But you can say that, looking back from the next time-warp, BAC will be seen to have moved in one or more of four broad directions:

1   It will be more embedded in the daily reality of the nation as it goes to work.
2   It will be seen as part (maybe even a distinguished feature) of the psycho-therapy landscape.
3   It will have disengaged itself from both these currents and be seen as some-thing distinct and validly distinct from either, while remaining related.
4   It will have disengaged itself to the point of creating a self-contained universe of its own.

These choices are not all mutually exclusive and to many of us it will appear to be a choice between positive alternatives. We are situated between the world of psychotherapy and the world of workplace counselling and thanks to some hard work BAC has acquired its own gravitational pull. The only choice we do not have is to pursue the present orbit. The coming celestial storm will leave nothing unchanged.

Looking back we will see that we have moved. That is the one thing we can say with certainty. But will BAC have moved of its own accord? Did it jump – or was it pushed?

We have been occupying the high ground for some years. No doubt about that. Occupying the high ground in clear weather is most rewarding. You can move about in freedom and safety. But once the waters start rising, isolation can come quite suddenly. You can soon find yourself with only two choices. Shin up the old ivory tower, out of harm's way, or swim for it.

This has been a short trip round the Counselling Galaxy. And a flood warning. 'Beam me up, Scottie . . .'

Discussion issues

1 Does the author succeed in making his case that counselling faces a 'celestial storm'?
2 Could counselling's main professional associations be sidelined by this revolution?
3 A central plank of the argument is that counselling will become more popular. What are the most persuasive reasons for you?
4 Should people pay for counselling – after all, one can get some excellent counselling from friends for nothing. If professional counsellors should be paid, should it be at a rate closer to an electrician or plumber – or to a lawyer or accountant?

76

Possible Future Trends in Counselling and Counsellor Training: a Personal View

Windy Dryden

In this chapter I wish to discuss some future trends that I would like to see happen in counselling and counsellor training. As such, this is a personal view. While preparing to write this I consulted a recent special issue of an American journal, *Psychotherapy: Theory, Research, Practice and Training*, which came out in 1992, entitled 'The Future of Psychotherapy'. I have sympathy with George Albee, who has an article in that issue listed on the contents page as two pages long. When I looked at the article, I was confronted with two blank pages! I thought 'I know exactly how he must have felt' in that talking about the possible future of counselling is rather grandiose. I don't know what is going to happen to me next week let alone what's going to happen to counselling in the foreseeable future. With that concern expressed I will now outline fourteen trends that I would like to see happen in the fields of counselling and counsellor training. Some of these will no doubt be controversial and that is fine. I hope to stimulate some lengthy debate for the future good of our field.

1 Developing a national register of counsellors

At the moment the British Association for Counselling has a voluntary scheme of accreditation. As such there is no compulsion for anyone to seek accreditation and anyone can say that they are a counsellor without achieving such accreditation. As is well known, some people try to pull the wool over other people's eyes by putting 'MBAC' after their names, implying that being a member of BAC is some kind of professional recognition. As we all know it isn't, as anybody can be a member of BAC.

A national register of counsellors might be organized along the lines of the new register of psychotherapists compiled by the United Kingdom Council for Psychotherapy (UKCP). This body comprises a number of member organizations divided into sections. In order to get on this register someone would need to be properly trained and acceptable to that member organization. I'm not quite sure how this model would work in the world of counselling because although there are member organizations of BAC, these are not all bodies which seek to train counsellors to professional standards and to sustain their members in ongoing professional development. However, I think if we extend the idea of accreditation, so that in

This chapter was first published in *Counselling, Journal of the British Association for Counselling*, vol. 5, no. 3, pp. 194–7 (1994).

order to practise it becomes mandatory to be accredited, this might be the way BAC may wish to go in future. In fact, BAC are currently holding discussions with other national counselling organizations on the possible development of a United Kingdom Register for Counselling. A mandatory register would, of course, raise the hackles of a lot of people. I can see Derek Gale, for example, frothing at the mouth and accusing me of 'intellectual fascism'. I also realize that being on the register of accredited counsellors is no guarantee that abuse of clients will not occur, although I think it will help to reduce it. However, if counselling seeks to be a profession it needs to take professional steps and the development of such a register is one such step.

2 Maintaining the interdisciplinary foundations of counselling

There is a dark cloud looming over the horizon for those of you who are not psychologists. The British Psychological Society is getting its act together and now has a Division of Counselling Psychology. This may be quite threatening for people who don't have a psychology degree, because there is a danger, albeit a slim one, that in the foreseeable future you may need to be a psychologist in order to practise counselling. I say 'Heaven forbid' . . . and I'm a psychologist! Indeed, I would fight to retain the present interdisciplinary foundations of counselling. To this end, I have edited a book with Brian Thorne (Thorne and Dryden, 1993) called *Counselling: Interdisciplinary Perspectives* in which various people from different subject areas/disciplines (even social anthropology, education, theology, philosophy, etc.) show how their particular discipline can enrich counselling. I would hate it if counselling were to lose the rich diversity and I doubt that it will. What is more likely to happen is that, in the minds of some, being a counselling psychologist will be seen as having more status than being a counsellor. Some employing agencies, for example the Health Service with its history of employing clinical psychologists, *might* be more likely to hire counselling psychologists rather than counsellors. I stress the word *might* here and again I hope that this doesn't happen. However counsellors may well have to heed the following point if there are to be plausible alternatives to counselling psychologists.

3 Increasing emphasis on audit and evaluation

I would like to see counsellors take an increasing interest in evaluation and audit. In future, employers will increasingly ask counsellors interesting questions like 'How do you know that your particular work is effective?' Now, you may wax lyrical about the fact that last year you had a bottle of whisky from one client and a box of chocolates from another and other such anecdotal examples. And you may point to the fact that most of your clients *say* that they have derived much from counselling, but this is hardly likely to suffice. Potential employers will want harder evidence and it is likely that counsellors will be required to provide such evidence in the not too distant future. Counsellors will therefore need to be trained how to properly evaluate their work and counsellor training courses will need to put evaluation and audit on their curricula.

In North America, as many readers will know, insurance companies are increasingly demanding evidence of the usefulness of counselling and psychotherapy. As such, practitioners are being asked to prove that they are using the most effective and efficient methods with their clients. This means that therapists are being forced by insurance companies to become more familiar with the research literature, a topic to which we now turn.

4 Developing respect for counselling research

I would also like to see an increase in the respect that practitioners have for research in the field of counselling. In a survey of BAC members published in 1978 (Nelson-Jones and Coxhead, 1978), research was given the lowest priority for BAC attention. In fifteen years the situation has changed somewhat but not appreciably. When I give talks to large audiences, I ask how many research articles people have read on counselling; the modal figure is zero. This, in my opinion, will not be acceptable in the future. Counsellors will be called upon to be cognizant of research work carried out both in North America and, increasingly, in Britain, and again employers may not hire practitioners who are ignorant of research developments in the field of counselling. If the development of counselling psychology in Britain provides the impetus for this shift then it will be all to the good. Of course, researchers will need to engage in an ongoing dialogue with practitioners to make research more meaningful to them, but there is enough meaningful research already being done on counselling to give the lie to the myth that counselling research has little to offer practising counsellors. It may well be that the increasing attention being given to qualitative research will also help to introduce reluctant counsellors to the world of research as it is less threatening to them and more in keeping with the spirit of counselling than quantitative research. (See Part Four.)

5 Increasing emphasis on providing counselling services to 'difficult to reach' client groups

In the next decade I think there will be increasing emphasis paid to providing counselling services for groups that are at present 'difficult to reach'. I'm thinking particularly about clients from ethnic minorities, those in prison (who will need to be seen by visiting counsellors) and other groups that tend to be unrepresented in our counselling services. Primarily, we need to do research to discover why these groups do not come forward for counselling. For that we need to have funding, but I'm confident that we might get it. As part of this process we will probably need to ask ourselves: 'in what ways do we need to change our counselling services to make these more applicable to these groups'? In parallel, we will need to consider how to modify our training courses to make the world of counselling more attractive to potential helpers from these groups. (See Chapters 20 and 21.)

6 Developing agreed standards on training at different levels

At present British counselling training is a mess. You can get a Diploma from one organization that has a number of teaching hours that on another course would count towards a Certificate. You can get a Master's degree in one educational establishment which if offered in another would grant you an advanced Certificate or a Diploma. Also, you can now get a BPhil in Counselling. How do all these qualifications equate? In short, they don't. We are in a complete and utter mess on this issue. Does this matter? I believe it does. For example, if you hold an Advanced Certificate in Counselling – which may have involved three years of study and practice – and you apply for a job, somebody else may apply for it who has a Master's degree which in reality is equivalent. Guess who will be more attractive to the employer? We need agreed national standards for training at different levels to enable us to know, for example, that a Certificate equals 'X' number of hours and covers these topics; a Diploma equals 'Y' number of hours and covers these further topics and so on. BAC is, I believe, in a unique position to take the lead on this issue.

At present I also believe that we need to train people who are not full professionals, the so-called 'para-professionals'. There is some research evidence which shows that para-professionals are as effective as trained professionals with certain groups of clients. This suggests the following question: what are we training people for, at what level and for which client groups? One development which I would like to see, which does not exist at the moment in Britain in our universities and colleges, is the formation of Departments of Counselling. At present, counselling is taught in Education Departments, Psychology Departments or Applied Social Studies Departments amongst others. As such it tends to be a marginalized activity since it does not lie at the heart of a department's central concerns. Counsellors are not going to be treated seriously as professionals, unless counselling becomes a more visible professional activity. So I would like to see the establishment of Departments of Counselling. This development would, of course, raise important issues, such as implications for the viability of smaller semi-autonomous counselling units, but these issues are worth grappling with.

7 Providing proper resources for counsellor training

What worries me about counselling training at present is that it seems to be losing sight of quality. When I was trained as a counsellor in the mid-1970s (I did the one-year full-time Diploma in Counselling in Educational Settings course at Aston University in Birmingham), we had skills training groups with a ratio of one staff member to three or four students. Now I've heard of staff–student ratios on counselling skills courses of one staff member to twenty-four students! What kind of feedback are students going to get from one poor counsellor trainer rushing around like a headless chicken trying to listen and give feedback to twenty-four students? It is very expensive to run a properly resourced counselling course and in the present climate institutions may be very reluctant to provide the necessary resources unless they charge students quite exorbitant fees. So, when you apply for a training course ask the organizers about the staff–student ratio, particularly on counselling skills training courses. If it is greater than one to twelve, forget it!

8 Increasing emphasis on competency in counsellor training

I would like to see greater emphasis on competency in counsellor training. Let's suppose you go into hospital to have an operation and learn that you are to be operated on by a newly qualified surgeon whom nobody has actually seen conduct an operation and who has never been given any kind of feedback on what he/she actually does in the operating theatre. Would you want to be operated on by such a person? Let's suppose he/she says 'I go to case discussion and I've talked about what I've done', would this make any difference to you? I doubt it. You would probably want to be assured that someone senior has seen the surgeon in question operate and given him or her ongoing live supervision throughout the operation. I believe that the same emphasis on competency is needed in counsellor training. Now, ongoing live supervision may well be impractical unless it is done by supervisors behind a one-way mirror, so audio taping will have to suffice. Incidentally, the emphasis on competency means that broad activities are broken down into discrete skills. We even need to break down psychodynamic skills which I believe can be done. I have asked trainers within the psychodynamic tradition 'What are the rules for making effective interpretations?' You would have thought I was asking for the Holy Grail! We need to be able to specify what the skills of effective counselling are and trainers need to be able to say to their trainees 'Yes I have heard you in a training situation and with a client and you have demonstrated this particular skill to an acceptable level of competence.' Now there are those who may well say: You can't break down the complex art of counselling into discrete skills. I would beg to differ. There are others who are against a use of audio tapes in counselling. Carl Rogers was the pioneer of making recordings of the counselling process, so if it is good enough for him . . .! Of course you need to be sensitive to the needs of particular clients and I am only suggesting using audio recording with the client's cooperation and informed consent. If this is given, it will enable trainees to be listened to by their supervisors who would be in a position to provide relevant skills-based feedback, a process which can only improve levels of competence.

9 Training counsellors in brief counselling

Most counselling that is done is brief, which can mean anything from one to twenty-five sessions. Yet a lot of counsellor training does not train counsellors to work briefly. I have been criticized in the counselling journals in that by advocating brief counselling I am seeking to deprive clients of what they really need, i.e. long-term counselling. Of course this is not my intention, nor is it the likely effect of my position. A minority of clients do require long-term counselling, and I believe they should be offered it. But most people, I believe, need a brief intervention. Incidentally, Budman and Gurman (1988) note that clients who receive brief time-limited counselling sometimes receive more sessions than those who receive counselling without time limits. So, we need to train counsellors to work briefly *by design*, if counselling is not going to be even more brief *by default*.

10 Bringing a client-centred focus to personal therapy

To what extent should personal therapy be mandatory for counselling trainees? Obviously trainees are (or should be!) interested in personal development otherwise they will not last long in the profession. So while I am in favour of personal development being an essential part of counselling training, I am against the idea that you *have to* be in personal therapy as part of your training. The available research does not indicate that it makes you a more effective practitioner. I think that one of the reasons for this is that generally personal therapy is not linked to client work. I have invented a term – client-centred personal therapy – which refers to the process where you go into personal therapy and talk about your feelings that are very much related to your work with clients. There is an approach in marital therapy, called 'Unilateral Marital Therapy', where one partner comes for counselling and the counsellor uses an empty chair to represent their partner who is absent. The therapeutic work is done with this absent individual in mind. If we had client-centred personal therapy, would this make personal therapy more effective? I believe it is worth a try and merits investigation.

11 Increasing emphasis on eclecticism and integration

Eclecticism and integration are the new buzz-words for counselling in the nineties. There will soon come a time when if you are not eclectic or integrative, other counsellors will think you terribly old-fashioned. However, eclecticism and integration are best developed from a base of sound training and much clinical experience and it is difficult to become eclectic or integrative if you have not been thoroughly trained in at least two approaches. Otherwise you will be putting things together in an uninformed way.

In addition, someone who wishes to be truly integrative or eclectic has got to read the counselling research literature to discover the treatments of choice for various problems. It is no good offering person-centred counselling, for example, to somebody with encrusted obsessive–compulsive problems, since this approach has insufficient potency with such problems. Such a person needs flooding and response prevention which needs to be carried out in an in-patient setting if the problems are very severe. I often refer to the 'bespoke counsellor', a term derived from the bespoke tailor. When you went to a bespoke tailor he would measure you and make a suit tailored just for you. Now we get suits off the peg and that's okay, but they are not especially tailored with you in mind. To become a bespoke counsellor and provide personalized counselling requires years of practice and you won't become one by attending a short course no matter how integrative or eclectic it is.

I use another term which is relevant to this discussion: shadchonim. Now a shadchen was a matchmaker. In order to survive, shadchonim had to have a very good knowledge of the young ladies and young men in a locality in order to make a suitable match. I would like to see therapeutic shadchonim. At present, if you want to see a counsellor, what do you do? You may ask a friend and he or she may say 'Oh yes, this counsellor was great for me, try her.' Just because the counsellor was helpful to your friend does not mean she will be helpful to you. If you consult a therapeutic shadchen he or she will have detailed knowledge of the counselling resources in your area. He or she will find out what your problem is, what kind of counselling you require, and match you with a counsellor who would be more or less right for you. This is, of course, a pipe-dream but I would like to see such people working in the counselling field.

12 Increasing emphasis on psycho-education

There is a real danger that counselling is losing touch with its roots. Increasingly, counsellors are working with people who are severely disturbed. Counselling was not developed for such work. It was originally developed for people who had vocational or educational problems, those with life crises and those who wished to explore and develop themselves further. Counsellors, at least in North America, then applied their skills to the area of deliberate psycho-education where they helped people prophylactically.

I believe that counsellors have much to contribute to the field of psycho-education. Here the emphasis is on helping clients to acquire skills for effective living rather than on overcoming severe disturbance. Richard Nelson-Jones' approach is an excellent example of such work. He has developed a model called 'Lifeskills Helping' where he helps people learn a variety of skills for effective living. This is done in small-group experiential settings with an increasing focus on generalizing such skills to everyday life (Nelson-Jones, 1991 and see Chapter 6).

13 Promoting the counsellor as consultant

Another way counsellors could be useful is as consultants to people who are involved in self-help. Counsellors could be quite useful to self-help groups by teaching them to use counselling skills and by being available to them as consultants, not in an elitist way but in an egalitarian manner when asked.

As is well known, counsellors have also got a lot to offer organizations and institutions as consultants, if only they will listen! Some of the ways in which people are treated in organizations and institutions and how they come to treat themselves are beyond belief. Let's take teaching. So many teachers don't take proper lunch hours. What kind of a job is it that deprives people of a lunch hour? You need a lunch hour to sit down, eat, digest and recover. If counsellors can encourage organizations to safeguard the mental health of their employees then this would be a real contribution. Some organizations may claim to practise 'Total Quality Management' and say they look after the well-being of their staff, but I am sceptical. I know someone who works in a TQM establishment; however, she has no lunch hour and shares a room with twelve to fourteen other people, where there is a broken window which lets in the cold. This is supposed to be a Total Quality Management environment!! Counsellors could make a very real difference to such organizations by emphasizing the word human in the phrase 'human resource management'.

14 Dryden to keep writing and editing

To end this look into the future, my final prediction is that I will keep writing and editing books on counselling, much to the consternation of some no doubt. However, I promise to stop when I reach 100 . . . books that is, not years!!

References

Budman, S.H. and Gurman, A.S. (1988) *Theory and Practice of Brief Therapy*. New York: Guilford.
Nelson-Jones, R. (1991) *Lifeskills: a Handbook*. London: Cassell.
Nelson-Jones, R. and Coxhead, P. (1978) 'Whither BAC: a survey of members' views on policy and priorities', *Counselling News*, no. 21, 2–5.
Thorne, B. and Dryden, W. (eds) (1993) *Counselling: Interdisciplinary Perspectives*. Buckingham: Open University Press.

Discussion issues

1 In what ways can counsellors demonstrate an increased interest in evaluation and audit of the effectiveness of their work?
2 What in your experience are the potential client groups that are difficult to reach and what might be the most effective ways of contacting them?
3 There is little research to demonstrate that personal therapy increases counsellor effectiveness. Comment on this using your own experience.
4 What are the advantages and disadvantages of using audio tapes of counselling sessions for the purposes of supervision?

77

New Directions in Counselling: a Roundtable

Edited by Ian Horton, Rowan Bayne and Jenny Bimrose

Contributors: Fiona Palmer Barnes, Judith Baron, Michael Jacobs, David A. Lane, Brian Thorne, Diana Whitmore and Ray Woolfe

We asked seven leading figures in British counselling, representing a variety of theoretical orientations and organizational allegiances, two questions:

1 What do you think is the most significant trend or issue in counselling today?
2 What trends would you like there to be?

Overall, their answers seem to us to give a predominantly positive and optimistic sense of counselling's present direction, but there is more than a hint of apprehension and despair too. Two broad trends seem to emerge from the contributors responses to the first question. One, referred to by three contributors, albeit from different perspectives, concerns the social and economic context of counselling. The other trend is about the expansion of counselling as a 'boom industry' and the related issues and implications for professionalism, complaints against counsellors' 'money-making' and the public image of counselling.

As expected, the second question produced more diverse and sometimes conflicting responses, including the need for a more preventive approach, re-evaluation of the whole purpose and efficacy of counselling, increased political and spiritual missionary zeal, greater understanding and more rigorous application of ethical and professional boundaries, expansion of free or low-cost counselling, stemming the flow of professional self-interest and raising the standards of training.

1 What do you think is the most significant trend or issue in counselling today?

Ray Woolfe

I don't think it makes much sense to talk about trends in counselling without acknowledging that the theory and practice of counselling is a part of the wider

This chapter was first published in *Counselling, Journal of the British Association for Counselling*, vol. 6, no. 1, pp. 34–40 (1995).

world of ideas and is influenced by and reflects these ideas. The concept which frames a great deal of contemporary academic discussion is that of 'post-modernism'. It is claimed by some that this is characterized by a move away from grand theories and a belief in overarching solutions towards a more pragmatic flexibility which allows for a variety of perspectives. It can be found across the whole field of human endeavour; in art, architecture, medicine, science, technology and politics. Kuhn (1970) coined the term 'paradigmatic shift' to describe major periods of upheaval in the world of ideas and this seems to describe appropriately the move from modernity to post-modernity.

Modernity emphasizes scientific objectivity and political-economic rationality. Counselling developed out of the modernist recognition that human behaviour is neither biologically programmed nor god-given and is, therefore, amenable to intervention and change. The major theories of counselling that we now work with derived from and in turn fuelled this development. It is hardly surprising, therefore, that the widespread breakdown in the modernist belief in a world of reason has been paralleled by widespread questioning within counselling of the relevance of many of the taken-for-granted boundaries between different approaches. In this process, Britain is following a trend already well-established and documented in the USA. The overall outcome appears to be a gradual move towards greater eclecticism.

This move has been motivated by a growing awareness that a key factor, namely the therapeutic alliance, is common to all approaches. In addition, there appears to be little evidence to suggest that one approach is inherently superior to another. Moreover, what evidence there is seems to support what to many counsellors is the uncomfortable finding that cognitive-behavioural methods appear to be widely effective across a range of conditions relating to the treatment of depression and anxiety.

The interest in eclecticism is often located within a debate about the respective merits of eclecticism versus integration. However, I would suggest that the significance of these concepts lies not so much in their difference as in the challenge they pose together to the old purist paradigms. Norcross and Grencavage (1989) suggest, along Kuhnian lines, that this can be envisaged as a process of transition which is characterized by three stages, beginning with the breakdown of old theories and the flowering of a multitude of new ones. They describe this as 'segregation'. This is followed by 'desegregation' in which all these ideas and methods mingle. The final step is 'integration' where the best bits of different systems are assimilated and accommodated into new principles and practices.

In my view this is the most significant trend in counselling today and it is reflected particularly in the development of a variety of brief-therapies, e.g. cognitive-analytic, solution-focused, etc. These are highly relevant in those key areas in which the development of counselling as a widely available resource is likely to take place, namely the workplace and primary health-care. The imperative in both of these settings is for counsellors to work pragmatically with clients on a time-limited basis against a continuous context of cost–benefit analysis. Moreover, there is likely (even after the demise of the present Conservative government) to be a continuing emphasis on auditing and evaluation of counselling services.

References

Kuhn, T. (1970) *The Structure of Scientific Revolutions*. Chicago: University of Chicago Press.

Norcross, J.C. and Grencavage, L.M. (1989) 'Eclecticism and integration in counselling and psychotherapy: major themes and obstacles', *British Journal of Guidance and Counselling* 17(3): 227–47.

David A. Lane

The basic assumptions and values of social policy throughout Europe are being re-evaluated in the light of economic decline. Counsellors are beginning to enter the debate on directions in social policy. Our contribution to that debate is the most significant trend today.

A revolution is happening in the provision of health, education and care in many countries, whatever their political persuasion. In the USA and Europe, for example, funding for health facilities has increasingly come under careful scrutiny. It is recognized that social progress is not possible without wealth creation and the competitiveness of those European economies which had traditionally spent highly on social policies has been overshadowed by the growth rate of Pacific Rim countries.

The importance of a socially responsible dimension to the provision of services, a matter of national pride in most European countries, is now being questioned. A series of reports from European governments and the European Union have forced member states to take a fresh look at the link between economic and social policies at national and European level. They question our ability to achieve sustainable social and economic progress. Fundamental questions are being asked. A European Social Policy Options paper (1993) questioned the type of society that Europeans wanted. Changing demographic patterns mean that a small labour force will have to support a growing number of inactive people, giving rise to possibly dangerous tensions. The existence and role of the welfare state is under review as a result of the growing number of people relegated to the fringes of society – the elderly, unemployed, refugees, minority groups.

In such periods of change it is common for marginalized populations to be under threat. Issues of social justice and equality of opportunities become paramount but may be neglected in the search for economic growth. It is recognized that for social integration to continue, the stereotyping of education, women, older people, ethnic groups, disabled people and children must be challenged. Counsellors are actively working at all levels of society and need to use that experience to influence the debate.

Calls for more funds to fight poverty and exclusion and to develop a preventive as well as a rehabilitative approach to well-being will not receive much sympathy. Funding will not be available. A new approach, indeed a revolution in practice, is needed to ensure effective options are developed. Projects will need to demonstrate that counselling makes an effective contribution.

The pressures faced by European governments are paralleled in the USA, and recent changes in priority through the review of social welfare by the Clinton administration point to possible responses. A move towards sustainable models for health and well-being extend beyond the rich nations to development projects in the rest of the world. Questions about the sustainability of the environment (Lane and Malkin, 1994) are now paralleled by the search for a sustainable social policy (European Union, 1993; European Association for Counselling, 1994).

The question arises as to whether counselling has anything to contribute to this debate. I believe we do offer a unique perspective drawn from our experiences of counselling with individuals, groups and organizations at all levels of society from the boardroom to the streets. That perspective enables counsellors to offer:

(a) clarification of the issues
(b) evidence to support debate
(c) practical strategies
(d) implemented projects of demonstrated value
(e) an increasing commitment to evaluation of service provision.

The willingness of many counsellors to enter this debate and offer counselling as something of value in the broader social context is the most significant trend in counselling today.

References

European Association for Counselling (1994) *An Invitation to Membership*. Rugby: EAC.
European Union (1993) 'European Social Policy: Green Paper'. Brussels: Commission of the European Communities.
Lane, D.A. and Malkin, J. (1994) 'The Challenge', in R. Samuels and D. Prasad (eds), *Global Warming and the Built Environment*. London: Chapman & Hall.

Brian Thorne

I am aware of a profound and exhilarating paradox in our society at the present time: barbarism and tenderness are both on the increase. The creeping contamination of almost all areas of our corporate life by the forces of the market place means that more and more people experience themselves not as persons but as consumers or providers and as potential victims on the altars of cost-effectiveness and efficiency. But the human spirit cannot bear it: people denied their personhood are breaking down under the strain; stress, anxiety and depression permeate our national life. And so it is, as I see it, that the age of the counsellors has ironically arrived. For me the most significant trend in the counselling world today is the astonishing and rapid increase of the activity itself. Training courses proliferate, practitioners multiply and the clients jostle each other on lengthening waiting lists. Most significantly, perhaps, the world of commerce and industry is taking counselling to its heart and the counsellor in the work place is an increasingly common figure. Institutionalized tenderness, it seems, responds to the ravages wrought by the barbarians, who sometimes inhabit the same institutions.

With this trend, where counselling is seemingly a 'boom industry', there comes a major issue. To what end is the counsellor's tenderness directed? Does the counselling process aim to restore sufficient worth to a battered identity so that the wounded client can once more return to the trenches of competitive materialism – or is something more profound at stake? At the moment I glimpse the signs of corruption in the ranks of the counsellors themselves and there are times when I know I am on the slippery slope myself. It is so easy to become a sleek counsellor at the court of the barbarians, where persons are employees, managers, expendable parts of the profit machine. Not to become so is to risk exposure as a subversive or even seditious agent serving a different authority and a different value system. I may seek comfort and reassurance in the concept of the counsellor as a change agent but right now the comfort is short-lived. I have an escalating fear that the change which is required is beyond the reformer or the revisionist. And I have never had the stomach for revolution nor the yearning for martyrdom. It would take a brave counsellor indeed to suggest, for example, that the worship of efficiency is a particularly perverse form of idolatry or that the 'professionaliza-tion' of counselling might be more the obsession of terrified materialists than the concern of compassionate carers.

Fiona Palmer Barnes

The most significant trend in counselling today is increasing professionalization. This can be seen in so many ways; from articles in the counselling press, to the setting of standards in training and supervision, to the refinement of Codes of Ethics and Practice. Codes have now been written for those who use counselling skills and these have been separated from codes for counsellors; we also have codes for trainers and supervisors. These are the benchmarks of standards and allow us to hear complaints in relation to them.

One of the trends of the past five years has been the increased number of complaints that have been brought to the British Association for Counselling's notice. This is in line with national trends of increased complaints linked with such developments as citizens' charters and an increased general encouragement for people to express grievance. I welcome this in that it exposes poor practice and will eventually encourage far higher standards; however, it causes far more work for the secretariat. Most grievances are resolved at an informal stage and only very few reach anything like a formal process.

Complaints can arise where there is a poor understanding between client and counsellor about the nature of contract and what each 'feels' has been agreed. I believe that this is an area in which many of our members are poorly informed and a clearer sense of what the law of contract involves is needed. Other common causes of difficulty are found in training courses where it is believed by the complainant that the goal posts have been moved during training. Again it is important that training providers are quite clear with course members about the extent of their commitment in terms of time and money before they start and are clear about what might hold up the qualifying process or stop it altogether for the candidate. Again, counselling services need to be clear about what they can offer, what the waiting period is for the initial session and what the probable waiting time is before being allocated for counselling. It is necessary for us always to hold in mind what a difficult task it often is for the client to pick up the phone and ring. Some services have very limited resources and need to be clear about this and not leave potential clients in limbo for a period of months without contact, since this can cause enormous distress to clients.

As the public demands a greater professionalization of counsellors, so counsellors, in their turn, are going to need to respond to the challenge and consider their practice in an increasingly professional way.

Michael Jacobs

An opposite number in New Zealand introduced me to the phrase 'claim-making'. There is apparently state money in that country for the counselling of sexually abused people. Some counsellors claim they are specialists in sexual abuse (and some are) so that they can get clients whose fees will be paid for them; and some clients claim to have been sexually abused (and some have been) in order to get free counselling. This is over-simplified, but the message is clear. Where there are rich pickings to be had, there will be many bids for it. Some claims are genuine; but some, my opposite number said, are dubious.

I am glad when I compare the claims for counselling and counsellors now with the defensive stance we had to take in the early 1970s, when the value of counselling in higher education was only seen by a few, and was derided and questioned by many. The early counsellors had to earn recognition. What was once the free domain of the few (students, or those who sought marriage counselling) has now spread into nearly every major sector of life, although sadly it is less and less a free service. With greater exposure, inevitably there has also come the need for counselling to be regulated, organized, evaluated and monitored. Counselling has grown up into the real world, where it must prove its claims and protect itself against false claims.

But exposure to the real world also means exposure to much else. There is money to be made. Newspaper advertisements, for example, in some cases include references to fulfilling requirements for NVQs, at a time when the NVQs for counselling have not even been agreed. Another organization in a full-page journal advertisement gives the impression that it is a major recognized accrediting body, when it is in fact a private company. Claim-making is rife. Where there is the potential for financial gain, counselling too can become prey to the entrepreneur. Thatcher's children have set up camp in this counselling field too, where the doctrine of the autonomy of the individual combined with the enterprise culture make it fertile ground.

The most significant trend in counselling must be its continuing expansion. While this is partly because it has earned a reputation, it is also because it is seen as a means of making money. It is difficult to know which comes first – is it the demand for counselling that gives rise to the demand for training, that gives rise to support for the expansion of courses in the private sector and in the new entrepreneurial world of higher and further education? Has there been a change of heart on the part of those who some years ago looked down on counselling as an unverifiable and woolly practice? Or are those same people (university administrators and, to be honest, some academic psychologists as well) now looking for new ways to make money by encouraging courses to recruit students who in turn expect their qualifications to bring them a stream of clients? Another feature of this expansion has been the flood of books on counselling on to the market, when before the 1990s only the occasional volume would have crept into the publishers' list (and very few publishers' lists at that) under the headings of psychology, education, sociology or women's studies. Now everyone is in on the act. This is neither a criticism nor a lament, but a statement that carries with it a certain degree of cynicism.

There is, of course, nothing wrong either with organizations or individuals finding new ways of supporting themselves financially, as long as clients (the objective of all this activity) are well served. It is difficult to believe that this greatly enlarged interest is not also self-interest, and that it must therefore affect the delivery of counselling – the way it is taught, sold and practised.

Judith Baron

As General Manager of the British Association for Counselling, I manage the Association's services pertaining to the promotion of counselling, answering queries about the nature of counselling and dealing with complaints about practice. All this has highlighted for me the need for an appropriate, adequate and coherent presentation to the public of the nature of counselling and the work of counsellors, in their wide variety of settings. On such a coherent picture hangs the public credibility of counselling and the future of the profession.

The eighteen years of BAC's life so far have been spent quietly and efficiently putting the parameters of counselling in place. Its success and the sense of identity thus created has brought about heightened visibility for the profession and a demand for its recognition from its members. Counsellors now want the public and institutions to see their service as an efficient viable tool amongst the range of interventions available in times of need. Users of services, in return, want information on standards, lines of accountability and descriptions of the service on offer. Any previous lack of a coherent public presentation has recently been seized upon by a media eager for stories of injustice and abuse at a moment in history when citizens' charters and litigations are popular. The onslaught of hostile media must be managed without resort to 'knee-jerk' solutions to publicity-driven criticisms. Counsellors need to show that abuse will not be tolerated and that the existence of a complaints process such as BAC's, which takes breaches of codes very seriously, is fundamental to the survival of the profession and does work fairly for all parties involved in the process.

The result of a coherent public picture and image should be a secure profession where individuals are able to place themselves within a career structure and/or amongst a range of services on offer. This, in turn, should give them confidence when dealing with the media and the public who approach them. The public will know whom to approach, when and how.

Amongst the items I list as providing the elements of the coherent picture are:

- A clear description of when one is acting as a counsellor, as opposed to another professional role using counselling skills, and the boundaries of that counselling contract.
- A clear description of the sufficient training/competence/experience required to work with the subject matter brought to the counsellor.
- A clear description of avenues to appropriate counselling help or services.
- A clear description of theoretical approaches and what can be expected to happen during a counselling session.
- A clear description of how a user can resolve differences with a counsellor or counselling service.
- A clear description of lines of accountability for the counsellor or counselling service.

Diana Whitmore

A person does not exist in isolation but in the context of the larger whole of society and in an intricate network of relationships. Great Britain is increasingly becoming a multi-cultural society but many counsellors today are not well equipped to be appropriately sensitive to, or skilful at addressing, this issue. Fortunately we are conscious of the important need to develop the awareness and skills necessary and the intention seems high, in the profession, to embrace this challenge. Many Counsellor Diploma courses are increasing their training elements in the areas of: multi-culture, gender, class, race and social issues. It is totally appropriate that this realm has become a conscious and international trend.

Moreover, after a significant period of work on self, many counsellors and clients alike are reaching for values that transcend egocentric concerns and affirm participation in the larger whole. Despite reaching authenticity and freedom, individual identity is not the end result but leads to a recognition of inter-dependence and a more creative response to life. We 'dis-identify' from ourselves as a separate unit, expand our identity to include the world around us and are motivated to make life choices that are consistent with this larger identity.

Consequently, feelings of responsibility for the state of society, for social issues, for global concerns, are not seen to be projections of self-interest but valued as authentic responses. An individual's deep inner response to social and global conditions will greatly affect his or her sense of well-being. There may be pain for the whole – for humanity – which is not a neurotic pain, but a genuine concern and a true desire for a life which both respects and is confluent with a greater good. For example, common feelings that may arise are despair and a sense of meaninglessness, fear of a lack of collective well-being, anger at the inequalities of society, guilt about one's own comfortable existence, frustration at a seeming inability to make a difference, and sorrow for others.

I believe that the above concerns represent a developmental step for the counselling profession and that we are being called upon to validate, include and embrace them. If we are to stay abreast of our rapidly changing world today, the profession needs to widen its vision, to recognize the issues and concerns of the day and work with them directly. Often these issues include but also go beyond childhood history and conditioning.

2 What trends would you like there to be?

Ray Woolfe

I seem to remember that once upon a time there used to be a lot of talk about the development as opposed to the remedial function of counselling. Perhaps this was related to what seemed in the 1970s and early 1980s to be a likely growth area: counselling in schools. However, this initiative, for all sorts of reasons, proved to be still-born.

Nevertheless, I think that the idea of counselling as having a developmental function remains of importance and should not be lost. So much of the work of counsellors today seems, of necessity, to be crisis-orientated and task-focused. While I would not wish to diminish the value of this work nor the resources devoted to it, I would also like to see counselling become more widely available within easily accessible community settings in which the developmental function is acknowledged.

In such settings, there would be some shift of focus away from responding to serious emotional or behavioural problems towards dealing with normal life-course issues such as becoming adolescent, starting work, living together, gender roles, becoming middle-aged, dealing with retirement. Alongside this would go a change of emphasis away from counselling the individual towards the family unit as the focus for the work.

To emphasize the developmental function of counselling within the family seems to me, if only in a small way, to counter the danger of its becoming part of a process whereby social problems and issues become reframed as personal, emotional problems. So much of what we call depression or other forms of emotional ill-health is a result of oppression of women by men, and children by adults. It would be nice if counsellors were able to work in such a way that they were able to contribute towards resisting the growth of oppressive forces rather than just dealing with their consequences.

Ray Woolfe, a Senior Lecturer in the Department of Applied Social Studies and Social Work, Keele University, is the author and editor of a number of books on counselling and related areas and has worked on key committees for both the British Psychological Society and BAC.

David A. Lane

Expectations of the type of services needed and offered by agencies have changed within society. The public, our clients, now demand a greater say in the setting of the priorities. Professionals no longer maintain a firm grip on the services provided and the process by which individuals seek and are offered support.

The changing climate is also reflected in the greater prominence given to the importance of rigorous evaluation of effectiveness and to ethical, gender, class, race and disability issues. Therapeutic services and the theoretical models which support them have been slow to deal with the criticism of their practice in relation to minority groups and the disempowered. Yet it is recognized that many transformations are taking place in society, the impact of which leads to a need for counselling for individuals, organizations and other groupings. Within Europe there are increasing examples of those transformations in the areas of the structure of employment, unemployment and the socially excluded, migration and refugees, the roles of men and women, regional and national identity and ethnicity. These transformations affect all societies and have involved a reduction in the function of social systems which have previously acted as defences against anxiety such as the family, school, places of work, religion, science and the military. It is now recognized that an interactive view of counselling is needed which approaches in a holistic way the social, cultural, economic and emotional issues facing us.

The revolution in service provision and need which is all around us has created challenges for the theoretical models which have traditionally supported counselling and therapeutic provision; for the contexts in which we seek to work and offer a service and to us as individual providers. The challenge is to ensure that we are part of a service leading to effective outcomes for our clients rather than simply a service which meets our own needs at the expense of our clients.

In order to meet the challenges we need to be clearer than we have been prepared to be in the past about our function. What does counselling set out to achieve? What is our purpose? Would it matter if we did not exist at all? What is counselling? What objectives can we legitimately meet? Are there criteria which enable us to assess the quality of the service provided? Questions of these types are increasingly being asked.

The changing agenda in counselling has generated a wider consideration of the purpose of counselling. In the past this question was largely addressed from the point of view of the practitioner or dictated by a theoretical model. It is now clear that the purpose must be defined by clients as well as practitioners and in terms of its function in society and not just the way it functions within a theoretical framework. A framework for classifying the counselling process and its relationship to other fields of activity, such as education and psychotherapy, is needed.

It is a trend towards evaluation in terms of the 'service-led' agenda that I would most like to see.

Professor David Lane, Director of the Professional Development Foundation, London, has written widely on counselling for children and adolescents.

Brian Thorne

I would like to see a trend towards the creation of a community of counsellors who are purposefully and overtly prophetic, political and spiritual. Those of us who are privileged day by day to accompany clients who often endure intolerable psychic pain are in possession of knowledge which could yet save the world. We know more than a little, for example, about birth and pre-birth and about the needs of the human infant. We are acutely aware of what destroys the human spirit and what heals and nourishes it. We daily practise empathy and are appalled at its rarity in our culture. The costly knowledge which we possess is often the outcome of relationships which have challenged us to extend ourselves to the limits of our own humanity. Such knowledge brings with it an increasing responsibility not unlike that borne in the past by prophets and seers. For an individual such a responsibility is well-nigh impossible to shoulder and that is why a corporate voice is required. I want to see a counselling community which is prepared to shout what it knows from the rooftops, to risk itself in the increasingly contemptible world of political discourse and to proclaim that persons are persons are persons – which means that we have bodies, minds and spirits.

Brian Thorne, Director of Student Counselling, University of East Anglia, has written and co-written extensively on person-centred counselling and has a long association with BAC.

Fiona Palmer Barnes

I would like to see counsellors working within far clearer boundaries, not only for themselves but also for their clients so that they may be better informed. I would look towards:

1 Counsellors all having a clear understanding of the various Codes of Ethics and Practice that apply to their work and an understanding of the arguments that led to the particular Code being written in the form it is. It would be helpful if changes became a matter of debate at Annual General Meetings as well as in the counselling press so that these arguments were well understood and rehearsed.

2 Counsellors understanding the nature of the contract they are making with the client and, whenever it is felt possible, working with a written contract. As it states in the Codes, the client needs to know the boundaries and limitations of the contract in terms of confidentiality, the practicalities of sessions and fees, and the support network of the counsellor in terms of training, supervision/ consultation and therapy. This would clarify many issues and I am sure reduce grievances expressed to the Clerk of the Complaints Sub-Committee and therefore eventual complaints.

3 Trainers and supervisors being able to encourage far higher standards by modelling good practice in their work and by challenging poor practice actively. As more trainers and supervisors become accredited this in itself should help raise standards and promote the principles behind the Codes of Ethics and Practice.

My hope is that there will be fewer complaints but I really wonder if this will be so. However, we will, hopefully, have a group of investigators who will have trained to carry out this task in a most professional and economical fashion. We already have considerable experience of adjudication and appeals and our experience will increase in this area also.

Most of all, I would hope that there was a growing confidence in the process of our management of complaints within the counselling world, so that it may be seen that BAC is synonymous with high standards and excellence. It is important in that process that the work of the Complaints Sub-Committee is seen as competent and fair and becomes the benchmark in the world of counselling and psychotherapy.

Fiona Palmer Barnes, Chair of the BAC Complaints Sub-Committee, trained through Jungian analysis and currently practises as a counsellor and therapist.

Michael Jacobs

A.J.P. Taylor said of the large amount of evidence available to the modern historian that there is 'often, one is tempted to say, too much'. Can there be too much counselling, too many courses, too many publications? I have myself benefited greatly from the expansion of this field, responding sufficiently to the demand to see my own career flourish. But I also know the temptation to take short cuts: to lower the demands on students, to recruit more of them and match the seemingly lesser requirements of rival training courses; to succumb to the pressure for brief work with clients, just because that is the way to make a living with employee counselling programmes; to write more to keep the publishers happy and the original books selling; to risk the quality of my preparation and thoughtfulness, because of the opportunities that need to be taken if I am to keep myself, my courses or any of my other counselling interests going. I sometimes find myself caught up in what seems like a tidal wave. Now, like the Sorcerer's Apprentice, I find myself wanting to hold it back, not just for my own integrity, but for that of counselling as well.

There are signs that the bubble may burst. Journalistic criticisms of counselling have joined those we smugly thought would only be directed at traditional psychotherapy. More serious criticisms must follow. Market forces will hopefully shake down the vast number of counsellors, as the thousands of hopefuls find less work than they imagined; publishers may become more discriminating when booksellers' shelves are overloaded with unmoved stock. Those of us with longer memories have seen it before, in the late 1970s, when career opportunities for counsellors in education waned. Some full-time postgraduate counselling courses went under, and others struggled to survive. Trained counsellors could not find jobs. It will not be long, I hope, before similar forces begin to regulate just how many can make a living from counselling, particularly in the private sector, amongst those who set up shop often without sufficient experience, supervision and training.

I suspect market forces will not help the trend I would most dearly like to see: the expansion of free and low-cost services. To achieve such an expansion requires the development of the voluntary sector, and the growth of salaried counsellor posts with no strings attached other than effective (not cost-effective) practice. My realism recognizes that while contraction of enthusiasm for counselling must come, it will not necessarily lead to the opportunities for extending help to the thousands who are still marginalized from access to it. My only hope in this harsh economic climate is that other voluntary groups and charities have similarly had to modernize and commercialize, without I guess too much loss to those they were originally set up to help. They have created jobs as well as encouraged voluntary activity. Let us make money to make counselling available; not make counselling available to make money.

Michael Jacobs, Director of Counselling and Psychotherapy in the Adult Education Department, University of Leicester, is the author and editor of several books on psychodynamic counselling.

Judith Baron

On first reading this question I read 'trends' in the singular and found it very difficult to pick out one. Having made a short list I decided that the items listed are some of the roots of professional activity. I was then relieved to see I can work in the plural and so can list them all. At this point I would like to say that a trend I do not wish to see is a move towards a profession that does not allow access to minority groups, which becomes rigid, self-perpetuating and applies unnecessary restrictive practices. This is a unique moment in time for counselling to model the values it promotes, such as autonomy, responsibility and equality.

Firstly, I would like to see funding for training of counsellors at the point of entry to their chosen career. This would help equal opportunities, enable training before practice, raise standards of practice and show government commitment to an activity that it is quick to call upon in times of crisis and emergency.

Secondly, there should be more research into the effectiveness of methods of counselling. In turn, this will improve practice and further the knowledge base and presentation of this emergent profession.

Thirdly, there should be more training for supervisors to improve the quality of supervision. This should be reflected in the number of BAC Recognized Supervisors. Supervisors have a unique role in maintaining these standards of counselling, protecting the client and ensuring part of the self-development of counsellors. They may have a considerable part to play in assessing for National Vocational Qualifications in counselling. I can remember the impetus in the late 1980s to ensure counsellors realized their obligation to be in supervision as a condition of being in membership of BAC and complying with the Codes of Ethics and Practice. Elisabeth Davies, my predecessor, helped many members find supervisors and dealt with indignant telephone calls when undertakings could not be made. Now the advantage of supervision is never questioned and there have been letters to BAC headquarters commenting on its beneficial effects.

Fourthly, I believe counsellors need to take more responsibility for the management of themselves and their practice. Many do so. However, at a time when contracting for services is common, counsellors need to manage proper record keeping, contracts of employment and accounting systems.

Lastly, I would like to see the acceptance of the proposed Register of Counsellors [BAC has been asked to facilitate the development of a UK Register of Counsellors – Ed.] by the wide field of those involved in counselling activity.

Unless this happens in an atmosphere of mutual understanding of the diversity of the field, that diversity will increase and this will not be to counsellors' benefit.

Judith Baron, General Manager of BAC, has been connected with the Association for many years.

Diana Whitmore

After twenty-five years in the counselling and therapy world, first as a client, then as a therapist and finally as a trainer of counsellors and psychotherapists, I find myself reflecting on 'counselling as a social issue'. I sometimes wonder about the efficiency of counselling, how long the process needs to be and how much of it is determined by the counselling culture itself. After all, 'we've had a hundred years of psychotherapy and the world's getting worse'.

My reflections were triggered several years ago when our trainees began practice counselling in placements with GP practices. Counselling in general practice must, by necessity, be short term, usually no more than six to eight sessions. While supervising these students, I was astonished by the positive results achieved, the amount of work done and the depths reached in such a short time. More research needs to be done to verify this, but I suspect it might shake the very foundations of many depth therapies, including my own. I would sincerely like to see the whole area of brief counselling and short-term therapy brought into the foreground in the development of our art.

Of course, the main concern regarding short-term counselling is for the retention of long-term benefits. In the long term, it is not valuable simply to *patch people up for the moment*. Perhaps the work of counselling needs also to become more educative. For many people, the most growthful times in their lives are moments of pain and crisis. It is on these occasions that we are potentially most open to learn and it is on these occasions that we tend to seek counselling. In times of crisis our personality is less firmly organized because old structures are collapsing.

Personal trauma can deeply damage a person and lead to states of psychological rigidity and depression, but it can also lead to insight and regeneration. Which of these alternatives occurs depends not on outer circumstances but on the inner responses of the individual. This attitude is not to negate the value and importance of outer change, but rather to foster the psychological freedom to address change transformatively.

Though seeming, to some extent, to be in conflict with the notion of short-term counselling, the counsellor can be less concerned with problem-solving than with fostering the conditions in which the problems can be addressed creatively. Rather than resolve a particular situation in the client's life, the counsellor can support the client while he or she learns *how* to deal effectively with problems as they arise. In this sense, the counsellor is helping the client develop the tools and inner resources necessary for growth rather than merely alleviating symptoms.

The key is how to practise short-term counselling in a way that transcends problem-solving and symptom alleviation. I would propose that the potential for doing this lies in our current practice. We are not as far from this possibility as we might imagine. What is required is to adapt creatively and adjust the methods, principles and techniques that we are presently skilful at using. Our aim should be for the client to develop the capacity to find his or her own answers, to be self-sufficient and to trust his or her emerging inner wisdom.

Lady Diana Whitmore, Founder and Director of the Psychosynthesis and Education Trust, London, is the author of *Psychosynthesis Counselling in Action*.

Discussion issues

1 What do you think is the most significant trend or issue in counselling today?
2 What trends would you like there to be?
3 What do you see as the main obstacles to those trends, and what are the positive factors encouraging them? Are there any actions (specific of course!) that you'd like to take?
4 How can pressures towards increased professionalization and increased support for clients within systems be reconciled with maintaining counselling as a profitable enterprise during a world recession?

78

The Development of the British Association for Counselling

Judith Baron

The reader of this book may wish to reflect on whether or not there is congruence between the chapters it contains, the development of counselling theory and practice over time, and the development of the British Association for Counselling (BAC), under whose auspices the articles were originally published. No doubt individuals will reach different conclusions. Those representing and working for BAC may ask themselves whether or not BAC has reacted adequately to the fields described in the various contributions or whether its proactive initiatives have been appropriate and understood. Here we address the development of BAC.

BAC – its aims

In 1987 BAC became a company limited by guarantee in addition to being an organization with charitable status. This gave it a recognized legal structure and identity within which to work. The move was seen as a necessary safeguard for members who would otherwise be legally liable for any losses the Association might sustain and made it more attractive to persons who might become its trustees or directors. The original aims, laid out in 1976, were incorporated into the Memorandum.

The Company is established:

i to promote and provide education and training for counsellors working in either professional or voluntary settings, whether full or part time, with a view to raising the standards of counselling for the benefit of the community and in particular for those who are the recipients of counselling; and

ii to advance the education of the public in the part that counselling can play generally and in particular to meet the needs of those members of society where development and participation in society is impaired by mental, physical or social handicap or disability.

BAC – the development of services

From its inception, BAC was concerned with standards of ethics and practice across the field. This was the concern that motivated the formation of the Standing Conference for the Advancement of Counselling which later grew into BAC. In being an organization that is *for* counselling instead of an organization *of* counsellors, BAC has been able to be a commentator on the wider field of provision. It has embraced those who use counselling skills in the course of another vocation or profession. It has embraced trainers, supervisors, counselling organizations and those who employ counsellors. Internecine war between those who use different theoretical models or approaches has been avoided by concentrating on the work settings in our society in which counselling has a part to play, reflected in Divisions, and in the needs of the client rather than in the interests of the counsellor.

BAC's Divisions are:

Association for Pastoral Care and Counselling (APCC)
Association for Counselling at Work (ACW)
Association for Student Counselling (ASC)
Counselling in Education (CIE)
Counselling in Medical Settings (CMS)
Personal, Sexual, Relationship and Family (PSRF)
Race and Cultural Education in Counselling (RACE)

The development of the divisions themselves reflects movement in our society. ACW now embraces an interest in the development of Employee Assistance Programmes. CMS is defining the difference in working arrangements between changing and varied medical settings. PSRF reflected changes in society's social relationship by changing its emphasis away from solely marital to other forms of relationship. RACE has developed from the growing recognition of the need for counselling to work with the cultural diversity inside our society. Its emergence has posed a question for the internal structure of BAC on how best the significant theoretical and social needs and requirements for counselling and counsellors can be interwoven across the length of settings of service delivery. RACE Division is a significant leader in meeting this challenge for BAC and appears to be avoiding the potential of forming an unintegrated group.

RACE Division developed from a Sub-Committee. Sub-Committees are set up to address specific areas of interest and need not be permanent. They advise on policy or undertake a specific piece of work. Two have come and gone. These were Counselling and Peace (1986), which addressed counsellors' needs in the nuclear age and Cold War, and Information Office Sub-Committee (1988), which developed policy on the information resources and directories of BAC. The current Sub-Committees are Accreditation and Recognition (1984), Complaints (1992), Disability Issues (DISC, 1988), European and International Affairs (1995), Professional (1993), Publications (1986), Research (1987), Standards and Ethics (1978), Training (1984), Trauma Care (1994) and the Interim United Kingdom Register Management Group (1994).

The dates of their formation, noted in the brackets, tell an interesting story in themselves. Many started as working parties of the Management Committee and have a slightly longer history. Standards for ethics and practice and managing the power balance between practitioner and client has underpinned the entire development of the Association. Putting those standards into practice through Accreditation and later Accreditation and Recognition services and enforcing them through a complaints procedure had high priority. The need to look at the effectiveness of counselling and the theoretical and research base for practice to underpin responses to a sceptical public gave rise to the emergence of the importance of the Research Sub-Committee and its ultimate inclusion in the Professional Sub-Committee which works across professional committees to address and define the professional voice of counselling. DISC addressed the aims of BAC outlined above. The European and International Affairs Sub-Committee is a response to the European Union and the highly significant part BAC played in establishing the European Association for Counselling (EAC) over a period between 1991 and 1995. Trauma Care Sub-Committee may be a Division in waiting. What it does reflect is how responses to traumas which have hit people in Britain in the past few years have almost catapulted the use of counselling as a tool in recovery into the public eye and enhanced claims that counselling is a profession based on a body of knowledge and bringing results that can be seen as effective in a high percentage of cases. Crisis, trauma and shock publicity is understandable to the public and can be used when describing counselling, the activity.

In developing BAC's services there has been a healthy and interesting interplay between the input of its members (the volunteers), paid staff and structures. Is this reflected in the articles? BAC has relied heavily, and in the early days almost completely, on voluntary input from its members in order to achieve its aims. In the early 1980s, membership was under 2,000 and incentives were given to staff to increase numbers, thereby increasing available funds and expertise to develop and implement policies. The Constitution Group of 1985 to 1987 which was a working party of the then BAC Executive Committee, were made acutely aware of members' wishes to keep policy-making in their hands and to retain their autonomy and control over their activities – a value reflected in BAC's codes of ethics and practice. This has led to headquarters staff acting as enablers and catalysts in the dissemination of information and the formulation of policy and to an organizational structure that can be described as staff supporting an organizational structure of members rather than members supporting the activities of the staff. The huge rise in membership (approximately 12,000 individual and 650 organizations in 1995) along with a rise in BAC's impact on society, has meant increasing strain on those volunteer members who give of their time. This can be in personal as well as financial terms. BAC is now in a much more secure financial position because people are joining with alacrity as they see the benefits of membership and the future might see either some form of recompense for volunteers, more work devolved to staff, or a combination of both.

The changes affecting members and services have in turn affected BAC headquarters. In 1991 there were 12 staff working from six rooms above a butcher's shop in Rugby, all reporting to one General Manager. In 1995 there will be 28 staff in two locations in Rugby linked by telephone and computer, grouped into six service departments. Amongst these staff will be a Registrar, reflecting the establishment of a new United Kingdom Register of Counsellors, and a Promotions and Publicity Officer, reflecting media interest and opportunities. These services will be different from those of the intervening few years where support for the development of a European policy and the development of National Vocational Qualifications (NVQs) was reflected.

BAC and the external world

Events outside BAC have influenced its services, structure and policies and the public perception of counselling. The fact that members work in many settings and thus interact with many other styles of life has enriched and informed its progress. Horizons have never been limited to the consulting room. This has made it easier for BAC to take part in the development of NVQs in Counselling because its members have a wide range of knowledge of work settings to bring to an employer-led process. However, it made it difficult to move swiftly to establish a BAC Register of Counsellors because of the wide range of existing registers amongst its varied memberships and allied professional colleagues.

It could be said that registration was an internally motivated move. However, it was essentially consideration of the effects of European Directives on the mobility of labour and qualifications that started serious consideration of registration. This was then compounded by demands from members, public and employers for guidance and accountability for service.

Europe, registration and NVQs have drawn attention to other things. The possibility of a European Association for Psychotherapy that might rule out lay therapeutic help in some parts of Europe was a threat to UK counsellors and psychotherapists. BAC and the United Kingdom Council for Psychotherapy (UKCP) reacted with different emphasis. Both went searching for colleagues in Europe. Both saw the need for registration and the recognition by the British government in some 'special' way of the expertise of their members. BAC took very active steps to form a European Association for Counselling but has moved more slowly on the path to registration of counsellors. As said before, this was mainly due to the much wider constituency that it serves and consideration of where and for whom a register might be appropriate. What was highlighted was that neither of these organizations serves the needs of all psychotherapists and counsellors and where should the individual best place themselves to describe their mode of working. This in turn has led to a wider debate, carried further in the NVQ forum on the possible differences between counselling and psychotherapy. Meanwhile there emerged chartered counselling psychologists. Where is the differentiating factor here between counselling psychology, and counselling and psychotherapy?

BAC – future developments

Do the articles chosen for publication here reflect the way BAC is currently heading? From the organization's viewpoint and listening to the views of its members, a number of areas in the world of counselling need to be addressed. Counselling skills may have been redefined by the NVQ process as high-level communication skills, and if accepted this change should lead to a new Code of Ethics and Practice for Counselling Skills. The needs of counselling organizations in tackling strict registration criteria are coming to the fore. Counsellors working inside organizations balancing contracts with clients against the contractual nature of their own employment, look for guidance. Employers of counsellors, be they organizations or the individual client, are grappling for an understanding of the wide range of models of counselling and therapy used. BAC may have a role in making them understandable. The need for a research base to underpin counselling and aid in its promotion is becoming clear. Individual Accreditation is becoming widely accepted and sought after. The establishment of the European Union will mean BAC and counsellors need to address a wider diversity of interests, modes of counselling and delivery. BAC will be questioned on whether it can sustain its current undoubted leadership in the field over the past 18 years in Europe. Emerging national associations and bodies might have learnt from Britain's mistakes and from its successes, and move on more quickly than BAC has been able to, to establish a professional framework for counselling. If this is the case, let BAC welcome it with a generosity of spirit whilst still moving forward itself in the light of the source knowledge and learnt wisdom.

Conclusion

BAC has metamorphosed from being an association of loosely federated interests to an organization that is taking the lead in setting the parameters of a professional activity. By a ruling in its favour at a Customs & Excise Tribunal, it has established itself as a Learned Society where members base their work on a body of knowledge and amongst whose members there are practitioners who can be called 'a professional counsellor'. The articles in *Counselling* played a large part in this historic ruling, and I quote:

> Taking into account the evidence we heard on the academic courses on counselling and the level of the articles in the *Journal of the [British] Association for Counselling*, we have no difficulty in concluding that counselling is a branch of knowledge for this purpose

(that is to say, an association, the primary purpose of which is the advancement of a particular branch of knowledge or the fostering of professional expertise, connected with the past or present professions or employment of its members).

Discussion issues

1 Plot the development of the BAC since its inception.
2 'The development of the Divisions themselves reflect movement in our society.' Discuss.
3 What are the advantages and disadvantages of relying on voluntary help by members for an organization such as BAC?
4 Why has BAC become involved in the setting up of a European Association for Counselling?

Notes on the Contributors

Tricia Allison has followed ten years as a professional counsellor with TSB Bank and the Post Office with work as an independent counsellor and an employee counselling consultant. Her counselling work is mainly within primary care.

Judith Baron is the general manager and company secretary of the British Association for Counselling (BAC). She was a director of BAC from 1980 to 1989 and chair of BAC from 1987 to 1989. She is a BAC fellow and has an independent counselling practice.

Rowan Bayne is admissions tutor and co-leader for the postgraduate diploma in counselling at the University of East London. He is the author of *The Myers–Briggs Type Indicator* (Chapman & Hall, 1995), and co-editor of *New Directions in Counselling* (Routledge, 1996).

Linda Beeley is a consultant clinical pharmacologist, a psychotherapist and counsellor in independent practice.

Anne Bentley works full-time as a counsellor with the Metropolitan Police Service. She formerly worked as a social worker with homeless people at St Martin-in-the-Fields Social Care Unit, London and at the St Giles Trust, Camberwell, London, providing resettlement and after-care to mentally vulnerable ex-offenders.

Scott Berry came to HIV work through grief overload in Australia. Originally trained as a group worker, he used theatre performance to raise awareness of HIV. In London Scott trained in one-to-one counselling and has worked in private practice, with groups at Body Positive and the Bereavement and Disability Service.

Jenny Bimrose teaches on the postgraduate diploma in counselling at the University of East London. She is co-editor of *New Directions in Counselling* (Routledge, 1996).

Jed Bland has researched gender identity for nine years, using self-analysis and case study approaches (a precedent set by Freud!) and as a participant observer. He founded the non-profit publishing venture the Derby TV/TS Group and is a trustee of both the Beaumont Trust and the Gender Trust.

Daphne Boddington is tutor on the MSc course in Couple Relationship and Sexual Therapy run by the Institute of Psychiatry at the Maudsley Hospital, London. She runs a private practice for individual, marital and family therapy and works as a counsellor in a GP surgery.

Tim Bond is staff tutor in counselling at the University of Durham and current chairperson of the British Association for Counselling. He has written extensively on professional, legal and ethical issues, including *Standards and Ethics for Counselling in Action* (Sage, 1993).

David Bott is senior lecturer in counselling and therapy at the University of Brighton and rotating course leader of the MA in Counselling Psychology jointly provided by the Universities of Brighton and Sussex. He also practises independently as a BAC accredited counsellor and a UKCP registered family and couple therapist.

Philip Burnard is Reader in Nursing Studies at the University of Wales College of Medicine, Cardiff. He is also a visiting lecturer in Sweden, the Netherlands and the West Indies. He has written a number of books on counselling and interpersonal skills training, including *Counselling Skills for Health Professionals* (Chapman & Hall, 1995).

Fergus Cairns works in private practice, at PACE, the counselling and training organization for lesbians and gay men, and has facilitated support groups for gay men and people affected by HIV for London Lighthouse and several other organizations.

Petrūska Clarkson is a consultant chartered clinical and counselling psychologist, psychotherapist, supervisor and organizational development consultant, who now works under the name of Physis. Past chair of the former BAC Personal, Family and Marital Division, she lectures internationally and has written extensively in these fields.

Sue Coles (formerly **Middlehurst**) now works as a freelance counsellor and trainer for the student counselling service and the continuing education department of Bristol University. She is associated with Advice and Counselling for Alcohol and Drugs, Off the Record and other charitable and statutory organizations.

Michèle Crouan is a trainer and voluntary counsellor with COMPASS, Liverpool, a senior lecturer in the School of Health Care, Liverpool John Moores University and a supervisor in private practice in Manchester.

Sheila Dainow is a counsellor, trainer and therapeutic massage practitioner. She is co-author with Gill Cox of *Making the Most of Yourself* (Sheldon Press, 1985) and *Making the Most of Loving* (Sheldon Press, 1987); co-author with Caroline Bailey of *Developing Skills with People* (Wiley, 1988); and author of *How to Survive your Teenager* (Sheldon Press, 1991) and *The Time of Your Life* (Boxtree Press, 1994).

Peter Dale is a BAC accredited counsellor, and has a private counselling and supervisory practice in Hastings. His PhD was for research exploring perceptions of therapy with adults who were abused as children.

Emmy van Deurzen-Smith is professor and dean of the School of Psychotherapy and Counselling at Regent's College, and she has published and lectured widely on the subject of existential psychotherapy, including her book *Existential Counselling in Practice* (Sage, 1988) and her forthcoming book *Everyday Mysteries* (to be published with Routledge). Emmy is a past chair of the UKCP and she presently serves as external relations officer to the European Association for Psychotherapy.

Merav DeVere is a counsellor, group facilitator and trainer with experience in social and voluntary organizations, currently working as a drugs counsellor for Turning Point. Merav is co-founder of the Photo-Language Workshop (PLW), which promotes and integrates the photo-language technique in existing group-work and counselling settings.

Windy Dryden is professor of counselling in the Psychology Department, Goldsmiths College, University of London. He is author and editor of numerous books on counselling and editor of Sage's *Counselling in Action* series and the *Brief Therapy and Counselling* series published by John Wiley & Sons.

Aisha Dupont-Joshua trained in inter-cultural therapy at London University, together with the Nafsiyat Inter-Cultural Therapy Centre, of which she is now a Professional Associate. She is a psychotherapist (UKCP), writer and trainer, presenting seminars and workshops on racial and cultural awareness within counselling training courses and a visiting lecturer at Southampton University. She is a member of the Executive Committee of the RACE division of the BAC, of whose *Newsletter* she is editor.

Ivan Ellingham is deputy manager of the counsellor education programme at Weald College, Harrow Weald, and lectures in counselling at North Herts College, Stevenage. He works as a counsellor/psychotherapist at St Anne's Opportunity Centre and for Residential Community Care, both in Reading.

Albert Ellis is president of the Institute for Rational Emotive Therapy, New York City. He is the founder of rational emotive behaviour therapy and grandfather of cognitive behaviour therapy. He is the author of over fifty books, including *Reason and Emotion in Psychotherapy* (Carol Publishing, New York, 1994).

Colin Feltham is senior lecturer in counselling at Sheffield Hallam University and a fellow of the British Association for Counselling. He edits two series for Sage Publications – *Professional Skills for Counsellors* and *Perspectives on Psychotherapy*. He is course leader of an MA which includes a module on controversies in and critiques of therapy.

Alan Frankland has been chair of the BAC Individual Accreditation Group since 1993. He is in independent practice as a counsellor/counselling psychologist/psychotherapist and supervisor with APSI (Nottingham), and is principal lecturer in counselling and psychotherapy, leading the counselling diploma/MA programme at the Nottingham Trent University. Recent publications include *Next Steps in Counselling*, co-authored with Pete Sanders (PCCS, 1995) and a number of papers and chapters exploring aspects of accreditation which are critical of NVQs in this area.

Fay Fransella is founder and director of the Centre for Personal Construct Psychology, London, and Emeritus reader in clinical psychology, University of London.

Kay Goddard is a qualified psychotherapist. She works at Leeds Women's Counselling and Therapy Service at Barnsley Psychology Department.

Mary Godden is a BAC fellow and accredited counsellor in private practice, a supervisor, trainer and lecturer on the diploma in counselling course at the University of Kent at Canterbury. She is a SPOD registered counsellor (Association to Aid Sexual and Personal Relationships of People with a Disability). Chair of BAC from 1981 to 1984, Mary is currently deputy chair of the BAC Accreditation and Recognition Committee.

Jack Gordon is a graduate member of the British Psychological Society and a rational emotive behaviour counsellor in private practice. He has co-authored six books with Windy Dryden. In 1994 he was elected honorary fellow of the Association of Rational Emotive Behaviour Therapists.

Antony Grey was secretary of the Homosexual Law Reform Society in the 1960s, and director of the Albany Trust (the pioneering counselling agency for sexual minorities) until 1977. He took a diploma in counselling skills at South West London College. Antony was an active member of BAC's executive committee in the 1970s and 1980s, helping to draft the association's constitution and code of ethics and to develop the PSMF division. He was convenor of BAC's AIDS counselling training panel. Since the mid-1980s he has concentrated on writing whilst continuing to counsel private clients.

Diane Hammersley is a chartered counselling psychologist in private practice.

James Hemming is an applied psychologist with experience in education, industry and counselling. His PhD was for research into adolescents' problems. He is a chartered psychologist and fellow of the British Psychological Society. Author of a number of books and papers, he has broadcast at home and overseas.

Carolyn Hicks is senior lecturer in Psychology/Research Methods in the School of Continuing Studies at Birmingham University. She is the author of several books on research methods, including *Research and Statistics: a Practical Introduction for Nurses* (Prentice Hall, 1990) and many articles.

Ian Horton is course tutor for the postgraduate diploma in counselling at the University of East London. He was chair of the BAC Scheme for the Recognition of Counsellor Training Courses from 1989–96. He is a BAC fellow and co-author of *The Counsellor's Handbook* (Chapman & Hall, 1994); *Issues in Professional Counsellor Training* (Cassell, 1995) and *New Directions in Counselling* (Routledge, 1996).

Alex Hossack is senior clinical psychologist in the Forensic Psychology Service in Merseyside. He is involved with research into treatment of post-traumatic stress disorder utilizing NLP principles.

Peter Jenkins is course tutor for the diploma in counselling at Stockport College of Further and Higher Education. He is the author of *Children's Rights* (Longman, 1993) and *Counselling, Psychotherapy and the Law* (Sage, in press).

Sue Emmy Jennings is a dramatherapist, counsellor and actress. She is professor of dramatherapy at the University of Ulster, and Director of the Rowan Theatre Company.

Helen Jones is a qualified counsellor who worked with Fay Fransella as Director of Education and Training at the Centre for Personal Construct Psychology, London. She has been an independent management consultant in the Northern and Yorkshire regions of the NHS, working with doctors and senior managers. She is now head of Leadership and Management Development Studies at the North Yorkshire College of Health, affiliated to York University.

Adam Jukes is a group analyst and psychotherapist in private practice in London.

Pat Justice is a BAC accredited counsellor, supervisor, trainer and debriefer (Docklands Bomb) practising in the east end of London. She is key tutor for the Introduction to Counselling course at Goldsmiths College, University of London, where she is currently taking an MA in applied psychoanalytic theory. Her expertise and interests lie in working with adults with learning difficulties and minority groups.

Marcia Karp is the co-director of training at the Holwell International Centre for Psychodrama, North Devon. She is co-editor of *Psychodrama Since Moreno* (Routledge, 1994) and *Psychodrama: Inspiration and Technique* (Routledge, 1992).

Caz Lack, a registered general and psychiatric nurse, is a clinical nurse specialist (substance misuse and HIV) working within Signpost, a substance misuse team managed by Lewisham and Guy's Mental Health NHS Trust. Caz wrote the original article whilst a volunteer for this project.

Jane Leslie wrote her article whilst a student adviser on the further education site of Bedford College of Higher Education. She has returned to her work as a probation officer and is taking a diploma in psychology with a view to pursuing further her interest in psychodynamic counselling.

Jennifer Mackewn is a counsellor/psychotherapist, consultant and trainer in Creative, Integrative and Gestalt approaches. She is a full teaching member of the Gestalt Psychotherapy Training Institute and trainer for the Metanoia Trust and Gestalt South West. She is co-author with Petrūska Clarkson of *Fritz Perls* (Sage, 1993) and author of *Developing Gestalt Counselling* (Sage, 1996).

John McLeod is professor of counselling studies at Keele University. He is interested in the cultural context of counselling and the relevance of research to counselling practice. His recent books, *Introduction to Counselling* (Open University, 1993) and *Doing Counselling Research* (Sage, 1994) examine these themes in contemporary practice.

Tony Merry works at the University of East London and is consultant to the Institute for Person Centred Learning. Publications include *What is Person Centred Therapy?* (with Bob Lusty, Gale Centre, 1993) and *An Invitation to Person Centred Psychology* (Whurr, 1995).

Pat Milner is a recent features editor of *Counselling*. She trained on the first counselling course at Reading University in 1965 and later as a Fulbright scholar at SUNY, Buffalo, USA. Founder chair of ASC, the oldest BAC division, she moved from student counselling at University College London to training at South West London College in the 1970s. Prior to recent retirement she worked at Goldsmiths' College, University of London, and the Centre for Stress Management. She wrote *Counselling in Education* (Dent, 1974; Milner, 1980).

Margaret Morgan was for 26 years responsible for the Spastic Society's (now Scope's) social services. Since retirement in 1983 she has worked in the UK and overseas with voluntary organizations concerned with people coping with brain damage.

Alan Naylor-Smith is a member of the Guild of Psychotherapists. He works as a psychotherapist in private practice and supervises and teaches on the postgraduate diploma course at Hertfordshire University.

Richard Nelson-Jones is associate professor of counselling psychology, Royal Melbourne Institute of Technology. He was a member of BAC's first executive committee and the first chairperson of the British Psychological Society's Counselling Psychology section. He holds dual British and Australian citizenship.

Ian R. Owen is an integrative psychotherapist and lecturer in counselling psychology at the University of Wolverhampton. He is interested in applying the ideas of equal opportunities and existentialism within the practice of counselling and psychotherapy.

Stephen Palmer is director of the Centre for Stress Management, London, and is an honorary visiting lecturer in psychology at Goldsmiths' College, University of London. He is editor of *Counselling Psychology Review*, co-editor of *The Rational Emotive Behaviour Therapist*, and former managing editor of *Counselling*. He has written over 80 articles and a number of books and training manuals on stress management and counselling.

Fiona Palmer Barnes, chair of the BAC Complaints Sub-Committee, trained as a Jungian analyst through the Association of Jungian Analysts, and currently practises as an analyst, therapist, teacher and supervisor.

Martin Payne gained Colchester Institute's diploma in counselling following early retirement from a career in further education. He is now a freelance counsellor working mainly in GP surgeries in Norfolk.

Hillary Ratna is a qualified counsellor and supervisor who is Organizing Tutor for Deaf Courses at the Westminster Pastoral Foundation in London. She has a private practice working with both deaf and hearing clients.

Michael Reddy has had a major impact on the development of workplace counselling in the UK, being influential at both the conceptual level and the practical level through the organization which he founded in 1987 – ICAS (Independent Counselling and Advisory Services Ltd). His long involvement in the counselling world has made him a credible representative of the counselling profession to employers, while influencing professional associations and national bodies which need to establish appropriate standards in workplace counselling.

Peter Reynolds is a senior partner with Westgate Specialist Training. He divides his time between consulting, designing and running training events and writing on a range of organizational issues.

Goldi Romm is a psychoanalytical psychotherapist and the founder and president of the Centre for Psychoanalytical Psychotherapy. She has worked for many years at the Kingston and Royal Free Hospitals as well as having experience in groupwork. She is in private practice.

Suzanna Rose is a clinical researcher based in the Cognition, Emotion and Trauma Group, Department of Psychology, Royal Holloway College, London University. She undertakes specialist counselling both privately and within the NHS. She is a member of the BAC Trauma Sub-Committee.

Peter Ross is director of the University of Reading Counselling Service. He is chair of the Heads of University Counselling Services. His main interests are in the evaluation of counselling and therapy.

John Rowan is a fellow of the British Psychological Society and a chartered counselling psychologist. His latest book is *Healing the Male Psyche: Therapy as Initiation* (Routledge, 1996). He is a founder member of the Association of Humanistic Psychology Practitioners, and teaches at the Minster Centre in London.

Dorothy Rowe is a consultant psychologist and author of 11 books, including *Dorothy Rowe's Guide to Life* (HarperCollins).

Janice Russell is an associate tutor at Durham University and a freelance consultant in training, supervision and research. She is currently researching the construction of intimacy within the counselling relationship.

Chris Scott is director of CS Training and senior lecturer and counsellor, Bolton Institute of Higher Education. He is a former editor of the BAC journal *Counselling*.

Julia Segal is currently senior counsellor at the CMH Multiple Sclerosis Unit, Central Middlesex Hospital, London. She also runs training sessions for professionals working with people with disabilities and teaches the ideas of Melanie Klein.

Geraldine Shipton is in private practice as an analytical psychotherapist and is a lecturer at the Centre for Psychotherapeutic Studies, Sheffield University. She has worked in student counselling and the NHS.

Liesl Silverstone has been a tutor, counsellor and art therapist in many settings. She is the founder of the Person Centred Art Therapy Centre, London where she teaches the person-centred art therapy courses certificated by Crawley College, offers supervision and runs workshops. She is the author of *Art Therapy – the Person Centred Way: Art and the Development of the Person*, published by Autonomy Books (1993).

David Smith is principal lecturer in psychotherapy and counselling at Regent's College, London, where he directs the MA in psychotherapy and counselling. He is the author of *Hidden Conversations: an Introduction to Communicative Psychoanalysis* (Routledge, 1991) and has published widely on psychoanalysis, psychotherapy and philosophy in the professional journals.

Karen Standidge is currently working as a social worker in an adult team for Wirral Social Services. She has a diploma in counselling.

Carole Sutton is principal lecturer in psychology at De Montfort University, Leicester, where she teaches psychology and counselling skills. She is a chartered counselling psychologist and a qualified social worker experienced in psychiatric settings. She is a former chair of the Research Panel of BAC and her interest is in the dissemination of research and evaluation of practice among the helping professions. She researches work with families experiencing difficulties in relationships. Publications include *Handbook of Research for the Helping Professions* (Routledge, 1987) and *Social Work, Community Work and Psychology* (British Psychological Society, 1994).

Kasia Szymanska is a chartered counselling psychologist who works as a counsellor, trainer and supervisor. She has a specialist interest in therapist–client abuse and has written several articles on this topic.

Gillian Thomas works as a specialist counsellor in the NHS seeing people affected by IBD. She is currently completing the final stages of her PhD thesis, 'The place of counselling in the care of people affected by inflammatory bowel disease' at the University of Reading.

Peter Thomas is currently working as a counsellor (part-time) for the West Lambeth Community Care Trust. He also works as a counselling psychologist in a general practice in East Dulwich and in private practice. The article is a synopsis of the research for his MSc in Counselling Psychology at the University of East London.

Barbara Traynor is a counsellor and UKCP registered psychotherapist. She supervises and trains students who are studying to become TA psychotherapists and is the editor of *ITA News*.

Verena Tschudin is a counsellor and writer/editor and a senior lecturer at the University of East London. She is the author of *Counselling Skills for Nurses*, *Counselling: a Training Package* and *Counselling for Loss and Bereavement*.

Tony Waring is a senior lecturer in psychology at Bolton Institute of Higher Education, involved with courses on clinical and counselling psychology. He helped to establish MOVE, a self-help group for men who batter their partners, and has worked with this client group for several years.

Tony Watts is director of the National Institute for Careers Education and Counselling (NICEC), a specialist centre for applied research and development work on careers guidance in Cambridge. He has carried out a variety of projects for government bodies and has written extensively on counselling at work, career development and educational and vocational guidance. He is editor of the *British Journal of Guidance and Counselling*.

Colin Weaver was a senior psychiatric social worker in a department of child and family psychiatry following his work after the Zeebrugge ferry disaster. He is now a freelance counsellor, debriefer and trainer.

Sue Wheeler is a lecturer in counselling at the School of Continuing Studies, University of Birmingham and a BAC accredited counsellor in private practice. She is co-author with Jan Birtle of *A Handbook for Personal Tutors* (OU Press, 1993) and author of *Counselling Training: The Assessment of Competence* (Cassell, 1996).

Ron Wilgosh works as a day hospital manager in the NHS, providing a family therapy service. He applies a solution-focused approach to his work with individuals, couples and families, after training in Milwaukee, USA, with Steve de Shazer. Ron and a colleague were winners of the Queen's Nursing Institute Annual Award for Innovation 1993, for achievements in the field of SFT. He currently provides training in the approach.

David I. Williams is senior lecturer in psychology and course director of the University of Hull postgraduate programmes in counselling and is responsible for Master's degrees in Kuwait and Vienna.

Jim Wilson was instrumental in setting up the MOVE group in Bolton, and has worked in this area with groups and with clients on an individual basis for more than five years. He has contributed to a number of workshops for professionals working in this area.

Ray Woolfe is course director for the diploma/MA in counselling at Keele University and is the author of many articles and a number of books on counselling and counselling psychology. He has recently co-edited, with Windy Dryden, a *Handbook of Counselling Psychology* (Sage, 1996).

Robert Wubbolding is director of training for the William Hasser Institute in the USA. He is professor of counselling at Xavier University, Cincinnati, Ohio and co-director of the Centre for Reality Therapy in Leighton Buzzard. He has written eight books on reality therapy and is a regular presenter at the BAC annual conference.

Index

models:
Biochemical.
Psychodynamic
Environmentalist